IN TRUTH

A History of Lies from Ancient Rome to Modern America

Matthew Fraser

 Prometheus Books

Guilford, Connecticut

Prometheus Books

An imprint of The Rowman & Littlefield Publishing Group, Inc.
4501 Forbes Boulevard, Suite 200
Lanham, Maryland 20706
www.rowman.com

Distributed by NATIONAL BOOK NETWORK

British Library Cataloguing in Publication Information Available

Library of Congress Cataloging-in-Publication Data

Names: Fraser, Matthew, 1958– author.
Title: In truth : a history of lies from Ancient Rome to modern America / Matthew Fraser.
Other titles: History of lies from Ancient Rome to modern America
Description: Guilford, Connecticut : Prometheus Books, [2020] | Includes bibliographical references and index. | Summary: "From the ancient Greeks and Romans to the modern era, how have people determined what is true? How have those with power and influence sought to control the narrative? Are we living in a post-truth era, or is that notion simply the latest attempt to control the narrative? The relationship between truth and power is the key theme. Moving through major historical periods, the author focuses on notable people and events, from well-known leaders like Julius Caesar and Adolf Hitler to lesser-known individuals like Procopius and Savonarola. . . . The author concludes optimistically, noting that we are debating and discussing truth more fiercely today than in any previous era. . . ."— Provided by publisher.
Identifiers: LCCN 2019054811 (print) | LCCN 2019054812 (ebook) | ISBN 9781633886247 (cloth) | ISBN 9781633886254 (epub)
Subjects: LCSH: History—Errors, inventions, etc. | Truthfulness and falsehood—Political aspects. | Truthfulness and falsehood—History. | Journalism—Political aspects—History. | Press and politics—History. | Political leadership—History.
Classification: LCC D10 .F815 2020 (print) | LCC D10 (ebook) | DDC 904—dc23
LC record available at https://lccn.loc.gov/2019054811
LC ebook record available at https://lccn.loc.gov/2019054812

For Oscar, Leo, Hugo, and Hector

CONTENTS

ACKNOWLEDGMENTS

My inspiration for writing this book was unexpected, accidental, serendipitous.

In early 2017, I was working on a novel, a psychological thriller about a British university professor in Paris who finds himself accused of the murder of one of his female graduate students. I'd been working on this novel for two years and was getting close to a final draft. One day at the American University of Paris, where I'm on faculty, a female student in my graduate seminar, Nicole Hanley, approached me with a request. She wanted to know if I would consider taking her on as a research assistant. She mentioned that other MA students at the university were working as research assistants, paid a stipend, to assist professors working on scholarly books.

A little embarrassed, I replied that I wasn't working on a scholarly book at the moment—in fact, I added, I was writing a novel. Needless to say, I carefully avoided the subject of the novel's plot.

I could see a vague trace of disappointment in Nicole's eyes and felt badly about letting her down. That sensation of guilt got me thinking about a possible work of scholarly nonfiction on which I could embark to justify a stipend paid to Nicole Hanley as my research assistant.

It occurred to me fairly quickly that there was indeed a book idea on which I had been ruminating for several months. Donald Trump had just been elected, and there was a great deal of talk of "post truth" in the media. I had been lecturing on the history of propaganda for several years, notably in a course called Media and War and, more recently, in preparing a new course titled From Gutenberg to Google. With Trump in the White House, I was starting to see patterns and connections between past and present. But I was too busy working on the novel to take the idea forward.

A few days later, I got back to Nicole to say that I might have a book idea after all.

That was how this book was born. In the early stage, Nicole spent many hours in Paris university libraries searching on databases for scholarly papers that corresponded to specific themes and topics I had drawn up on a list. Within a few weeks, I could see the clear outlines of a book. The casualty of this new project was my novel. It was put on hold for the three years on which I focused and worked on this book.

A word on my approach and style in this book. I am a political scientist, which in the academic world assigns my scholarly interests and methodology to a specific discipline. My approach in researching and writing this book, however, was deliberately expansive and open-ended, ranging across several fields—history, philosophy, sociology, politics, economics, communications, and others. It's an approach I grew to admire many years ago when, as a graduate student in Paris, I first encountered the seminal works of the German-born economist Albert O. Hirschman, notably *Exit, Voice, Loyalty* and *The Passions and the Interests*. What fascinated me in Hirschman's books, now recognized as classics, was how he made unexpected and insightful connections between ideas and their far-researching consequences, often unintended. I took a similar multidisciplinary approach in writing this book, which is expansive in scope and multi-layered in ideas, themes, and arguments. I should also insist here that this book was not written for specialists. While I endeavored to conduct the research with scholarly rigor, the book is aimed at a wide audience of educated readers.

My gratitude to Nicole Hanley for prodding me to come up with a book idea so she could secure a stipend as my research assistant. I wish also to thank my old friend Adam Ostry for going through early chapter drafts and offering helpful feedback and advice. Many thanks to my agent, Amanda Jain at Bookends Literary Agency, who placed the book with Jake Bonar at Prometheus Books. I am grateful to Jake and his colleagues at Prometheus's parent company, Rowman & Littlefield, for their professionalism and efficiency throughout the design, editing, and proofreading.

Now that this book is in the hands of readers, I can return to my novel about a gruesome murder in Paris.

INTRODUCTION

At the end of August in 1835, the *New York Sun* published a story that stunned the world.

The newspaper revealed that the eminent British astronomer Sir John Herschel had just discovered life on the moon. Herschel's powerful telescope had observed with astonishing clarity a lunar landscape teeming with animal life—herds of bison-like beasts, single-horned goats, two-legged beavers, and even more extraordinary, humanoid creatures that resembled large bats about four feet tall.

At first blush, there was no reason to doubt the veracity of the *Sun*'s extraordinary revelation. Sir John Herschel, L.L.D., F.R.S., founder of the Royal Astronomical Society, was the world's most distinguished name in his field. His illustrious father, renowned astronomer William Herschel, had discovered the planet Uranus and was known for his belief in the possibility of extraterrestrial life. What's more, the source for Sir John Herschel's astounding discovery was a scientific article published in the prestigious *Edinburgh Journal of Science*. Everything added up. It had to be true.

The *Sun*'s scoop was a massive coup for the upstart penny paper struggling to survive in the crowded New York newspaper market. The *Sun* stretched out the story over an entire week, adding fantastic details with each edition. Thousands of New Yorkers clamored to get their hands on the latest installment about Sir John Herschel's "Great Astronomical Discoveries." Other American newspapers, embarrassed to have missed the story of the century, scrambled to catch up. The *New York Times* conceded that the *Sun*'s story was "possible and probable." The *New Yorker*, for its part, declared: "The promulgation of these discoveries creates a new era in astronomy and science generally." Soon European papers were offering the *Sun* large sums to reprint the original six-part series.

The story was, of course, a complete fabrication—the first silly-season hoax in the history of journalism. Not a word of it was true. Sir John Herschel was real, but he had never made any claim about discovering life on the moon. The prestigious *Edinburgh Journal of Science* was authentic too, but was now defunct. The "Great Moon Hoax," as it became known, was an extravagant pseudo-science satire, mocking widespread credulity in an era when people were prepared to believe just about anything—including, apparently, that herds of bison, reindeer, and zebra were roaming through lush lunar valleys.

For the *Sun*, the Great Moon Hoax was a huge commercial success. Circulation shot up to more than 40,000 copies, making the *Sun* the biggest-selling newspaper in the world. The Great Moon Hoax was so successful, in fact, that it gave birth to a whole new genre in journalism. For decades, hoax stories flourished in newspapers, filling their pages with alarming tales of bloody massacres, escaped zoo animals, and the unearthing of petrified men. Journalists didn't let facts get in the way of a great story. By the end of the century, fabricated news would provoke diplomatic incidents, even wars, between nations.

In today's internet era of "fake news," the outlandish stories hatched in Victorian-era newsrooms seem oddly familiar. And yet we debate the proliferation of false information as if it were an alarming new trend. Today, fabricated news does more than astound, shock, and distract. Many claim pervasive misinformation is debasing public discourse and corroding democracy. Over the past few years it has become commonplace, even clichéd, to observe despairingly that we are living in a "post-truth" age.

According to the accepted chronology, the post-truth era emerged from the political turmoil of 2016. It was indeed an *annus horribilis* for the truth. The year started with a carnival of deceptive claims and outrageous lies in the run-up to the Brexit referendum in Britain and ended with the spectacle of falsehoods and slander during the American presidential election campaign. Donald Trump's stunning victory appeared to demonstrate that truth no longer mattered in politics. People believed what they wanted to believe. News wasn't fact-checked; it was gut-checked.

Trump was a perfect icon for the post-truth era: real-estate tycoon, casino magnate, Wrestlemania showman, and reality TV celebrity. His media persona belonged to the realm of fantasy. He made no bones about his disregard for truth; he professed it as a virtue. Throughout his flamboyant business career, Trump's motto had been "truthful hyperbole." As he boasted in his autobiography, *The Art of the Deal*: "I play to people's fantasies. People may not always think big themselves, but they can still get very excited by those who do. That's why a little hyperbole never hurts. People want to believe that something is the biggest and the greatest and the most spectacular. I call it truthful hyperbole. It's an innocent form of exaggeration—and a very effective form of promotion." Twenty years later, Trump brought his "truthful hyperbole" credo to politics. And it worked. Americans who voted for Trumped believed—or wanted to believe—his inflammatory rhetoric. Once installed in the White House, his penchant for hyperbole, exaggeration, and outright falsehoods continued, unrestrained by the duties of high office. His boasts and tirades on Twitter became the object of satire. Newspapers such as the *New York Times* and *Washington Post* began publishing tallies of his steady flow of false statements.

Donald Trump was not, of course, the first American presidential candidate to arrive in the White House on a wave of false promises. Politics, in America and elsewhere, has long been animated by hype, distortions, and lies. In may be a regrettable fact of modern democracy, but deception and dishonesty are indispensable to winning and exercising power. As Hannah Arendt observes in her essay "Lying in Politics": "Truthfulness has never been counted among the political virtues, and lies have always been regarded as justifiable tools in political dealings."[1]

For Donald Trump's critics, however, he was in a league of his own. Trump took lying to a whole new level. Hillary Clinton, his rival for the White House in 2016, accused Trump of waging an "all-out war" on truth, facts, and reason. "When leaders deny things we can see with our own eyes, like the size of a crowd at the inauguration," said Clinton, "when they refuse to accept settled science when it comes to urgent challenges like climate change. . . . It is the beginning of the end of freedom. And that is not hyperbole. It's what authoritarian regimes through history have done."[2]

At the end of 2016, the *Oxford English Dictionary* declared *post-truth* as Word of the Year. Two months after Trump's inauguration, *Time* magazine's cover was solid black featuring three words in large scarlet letters: "Is Truth Dead?"

The question was almost apocalyptical. Donald Trump's presidency, it seemed, was a symptom of a malaise that went much deeper than the crass claims of political contests. The curtain had come down on an entire epoch. Nearly three centuries ago, Enlightenment thinkers had framed our modern constitutions proclaiming truths as self-evident. The Latin word for truth—*veritas*—was embedded in the mottos of our great universities. Our understanding of what is true and false was shaped by unwavering adherence to values based on reason and verifiable facts. Now the consensus around those cherished values was shattered.

In our "post-truth" age, it seems the distinction between truth and falsehood is no longer discernible. Worse, it is considered irrelevant. Values are relative, subject to personal opinions. In politics, widespread suspicion of facts has opened a breach for demagogues—in America and elsewhere—to come peddling their dangerous fictions. The fundamental values that underpin liberal democracy, with all its imperfections, are under threat. Some claim that the liberal model is obsolete. Religious fanaticism and populist nationalism are spreading throughout the world with passionate intensity. Authoritarian regimes appeal to those who have abandoned values based on reason. Convinced that there is no such thing as objective truth, they are embracing subjective identities based on group belonging—tribe, nation, religion, race—and their moral reasoning is shaped by these loyalties.

How did our relationship with truth become so troubled?

Many blame social media—Twitter, Facebook, Google, YouTube—for our "post-truth" crisis. Online networks provide a powerful platform for the dark, irrational impulses of the human psyche. The obsession with clicking, liking, commenting, sharing, and retweeting has unleashed a vortex of slander, hatred, falsehoods, and lies. The internet has pushed opinion toward the fevered extremes where conspiracy theories thrive and irrational arguments overwhelm reasoned discourse. The result is a polarized culture of distrust, anger, even violence. Democratic elections are manipulated, sometimes by agents of foreign states, by spreading disinformation on Facebook. Political advertising, once a game of familiar boasts and exaggeration, is now a sinister sphere of viral deception and lies. The solution, many believe, is to regulate social media by policing speech and banning falsehoods. But who decides what is true and false?

Others attribute our "post-truth" crisis to distrust in experts and institutions. Putting trust in professional elites was no small achievement in modern societies. Trust is essential for social cohesion because it establishes a consensus about collective truth. We count on trusted sources—teachers, doctors, scientists, judges, journalists, priests—to tell us the truth. Today, however, people are suspicious of truths that come from experts. The devastating consequences of global financial crises on the lives of ordinary people, and the cynical spectacle of political corruption, exacerbate these attitudes. People are also distrustful of the media, which they lump in with the elites that they deeply resent. Donald Trump's tirades against "fake news," and his promises to "drain the swamp," tapped into these hardened feelings of distrust toward the establishment. The terms *fake news* and *post truth* have become weaponized in a bitter culture war between the disenfranchised and the entitled.

Still others point to the influence of "postmodern" culture to explain our disavowal of truth. In the postmodernist worldview, there are no objective truths. Its adherents claim that the only thing we can rely on is our subjective perspective. They reject the rationalist foundations of the Enlightenment—reason, facts, objectivity—as a coercive system of Western "neoliberal" domination. Even scientific truths are suspect. The evidence behind climate change and vaccinations is disputed. Many today, especially young people, have embraced this cultural hostility toward objective truth. They have retreated into personal beliefs, subjective feelings, emotions, and group identity as the basis for truths they feel they can trust.

If this seems despairing, it might be asked: What is wrong with subjectivity, feelings, and emotions? No one disputes that modern rationalism has produced great achievements in science, medicine, and technology. Yet rationalism has also driven us to dominate the natural world to satisfy our own selfish aims. The social consequences of unbridled capitalism, the catastrophe of climate change, the devastation of forests and wildlife, the horrors of factory farming—all are the brutal legacy of uncontrolled rationalism. Perhaps our grave error has been to neglect our subjective, instinctive, and emotional connection with the world we inhabit.

Like reason, emotions have a cognitive basis in the human psyche. Our imagination and feelings provide access to profound truths, self-transcendence, and the sublime. When we engage with works of art, we are immersed in deeply subjective experiences. Reading the poems of Baudelaire and the novels of Virginia Woolf, listening to the symphonies of Mozart and Mahler, contemplating the paintings of Van Gogh and Edward Hopper—all bring us just as close to truths about life as scientific knowledge does about the objective world. As the German romantic poet Goethe wrote, "Each sees what is present in their heart." The entire thrust of the Romantic movement in the nineteenth century—which gave us the poetry of Byron and the symphonies of Beethoven—was an emotional rebellion against the excesses of rationalism. If poetry, art, and romantic passions belong to the realm of unreason, surely it is an irrationality that we cannot easily live without. Artists are the most powerful commanders of human aspirations because they create values and truths. As the poet Shelley famously asserts, "Poets are the unacknowledged legislators of the world."[3]

It may be comforting to know that these questions have been debated for a very long time. We have been attempting to understand the nature of truth—and the temptation of lies—since the cradle of every civilization. In ancient Greece, philosophers regarded truth as the loftiest goal of all knowledge. Yet the Greeks held different views on the nature of truth.

Plato, who believed in objective values, associated truth with abstract ideals independent of both the physical world and our consciousness—an idea that would later sit well with Christian theologians. Aristotle oriented the question of truth toward the empirical, practical, and rational. The Stoics, like Aristotle, advocated a virtuous life, though warning against excessive emotions, cautioning that they lead to errors in judgment. The Epicureans, on the other hand, believed we should maximize pleasure and minimize pain. The Sophists, for their part, were skeptical toward religion and contended that nothing can ever be known and truth is an illusion. One of the most famous Sophists, Protagoras, stated that "man is the measure of all things." In other words, there are no absolute truths, only truths we construct for ourselves.

Another enduring insight into truth comes from the ancient Greek poet Archilochus, who gave us the familiar comparison of the fox and hedgehog. "The fox knows many things," stated Archilochus, "but the hedgehog knows one big thing." The fox is known for its guile in the pursuit of practical goals, adaptable in different circumstances. The hedgehog, by contrast, steadily stays the course, emboldened in its ability to roll up into a ball with its spines facing outward. The fox has many modes of survival; the hedgehog has only one. Archilochus's fox-and-hedgehog metaphor inspired the modern philosopher Isaiah Berlin to formulate a model that helps us understand the different ways we think, feel, and act. Many of us are like the cunning fox, pursuing many ends but through actions based on partial knowledge. Practical truths, while useful, are disconnected from a coherent moral principle. Others are like the hedgehog, behaving according to a single principle that provides unifying purpose. Their lives are guided by one coherent vision. The story of the fox and hedgehog illustrates the human dilemma: Should we accept our incomplete knowledge, or should we persist in our quest for certainties procured by truth? In our "post-truth" era, it seems that foxes far outnumber hedgehogs; or, at least, their vision of truth is more in fashion. The acceptance of partial truths, even a wholescale rejection of the possibility of truth, appears to be the hallmark of our age. The hedgehog nonetheless has its defenders. They insist that life with moral purpose must be based on a coherent system of values. What separates foxes and hedgehogs is how they perceive the world, and how their perceptions determine their actions.[4]

A simpler approach to truth, also stretching back to the ancient Greeks, asserts that something is true if it corresponds to reality. When we agree that we see the same thing, and it exists as we see it, it must be real—and therefore is true. That sounds reasonable enough. But can we really trust what we see? Take, for example, the famous photo of a woman's dress that went viral on the internet. Millions of people were puzzled by the photo because they did not see the same thing. Some saw a white and gold dress; others saw a blue and black dress. The issue remained unresolved when the celebrity couple Kim Kardashian and Kanye West announced to the world that they could not agree on the color of that dress. Kim saw white and gold, Kanye saw blue and black. How is it possible that people can observe the same object and yet see something completely different? Can we rely on our own perceptions to ascertain what is true? Perhaps this can help explain why there are so many disputes over how we perceive political leaders and interpret the declarations they make.

It is also argued that truth not only is what we see but also must be coherent with what we already know to be true. Things are true when they are consistent with our prior knowledge. If told that the sun will rise tomorrow morning, we don't doubt it. But if told the moon is teeming with intelligent life, we probably will disbelieve it. The sun rising every morning is coherent with what we know to be true. Intelligent life on the moon, however, is inconsistent with established knowledge. And yet, as the Great Moon Hoax demonstrated, people sometimes show astounding credulity against their better judgment. Others prefer to see truth as pragmatic, the result of our practices, commitments, and engagements in the world. Truth, in short, is what has withstood the test of human inquiry. We simply know things to be true. This view sees truths as useful tools that help us navigate through reality.

It could be argued, however, that some falsehoods can be useful. Those who believe in astrological predictions, or in the medicinal benefits of powdered rhino horns, may well claim that, despite all scientific evidence to the contrary, they "work" for them. People often turn to astrology and spiritualism in times of crisis when they are searching for something to believe in. It might be asked, therefore, whether assertions of truth based on personal belief can be accepted as valid given that they are outside the parameters of rational, evidence-based inquiry. In the public sphere of reasoned discourse, what status should be accorded to personal convictions based on "faith" and proclaimed as truth? The question is especially pertinent today. Astrology is enjoying a resurgence of popularity with millennials.[5] Religious fundamentalism, too, is surging back as a powerful political force in many parts of the world, including the United States.

What is accepted as true, and rejected as false, changes over time. For centuries, the Catholic Church asserted as doctrine that the earth stood at the center of the universe. This truth found its source in biblical Scripture. Anyone who dared refute this dogma—such as the astronomer Galileo—risked persecution, torture, even death. Today, no rational person believes that our planet is located at the center of the universe. Galileo's vindication appears to demonstrate that, in the end, truth always prevails. Or as the nineteenth-century philosopher Arthur Schopenhauer observed, truths are at first ridiculed, then triumphed as self-evident. When all is said and done, we always get it right. The march of civilization is a narrative of constant self-correction. It's a reassuring thought, but it doesn't quite happen that way. Errors in science are corrected and never return to reassert themselves as true. But history demonstrates that we stubbornly fail to learn moral lessons from the past—and indeed keep repeating them. The quest to discover truth has not followed a trajectory of constant linear progress. It has been a tortured journey down a twisted path with false prophets lying in wait at every turn. Schisms over the question of truth have triggered great upheavals, ignited revolutions, toppled monarchies, shaken entire civilizations, and inflicted horrendous suffering on the world. The march of folly is alarmingly persistent.

The chapters that follow attempt to untangle the threads of history's vast narrative tapestry—from ancient Rome to the present—with an aim to help better understand our own "post-truth" crisis. The book is organized in six periods. The first section, "Caesar's Things," covers ancient Rome starting with Julius Caesar's conquests, the collapse of the republic, the imperial rule of Augustus, and the irrational reign of Nero. The second section, "Icons and Iconoclasts," examines the rivalry of popes and Byzantine emperors in early Christianity, the myths of sacred kings Charlemagne and Alfred the Great, and the fanatical monk Savonarola's assault on papal authority. The third section, "Twilight of the Icons," focuses on the Renaissance period when the printing press unleashed a vortex of dissent, starting with Martin Luther's religious rebellion and the English Civil War through to Enlightenment ideas and their consequences for France's divine-right monarchy. The fourth section, "Empire of Lies," covers the post–Industrial Revolution era of scientific discovery and commercial newspapers that manipulated public opinion at a time of emerging nationalism—Bismarck's Germany, France under Napoleon III, and the Spanish-American War. The fifth section, "Supermen, Supermyths, Superpowers," examines the twentieth century of mass media and propaganda techniques exploited by the "big lie" ideologies of Nazi fascism and Soviet communism. The final section, "The War on Truth," brings the book to the present, analyzing our current "post-truth" crisis and the cultural zeitgeist that facilitated the astounding rise and political triumph of Donald Trump.

The juxtaposition of *truth* and *lies* in the book's title is deliberate. The book explores the question of truth by tracing the history of lies. Our approach is not didactic: the narrative does not compile a catalog of lies and examine each example to draw lessons for our own age. The astute reader will grasp the connections between past and present. Also, we use *lies* in the broadest sense of the term—myths, tales, legends, superstitions, ideologies, propaganda, disinformation, and so on. The book's main premise is that, throughout history, truth and lies have been opposite sides of the same coin, double-faced, intimately connected, difficult to distinguish, circulated as legitimate currency. They have cohabited the same space, like strange bedfellows, in our collective psyche. The dilemma between truth and falsehood is not always presented as a clear choice. Both are intertwined in the same narrative, each making claims on our values, loyalties, commitments, and conduct. It is often said that people lie for a reason; otherwise they would tell the truth. This book endeavors to discover those reasons and their consequences.

This central argument is explored on three levels—or three "battlefields" in our collective psyche. First, the tension between reason and irrationality. Second, the rivalry between competing narratives about truth. Third, the combat between authority and dissent.

First, the tension between reason and irrationality is deeply embedded in our collective experience. For the ancient Greeks, reason was associated with the sun god Apollo, who represented the rational principle of *logos*. In contrast to reason's luminosity was the dark zone of *mythos*, embodied by the god Dionysus, who represented irrational impulses and bodily indulgences. Logical and objective, *logos* inhabits our minds. Emotional and subjective, *mythos* fills our hearts. *Logos* produces reasoned discourse; *mythos* inspires tales, legends, and myths.

On the surface, reason and irrationality are counter-forces battling in the human psyche, like the split personality of Dr. Jekyll and Mr. Hyde. One is reasonable, civilized, and respectable; the other irrational, unstable, and monstrous. When we turn to history, some epochs (such as the Enlightenment) appear to have been shaped by values based largely on reason, while other periods (like Nazi Germany) were animated by mass hysteria and collective madness. The argument in this book is that reason and irrationality are not turned on and off like a light switch. They are both constantly present, operating simultaneously, embedded in the psyche of every epoch. The Romans were profoundly rational, with codified laws and spectacular feats of engineering; yet at the same time they remained extraordinarily superstitious. Early Christianity asserted religious doctrine as truth, yet Church theologians integrated principles of reason into arguments for the existence of God. The Enlightenment was, like ancient Rome, rational and humanist, though religious fanaticism persisted. In France, Louis XIV was known as the "Sun King" because of his commitment to the Apollonian principles of reason. But as we shall see, his Versailles court was rocked by a sordid scandal about sorcery, soothsayers, palm readers, and poison plots in the king's most intimate circles.

Some eras, it cannot be doubted, are drawn more toward rationalism while others fall under the spell of collective hysteria. At certain points in history, the interplay between reason and irrationality breaks down and one side overwhelms the other. At the height of the Italian Renaissance, the illuminated monk Savonarola mesmerized the citizens of Florence to the point where they submitted themselves to a fanatical theocracy. In modern Germany, the evil ideology of Adolf Hitler entranced an entire population from the same German culture that had produced Mozart, Immanuel Kant, and Albert Einstein. The lessons of history leave no doubt: reason can be defeated by irrational passions, frequently with tragic consequences. These lessons can help us understand the assault on truth today that, it is feared, is undermining the cherished values of liberal democracy. Many deplore the rise of populist demagogues in our politics, but it has been the inevitable consequence of values that prepared the ground for their triumph.

Second, rivalry between competing claims on truth, each with its own propaganda narrative, has been an enduring dynamic throughout history. Here the tension is between truth and lies. Dressing up falsehoods in the guise of truth is a powerful human impulse. As we have noted, people lie for a reason.[6] In ancient Greece, Plato cautioned that truths are dangerous. He argued that rulers must invent stories—or "noble lies"—to hold society together in a common purpose. As we shall see in this book's first section, Julius Caesar penned a chronicle of his military conquests to fabricate his own heroic legend in a political rivalry with his enemies in the Roman Senate. Later, emperor Augustus commissioned the poet Virgil to write an epic narrative, *The Aeneid,* to celebrate the imperial glory of Rome. Both works of literature were *mythos* at the service of Roman propaganda. Centuries later, monks were Christian spin doctors spreading Church propaganda in the form of tales about miracles, the intercession of saints, and the heroic exploits of sacred kings. Throughout Christendom, any narrative that challenged official Church dogma, defended as the "gospel truth," was punished as heresy. This was Galileo's fate, forced to recant even though objective truth was on his side. It may explain, at least in part, why later scientists such as René Descartes accommodated religious dogma in their metaphysical speculations.

Machiavelli took Plato's "noble lie" further by advising the prince that he must be duplicitous, forge myths, and deceive when it was necessary for the greater good. The spirit of Machiavelli's cunning advice is still present in today's backrooms, boardrooms, and war rooms. Over the past century, despite professional journalism's claims on objective truths, we have been bombarded with a dizzying onslaught of false narratives in the form of propaganda, disinformation, PR hype, media bias, false advertising, and spin doctoring. The Soviet regime's propaganda newspaper was titled *Pravda*, which in Russian means "truth." Stalinist truths were Orwellian doublespeak: anything can mean its opposite. In the Soviet Union, communist ideology was proclaimed as a science. Thus, the horrendous lies behind a brutal dictatorship sought legitimacy in the claims of scientific rationalism. In our modern democratic politics, falsehoods are sometimes called "alternative facts." They may be false, but no matter, so long as they are believed to be true.

We are indeed often attracted more to compelling lies than to rational truths. One has only to follow the irrational exuberance that drives stock market speculation to euphoric heights before the inevitable crash. And yet every stock, however dubious, had a great story. Our cultural attraction to a great story can render us susceptible to believing just about anything. Some argue that history itself is little more than an elaborate narrative of falsehoods.[7] We delude ourselves in the present and commit the same self-deception when reconstructing the past. History is a self-deceiving act of the imagination. Or as Napoleon Bonaparte observed, it is "a set of lies, agreed upon." Legends and myths have remarkable tenacity. We still repeat the myth that Nero "fiddled while Rome burned," even though it never happened. And many believe that Marie-Antoinette uttered the supercilious remark, "Let them eat cake," despite the lack of any historical evidence. We believe it, and keep repeating it, because we want to believe it's true.

Third, the combat between authority and dissent plays out in an inexorable power struggle to impose values about truth. Disputes over truth are fractious, and often violent, because much is at stake. Monopolizing truth confers power. But as Shakespeare warned, uneasy lies the head that wears the crown. Forces of dissent inevitably mobilize around rival claims on truth. Following the collapse of the Roman Empire, Christianity emerged as its successor, whose power was founded on a new ideology. It took a thousand years, but the Church finally began to lose its grip on power in the Renaissance. One group of dissenters were scientists such as Galileo, who challenged the official Church narrative about the cosmos. Another assault was led by determined religious reformers—first Savonarola in Italy, then Martin Luther in Germany, followed by Henry VIII in England. During the Enlightenment, scientists and philosophers rejected the supernatural and challenged religious dogma with arguments based on reason.

In the modern era, bureaucracies and professions accumulated tremendous power by monopolizing information and expertise based on objective truths. One of those professions was journalism, which in liberal democracies controlled the news agenda as a powerful "fourth estate." In today's internet era, the power of these professional elites has been undermined by rival voices on social media. These mobilized forces of dissent—and disinformation—are frequently hostile to the values of objective truth and the elites who proclaim them. It was against this turbulent backdrop that Donald Trump triumphed politically in America by promising to "drain the swamp" of corruption that many of his supporters associated with traditional elites. This book's final chapter explores how Trump was not a false prophet of a "post-truth" age, but rather an inevitable political apotheosis in a culture that had already rejected and abandoned the possibility of truth.

The book concludes with reflections on a way forward as we consider new approaches to the question of truth and the future of liberal democracy. If the past teaches us anything, it is that democracies do die.[8] Democracy died in ancient Greece. It died in ancient Rome. And it died in modern Germany. Today it is increasingly under threat in many countries in the grip of authoritarian populism—Russia, Turkey, Venezuela, Brazil, Hungary, to name only a few. Some would add the United States to the list. Corroded trust and rising intolerance are pushing politics in many countries toward demagoguery. The pendulum, it seems, is swinging from reason to unreason, from truth to falsehoods, from the trusted authority of established institutions to the passionate intensity of dissent. Going forward, how can we affirm values around truth in a public sphere of reasoned discourse in which diverse voices and values can be acknowledged?

Our anxiety about a post-truth era is perhaps a reason for optimism. The fact that we are so fiercely debating truth is a sign that we recognize its vital importance. Despite our stubborn instinct for distorting, concealing, and rejecting truth, we have remained just as steadfastly committed to affirming its existence. That extraordinary paradox is the subject of this book.

Part I

Caesar's Things

I

I CAME, I SAW, I PUBLISHED

Julius Caesar is recognized as one of the greatest military commanders in history. He conquered Gaul, invaded Britain, then prevailed in a bloody civil war to emerge as unrivaled master of Rome.

More than two thousand years later, we still pay tribute to Caesar's legend in our daily lives. The month of July is named after him. We use his famous expressions—"the die is cast" and "cross the Rubicon"—in everyday situations. The words *kaiser* and *czar* for "king" are derived from his surname.

Julius Caesar is less known for something else that secured his exalted place in historical legend. He was a master of PR and spin.

Caesar famously declared, *"Veni, vidi, vici"*—I came, I saw, I conquered—to describe his conquests. But he neglected to insert a fourth verb, much more important than the famous three. Caesar not only came, saw, and conquered—he *published*. He observed, assessed, noted, and recounted his saga to a multitude of admiring fans among ordinary Romans. Caesar was the first major figure in history to leave behind a detailed written account of the events in which he was the protagonist.

Caesar's decade-long conquest of Gaul produced his most famous tome, *The Gallic Wars*.[1] The book remains a classic, admired for its terse and unadorned Latin. Caesar's chronicle is an ethnographic treasure trove, brimming with detailed observations about the Celtic and Germanic tribes that he encountered and vanquished. The book is also a horrifying narrative of unspeakable brutality and quasi-genocidal slaughter. It is estimated that Caesar's armies killed 1 million people and sent another million into slavery. Yet contemporary Romans who followed the *Gallic Wars* chronicles did not react with moral outrage. Caesar's military victories in "barbarian" Gaul were a triumphant assertion of the superiority of

Roman civilization. They also won Caesar the adulation he craved. In that respect, *The Gallic Wars* remains one of the greatest PR coups ever. It could be claimed that Caesar achieved another historical first in pioneering the art of personal branding.

A question that constantly comes up, however, is Caesar's reliability as a narrator, or to put it more bluntly, his credibility. Was Caesar telling the truth? How much of what he described in *The Gallic Wars* can we trust as factually accurate?

A careful reading of Caesar's chronicles provides us with insights into his character. Most published memoirs are motivated to some degree by vanity and self-justification. Julius Caesar was no different. He had a massive ego. He was also excessively vain, combing over his bald spot and constantly fussing over his physical appearance. He was notoriously thin-skinned, quick to anger, rebutting his critics with vitriolic attack. *The Gallic Wars* chronicles also reveal a great deal about Roman values and attitudes toward truth. Ancient Rome, with its codified laws and vast network of aqueducts, was a highly rational civilization. At the same time, however, Romans turned to superstitions, legends, and myths for truths that shaped their understanding of the world. The collective Roman psyche was simultaneously inhabited by rational designs and irrational impulses. Caesar understood this dichotomy in the Roman zeitgeist. As a chronicler of his own military conquests, he was attuned to the power of heroic mythology in Roman culture.

Officially, Caesar wrote his chronicles as an annual report to the Roman Senate. In Caesar's day, the Senate was stacked with his enemies in the patrician oligarchy, called "Optimates." Though Caesar was a patrician by birth (his family claimed to be descended from the Trojan hero Aeneas and the goddess Venus), in politics he was a reformist member of the opposing populist part, called the "Populares."[2] His family clan may have been illustrious, but Caesar was far from rich—in fact, he was often in debt. This put him at great disadvantage in electoral politics. Politics in the Roman republic was driven by money. Only the rich could afford to stand for elected office. This explains Caesar's early career dependency on his rich and powerful sponsor, Crassus. A military commander who had gained glory by putting down Spartacus's slave revolt, Crassus was the wealthiest man in Rome—a classic example of the "millionaire soldier-politician" tradition in the Roman republic. Caesar needed Crassus's patronage to rise in politics. Winning elections usually involved massive vote-buying. Politicians lavished gifts on voters, including wine distributed in commemorative cups. After the happy beneficiary drank the wine, the name of the politician to vote for was clearly inscribed at the bottom of the cup. This subtle form of corruption was difficult to police due to a blurred legal distinction between electoral bribery (*ambitus*) and generosity (*benignitas*). Vote buying was so rampant in the Roman republic that, as the statesman Cicero noted, the massive inflow of dirty money during elections made interest rates soar.

Caesar was no stranger to these corrupt practices. A nephew of the great Roman general Gaius Marius, from an early age Caesar had been battle-hardened in the cut-throat world of Roman politics. As a young man, he had been forced to go into hiding during a bloody political purge. Later in life, he was elected Pontifex Maximus, chief priest of Rome's state religion. He also served as governor of Hispania Ulterior in modern-day Spain. He was first elected consul, putting him at the pinnacle of Roman political power, in 59 BC when he was entering mid-life at age 41. It marked the beginning of his alliance of convenience with Crassus and the powerful Roman general, Pompey, another rich soldier-politician. Their triumvirate was cemented by Pompey's marriage to Caesar's daughter, Julia.[3]

Caesar's first political act as consul was to decree that all senatorial proceedings be published in the daily political bulletin, the *acta diurna populi Romani*. He also ordered that all Senate speeches and votes be posted publicly in the Roman forum. This bold reform threatened to pry open the Senate's closed-door proceedings and secret votes. It also transformed Roman politics by creating an open public sphere where information, buzz, and gossip circulated freely. Wealthy Romans began sending scribes to the forum to read the *acta* and take notes, jotting down bits of news, sometimes copying entire speeches. Information was power. The *acta* was, in effect, the first "newspaper" in Western history.

Caesar's reformist legislation and strong-arm political tactics made him many enemies, especially among the patrician Optimates in the Senate. The senatorial oligarchs were hugely relieved when, a year into his consulship, Caesar left Rome to take up the governorship of Transalpine Gaul. The move put Caesar out of the loop. Some believed his motivation for seeking the post in Gaul was financial. By plundering barbarian territories in northern Europe, he could pay off massive debts accumulated during his office-seeking career. That was undoubtedly true, but Caesar had another agenda when he arrived in Gaul in 58 BC. If his enemies in Rome believed he would vanish into obscurity, they were cruelly mistaken. For Caesar, his rustication was a fabulous opportunity not only to build a war chest but also to produce a heroic narrative that would prepare the ground for his political comeback. More than just an annual report to the Senate, his chronicles from Gaul were published as an epic saga worthy of Homer and Virgil. And Julius Caesar was the hero of his own story.

Caesar's literary project showed that he shrewdly grasped the media dynamics of his day. Romans were profoundly humanist, passionately engaged in the here and now, driven by a lust for fame, obsessed with leaving to posterity a trace of their time in this world. Ancient Rome was also an information-rich society. Romans had a voracious appetite for news, gossip, myths, legends, and exotic tales. Authors pandered after notoriety by writing in every form—novels, poems, satires, dramas, epic poetry. Statesmen such as Cicero—who wrote classics on politics, morality, and philosophy—carefully managed the publication of their own works and orchestrated publicity campaigns to generate public interest. Cicero once urged a historian friend to write up a flattering account of his consulship, adding: "The idea of being spoken about by posterity pushes me to some sort of hope for immortality."[4] Julius Caesar, too, had cultivated literary ambitions since his youth. He had even tried his hand at a dramatic tragedy about Oedipus. As a politician many years later, he was instinctively keyed into the power of storytelling.

Rome's buzzing literary culture received a boost from new publishing technologies. The Greeks had been attached to the oral tradition, producing spoken-word epics such as Homer's *Iliad* and *Odyssey*. During Caesar's lifetime in the first century BC, the Roman republic was emerging as a print culture. Oratory remained important, but public life was increasingly structured around the written word. In Caesar's day, a new type of retail merchant (called a *librarius,* from Latin *liber* for book) was driving a burgeoning book trade. Rome didn't have a "book industry" in the modern sense. With no mechanized printing presses, Roman books were copied by hand, a task usually assigned to literate slaves and freedmen. Copies of all forms of writing—letters, speeches, books—were circulated, read, and declaimed in public forums. Romans even had book format wars: the choice was between parchment and papyrus. For documents and books sent over long distances, papyrus was favored. Reed pens dipped in ink were used to write on sheets of papyrus before rolling them up into cylinder scrolls around a rod with knobs at both ends. For shorter distances, Romans scribbled messages written with a stylus on waxed parchment tablets mounted in wooden frames. For educated Romans, the exchanged notes and letters with these new technologies were in many respects engagement in ancient "social media."[5]

When Caesar arrived in Gaul as a military commander, he had an intimate knowledge of how buzz worked in Rome. He published *The Gallic Wars* chronicle not as a single-volume memoir published after the fact. He wanted his followers to experience his military expeditions in real time. He recounted battles on the fly, reporting from the front line, sending dispatches back to Rome in staggered installments, knowing they would be read and declaimed in public forums. Caesar was careful to build suspense, publishing *The Gallic Wars* as a serialized book, with each new installment eagerly awaited by readers.[6]

The book was not a solo project. Caesar benefited from a loyal team of aides to produce and promote his narrative. During his eight years in Gaul, he spent the cold winter months dictating his exploits to his trusted general, Aulus Hirtius. Hirtius sent Caesar's texts to two loyal lieutenants back in Rome, Lucius Balbus and Gaius Oppius, who were in effect Caesar's image handlers operating a well-oiled publicity machine. In their marketing campaign for *The Gallic Wars,* nothing was overlooked. The manuscript in hand, Balbus and Oppius ensured that copies of Caesar's chronicles were widely distributed throughout Italy. They also organized public readings of each new installment. This was common practice in literary circles in ancient Rome. Ordinary citizens gathered in public squares to hear readings, called *recitatio.* Many Romans knew *The Gallic Wars* chronicles from these public performances. Caesar shrewdly understood his target audience. His story was aimed at ordinary Romans. By appealing directly to Roman public opinion, Caesar cut through the senatorial elites who regarded him with resentment and fear. Caesar's chronicles were, in that respect, a masterful storytelling exercise in political spin targeting a specific segment of the population.

With a careful eye on his own image, Caesar scrupulously justified his motives and actions in Gaul. He insisted that his legions were intervening in Gaul out of necessity and duty. His military campaigns, he claimed, were a response to urgent requests for aid from friendly Celtic tribes under attack from rival barbarian peoples. The necessity to morally justify his military conquests can be measured by the magnitude of human slaughter inflicted by Caesar's army. According to his own account, in the aftermath of a battle against Germanic tribes pushing into Gaul from modern-day Switzerland, his Roman armies killed or enslaved some 250,000 people. In the spring of 55 BC, Caesar's legions were ambushed by another wave of Germanic tribes marauding into Gaul. The Germans killed seventy Roman soldiers in their attack. Caesar took immediate revenge, showing no mercy. His armies massacred every single man, woman, and child in the German camp. Caesar's narrative speaks of horrific cries as his soldiers butchered thousands of Germans fleeing in panic. His legions slaughtered more than 400,000 people as revenge for seventy dead Roman soldiers. To justify butchery on this scale, Caesar played the "us and them" card. His chronicles portrayed the Germanic tribes as a bellicose and uncivilized people who, lacking agriculture, were constantly attacking neighbors for plunder. It was Rome's duty to stop them.[7]

Was Caesar's narrative accurate? Or was he exaggerating the extent of Roman slaughter to excite bloodthirsty patriotism back in Rome? It is impossible to confirm or dispute Caesar's claims, if only because he was the unique witness to the events he described. The only modern means of corroboration are archaeological digs of ancient battlefields. After one Roman battlefield was unearthed near Kessel in modern-day Netherlands, archaeologists estimated that Caesar's armies had slaughtered between 150,000 and 200,000 people belonging to two Germanic tribes—roughly half the number claimed in Caesar's chronicle.[8] Still, the massacre of nearly 200,000 people—men, women, children—is horrifying to contemplate.

Caesar's narrative reached its crescendo with the historic defeat of the Gallic warrior Vercingetorix at the Battle of Alesia in 52 BC. Vercingetorix came closer than any other Celtic ruler to defeating Julius Caesar. Vercingetorix made the fatal mistake, however, of retrenching in the citadel town of Alesia, giving Caesar an opportunity to starve him out through siege warfare. Caesar's legions constructed twenty-foot-wide fortifications and dug water-filled trenches around the elevated Celtic town. It was an extraordinary feat of tactical engineering that included gruesome details. The Romans mined the no-man's zone around the citadel with spikes, traps, spurs, and lily-covered pits concealing sharpened logs that mortally impaled anyone who fell in. In his chronicles, Caesar glossed over these grisly aspects of the Alesia siege. Fortunately, a fuller story was later provided by the ancient Roman historian Cassius Dio. The encircled Gauls, worn down by the siege, released hundreds of women, children, and elderly onto the mined no-man's land between the walled city and Caesar's fortifications. Vercingetorix was hoping the Romans would show them mercy. But Caesar was unmoved. Unable to escape or return to the citadel, the women, children, and elderly perished slowly, dying of starvation in full sight of their Celtic loved ones. Vercingetorix finally surrendered, laying down his arms and prostrating himself before Caesar. Caesar had Vercingetorix put in irons and sent to Rome, where he was later strangled to death, the customary fate of trophy prisoners.

Following the Roman victory at Alesia, Caesar informed the Senate that Gaul was subdued. All the Gallic peoples had been brought under Roman domination. It marked the end of an entire civilization. The Gauls were, over time, assimilated into the culture of their new masters, adopting Roman manners, religion, culture, art, institutions, and the Latin language. But the birth of the Gallo-Roman society came at great human cost. Caesar's armies massacred 1 million human beings. His conquest of Gaul was a genocidal crime. But there was no controversy, no outrage, no war crimes tribunals. Only victory and glory for Julius Caesar.

As a work of literature, Caesar's chronicles were a smashing success. As one ancient historian reported: "The impact of his adventures in Gaul was immediate."[9] Influential figures such as Catullus and Cicero were extravagant with praise. Cicero gushed that Caesar's memoirs were "cleanly, directly and gracefully composed and divested of all rhetorical trappings."[10] Caesar's friend and ghostwriter, Aulus Hirtius, observed that "these memoirs are so highly rated by all judicious critics" that historians could never improve upon them.

The question of Caesar's reliability as a narrator remains a puzzle. How much of *The Gallic Wars* was true? Or to put it inversely, how much was fabrication, exaggeration, and blatant lies?

That Caesar was describing real events cannot be doubted. It is almost certain, however, that he was selective with facts. The ancient Roman historian Suetonius, who admired Caesar's chronicles, noted however that, according to the soldier-historian Asinius Pollio, they "were put together somewhat carelessly and without strict regard for truth; since in many cases Caesar was too ready to believe the accounts which others gave of their actions, and gave a perverted account of his own, either designedly or perhaps from forgetfulness."[11] Caesar played up his victories, but was less loquacious about his setbacks. He was sketchy, for example, about his invasion of Britannia, even though it was the first time a Roman had ever set foot on British soil. This can perhaps be explained by his motives for invading the British Isles. Suetonius tells us that Caesar crossed the channel in the hope of finding pearls; but the main reason was probably plunder and pillaging to bring slaves and minerals back to Rome. He certainly encountered the local Britons at close range, describing them as a strange and exotic race with woad-dyed blue skin and shaved bodies except for head and upper lip. He also observed that British women kept their hair long and loose and were sexually shared between groups of ten or twelve men. Caesar put a brave face on two separate Roman confrontations with the Britons, recounting skirmishes along the coast and inland. It appears, however, that he retreated hastily after his fleet was partially destroyed in gales. Caesar nonetheless recounted his invasion of Britain as a great military victory. Back in Rome, a public twenty-day Thanksgiving was decreed to celebrate his conquest of the cold and rainy island that, a century later, would become a Roman province.

Whether Caesar's chronicles were factual was not of paramount importance to his contemporary Roman audience. For all their great achievements in the arts and sciences, Romans were not scrupulously attached to factual truth. While Romans ranked *veritas* among the greatest virtues, their relationship with the truth was ambiguous. That ambiguity was symbolized in the Roman goddess of truth, Veritas, depicted as a young virgin dressed in white and holding a hand mirror. She was believed to be hiding at the bottom of a sacred well—elusive, like the truth. The goal of virtuous Roman citizens was to pursue and discover the truth. But they were ready to make allowances for fiction, especially regarding their own history.

This indulgence also applied to ancient Roman historians, who were not particularly devoted to factual truths. The Roman satirist Lucian wrote a book, *How to Write History*, in which he criticized "the fashion to neglect the examination of facts."[12] Roman historians were not fussy about excavating archives, poring over documents, and examining artifacts. Some historians, such as Tacitus, did painstakingly consult documents. Tacitus embraced the motto *sine ira et studio* ("without anger and fondness") to underscore his dispassionate objectivity. Most Roman historians, however, were not meticulously interested in fact-based truths. They regarded truth not as factual, but as essentially moral. Roman histories were designed to arouse patriotic emotions with legends and myths about heroism and reversals of fortune. This blurred distinction between fact and fiction in Roman culture was inherited from the Greeks. In Plato's *Republic*, Socrates asserts that, while it is preferable to be truthful in writing about historical events, it is acceptable to invent stories (or "lies") so long as they are useful. Romans took the same attitude toward historical writing. As classicist Mary Beard observes in her book *SPQR: A History of Ancient Rome*: "There is often a fuzzy boundary between myth and history (think of King Arthur or Pocahontas). . . . Rome is one of those cultures where that boundary is particularly blurred."[13] In a word, Roman histories contained a heavy dose of *mythos*—stories and legends whose goal was not factual accuracy, but moral edification.[14]

A classic example of Roman history as myth is the legend of Lucretia, the beautiful wife of a nobleman who was raped by the Roman prince Tarquin. Lucretia denounced her rapists and committed suicide by stabbing herself to preserve her virtue. That dramatic event triggered the overthrow of the Roman monarchy and creation of a republic whose leaders henceforth swore that Rome would never again be ruled by kings. The rape of Lucretia—later immortalized by Botticelli and Shakespeare—thus became the founding act of the Roman republic in 509 BC. Whether Lucretia was a real figure from history was uncertain. But for Romans, the legend's basis in fact was unimportant. The history of Rome itself took inspiration from a founding myth about twin brothers, Romulus and Remus. According to legend, the two boys were the offspring of a raped vestal virgin, Rhea Silvia, daughter of King Numitor, a descendant of the great Trojan warrior Aeneas. Offspring of a rape, the infants were abandoned in a basket on a bank of the Tiber. Suckled by a she-wolf called Lupa, they were later adopted by a shepherd named Faustulus. Later in life, Romulus killed his brother Remus and went on to found the city of Rome. For Romans, this legend gave meaning to their collective existence and established a mythic connection with ancient Troy.

When writing his chronicles, Julius Caesar was acutely aware that his tales of conquest fit into this literary convention that blended history, legend, and myth. He knew that he was writing in a genre that was not scrupulous with facts. The full title of the work, *Commentaries on the Gallic Wars*, made it clear that his chronicles were based on his personal interpretations of events. The moral tone of *The Gallic Wars*, moreover, was consistent with other Roman historical writings about battles with the volatile barbarians. In Caesar's day, there was a great popular appetite for tales of Roman military heroes vanquishing the barbarian Celts. Generations of Romans were raised with terrifying tales about the Celtic warlord Brennus, who, in the year 390 BC, had invaded Italy, sacked Rome, and occupied the city for months.

Caesar's audience would have been familiar with these tales. They were indifferent to the exigencies of factual truth in *The Gallic Wars*. Romans wanted a cracking good story. And Caesar delivered.

***

Following his conquest of Gaul, Caesar was rich, powerful, and famous; his military campaigns in northern Europe were the stuff of legend. He expected to return to Rome cheered by the masses in a triumphal procession.

The conservative Optimates in the Senate saw things differently. They had resented Caesar since the days of his consulship when he issued meddling decrees that checked their prerogatives. Caesar was now politically isolated. After the violent death of Crassus on the battlefield in 53 BC—the enemy Parthians had poured molten gold down his throat—the triumvirate was over. Pompey no longer considered himself Caesar's ally. Their family connection had been extinguished by the death of Caesar's daughter Julia—Pompey's wife—five years earlier in 54 BC. Pompey was now on the side of the senatorial Optimates, who were hostile to Caesar.

Caesar's fiercest critic in the Senate was Marcus Cato, a powerful voice among the conservative Optimates. Great-grandson of the great Roman statesman Cato the Elder, the young Cato was a champion of liberty who had built his reputation combating corruption and defending the constitution. He and Julius Caesar had a long and complex relationship. Cato's half-sister Servilia had been Caesar's mistress and confidante. Caesar was also a surrogate father to Servilia's son, Brutus. But these intimate family connections did little to endear Caesar to Cato. The two men despised each other. Cato did not count himself among the fans of Caesar's *Gallic Wars* chronicles. In fact, he was so horrified by Caesar's accounts of slaughtering Germanic tribes that he threatened to have him arrested, impeached, and turned over to his barbarian enemies. But Caesar commanded legions. And there was nothing more threatening to the Senate than a triumphant military commander marching on Rome. Warning his fellow senators that Rome had more to fear from Julius Caesar than from the Celts and Germans, Cato obtained a Senate resolution ordering Caesar to disband his armies and return to Rome as a private citizen.

At first Caesar attempted to negotiate the terms of his return to Rome. But he feared a trap that would lead to a trial and exile, if not execution, for longstanding allegations of corruption against him.[15] After Caesar refused to make any concessions, the Senate declared him an enemy of the people. Now Caesar's hand was forced. In early January of 49 BC, he made his famous decision to march on Rome with one of his legions. That historic moment gave birth to two famous metaphors signifying a point of no return. When Caesar "crossed the Rubicon," there was no going back. And while crossing the narrow river in northern Italy, he declared, "The die is cast!" (in Latin, *alea iacta est!*).

Caesar's march on Rome triggered a five-year civil war that opposed his legions and the Optimate army commanded by his former ally Pompey. True to form, Caesar seized on the new conflict as another opportunity to spin a narrative in his own favor. This time his chronicle was titled *The Civil War*.[16] Shorter than *The Gallic Wars*, his account of the Civil War was written in the same tone of self-justification, omitting events that might call into question his own motives. Caesar portrayed himself as a great hero of the Roman people who had been double-crossed by the old elitists in the Optimates camp—notably Pompey, Cato, and Cicero.

The book's climactic episode was Caesar's victory over Pompey at the Battle of Pharsalus in Greece in 48 BC. Pompey fled to Egypt to seek the aid of the Egyptian boy king Ptolemy, brother of Cleopatra. But Ptolemy, under the influence of his eunuch regent Pothinus, decided to placate Julius Caesar with the corpse of Pompey. When Pompey was in a small boat coming to the Egyptian shore to be received by Ptolemy, he was murdered by officers guarding the Egyptian king. They hacked off Pompey's head and threw his body into the sea. The decapitated head was presented to Caesar. Instead of receiving the gruesome trophy with satisfaction, Caesar recoiled in horror. But with Pompey out of the way, Rome was finally at his feet.

Caesar now had only one enemy left: Cato the Younger, his old adversary in the Senate. In 46 BC, Cato was in North Africa raising a mercenary army to fight Caesar's legions. Caesar tracked Cato down in modern-day Tunisia and cornered him in the town of Utica. Realizing there was no way out, Cato preferred to die honorably than beg for Caesar's clemency. On the final night of his life, he quietly read Plato's *Phaedo*, which recounts the suicide of Socrates. The following day, Cato retreated to an empty room and, pulling out a dagger, ripped open his stomach until his bowels spilled out.[17] Cato was dead at age 48. Learning of Cato's suicide, Caesar remarked, "Cato, I grudge you your death, as you would have grudged me the preservation of your life."[18]

News of Cato's death quickly reached Rome. Cicero was so moved by the tragic news that he dashed off a panegyric, titled *Laus Catonis*, celebrating Cato's honor and heroism. When Caesar returned to Rome, Cicero's pamphlet was feverishly circulating in the capital—today we would say it was "going viral." Exasperated at being upstaged by Cato's dramatic suicide, Caesar fired off a rebuttal, titled *Anticato*, and published it immediately. The *Anticato* has not survived, but we know its contents through references and citations in Caesar's lifetime. It was a vitriolic diatribe pouring scorn on Cato's entire life. Caesar cataloged Cato's vices, including his fondness for wine, his alleged avarice, and his failed marriage. He repeated a vile rumor that Cato, following the death of his brother Caepio, had passed his sibling's ashes through a sieve looking for traces of gold. Caesar's pamphlet was odious slander.

It might be wondered why Julius Caesar, at the very moment he was about to seize power in Rome, took the trouble to dash off a mean-spirited pamphlet that smeared the reputation of a greatly admired Roman who was no longer alive to defend his own honor. Surely the moment called for dignified silence. Caesar's outburst, if morally questionable, was not an egregious gesture in ancient Rome. Innuendo, slander, and character assassination were standard weapons in Roman politics. On the level of tactics, Caesar doubtless realized that, while he'd won the civil war, he was losing the PR war. Cicero's tribute to Cato was creating negative buzz. Caesar had no choice but to go on the offensive.

When Caesar finally returned to Rome, the republic was no more. Proclaimed dictator for ten years, Caesar carefully created a cult of personality around his own person. Public celebrations featured elaborate spectacles, entertainments, and a triumphal procession. In Caesar's parade, prisoners from Gaul, Egypt, Africa, and Asia were marched in chains before cheering Romans. And as Suetonius tells us, crowds applauded the words "*Veni, vidi, vici*," displayed on a massive placard held aloft over Portus. Suetonius adds that the slogan was Caesar's boast that his victories had been so decisively swift.[19] Another Roman tradition during triumphal processions was the presence of a slave seated in the carriage behind the victorious general, whispering in his ear, "*sic transit gloria mundi*"—a reminder that he was mortal and glory was fleeting.

It was advice that Caesar should have heeded. But it was too late. Corrupted by absolute power, he was carrying himself like a monarch. When returning to Rome from a Latin festival in Alban Mount, a crowd cheered him, shouting, "Long live the king!," using the word *rex* for king. Caesar replied, "Caesarem se, non regem esse " ("I'm Caesar, not king").

The ancient historian Plutarch tells us that Caesar was troubled when the crowd fell silent after his response. It's possible that Caesar was simply clarifying his name. He could not have been unaware, however, of the longstanding Roman hostility toward kings embedded in their collective imagination by the rape of Lucretia legend. Suetonius recounts that Caesar made a great display of false modesty by eschewing the title "king," and ensured that his avowed humility was written up in the *acta* so it was known publicly. But in private, Caesar did not oppose statues of himself being placed next to those of ancient Roman kings. [20]

For the Roman senators who had long resented Caesar's ambitions, his attitude toward the title "king" was suspiciously ambiguous. So was Caesar's new habit of wearing high red boots that, evoking the traditional footwear of Rome's early kings, caused offense in republican Rome. Caesar was also said to have reacted with anger when a diadem on one of his statues was removed. At the festival of Lupercalia, when Caesar's trusted lieutenant Mark Antony attempted to place a golden crown on Caesar's head, his gracious refusal of the honor appeared suspiciously rehearsed. These were mistakes that Caesar could have avoided. His biggest mistake, though, was accepting the title of *dictator perpetuo*—dictator in perpetuity. For his enemies in the Senate, it was a bridge too far. They realized that the only way to curtail Caesar's power was by eliminating him.

The Ides of March in 44 BC is the most famous assassination in history. But did it really happen as described in the annals of history? Or was Caesar's murder, like so many events in ancient Rome, another legend mixing historical fact and fiction?

According to legend, Caesar ignored omens of plots against his life. A month before the assassination, an Etruscan soothsayer named Titus Spurinna had warned him that he should fear for his life for the next thirty days. The bad omen, he warned Caesar, came from the entrails of a sacrificed bull earlier that day: the animal had no heart.

Romans took omens seriously. Soothsayers such as Spurinna were well-connected and enjoyed high status. For a civilization whose philosophy, institutions, science, and architecture were based on the principle of reason, Roman belief in oracles and divinations was on the surface paradoxical. Superstition was pervasive in Roman society. Romans also interpreted natural events—comets, thunderbolts, flight patterns of birds—as unfavorable portents. The ancient writer Petronius, in his famous *Satyricon*, gives an account of several Roman superstitions, including tales of werewolves and witches and belief that a rooster's crowing is a bad omen. The Roman satirist Juvenal published scornful commentaries on the attraction of astrologers and fortune-tellers who, he remarked sarcastically, foretold the future in the entrails of frogs. [21] Romans also believed that dreams provided forebodings. In Roman mythology, King Latinus learns in a dream oracle that his daughter Lavinia will not marry a Latin, setting the stage for her marriage to the Trojan hero Aeneas, who will go on to found Rome. In the official Roman religion, augurs and sibylline oracles acted as official priests. It was not uncommon for Roman rulers to consult soothsayers, or *haruspices*, who read omens in the warm entrails of freshly sacrificed animals.

On the morning of the Ides of March, thirty days after the original omen, Caesar had a disquieting dream in which he shook the hand of the god Jupiter. Caesar's wife Calpurnia begged him not to leave the house. She herself had a premonition in a dream the previous night. But Caesar, known to reject superstitions, brushed aside these omens. His business at the Senate was too important.

By coincidence, that morning Caesar came across the soothsayer Spurinna again.

"The Ides of March have come," said Caesar with a smile, dismissing Spurinna's prophecy.

Spurinna replied that the Ides of March had come, but they had not gone.[22]

As a final precaution, Spurinna performed more animal sacrifices and read more entrails. The omens were still bad.

That is the legend. It is gripping ancient crime drama, even though we know how it ends. But did it really happen? There is a strong probability that it was yet another example of Roman historical fiction. The role of the *haruspex,* reading entrails of sacrificed animals and making dark prophecies, was a standard literary device in ancient Rome.

If it did happen, Caesar dismissed Spurinna's final omen. He proceeded to the Senate that afternoon dressed in a purple toga embroidered in gold, unconcerned about a possible attempt on his life.

Some sixty senators were involved in the assassination plot, its leading conspirators Gaius Cassius and Marcus Brutus. Caesar loved Brutus—the child of Cato the Younger's half-sister Servilia—as his own son. But Brutus had turned against Caesar and sided with Pompey during the Civil War. Caesar had forgiven Brutus's betrayal, however, appointing him as governor of the newly conquered Gaul. On the Ides of March, Caesar had no reason to suspect Brutus of treachery.

One final alarm bell sounded just before Caesar entered the Senate house. A man pushed through the crowd and approached Caesar, handing him a scrolled note. The message warned of a plot against his life. Caesar took the note but, since he was running late, did not read it.

Inside the Senate, Caesar mounted his golden throne. A group of senators approached the dais and surrounded him. Caesar sensed that something was not right. The air was fraught with a strangely expectant tension.

One of the conspirators violently grabbed Caesar by the shoulder.

Caesar cried out, "This is violence!"

A dagger came down and stabbed him just below the throat.

Caesar drew his gown over his head and collapsed to the floor. Twenty-three dagger blows rained down on him. It was claimed that Brutus, avenging his uncle Cato's death, plunged the lethal blow into Caesar's chest.

Mortally wounded, Caesar turned to Brutus and, astonished by his betrayal, uttered the famous words, "*Et tu, Brute?*"

It's poignant historical drama, but utterly false. Caesar never said those words. That line comes from Shakespeare's play, *Julius Caesar.* The Roman historian Suetonius, who was much closer to the events, tells us that Caesar "did not utter a sound" after the first blow to his neck (though he adds that some claimed Caesar looked at Brutus and said, "You too, my child?"). The assassins immediately fled from the scene, leaving Julius Caesar on the Senate floor, where he bled to death.

A few days after the assassination, Caesar's body was displayed in the Roman forum before a throng of mourners wailing in a public ritual of grief. On the funeral bier guarded by a phalanx of soldiers, a wax effigy of the murdered dictator concealed the corpse. Caesar's trusted lieutenant, Mark Antony, commanded the podium. Making a gesture toward Caesar's body, Antony launched into a funeral oration filled with indignation.

"Our future, and indeed our present," he declared, "is poised on a knife-edge above great dangers and we risk being dragged back into our previous state of civil war, with the complete extinction of our city's remaining noble families."[23]

Antony turned and stripped the clothes from Caesar's corpse and held them aloft on a pole, waving them back and forth so the amassed crowd could gaze upon the blood-stained garments. The mob let out a groan of agony and fury. The crowd turned violent, rampaging through the streets of Rome to hunt down Caesar's assassins. Soon the Senate house where Caesar had been murdered was in flames.

Shortly after the Ides of March, Romans turned their eyes to the sky with astonishment and wonder. A blazing comet was burning bright. It illuminated the sky for seven days. Romans believed the comet was Caesar's soul soaring to the heavens. He was now a god. The first Roman ruler to be deified, Julius Caesar was transformed from worldly figure of history to mythic character of legend.

2

SHOW ME THE MONEY

Julius Caesar's last will and testament left Romans stunned and perplexed. Since he had no legitimate children under Roman law, most expected his trusted right-hand man Mark Antony to be named as heir.

Mark Antony was a hard-charging, high-testosterone figure known for his volatile temper. He was also a prodigious seducer of women, including Caesar's own mistress, Cleopatra. Antony possessed undoubted leadership abilities. After the assassination, he had the blessing of Caesar's wife, Calpurnia. She bestowed her husband's personal papers on Antony along with custody of his property. He was Caesar's obvious successor.[1]

But Julius Caesar apparently had changed his mind about Mark Antony. Prior to his death, he had redrafted his will before depositing it with the Vestal Virgins. In the revised document, Caesar designated as heir his eighteen-year-old great-nephew, Gaius Octavius. Octavian, as he was later known, was the grandson of Caesar's sister Julia.

Young Octavian had accompanied his famous great-uncle on one military campaign. Beyond that apprenticeship, he was completely unknown in Roman political circles. On the day of Caesar's assassination, Octavian was on the other side of the Adriatic training in the Roman army. He must have been stunned to learn, in the same breath, that Julius Caesar was dead, had adopted him posthumously, and had named him as his sole heir. In a single instant, his life changed forever.[2]

Octavian was clever enough to grasp that Caesar's assassination had laid before him a magnificent destiny. But he faced a terrible dilemma. Should he hide for his own safety, fearing Caesar's assassins? Or should he return to Rome to claim Caesar's throne and avenge his murder?

Cautious and calculating by nature, Octavian consulted those around him, weighing every option. Finally, he decided to return to Rome to

assess the political mood. As Caesar's newly adopted son, his first gesture was to change his name to "Gaius Julius Caesar" in accordance with
custom. It also sent a strong political message. His new name let it be
known that he was Julius Caesar's legitimate heir.

Despite his exalted name, few in Rome took young Octavian seriously. Mark Antony, the man everyone regarded as Caesar's natural heir,
was twenty-two years older and boasted high-ranking experience as a
consul and military commander. When Octavian sought a meeting with
Mark Antony to discuss legal matters concerning his inheritance, Antony
kept putting him off before, after an indecent delay, finally according the
boy a cursory audience in his gardens. The historian Suetonius tells us
that Octavian was enraged by Mark Antony's condescending manner.
Octavian later hired an assassin to murder him.[3] It was a sign that Octavian, despite his youth, was capable of cunning. The murder plot was
discovered, however, forcing Octavian to hire bodyguards for his own
protection. The two men got off to a bad start—and things were about to
get much worse.

The rivalry between Mark Antony and Octavian quickly degenerated
into a full-scale civil war. Mark Antony and Octavian were opposites in
just about everything, except their attachment to Julius Caesar. They
embodied conflicting sides of Rome's collective psyche. Octavian was a
methodic, logical, and rational figure who carefully plotted his moves.
Even his diet was disciplined, limited to bread, cheese, dates, and berries.
Mark Antony, by contrast, was a creature of passions and physical impulses, including the seduction of women. Octavian was the embodiment
of the principle of rational *logos*. Mark Antony was a Dionysian force of
nature who embraced the irrational spirit of *mythos*.

The epic contest opposing Mark Antony and Octavian remains one of
history's great dramas. In its early phase, before the outbreak of full-scale
war, its weapons were gossip, innuendo, and slander in an ugly smear
campaign. Mark Antony and Octavian provided an ancient template for
political dirty tricks that would, when the hostilities ended, produce the
sole ruler of Rome.

Octavian had the upper hand at the outset, at least symbolically. He
could legally call himself Caesar, a name that inspired awe. Antony was
aware of his disadvantage on this score. According to Cicero, he dismissed Octavian as a boy "who owes everything to his name."[4] Antony
could boast a much more impressive curriculum vitae: consul, military
commander, leader of the Caesarian faction in Rome. Octavian had no
political experience. He occupied no public office. He lacked the support
of a political faction. He had no armies at his command. His "Caesar"
name-branding advantage was the only card he could play.

Octavian played it for everything it was worth. When Julius Caesar was deified a few months after his assassination, Octavian began referring to himself as *divi filius*, or "son of the god." It was an exaggerated boast, though legally justifiable. Julius Caesar had been made a god, and Octavian was his adopted son. But Octavian needed more than divine titles to outmaneuver Mark Antony. He was lacking solid experience and credentials. So he organized his own election as consul. He was the youngest man ever to hold that office. More importantly, it suddenly made him Antony's equal in official status.

In the Roman Senate, still stained with Caesar's blood, the hatred between Octavian and Mark Antony was a source of mounting anxiety. Senators had to choose between the two men. Not surprisingly, they preferred the one who was least threatening—and, more to the point, most likely to affirm the powers of the Senate. The choice was easy. The Senate was fearful of Mark Antony, who had no interest in restoring the republic. As Caesar's henchman, he possessed the same autocratic personality as his mentor and had a long record of violence and brutality. Octavian, inexperienced in the cut-throat world of Roman political intrigue, appeared more malleable. He would be useful to remove Antony as a threat to the Senate.

The great orator Cicero, the most powerful figure in the Senate, took up Octavian's cause. A veteran politician at sixty-four, Cicero belonged to the old senatorial class attached to the republican values that reinforced their own powers. Like other senators, he believed Octavian would restore the republic. Mighty with the pen and fearless in public debate, Cicero put his formidable talents to work for Octavian. He also unleashed a torrent of invective against Mark Antony in fourteen published orations known as the *Philippics*. [5]

The bad blood between Cicero and Antony had a long history. When consul, Cicero had ordered the execution of Antony's stepfather, Cornelius Lentulus, as one of the ringleaders in the infamous Cataline conspiracy to overthrow his consulship. In his *Philippics* orations, Cicero dropped vile innuendo about Antony's depravity, homosexual escapades in his youth, and sexual intrigue with a courtesan called Volumnia Cytheris. "You are a drink-sodden, sex-ridden wreck," accused Cicero. "Never a day passes in that ill-reputed house of yours without orgies of the most repulsive kind." [6] Cicero moreover suggested that Antony had married his wife, Fulvia, only for her money. More concretely, he proposed that the Senate declare Antony *hostis publicus*, or public enemy. Given Cicero's prestige and power, the Senate endorsed the motion.

Young Octavian could not have been entirely displeased by Cicero's invectives against his rival. But in an unexpected turn of events in 43 BC, Octavian was pushed into an alliance with Antony to form a ruling triumvirate with a third ally, Marcus Lepidus. According to the truce, Octavian governed Italy and the western provinces in Europe; Mark Antony took the eastern empire including Greece, Turkey, Syria, and Egypt; and Lepidus oversaw North Africa. The triumvirate—in effect, a three-man dictatorship—was a tactical arrangement of convenience that would last a decade. It shifted power from the Senate to the armies controlled by Antony and Octavian. This reversal of fortunes proved fatal for Cicero.[7] When Octavian and Antony made common cause to track down and execute Julius Caesar's assassins, Antony added Cicero's name to the proscribed hit list.

Fearing for his life, Cicero retreated to his country residence in Formia, halfway between Rome and Naples. His seaside villa, called "Formianum," boasted frescoes, mosaics, fish ponds, and a marble nymphaeum. Once on the coast, he attempted to escape by boat to Macedonia, but was forced to turn back due to a storm at sea. According to accounts by ancient historians, the following morning Cicero was roused from his sleep by the squawking of crows that had flown into his bedroom (a classic literary device deployed to evoke the importance of omens). The same day, he attempted to join the sea again, carried on a litter by his attendants. This time, Antony's men intercepted him. Cicero knew his hour had come. Defiant in death, he looked steadfastly at his slayers as they fell upon him with their swords. What happened next was gut-wrenching. Following Mark Antony's strict instructions, the assassins hacked off Cicero's head with three blows, sawing through the neck and ripping the skull from the torso. They also chopped off Cicero's right hand—the one he'd used to write the defamatory *Philippics*. The assassins fled the scene clutching Cicero's blood-dripping body parts, leaving his mutilated corpse at the edge of the road, where his attendants looked on in horror.[8]

When Cicero's body parts arrived in Rome, Antony received the gruesome trophies with elation. But he was not content knowing Cicero was dead; he wanted to exact revenge on the murdered senator's corpse. According to historian Cassius Dio, Antony placed Cicero's head on his table at meals so he could stare at it with contempt. Sometimes he screamed black rage at the head. Even more gruesome, Antony's wife Fulvia, a powerful figure in her own right, spat in Cicero's cadaverous face. She put the head on her lap and, opening the mouth, repeatedly pierced the tongue with a hairpin—morbid revenge for his malicious speeches against her husband. Cicero's head and hand were later displayed publicly on the rostra in the Forum. The historian Plutarch tells us that Romans shuddered at the sight of the great statesman's decapitated head. It was a grisly warning that speaking truth to power was no longer tolerated. Roman democracy was over.[9]

Though officially political partners in the triumvirate, the rivalry between Octavian and Antony continued. The mutual distrust, at this phase, was largely a combat of egos. One battlefield in which they attempted to outmaneuver each other was most unexpected: coins in Romans' pockets.

Coinage was a powerful propaganda tool in ancient Rome. Coins functioned as "monuments in miniature" inscribed with the profiles of great personages and events of the Roman political drama. For Romans, coins were not only a currency but also a communications medium with the stamp of their collective identity and memory. The words *money* and *monetary* come from the Latin *moneta*, whose origin is the Greek word for the goddess of memory, Mnemosyne.[10] The Temple of Juno Moneta was the place on Rome's Capitoline Hill where coins were minted. For Roman rulers, minting coins was a way of shaping the message. Inscriptions and portraitures on coins were used as political spin. Consuls put their profiles on denarius coins to enhance their visibility and reinforce their legitimacy. Coins were a powerful form of political advertising. The profile on the face of a denarius told you who was in power. Both Octavian and Antony grasped the symbolic importance of coins for winning the show-me-the-money propaganda war.[11]

Only a year after Caesar's assassination, Antony minted coins featuring his strong-chinned profile with the inscription "M Antonius IMP," signifying *imperator* (or "leader of the army"). He also minted coins with a portraiture emphasizing his religious status as a priest in the clemency cult of Julius Caesar. For Antony, the implied connection to Caesar as a member of the priestly college of *luperci Iulii* would have underscored his putative status as Caesar's heir.

Octavian, lagging in coinage bragging rights, quickly caught up. Like Antony, Octavian exploited coin inscriptions to underscore his personal connection to the deified Julius Caesar. One denarius featured Octavian's comparatively boyish profile with the inscription "Caesar III VIR RPC," boasting his adopted name and an abbreviation for *Triumvir Republicæ Constituendæ* (his Triumvirate credentials). In 43 BC, Octavian struck coins with double portraits showing himself with Julius Caesar and their religious offices inscribed. His coins were inscribed "Caesar IMP PONT III VIR RPC," combining *imperator* and pontifex maximus (head of Rome's state religion), a title inherited from Julius Caesar. It was a rare privilege to boast such an exalted rank (Catholic popes today still claim the title pontifex maximus). Octavian also pulled out his divine trump card with coins showing his portrait and the inscription "CAESAR DIVI F"—*Caesar divi filius* ("son of the god"). Outmaneuvered, Antony had no choice but to counter-program his coinage, emphasizing his down-to-earth republican credentials with the inscription "COS" for consul. It was a sly wink to the Senate, which he knew would look askance at Octavian's quasi-divine pretensions.

After the triumvirate eventually dissolved in 33 BC, more than a decade after Julius Caesar's assassination. Octavian was now an experienced political operator and battle-hardened commander of armies. As his rivalry with Mark Antony grew increasingly poisonous, Octavian also proved to be astute in the black arts of political defamation. He circulated letters and pamphlets filled with insinuations that tarnished Antony's reputation. Some alluded to Antony's debauched youth; others appealed to Roman suspicion of foreigners by portraying Antony as a besotted lover of his Egyptian mistress Cleopatra. Octavian must have taken great satisfaction in the effect produced by his campaign of calumny. Antony had wed Octavian's sister, called Octavia, as a diplomatic gesture to forge peace during the shaky triumvirate. The marriage had been a political expediency, not a love match. Antony carried on his torrid affair with Cleopatra while married to Octavia. Octavian knew this. The innuendo impugning Antony's character was revenge served cold.

Antony struck back with his own epistolary smear campaign aimed at Octavian. He could find no fault in his opponent's character. Octavian carefully projected a public image of great simplicity in his tastes and manners—disciplined diet, modest clothing, unpretentious furnishings, conservative morals. Antony found his rival's Achilles' heel in Octavian's social origins. Antony's letters referred to Octavian's paternal grandfather as a crass money-changer and mentioned that his great-grandfather ran a perfume shop. In ancient Rome, where the Senate was dominated by old aristocratic families, this sort of snobbery resonated in a culture that placed high value on social rank. Antony also put it about that Octavian had ingratiated himself with Julius Caesar through sexual favors. Rome was an aggressively masculine culture, and accusations of homosexuality were an often-used weapon in the arsenal of Roman political mudslinging.[12] Julius Caesar himself had been dogged by rumors that he had gay lovers in his youth. Cicero had even accused Antony, an ardent seducer of women, of homosexual liaisons. Now Antony was suggesting that Octavian had won Julius Caesar's paternal affections through lecherous relations. It was an extraordinary accusation given that Antony had been Caesar's most loyal lieutenant, and moreover the murdered dictator was now revered as a god.

It is difficult to assess the veracity of these defamatory claims. Antony's vile rumor about Octavian and Caesar was almost certainly false. Most of these libels were, at best, exaggerated half-truths or odious fabrications. But in ancient Rome, mendacious attacks on a political rival's character were a standard tactic. Octavian and Antony were engaged in a battle for power, and appealing to Roman public opinion was critical for victory. Lies were accepted weapons in their propaganda war.

In 32 BC, a year after the dissolution of the triumvirate, Octavian got his hands on a deadly weapon. After learning that Antony's last will and testament was being kept in the temple of the Vestal Virgins, he committed sacrilege by trespassing on the religious sanctuary to seize the document. What he discovered must have startled and delighted him. In his will, Antony had named his children with Cleopatra as his heirs, gifting them large territories in the Mediterranean. The document, moreover, stipulated that Antony was to be buried not in Rome, but in Alexandria. The most alarming clause was Antony's wish to posthumously adopt the boy Caesarion, born from Cleopatra's affair with Julius Caesar. This presented the prospect of Rome one day being ruled by the offspring of an Egyptian queen.

Antony had already broken politically with Rome in 34 BC after his military victory in Armenia. At a Roman-style triumphal procession in Alexandria, now called the "New Rome," a troop of Roman soldiers held shields emblazoned with the letter "C" for Cleopatra. Antony was joined in the procession by the thirteen-year-old Caesarion, officially recognized as his father Julius Caesar's legitimate heir. At a lavish banquet where Antony and Cleopatra were installed on golden thrones, Caesarion was declared "King of Kings." Titled Ptolemy XV Caesar, he would now co-rule over Egypt with his mother Cleopatra. While Antony legally ruled over Rome's eastern empire, his extravagant celebrations in client state Egypt had been an unacceptable affront to the sensibilities of many Romans. The contents of his will—even though the authenticity of the document was questionable—was the final nail in his coffin. It was just what Octavian needed to convince Romans that Antony had lost the habits of Rome. [13]

Octavian went straight to the Senate and, surrounded by armed guards, read the document aloud. He also ensured that the details of Antony's will were spread throughout the Roman world. This set in motion a furious rumor mill. It was murmured everywhere that Mark Antony, enslaved by his passion for Cleopatra (a *peregrina*, or non-Roman), had disavowed Rome. There was innuendo about the two lovers leading lives of shocking decadence in Egypt. Romans heard stories about Antony and Cleopatra posing together for paintings and statues. At the victory banquet where the boy Caesarion had been declared "King of Kings," Antony was dressed as the Greek-Egyptian god Dionysus-Osiris, and Cleopatra as the goddess Aphrodite-Isis. This mental image would have been profoundly offensive to Romans. [14] Octavian's malicious rumor campaign was a nasty stitch-up, but it worked. The divulgation of Antony's will turned Roman public opinion against him. The Senate voted to strip Antony of his consulship and declared war on Cleopatra. The final phase of the Roman civil wars was now on.

In the end, Octavian defeated Antony not with vile slander or glorified coinage, but with military force. In 31 BC, his warships destroyed Antony's fleet in the historic Battle of Actium off the Ionian coast in Greece. Antony fled with Cleopatra back to Egypt to play out the final act in the drama that would become the stuff of legend. Antony stabbed himself and expired in Cleopatra's arms. She famously committed suicide by holding a poisonous asp to her breast. In his final gesture, Antony was true to his Dionysian passions, a creature of *mythos*, the flawed hero of a tragedy whose poignant end would resonate throughout history.

Octavian, true to his own nature, arrived on the scene in Egypt to look upon Antony's corpse with his own eyes. Cleopatra's death displeased him, not because he wished to show her mercy, but because he was hoping to drag her alive through the streets of Rome as a victory trophy in a triumphal procession. Her suicide deprived him of that glory. There was one last grisly piece of unfinished business. Octavian ordered his soldiers to capture the boy Caesarion, the offspring of Julius Caesar and Cleopatra. Caesarion was then sixteen. The boy was Caesar's only biological son, declared "King of Kings." Octavian could take no chances. He had the boy tracked down and put to death. Octavian owed Julius Caesar everything. No matter, he had Caesar's only son murdered to remove him as a potential rival.

Rome now swore allegiance to Octavian. He had finally consolidated power in his own hands as the sole ruler of Rome, whose territories stretched from Syria to Spain. His victory had been the triumph of cold calculation over unruly passion.

***

Following the double suicide of Mark Antony and Cleopatra, Octavian treated himself to a magnificent triumphal procession through Rome.

Dressed in purple robes with his face painted red, Octavian rode aloft a chariot proceeding through the eternal city's Via Sacra. Among his human trophies were the teenage twins of Antony and Cleopatra, prince Alexander Helios and princess Cleopatra Selene, both paraded in golden chains. The boy had been jointly named for Alexander the Great and the Greek sun god Helios; Selene was the Greek goddess of the moon—thus the twins were named for the sun and moon.[15] In the procession, they were accompanied by an effigy of the deceased Cleopatra herself, along with a painted portrait of the Egyptian queen holding a snake to her breast. Several other kings and princes of conquered territories were similarly dragged through the streets, some of them ritually murdered later

(Cleopatra's twins were spared execution). The celebrations ended with public games and entertainments for the masses—gladiatorial contests, horse races, and a political spectacle where hunters slaughtered exotic beasts including a rhino and hippopotamus. Octavian lavished 100 denarii on every adult male citizen and gave 1,000 sesterces each to the 120,000 soldiers in Rome's provinces. Loyalty was thus secured with entertainments and largesse. Octavian's triumphal procession was spectacle on a grand scale.

The Senate, too, had to be placated. Knowing that senators were hostile to kings and dictators, Octavian made a great display of refusing exalted titles. He humbly insisted that his only ambition was to restore the republic. He even declared that he intended to retreat from public life, a promise that must have seemed implausible given that he was only thirty-four. But Octavian's blandishments worked. He played the Senate so skillfully that senators agreed to their own political emasculation. When the Senate insisted that he remain as head of state, Octavian graciously accepted. After some back and forth on the question of his title, he finally agreed to accept *princeps Senatus*, or "leader of the Senate." He also took a new name: Augustus ("the illustrious one").

Octavian's transformation from consummate manipulator to the enlightened emperor, Augustus, remains one of the history's great enigmas. He was, by nature, a young man in full command of his temperament, notoriously cautious and calculating. But he had other formidable qualities. Like his adopted father Julius Caesar, he proved to be a master at self-promotion and storytelling. Augustus had a clear and determined idea about truth and lies, especially how they could be manipulated to serve his own purposes. From the very outset of Octavian's long rule as Augustus, he carefully constructed his own cult of personality in a tightly controlled regime of censorship. It was this aspect of his personal rule that marked a definitive rupture with the free-for-all Roman republic. In imperial Rome, truth was tightly controlled propaganda.

Augustus quickly grasped that Roman religion could be manipulated as an instrument of social control. He integrated traditional deities into the cult of the imperial regime—in effect, merging state and religion. Augustus's inherited title of Pontifex Maximus came in handy for his new role as head of Rome's official state religion. It served a double purpose. First, it legitimized his imperial dynasty through direct lineage to the gods. Second, it created a cult of personality around Roman emperors—starting, of course, with Augustus himself. Augustus thus concentrated both civic and religious powers in his own hands. He also used his authority to regulate Roman social customs right down to dress codes, which henceforth had to conform strictly with religious principles.

Official propaganda under Augustus also marked a shift from rhetoric and writing toward visual representations in icons and idols. Under the Roman republic, oratory and writing had been the political lifeblood. Truths and falsehoods battled in the public forum. Augustus had experienced firsthand how open conflict of ideas and egos pushed Rome into civil war. He had been an active belligerent in those battles. As emperor, however, he was the embodiment of a Pax Romana. His primary mission was order, stability, and peace. Augustus therefore launched a propaganda campaign through media—coins, statues, temples, monuments—that was durable and, above all, controllable. Imperial propaganda would be visible to all—especially images of Augustus himself. He fashioned a cult of personality around his own iconography throughout the Roman world: on coins, in life-size marble statues displayed in public squares, even on embossed portraits, rings, and silverware. [16]

Augustus's cult of personality was the first time a Roman ruler disseminated his own image on a massive scale. Few statues of Roman kings and statesmen pre-dating Augustus—including Julius Caesar—have been unearthed by archaeologists. Yet roughly 250 statues of Augustus have been discovered throughout the Roman Empire from modern-day Turkey to Spain. Statues of Augustus were aesthetically stylized in the Greek tradition, portraying him in one of four personae: statesman, military commander, high priest, and god. He covered all the bases. The most famous statue was the white marble "Prime Porta" representing Augustus as god-like military commander. An extraordinary piece of propaganda, the Prima Porta statue is an idealized portrait of deified Augustus. It shows the young Augustus, his hair cropped short, his expression solemn, wearing a cuirass breastplate emblazoned with figures representing the emperor's great military achievements. Augustus's right hand is raised in an *adlocutio* rhetorical pose, addressing his troops, a cherubic Cupid at his feet to underscore the emperor's connection to the goddess Venus. [17]

Visual propaganda under Augustus broke with the artistic practice under the Roman republic of depicting rulers realistically. This explains why Augustus remained forever young in his iconography. Over the four decades of his imperial rule, he never aged in portraits and statues. All represented him as a youthful emperor, perfectly conserved, god-like, in a timeless pose. For this reason, it's difficult to know how Augustus looked in real life, though he was described as somewhat short (he wore high heels to compensate) with disheveled sandy hair and bad teeth. [18] In his iconography, however, he was the physical embodiment of divine perfection. Augustus regarded icons and idols of his own image not as works of art, but as expressions of official Roman ideology.

There were no more coinage wars with political rivals, but Augustus continued to use coins for propaganda purposes. Silver coins showed his profile on the obverse side and, on the reverse, featured a crocodile image with the words "AEGYPTO CAPTA" ("captured Egypt"). This denarius signaled that Augustus was now ruler of Cleopatra's kingdom. Other coins featured the apotheosis *Sidus Iulium* star, evoking the emperor's connection to the deified Julius Caesar. Images of the Temple of the Divine Julius were engraved on coins with the inscription "CAESAR DIVI F" ("son of the god") next to Augustus's profile. On other coins, Romans saw a full portrait of Augustus as warrior with his foot on the conquered globe, holding a lance in one hand and the stern of an enemy ship in the other. Some coins featured Augustus in *adlocutio* posture, arm raised, with the goddess Pax (for peace) on the reverse side. After the pacification of Parthia in modern-day Iraq and Iran, he issued new coins celebrating the event, which also inspired his Prima Porta statue. Augustus was portrayed on coins as a supreme ruler who had conquered enemies and brought peace to the Roman world. The letters "S. C." etched on his coins signified *Senatus Consulto*—by decree of the Senate. This revealed that Augustus was still careful to create the impression that he was restoring the republic.

Augustus was also an ambitious builder of temples, altars, triumphal arches, monuments, and buildings. During the Roman republic, the capital had been badly designed, and much of the city was dilapidated. The Greeks openly ridiculed Rome's ugliness. Augustus rebuilt Rome into a grand imperial capital. As he famously remarked, "I found Rome made of brick and left it a city of marble." This legend comes to us from Suetonius, who observes, "Since the city was not adorned as the dignity of the empire demanded, and was exposed to flood and fire, he so beautified it that he could justly boast that he had found it built of brick and left it in marble."[19] Augustus's architectural achievements were indeed considerable, including the Forum Augustum with its enormous statue of Mars Ultor, the avenging god of war. Rome's triumphal arches, Coliseum, Pantheon, and other great monuments date to the Augustan period and first century AD immediately following his reign.

Augustus's attitude toward freedom of speech was less enlightened, more in keeping with his cautious and controlling personality. He did not brutally repress Rome's flourishing culture of rhetoric and oratory. His regime of censorship was imposed gradually, slowly suffocating free speech. Some specific measures were taken to shut down public debate. The publication of senatorial proceedings in the daily *acta*—instituted by Julius Caesar—was discontinued. Under Augustus, politics quietly retreated from the public forum into the corridors of his imperial palaces. Almost imperceptibly, Rome was transformed from republican democracy to imperial autocracy.

Roman literature continued to flourish in the Augustan age, but often served the emperor's propaganda goals. The emperor was a highly literate man who genuinely appreciated the company of literary figures. He even wrote his own autobiography (unfortunately, it has not survived) and a play based on the Trojan hero Ajax. Augustus nonetheless regarded literature as an extension of Roman ideology. This left no place in Rome's literary culture for satire. Writers became court flatterers seeking favor at court. Augustus spent a great deal of time inquiring about possible literary commissions, usually through his influential advisor Gaius Maecenas, a wealthy patron of the arts who sponsored poets including Horace and Virgil. Sometimes Augustus wrote directly to famous authors to encourage them to glorify his name. Exasperated that the poet Horace was not mentioning him directly in his poems, Augustus chided him in a letter: "Are you afraid that your reputation with posterity will suffer because it appears that you were my friend?"[20]

The emperor scored a major coup when he convinced Virgil to write an epic paean to the glory of the Augustan age. The result was *The Aeneid,* which ranks among the greatest literary masterpieces of the ancient world, along with Homer's *Iliad* and *Odyssey.* The poem follows the Trojan warrior Aeneas who, after the Fall of Troy, undertakes a long journey to Italy, where he eventually becomes the mythic founder of Rome. Virgil's epic, drawing a close parallel between Aeneas and Augustus, provided Rome with its own epic of imperial grandeur.[21]

This was Augustus in *mythos* propaganda mode. The choice of Aeneas fit perfectly into his own family mythology. His adopted father, Julius Caesar, claimed direct lineage to the famous Trojan hero. *The Aeneid* became an instant classic after its publication, read by all learned Romans, even schoolchildren. Virgil enjoyed extraordinary fame during his lifetime thanks to his celebrated epic. The historian Tacitus tells us that, when Virgil showed up at public readings of *The Aeneid*, audiences rose to their feet and cheered him "as if he were Augustus himself." Augustus makes an appearance in the epic poem during the scene celebrating his victory over Mark Antony at the Battle of Actium. Virgil certainly knew his subject. He was an intimate friend of Augustus, gave him personal recitations of his work, and accompanied the emperor on trips. When Virgil died in 19 BC, he named Augustus as his heir.

The status of Roman historians under Augustus was similar to that of poets. They were essentially courtiers writing authorized works that glorified Rome. The greatest historian of the era was Titus Livy, whose history of Rome remains a masterpiece today. Like Virgil, he was a close friend of the emperor. He was also tutor to members of the imperial family. Livy's *Ad Urbe Condita Libri* (*Books from the Foundation of the City*) was the prose equivalent of Virgil's poetic epic. It traced the entire history of Rome from its origins to the Augustan era. Like Virgil, Livy enjoyed tremendous acclaim in his own lifetime. It paid to be close to the emperor. Later Roman historians such as Tacitus, who himself was well-connected at court, criticized his forerunners as the emperor's PR agents. Tacitus observed that, under Augustus, writers were sycophants. "After the battle of Actium, when the interests of peace required that all power should be concentrated in the hands of one man," noted Tactitus, "writers of like ability disappeared; and at the same time historical truth was impaired in many ways: first, because men were ignorant of politics as being not any concern of theirs; later, because of their passionate desire to flatter."[22]

While Augustus enjoyed the company of writers, he was quick to punish any scribe who displeased him. The poet Ovid, famous for his *Metamorphoses*, learned this the hard way. In the year 7 AD, Augustus was an old man near the end of his reign, plagued by a scandal over his promiscuous granddaughter Julia. The emperor kept mistresses, including much younger girls, but was hypocritically severe with women in his own family. Discovering that Julia, who was married, was pregnant with a lover's child, Augustus had the suitor exiled. When his granddaughter gave birth to the child a few months later, Augustus ordered that it be killed by exposure. For reasons that remain unclear, the poet Ovid somehow got dragged into this scandal. Some believe Augustus had been offended by Ovid's parody *Ars Amatoria* (*The Art of Love*), which gave advice on sexual seduction. Whatever the reason, Ovid's works were expunged from the imperial libraries, and the poet was sent into exile on the Black Sea. We may never discover why Ovid was exiled, but we know that he endured it as torture inflicted on his soul. Languishing in exile in modern-day Romania, he wrote a long poem titled *Tristia* (*Sorrows*) begging the emperor for forgiveness. Augustus was deaf to his entreaties. Ovid never saw Rome again.

Literary censorship in the Augustan age had a darker side: Augustus institutionalized book burnings. The burning of books was in practice during the Roman republic, but accelerated under the empire. Book burning was a quasi-religious ritual. Occult and divinatory books from foreign religions were often targeted. The historian Suetonius tells us that Augustus, in his role as Pontifex Maximus, had some two thousand books of prophecy in Greek and Latin collected and burnt.[23] No books, especially foreign ones, could compete with Rome's official state religion. Augustus also ordered the burning of incendiary pamphlets, lampoons, and satires that he considered defamatory. Their authors were punished. This created a pervasive atmosphere of paranoia in Roman literary circles, where snitches (*delatores*) turned in authors whose works gave offense.

The historian Titus Labienus, a republican whose works castigated the imperial regime, was found guilty of literary treason. On orders of the Senate, his works were incinerated. In an act of defiance, Labienus locked himself in his family crypt and committed suicide by starvation—a Roman martyr to the cause of freedom of speech. The Roman orator Cassius Severus defiantly declared: "If they really want to destroy the works of Labienus, they must burn me alive. For I have learned them by heart!" Augustus was unmoved. The works of Cassius Severus were, like those of Titus Labienus, turned to cinders. Augustus even ordered the destruction of Julius Caesar's early literary works, a collection of poems and a play. Caesar's youthful literary efforts presumably didn't fit into the official imperial narrative. This regime of censorship was a far cry from the culture of rhetoric, oratory, satire, and public sparring during the Roman republic.

The book burnings didn't end with Augustus. They became established practice in imperial Rome following his reign. His successors, Tiberius and Nero, ordered many book burnings, as did later emperors, including Domitian and Diocletian. The motive for burning books was sometimes spurious, but usually the offense was libel or literary treason. Despite the great burst of literature in the first century AD—Petronius, Juvenal, Martial, Pliny, Tacitus, Seneca, and many others published during this period—authors lived under constant threat of censorship, exile, and worse. Suetonius describes the climate of paranoia in his portrait of Augustus's successor, Tiberius: "Every crime was treated as a capital offence, even when it was just a matter of a few simple words. . . . Authors were attacked and books banned, even though some years previously they had been well received by audiences which had included the emperor Augustus."[24] Under Tiberius, the poet and senator Mamercus Scaurus was charged with literary treason for a single line in his play *Atreus*, in which a man is advised to "bear the follies of the reigning prince with patience." To avoid disgrace, Scaurus committed suicide.

During Augustus's long rule, one literary work that never feared censorship was written by the emperor himself. Unfortunately for history, his autobiography met another fate. It never survived. We know that Augustus wrote his memoirs, probably around 25 BC, through fragments and contemporary references. But no copy of the work has ever been found. Historians believe the book was largely apologetic, which isn't surprising given Augustus's cautious, controlling nature.

We do, fortunately, have a copy of Augustus's final great work, *Res Gestae Divi Augusti*, written in his declining years. Unlike his memoirs, the *Res Gestae* survived because it was inscribed on durable material. The text was etched on two bronze pillars buttressing the entrance of Augustus's tomb. They both vanished, possibly melted down in the Middle

Ages, but we have the complete text thanks to discoveries of versions inscribed on stone throughout the empire. The most famous one was found near modern-day Ankara, chiseled on the stone wall of a temple in honor of Augustus.

The *Res Gestae*—which means "things done"—was an account of what Augustus accomplished in his long and illustrious life. The full title, *Res Gestae Divi Augusti*, is usually translated as *The Deeds of Divine Augustus*, underscoring that the emperor was a god. Augustus chose the first-person perspective—"I restored liberty to the republic"—for his narrative, eschewing the distant third-person employed by Julius Caesar. As memoirs go, the *Res Gestae* is not a thrilling read. Augustus lacked Julius Caesar's flare for narrative. Augustus, moreover, was not interested in truth. The *Res Gestae* revealed the conservative side of an elderly emperor who, as he looked back on his long rule, saw only virtue. It reads like a boastful catalog of personal achievements—his glorious military victories, his generous benefactions, his great architectural projects. The classical scholar Mary Beard has described it as a "self-serving, partisan and often rose-tinted piece of work, which carefully glosses or entirely ignores the murderous illegalities of his early career. . . . It is a unique account, in roughly ten pages of modern text, of what the old reptile wanted posterity to know about his many years as *princeps*."[25] Augustus, it might be said, was the ancient initiator of the unapologetically self-justifying, and excruciatingly dull, political memoir.

In the year 14 AD, when Jesus was a teenager in the Roman province of Judea, the emperor Augustus died of natural causes at seventy-five. He had ruled Rome for more than four decades. His last words, citing a Greek play, were: "If I have played my part well, then give me applause."

Augustus died a paradox. He was, by any measure, the greatest of all Roman emperors. Yet he was the emperor who extinguished the flame of liberty to impose an autocratic regime of official propaganda, censorship, and cult of personality. For Augustus, there was only one truth—imperial Roman ideology.

Perhaps that is why Augustus remains such an enigma. He lived and died true to his own symbol, the sphinx. For the vast Roman Empire left to his heirs, the troubles were about to begin.

3

THE NERO UNREALITY SHOW

Nero is the most infamous of all Roman emperors. He was accused in his own lifetime of monstrous crimes. His name is still synonymous with shocking depravity. Nero was the worst of all tyrants.

There is almost nothing that redeems Nero's reputation. He murdered his own mother. He kicked his pregnant wife to death. He persecuted Christians, watching them tortured before ordering their dead bodies to be fed to ravenous dogs. He fiddled while Rome was destroyed by flames. In the end, his troubled reign brought the final curtain down on the dynasty founded by Julius Caesar.[1]

But who was the real Nero? Was he really the depraved tyrant who has come down to us in the annals of history?

Nero was a complex personality whose reign is still largely misunderstood. His portrait has been disfigured by so many legends and myths that it's almost impossible to separate fact from fiction. We cannot be indifferent to Nero's legacy if only because he was, in many respects, a thoroughly modern figure. The ancient historian Suetonius tells us that Nero was driven by a longing for immortality and undying fame.[2] Nero regarded everything as performance and was addicted to public acclaim. He was the exalted star of his own imperial drama. His tragedy is a cautionary tale for our own age.

Nero was the only child of Agrippina Minor, the great-granddaughter of emperor Augustus. A formidable force in her own right, Agrippina was the most powerful woman in the Julio-Claudian dynasty. She was the daughter of the great Roman general Germanicus, who had been heir to the imperial throne until his tragic death at age thirty-three. Agrippina's brother was the emperor Caligula, who was assassinated at age twenty-eight. Through his mother, Nero was a direct descendant of one emperor, Augustus, and nephew of another, Caligula.[3]

Agrippina was determined to put her only son on the throne. Her ambitions for him made Nero, from early childhood, a pawn in his mother's sinister schemes to position him at the top of the imperial pecking order. Succession in the Julio-Claudian dynasty was based on a practice of "adopted" heirs from a wide family circle. In some respects, this system was sound. It avoided the pitfalls of direct genetic inheritance producing unfit emperors. Julius Caesar had adopted his successor Augustus. Augustus had, in like manner, designated his stepson Tiberius as his heir. In other respects, however, the system was dysfunctional. It created a climate of constant rivalry for succession in a permanent atmosphere of suspicion and betrayal. Potential heirs lived in fear of being bumped off to make way for a more conniving aspirant to the throne.

In 41 AD, Nero was a small child of barely four when his uncle, Caligula, was murdered. Caligula was succeeded by Claudius, younger brother of the late general Germanicus. Nero grew up at Claudius's court watching his mother hatch plots and manipulate events to position him as next in the line of succession.[4] Agrippina got closer to achieving this ambition by seducing Claudius into marriage, despite the inconvenient fact that she was his niece. Agrippina later arranged the marriage of young Nero to Claudius's daughter from a previous marriage, Octavia. This double incestuous configuration—Agrippina betrothing her uncle, Nero marrying his stepsister—secured Nero's position as imperial successor. Agrippina had been careful to consult Chaldaean astrologers to know her son's destiny. Like an oracle in a Greek tragedy, the astrologers had prophesied that Nero would rule as emperor, but that he would also kill his own mother. According to Tacitus, Agrippina was unflustered. She replied: "Let him kill me, provided he becomes emperor!"[5]

In 54 AD, the emperor Claudius suddenly died of a violent fever. Agrippina was suspected of murdering her husband with a dish of poisonous mushrooms. The timing of the emperor's death was certainly suspicious. Claudius's own son, thirteen-year-old Britannicus, was too young to be proclaimed emperor. That made Nero, the late emperor's seventeen-year-old stepson who was already wearing a *toga virilis* to mark his manhood, the obvious successor. Nero was thus proclaimed Roman emperor on the same day of Claudius's death. The boy Britannicus would soon be poisoned, like his father, to remove him as a potential rival to Nero.

Nero ascended to the throne on a wave of popular acclaim. It wasn't difficult to be popular following the turpitudes of his predecessors. Tiberius, who had been emperor when Jesus Christ was crucified, gloomily withdrew into a life of reclusive depravities at his villa on the island of

Capri. Caligula was a sadistic tyrant who was said to have appointed his favorite horse Incitatus as consul (that legend was almost certainly false). Claudius, the first Roman emperor to set foot on British soil, was an unlikely ruler who suffered from partial deafness, stammered speech, and physical deformity. He spent much of his reign dodging assassination attempts and executing suspected plotters—until his fatal meal of mushrooms. When Nero ascended to the throne, Romans were ready for a change.

At the beginning of his reign, Nero appeared to take his duties seriously. He scrupulously followed the advice of two key advisers: the philosopher Seneca and Sextus Burrus, a prefect of the Praetorian Guard who was hand-picked by Nero's mother. The young emperor declared to the Senate that his model was his glorious ancestor Augustus. It was the right thing to say following a succession of emperors whose attitude toward the Senate had been hostility and contempt. Seneca, who belonged the stoical school of philosophy, impressed upon young Nero the need to embody the virtue of clemency (*clementia*) because it would bring glory. The historian Suetonius, who normally never missed an opportunity to defame Nero, tells us that, when a warrant for the execution of a condemned man was presented for the emperor's signature, Nero said: "How I wish I had never learned to write!"[6] His foreign policy also appeared judicious. In the aftermath of the Roman repression of Boudicca's revolt in Britain, Nero recalled the governor on the island as punishment for his abusive treatment of the local Britons. Under Seneca's tutelage, Nero appeared to embrace the virtues of reason.[7]

Nero made one big mistake, however. He left important affairs of state to his domineering mother. Having succeeded in putting her teenage son on the throne, Agrippina had no intention of fading into the background. She saw her role as regent. That must have been obvious to Romans when they looked at the profiles stamped on Roman coins. In the early years of Nero's reign, the emperor and his mother appeared together on coinage. Agrippina's inscription was: AGRIPP AVG DIVI CLAVD NERONIS CAES MATER EX SC ("Agrippina, wife of the divine Claudius, mother of Nero Caesar, by decree of the Senate"). Nero's profile made him appear thin and boyish with long hair at the back. By most accounts, he was not physically prepossessing: average height with blond curly hair, deep-set blue eyes, a thick neck, protuberant stomach, and spindly legs. On later coins, Nero's profile showed his stocky neck, puffy face, and double chin.[8] Sharing top billing on coins with his mother created the impression that they were co-rulers.

Not surprisingly, Nero and his mother quarreled constantly. The worst feuds were over Nero's sexual escapades. Agrippina strongly opposed her son's wish to divorce Octavia after he'd fallen in love with an ex-slave girl called Acte. A divorce with Octavia was out of the question. She was the daughter of the late emperor Claudius, now deified. Nero obeyed his mother's command, but soon he was infatuated with an older woman called Poppaea Sabina. The glamorous daughter of a wealthy provincial governor, Poppaea was described as beautiful, flirtatious, manipulative, and fond of taking baths in donkey's milk to prevent wrinkles. She was also married to a praetorian prefect. To push Poppaea's cuckolded husband out of the picture, Nero appointed him governor of Lusitania (in modern-day Spain and Portugal). It was said that Nero was attracted to Poppaea because she resembled his mother.[9] His obsession with an older, married mistress did little to improve relations with Agrippina.

In the short term, Nero avoided his mother's meddling by escaping into distractions, especially sports competitions and musical performances. He competed in four-horse chariot races and trained to become a lyre player and singer. Though Nero's voice was described as weak and husky, he was passionate about music and devoted countless hours to singing exercises, lying flat on his back with a leaden plate on his chest while strengthening his vocal chords. He also restricted his diet to dried figs, chives preserved in oil, leeks, and garlic in the belief that they would strengthen his voice. He also purged himself with vomiting and refrained from loud speaking, eventually giving up public speeches to preserve his voice. After rigorous training and growing confidence, Nero started participating in public singing competitions.[10] Ordinary Romans were astonished to see the emperor in the flesh on stage. Ironically, Nero was invariably nervous in front of audiences and scrupulously followed competition rules. He also appeared genuinely surprised when, unfailingly, he took top prize every time to cheers and applause. Whenever Nero was in a competition, the jury declared the same verdict: "Nero Caesar wins this contest and crowns the Roman people and his world empire."

Nero's growing obsession with performing in public was not only eccentric but also inappropriate for a man of his exalted station. But Nero's craving for attention and applause was unstoppable. He soon initiated his own festival—called the "Neronia"—that featured Greek-style gymnastics, chariot-racing, and musical performances. He personally performed at these events. The nobles in the Roman Senate were so appalled by the emperor's conduct that they attempted to dissuade him from these public displays by offering him the top prizes before the games took place. Nero rejected the Senate's offering, insisting that his talents should be judged fairly. He had a particularly strong passion for singing arias and playing roles in Greek tragedies, including *Orestes* and *Antigone*. Intoxicated by his own celebrity, he soon changed his coiffure to rows of curls flattened on his forehead, modeled on Greek actors and charioteers—a style that later became known as "Neronian."

While Nero was sincerely devoted to the stage, it appears he was not a particularly gifted singer. He also could be thin-skinned and fretted about being upstaged. Suetonius tells us that Nero "was obsessed by a desire for popularity and was the rival of anyone who, in any way, stirred the feelings of the mob."[11] Nero had a famous feud with his friend Lucan, author of the epic poem *Pharsalia*. When Lucan won a prize for extemporizing *Orpheus* at a Neronia festival, Nero was so jealous that he banned him from seeking publicity for his work. This suggests that Nero's exhibitionism was driven by deep insecurity. Escaping his mother Agrippina's domination, he sought refuge in the approval of audiences.

Nero became so addicted to applause that he hired his own retinue of professional clappers, called "Augustiani." At his performances, their clapping emulated a rhythmic style of applause that combined flat-palm and cupped-palm with voice trilling. It's said Nero had as many as five thousand clappers in amphitheaters during his performances, all paid handsomely for their extravagant enthusiasm. The ambiance must have been strangely tense. Nero's guards were posted everywhere, inspecting the audience for their reactions, nudging them to cheer the emperor. No one could leave the theater under any pretext while Nero was performing. Suetonius tells us with his usual flare for gossip that, on some occasions, members of the audience were so bored by Nero's singing that they pretended to die so they could be carried out of the auditorium.[12] The military general Vespasian, a future emperor himself, once insulted Nero by snoring in the front row during his recital.

There can be little doubt that Nero's artistic sensibility was deeply authentic, and it produced benefits beyond his own vanity. Thanks to Nero's devotion to the arts, his reign witnessed a great "Neronian renaissance" in literature. This made Nero fundamentally different from his imperial predecessors, notably Augustus, who regarded writers as court propaganda glove-puppets. Nero, by contrast, sincerely regarded himself as an artist. He actively cultivated other artists as his equals. His sensitive temperament sometimes ruined those relationships, however. Poets who wrote satirical verses about him were banished.

The wealthy Roman writer Petronius, who had served as consul, had been so influential in Nero's closest circle that the emperor named him court *arbiter elegantarium* ("arbiter of elegance") on all matters of taste. Petronius's influence on Nero was defiantly epicurean, a Dionysian contrast to the rational and tempered advice the emperor received from the Stoical philosopher Seneca. Some believe Petronius's satire of debauchery in his *Satyricon* contained subtle allusions to Nero. He eventually fell out of favor with Nero, but not over his writings. Nero was hearing rumors that Petronius had been involved in a plot against him. Fearing for his life, Petronius committed suicide by slitting his veins—

but before taking his own life, exacted devious revenge on Nero. He appended to his will a list naming Nero's many sexual conquests. The historian Tacitus tells us that Petronius provided names of "each male and female bed-fellow and details of every lubricious novelty—and sent it under seal to Nero."[13] Following Petronius's death, Nero was so astonished by the accuracy of Petronius's list that he ordered that the informant be found. He suspected a former lover, Silia, the wife of a senator and friend to Petronius. For her alleged indiscretions, she was exiled.

Despite his authentic passion for the arts, Nero's craving for public adulation blinded him from the rational demands of his role as emperor. Increasingly absorbed into the emotional turmoil of the Greek tragedies in which he performed, he gradually became unplugged from reality. On his theatrical tours, adoring fans thronged to see him. But back in Rome, he had powerful enemies in the Senate. The Roman nobility regarded his obsession with performing in public as degrading, especially Nero's Greek-style spectacles where dancers cavorted in the nude. In answer to his critics, Nero remarked, "The Greeks alone know how to appreciate me and my art."[14]

The final straw came when, following one of Nero's sensational tours of Greece, he organized an extravagant return to Rome that was insanely over the top. In a triumphal procession in Emperor Augustus's chariot, Nero was outfitted in a Greek cloak and Olympic crown on his head. Eschewing the customary entrance into the eternal city via Rome's triumphal arch, Nero passed through a breach in the walls to mimic a Greek victor in the sacred games. Even more astounding, he spurned the custom of carrying aloft the names of cities he had conquered. Instead, Nero held up a record of his trophies won in singing competitions. The final self-indulgent touch was his massive retinue—not legionnaires, but a throng of clappers who rhythmically applauded the emperor as the parade proceeded through the capital. Nero's triumphal procession was not that of a victorious emperor; it was the outlandish conclusion of the Nero unreality show. In the eyes of his powerful adversaries in the Senate, enough was enough.

For those who believed Nero was unhinged, there had been signs of mental instability throughout his reign. He had accumulated psychological traumas from an early age, most of them inflicted by his controlling mother Agrippina. There were even rumors that he and his mother had an incestuous sexual relationship. Mother and son were in constant conflict, especially over his resistance to her disapproval of his relationship with Poppaea Sabina. The tensions grew so bitter that Nero suspected Agrippina of plotting his assassination. Having witnessed emperor Claudius's death by mushroom poisoning, Nero knew his mother was capable of murder. He became increasingly convinced that he needed to move first to get rid of his mother. Suetonius tell us that he had attempted to poison Agrippina three times, but abandoned these plans when he learned that his mother, a veteran of palace murder plots, always fortified herself with antidotes against poisons. [15]

In 59 AD, Nero heard a rumor that his mother was boasting of incestuous relations with him. Fearing that gossip about sexual perversions would undermine his authority with the Roman army, he decided that Agrippina was a burden he could no longer bear. Looking for a fool-proof matricidal plan, Nero finally seized on the pretext of the feast of Minerva in late March. He invited his mother to join him for the festivities in Baiae, on the Bay of Naples. At a banquet at a nearby villa called Bauli, Nero made a great display of affection toward his mother to create the impression of a reconciliation. He presented Agrippina with a lavish gift of a yacht, which, following the festival, would take her back up the coast to her villa in Antium. The vessel was rigged to self-destruct and sink at sea. It was a death trap.

Nero's plan backfired, however. When the vessel set sail with Agrippina and her servants on board, it partially collapsed but failed to sink. Agrippina, only wounded in the accident, managed to swim back to shore, where she was rescued by local boatmen. She had no doubt about who had been behind the incident. When news reached Nero that his mother was alive, he panicked. Knowing his mother's wrath, he was certain that Agrippina would seek revenge. The historian Tacitus tells us that he was "out of his mind with fear." [16] She could appeal to the Senate to have him deposed. Or more likely, she would send her own assassins to murder him. He had to act to preempt his mother's vengeance.

Nero turned to his two lieutenants, Sextus Burrus and the philosopher Seneca. Burrus advised Nero that he could not count on the Praetorian Guard to kill Agrippina, as she was a direct descendant of deified emperors. Nero therefore dispatched henchmen to find her and finish her off. The assassins tracked Agrippina down in her villa. She knew why they had come. Defiantly pointing at her womb, she shouted, "Strike here!"— a spiteful allusion to the part of her body that had given birth to her ungrateful son. Nero's assassins followed her instructions, thrusting their swords into her stomach. Agrippina, the most powerful woman in the Julio-Claudian dynasty, was dead. [17]

Nero was paralyzed by news of his mother's murder, as if he couldn't believe that Agrippina was actually dead. He knew his horrible act would have grave repercussions if a convincing story was not concocted. This time he turned to the philosopher Seneca, who carefully drafted a letter to the Senate justifying the murder. The letter claimed that Agrippina had dispatched a slave to assassinate the emperor but the plot was thwarted. Seneca added to this a litany of other crimes committed by Agrippina over the years, including the usurpation of Nero's power, her humiliation of the Senate, her disregard for the army, and her contempt for the Roman people. The description of Agrippina's murder was a brazen lie, written by the hand of Rome's greatest living philosopher. And yet, surprisingly, nearly everyone believed it. The Roman cult of the emperor prevailed over the traditional reverence due to Agrippina as great-granddaughter of the divine Augustus. Senators congratulated Nero for discovering his mother's vile assassination plot. Nero triumphantly returned to Rome greeted with ecstatic acclaim and joyous celebrations.

With his mother out of the picture, Nero now had his hands free. But he fell into irrational despair, regretting his sickening crime. Something in Nero's mind snapped. There had been signs of Nero's mental instability throughout his reign. It was now obvious, however, that the emperor was becoming unhinged. It may have been the ghost of his murdered mother. Inside the imperial court, the death of his powerful adviser Burrus, and the diminishing influence of the philosopher Seneca, left Nero without a trusted inner circle. He increasingly depended on the advice of ruthless Praetorian Guard commanders, who created a climate of paranoia around the emperor.

Nero suddenly saw plots everywhere. He had people put to death on the slightest pretexts, including superstitions. When a comet appeared in the sky, Suetonius tells us, Nero was worried because such celestial events were believed to portend the deaths of great rulers.[18] He consulted an astrologer, who told him that he could avoid this fate through the deaths of other distinguished men. Upon learning this, Nero began ordering the murders of men holding high offices of state. A senator was executed for speaking ill of Nero at a dinner party; others were killed on suspicion of conspiring against him.

In his private life, Nero succumbed to shockingly depraved impulses. Rumors circulated about the emperor wandering through the streets of Rome at night, randomly stabbing men who were returning home from dinners. There was gossip that Nero defiled married women along the river, raped a Vestal Virgin, and abused freeborn boys. Graffiti appeared on Roman walls, sometimes in verse, accusing Nero of every imaginable depravity and evil act. In an imperial dictatorship where one could be executed for the slightest murmur against the emperor's name, this sort of graffiti served as a subversive form of public truth, scribbled anonymously, uttering what nobody dared to say in public.

Nero's most unspeakable crime was the murder of his ex-wife Octavia, who was living in exile after their divorce. Under pressure from his new wife, Poppaea, he ordered Octavia to be killed by suffocation in a steaming bath. Her severed head was returned to Rome so Poppaea could look upon it with satisfaction. Now that Agrippina was dead, Poppaea's profile joined his on Roman coins. When Poppaea gave birth to a girl in the year 63 AD, Nero was overjoyed. The Senate commended Poppaea's womb to the gods and a constructed a temple dedicated to the god of fertility, Fecunditas. But the child, named Claudia Augusta, died in infancy. Poppaea became pregnant again, but the second child would never be born. According to ancient sources, during a violent argument about Nero's addiction to chariot-racing, he kicked Poppaea in the stomach, killing both her and the unborn child. This story is almost certainly a fabrication. Modern historians believe Poppaea likely died from a miscarriage, not a violent beating. For contemporary Romans, however, Nero was guilty of two unspeakable crimes: the murder of his own mother (*matricide*) and the killing of two wives (*uxoricide*).

Nero's paranoid psychosis spilled onto the stage. On a tour of Greece, he insisted on performing in tragedies that eerily evoked traumatic events in his own life. One was *Orestes the Matricide*, which recounts the story of Orestes, the son of Agamemnon and Clytemnestra. Orestes's mother conspires with her lover Aegisthus to murder her husband, Agamemnon. When Orestes returns from the Trojan War, he slays both his mother and Aegisthus to avenge the death of his father. Given Nero's murder of his own mother, the connection between myth and reality must have been screaming in his mind on stage. Off stage, he was constantly haunted by the murder of his mother, terrified that the Furies would come to avenge her death.

The Furies would eventually find him. They were not the furies of mythology, however. They were infuriated Romans sickened by Nero's shocking conduct.

***

We may never know who set Rome ablaze in late July in 64 AD.

The fire started near the Circus Maximus and spread rapidly through the narrow streets where shops were packed with inflammable goods. The flames quickly overran much of the city. Rome was a massive inferno. Terrified shrieks filled the air as thousands of men, women, and children ran in confused panic. Looters grabbed what they could. When the fire finally died out, only four of Rome's fourteen districts remained intact.

Roman historians blamed Nero. They claimed he ordered his henchmen to set the fire so he could reconstruct Rome in his own image and rename it "Neropolis." This rumor was based on Nero's well-known construction plans for his "Domus Aurea," or Golden Palace, a vast architectural project featuring an imperial residence surrounded by parks, gardens, fountains, and wide avenues.

There is no evidence that Nero had anything to do with the fire. Neither did he have any concrete motive to set the blaze. His Domus Aurea was constructed a half mile away on the other side of the Palatine Hill. Still, rumors circulated that Nero's arsonists had deliberately burned the city to the ground so he could build his own private Xanadu. It was ancient Roman fake news. But the myth of Nero the arsonist persisted.

The second accusation against Nero was the famous tale that he "fiddled" while Rome burned. That legend is more easily contested. Nero never played a fiddle; his instrument was the lyre. The fiddle story was a fictitious embellishment added centuries later (possibly due to a confusion with the Latin *fides* or *fidicula* for stringed instruments).[19] The rumor in Nero's day, passed along by ancient historians, was that the emperor had climbed on his palace roof during the blaze and had sung "The Sack of Troy" while playing his cithara. There were other variations of this story, all of them false. But the intention was obvious. They were meant to portray Nero as a supercilious emperor engaged in idle distractions while his capital was in flames.

The truth is that, when the fire broke out, Nero was at his villa in Antium, outside of Rome. When news of the conflagration reached him, he rushed back to the capital and joined relief efforts unattended by bodyguards. He hunted through the debris in search of survivors and opened his imperial gardens to victims. In the aftermath of the blaze, Nero's conduct and decisions were entirely sensible. He used his private funds to build emergency accommodations for those left homeless. He introduced new building regulations for Rome—wider streets and ground-floor porticoes—to minimize the risk of fires in the future. He imported food for the destitute and cut the market price of corn. These actions were in character for Nero, who had a reputation for sensitivity and empathy. There were nonetheless rumors that, while Romans faced corn prices in the chaotic aftermath of the fire, Nero was importing sand for court wrestlers. He was also accused of pillaging the treasuries of temples to pay for the reconstruction of Rome.

Nero was aware of the malicious rumors circulating about him. He knew Romans believed he had torched the city to clear the ground for his imperial palace. And like all Roman emperors, he feared the wrath of the mob. In damage-control mode, Nero organized religious ceremonies to appease the angry gods with supplicatory prayers and propitiatory ceremonies. But if the gods were appeased, Romans were not. The nasty rumors continued. Tacitus tells us that Nero, to placate the mounting anger, looked for a scapegoat.[20] The designated culprits were the members of a new religious cult who called themselves Christians.

In Nero's day, Christians were a despised sect of religious zealots who were devoted to the teachings of a Jewish preacher crucified thirty years earlier in Judea. The disciples of Christ, including the apostle Paul, had recently arrived in Rome, where they were proselytizing and predicting the Last Judgment. They were known to be a violent sect, attacking Roman religion and smashing pagan idols. In the eyes of most Romans, Christians were illuminated fanatics. Suetonius called them "a class of men given to a new and mischievous superstition."[21] Even Tacitus, usually even-handed, described Christians as "notoriously depraved." He gave the following account of their religion: "The originator, Christ, had been executed in Tiberius' reign by the governor of Judea, Pontius Pilate. But despite this temporary setback, the pernicious superstition had broken out afresh, not only in Judea, where the evil had started, but even in Rome where all degraded and shameful practices collect and flourish."[22]

On Nero's orders, Roman authorities arrested and interrogated Christians suspected of being implicated in the fire. Few in Rome would have been surprised to discover that these strange religious fanatics had set the blaze. Tacitus tells us that some of the Christians confessed. Their punishment was horrific. They were whipped, tortured, and torn to pieces by wild dogs. Some ancient sources claim Nero had Christians nailed to crosses and set aflame, using their bodies as human torches to light up his gardens at night. The torture was so cruel, it was said, that Romans took pity on them.

This familiar tale of persecuting Christians forever cemented Nero's image as an evil tyrant. But does Nero deserve his monstrous reputation as a persecutor of Christians? There is reason for doubt. Tacitus tells us that Nero had no malice against Christians. Nero did not have Christians punished for the fire, noted Tacitus; they were persecuted because of their "hatred of the human race" (*odium humani generis*).[23] In other words, Christians were punished not for arson, but for religious fanaticism and subversion.

Nero's public relations campaign after the Great Fire continued with the burnishing of his image—literally, on Roman coinage. On freshly minted coins, Nero was portrayed as the Sun King: the radiant, all-seeing god, Sol, driving his brilliant chariot toward a new Golden Age. He also commissioned a towering, self-glorifying bronze statue of himself, called the "Colossus Neronis," which was erected on the Sacra Via. Standing 120 feet high, it showed Nero with a luminous crown and outstretched arm. The radiant Sun King makeover was an old trick that had worked for Augustus but backfired on Caligula. For Nero, it was too late. His dark reputation as an irrational Dionysius was irredeemable. He was under attack from all sides, especially in the Senate. The senatorial nobility was fed up with Nero's nonstop musical tours; and what's more, many had never forgiven him for the murder of his mother, Agrippina.

Only a year after the Great Fire, a powerful senator called Gaius Calpurnius Piso initiated a secret plan to assassinate the emperor. The plot was discovered, however, and Nero ordered the executions of nineteen conspirators. Piso was forced to commit suicide. Even Nero's longtime tutor Seneca was suspected of being involved in the conspiracy. Forced to commit suicide, Seneca sliced his veins in a warm bath. The same fate awaited Nero's literary friends, including Lucan and Petronius. The imperial vendetta sent a chill throughout Roman society.

Nero's ruthless purge might have worked, but he went a bridge too far by ordering high military commanders to commit suicide. Now it wasn't only the Senate against him; he lost the support of his legions. When Nero returned to Rome covered with garlands after yet another triumphant theatrical tour of Greece, he received alarming news. The Roman governors in Gaul and Hispania were in revolt. A military coup had been set in motion. Nero, who had never been a military commander, at first threatened to have the conspirators executed. This time, however, nobody was listening. Even the Praetorian Guard switched allegiances to the army.

In early June of 68 AD, Nero was isolated and panicking as rumors about plots against him grew more ominous. He took refuge outside Rome in a villa belonging to one of his servants. His only way out now was suicide. But the flamboyant emperor with a flair for drama lacked the nerve to play out his own final act. The gruesome task fell to his private secretary. At Nero's command, the servant took a dagger and stabbed the emperor in the neck.

Nero was dead at age thirty. Faithful to his image as a stage performer, his last words were: "*Qualis artifex pereo*" ("What an artist I die!"). True to himself, he turned even his death into a dramatic performance.

Nero's suicide marked not only the end of his own turbulent reign but also the collapse of the entire Julio-Claudian dynasty founded more than a century earlier by Julius Caesar. Unlike his great-great-grandfather Augustus, Nero was temperamentally incapable of seeing the world with the sober clarity of reason. He was more interested in performing on a stage than in ruling over an empire. While Augustus commissioned *The Aeneid* to celebrate the glory of Rome, Nero starred in a Greek tragedy about a man who murders his mother. Unable to liberate himself from the dictates of his exalted rank, Nero escaped into the leading role in a tortured drama of his own making. And like all great tragedies, it ended in his own violent death. Nero failed miserably as emperor of Rome, but succeeded magnificently as a performer on the stage of history.

The truth about Nero remains a mystery after two thousand years. The myths about him began almost immediately following his death. Most were concocted by those with the most to gain from his image as an insane tyrant. The Roman elites who had plotted his assassination had every reason to portray him as a monster. Roman historians, too, constructed a myth about Nero that suited the prevailing biases of the day. Most ancient accounts of Nero's reign were written by a small number of historians—notably Tacitus and Suetonius—during the new Flavian dynasty following Nero's death. These historians were personally connected to Flavian emperors—Tacitus to Vespasian, Suetonius to both Trajan and Hadrian. They had a strong motive to portray the entire Julio-Claudian dynasty in a negative light. The official script was easy to follow: the Julio-Claudian dynasty had collapsed because it was corrupt; the Flavian dynasty was now flourishing because it was virtuous. Tacitus even acknowledged that historians of his own time were biased: "The reigns of Tiberius, Gaius, Claudius, and Nero were described during their lifetimes in fictitious terms, for fear of the consequences; whereas the accounts written after their deaths were influenced by still raging animosities."[24] In the imperial rivalries of first century Rome, Nero was the ultimate fall guy.

Nero's posthumous legend took strange twists and turns that probably would not have displeased him. Immediately after his death, he became a mythic cult figure whose admirers refused to believe he was truly dead. Rumors spread that the body buried in the imperial family's Augustan mausoleum was not Nero. A "Nero Redivivus" cult sprang up, claiming that Nero had in fact fled to Parthia (modern-day Iran) and would return to destroy Rome, slaughter his enemies, and rule his empire again.[25] As this strange cult of Nero spread, so did sightings of the emperor. At least three Nero imposters surfaced, each with his own following. Two of them played the lyre to prove their authenticity. The third was so convincing that the king of Parthia backed him and came close to declaring war on Rome under the pretext of restoring Nero to power.

If tales of a resurrected Nero sound oddly Christian for a pagan emperor, this was not a strange coincidence. It is a tribute to Nero that his legend persisted deep into the Christian era, even if it took on a sinister aspect that was adapted to the new religion. Early Christians resurrected Nero to repurpose him as the Antichrist.

In the early fifth century, Saint Augustine wrote in *The City of God* that many believed Nero would return and be restored to his kingdom. Saint Augustine's work, a cornerstone of Christian theology, was written in the aftermath of the barbarian sack of Rome in 410 AD. The shock of that event threw many Christians into despair. They regarded the chaos as punishment for abandoning the old Roman religion. Saint Augustine, as suggested by the Latin title of his work, *De Civitate Dei contra Paganos* (On the City of God against the Pagans), was defending Christianity as the new theology with a more compelling narrative for the faithful. For

Augustine, the fall of Rome was part of God's unfolding plan. Rome was a worldly city, he observed; the heavenly city was the New Jerusalem and divine providence would triumph in the City of God. He added that it was believed that, on the day of judgment, Nero would be revealed as the Antichrist.[26] "Some think that the Apostle Paul referred to the Roman empire, and that he was unwilling to use language more explicit, lest he should incur the calumnious charge of wishing ill to the empire which it was hoped would be eternal," writes Saint Augustine, "so that in saying, 'For the mystery of iniquity doth already work,' he alluded to Nero, whose deeds already seemed to be the deeds of the Antichrist. And hence some suppose that he shall rise again and be Antichrist. Others, again, suppose that he is not even dead, but that he was concealed that he might be supposed to have been killed, and that he now lives in concealment in the vigor of that same age which he had reached when he was believed to have perished, and will live until he is revealed in his own time and restored to his kingdom."[27]

Many believed Nero was the "eighth king" cited in this passage of the Book of Revelation: "There are also seven kings. Five have fallen, one is, and the other has not yet come. And when he comes, he must continue a short time. The beast that was, and is not, is himself also the eighth, and is of the seven, and is going to perdition."[28] This passage, it was believed, drew a connection between Nero and the "Beast" in the Apocalypse. Nero fit the profile perfectly. It was Nero who had mercilessly persecuted Christians. The early Christian chronicler Selpucius Severus writes that Nero was "the basest of all men, and even of wild beasts . . . who will yet appear immediately before the coming of Antichrist."[29] Some theologians claimed that, when using Hebrew gematria assigning numeric values to letters, Nero's name equaled 666—the number of the Beast of Revelation.[30]

Like Roman historians of the Flavian period, early Christian theologians constructed a myth around Nero that reflected their own biases. For Roman historians, Nero was the emperor who had destroyed the Julio-Claudian dynasty; he was therefore portrayed as depraved and corrupt. For early Christians, Nero had executed the apostles Peter and Paul and persecuted Christians; he was therefore the incarnation of evil. Nero's dark image as the Antichrist endured for centuries. In late-nineteenth-century France, Ernest Renan wrote *The Antichrist*—part of his larger work on the origins of Christianity—which portrayed Nero as the Antichrist who persecuted Christians. Fifteen years later, the German philosopher Friedrich Nietzsche wrote his own *Antichrist* as a response to Renan, arguing that Christianity—with its emphasis on modesty, self-denial, and pity—is a religion for the weak. In many respects, Nietzsche was the kind of philosopher who Nero would have appreciated for his interest in the

Dionysian aspects of the Greek tragedies.[31] Nietzsche's motto, borrowed from the ancient Greek poet Pindar, was "become what you are."[32] Nero's entire life, it could be argued, was a quest to realize the truth of that credo. Nero was passionately committed to his true self, the man he really was—not an emperor, but the stage performer.

Today we still regard Nero as the Antichrist emperor who relentlessly persecuted Christians, and we still repeat the cliché that he fiddled while Rome burned, even though both myths are disputed, or at least nuanced, by historical facts. Like all myths, they were constructed to reinforce the biases of those who fabricated them. What we have believed about Nero over the centuries reveals more about ourselves than it does about Nero himself.

In the end, Nero landed a role to last for all eternity—star billing as the Antichrist. It was not the role he desired; he preferred Greek tragedies. One can nonetheless imagine Nero, who craved attention more than anything else, strangely delighted with his enduring legend.

And yet he remains an enigma. Two thousand years after Nero's death, we are still struggling to understand him.

Part II

Icons and Iconoclasts

4

SECRETS AND LIES

The name Procopius is largely unknown today. His obscurity in the annals of history is a puzzling injustice, for the sixth-century historian left us one of the most fascinating books in Western civilization.

Procopius's *Secret History* could be described as the first "unauthorized" biography ever written.[1] It was an unflattering behind-the-scenes account of court intrigue under the great Byzantine emperor Justinian I. That it took more than a thousand years for Procopius's defamatory narrative to come to light tells us something about its potential for scandal.

The book's Latin title, *Anecdota*—from the Greek *anékdota* for "unpublished work"—is fitting because the book is a series of anecdotes revealing the scurrilous secrets behind the Byzantine throne. Others refer to the book as the *Historia Arcana*. Procopius's motive for writing *The Secret History* is often interpreted as mischievous. Filled with personal loathing, the work is a virulent invective that dishes the dirt on Justinian and his empress Theodora. Some regard it as a poisoned work of satire that exposes the hypocrisy behind official Byzantine propaganda. Whatever his motive, Procopius was handing down to posterity the unedited truth—or, at least, his version of the truth.

Procopius's privileged vantage point inside the Byzantine court made his infamous tome doubly remarkable. He was Justinian's court historian—in effect, the emperor's propagandist-in-chief. Justinian hand-picked Procopius to write an officially sanctioned history praising the emperor's great works. Procopius discharged this duty faithfully. Those works are invaluable historical documents rich in information about the reign of Justinian and Theodora. His *Secret History* is a more intriguing work. It sketched, in lurid detail, a warts-and-all portrait of his two exalted subjects. Procopius's double-tracked literary project was extraordinarily brave for a Byzantine court historian.[2] It offered two versions of the same history—one noble lies, one naked truth.

Justinian, known in his day as "the emperor who never sleeps," was an ambitious leader with big plans. He ruled the Byzantine empire at a critical juncture, from 527 to 565 AD, in the aftershock of the western Roman Empire's collapse following barbarian invasions. As Byzantine emperor in Constantinople, Justinian was determined to restore the western empire in Italy, Spain, and North Africa. His aggressive foreign policy, called *renovatio imperii*, consisted of relentless military campaigns to defeat the Germanic tribes who had smashed apart the empire. He also commissioned a redrafting of Roman law, the *Corpus Juris Civilis*, and undertook massive building schemes, including the magnificent Hagia Sophia basilica in Constantinople. While Byzantium was an essentially Greek sphere, Justinian's culture was Latin. His official name underscored his attachment to Rome: Flavius Petrus Sabbatius Iustinianus Augustus. His tireless efforts to restore the Roman Empire earned him the status of "last of the Romans."[3]

Justinian inherited another Roman trait: an obsession with propaganda to glorify his own name. For that task, the top job fell to Procopius. If Justinian was the last emperor of Rome, Procopius was the last historian of the Roman world. He is often described as a chronicler who lived at the cusp between classical antiquity and early medieval Christendom. He came from Caesarea, a town in modern-day Israel named after Caesar Augustus. In Procopius's lifetime, Caesarea was the Byzantine capital in the province of Palaestina Prima. After receiving an elite education in Greek and Latin and studying law, he rose steadily in the ranks of the Byzantine power system. He was notably legal adviser to Justinian's military commander, Belisarius, who was leading campaigns to crush the Ostrogoths in Italy and the Vandals in North Africa.

Through his proximity to Belisarius, Procopius became a firsthand witness to numerous battles and massacres, including the captures of Carthage and Ravenna. Reporting on the wars against the Vandals, Procopius documented the mysterious "black sun" during the winter of 535–536 AD, a catastrophic event that nearly switched off the lights of Western civilization. Modern scientists believe the extended darkness was caused by volcanic eruptions, perhaps a comet striking earth, or possibly an intergalactic collision. Procopius left us an account of the events that gave literal meaning to the term *Dark Ages*: "And it came about during this year that a most dread portent took place. For the sun gave forth its light without brightness, like the moon, during this whole year, and it seemed exceedingly like the sun in eclipse, for the beams it shed were not clear nor such as it is accustomed to shed. And from the time when this thing happened men were free neither from war nor pestilence nor any other thing leading to death."[4] The cataclysm of 536 AD caused pestilence and famine that wiped out much of Europe's population, human and animal. The devastating impact was felt as far away as China and Peru. Old Norse literature documented the same volcanic winter, during which sacrificial offerings of gold were made to placate the wrath of the gods.

When he returned to Constantinople, Procopius advanced quickly in the Byzantine court to the rank of *illustrius*. Some historians believe he was also a senator. His obvious talents earned him privileged access in the highest circles at court. Justinian and empress Theodora must have been impressed by Procopius's abilities, for his position as chief propagandist was not a minor appointment. Procopius himself regarded his vocation at the Byzantine court as official historian, and we know from his writing that his lofty model was the great Greek historian Thucydides.

Procopius is known chiefly for two historical works: *Wars of Justinian* and *Buildings of Justinian*. The titles reveal their purpose and—above all—the star of the narrative. The two books portrayed Justinian as an idealized Christian emperor who crushed the heathens and built great churches to the glory of God. Though written in Greek, both works were Roman in form and style.[5] Procopius was to Justinian what the poet Virgil was to Augustus: a court scribe with a literary commission to glorify the emperor. Virgil's epic, *The Aeneid,* took inspiration from the Trojan War saga to associate Augustus's name with the founding of Rome. Procopius, despite his classical culture, recounted his chronicles as a Christian narrative to portray Justinian as the pious ruler who built Hagia Sophia. The narrative frames were different, but the propaganda message was the same.

The Secret History was a very different kind of literary project. Procopius claimed it had been written as a sequel to the *Wars of Justinian.* Part of the book indeed is devoted to discrediting Procopius's former military boss, Belisarius (and his influential wife Antonina), but the real target was clearly Justinian. Luckily for the Byzantine emperor, the book was not read in his lifetime. *The Secret History* lived up to its title, literally—it was an unpublished secret. Procopius probably wrote the book around 550 AD, when Justinian was an old man approaching the end of his long thirty-eight-year reign. Some have contested the book's authenticity, disbelieving that Procopius could have put his name to such a mean-spirited invective against his imperial masters. Others argue that Procopius, disillusioned in his role as court flatterer, vindictively penned *The Secret History* to get the truth out, albeit posthumously. The wait would be long. While there were mentions of the work in the Byzantine lexicon, it took more than a thousand years for the book to surface. Only one manuscript survived, discovered in the Vatican library and published in the early seventeenth century.[6]

The Secret History reads like a legal brief presented methodically in a courtroom. This is not surprising given Procopius's legal background. The case he made against Justinian was devastating. Far from the pious emperor portrayed in Procopius's official propaganda, in *The Secret History* Justinian comes off as a wicked and rapacious tyrant. Even Procopius's physical description of Justinian was unflattering. He noted that Justinian resembled the despotic Roman emperor Domitian. Since Domitian ruled in the late first century, there was no way Procopius could have known what he looked like, except through statue busts. But that wasn't the point. Procopius had obviously read historian Suetonius's biography depicting Domitian as a megalomaniacal tyrant who put to death senators who made jokes about him and, when alone, enjoyed catching flies and stabbing them with a needle. By informing his readers that Justinian looked like Domitian, Procopius was inflicting a severe moral judgment on his master's character.

If Procopius's anecdotes can be believed, Justinian's main character flaw was greed. He looted the fortunes of the wealthy through property seizures and, if necessary, through murder. "When he had without any excuse got rid of thousands and thousands of people, he promptly devised schemes for doing the same to others more numerous still," writes Procopius. "With a friendly expression on his face and without raising an eyebrow, in a gentle voice he would order tens of thousands of innocent people to be put to death, cities to be razed to the ground, and all their possessions to be confiscated for the treasury." Even Justinian's piety was suspect. Procopius described him as a persecutor of pagan non-Christians for reasons that had little to do with faith. Justinian was less interested in punishing their impiety than in despoiling their fortunes. In short, Christianity provided Justinian with religious cover for a massive extortion racket.

Procopius was harsher still toward Justinian's wife, empress Theodora. Depicted as a Cleopatra-like figure in famous church mosaics, Theodora remains a mysterious figure in history.[7] Almost everything we know about her personal life comes to us from Procopius. She was born in Cyprus into a humble family (her father was a bear tamer in Constantinople and her mother was a dancer). In her childhood, she and her sister followed their mother onto the stage, dancing at the hippodrome with a capacity of 30,000. She was probably a child prostitute in these early years. It was not unusual for young female dancers in Byzantium to prostitute themselves. By her late teens, Theodora had already had several abortions and traveled widely as the mistress of powerful men, including the governor of modern-day Libya. When she was twenty-one, she was back in Constantinople, where, thanks to her rich lovers, she caught the eye of the heir to the throne, Justinian. He was two decades older. They married despite the mismatch and official disapproval.

In his airbrushed propaganda, Procopius portrayed Theodora as a pious empress and praised her great beauty. In *The Secret History,* he painted a very different portrait. He reminded readers that Theodora was little more than a jumped-up harlot whose personality was vulgar, self-indulgent, wanton, and manipulative. His descriptions of her sexual indecencies—dubbing her "Theodora-from-the-Brothel"—left no doubt what he thought of her moral character. Theodora had once confided, he revealed, that she regretted having only three orifices and once enjoyed forty men in a single evening. Despite her wanton conduct, she was clearly the one in charge at the imperial court. Procopius tells us that she insisted that all senators prostrate themselves in her presence. Anyone who dared cross her was removed or executed.

Was Procopius telling the wicked truth about Theodora? Or was he writing up a misogynist character assassination? Or perhaps he was defaming the wife to get at his real target: Justinian. [8]

There is evidence Procopius's scandalous portrait of Theodora was recklessly malicious. Theodora worked tirelessly to champion women's rights throughout the empire, including divorce and property rights. Some claim she was an early medieval feminist. Having suffered the indignity of prostitution as a girl, she passed laws making pimping illegal and instituted the death penalty for rape. She also constructed a convent as a refuge for girls escaping the slavery of prostitution (though, Procopius noted, she had the girls "rounded up" and forced into the convent). Theodora was undoubtedly a complex character, driven by different ambitions, agendas, and motives at different points in her eventful life. When she died of cancer at age forty-eight in 548—seventeen years before Justinian's death—Procopius had not yet started to write his *Secret History.* [9]

Some historians have speculated that Procopius wrote his *Secret History* to protect himself if Justinian were overthrown. He knew Justinian was not a popular emperor. He'd barely survived being toppled in 532 AD after a popular revolt against high taxes. Some 30,000 protestors were slaughtered in a week of rioting that destroyed much of Constantinople. *The Secret History* may have been Procopius's literary insurance policy to save his own skin. It's more likely, however, that he wrote the book because, near the end of his career, he had gradually turned a critical eye on everything he witnessed at the imperial court.

In the final analysis, Procopius's anxieties were in vain. He went to his grave a decade before Justinian. The emperor died at the grand age of eighty-two in the year 565, blissfully unaware that the man he trusted as his chief propagandist had cruelly defamed him for posterity. The medieval poet Dante was kinder to Justinian. In the *Divine Comedy*, the Byzantine emperor enters paradise penitent, confessing that he had loved fame more than honor.

"Caesar I was, I am Justinian," he declares, indicating that, though he was once an emperor, he is now merely a humble man before God.

So who was the real Justinian—pious emperor or ruthless tyrant? And who was the real Theodora—courageous saint or wicked courtesan? We may never know.

***

Justinian's appearance in Dante reminds us that, in the sixth century, Christendom still had one foot firmly planted in ancient Rome.

Justinian regarded himself as a Christian theologian, yet he also self-identified as a Caesar. The "last of the Romans," he embodied the connection between the classical Roman and medieval Christian worlds. Procopius, too, straddled these two worlds. Historians have debated whether Procopius was a pagan influenced by Christian theology, or a Christian carrying pagan cultural baggage.

How the upstart Christian religion ended up becoming the official religion throughout the empire remains one of Western history's most astounding chapters. The spectacular success of Christianity, against all odds, raises the question of how religions emerge and, facing competing narratives, end up prevailing as accepted truth.

The success of Christianity could not have been a mere accident. There must have been something powerfully compelling about the Christian narrative, even for pagan Romans whose emperors eventually converted to the new faith. Consider that, in the decades following the crucifixion of Christ, most Romans regarded Christians as dangerous fanatics suffering from mental illness. Romans turned their anger toward Nero because they believed he had set Rome ablaze, but few hated him for persecuting Christians. A half century later, under Emperor Trajan in 112 AD, Pliny the Younger, as Roman governor of a region in modern-day Turkey, matter-of-factly reported to Trajan that he had tortured and executed a group of Christians for refusing to recant their faith and sought the emperor's advice. Trajan replied that Pliny was doing the right thing, but counseled him to pardon any suspected Christians who could prove they were worshipping Roman gods. Sporadic persecution of Christians persisted until the reign of emperor Diocletian, when it became official policy, at the outset of the fourth century.

How did a despised religious sect end up conquering every corner of the Roman Empire and beyond?

The most familiar reason is that the Roman Empire collapsed, opening a massive opportunity for Christian theology to spread in the ruinous aftermath. Various reasons have been given for the empire's decline and fall.[10] Some historians argue it was imperial overstretch and barbarian invasions. Others point to moral decadence, rivalry among elites, mass migrations, and chronic political instability. In his monumental *The History of the Decline and Fall of the Roman Empire*, Edward Gibbon observes that the rise of Christianity hastened the collapse of pagan Rome.[11] There was something unstoppable about this new religious faith in Jesus Christ as God. Or as Gibbon noted, Christianity was driven by an "exclusive zeal for the truth of religion."[12] The old Roman pagan deities simply couldn't compete with Christ. It is also possible that the Christian narrative was appealing precisely because the old Roman state religion was declining along with the empire itself in the early fourth century.

Before the emergence of Christianity, Roman religion had served an essentially civic purpose. The Romans had no theological concept of blasphemy or sacrilege in the Christian sense of those terms, except the physical destruction of their temples.[13] Religion was embedded in Rome's political system and served the interests of the state. The Roman pantheon of gods—Jupiter, Apollo, Mars, Dionysus—interplayed with humans and influenced their destiny. The Trojan hero Aeneas, founder of Rome, was said to be the child of the goddess Venus. Some Roman rulers claimed to be descended from the gods. Julius Caesar boasted Venus and Aeneas as ancestors, thus claiming a direct mythological connection to the founding of Rome. After Caesar's assassination, his adopted heir Augustus made the same claim on ancestry to the Trojan Aeneas. Caesar was deified after his death, a sign that the Romans were highly flexible about the status of divinity. Following Caesar's example, it became customary for Roman emperors to be defied upon their deaths. According to some sources, the emperor Vespasian's famous last words on his deathbed were, "Oh dear, I think I'm becoming a god." In ancient Rome, you could aspire to deification.

In the new Christian religion, there was no place for Rome's creatively flexible approach toward divinity. Whereas the Roman gods were like flamboyant rock stars who meddled in the lives of humans, the Christian faith had only one superstar: Jesus Christ. True, saints would later show up and intervene in human affairs with miraculous intercessions, but Christian faith was a monotheistic faith based on revelation. There was no possibility for imperial apotheosis in Christianity; only Christ was God. Whereas Roman religion was objective and unmystical, Christian faith was subjective and emotional. And whereas Roman religion was essentially pragmatic, Christianity was based on a strict dogma. In the Gospels, Christ declares, "I am the way, the *truth*, and the life: no man cometh unto the Father, but by me." The message was clear: there is only one truth.

It was this aspect of Christianity that made its early adherents doctrinaire and sometimes violent.[14] Romans regarded Christians as a dangerous, wide-eyed religious cult. As Edward Gibbon noted, Roman society was based on "religious harmony" devoid of orthodoxy. Christianity, by contrast, was zealously intolerant, and many of its early followers were illuminated mystics who regarded pagan Roman society with hostility.[15] Early Christians waged a fanatical culture war against the pagan religion of the Romans. Adherents of the new religion defaced and destroyed pagan temples, demolished altars, and smashed statues in the Parthenon on the Acropolis in Athens. In the year 385 AD, Christians sacked the temple of Athena at Palmyra, in modern-day Syria, and decapitated the statue of the goddess. Much of this violence was incited by the overheated, metaphor-laden rhetoric of early Church theologians. This undoubtedly explains why Gibbon, a product of the Enlightenment, was so skeptical about the early Christian church. Like many educated Englishmen of his day, his intellectual culture was turned nostalgically toward classical Antiquity. He regarded the triumph of Christianity over pagan Rome as a victory of superstition over reason.[16]

The emergence of Christianity was in fact a gradual process extended over centuries. The slow collapse of the Roman world was caused by several converging factors, including barbarian invasions. The combination of chronic war and pestilence also brought tremendous suffering throughout the Roman world. A smallpox pandemic from 165–180 AD wiped out a third of the empire's population. Two Roman emperors, Lucius Verus and Marcus Aurelius, were among its victims. A century later, another epidemic struck, adding plague to war and economic depression. As disparate populations throughout Europe struggled with the afflictions of violence and chaos, the crippled empire lurched toward collapse. At a time when life was misery, fear, and suffering, Christianity provided an appealing counter narrative that held out a new "truth." Christian faith promised spiritual consolation in an order that was falling apart. That was the key to Christianity's success. In a Roman world plagued by pestilence and violence, Christianity offered salvation and eternal life. Politically, Christianity was a new religious ideology that promised to revitalize a crumbling imperial order.[17]

Spreading the Christian message was a monumental challenge in a vast Roman space with a powerful cultural legacy stretching from Babylon to Britain. Fortuitously, the Romans had constructed a sophisticated network of roads and aqueducts, providing an efficient communications system that wouldn't be matched for more than a thousand years. Rome's imperial propaganda was physically omnipresent in architecture, amphitheaters, statues, and military outposts. The early Church grafted itself on the remnants of the Roman infrastructure and administration while taking pains to eradicate Rome's pagan propaganda. There was a new message with only one truth: Christian dogma.

Saint Augustine was the first Christian theologian to undertake the task of propagating religious doctrine. His classic work, *The City of God*, published shortly after the Visigoth sack of Rome in 410 AD, was a response to those who claimed Christianity had been responsible for the Roman empire's decline. Augustine blamed pagan Rome for its own destruction through moral corruption. Christianity had triumphed over paganism, he argues, because Christian theology was "truth." Pagan gods had failed Rome in the City of Man. Through Christ, the faithful would find the City of God. Since the contemplation of philosophical questions was henceforth a matter of religious faith, early Christian theologians largely ignored pagan Greek and Roman philosophy, though they cherry-picked concepts from Plato and Aristotle, such as natural theology, when they proved harmonious to Christian doctrine. Natural theology argued for the existence of God by appealing to human experience of the world. While revealed theology appeals to faith, natural theology appeals to reason. This idea resonated with Saint Augustine's theological philosophy. His evocation of natural theology makes a case, picked up centuries later during the medieval period, for both faith and reason as sources of religious truth.

In the early phase of the Church, these questions of religious truth were heatedly disputed. The most contentious issue related to the figure of Christ—or the question of "Christology." Was Christ human, divine, or both? The Church held seven Ecumenical Councils over two centuries to reconcile conflicting views on this and other doctrines. Theological disputes entailed enormous power stakes. In many cases, tensions over doctrine masked jurisdictional power struggles among competing Church patriarchs, especially between Rome and Constantinople. The God-or-man question about Christ, fundamental to Christian theology, was so divisive that finding a consensus was impossible.

The Byzantine emperor Justinian adhered to the prevailing conception of Christ as having "two natures"—the incarnation of God, made flesh as human. In short, Christ was both God and man. Justinian's empress Theodora opposed her husband on this point. During her youth in Alexandria, she converted to the "Miaphysite" Christian sect—today known as the Coptic Orthodox Church—which held that Christ was entirely divine, God and man united as one. For many in Justinian's court, Theodora's unorthodox conception of Christ made her a heretic. Beyond Byzantium, the rivalry over this God-or-man point of Christian doctrine became so fractious that, in the eleventh century, it provoked the Great Schism between the Roman Catholic and Orthodox faiths.

Besides questions of theology, Christian propaganda also created sacred legends around secular rulers. Emperor Constantine's religious conversion was a classic in this genre. Constantine is famously known as the first Roman emperor to convert to Christianity.[18] It is less known, however, that the legend of his "conversion" contains a good dose of Christian myth. The background to Constantine's conversion legend was the imperial rivalry between him and Maxentius, both sons of former emperors, in a collegiate tetrarchy of four emperors ruling over the Roman empire. Constantine was promoted to the rank of full "Augustus" after the death of his father, Constantius, in the British town of York in 306 AD. As co-emperor, Constantine ruled over Britain, Gaul, and Spain. But a full-scale civil war broke out with Maxentius over their rival claims to the western empire. The fact that Constantine was Maxentius's brother-in-law (he was married to Maxentius's sister, Fausta) did little to appease their competing ambitions.

In 312 AD, before his army marched against Maxentius's much larger forces in Italy, Constantine had a vision. He beheld an enormous cross of light in the sky with a message: *in hoc signo vinces* ("In this sign, you will conquer"). That same night, Constantine had a dream—another classic device in Christian legend—in which Christ appeared and instructed him to use the cross against his enemies. Emboldened by this revelation, Constantine sent his soldiers into battle with a vexillum military standard featuring the first two Greek letters of Christ's name, *Chi Rho*. Divine inspiration proved decisive on the battlefield. Constantine's army defeated Maxentius in the famous Battle of Milvian Bridge near Rome. Maxentius drowned in the Tiber during the battle. His body was dragged from the river and decapitated, and his severed head was paraded through Rome as a victory trophy. Constantine posthumously condemned Maxentius to *damnatio memoriae:* his name and legacy were disgraced and erased from history. Constantine was now the sole ruler of the Roman Empire. He owed his historic military victory to Christ.

Thus was born the myth of Constantine, the first Roman emperor to convert to Christianity. Part of the story is based on historical fact. As emperor, Constantine made Christianity legal throughout the empire, officially ending the persecution of Christians. He also sponsored the construction of basilicas, promoted Christians to high offices, gave tax exemptions to the Christian clergy, and convened a council of bishops in the French town of Arles in 314 AD.[19] Constantine's generosity toward the new religion was truly remarkable—especially since he was not, in fact, a practicing Christian. Constantine remained a pagan.

To commemorate the emperor's victory over Maxentius, a triumphal Arch of Constantine was erected in Rome in 315 AD. Constantine dedicated the triumphal arch to the Roman Senate, not to Christ, and it featured no explicit Christian symbols or iconography. This would suggest that Constantine, contrary to the legend, did not attribute his victory over Maxentius to divine inspiration. The legend of Constantine's visions of Christ came from two Christian apologists, Eusebius and Lactantius, both of whom were councilors to the emperor. They were the emperor's spin doctors. Eusebius's unfinished biography of his master, *Vita Constantini*, was a panegyric intended as Christian propaganda.[20] Eusebius claimed that Constantine was made emperor by God and, once in office, banned heretic books and prohibited pagan sacrifices. In fact, when Constantine was promoted to emperor, he was saluted by his father's army as "Augustus." Like other Roman emperors before him, Constantine identified with the god Apollo. He made lavish gifts to the temple of Apollo in Gaul, and his official coinage represented Constantine as *Sol Invictus* ("unconquered son") with a radiant crown. In Rome, the Sol Invictus image figured on the triumphal Arch of Constantine, which was aligned with Nero's statue of Sol near the Coliseum. Constantine's Sol Invictus image continued to appear on Roman coins until 325 AD, more than a decade after his "conversion," and yet no explicit Christian symbols appeared on his coins.[21] In 321 AD, Constantine dedicated a day of the week as *dies Solis*—"Sun" day, or Sunday—as the Roman day of rest. The Roman holiday known as *Dies Natalis Solis Invicti* ("Day of the Unconquered Sun") eventually became, for Christians, the holy day of Christmas on December 25. Constantine was brought up on the pagan side of these traditions and observed them well into his reign.

The legend of Constantine's "conversion" to Christianity was an invented narrative that owed more to political expedience than to religious epiphany. The emperor wasn't baptized a Christian until his deathbed, when he ordered bishops to perform the ritual. He promised to lead a more Christian life if he survived his mortal illness. But he expired, age sixty-five, on May 22 in 337 AD. His sins were finally absolved.[22]

Whatever the authenticity of Constantine's demonstrations of Christian piety, his reign marked a turning point for religious art as propaganda. Sacred iconography that is universally familiar—Christ sitting solemnly on his throne, surrounded by angels, his hand gesture making a signal of benediction—first appeared in the time of Constantine. The use of icons was controversial because Biblical scripture explicitly prohibited them. In Exodus 20:4, the second commandment stipulates: "Thou shalt not make unto thee any graven image."[23] In the New Testament, the Book of John warns in 5:21 KJV, "Keep yourselves from idols."[24] Given this scriptural interdiction, early Christians rejected all icons and idols. No

Christian images, icons, or idols can be dated to the first three centuries of the new religion. Zealous Christians of this period interrupted Roman festivals, kicked over altars, and smashed pagan idols.[25]

It took until Constantine's reign in the early fourth century for Christian icons to appear. Here too, early Christian icons were heavily imprinted by pagan tradition. Sacred iconography took inspiration from Greek and Roman themes. Visualizations of Christ in this period were often inspired by Roman monumental models. Frequently, Christ appeared rigid and solemn like a Roman emperor—referred to as "Emperor Mystique" iconography.[26] He was sometimes represented as Apollo, following the Roman tradition of emperors venerating the sun god, including Augustus, Nero, and Constantine himself. The depiction of Christ as a shepherd tending to his flock was also borrowed from Greek and Roman mythology. The figure of Orpheus, taming beasts with his music, was also a good shepherd. So was the Trojan warrior Aeneas, the founder of Rome in the poet Virgil's epic. Early Christian iconographers would have been intimately familiar with these pagan traditions of deities and symbols. Christianity was rising as a new religion in the late Roman Empire, but its symbolic inspiration owed a great deal to the pagan world.

Two centuries later, Justinian and Theodora were ardent believers in the power of iconography. The famous Byzantine mosaics in the church of St. Vitale in Ravenna, built in 547, show Justinian as a Christ-like figure: dressed in a Tyrian purple robe, his dark eyes gazing at the viewer, his head surrounded by a glowing halo, holding a bowl for the bread of the Eucharist. Imperial administrators and soldiers are positioned on his right, the white-robed clergy to the left. Justinian is thus represented as a Christian emperor, both worldly and divine. On another mosaic panel in St. Vitale, we see Theodora, haloed like a goddess, wearing a jewel-encrusted crown. Remarkably, Justinian and Theodora are represented just as prominently as Christ, perhaps revealing something about their exalted self-importance.

Justinian also constructed self-glorifying idols and statues that used Christian symbolism. The most visible was the great Column of Justinian erected in Constantinople in 543 to celebrate his military victories over the barbarians. The massive marble-pedestaled column, erected in the Augustaeum public square, rose so high that it could be seen from the sea. It was topped by a massive bronze equestrian statue of Justinian dressed as the ancient Greek hero Achilles, breast-plated and his helmet plumed with peacock feathers. Justinian's portrayal as Achilles revealed that, like Constantine two centuries earlier, he still had one foot firmly planted in the classical world.[27] The main symbolism, however, was manifestly Christian. In Justinian's left hand, he was holding a *globus cruciger*—or "cross-bearing orb"—a symbol of Christ's dominion over the world. The bronze statue depicted Justinian as the secular *Salvator Mundi*, ruling over the world on behalf of Christ the Savior. The column stood majestically for nearly a thousand years, until 1425, when the *globus cruciger* fell from Justinian's hand. The people of Constantinople interpreted it as an omen of the city's doom. Less than three decades later, in 1453, the Muslim Ottomans captured the city and destroyed the column. The toppling of Justinian's statue marked the end of Christian rule over Byzantium.

Like Byzantine emperors, the early popes in Rome understood that images, idols, frescoes, stained glass, tapestries, ceramics, and paintings were effective marketing tools for religious propaganda. Basilicas were constructed as magnificent architectural tributes to Christian iconography. Certain biblical scenes, such as the Resurrection of Christ, became popular icons in churches. At the same time, the veneration of physical representations of Christ, the Virgin, and the Saints were integrated into Christian ritual. Icons and idols gave illiterate worshippers a visible, tangible connection to the Christian narrative. The inconvenient fact the icon veneration violated the Sacred Scriptures was overlooked in the interest of propagating the faith. Iconography was especially useful with the growing belief in the intercession of saints. The practice of pilgrimages to holy places created cults around holy relics associated with saints. Contemplation of icons provided the faithful with an intimate connection, allowing prayer to be addressed directly to the saint represented. The growing Christian fixation on contact relics boosted the value placed on images, objects, and idols—and, inevitably, created a lucrative market for relics, though many of them were bogus.[28]

Inevitably, the propaganda exploitation of icons and idols provoked controversy within the Church. Tensions reached a breaking point in the eighth century with the famous Iconoclastic Controversy.[29] The word *iconoclast*, understood as someone who goes against prevailing beliefs and institutions, finds its origins in this early medieval religious dispute. In the early Christian period, iconoclasts were those who opposed the veneration of religious icons. The most powerful iconoclast was Byzantine emperor Leo III "the Isaurian" (a reference to his Syrian roots). The underlying reason for Leo III's hostility toward icons and idols has been the subject of debate. Some claim his motives were theological. The Eastern Church regarded Christ as divine; therefore all images of the Savior were forbidden. It has also been argued that Leo III, like other Byzantine rulers, was interested in spreading his own cult and did not wish to compete with religious iconography. Others argue it was Leo III's defensive reaction to external pressures from the invading Muslim armies who were menacing Byzantium. Muslims were stridently opposed to all forms of idolatry. Shortly after Leo III was proclaimed emperor, he spent months fending off a massive Caliphate-sponsored land-and-sea siege of Constantinople that eventually failed. It is possible that he embraced iconoclasm—Greek for "breaker of icons"—to avoid aggravating further tensions with the icon-smashing Muslim invaders. Those tensions would not subside, of course, eventually provoking full-scale religious wars during the Crusades, triggered by Byzantine emperor Alexios I in 1095, when he called on Pope Urban II and European kings to come to his aid to drive out the Turks.

In 730 AD, Leo III banned all icons and idols, decreeing that all images of saints, martyrs, and angels were accursed. According to legend, Leo took his decision to interdict icons a violent volcanic eruption that extinguished the sunlight. Convinced that the darkness was a sign of God's wrath over the growing Christian culture of image veneration, Leo banned icons and ordered the removal of Christ's image from the entrance of his Sacred Palace in Constantinople. Following a backlash riot led by pro-icon worshippers, Leo initiated a policy of persecution, torture, and murder of Christians guilty of icon veneration. Monks, who generally supported icons, were arrested and forced to break their monastic vows. Many went into exile in the west, where the early popes were much more sympathetic to icons.

Leo's great adversary in the Iconoclasm Controversy was Pope Gregory II. Born into a Roman noble family in 669, Gregory had much experience in the back rooms of the Vatican. Elected pontiff in 715, he immediately became known as a pope with an eye for details. Gregory II meddled in everything. He was particularly attentive to missionary work, which, spreading Christianity throughout Europe, expanded the Vatican's influence into Germany and Britain. Gregory was adamantly in favor of icons. He understood that the symbolic power of images, notably stained-glass depictions of Biblical scenes, inspired awe and wonder in the hearts of the faithful. Stained-glass iconography in churches was an early Christian form of television, providing visual stories with Christ at the center of the narrative.

Gregory II could find support for his pro-icon stance in the works of John of Damascus, a Syrian monk (later St. John Damascene) who wrote the famous treatise *Apologia against Those Who Decry Holy Images.* His argument was based on a clever technicality that escaped the reproach of scripture. Since Christ was a man, representations of him were allowed. It is through images of Christ that we have access to God. John of Damascus also insisted on a distinction between veneration and worship: icons can be venerated, but not worshipped. By venerating the cross, one is not worshipping the wood of which it is made, but rather worshipping Christ through a representation image. In a famous concluding argument, John argued: "I do not worship matter; I worship the Creator of matter who became matter for my sake, who accepted to dwell in matter, who worked out my salvation through matter. Never will I cease adoring the matter which wrought my salvation!"[30]

Pope Gregory refused to be bullied by the Byzantine emperor. He certainly had reasons to despise Leo III. Leo had attempted to drain Gregory's monastic revenues by taxing papal territories in Italy. More troubling, Leo was involved in a sinister conspiracy to have Pope Gregory murdered. The plot was discovered, however, and the assassins executed. After Leo issued his edict banning icons, Gregory moved quickly to put the Byzantine emperor in his place. He convened a synod to condemn the Byzantine emperor's iconoclasm and dispatched letters to Leo III curtly reminding him that the Byzantine emperor had no authority over Church dogma.[31]

Enraged, Leo set in motion another conspiracy to assassinate Gregory. But this second attempt also failed.

Pope Gregory II prevailed in the end. The image henceforth enjoyed pride of place with the word in the Christian narrative. An old Roman propaganda technique, deployed by emperor Augustus, who had spread his own image throughout the empire, was dusted off and repurposed to propagate the Christian faith. The entire medieval age witnessed a massive boom in the veneration of Christian icons, idols, and sacred relics. It proved that, for the Church, the pragmatic gains of effective marketing outweighed strict adherence to biblical scripture.

The iconoclasm controversy did not go away however. It simply went dormant for several hundred years. When it resurfaced during the Reformation, it triggered religious wars that would rage for centuries.

5

PR MEN IN THE MONASTERIES

Charlemagne bestrides European history like a colossus. King of the Franks, he conquered most of Europe during a reign that lasted nearly half a century, from 768 to 814 AD.

Anointed "Emperor of the Romans" by the pope, Charlemagne was Europe's greatest ruler since imperial Rome. During his reign, the continent achieved stability and experienced a great cultural revival in learning and the arts. Even today, many consider Charlemagne to be the "Father of Europe."

Yet Charlemagne remains strangely elusive. His legend resonates like a saga from historical fiction, emerging from the mists of a distant epoch that resembles an episode of *Game of Thrones*. He inhabits our collective imagination like King Arthur and his Knights of the Round Table. Even in his own day, Charlemagne was the stuff of legend, a sacred king vanquishing the heathen hordes. The chivalric *chanson de geste* narratives in medieval French literature were devoted to the age of Charlemagne. The eleventh-century "Chanson de Roland" epic fabricated the Charlemagne myth in the same way Virgil's *Aeneid* glorified emperor Augustus.

Over the centuries, the Charlemagne of legend has become merged with the Charlemagne of history. His myth is such a richly embroidered narrative that it's difficult to distinguish historical fact from fiction. Charlemagne is part real, part fantasy, part truth, part myth. [1]

So who was the real Charlemagne?

There are biographical facts, of course, such as his birth in 743 AD, the son of the Frankish king Pepin III (known as "Pepin the Short"). The Franks, whose leader had been integrated into the Imperium Romanum, established their power base in northern Europe following the collapse of the empire at the end of the fifth century. When Pepin III died in 768 AD, Charlemagne jointly inherited the Frankish throne with his younger brother, Carloman. The two brothers disliked each other intensely, a rivalry that strained their shared rule, which was refereed by their mother, Bertrada. The fraternal tensions came to a boiling point when Charlemagne abandoned his first wife, a Lombard princess called Desiderata, to marry a thirteen-year-old German aristocrat named Hildegarde. In 771, Carloman suddenly died at age twenty in unexplained circumstances. It left his older brother as sole ruler. [2]

Charlemagne is often believed to have been French, a mistaken impression reinforced by the fact that his Frankish kingdom extended over a vast portion of modern-day France. His enormous equestrian statue in front of Notre Dame Cathedral in Paris further strengthens the idea that Charlemagne stands at the epicenter of French history. His French name also makes this connection, though that too is misleading. His real name was Carolus. Charlemagne is from Latin, *Carolus Magnus,* or "Charles the Great." Charlemagne was not French by any modern standard. He didn't speak French, for one thing. And his capital—which the French refer to as Aix-la-Chapelle—was the modern-day German city of Aachen. His wife, Hildegarde, was from Swabia, which today corresponds to southwestern Germany. If we could be transported back to Charlemagne's time to meet the emperor in the flesh, there would be almost nothing "French" about him. His Frankish speech would sound like a strange German or Dutch dialect. Ironically, the words for France in those two languages make a clear connection between the Franks and the French. In German, France is *Frankreich*. In Dutch, France is *Frankrijk*. And so the image of Charlemagne as French has stuck despite the historical facts.

Charlemagne was, above all, a military conqueror. Like Julius Caesar, he spent most of his career leading campaigns against foreign armies and putting entire populations to the sword—Saxons, Lombards, Moors, Basques. [3] If Caesar's conquest of Gaul was genocidal, Charlemagne's military legacy was equally horrific. His long wars in Germany earned him the nickname "butcher of the Saxons." The Saxons, pagans who stubbornly held on to their old German religion, worshipping gods such as Wodan, had long been enemies of the Franks. In Charlemagne's reign, the Saxons were rebelling against the Franks by attacking and destroying Christian churches. In retaliation, Charlemagne gave no quarter. At the infamous Massacre of Verden in 782, he had 4,500 Saxon prisoners beheaded on the banks of the Weser in a single day. The motive for this bloodbath was Christian faith: the decapitated Saxons were pagan prisoners who refused baptism. Charlemagne found justification for this slaughter in the Bible. He was emulating the Israelite king Saul's massacre of the Amalekites. In the Old Testament, the Amalekites were the enemy of the Israelites. In the Book of Samuel 15:3, Saul is commanded to destroy the Amalekites: "Now go and smite Amalek, and utterly destroy all that they have, and spare them not; but slay both man and woman, infant and suckling, ox and sheep, camel and ass." Once the Saxons were subjugated, Charlemagne used the death penalty to curtail their traditional religious rites, including cannibalism and human sacrifice. The Saxon king, Widukind, finally surrendered and agreed to be baptized. Charlemagne personally acted as his godfather.

Despite his brutality as a warlord, the legend of Charlemagne that persisted for centuries was based on his image as a pious Christian conqueror who annexed and spread the faith through most of Europe. He also established a solid administrative system and was patron to a great flourishing of learning, literature, and art. He attracted to his court in Aachen some of the most learned minds of his day, notably the English scholar Alcuin of York.[4] Charlemagne is credited as the medieval ruler who dragged Europe out of the Dark Ages and laid the Christian foundations of Western civilization. With an achievement of that magnitude, it was easy—and convenient—to overlook his blood trail of monstrous atrocities. The Christian narrative, often taken directly from biblical passages, put a radiant halo on the harsher realities of Charlemagne's military expeditions.

Chroniclers in Charlemagne's day were the first to blur the lines between fact and fiction. Historical writing in the early Middle Ages operated according to the same method—part fact, mostly fiction—employed in ancient Roman histories. Like their ancient forbearers, medieval chroniclers used mythology to impart moral lessons. The difference was that, in medieval Europe, morality tales were Christian. As religious propaganda, medieval chronicles were constructed around the same narrative: divinely inspired kings, martial defense of the faith, and religious conversion of heathens.

The Church's propaganda machine was its vast network of monasteries. Following the collapse of the Roman Empire, the production of knowledge retreated into monastic cloisters where monks enjoyed a quasi-monopoly on the production, packaging, and dissemination of "truth." The standard cliché of the medieval monastery is a cloistered place where cowled monks led ascetic lives of seclusion (the word *monastic* comes from the Greek, *monachos,* for "alone"), bent solemnly over manuscripts, laboriously transcribing illustrated copies of the Bible. This stereotype underestimates the real status and power of monasteries. Monks were the Church's brain trust empowered with the production and preservation of religious and secular learning, including classical texts in Greek and Latin. At the height of monastic power, before the emergence of universities, influential monasteries attracted the most important scholars throughout Christendom. They were, in effect, the think tanks of medieval Christendom. Some well-connected monastic leaders, such as the Cistercian monk Bernard de Clairvaux in Burgundy, were powerful political players who had the ears of popes and kings.

The monastic system's power was based on information. Monks did devote their labors to transcribing copies of the Bible in luminous illustrated editions. But they were also chroniclers and propagandists. The earliest historical chronicles in Europe were almost always written by monks. A famous example is the Venerable Bede, author of the *Ecclesiastical History of the English People.*[5] Monastic historians like Bede were educated in Latin and familiar with Roman writers—Virgil, Pliny, Ovid, Tacitus—whose works they would not have considered as "ancient." Bede's famous history began with Julius Caesar's invasion of Britain. Monastic writers considered the Roman world as part of their history. But while Roman historians Tacitus and Suetonius were largely interested in worldly vice and virtue, monastic historians were more focused on Christian piety. Bede's tome was not billed as a history of the English people, but as an *ecclesiastical* history. This religious bias produced serious consequences for the way these historical chronicles portrayed events. They were not rigorously interested in factual truth. Monastic narratives invented pious legends at the service of Christian doctrine. Monks were the Church's PR men in the monasteries.

Charlemagne, like Julius Caesar, carefully managed his own image and personal mythology. Caesar dictated his chronicles of conquest to aides who organized their publication to spread news of his conquests. Charlemagne took a different approach. He hired his own court propagandist. The scribe's name was Einhard, a Frankish scholar educated by monks. Einhard was, in effect, Charlemagne's official biographer—not unlike Procopius to Byzantine emperor Justinian. There were two important differences, however. First, Einhard wrote *Vita Karoli Magni* (*Life of Charlemagne*) after the emperor's death. Also, so far as we know, Einhard never slipped into the shadows to pen a "secret history" for posterity, giving us the behind-the-scenes dirt on Charlemagne.

As biographical literature, *Life of Charlemagne* was styled on Suetonius's life of the Roman emperor Augustus, a book that Einhard knew well. But whereas Suetonius indulged in juicy gossip about his imperial subjects, Einhard's biography of Charlemagne was largely propaganda written by a close confidant who had benefited greatly from the emperor's generosity. In the Prologue, he refers to the "unbroken friendship which I enjoyed with the King himself and his children from the time when I first began to live at his Court."[6] In that respect, Einhard's literary project shared the traits of Eusebius's panegyric about emperor Constantine, *Vita Constantini*.

Einhard confesses unapologetically that his motive for writing *Life of Charlemagne* was to ensure that "the illustrious life of the greatest king of the age and his famous deeds, unmatched by his contemporaries," did not "disappear forever into forgetfulness."[7] His literary mission was to praise Charlemagne's virtues, not to recount his vices. Einhard did not spurn facts entirely, however. Indulging in a Suetonian touch, he provided a detailed description of the emperor's physical appearance, habits, and preferences. Charlemagne, he observed, was "heavily built, sturdy, and of considerable stature" with a "round head, large and lively eyes, a slightly larger nose than usual, white but still attractive hair, a bright and cheerful expression, a short and fat neck."[8] Einhard also informed his readers that, while Charlemagne enjoyed good health, toward the end of his life he dragged one leg, presumably after being wounded in battle.[9] Still, Einhard's portrait of Charlemagne was essentially an encomium. He portrayed Charlemagne as an enlightened emperor in both the city of man and city of God. He recounted, in fact, that Charlemagne was profoundly influenced by Saint Augustine's *City of God* and had passages read aloud to him.[10] This reinforced the image of the pious Charlemagne who, despite the vastness of his worldly realms, aspired only to salvation in the kingdom of heaven.

The Charlemagne myth was fabricated around two legends. The first was the warrior Charlemagne of epic poetry in "Chanson de Roland," the heroic Christian conqueror, followed by his loyal paladins, battling the Muslim heathens. The second was pious Charlemagne, inspired by divinations, devoted to Christian truths, propagator of the faith, protector of the pope. Einhard spun both these legends, describing how Charlemagne had Christianized former barbarian territories whose people now opened their eyes to God's illumination. On the more gruesome aspects of his military conquests, Einhard evoked the same sacred rationale: Charlemagne's zeal for this Christian faith. Einhard described the pagan Saxons as "devoted to the worship of demons and hostile to our religion." When Charlemagne finally subjugated them, he added, the Saxons abandoned their worship of devils and received the sacraments of the Christian faith.

Charlemagne's legendary battle against Muslims in Spain in 778 AD offers a revealing illustration of how Christian narratives glossed over the facts of historical events. According to medieval legend, Charlemagne invaded Spain to recapture the sacred site at Compostela where the body of the apostle James was buried. Saint James was beheaded in Judea by King Herod Agrippa in 44 AD, but according to tradition he had preached Christian faith in Spain. After his martyrdom, his disciples brought his body back to Compostela. By Charlemagne's day in the ninth century,

Compostela in Galicia was a pilgrimage whose route was called "Saint James Way," though it was controlled by the peninsula's Muslim oppressors.

Charlemagne was said to have received a vision of Saint James in a dream. In the dream, apostle James urged Charlemagne to free Spain from the heathens. The call-to-arms vision inspired Charlemagne to lead his army on an invasion of the Iberian Peninsula to reopen the pilgrim road and punish the heathen Muslims.[11] Accompanied by his chivalrous knight Roland, Charlemagne's soldiers laid siege to Pamplona. When the Muslims refused to surrender, Charlemagne called on God's help. Miraculously, the walls of Pamplona collapsed—like the walls of Jericho in the biblical story—allowing Charlemagne to capture the city. In victory, Charlemagne showed mercy to all defeated Muslims who converted to Christianity. Those who refused Christ were put to the sword. Crossing the Pyrenees on their way home, Charlemagne's soldiers were ambushed in a surprise attack by vengeful Muslims forces. Charlemagne had been betrayed to the Muslims by one of his own, Roland's own stepfather Ganelon. Tragically, the brave Roland, famous for his ivory oliphant horn, was killed in the battle. Despite this poignant loss for Charlemagne, his soldiers valiantly fought off the heathens and, after scattering the Muslim armies, returned safely to his capital in Aix-la-Chapelle. Ganelon was punished for his treachery by being dismembered. His limbs were ripped from his torso by four galloping horses.

That is the Charlemagne myth found in epic narratives like the eleventh-century "Chanson de Roland."[12] The historical facts are less heroic. Charlemagne did not invade Spain to save the sacred shrine of Saint James. His military expedition was, in fact, a response to pleas by a local Muslim governor, Suleiman Ibn Al-Arabi, offering his submission to the Frankish king in return for his help against rival Saracens in Spain. Muslims were fighting other Muslims in Spain. For Charlemagne, the invitation was an unexpected opportunity to make a land grab and extend his realms. An invasion of Muslim-controlled Spain was also encouraged by Pope Adrian I. Charlemagne's expedition in Spain started with a siege of Zaragoza, but had to be aborted when he was forced to return to Germany to put down a Saxon revolt there. As for the surprise attack in a Pyrenees mountain pass, it was not launched by Muslims. It was an ambush by Basques avenging Charlemagne's destruction of their capital, Pamplona. For purposes of Christian propaganda, however, the story of Charlemagne's expedition in Spain was transformed into a morality tale of valiant Christian knights vanquishing the heathen Saracens. The bonus happy ending was that the defeated Muslims converted to the worship of Christ.

The romanticized legend was a fantastic press release, riddled with false information, and carried forward in epic poetry and chronicles that amplified the Charlemagne myth. Christian propaganda was the function of the *chanson de geste* verses, which were recited and sung by minstrels. Breaking with the tradition of celebrating heroes from Antiquity, the *chansons* created legends around medieval Christian crusaders fighting the Muslims. The "Chanson de Roland," recounting Charlemagne's battles against the Saracens in Spain, was religious propaganda during the early Crusades when Christian kings were invading the Holy Land to drive out the Muslim infidels. Later poems, such as "La Chanson d'Antioche," put other protagonists in the starring role, such as Frankish knight Godefroy de Bouillon, who led his army down "Charlemagne's Road" on their way to Jerusalem. The road was a reference to another *chanson de geste*, "The Pilgrimage of Charlemagne," recounting his journey to Jerusalem with his twelve paladins (the number corresponds to the Twelve Apostles).[13] In Dante's *Divine Comedy*, written in 1320, Charlemagne and Roland are rewarded with a place in the heavenly circle of Mars for their valiant battles against the heathen. The treacherous Ganelon, for his part, is banished to the ninth circle of hell.

For the real medieval armies and knights embarked on the Crusades, these myths provided a pious pretext for a much less romantic enterprise: plundering, pillaging, and pogroms. Many of the early crusaders were desperate European populations afflicted by drought and famine. Some were suffering from a disease known as ergotism, or *ignis sacer* (also called "Saint Anthony's Fire"), caused by eating fungus-infected rye bread. The outbreak of its terrifying symptoms, including convulsions and insanity, triggered a religious fever of millenarianism that brought widespread belief that the Day of Judgment was imminent. The end of days was confirmed by the sight of a comet, a meteor shower, and a lunar eclipse. Religious hysteria thus emboldened military expeditions against the Antichrist heathens in the Holy Land.

The Charlemagne myth as valiant Christian king reached its apogee with his anointment as Holy Roman Emperor in the year 800. Once again, the myth didn't quite correspond to historical facts. Pope Leo III anointed Charlemagne as Defender of the Faith, thus conferring a sacred aura on his worldly conquests. Charlemagne, as a humble Christian warrior, was said to have accepted the title reluctantly. That's the myth. In truth, Pope Leo was in a spot of bother and desperately needed Charlemagne's help. Leo had many enemies, especially Roman nobles who had been close to his predecessor, Adrian I. Whereas Pope Adrian had been born into the nobility, his successor Leo was a low-born Greek cleric who lacked aristocratic poise. He also found himself surrounded by his predecessor's powerful relatives, protégés, and cronies who were entrenched in key positions after Adrian's long pontificate. They regarded Pope Leo as a parvenu unfit for office.[14] Looking for a pretext to destabilize the new pontiff, they accused him of perjury and sexual misconduct. More troubling, they began plotting his overthrow. In April 799, when Pope Leo was making his way to Rome's Flaminian Gate during the Greater Litanies procession of exorcism and blessing, one of the late Pope Adrian's nephews orchestrated a physical assault on the new pontiff. The attackers threw Leo III to the ground and attempted to gouge his eyes and rip out his tongue. Thanks to quick intervention by guards, Pope Leo's life was saved, but the pontiff was imprisoned in a monastery.

Leo managed to escape and, fleeing Rome, went into hiding in Paderborn, Germany. He turned to Charlemagne for assistance on the strength of a longstanding alliance between the papacy and Frankish kings as the pope's protector. Charlemagne had his army escort the shattered pontiff back to Rome and held a synod to examine the accusations against the pontiff. After Leo swore his own innocence by taking an oath of purgation, Charlemagne restored him as pope, sentenced his attackers to death for *lèse majesté*, and exiled the pontiff's enemies. On Christmas Day in 800, Leo grandly demonstrated his gratitude by anointing Charlemagne Holy Roman Emperor in St. Peter's Basilica. Despite Charlemagne's humble display of modesty upon receiving his sacralization, there could be no mistake about who was the stronger player in the bargain.[15]

After his papal anointment, Charlemagne was no longer a Frankish king only. He was now a Christian "Emperor of the Romans." Pope Leo even bestowed on him the title "Augustus." Four centuries after the collapse of Rome, nostalgia for the old empire was still powerful. The symbolic connection to ancient Rome must have been a magnificent vindication for Charlemagne. The Frankish people, like the Romans, believed they were descended from the ancient Trojans. According to an eighth-century Frankish history, *Liber Historiae Francorum*, the Franks had their own Aeneas myth claiming that, following the Trojan War, some 12,000 soldiers settled in Germany along the Rhine. Now under Charlemagne, the Franks dominated all of Europe. By taking the Roman title "Augustus," Charlemagne was joining up two glorious myths in his own exalted person.

Charlemagne's domed Palatine Chapel standing next to his palace in Aix-la-Chappelle was his most powerful Christian symbol. Consecrated in 805 by the ever-grateful Pope Leo III, the chapel was modeled on the Byzantine church of St. Vitale in Ravenna, once capital of the Roman Empire in its final decline. Charlemagne had visited Ravenna three times and marveled at the magnificent mosaics of Justinian and Theodora. Building his Palatine Chapel symbolized the relocation of the Holy Roman Empire's capital from Ravenna to Aix-la-Chapelle. The pope even authorized Charlemagne to help himself to anything he needed in Ravenna for his construction project. Charlemagne took up the offer. A vast quantity of Roman columns, statues, mosaics, and other artifacts were crated up and hauled off to Aix-la-Chapelle. The Palatine Chapel, which still stands today, became a sacred place after Charlemagne's death. For more than five centuries, all Holy Roman Emperors were crowned in the chapel. Charlemagne's body was entombed there after his death in 814.

The Charlemagne myth as sacred king and proto-crusader was amplified in many chivalric romances throughout the late Middle Ages. It was said that William the Conqueror and his soldiers sang the "Chanson de Roland" on the eve of their historic victory against the Anglo-Saxons at the Battle of Hastings in 1066.[16] Charlemagne was canonized in 1165, only four years after the canonization of English king Edward the Confessor, adding royal sainthood to his idealized legend. Throughout the Middle Ages, the Charlemagne myth flourished in chivalric romances in parallel with British folklore about King Arthur and the Knights of the Round Table. While tales of knights errant and courtly love fell out of fashion in the early Renaissance (Cervantes parodied the genre in *Don Quixote*), the attraction of medieval legends like the "Song of Roland" endured into the Enlightenment. Handel's famous opera *Orlando* (Italian for "Roland") was based on the sixteenth-century Italian epic poem "Orlando Furioso," recounting the romantic travails of Charlemagne's chivalrous knight who falls in love with a Saracen princess, Angelica.

Charlemagne's major comeback in the popular imagination came in the nineteenth century. Two things happened in that century that catapulted medieval legends into the spotlight. First, the Romantic movement's rebellion against Enlightenment rationalism triggered a fascination with all things gothic. The gothic revival movement, which spread from literature to architecture, took inspiration from pre-Enlightenment themes associated with the medieval age. In literature, the movement began as early as 1764 with Horace Walpole's *The Castle of Otranto*, continued in the early nineteenth century with Mary Shelley's *Frankenstein* and Sir Walter Scott's *Ivanhoe*, followed by the tales of Edgar Allen Poe and Bram Stoker's *Dracula*.[17] The second event happened not in the sphere of popular imagination, but on the battlefield. In the nineteenth century, Europe was once again soaked in blood as French and German rule—first Napoleon, then Bismarck—attempted to dominate the continent just as Charlemagne had done a thousand years earlier. But was Charlemagne a German or French emperor? Napoleon hero-worshipped Charlemagne. For Germans, Charlemagne had ruled over the Germanic Holy Roman Empire that was dissolved by Napoleon in 1806. Thus Charlemagne became an idealized Teutonic symbol of German national aspirations throughout the nineteenth century. His double Frankish-Germanic identity made his myth popular in both France and Germany. Each could claim him as their own. [18]

In France, the equestrian statue of Charlemagne in front of Notre Dame stands there for a good reason. The statue, showing Charlemagne with a Nuremberg crown on his head, was commissioned in the 1850s shortly after Napoleon III overthrew the French republic. Charlemagne was a potent symbol for France's Second Empire, even though the statue remained unfinished until after Napoleon III was defeated by Bismarck in 1871. In the subsequent years, France's secular Third Republic was not particularly interested in images of sacred kings. So the Charlemagne statue was bolted down in front of Notre Dame.

During the Nazi occupation of Paris in the early 1940s, the Germans melted down bronze statues throughout the French capital. The statue of Charlemagne presented a dilemma. Some top Nazis despised Charlemagne—"Karl der Grosse " in German—for his massacre of Germanic Saxons. Hitler personally intervened and ordered that Charlemagne was never to be described as the "butcher of the Saxons." In the Third Reich, Charlemagne was a symbol for the German Empire. [19] Charlemagne was like a Teutonic hero from the Wagnerian operas admired by the Führer. One of Hitler's SS divisions was named "Charlemagne." In 1942, when the Nazis were attempting to boost national resolve in the middle of the Second World War, Germans held celebrations to commemorate the 1,200th anniversary of Charlemagne's birth. In Nazi-occupied France, melting down a statue of Karl der Grosse, even in Paris, was out of the question. So the equestrian statue of Charlemagne remained untouched— and still stands in front of Notre Dame today.

After the Second World War, Charlemagne was resurrected yet again as the "Father of Europe." The founding fathers of a united Europe saw in him a glorious symbol of continental unity. Charlemagne had forged a European union through the force of arms and Christian faith. The new modern Europe was to be a more rational construction. Peace would be achieved through mutual economic interests and goodwill. The legacy of Charlemagne was integrated into Europe's new political project. In 1965, the 800th anniversary of Charlemagne's canonization, the Council of Europe sponsored an ambitious exhibition in his medieval capital of Aachen. [20] When the European Union finally came into existence in 1992, the location selected for the official EU signing ceremony was Maastricht, a city at the heart of Charlemagne's empire. So were the European Union's capitals, Strasbourg and Brussels. Further recognition came from *The Economist* magazine, which gave a fitting name to its regular column on European affairs: "Charlemagne."

In today's post-Brexit world, the European Union appears to be floundering, torn apart from within, doubting its own future, proving that national myths are more powerful than supranational ideals. Still, the parts of Europe once governed by Charlemagne—stretching from modern France through the Netherlands and Germany—remain solidly committed to the European ideal that he consolidated under his rule.

In the spring of 2018, French president Emmanuel Macron was awarded the Charlemagne Prize for his "vision of a new Europe." Macron traveled to Aachen to receive the prize in Charlemagne's coronation room. The citation praised the French president as a "courageous pioneer for the revitalization of the European dream."

***

Alfred the Great is widely regarded as the founder of the English nation. Winston Churchill, himself a great figure in history, called Alfred the greatest Englishman who ever lived. In polls about the greatest figures in British history, Alfred always ranks near the top.

Alfred is the only British monarch who has been honored with the exalted sobriquet "Great." His heroic legend as hammer of the Danes is one of the most familiar stories in the annals of British history. During the Victorian era, Alfred was the revered icon of an Anglo-Saxon cult that legitimized the ambitions of the British Empire. In 1899, a statue of Alfred, holding his sword aloft, was erected in Winchester for the millennium commemoration of his death in that English town. Stained-glass images of Alfred can still be viewed in many English churches, and he is venerated in the Anglican Communion as a Christian hero whose feast day is October 26. Children in Britain still learn the affectionate tale of King Alfred being scolded by a peasant woman for unwittingly burning her cakes on a stove.

In his own lifetime, Alfred was described as *veredicus*, Latin for "truthful." He was regarded as a man who loved wisdom and did not shun the truth. It is ironic, therefore, that so much of what we know about him is myth.

Alfred the Great is England's Charlemagne. His legend over the centuries was based on the same double narrative that inspired the Charlemagne myth: Christian piety and military prowess. Alfred was portrayed as the pious English king who drove away pagan Viking invaders and forged England as a Christian people. But as with Charlemagne, what was frequently accepted as fact about Alfred was in fact historical fable. Alfred was the first English king to benefit from a meticulous theological airbrushing by the Church's PR men in the monasteries.[21]

Most of what we know about Alfred comes from a Welsh monk called John Asser, who became a bishop around 890 AD. Like Charlemagne's official scribe Einhard, Asser was an insider on Alfred's payroll. His *Life of King Alfred*—written in Latin under the title *Vita Ælfredi regis Angul Saxonum*—had no pretense to objectivity.[22] Asser was to Alfred what Eusebian was to Constantine, Procopius to Justinian, and Einhard to Charlemagne. He was king Alfred's court propagandist whose purpose was lavish encomium.

Asser wrote *Life of King Alfred* around 893, six years before Alfred's death. It was not, therefore, a posthumous biography or a "secret history." It was written while its regal subject was very much alive. More to the point, Alfred could read and approve every word of the manuscript. Alfred not only commissioned his own biography but also devoted great attention to its publication. He was, like Charlemagne, a shrewd self-publicist keenly aware that he was creating a cult of personality around his own kingship. He had already commissioned the *Anglo-Saxon Chronicles* as official propaganda. He must have regarded Asser's biography as a key document in further self-publicity efforts.

Alfred had hand-picked Asser among many other learned men he attracted to his Anglo-Saxon court. He must have found the educated Welsh bishop extraordinarily useful. He turned to Asser to produce a translation of Pope Gregory I's *Regulae Pastoralis* (*Pastoral Care*) from Latin into Old English. Alfred was deeply interested in Pope Gregory— for whom the monophonic "Gregorian Chant" was named—due to the pontiff's connection to England. Gregory I was the pope who, in 597 AD, had sent the Benedictine monk Augustine to England to evangelize the pagan Anglo-Saxons.

Asser's *Life of King Alfred* belonged squarely in the medieval tradition of monastic writings interpreting history through the filter of Christian theology. He almost certainly had read Bede's *Ecclesiastical History of the English People*.[23] Bede's ambitious history, completed in 731, recounted the Christian evangelization of England from Roman times to his own day. More didactic than historical, Bede's book recounted the transformation of Anglo-Saxon Britain into a Christian nation thanks to missionaries such as Augustine. Bede's point was that the disparate peoples on the British Isles—Anglo-Saxons, Britons, Picts, Irish—had been brought together in a single purpose through the Christian faith. Later medieval historians, such as Geoffrey of Monmouth (he too was a monk), nurtured the same legend of Alfred. Monmouth's *History of the Kings of Britain*, written circa 1136, was read as factual history for several centuries, though today it's considered largely unreliable, probably fictitious, more fantasy than fact.[24] Monmouth, like Virgil in ancient Rome, attempted to establish a heroic connection with the Trojan warrior Aeneas, this time as founder of the British nation. Monmouth claimed that the founder of Britain was Brutus of Troy, a descendant of Aeneas. The myth of direct lineage from ancient Troy—also part of Charlemagne's Frankish historical mythology—was a cultural infatuation inherited from the Romans. It was pure historical *mythos*.

Monmouth also spun the Arthurian legend—evoking Guinevere, the wizard Merlin, the Knights of the Round Table, the magical sword Excalibur—about the legendary sixth-century British king who defended the island from the Anglo-Saxon invaders. There were many other myths about early British kings. Perhaps the most famous was Vortigern, the British warlord whose legend was fabricated by the sixth-century historian (and monk) Gildas in his book *On the Ruin and Conquest of Britain*. The title left little doubt how his story was going to end. According to the legend, Vortigern invited the Saxons to Britain to help him fight the Scots and Picts. But the Germanic invaders turned against him and seized control of modern-day Kent. According to Gildas, the invasion of Britain by impious Saxons ("a race hateful both to God and men") was punishment for Britons' sin of resisting conversion to Christianity. The moral lesson was thus religious. So was the prescription: strong Christian kingship was necessary to defeat heathen invaders.

Asser's *Life of King Alfred* was likely inspired by Bede. His portrait of Alfred as a pious king driving off pagan invaders carried forward Bede's Christian narrative. In Asser's treatment of Alfred's life, biographical facts invariably advanced the cause of Christian theology. He recounted how Alfred's father, the Saxon king Æthelwulf of Wessex, sent young Alfred to Rome when he was only four years old to be confirmed by Pope Leo IV. The pontiff adopted Alfred as his spiritual son and anointed him as a future "king." This sacred legend created the impression that Alfred's destiny as a great king had been pre-ordained by the pope. It's almost certainly an invented story, however. Alfred was the youngest child in a family of six children. His older brothers, not him, were in line to become king of Wessex.

Alfred obviously was not loath to provide his friendly biographer with intimate details of his personal life. He confided to Asser, for example, that as a youth he was so overcome with carnal desires that he prayed to God to be afflicted with an illness that would prevent his lust. His prayers were answered when he came down with "ficus," or piles. According to Asser, however, the hemorrhoids were so painful that he prayed to God to afflict him with a less agonizing illness.[25] Those prayers were answered too, though the precise nature of Alfred's lifelong disease was never made explicit. The point here is that Asser exploited the embarrassing anecdote to put a classic theological spin on Alfred's dilemma. Alfred turned to God to master his carnal sins through painful denigration of the flesh.

The other section of Asser's biography was devoted to his great achievements and martial defense of the faith. The tales of Alfred's military campaigns were more entrenched in historical fact, though often embellished. Alfred earned his mythic reputation as Defender of the Faith by defeating impious Viking pagans. In 878, Alfred defeated the so-called Great Heathen Army at the Battle of Edington in Wiltshire. Recounting this historic victory, Asser was careful to spin the story with a religious message. The Danish pagans had attacked Alfred's troops on the Epiphany—January 6, 878. Forced into exile, Alfred raised an army to take back his kingdom. At Edington, Alfred finally defeated the Viking king Guthrum, whom he forced to convert to Christianity. Alfred even stood sponsor at Guthrum's baptism to ensure that his defeated Danish enemy was a truly converted Christian. Guthrum took the name Æthelstan and returned to rule over East Anglia, leaving the western part of England to Alfred. In the end, the battle against the Vikings ended in a truce and peace treaty. But the battle was a decisive victory for the Christian faith.

The parallels between the Alfred and Charlemagne legends are remarkable. Both kings were divinely inspired to battle the heathens after the intercession of a saint. The Apostle James appeared before Charlemagne in a dream; Saint Cuthbert called upon Alfred in a vision. And both Charlemagne and Alfred converted enemy heathens to the Christian faith. The conversion of Guthrum mirrored the tale of Charlemagne defeating the Saxon king Widukind, forcing him to convert to Christianity, and personally assisting at his baptism. These parallels were not a coincidence. For the monks writing historical chronicles, they were well-established literary conventions in Christian narratives about sacred monarchs. Heroic Christian kings were inspired by visions of saints to battle the heathens and convert them to the cross.

The secular aspects in Alfred's legend were constructed to portray him as a king with a common touch. The most famous tale about Alfred's character is the "burnt cakes" story. After being routed by the Vikings, Alfred retreated to the Somerset marshes, where he was short of food. One day he came upon a swineherd's hut where a peasant woman offered him shelter. Not realizing who Alfred was, she asked him to watch over some wheaten cakes cooking on the fire. Alfred graciously complied, but was so distracted tending his weapons that he forgot to turn the cakes over. When the peasant woman returned and saw the burnt cakes, she scolded Alfred for his carelessness. Another version of the tale, more in keeping with religious propaganda, claims Alfred had been distracted with meditations on holy scripture. The endearing burnt cakes story was, in fact, fabricated by monkish chroniclers more than a century later. It was a post-facto invention, possibly lifted from an old Norse saga.[26]

Another aspect of Alfred's character recounted by Asser was his remarkable intellectual gifts as an ecclesiastical scholar. The image of Alfred as a man of great learning took hold early and endured for centuries. In the fourteenth century, Oxford University designated Alfred as its founder. In 1384, fellows at the university submitted to King Richard II a petition (written in Old French) referring to itself as "the Great University College in Oxford, which College was first founded by your noble ancestor King Alfred." The claim that Alfred had founded the college was a convenient fiction. The University College fellows were buttering up Richard II in a bid to secure title to property in Oxford. Centuries later, Oxford colleges boasted their connection with King Alfred's patronage. At Brasenose College, a seventeenth-century bust of Alfred stood above the door of the refectory. At University College, a life-size statue of the venerated Anglo-Saxon king was placed over the outer arch of the gate tower in the late seventeenth century, though it was later taken down and moved to the doorway leading to the college hall.[27] A marble bust of wise king Alfred was displayed in the college's Poynton Reading Room.

It is undoubtedly true that Alfred, like Charlemagne on the continent, had a great thirst for learning and recruited bishops and abbots to foster a revival of learning in his kingdom. There is little evidence, however, that Alfred himself was a great scholar. He didn't learn to read until he was twelve. His lack of formal education was typical of cultural attitudes toward education in the early Middle Ages following the collapse of Roman civilization. Outside of monasteries, the level of learning in England in Alfred's day was astoundingly poor. Even kings had little grasp of Latin and Greek. Alfred spoke Old English. He relied on John Asser to translate Pope Gregory's *Pastoral Care* from Latin. To Alfred's credit, he sought to elevate learning in England by producing translations of Latin works into Old English, including Saint Augustine's *Soliloquies* and Bede's *Ecclesiastical History*. Asser humbly gave credit to Alfred for the *Pastoral Care* translation, stating that the king had suddenly learned Latin by "divine inspiration." This may have seemed plausible in the Middle Ages when many things were attributed to divine intervention. But the story of Alfred's miraculous mastery of Latin through an epiphany-like flash was historical fantasy.

Alfred the Great's most enduring legend, as father of the English nation, was born of historical convenience following the Reformation. In Tudor England, after four turbulent centuries under the "Norman yoke," the English were turning nostalgically back to their Anglo-Saxon past. Alfred's lack of sainthood made him—in contrast to Edward the Confessor—a palatable post-Reformation symbol for an idealized period in English history before the Norman Conquest. William the Conqueror had transformed England after 1066, but his authoritarian Norman legacy was unappealing. From a Tudor perspective, the Normans had suppressed the Anglo-Saxon culture of personal liberty and replaced democratic trial-by-jury legal institutions with trial by ordeal, feudal tyranny, and Roman Catholicism.[28] This sentiment was based partly on Anglo-Saxon nostalgia that defied historical facts. The Normans had put an end to slavery, which, after the Romans left, had flourished in Britain under the Anglo-Saxons. At the time of the Norman Conquest in 1066, some 10 percent of the entire British population were slaves, sold abroad in port cities such as Bristol, just as Dublin had been a Viking slave-trading center. No matter, by the Tudor-era sixteenth century, the English had had enough of the Normans and their dynastic wars in France. Alfred symbolized Tudor England's reconnection with an old Anglo-Saxon identity. Politically, his impeccable Anglo-Saxon credentials made him a perfect candidate for Protestant propaganda after Henry VIII's break with Rome and determination to establish his own English church. It was during the Tudor period that people started referring to him as "Alfred the Great," a title that had never been used in his own lifetime. A testimony to his fame in Tudor England was the publication in 1574 of a new edition of Asser's *Life of King Alfred*.

Following the revival of Alfred's legend in Tudor England, British monarchs sought to associate their rules with his legacy. During the Stuart period, a biography of Alfred in 1634 drew a comparison between Charles I and Alfred the Great, claiming that Charles embodied Alfred's respect for English law. The timing was unfortunate. Charles's battles with parliament were just beginning, and the Civil War was on the horizon. In the eighteenth century, the Hanoverian kings enthusiastically embraced Alfred the Great's legend—not surprisingly, given their shared Germanic ancestry. Particularly active in the Alfred revival movement was Frederick, Prince of Wales, eldest son of George II. The eighteenth century witnessed a flourishing of patriotic manifestos, plays, and operas based on Alfred the Great, especially after the wars with France. Alfred was the Anglo-Saxon king who had driven out foreigners—Danes in his day, but a useful symbol against the French too. In 1762, Scottish philosopher David Hume effusively praised Alfred in his *The History of England from the Invasion of Julius Caesar to the Revolution in 1688*. Seizing on a principle dear in his own era, Hume lauded Alfred as the first champion of individual liberties. Alfred, he noted, fought to ensure that the English "should forever remain as free as their own thoughts."[29]

Alfred the Great's legend soared to the status of apotheosis in the nineteenth century. In the Victorian era, popular histories of Alfred turned the Anglo-Saxon king into a schoolboy hero. Not only did Victorians cherish Alfred as the embodiment of England's Christian virtues, but he also became venerated as the symbol of a national cult of Anglo-Saxonism. Fascination with Alfred in the nineteenth century can be partly explained by that era's romantic nostalgia for everything gothic. Charlemagne's myth had benefited from the same nineteenth-century fascination with the medieval period. In Victorian Britain, Alfred's legend also provided a heroic narrative that gave legitimacy to British superiority in a great era of progress and imperialism. The Anglo-Saxon race, boasting a pedigree stretching back a thousand years to Alfred the Great, richly deserved their status as rulers of an empire on which the sun never set.

In the early 1850s, Charles Dickens published a *Child's History of England* that praised Alfred the Great as the embodiment of the Anglo-Saxon race that was a model to the world. "Under the great Alfred, all the best points of the English-Saxon character were first encouraged, and in him first shown," writes Dickens.

> Wherever the descendants of the Saxon race have gone, have sailed or otherwise made their way, even to the remotest regions of the world, they have been patient, persevering, never to be broken in spirit, never to be turned aside from enterprises on which they have resolved. In Europe, Asia, Africa, America, the whole world over; in the desert, in the forest, on the sea; scorched by the burning sun, or frozen by ice that never melts; the Saxon blood remains unchanged. Wheresoever that race goes, there, law, and industry, and safety for life and property, and all the great results of steady perseverance, are certain to rise.[30]

At the height of the Victorian period, there was a veritable "Alfredophilia" cult in England. The Christian name "Alfred" became hugely popular. The era's greatest poet, Lord Tennyson, was called Alfred. Tennyson's successor as Poet Laureate was Alfred Austin. Queen Victoria's second son was also named Alfred. At a time of suspicion toward the German origins of the Queen's consort, Prince Albert of Saxe-Cobourg and Gotha, the monarchy could romanticize their Saxon bloodlines stretching back to Alfred the Great. In 1899, the bishop of London declared that "the blood of Alfred still ran in the veins of her Most Gracious Majesty Queen Victoria."[31] Arthur Conan Doyle, creator of Sherlock Holmes and great supporter of British imperialism, declared in 1899 on the occasion of Alfred the Great's millennial commemoration:

> What we are really commemorating is not merely the anniversary of the death of King Alfred but the greatness of those institutions which he founded. This anniversary may be said to indicate the thousandth milestone in the majestic journey of our race. . . . From that, the greatest of English kings, to this the greatest of British queens, there extends that unbroken record, the longest which the modern world can show.[32]

The twentieth century was less enthusiastic about Alfred the Great. Things got off to a bad start in 1914 when Britain went to war against the German Kaiser, who was the favorite grandson of Queen Victoria. After the war, the British monarchy hastily changed their German name, Saxe-Cobourg-Gotha, to the more acceptably English "Windsor." The decline of the British Empire following the Second World War didn't help matters. Victorian values were out, and with them Alfred the Great as a glorious Anglo-Saxon symbol of British imperialism. Britain's membership in the European Union starting in the 1970s marked a turn toward the Continent. The legend of Alfred the Great, hammer of the Danes, had been inspired by his valiant defiance of invasions from Europe. The moment belonged to Charlemagne, not Alfred.

Today, the legend of Alfred the Great has become blurred in the popular imagination. King Alfred, ironically, is often confused with King Arthur, famous for fighting off the Saxon invaders. Alfred the Great's legend is part fact, part fiction; the historical romance of King Arthur is entirely fiction. Most prefer the fantasy. The venerated Anglo-Saxon ruler has been upstaged by a folkloric Celtic king and his Knights of the Round Table. Camelot is a more compelling narrative than a story about burnt cakes.

It's possible that Alfred could make a comeback, especially in the post-Brexit era of populist nationalism and Euro-skepticism in England. But the resurgence of an Anglo-Saxon identity would inevitably splinter the British nation, returning to traditional cultural cleavages between English and Celtic—and possibly break up the United Kingdom.

6

BONFIRES OF VANITIES

The Cadaver Synod was undoubtedly the most gruesome episode in the history of the Catholic Church.

The *Synodus Horrenda*, as it's known in Latin, was the ecclesiastical trial of a dead pope. The pontiff was put on trial not just in name, posthumously. His rotting corpse was dug up and dragged into an ecclesiastical court.

The event was so macabre that it's difficult to believe that it actually happened. No official record of the Cadaver Synod exists. It was so horrifying that the Vatican quietly expunged this shameful chapter from its own history. Too unspeakable to be known, it was a truth that the Church wanted suppressed.

The macabre event took place in the St. John Lateran Basilica in Rome. The year was 897 AD. The chief prosecutor was the sitting pope, Stephen VI, elected pontiff a year earlier. The defendant was the late Pope Formosus, accused of crimes committed during his papacy. His putrefied cadaver was exhumed and hauled into court, where the body was propped up on a throne. Pope Stephen shouted out the charges against the deceased pontiff: perjury, coveting the papacy, and violating Church canons.[1]

The name of the accused, Formosus, meant "good looking" in Latin. One can imagine, however, his ghoulish physical appearance while Pope Stephen fulminated at his corpse in an advanced state of decomposition.[2] Since Formosus was in no condition to speak for himself, a young deacon had been appointed to defend the corpse. Terrified, the novice cowered behind his dead client as Pope Stephen hurled abuse at the cadaver. At one point during the trial, an earthquake struck Rome, shaking the basilica and causing part of the structure to collapse. It must have seemed like a dark omen presaging the fall of the papacy itself.

A shocking deviance from the pious image of the Church as heavenly kingdom, the Cadaver Synod exposed the dark irrationality of a corrupt papacy mired in the worst excesses of the Earthly City. It marked the beginning of the Church's so-called Dark Age, or *saeculum obscurum*, through most of the tenth century. This was the scandalous chapter of the "bad popes."[3]

It is impossible to grasp the horror of the Cadaver Synod without understanding the historical backdrop that made it possible. The ninth century was a period of ceaseless turmoil and upheaval throughout Christendom. Following the death of Charlemagne in 814 AD, his Holy Roman Empire gradually unraveled and slipped into violence and chaos. The Frankish kings, and Charlemagne in particular, had provided the papacy with protection and stability. Charlemagne had saved Pope Leo III from assassination by Roman nobles, restored him as pontiff, and sent a strong message that the papacy was under Frankish military protection. The Church's alliance with, and dependency on, Charlemagne had been sacralized with his coronation as Holy Roman emperor. Following Charlemagne's death, however, his *divisio regnorum* policy split his empire among his heirs. The result was power struggles, civil war, and warring fiefdoms. The incompetent reign of Charlemagne's lethargic great-grandson, known as Charles the Fat, effectively dissolved the empire after he was deposed in 887 AD.[4] Europe was now a rough patchwork of rival potentates, *multi reguli* in Latin, with no overarching structure of temporal power. They were not only quarreling among one another but also preoccupied by foreign threats from invading Muslims, Magyars, and Vikings.

The breakdown of Charlemagne's empire meant that the papacy could no longer count on the protection of Frankish kings. Popes lost their aura and prestige. Worse, the power vacuum rendered popes vulnerable to foreign invasions and usurpers inside Italy. In 853, when the future Alfred the Great visited Rome as a small child of four, the pontiff who anointed the boy was busy constructing a forty-foot wall around the Vatican to fend off assaults by marauding Muslims who had attacked Rome and desecrated the graves of apostles Peter and Paul. In the snakepit of Italian politics, the powerful aristocratic dynasties who had imprisoned Pope Leo III now had their hands free to take control of the papacy. Popes became the puppets of powerful Roman families who fixed papal elections and, if necessary, had recalcitrant pontiffs deposed or murdered. Popes rarely lasted long; many died in suspicious circumstances, usually violently. Deposed pontiffs were usually replaced by even more sinister characters. As the sacred surrendered to the profane, pontiffs lapsed into shocking corruption—selling offices, nepotism, concubinage, financial malfeasance, and murder plots. At the end of the ninth century, more than two dozen popes died violently—bludgeoned, poisoned, strangled, smothered, mutilated. Fifteen years before the Cadaver Synod, plotters inside the papal court attempted to poison Pope John VIII. When the poison didn't produce the desired result, the assassins smashed in his skull with a hammer. That did the job.

It was in this paranoid climate of political rivalry and corruption that, in 897 AD, Pope Stephen ordered the exhumation of his penultimate predecessor. Pope Formosus had been pontiff from 891 to 896, during the period of turmoil and chaos following the disintegration of the Frankish-controlled Holy Roman Empire. Before his elevation to the papacy, Formosus had enjoyed an excellent reputation as a brilliant missionary. He was, perhaps, too successful as a cleric. He muscled in on the turf of other bishops. His ambition attracted resentment. He was a cleric with his eye on the prize—and it finally came. Following the murder of Pope John VIII—the pope who had his head bashed in—the papal turnover rate had been terrifyingly high. In 891, it was Formosus's turn.

Formosus had been dead for seven months when his corpse, ripped from a crypt at St. Peter's Basilica, was hauled before the pontifical court. The decaying cadaver was still clad in papal vestments, propped up on its throne like a broken puppet. The gruesome trial concluded with a verdict. Guilty of perjury. Guilty of coveting the papacy. Guilty of violating Church canons.

These accusations were trumped-up charges against Formosus. The real reason he had been subjected to posthumous humiliation was political. Formosus had made the mistake of crossing the most powerful dynasty in Italy, the Spoletos. The dukes of Spoleto had ruled much of Italy outside the Papal States since the sixth century. They boasted the exalted titles of *dux et marchio* (duke and margrave) and had married into Charlemagne's dynasty. It was thanks to the Spoletos' military power that the Saracen invasion of Italy in 846 had been repelled. That attack had almost been catastrophic for the papacy. Muslim forces had surrounded Rome and plundered the treasures of the old St. Peter's Basilica.

The routing of the Saracens tremendously enhanced the Spoletos' prestige in Italy. They were richly rewarded in 889 when Pope Stephen V crowned Guido Spoleto as king of Italy, taking the name Guy III. But the Spoletos had set their sights higher. They coveted an imperial title. And after Charlemagne's great-grandson Charles the Fat's overthrow in 887, the exalted title of Holy Roman Emperor was up for grabs. In 891, Guido had himself duly crowned Holy Roman Emperor with the complicity of the same friendly pope, Stephen V. Now the Spoletos were the most powerful dynasty in Europe. Except for one caveat: they were still vassals of the pope. And shortly after Guy Spoleto's coronation as Holy Roman Emperor, the new pontiff was Pope Formosus.

Pope Formosus distrusted the ambitious Spoletos, but had to recognize their formidable political power. Formosus therefore ceded reluctantly to their pressures to appoint Guido's son, Lambert, as co–Holy Roman Emperor, thus ensuring dynastic succession. But Formosus, fearing that the Spoletos were attempting to outmaneuver him, immediately regretted his decision. He began plotting behind their backs to break the Spoletos' hold on the imperial throne. Looking for a rival candidate for Holy Roman Emperor, he turned to a direct descendant of Charlemagne: Arnulf of Carinthia, king of East Francia, the man who had deposed his uncle Charles the Fat.

Dangling the imperial title before Arnulf, Formosus convinced him to invade Italy and oust the Spoletos. When Guy suddenly died in 894, Formosus found himself in direct conflict with the real power behind the Spoleto throne: Guy's widow, empress Algitrude Spoleto. An attractive blonde, Algitrude was a Lady Macbeth character who had masterminded her son Lambert's anointment as co–Holy Roman Emperor. When news of Arnulf's invasion reached the Spoletos, she moved quickly to have Formosus arrested and imprisoned. But Arnulf's Frankish army smashed through the gates of Rome and released Formosus. The Spoletos were defeated. In gratitude, Pope Formosus crowned Arnulf as Holy Roman Emperor before the crypt of St. Peter. Arnulf took the supplementary title "Caesar Augustus."

The Spoletos never forgot their humiliation. They wanted revenge. Good news came much sooner than they could have imagined. Formosus died shortly after Arnulf's coronation as Holy Roman Emperor. The papacy was suddenly vacant again. Now the Spoletos redoubled their efforts to secure the papacy for one of their glove-puppets, the bishop of Anagni. He was elected pope as Stephen VI.

With Stephen VI as pontiff, the Spoletos could now exact revenge on Formosus—even though he was dead. Pope Stephen would do what he was told. The fact that Stephen VI was likely insane, or suffering from a serious mental illness, was only a minor inconvenience. When Pope Stephen put Formosus's dead body on trial, the spectacle was a Spoleto-orchestrated vendetta whose intention was to humiliate and destroy Pope Formosus utterly, including what remained of his corpse.

Found guilty on all charges, Formosus was sentenced to *damnatio memoriae*, Latin for "condemnation of memory."[5] *Damnatio memoriae* had a long history stretching back to the Roman Empire, when it was required punishment for anyone found guilty of betraying the state. Roman elites dreaded a *damnatio* sentence. It meant you were effectively a non-person, erased from history. In the reign of Tiberius, his second-in-command Lucius Sejanus was executed and condemned to *damnatio* for his conspiracy to assassinate the emperor. Sejanus's name was removed from all records. The punishment was sometimes inflicted on deceased emperors. Following an emperor's death, the Roman Senate could either vote for *consecratio* (proclaiming the emperor as divine) or opt for *damnatio* (condemning him to perpetual disgrace). The emperors Caracalla, Commodus, and Alexander Severus were thus condemned, posthumously, as enemies of the Roman state. Constantine posthumously condemned his arch-rival Maxentius to *damnatio memoriae*. The sentence was enforced through wholesale destruction of statues of Maxentius, removal of his name from public inscriptions on monuments, and scratching his image from Roman coins.

Pope Formosus was, in like manner, consigned to oblivion for all eternity. His entire papacy was erased from history. But his accusers did not stop there. They insisted that the dead pontiff be punished physically, too. His putrefied flesh was to be desecrated. His cadaver was stripped of its papal robes before the mutilation began.[6] First, the three fingers Formosus had used for papal blessings were chopped off. Then his body was dragged through the corridors of the basilica and flung off a balcony. The crowds below gasped in horror. The corpse was finally buried in a common grave. Some claimed it was re-exhumed, tied to weights, and thrown into the Tiber River.

Rumors soon circulated that Formosus was resurrected and performing miracles. This "miracle performing" superstition was not uncommon in medieval Christendom—not unlike the revival legends about Nero during the early Christian era. Outraged by the posthumous cruelty inflicted on Formosus, public opinion in Rome quickly turned against Pope Stephen. The outcry soon turned violent. Pope Stephen was tracked down, deposed, imprisoned, and strangled to death.

While this was hardly the first time a pope had been brutally murdered, it was a serious crisis for the papacy. The Spoletos had gone too far. The next pontiff, Theodore II, hastily convened a synod to invalidate Formosus's *damnatio* sentence. Formosus's remains were solemnly reburied in St. Peter's Basilica in a ceremony officiated by Pope Theodore himself.

But the gruesome saga was still not over. A decade later, a new pope, Sergius III, overturned the exculpations and found Formosus guilty yet again. Pope Sergius had Formosus's body—ten years dead at this point— disinterred, put on trial again, found guilty, and decapitated. The headless cadaver was once again thrown into the Tiber, where it became entangled in a fisherman's net.

Like the actions of Pope Stephen, Sergius III's motives were ignoble. He was, even by the shameful papal standards of the era, an irredeemably wretched man. Like Stephen VI, he was a puppet of a powerful aristocratic dynasty, in his case the Theophylact family, who dominated Roman politics as counts of Tusculum (they were intermarried with the Spoletos). Sergius III became pope by plotting the murders of his two immediate predecessors, one by strangulation. Once installed as pontiff, Sergius took Count Theophylact's fifteen-year-old daughter, Marozia, as his mistress with the approval of her mother Theodora, herself the mistress of a previous pope. The bastard son of Sergius and Marozia later became Pope John XI. With Sergius III, the Church's dark age *saeculum obscurum* had begun.

Sergius III's papacy was also known as "Pornocracy" because of the powerful role of Theophylact women as the real powers behind the pontifical throne.[7] Besides her son Pope John XI, Marozia became a dynastic matriarch who produced a long line of future popes: two grandsons, two great grandsons, and one great-great grandson. One was Pope Benedict IX, arguably the most dissolute and corrupt pope in history. Anointed pope in 1032 when he was only twenty, Benedict sold the papacy for a large bribe paid by his godfather, who became Pope Gregory VI (but later decided he wanted to be pope after all so attempted to depose Pope Gregory). The stinking corruption of the entire era led to the Gregorian Reforms, circa 1050, shortly after the expulsion of Benedict IX.

Despite the gruesome brutality inflicted by Sergius III on Formosus's mutilated corpse, the victim of the Cadaver Synod was vindicated in the end. The Vatican invalidated Pope Sergius's charges against Formosus and had his remains buried, this time for good, in St. Peter's Basilica.

But while Formosus's reputation was rehabilitated, his name was forever cursed. No future pontiff ever took the name Formosus.

***

At the end of the fifteenth century, the city of Florence was seized by a convulsion of religious fanaticism that bordered on mass delirium. This episode in history remains an enigma, as does the man who fomented the collective hysteria: Dominican friar Girolamo Savonarola.

It is generally believed that the Reformation was triggered by the German theologian Martin Luther. While that is not historically inaccurate, it is often overlooked that the first rebellion against the Catholic Church came a generation earlier in Florence. The fanatical monk Savonarola incited a religious revolution that shook the papacy like a volcanic eruption.

Savonarola remains one of the most perplexing characters in history. For some he was a divinely inspired prophet who revolted against corrupt papal power. For others, he was an illuminated lunatic whose tragedy foreshadowed centuries of irrational violence inflicted on the modern world by religious fanaticism. It is difficult to assess the moral lesson of Savonarola's short-lived theocratic republic in Florence. We know how it ended, of course. In 1498, Savonarola was hanged and burned at the stake before a Florentine mob in the city that he'd proclaimed as the New Jerusalem. Machiavelli, who witnessed the execution with his own eyes, observed that Savonarola was an opportunist who "colored his lies." Though in his famous treatise, *The Prince,* Machiavelli dignified the fanatical priest's memory by citing his downfall as a lesson in the cruel realities of politics.[8]

Machiavelli's assessment of Savonarola's failed Florentine republic was intended as a lesson in statecraft for Renaissance princes. Understanding how a figure like Savonarola emerged as a powerful force in Italian politics requires a grasp of wider historical dynamics that Machiavelli himself, as a contemporary who attended the fanatical monk's sermons, was living through in the present. Three key factors can open insights into Savonarola and the epoch that produced him. First, his religious fanaticism was a reaction to the burst of humanism in the early Italian Renaissance, especially the revival of pagan Antiquity as a revered cultural reference. Second, the perceived corruption of the Roman popes and powerful dynasties like the Medicis gave Savonarola symbolic targets for his Apocalyptic fulminations against the depravity of his age. Finally, the explosion of the printing press in his own lifetime put a powerful new medium in Savonarola's hands to propagate his religious and political agendas. Savonarola smashed to pieces the traditional mold of the monk serving as official Church propagandist. His illuminated zealotry was a radical message of dissent against the papacy.

Florence in the late fifteenth century was at the center of the Italian Renaissance that owed much to rich benefactors such as the Medicis and other Florentine fortunes. Humanism flourished, and the greatest artists of the era, including Leonardo da Vinci and Michelangelo, converged on Florence. The Vatican, too, was a great patron of the arts, commissioning works by Botticelli, Perugino, and Rosselli. It was also an age of decadence, depravity, and political violence.

In some respects, Savonarola was a pure product of Renaissance Italy . Born in Ferrara in 1452, he received a classical education, studying not only the Sacred Scriptures but also logic, Aristotelean philosophy, and humanist writers such as Petrarch. He was meant to follow his father into the medical profession. Some accounts claim he turned to religion after romantic rejection by a Florentine girl living in Ferrara. In 1475, he entered a Dominican monastery in Bologna, where he remained cloistered for several years. After a few years preaching throughout Italy, in 1490 he ended up in Florence to take up a teaching position at the San

Marco convent, which depended on the patronage of the powerful Medici dynasty.[9]

As a young priest, Savonarola saw "blind wickedness" wherever he looked in Italy. He was revolted by the worldly excesses and corruption he saw everywhere. He had been writing poems with titles such as "On the Ruin of the Church" and, even more apocalyptic, "On the Ruin of the World." He was outraged that religious truths were, in his view, being usurped by values celebrating the glory of man. He believed that the Renaissance celebration of humanism—embodied by the Medici dynasty—was driving Christians from the City of God. He was convinced that the Church in Rome was a corrupt abomination that needed to be cleansed and purified. As a fanatical priest at the height of the Italian Renaissance, Savonarola was on a collision course with his own epoch.

Savonarola was a religious fanatic even by the standards of Church doctrine. Before Savonarola's day, medieval theologians had transformed Christian theology. In the thirteenth century, Thomas Aquinas had argued that both faith and reason were the source of religious truth. His "two truths" assertion marked a rupture with the Platonic inspiration for Christian theology, based largely on idealism and mysticism. Aquinas embraced Aristotle's empirical philosophy based on logic and the physical world. According to Aquinas, religious truth was not only revelation and faith but also accessible through reason and intellectual inquiry. Aquinas reconciled both traditions, asserting that there are two sources of truth—faith and reason.[10] Savonarola had studied Aquinas's theological writings. But he embraced a reactionary theology hostile to the flourishing humanist values of the Renaissance. He regarded humanism as corrupt paganism that would be destroyed by the wrath of God. Truth for Savonarola was divine revelation.

Savonarola's denunciations of the wickedness of his age was not a lonely enterprise. He belonged to a larger movement of religious fundamentalists in fifteenth-century Italy who excoriated the sinful influence of Renaissance humanism, inspired by classical Antiquity's "pagan" culture, on Christian morality. A major figure in this movement was Bernardino da Feltre, a Franciscan monk who, two decades before Savonarola, was stirring up large audiences with impassioned sermons denouncing worldly turpitudes. He organized massive bonfires at which the faithful tossed onto the flames their worldly objects of sin—jewelry, wigs, charms, cosmetics, playing cards, and so on. In his sermons, Bernardino da Feltre vilified Jews for their practice of usury and called for their expulsion from Italy. His name is forever associated with a horrifying incident in the northern Italian town of Trent, where, in 1475, a two-year-old Christian infant called Simonino went missing. The boy's dead body was reportedly found on Easter Sunday in the basement of a local Jewish money lender called Samuel. Bernardino da Feltre delivered a series of inflamed sermons claiming that Jews had kidnapped and butchered Simonino to drink his blood at Passover. Stories about Jews ritually murdering Christian children at Passover had deep roots in medieval Europe. On the strength of vile rumors about the boy in Trent, local Jews were rounded up, tortured, and forced to confess to blood libel. Seventeen Jews were found guilty and burned at the stake. A Christian legend grew around the murdered boy, Simonino, who was said to be responsible for hundreds of miracles. He was later canonized as Saint Simon of Trent and venerated as a holy infant martyr.[11]

It was in this wider climate of religious fanaticism that Savonarola began attracting notoriety for his firebrand sermons in Florence. He must have been an extraordinary sight—gaunt expression, angular facial features, strong aquiline nose, eyes burning with intensity—as he electrified audiences packed into cathedrals. He exhorted Florentines to take Christ as their king. He declared that Florence had been chosen by God as the new Jerusalem—on condition that the city cleanse itself of sin. His blistering attacks spared no one. He excoriated the Church, whose sacred art portrayed the Virgin as a sensual feminine figure, exciting lust. He prophesied that, for these sins, the "sword of God" would bring terrible tribulations to Italy. He warned that the Day of Judgment was imminent and that horrendous catastrophes were coming. His fulminations were a direct attack on the papacy.

Savonarola's apocalyptical message struck a chord with Florentines. His doomsday sermons tapped into the early Renaissance *contemptus mundi* ("contempt for this world") zeitgeist that sought to expunge worldly sins. From early medieval times, Christians believed that life in this world was nothing but pain, misery, and suffering. The *contemptus* ethos flowed from medieval values about truth. Truth resided in the supernatural sphere and was accessible only through revelation and faith. The natural world was sin, pestilence, and agony. A constant reminder was the Black Death. The plague had arrived in Italy in the mid-fourteenth century and rapidly spread throughout Europe. It decimated roughly half of Europe's population and provoked catastrophic economic and social upheaval. In Florence where Savonarola was preaching, the plague had killed half of the city's population of 100,000. Little wonder that this horrific trail of devastation fueled religious fanaticism. Since people believed that everything in this world was God's will, the plague was accepted as divine punishment for wickedness. Flagellants whipped their bodies to purify their sins, hoping to escape God's wrath. Only religious faith held out the promise of redemption, salvation, and eternal life.

Savonarola's sermons quickly became so popular that they had to be moved to Florence's Duomo Cathedral, where he drew zealous audiences of 15,000 worshippers. He was a medieval celebrity, filling bigger and bigger venues. Savonarola prophesied that a "new Cyrus" from the Bible—the Persian king who ended the Babylonian captivity of the Jews and rebuilt the Temple in Jerusalem—was coming over the mountains to scourge Italy of its sins and purify the corrupt Roman papacy. He entranced his audiences with his emotional fulminations. As he warned of the coming Apocalypse and foretold of horrendous punishments for worldly sins—fornication, adultery, sodomy, envy—worshippers wept and wailed in the cathedral.[12]

One regular attendee at Savonarola's sermons was the painter Sandro Botticelli, famous for his "Birth of Venus" masterpiece. That work and its sister painting, "Primavera," were commissioned by the powerful Medicis. The painter's brother, Simone, was a devout follower of the radical Dominican friar. Simone brought his brother Sandro to Savonarola's sermons and introduced him to the charismatic priest. Historians dispute whether Botticelli himself shared his brother's religious zeal, but there can be no doubt that Savonarola exercised tremendous influence on the artist. When previously working under the Medicis' patronage, Botticelli produced works of sensual beauty that inspired the later Pre-Raphaelite and Art Nouveau movements. After meeting Savonarola, he began executing austere works inspired by the friar's apocalyptical sermons. His "Lamentation over the Dead Christ" was a sorrowful icon of Christ's body collapsed in the arms of the Virgin Mary consoled by the disciple John. Botticelli fell under Savonarola's spell.

Emboldened by his growing notoriety, Savonarola turned God's wrath on the most powerful figures and institutions in Italy. He called the Roman Curia a "whore," evoking the Whore of Babylon in the Bible. He expressed outrage at the complicity between Pope Innocent VIII and the powerful Medici dynasty. His audiences were astonished when he prophesized that patriarch Lorenzo de' Medici and Pope Innocent would both die in the same year: 1492. Such a macabre prediction about the two most powerful men in Italy was tantamount to treason, if not heresy. The precise date—1492—made Savonarola's prophecy even more astonishing.

Lorenzo de' Medici was also astounded, especially after he fell gravely ill in April 1492—just as Savonarola had predicted. The Medici patriarch had a gangrened leg and was on his deathbed. The accuracy of Savonarola's prediction now silenced his detractors. Lorenzo de' Medici summoned the priest to receive absolution from him. Some claim Savonarola damned the Medici patriarch on his deathbed; others say he blessed Lorenzo and administered last rites. Lorenzo de' Medici died on April 9, 1492. He was only forty-three.

When Pope Innocent VIII fell into a terrible fever a few months later, Florentines were stunned. Pope Innocent was one of history's less saintly pontiffs. A devious character motivated primarily by money and mistresses, his papacy was notable for its venality and sexual licentiousness. He was said to have fathered many children (eight sons and eight daughters) and placed them in influential positions in the Vatican power system. Lorenzo de' Medici consented to give his daughter Maddalena in marriage to one of Innocent's sons in exchange for appointing Lorenzo's son Giovanni a cardinal (he later became Pope Leo X, famous for his standoff with England's Henry VIII). When not busy selling Vatican offices and bartering his children, Pope Innocent was eradicating sorcery by dispatching papal inquisitors throughout Christendom to put witches on trial.

In late July 1492, when Innocent suddenly fell ill, his physician attempted to save the sixty-year-old pontiff's life with a blood "transfusion." The operation was evidently the first blood transfusion ever performed. According to one legend, Pope Innocent drank the infused blood drawn from three ten-year-old boys. The boys, each paid a ducat for their participation in the medical experiment, died during the infusion—and so did the Pope. This vampire story was undoubtedly apocryphal, invented centuries later. It even had a tinge of anti-Semitism, for the doctor who allegedly performed the deadly operation was said to be a Jew, described in one account as "a deceiver." What is beyond dispute, however, is that Pope Innocent died in late July 1492. [13]

Both Lorenzo de' Medici and Pope Innocent VIII had died in the same year, 1492. Savonarola's followers were in awe. There could be no doubt that the Dominican priest was the true prophet he claimed to be.

Following Innocent VIII's bizarre death in 1492, he was succeeded by Rodrigo Borgia, who ascended to the papacy as Pope Alexander VI. If Pope Innocent's conduct had been shockingly corrupt, he was quickly outdone by his successor. Although the dark chapter of the Cadaver Synod and Church's *saeculum obscurum* was five centuries in the past, the papacy was still controlled by powerful family dynasties who regarded the Holy See as a political prize.

Pope Alexander VI was from the Spanish Borgia clan, infamous for their ambition, cunning, and cruelty. Alexander VI, born in 1431, was not a figure of admirable Christian piety. A Renaissance embodiment of the Machiavellian spirit, he bribed his way to the papacy. As pope, he was more interested in plots, power, and self-aggrandizement than in the souls of the faithful. He extorted and murdered the rich to despoil their fortunes. There were many scandalous stories of depravity at the Borgia papal court, before and after Savonarola's rebellion. The most notorious was the so-called Ballet of Chestnuts in 1501. Fifty prostitutes were hired for the entertainments at a lavish banquet held at the papal palace by the

pope's notorious son Cesare Borgia and attended by his father. The har-
lots danced naked on a floor covered in chestnuts and performed sexual
acts with guests. A contest was held to see which guest could perform sex
the most times. Prizes were distributed to the winners.

Alexander VI fathered bastard children, notably his ambitious son
Cesare Borgia, whose reputation for double-dealing, treachery, and murder was legendary. Alexander VI concealed his illegitimate offspring,
passing off Cesare as his "nephew." This was not unusual in the era of so-
called *cardinalis nepos*, or "cardinal-nephews." High office in the Church
was a quasi-hereditary privilege (the word *nepotism* comes from Latin
nepos for "nephew"). Earlier in his career, Alexander VI had been a
beneficiary of the *cardinalis nepos* tradition: he was appointed to the
College of Cardinals by his uncle, Pope Callixtus III. As pope, Alexander
VI took this tradition a step further by appointing his "nephew" Cesare a
cardinal when he was only seventeen years old. [14]

Alexander VI's corrupt papal court provided Savonarola with a perfect target for his sermons against corruption. Shocking tales of papal
depravity almost certainly reached his ears. The political climate in Italy
also gave credence to Savonarola's "sword of God" prophecies that Italy
would soon be invaded as punishment for its sins. In 1494, French king
Charles VIII invaded Italy with an army of 25,000 men to make his claim
on the crown of Naples. The French troops cut a devastating path through
the country, sacking and plundering Tuscany. The Medicis capitulated
and paid the French a massive indemnity. The French nonetheless drove
the Medicis out of Florence. An anti-Medici uprising in the city saw their
palace sacked and most of their precious art stolen. Giovanni de Medici—
later Pope Leo X—saved his own skin by fleeing the city disguised as a
monk.

In Florence, an authentic monk, Savonarola, showed more courage.
He sent an emissary to request a tête-à-tête with the French king. Charles
VIII agreed to receive the eccentric Italian priest in Pisa. Charles was a
relatively young king at only twenty-four (he would die suddenly only
three years later after accidentally banging his head against a doorway on
his way to play a game of *jeu de paume* at the chateau d'Amboise).
Savonarola was two decades older at forty-two. At their meeting, Savonarola presented himself to the young French monarch as a prophet who had
come to tell Charles he was the instrument of God's divine plan. He
proclaimed Charles VIII as the "new Cyrus" prophesied in his sermons.
Like the great Persian king in the Bible, declared Savonarola, the French
king had come to cleanse Italy of its sins. Savonarola urged Charles VIII
to be merciful, however, especially with his city of Florence. The French
monarch was impressed. It was thanks to Savonarola's intercession with
Charles VIII that the city was spared destruction by the French army.

Florentines were, once again, awed by Savonarola's powers of foresight and persuasion. There could be no doubt that he was a true prophet sent by God.

Revered as a prophet, it was inevitable that Savonarola would shift his attention to worldly affairs. In the New Jerusalem of Florence, he would build his own republic as a City of God. Political rivalries in Florence, divided into political factions, guilds, and powerful families, were fractious. The instability helped a figure like Savonarola to break through with his own populist movement, called the "Piagnoni" party (named after the weepers and wailers at his sermons). His Piagnoni movement handily triumphed at the ballot box, defeating the "Arrabbiati" (or "angry ones"), who had dismissed Savonarola as a lunatic. Once in power, Savonarola declared the city a Christian republic and drew up a new constitution that gave every citizen the right to vote for the city's Consiglio Maggiore, or Great Council. He also adopted a raft of populist policies to improve the condition of the common people. One was the creation of a bank to lend money to the poor at low rates, liberating them from the clutches of money lenders.

For many, Savonarola's republic was a refreshing change after decades of the Medici oligarchy. There was, however, a darker side to the city's new regime. Savonarola's religious fanaticism quickly turned his Florentine republic into an oppressive theocracy. He passed legislation prohibiting gambling, swearing, and singing bawdy songs. Blasphemers had their tongues cut out. Homosexuality was severely punished. Torture was used to extract confessions. To enforce Savonarola's policies of moral purification, Christian shock troops called "Bands of Hope" patrolled the streets of Florence and punished any sign of immodesty in dress or manner. Many of these boys had previously been in teenage gangs, or *fanciulli*, who Savonarola reformed and turned into a disciplined confraternity of Christian morality enforcers. On Palm Sunday, a procession of these boys, accompanied by girls with olive garlands on their heads, marched through the Piazza della Signoria as lauds were sung to the chant "Long in our hearts, King Christ, leader and Lord!"[15]

The most notorious ritual in Savonarola's theocracy were the bonfires of vanities. His Band of Hope enforcers charged through the city knocking on doors, bullying people into handing over their "vanities." They collected all sinful objects—books of poetry, cosmetics, perfumes, mirrors, masks, playing cards, dice, jewelry, harps, guitars, nude paintings, sculptures, ornaments of any kind—and carried them to the Piazza della Signoria for purifying incineration. The date for their ritual burning was chosen for its symbolic significance: the annual spring carnival. During carnivals in the Medici era, it was customary to wear masks and indulge in libations and lewd behavior. Savonarola, who deplored this tradition as licentious pagan antics, turned the annual carnival into a Christian ritual of purification before the holy Lent. The cursed objects were tossed onto one of seven pyres, each representing one of the deadly sins. The heaped piles of earthly indulgences were then torched in a massive bonfire. Among books incinerated were volumes of Boccaccio, Dante, Petrarch, and Ovid. Female statues by Donatello were also tossed into the flames. It was said that Botticelli, still under Savonarola's spell, threw his own paintings onto the bonfires.

Meanwhile in Rome, Pope Alexander VI was, at the outset, more intrigued than anxious about the fanatical friar in Florence. The pontiff took the precaution of dispatching a Dominican priest to Florence to discreetly investigate claims that Savonarola had been receiving revelations directly from God. As the illuminated friar's power grew, however, Alexander VI became increasingly worried. He was especially troubled by rumors of Savonarola's claims of performing miracles and his prophesies of the scourging of Italy and reforming the Church.

The pontiff now attempted to win over the Dominican friar with blandishments, dangling the prospect of a cardinal's red hat.

"A red hat?" Savonarola replied publicly in a sermon before his congregation. "I want no hats, no mitres either large or small. I want nothing but what you God have given to your saints: death. A red hat, a hat of blood; this is what I want!"[16]

Savonarola sent the pontiff a copy of his book, *Compendium of Revelations*, a sort of apocalyptical calling card containing his visions and prophecies. Among the passages in the tome was: "Almighty God, seeing that sins of Italy continue to multiply, especially those of her princes, both ecclesiastical and secular, and unable to bear them any longer, I decided to cleanse His church with a mighty scourge."[17] It was clear to Alexander VI that Savonarola was not one to succumb to flattery. His religious zeal was a belligerent expression of dissent.

Savonarola's clever use of published books was a key factor in spreading his message and amplifying his notoriety. He was born only a few years after Gutenberg's invention of the printing press in the middle of the fifteenth century. The emergence of printing in Savonarola's lifetime put him on the vanguard of a media revolution that was about to shake the foundations of the Church. Savonarola was ideally placed to take advantage of the new print medium. Priests in Florence had been using the printing press for at least a decade before he arrived in the city. Access to presses was one of the advantages of being located at the center of the Italian Renaissance—an irony that Savonarola doubtless overlooked. He despised Renaissance humanism, but that didn't stop him from using its printing presses to churn out his fanatical religious propaganda.

Savonarola was also among the first polemicists to exploit the potential of the printed book.[18] And like Julius Caesar in ancient Rome, Savonarola was quick to print. He packaged his fiery sermons into one-sheet tracts and published them straight away, on the fly, in the heat of the action. He distributed his "open letters" addressed to everyone in Florence to mobilize public opinion behind his cause. The great artist Michelangelo was among those who read his tracts and attended his sermons. Thanks to his canny talents for self-publicity, Savonarola quickly became the most-read author of his day. At the height of Savonarola's influence, at least a hundred editions of his sermons were circulating in Florence. What's more, he wrote in Italian to appeal to supporters among the lower and middle classes. The book he offered to the pope was published in Latin, but it was also published in Italian under the title *Compendio di rivelazioni*. Savonarola also understood the power of the image as a marketing tool. With a sharp eye on the visual dimension of his publications, he pioneered the use of decorated woodcarvings for illustrations. The illustrated tracts were so popular that they were quickly reprinted in Paris, the Netherlands, and Germany in both Latin and German.[19]

Pope Alexander VI, meanwhile, was running out of patience with the canny Dominican priest. The breaking point came when Savonarola refused to commit Florence to the pope's Holy League against the French king, Charles VIII. Enraged, the pope summoned Savonarola to Rome. Suspecting a plot against his life, Savonarola spurned the invitation, though he pleaded ill health. The pontiff, infuriated by the friar's insubordination, banned him from delivering sermons. Savonarola initially submitted to the interdiction, but soon was giving even more animated sermons and whipping up his "Weepers"—as his audiences were called—into a groundswell of moral indignation against the evils of the papacy.

In early May 1497, Alexander VI finally played his most formidable card: excommunication. Even during the humanist Renaissance, people feared divine retribution. Excommunication was a terrifying punishment. The pope's order of excommunication was read out in five churches in Florence. Savonarola lashed out against his excommunication in an "open letter" against the papacy. But the Pope's move against Savonarola proved effective in turning public opinion against him. The people of Florence had already been growing tired of the Dominican priest's oppressive theocracy. His adversaries were emboldened by the excommunication, especially Franciscans, who accused him of being a false prophet. A riot had erupted during his Ascension Day sermon.

Savonarola responded at greater length in an apologetic treatise, *Triumphus Crucis* (*Triumph of the Cross*), which celebrated the victory of the cross over sin—especially the sins of his accusers. Answering the accusations against him, which he called "the impious garrulousness of the wise of this world," Savonarola used the book to put forward an exposition of the "true religion" as taught by Jesus Christ. Interestingly, Savonarola seized on the metaphor of a Roman chariot, borrowed from the ancient literature, as an image of Christ's triumph.[20]

The standoff with the pope was complicated by two events. First, Alexander VI's favorite son, Giovanni Borgia, Duke of Gandia, was murdered and his body found floating in the Tiber. The pontiff was inconsolable. Second, the plague struck Florence, and thousands were dying. Many were fleeing the city. Still, it was too late for Savonarola. The Church could not countenance an illuminated priest openly defying papal authority.

On Palm Sunday in 1498, Savonarola and two friars among his most ardent followers were arrested for heresy and imprisoned. Alexander VI sent emissaries to Florence to watch over the proceedings. Savonarola's initial interrogation included torture, or *tormento*, using an infamous method known as *strappado*. His hands were bound behind his back and he was yanked up by a pulley so that his arms were drawn over his head, causing agonizing pain as his shoulders dislocated. At the end of his ecclesiastical trial, Savonarola confessed that he was a false prophet. All his prophecies, he admitted, were inspired by his lust for worldly glory, or so his inquisitors reported in the official transcript of the trial.

Declared a heretic along with his two loyal friars, all three were sentenced to death. On May 23, 1498, they were dragged to the scaffold in Florence's main square, the Piazza della Signoria, where he had once held bonfires of vanities and led processions chanting "Long live Christ who is our King!" This time, Savonarola was taken here as a condemned false prophet. He and his two followers were dressed in simple white tunics, their feet bare, their hands tied. Their heads were shaved, a customary degradation ritual, before they were led to the cross-shaped gallows. Savonarola was positioned between the other two condemned friars. After they were hanged, their limp bodies, dropping from chains attached to the cross, were suspended over a massive fire that must have resembled one of Savonarola's own purification bonfires. As the bodies were slowly consumed by flames, the Florentine mob screamed insults. Some in the crowd, transfixed, gazed in wonder, waiting for a miracle to happen as the fulfillment of Savonarola's prophecies. A few said they saw Savonarola's right hand moving in a gesture of blessing. When the ordeal was over, some in the audience swept up bits of bone and ash to keep as relics.

Niccolo Machiavelli, who was in the crowd witnessing the execution, would later reflect on the ill-fated priest in his masterpiece, *The Prince,* and later in *Discourses on Livy.*[21] Machiavelli drew lessons from Savonarola's short-lived Florentine republic, which had lasted less than four years. He observed that Savonarola's catastrophic error was that his religious regime lacked armed force. Unlike Moses, Cyrus, and Theseus, Savonarola was an "unarmed prophet." He had come to grief because he neglected a key tenet of power: founders of new orders must impose their constitutions with force, and be prepared to use violence against envious rivals. Savonarola succeeded in mobilizing the people of Florence around his claims of divine guidance, but his political project failed because he lacked the instruments of physical coercion to back up his will. Savonarola spoke his truth to power, but that wasn't enough. He neglected to grasp that the Church's monopoly on truth was reinforced by a powerful system of propaganda and coercion. Hectoring his adversaries in impassioned sermons was not sufficient to challenge the blunt force of the Church's temporal power. Machiavelli, in his counsel to the princes, took the lesson of Savonarola's downfall to remind them of the primacy of human truths in the sphere of political action.

"Since my intention is to say something of practical use to the enquirer," Machiavelli writes in *The Prince*, "I have thought it proper to represent things as they are in *real truth*, rather than as they are imagined."[22] In short, man does not live in imagined republics; we must take man as he is.

Following his execution, Savonarola's ashes were scattered in the Arno River so there could be no sacred relics. Despite the lack of a tomb, a martyr cult grew around his name. Every year on the anniversary of Savonarola's death, fresh flowers were placed on the spot in the Piazza della Signoria where he had been hanged and burned at the stake. The painter Botticelli, meanwhile, was so devastated by Savonarola's execution that he produced very little art afterward and died in poverty in 1510.

The growing cult around Savonarola troubled the Church. Fifteen years after his death, the Florentine archdiocese issued proclamations banning his tracts and forbidding any preaching that venerated him. Savonarola's works were later put on the Church index of banned books in the most severe category of *opera omnia*. Those who continued to preach Savonarola's message were tortured and murdered, but his most fervent devotees in the Piagnoni movement established a Savonarola cult. They claimed that his death had been an apocalyptical event and that his prophesies were being fulfilled.

For the exiled Medici dynasty, Savonarola's downfall was a blessing. The Medicis were restored to power not only in Florence but also in Rome. In 1513, Giovanni de Medici was elected pontiff as Pope Leo X. When Machiavelli completed *The Prince*, he dedicated the book to Lorenzo de Medici, grandson of the dynasty patriarch who had died in 1492 with Savonarola at his deathbed.

Savonarola failed to topple the papacy and build his New Jerusalem in Florence. But the flame of his burning truths had not been snuffed out. His revolt was far from over. In fact, it was only just beginning.

Part III

Twilight of the Icons

7

SELLING INDULGENCES

It was a dramatic moment that changed the world: On October 31, 1517, on the eve of All Saints' Day, a little-known German theologian called Martin Luther took a hammer and banged a list of religious grievances onto a Wittenberg church door. In one dramatic gesture, the Protestant faith was born.

That's the myth. But it didn't happen. Luther did draw up his famous "95 Theses" listing his complaints against the Catholic Church. But the story of him nailing them to the door of All Saints' Church is a legend whose basis in historical fact is disputed. [1]

Religions, like nations, need founding myths. The legend of Luther hammering his complaints onto a church door was a perfect narrative for hard and determined protest. Luther was challenging Church doctrine with his own truth. His rebellion against the papacy unleashed a fury of icon smashing, idol destruction, and bloody wars of religion.

Martin Luther was an unlikely figure to challenge the Catholic Church. Unlike the illuminated monk Savonarola, who whipped up hysterical devotion with apocalyptical sermons, Luther was a colorless German priest interested chiefly in the academic points of religious doctrine. Savonarola was gaunt, ascetic, flesh-denying, and outraged by the corruption and depravity that he saw all around him in humanist Italy. Luther was portly, cantankerous, unashamed of his bowel movements, enjoyed drinking beer, and broke his vows of chastity for the carnal pleasures of marriage.

But Luther was, in many respects, carrying forward Savonarola's combat. He was intimately familiar with the firebrand Italian monk's writings and tragic fate. He had read Savonarola's pamphlets; he had even written a preface to Savonarola's meditations. Luther shared Savonarola's outrage at papal corruption, but his rebellion was not inflamed with bonfires consuming the sins of human vanities. Savonarola had wanted to build a New Jerusalem in Florence. Luther's revolt was focused on corrupt Church practices throughout the Holy Roman Empire. He also opposed the Church on questions of theological doctrine. For the papacy, that made Luther even more dangerous.

Luther's timing was propitious. He lived in an age when Church doctrines were being challenged on different fronts. The fractures had begun in the fourteenth century with reformers such as the English theologian John Wycliffe, who opposed icons, attacked monasteries, condemned indulgences, and rejected the veneration of saints. He frontally challenged Pope Gregory XI and even contested the need for a papacy. For Wycliffe and his followers, the Lollards, the only thing that mattered was the Scriptures. Wycliffe further defied the Church by translating the Bible into Middle English. In 1415, the Church declared Wycliffe a heretic and excommunicated him—even though he was already deceased. The Church decreed that Wycliffe's remains be removed from consecrated ground, his body exhumed, burned, and his ashes thrown into the river Swift in Leicestershire. Five centuries after the Cadaver Synod, the Church was still exacting revenge on putrefied corpses.

A century before Savonarola's religious revolt in Florence, the Devotio Moderna movement—stressing simple piety and humility imitating the life of Christ—took off in the low countries in protest to the wealth of the monasteries, the simony of the clergy, and the worldly corruption of the Church.[2] In Bohemia, the religious reformist Jan Hus foreshadowed Savonarola's fulminations with his own pulpit denunciations of the papacy. Like Savonarola, Jan Hus was burned at the stake for heresy, but the Hussite wars against the Church raged for decades in the early fifteenth century. At the end of the century, a young Prussian astronomer called Copernicus was formulating a revolutionary theory of celestial bodies. Copernicus repudiated the geocentric view that the earth stood at the center of the universe, asserting that the earth revolved around the sun, not the opposite. Copernicus shattered the Church's official doctrine on celestial bodies, inspired by ancient theories stretching back to Aristotle. The Church used excommunication, inquisitions, and an index of banned books to prevent these threatening ideas from spreading. Savonarola's pamphlets would also be indexed.

It was into this climate of dissent that Martin Luther was born in 1483. When Savonarola was founding his theocratic republic in Florence, Luther was a boy of eleven. When Luther entered a St. Augustine's monastery as a young man in 1505, Savonarola had been hanged and burned at the stake only seven years earlier. Luther's decision to take vows apparently disappointed his ambitious father, Hans Luther, a wealthy manager of a copper smelter and local town counselor who was expecting his son to go into the law.[3] Luther later recalled that his decision to enter the holy orders was triggered by a traumatic event. Returning home on horseback from university, where he was studying law and philosophy, he got caught in a thunderstorm. A lightning bolt almost struck him dead. Luther took his brush with death as divine judgment. He cried out, "Help, Saint Anna, I will become a monk!" So he gave up his law studies and entered the monastery. His choice of the Hermits of Saint Augustine proved fateful. Unlike other holy orders where monks retreated from the world to devote themselves to prayer, meditation, and copying books, Augustinians lived with the wider population and traveled to preach in vernacular languages.

In 1512, at age twenty-nine, Luther received his Doctor of Theology from the university in Wittenberg, a small provincial town between Leipzig and Berlin. Three years later, he was appointed vicar with oversight of twelve monasteries in the province of Saxony and Thuringia. In 1516, however, things took a different turn that would radically change Luther's life mission. A local Dominican friar called Johann Tetzel came through Saxony selling "indulgences" on behalf of the Church.

Religious indulgences were standard practice in various forms in late medieval Christianity. Indulgences found justification in the sacrament of penance: all souls are stained by sin and therefore must be cleansed before entering heaven. Original sin was cleansed by baptism. Venial sins, although they weakened the soul, could be absolved by confession to avoid purgatory. Mortal sins (or *peccatum mortale*) were the most grievous of all. If they went unrepented, the sinner forfeited entry into heaven and the soul was condemned to perpetual hellfire. Penance was not sufficient to absolve sins, however. One also had to undergo temporal punishment. In Church practice, an indulgence was remission of temporal punishment for one's sins. Church indulgences were based on a theological notion called "treasury of merit," which was a repository of unused holiness attained by the saints. The pope could draw on this spiritual stockpile of "merits" to reduce the temporal punishment of the penitent if they performed pious acts. An indulgence was usually received in return for penitence in the form of prayer, giving alms, serving the poor, or going on a pilgrimage. In 1095, Pope Urban II issued a decree offering plenary indulgences, or complete remission of penance for sin, for all Christians who joined the first crusade to rescue the Holy Land from the heathen Turks.

Over time, the granting of indulgences became corrupted by abusive commercial practices. Pilgrimages became an economic enterprise for the Church. Major pilgrimage sites—Christ's tomb in Jerusalem, St. Peter's tomb in Rome, and St. James's tomb in Santiago de Compostela in

Spain—provided lucrative sources of revenue for the papacy and the network of monasteries on their routes. It is estimated that some 500,000 pilgrims journeyed to Santiago de Compostela every year throughout the fourteenth century. In England, Geoffrey Chaucer's *Canterbury Tales*, written circa 1400, recounted the story of a group of pilgrims on a journey to visit the shrine of Saint Thomas Beckett at Canterbury Cathedral. The most dubious character in Chaucer's tale is the Pardoner, a cynical seller of indulgences whose theme is *radix malorum est cupiditas* ("greed is the root of all evil"), though he admits his own avarice and hypocrisy. Chaucer's Pardoner embodies the morally questionable side of indulgences and pilgrimages. Pilgrims often paid large fees to the Church for plenary indulgences before embarking on their journeys, followed by donations to the shrines upon arrival.[4] Indulgences, in short, were tariffed. No longer the performance of pious acts, penitence became cash payments to the Church. The transaction was simple: you gave money to the Church to have your sins absolved. Indulgence payments were, in short, a fast track out of purgatory to secure a spot in heaven.

For the Church, indulgences were a lucrative tax on souls. In 1507, Pope Julius launched a "Jubilee Indulgence" campaign to raise funds for the reconstruction of St. Peter's Basilica in Rome. Greedy papal commissioners fanned out throughout Europe to flog indulgences like pestering salesmen. Their sales pitches were almost always convincing, if only because they came with a terrifying implied threat. If the faithful didn't cough up, their souls risked eternal damnation. Secular rulers had a finger in the pie, too, through commissions for their complicit support of indulgence schemes. For ecclesiastic and secular authorities alike, selling indulgences was an efficient way to replenish their treasuries. Everyone got their cut.[5]

The Dominican priest Johann Tetzel was, in effect, Pope Leo X's tax farmer in Germany. Pope Leo X, notorious as a big spender, was using the sale of indulgences to raise funds to complete the construction of the new St. Peter's Basilica. When Tetzel arrived in town, he was treated to an official procession by local ecclesiastical and government leaders. The papal coat-of-arms and papal bull decreeing the indulgences were prominently displayed for all to see while church bells sounded in an atmosphere of pious solemnity. Then Tetzel would begin his stump-preacher sales pitch, flogging remission from purgatory to the sin-stained faithful seeking a passport to the "celestial joys of Paradise."

By Martin's Luther's day, resentment toward the practice of selling indulgences was growing. In 1515, Leo X sent a papal legate to Scandinavia to collect money for the refurbishing of St. Peter's Basilica. More than 2 million florins were drummed up in Denmark, Norway, and Sweden, the poorest kingdoms in Europe at the time. But the local population in Scandinavia deeply resented being bilked. In Germany, the Pope's taxman, Johann Tetzel, was a particularly aggressive salesman. He not only targeted sinners but also sold indulgences to the deceased—or, rather, to their living relatives. The dubious practice of selling indulgences to save the souls of the deceased had been initiated by Pope Sixtus IV in 1476. If you paid for an indulgence for, say, your late father, who you knew had left this world an impenitent sinner, the cash payment would spring his tortured soul from the eternal torment of purgatory. Tetzel had a crass rhyming slogan to describe this abusive racket: "As soon as the coin in the coffer rings, so the soul from purgatory springs." Tetzel's hard-sell tactics contributed to the growing resentment toward indulgences as "Roman bloodsucking."

Martin Luther was scandalized by the Church's organized extortion of the faithful. His opposition to indulgences was based on Christian doctrine. He argued that remission from God's punishment for sin could not be purchased. It was Luther's opposition to the selling of indulgences that triggered his famous "95 Theses," titled *Disputation for Clarifying the Power of Indulgences.*[6] Luther did not nail his list of complaints to the door of the Schlosskirche in Wittenberg. He made the less dramatic, but more courageous, gesture of dispatching his complaints directly to the archbishop of Mainz, Albrecht of Brandenburg. Luther was sending his grievances up the chain of command.

Martin Luther was hardly a power in the Church system, but his challenge was a serious provocation. Not surprisingly, Albrecht of Brandenburg was alarmed by what he read, if only because he was pocketing a 50 percent commission on the proceeds from Tetzel's sale of indulgences. Brandenburg desperately needed the cash to pay off loans used to purchase benefices from Pope Leo X: the archbishoprics of Mainz and Magdeburg along with the bishopric of Halberstadt. Luther's attack on indulgences was a direct assault on Brandenburg's own financial interests. Luther moreover took direct aim at the pope with the following question: "Why does the pope, whose wealth today is greater than the wealth of the richest Crassus, build the basilica of St. Peter with the money of poor believers rather than with his own money?" Luther was alluding to Pope Leo X's personal fortune as a scion of the Medici banking dynasty. The implicit hostility toward the pope revealed an ambivalent attitude toward the papacy. Luther had in fact dedicated his "95 Theses" to Pope Leo X to send a signal that his protest was not against the papacy, but specifically against the practice of selling indulgences. But the Vatican was in no mood to accept the German monk's blandishments. Pope Leo was counting on taxation revenues from indulgences to build his new St. Peter's Basilica.

Pope Leo X, born Giovanni de Medici, was the second son of Lorenzo the Magnificent, the powerful Medici patriarch whose death Savonarola had predicted in 1492. Thanks to his powerful family's connections, Giovanni de Medici had benefited from a spectacular rise in the Vatican system. In 1488, he was appointed cardinal at the age of thirteen. He never even bothered becoming a priest. When the Medicis were driven out of Florence before Savonarola's theocratic interlude, Giovanni barely escaped with his own life, forced to flee the city disguised as a monk. In 1513, after his family was restored to power in Florence, Giovanni was elevated to the papacy as Leo X at age thirty-seven.[7] As the first Florentine pope, Leo's elevation was a triumphant vindication for the Medici dynasty. He would be the first of four Medici popes over the following century.

Pope Leo X was short and flabby with a reputation for hedonism, though he was personally affable and highly cultured, a great lover of music and the arts. He was famous for saying, "God has given us the papacy, let us enjoy it." Like a Roman emperor, Leo enjoyed great spectacles in the Coliseum that combined pagan rites and Christian feasts. In one procession, a howdah-bejeweled elephant bearing gifts from the king of Portugal bowed down three times before Leo and sprayed the surrounding audience with water.[8] Having benefited from family connections his entire life, Leo displayed the same instincts as pontiff. In the time-honored *cardinalis nepos* tradition of papal nepotism, he was determined to appoint his cousin, Giuliano de' Medici, as a cardinal. He also drained the papal treasury by raising troops for a costly war to have yet another Medici relation installed as Duke of Urbino. And he spent lavishly on renovating St. Peter's Basilica, commissioning artists such as Raphael to produce work for the Vatican rooms. Raphael also painted a portrait of Pope Leo in his purple robes, seated before an illuminated Bible, his cousin Giuliano standing to his right (Giuliano would later be elected as Pope Clement VII, the pontiff who would come into direct conflict with England's Henry VIII).

Leo X was forty-one years old, and had been pope for four years, when Martin Luther banged off his "95 Theses." When Luther's protest reached Rome, it was concluded that the German priest was an ecclesiastical dissident spreading *nova dogmata*, or new doctrines.[9] The archbishop of Mainz and his Dominican supporters denounced Luther in the strongest possible terms, describing the German monk as a dangerous heretic. Pope Leo took a more cautious approach. He ordered the head of the Augustinian Hermits—Luther's monastic religious order—to keep a close eye on the recalcitrant German monk and write up an opinion that could be used in a trial against him. Pope Leo believed Luther could be swayed or, if needed, marginalized by prosecution. That was the classic

Church tactic to eliminate threats—used by Pope Alexander VI against Savonarola.

Pope Leo underestimated the power of Luther's ideas. The pontiff failed to see, or perhaps refused to accept, that the tide had been turning against papal power. By the early sixteenth century, the Church's monopoly on truth was weakening. The rise of scholasticism and founding of universities had created a space for open intellectual inquiry. Many were reconnecting with ancient Greek learning to argue that truth was accessible through reason. Luther himself had received a classical education at the University of Wittenberg, which was at the center of the reformist movement in his day. While he expressed objections to Aristotle's influence on scholasticism, he was thoroughly schooled in Aristotelian philosophy. And though he distrusted the role of logic in leading men to God, Luther was a rigorous theologian trained in law. It was Luther's mastery of logic and reasoning that made his critique of Church practices and doctrines so persuasive. Luther articulated winning arguments.

The big game-changer, however, was his mastery of a new technology—the printing press—to spread his ideas.

***

Johannes Gutenberg and his colleagues started commercializing printing presses in the 1450s. Previously, the production of a single manuscript book—the Latin Bible, for example—took months, even years, to complete in the monastic scriptoria. The printing press could churn out hundreds of copies in a period of several weeks.

Printing presses sprouted all over Europe within two decades—in Rome, Paris, London, and other cities. In the hands of reformists and critics of the ecclesiastical establishment, the printing press was a powerful new weapon. In the 1490s, Savonarola seized on the new technology to publish his inflammatory sermons against the papacy. A generation later, the great Dutch humanist Erasmus observed in 1525: "Not everyone is allowed to be a baker, yet making money by printing is forbidden to nobody."[10]

Luther's religious rebellion harnessed this media revolution. He grasped the power of the press. When he dispatched his list of grievances to the Archbishop of Mainz, he was also careful to arrange for his "95 Theses" to be published by the University of Wittenberg under the Latin title *Disputatio pro declaratione virtutis indulgentiarum*. It became a bestseller almost immediately. Print editions quickly appeared in other German cities such as Leipzig, Nuremberg, and Basel, followed by a translation into German the same year. Within two years, Luther's grievances were being read in England, France, and Italy.

Luther's own associates were astounded by how quickly the *Disputa-tio* took off. His friend Friedrich Myconius observed: "Hardly 14 days had passed when these propositions were known throughout Germany and within four weeks almost all of Christendom was familiar with them. It almost appeared as if the angels themselves had been their messengers and brought them before the eyes of all the people. One can hardly believe how much they were talked about."[11] Luther's adversaries were equally impressed. The churchmen who opposed his ideas noted with resignation that "every day it rains Luther books."[12] Luther himself was astounded by the buzz, positive and negative, around his published works. "They are printed and circulated far beyond my expectation," he wrote in March 1518.[13] Luther's ideas, it might be said, had gone viral. Savonarola had gained notoriety thanks to the diffusion of his printed tracts. But Luther took publishing to a whole new level. He quickly became a Renaissance literary sensation.

Luther's celebrity made him an object of curiosity, by both disciples and detractors. Students flocked to his university lectures to hear the great man speak. Those opposed to his ideas seized copies of the *Disputatio* and torched them. Like many bestselling authors, Luther felt pressured to churn out a follow-up book. A year later, he released *Sermon on Indulgences and Grace*, this time publishing in vernacular German. By eschewing Latin, Luther was taking his cause beyond the academic sphere of theological discussion to reach the widest possible audience. There was a good reason for this. Literacy rates in Holy Roman Empire towns were roughly 30 percent, six times higher than in the countryside. Published in German, Luther's ideas found an audience among literate clerical, craftsmen, and merchant classes. The price was also right. Buying a pamphlet cost only a few pennies, within reach for the German reading public. There was also a strong spoken word—gossip and buzz—dimension to Luther's evangelical movement. Many learned about his ideas from sermons, conversations, and readings in taverns, spinning bees, and bakeries.[14]

Luther's *Sermon on Indulgences and Grace* was a huge success, going through fourteen printings of one thousand copies in a year. Within a couple of years, his works dominated the market. Of the 7,500 first-edition pamphlets published in Germany between 1520 and 1526, roughly 20 percent of them were by Martin Luther. In 1523 alone, four hundred editions of Luther's works were published. Besides Luther's own works, many other pamphlets of this period were produced by evangelicals supporting Luther. The format of pamphlets—in German called *büchlein*, or booklets—was also crucial to their subversive impact. Pamphlets were printed in quarto format (sheets folded twice to make four leaves or eight pages) with no hard cover. They were cheap to buy, convenient to transport, and easy to conceal.[15]

Luther's published works took advantage of the latest publishing technology, notably woodcuts to add vivid graphics to enhance the written message. Luther was not unaware of the impact of these embellishments. "Without images we can neither think nor understand anything," he wrote.[16] He even recruited the talented artist Lucas Cranach—Prince Frederick III's court painter—to make the woodcuts for his "Wittenberg editions." Some woodcuts were obviously intended as provocation. One image, for example, contrasted the piety of Christ with the corruption of the pope. Cranach's woodcut portraits of Luther made the German monk one of the most recognizable faces in Europe. The distribution of his portrait elevated Luther's image and name to the same level of recognition enjoyed by ruling monarchs.[17]

One of those monarchs was England's Henry VIII. Henry was a young man of twenty-six, barely eight years into his four-decade reign, when Martin Luther's revolt against the Church erupted. Henry had been following Luther's assaults on the Church with intense interest. In 1519, he drafted a rebuttal to Luther's *Disputatio* and consulted his chief minister, Cardinal Wolsey, about the manuscript. Its publication was delayed, however, while the papacy was taking steps to silence the German priest. In the meantime, Henry read Luther's latest invectives rolling off the presses. One was *To the Christian Nobility of the German Nation*, in which he called on secular rulers to break with the Church in Rome. Luther evocation of a "German nation" was an implicit political threat to the papacy, which regarded German princes in the Holy Roman Empire as their vassals. Another tract was *On the Babylonian Captivity of the Church*, in which Luther didn't mince his words: he accused the pope of being the Antichrist.

In 1521, Henry VIII finally published his own treatise, titled *Defense of the Seven Sacraments* (in Latin, *Assertio Septem Sacramentorum*). The tract attacked Luther and defended Pope Leo X. As its title indicated, Henry's *Assertio* was a defense of the seven sacraments in Catholic rites: baptism, confirmation, communion (Lord's Supper), penance (confession), anointing of sick, matrimony, and holy orders. Luther, in his *Babylonian Captivity of the Church*, had called for them to be reduced to only two: baptism and communion. A year after Henry's stinging rebuttal appeared in Latin, it was translated into German, attacking Luther on his home turf. The same year, Luther's books were ceremoniously burned in the churchyard of St. Paul's Cathedral in London.

Henry VIII's motivations for defending Pope Leo may seem puzzling. In 1521, however, his famous rift with the papacy was still in the future. Also, the *Assertio* was likely written by Henry's counselor, Sir Thomas

More, a strident opponent of the Reformation. More was likely worried that Luther's religious revolt on the continent might reach King Henry's shores in England. By coming down resolutely on the side of ecclesiastic authority, Henry VIII was sending a message to potential reformists in his own kingdom. His *Assertio* held out the added advantage of endearing himself with Pope Leo X. Henry even dedicated his treatise to the pontiff. Pope Leo showed his gratitude by conferring on Henry the title *Fidei defensor* ("Defender of the Faith").

Luther promptly rebutted Henry VIII in a tract titled *Against Henry, King of the English*, to which Thomas More dashed off a reply, *Responsio ad Lutherum*. The sparring match between an English king and German monk was fascinating—and a testimony to Luther's immense fame. Luther was indeed increasingly conscious of his own power and influence, and how it was driving the success of his movement. He not only spent an extraordinary amount of time focused on the technical aspects of his published works but also ensured that they were distributed to key thought leaders. Luther's name was prominently featured on the title page of each edition. This was a major innovation in Luther's day, when authors' names were rarely highlighted on books.

Luther's assaults on the Church became intolerable for the papacy. He was now taking direct aim at the pontiff by calling Pope Leo X the Antichrist and comparing the Church to the Whore of Babylon. He was challenging fundamental tenets of Church dogma by insisting on the primacy of faith alone, or *sola fide*, for salvation. He objected to the role of the Church—notably through the intercession of priests in confessions— as an intermediary between God and the faithful. How to deal with the rebellious German monk presented a dilemma. Ecclesiastic authorities, accustomed to unquestioning obedience to Church dogma, were disarmed by Luther's notoriety. He was famous throughout Europe. The Church, moreover, had no structured experience in engaging debate in vernacular languages such as German. Luther, on the other hand, had been turning over these questions in his mind for years.

Luther also enjoyed the support of followers who were passionately committed to reform and ready to use pamphlets to voice their opposition to the "papal Antichrist." Luther could count on friends in high places, too. His most powerful supporter was the elector prince Frederick III, known as Frederick the Wise. Frederick was something of an eccentric for his time. Never married, he spent a fortune on thousands of holy relics, including a twig from Moses's burning bush and a collection of hay said to be from the holy manger. A generous patron of the arts, Frederick financed the painter Albrecht Dürer, who executed a portrait of Frederick at age thirty-three, bearded with long, shoulder-length hair, a dark beret on his head, holding a small scroll in one hand. He was also a patron of Lucas Cranach, who did the illustrations for Luther's books. Frederick was, moreover, the founder of Luther's alma mater, the University of Wittenberg. The prince would prove to be a key reform-minded supporter of Luther's reformist agenda.

Pope Leo X had unsuccessfully attempted to summon Luther to Rome. It was the same tactic that Leo X's predecessor, Pope Alexander VI, had tried with Savonarola. Luther's message to the pope was less defiant, though similarly noncommittal. He responded by writing another tract elaborating on his opposition to indulgences. The Church decided to counter Luther with its own published rebuttals. If the printing press was making Martin Luther famous, it could also be used to contradict his dangerous ideas.

In Rome, a Dominican theologian, Sylvester Prierias, drafted a refutation of Luther's "95 Theses" as part of a legal case against the German priest. As Pope Leo X's master of the sacred books, Prierias was the official papal theologian and censor. His rebuttal of Luther's complaints was titled *Dialogue against the Presumptuous Theses of Martin Luther Concerning the Power of the Pope*. Citing the doctrine of papal infallibility, Prierias dismissed Luther as a "leper with a brain of brass and a nose of iron."[18] Other rebuttals were more diplomatic, combining courtesy with reproach. The Franciscan jurist Thomas Murner published several treatises with similarly long titles, such as *A Christian and Fraternal Admonition to the Highly Learned Doctor Martin Luther of the Augustinian Order*. Murner warned that Luther's views were a dangerous mixture of truths and falsehoods that could mislead Christians into rebellion. "Matters of faith," he wrote, "should not be disputed before the ignorant common folk."[19] Murner was essentially making a "noble lie" argument. Members of the clergy should not wash their dirty linen in public because the ordinary people were incapable of understanding complex questions of theology. Another Murner treatise, answering Luther's call to the German nobility, called on the same secular rulers to "protect the Christian faith against the destroyer of the faith of Christ, Martin Luther, a seducer of simple Christians."[20]

In this jousting match of published arguments and rebuttals, others jumped into the fray with tracts supporting and denouncing Luther. The controversy was an unexpected boon for German printers. It's estimated that, between 1518 and 1526, some 8 million copies of religious tracts were circulating in Germany. About 90 percent of them were generated by Martin Luther and his supporters.

As Luther's attacks on the Church spread throughout Europe, the papacy realized that contradicting the irksome German monk was not sufficient. The Church was losing the argument. Luther's "true Church" counter-narrative was seriously threatening to the papacy's monopoly on truth.

The Church traditionally protected its monopoly with specific means of coercion: censorship, inquisition, and excommunication against internal threats; crusades against external threats.[21] Luther was a famous and influential priest threatening Church dogma from within ecclesiastical authority. Something had to be done about him.

In 1520, Leo X issued a papal bull comparing Luther's ideas to a "cancerous disease." The pontiff threatened Luther with excommunication unless he recanted his criticism of the Church within sixty days. Defiant, Luther responded by publishing more pamphlets, notably *On the Freedom of a Christian*, in which he repeated his denunciation of Pope Leo as the Antichrist. The final straw for Pope Leo came when Luther publicly burned his papal bull in Wittenberg. In January 1521, the pope excommunicated Martin Luther.

Leo X needed secular authorities to enforce the papal ban on Luther's writings. For that task, the pope turned to the Holy Roman Emperor, Charles V, one of the most powerful rulers in Europe. Charles V was the heir of three European dynasties that made him simultaneously ruler of Spain, the Netherlands, and the Holy Roman Empire. Famous for his abnormally long chin, he spoke so many languages that he once remarked: "I speak Spanish to God, Italian to women, French to men, and German to my horse." In 1521, Charles V summoned Luther to the Diet of Worms, where Holy Roman Empire rulers were convening. Luther suspected that the summons was a death trap. But he was not politically naïve. He knew that, a century earlier, the reformist theologian Jan Hus had been lured to an ecumenical council at Constance and, when he refused to recant, was summarily tried, sentenced to death, and burned at the stake. Fearing for his life, Luther agreed to appear at the Diet of Worms, but he made the trip under the protection of an escort provided by his protector, Frederick III. When Luther arrived in Worms, he was given celebrity treatment. As a throng of two thousand people escorted him through the city gates in an official procession, the local population rushed into the street to get a look at the famous monk.[22]

Luther's anxiety was justified. Many present in Worms wanted the German monk tried and executed as a heretic. Pressured under interrogation to recant his views, Luther refused. "I am bound by the Scriptures I have quoted and my conscience is captive to the Word of God," he declared. "I cannot and will not recant anything, since it is neither safe nor right to go against conscience. I cannot do otherwise, here I stand. May God help me. Amen."[23] The meeting ended in disaster. Luther made his escape thanks to safe conduct provided by Frederick III. The German prince's men even staged a fake kidnapping so they could spirit Luther to safety in Wartburg Castle at Eisenach. Charles V, for his part, issued an Edict of Worms condemning Luther and offering a reward for his capture.

The edict stated that, if the spread of Luther's ideas was not stopped, "the whole German nation, and later all other nations, will be infected by this same disorder."[24]

Disgraced and on the run, Luther hid incognito at Wartburg Castle, growing his hair and beard and taking the aristocratic pseudonym Junker Jörg. These difficult circumstances did not diminish his energy, however. He was emboldened by his persecution and threw himself into a feverish burst of writing. It was during this period that Luther translated the New Testament from Greek into German. His German Bible became an instant bestseller, going through numerous reprints that totaled some 86,000 copies sold. He also continued publishing critiques of the Church, including *On Confession, Whether the Pope Has the Power to Require It*. Luther opposed confessions and absolution on the grounds that "every Christian is a confessor." He condemned Catholic mass as idolatry and argued that priests and nuns could break their monastic vows without sinning.

Luther professed other views that were contradictory, and profoundly contestable, beyond matters of Church dogma: his attitudes toward Jews, for example. In his early career, Luther's opinions about Jews had been relatively sympathetic, especially in his 1523 tract, *That Jesus Christ Was Born a Jew*. In that work, he wrote, "For our fools the popes, bishops, sophists and monks, all stupid donkeys, have treated the Jews in such a way that anyone who was a good Christian would have been apt to become a Jew." Luther believed, however, that Jews should be convinced of the truth of Christianity. Later in life, his views on Jews grew intolerant. Some historians claim Luther was influenced by the anti-Semitism of his aristocratic patron Frederick III, who banned Jews from his realms. Expulsion of Jews was common throughout the Middle Ages and early Renaissance, and Luther was certainly aware of this. His own region of Saxony counted very few Jews (they had been expelled in the early fourteenth century). It's doubtful, therefore, that Luther had any personal contact with Jews, though by the late 1530s he was calling for their expulsion from German towns. Some believe his anti-Semitism was influenced by Anton Margaritha's *The Whole Jewish Belief*, published in 1530. The son of a rabbi, Margaritha was a Jew converted to Christianity. His book ridiculed Jewish religion, customs, and habits. In 1543, Luther published a 65,000-word, anti-Semitic tract titled *On the Jews and Their Lies*, which extensively quoted Margaritha's diatribe. In his invective, Luther described Jews as "miserable and accursed people," expounded on their alleged lies, and called for the destruction of their synagogues. Some have argued that Luther's virulence towards Jews in this, and other, widely circulated tracts embedded anti-Semitism in German culture over the following centuries.[25]

Luther's views on Muslims revealed the same ambiguity that hardened into hostility. Early in his career, Luther regarded Islam as divine punishment visited on the corrupt Church. This view echoed Savonarola's praise of the invading French king Charles VIII as the "new Cyrus" who had come to cleanse Italy of its sins. Luther likewise cautioned against war with the "Turks," the word he used to describe Muslims. "To fight against the Turks is to oppose the judgment God visits upon our iniquities through them," he declared. He changed his mind, however, after the Turkish invasions that ended with the siege of Vienna in 1529. In his essay *On War against the Turk,* Luther made specific observations about Muslims and their religion. He regarded Islam as the work of the devil aimed at destroying Christianity. He observed that Muslims ruled by the sword, not through preaching and miracles. And he condemned their custom of polygamy as an abomination that reduced women to cattle to be bought and sold. Luther was nonetheless opposed to a Church-led holy war against Muslims. He encouraged the Holy Roman Emperor—not the pope—to wage a secular war against the Turks.[26]

In Germany, Luther's rebellion against the Church spread like wildfire and quickly became an out-of-control conflagration. One of his supporters, scholastic theologian Andreas von Karlstadt, was inciting an idol-smashing movement—called *Bildersturm,* or "statue storm"—that was a Renaissance replay of the iconoclastic fury in the early Christian period. *Bildersturm* violence erupted in Wittenberg and spread to other German cities, where religious zealots smashed icons and idols in churches and burned convents and monasteries. The rebellion provoked widespread upheaval among peasants, especially after crop failures and the threat of starvation. Luther had declared that Christians were free; now German peasants were taking him at his word. This was the great leveling effect of Luther's teachings that would lay the foundations for democratic values. Invoking divine law, peasants denounced serfdom as incompatible with Christian liberty and clamored for freedom from oppression by nobles and landowners. In 1525, the year Luther married former nun Kattarina von Bora, a full-scale Peasants' War broke out and swept through Germany. Luther's religious rebellion against the Church was now a class war against the entire feudal system. Peasants organized armies and burned convents, monasteries, libraries, and palaces.

Luther was sympathetic to some peasant demands, but was horrified by the violence perpetrated in his name. "During my absence, Satan has entered my sheepfold," he wrote.[27] Luther was also sensitive to the political interests of his princely protectors. Attempting to temporize, he published a tract whose title made its purpose clear, *Against the Murderous, Thieving Hordes of Peasants.* Luther justified his opposition to the Peasants' Revolt by quoting the Bible: "Render unto Caesar the things that are

Caesar's." The Peasants' War was eventually put down, but not without horrendous bloodshed. More than 100,000 German peasants were slaughtered. The rebellion's most zealous supporters found a religious home in Anabaptism, some of them migrating to America.

These radical fringes of his reformist movement made Luther's ideas seem acceptably mainstream. His was now a voice of moderation. This perception helped Luther as he turned his attention to building the reformed church that announced the Protestant Reformation. When he died quietly in 1543, at age sixty-two, he was secure in the knowledge that he had changed the world. Luther proved wrong Machiavelli's adage about unarmed prophets being doomed to failure. Luther lacked instruments of coercion to enforce his "true Church" constitution. He prevailed because he was armed with the rigor of his convictions—and the power of the printing press.

On his deathbed, Luther's last words were, "We are beggars, this is true."[28]

8

LÈSE MAJESTÉ

It is easy to regard Henry VIII's passionate defense of the seven sacraments as royal hypocrisy. Not long after he published his anti-Luther tract, *Assertio Septem Sacramentorum,* Henry openly flouted one of the sacraments: matrimony.

When Anne Boleyn arrived at the English court in 1522, she immediately caught married Henry's eye. We know how the story ends.

Henry's conflict with Pope Clement VII (another Medici pope, nephew of Leo X) is often depicted as a religious standoff about divorce. That is the familiar historical narrative that has become legend. Henry VIII wanted a male heir, so he divorced Catherine of Aragon. He broke with the pope, who refused an annulment. He married Anne Boleyn, who failed to provide him with a male heir, so her head was chopped off while Henry impulsively worked his way through four more wives.

That's only part of the story. Henry's rupture with the papacy was driven not only by the dictates of dynastic sex. It was largely about money and power. In the end, all three narratives—sex, money, power— would leave England with a bloody legacy of political strife, religious tensions, civil war, and the decapitation of a monarch.

When Henry VIII became king in 1509, the Church controlled about a quarter of the landed wealth in England. Henry, for his part, was not a shrewd money manager. He catastrophically managed his kingdom's finances and was soon desperate. Henry needed money, especially for his wars. The Church's religious houses in England produced revenues of roughly £130,000 a year in the early sixteenth century. That was double the amount yielded by Henry VIII's vast crown estates. Picking a fight with the pope over his divorce gave Henry a timely pretext to confiscate the Church's assets in his realm. The infamous Dissolution of the Monasteries, as it was called, was a smash-and-grab asset seizure that, as one observer has put it, was "surprisingly short of ideology, let alone theology, and almost entirely a story of greed."[1]

Henry VIII laid the groundwork for his strike against the Church with laws that neutralized papal power in England. In 1532, parliament passed a law that halted papal annates paid to Rome, followed by an act enforcing the submission of the clergy. A year after he married Anne Boleyn in 1533, the Act of Supremacy formalized Henry's power by asserting that the king was "the only supreme head on Earth of the Church of England." The same year, the Treason Act of 1534 provided the death penalty for anyone who refused to take the Oath of Supremacy acknowledging the king as the legitimate head of the Church. Armed with these new statutory powers, now Henry was ready to make his move on the pope's assets in his kingdom.

The Church had a massive physical presence in England—some nine hundred religious houses counting four thousand monks, three thousand canons, three thousand friars, and two thousand nuns. In the early sixteenth century, monasteries were uncontroversial in England. While the Church was a major landowner, monasteries had lost much of their power and were out of fashion as purgatorial institutions. Many still performed their monastic obligation of offering food and lodging to travelers and providing succor and spiritual comfort to the poor. Some were small and modest, with only a few monks; others were larger, well-endowed houses. Monks, nuns, and friars were a familiar aspect of everyday life in most parts of the country. There had been some impetus to reform monasteries, but it could hardly be said that there was a great public outcry against monasteries in England. That was inconvenient for Henry VIII. He needed a convincing moral justification to take possession of Church assets. Ironically, he found just what he was looking for in the writings of his old rival, Martin Luther.

Luther, as an Augustinian monk and doctor of theology, was well qualified to have an opinion on monastic life, even if he was not deeply committed to the traditions of his order. His tract, *De Votis Monasticis,* published in 1521, was a frontal attack on monastic vows. He argued, among other things, that monasteries had no basis in scripture. That armed Henry VIII with a powerful theological justification for evicting monks and nuns from monasteries in his own kingdom. There were also rumors and tales about monks and nuns engaged in secret lives of moral depravity and indulging in superstitious practices. In 1536, Henry's influential counselor, Thomas Cromwell, orchestrated "visitations" ostensibly to assess the monastic wealth of the Church for tax purposes. The *Valor Ecclesiasticus* had another, more covert agenda: the collection of salacious and damning information that cast doubt on the chastity and moral rectitude of monastic life. The shameful sins lodged in margins of reports included sodomy and *incontinentia* for monks guilty of sexual misconduct with women. The combination of scripture and scuttlebutt armed the English monarchy with enough justification to make a move on monastic lands. Monasteries needed be purged.

When the dissolution of Church assets in England began in the late 1530s, the land grab didn't target just monasteries; it also included abbeys, priories, and nunneries. Between 1536 and 1540, more than eight hundred religious houses were suppressed, and roughly seven thousand monks, nuns, and friars were turned out into society at large. The devastation was also cultural. On the king's orders, monastic libraries were pillaged or destroyed. Priories containing hundreds of volumes of medieval illuminated texts were burnt to ashes. In 1538, Henry VIII issued a royal injunction banning pilgrimages, religious icons, and "the most detestable sin of idolatry." Throughout England, Catholic icons, idols, frescoes, and statues were smashed to pieces, and shrines to saints were despoiled. At Canterbury Cathedral, not only was Saint Thomas Becket's shrine despoiled but also his body was desecrated and burned in public.[2] The violence was reminiscent of the idol-smashing *bildersturm* vandalism perpetrated by Martin Luther's followers in Germany a decade earlier. Iconoclastic violence was not new in England. Religious reformers such as William Tyndale and the Lollards had already been attacking icons and idols. This time, however, the icon-smashing destruction was sanctioned by royal decree. Henry VIII was not personally opposed to icons. The injunctions were issued by his minister, Thomas Cromwell. By 1540, the royal campaign against Church icons and idols had wiped out much of England's cultural heritage.

Henry had no long-term strategic plan for the Church's despoiled assets. He treated his financial gains as a one-time windfall. The seized lands were either sold off to the aristocracy, transformed into English churches, or left as ruins. Henry used a portion of the funds to pay for additions to his Hampton Court Palace and to fund Trinity College, Cambridge, and Christ Church, Oxford. Most of the proceeds, however, were used to finance wars against France in the 1540s. This would appear to indicate that greed could not have been Henry's only motive, for he quickly burned through the proceeds.

If the dissolution of the monasteries had other motives, one was ego. Henry was showing the pontiff in Rome who was boss in England.[3]

Henry had good reason to suspect the Church's power in his kingdom. When he had been attempting to obtain his divorce from Catherine of Aragon, organized resistance to his plans came from the religious orders in England. Famous among them was a nun called Elizabeth Barton, known as the "Holy Maid of Kent" because she was protected by the

Franciscan friars at Christ Church in Canterbury. A hangover from the medieval age of female visionaries in the style of Joan of Arc, Barton had gained notoriety through her religious visions and foretelling of events. Intrigued by her prophecies, Henry VIII had even accorded Barton an audience on two occasions, doubtless because he regarded the Canterbury nun as politically useful. But Barton turned against the king during his rupture with the pope. She prophesied that, if Henry married Anne Boleyn, he would not be king a month afterward and would find a place in hell. The nun also tarnished Henry's foreign policy initiatives. When the king and Anne Boleyn were on the continent in Calais to meet with the French king François I to seek his diplomatic support against the pope, Barton announced yet another revelation from Canterbury, claiming that God was displeased with Henry's impending marriage to Anne Boleyn. Her prophesies proved both wrong and fatal. Henry married Anne Boleyn and lived for many years afterward. Elizabeth Barton, for her part, was arrested for treason and hanged in 1534 along with the friars who had supported her. It was in the wake of this incident that Henry VIII's Treason Act was passed with explicit wording making it a high crime of treason to "slanderously and maliciously publish and pronounce, by express writing or words, that the King our sovereign lord should be heretic, schismatic, tyrant, infidel or usurper of the crown."[4]

For Henry VIII, the Holy Maid of Kent episode was a reminder of how monastic orders could be a serious irritant. Religious orders like the Franciscans were international networks that reported to the pope in London, not to the king of England. After Henry VIII's break with Rome, these orders were potential networks of resistance to his authority. By smashing apart the monastic system in England, Henry was asserting his power as a new kind of sacred king.

The decimation of Church power in England also marked a profound shift in values about truth. By merging secular and religious power in his own person as English monarch, Henry announced the overthrow of theology as the prime source of truth. Henry VIII was henceforth the virile embodiment of a new political order in which truth resided with kings. Whereas in the past the gravest crime was *heresy*, in Tudor England the most dangerous threat to the new order was *sedition*. Falsehoods and lies were now crimes of *lèse majesté*.

After the dissolution of the monasteries, Henry VIII could no longer, like previous monarchs, count on monastic scribes to propagate his legend as a great Christian king. He had to take control of the narrative by orchestrating his own publicity machine. Keen to promote his image as a sacred king in the chivalric tradition, Henry oversaw an ambitious propaganda initiative that included everything from Tudor coinage and elaborate jousts and tournaments to royal portraits and published panegyrics.

It was somewhat ironic that the monarch who had issued decrees banning icons was inordinately fond of his own painted image. In royal portraits, Henry was the iconic object of obedience and veneration. He put court painters on retainers and commissioned artists such as Hans Holbein to execute portraits depicting him in full sovereign majesty— chest thrust forward, arms akimbo, fists clenched, feet spread apart, codpiece bursting out. Henry ordered copies of these paintings to be spread beyond his own palaces so his portraits could be revered in the great houses of his realm. Another propaganda image was the vast tableau, displayed at Hampton Court Palace, depicting the extravagant pageantry of Henry VIII's diplomatic summit in Calais with the French king François I. The painting put Europe's ambitious kings, with their larger-than-life personalities, squarely at the center stage of history in all their grandeur.

Henry's attitude toward books was, like almost everything about him, rife with contradiction. On one level, he was an intellectual who had received a broad humanist education. And yet he regarded books and pamphlets as instruments of his own propaganda. This was the era, following Savonarola in Italy and Martin Luther in Germany, when the printing press was unleashing a torrent of pamphlets and tracts throughout Europe. Henry VIII himself had authored published treatises, including his rebuttal to Luther's work on the sacraments. In England, Henry had all references to the pope erased from official church books, replaced by himself as king and supreme head of the Church in England. The king's chief minister, Thomas Cromwell, meanwhile hired "official" priests who defended and promoted the king's authority from the pulpit.[5]

On matters of English politics, Thomas Cromwell discreetly censored books while using the king's printer to promote works praising the king's royal authority. One prolific Tudor propagandist was Oxford-educated scholar Sir Richard Morison, who published at least nine tracts in support of Henry's royal supremacy. At a time when Henry was increasingly paranoid about seditious uprisings, Morison played a key role in creating a cult of personality around him with the message "Obey ye your Kynge." In 1536, when a popular uprising erupted in northern England to protest Henry's dissolution of the monasteries, Morison rushed to the king's defense with several tracts, including *A Remedy for Sedition*. Henry VIII and Thomas Cromwell were personally involved in overseeing the publications of Morison's pamphlets. Cromwell, a shrewd student of Machiavellian political tactics, managed a whole stable of quick-witted scribes to spin the news in the king's favor. In the end, the protest in Yorkshire was put down and its leaders executed; one was hanged, drawn, and quartered. Henry VIII richly rewarded Morison for his loyal services. The king granted him properties in London's Fleet Street and lands in Hertfordshire, named him gentleman of the Privy Chamber, selected him to sit as an MP in parliament, and appointed him as ambassador to the court of the Holy Roman Emperor, Charles V. Morison died a very rich man.[6]

The power of the printing press cut both ways. Pamphlets and tracts could serve as propaganda for sitting monarchs, but they could also destabilize even the most powerful rulers. Luther had demonstrated that in his assaults on the pope. Henry VIII, who had carefully followed Luther's war against the pope, regarded books by religious reformers as particularly dangerous. One English author in this category was the scholar William Tyndale, who was exiled on the continent. Like so many of Henry's relationships, his attitude toward Tyndale began auspiciously and then turned sour. Tyndale was an Oxford-educated theologian whose English translation of the Bible, inspired by Luther's Bible in German, became a bestseller after it was published in 1526 and arrived in England via Amsterdam. Vernacular Bibles were considered suspect as "heretical," especially following Luther's example with his German Bible in the Holy Roman Empire. Henry was nonetheless greatly pleased by Tyndale's tract in 1528, *The Obedience of a Christian Man*, if only because it articulated the principle of divine-right kingship and thus emboldened Henry in his resolution to defy the pope.

Henry was much less pleased, to put it mildly, when Tyndale published *The Practyse of Prelates* in 1530. Here Tyndale argued that Henry VIII's annulment of his own marriage violated the Scripture. Henry declared Tyndale's vernacular Bible as a corruption of Scripture. All of Tyndale's books were banned by royal proclamation. The Bishop of London had thousands of copies burned on the steps of St. Paul's Cathedral. Henry meanwhile appealed to Holy Roman Emperor Charles V to have Tyndale arrested and extradited to England. Charles V, the nephew of Henry's abandoned ex-wife, Catherine of Aragon, spurned the request. Tyndale was finally arrested in Antwerp and, in 1536, tried for heresy, found guilty, and sentenced to death.

Henry's queen, Anne Boleyn, was sympathetic to Tyndale and pleaded his case with the king. Henry dispatched Thomas Cromwell to intercede on Tyndale's behalf. But it was too late. Tyndale's execution at Vilvoorde castle, near Brussels, was particularly gruesome. He was tied to the stake and strangled to death. His final words were for Henry VIII: "Lord! Open the King of England's eyes."[7]

Tyndale was vindicated only three years later when, in 1539, Henry VIII finally authorized an official Bible in the English language. The Church of England's "Great Bible," as it was known, borrowed heavily from Tyndale's Bible. Eight years later, in 1547, Henry VIII finally expired, grotesquely obese, at age fifty-five. It is recorded that he died of natural causes, but the king had suffered from many ailments all his life, including smallpox, malaria, and varicose ulcers on his legs, possibly diabetes and high blood pressure. Some speculate that Henry's violent mood swings and irrational conduct were symptoms of syphilis, or the "French disease," as it was called in the early sixteenth century. The precise cause of his death remains unknown.[8]

According to legend, on his deathbed Henry VIII, in a delirium, turned his eyes to the dark recesses of his chamber and exclaimed, "Monks! Monks! Monks!" It seemed Henry, even on his deathbed, was haunted by the dissolution of the monasteries. The story is almost certainly apocryphal, a nineteenth-century embellishment adding poetic justice to Henry's final act. The truth is likely much more banal: Henry VIII quietly lapsed into a coma and expired.[9]

Henry's daughter Elizabeth I—the child born to Anne Boleyn, the latter executed for not producing a male heir—displayed the same personal vanity as her volatile father. Her reign tends to be romanticized as the golden age of the Tudor dynasty, perhaps because her era is associated with the great flourishing of Shakespearean literature. Yet Elizabethan England was just as repressive as the reign of Henry VIII. The Elizabethan Age was a time of propaganda, censorship, and surveillance throughout England.

Elizabeth found herself—unexpectedly, after the reign of her Catholic sister Mary—ruling over a bitterly divided kingdom. She was, like her father, acutely conscious of the importance of propaganda to forge allegiance to her royal authority. And like Henry, she understood the need to create a cult of personality around her own image. Hence her portraiture iconography as the Virgin Queen, an image that encouraged a secular cult around the female monarch, Gloriana, wedded only to her nation. The famous Sieve portrait of Elizabeth showed the queen with the temple of the Vestal Virgins in the background. Elizabeth cultivated other images in many different paintings. Her father Henry VIII loved posing for virile portraits of himself, but Elizabeth sat for even more artists than her father. The proliferation of iconic images of Elizabeth I—not only in painted portraits but also on ring cameos, jewels, and medals—revealed the high demand for her image as an object of veneration.[10] Each portrait was carefully designed to convey allegorical significance that inspired loyalty and devotion. And like the portraits of Henry VIII that airbrushed his grotesque physical traits, pictures of Gloriana showed a pale and majestic figure that was an idealization of the real Elizabeth. The famous *Rainbow Portrait* of 1600—when she was an old woman—depicted a still-young Queen, gloriously bejeweled, with the inscription *non sine sole iris*—"no rainbow without the sun."

Elizabeth's self-aggrandizing propaganda included the printed word. She made sure her public appearances were written about in pamphlets and spread widely throughout the realm. She commissioned poetry and plays to embellish her cult of personality. The most famous work of literary propaganda was Edmund Spenser's allegorical poem *The Faerie Queene,* a panegyric celebration of the Protestant Tudor dynasty. *The Faerie Queene* was to Elizabeth I what Virgil's *Aeneid* was to the Roman emperor Augustus. Elizabeth was aware of these associations with ancient epics. In one portrait, she was painted posing before a scene showing Aeneas walking away from burning Troy. Another portrait, "Elizabeth I and the Three Goddesses" showed the queen with Venus, Juno, and Minerva replicating the famous Judgment of Paris before the Trojan War.

Elizabeth was implacable with any hint of published slander against her person. She had grown up deeply suspicious of gossip. When she was only thirteen, a rumor had spread throughout the court that she had been deflowered by Thomas Seymour, the forty-year-old brother of Henry VIII's late wife Jane Seymour. That traumatic experience was Elizabeth's first cruel lesson of the damaging power of innuendo. When she ascended to the throne, she dealt severely with vitriolic pamphlets attacking her Protestant monarchy. During her long reign, England was a veritable surveillance state run by her principal secretary, Sir Francis Walsingham. Like Thomas Cromwell to her father Henry VIII, Walsingham acted as Elizabeth's chief spin doctor and spymaster. He had been Elizabeth's ambassador to the French court in the 1570s and had witnessed the St. Bartholomew's Day massacre with his own eyes, watching thousands of Protestants butchered in the streets of Paris. His motto—"There is less danger in fearing too much than too little"—was a justification for a permanent state of paranoia.[11]

The paranoia was partly based on Elizabeth's standing with the Catholic Church. In 1570, Pope Pius had issued a papal bull excommunicating Elizabeth ("the pretended Queen of England and the servant of crime") as a heretic and commanded her subjects to stop obeying her "orders, mandates, and laws." In retribution, Catholics in England were arrested and tortured; and if they refused to recognize Elizabeth I as the head of the Church in England, they were executed. Some Catholics found guilty of treason, like Jesuit priest Edmund Campion, were hanged, drawn, and quartered in pubic. Campion was an Oxford-educated Anglican deacon who converted to Catholicism and distributed copies of his pamphlet, "Ten Reasons," denouncing the Church of England. Charged with sedition, he was tortured in the Tower of London before being hanged and dismembered, a gruesome end that earned him beatification as a Catholic martyr in 1886, followed by canonization in 1970.[12]

Elizabeth I's police state extended surveillance beyond questions of religion. Punishments, including execution, were provided for anyone writing or publishing "false, seditious and slanderous matter to the defamation of the Queene's Majesty."[13] A Puritan lawyer named John Stubbs was arrested for his scurrilous pamphlet spreading rumors about Elizabeth's possible marriage to the French prince François, Duc d'Alençon, younger brother to France's king Henri III. Stubbs argued that the queen's marriage to a Catholic was a breach of God's law. The Duc d'Alençon had indeed been courting Elizabeth, and moreover, she'd been quite smitten by him (she affectionately called him "Frog"). But a serious prospect of marriage was highly unlikely, if only because of the considerable age difference: he was only twenty-four years old while Elizabeth was a mature woman of forty-six. No matter, Elizabeth issued a proclamation against Stubbs's "lewd, seditious book," which, she claimed, contained "false statements" and "manifest lies." Stubbs was arrested and sentenced to have his right hand—the one used to write the slander against Her Majesty—severed with a cleaver. Stubbs stepped onto the scaffold in Westminster before an assembled crowd. After his hand was sliced off, he raised his intact left hand to his head, removed his cap, and exclaimed "God save the Queen!"[14]

The extinction of the Tudor dynasty with Elizabeth I did little to further the cause of free speech in England. Following her death in 1603, the Stuart dynasty, closely connected to French Catholicism, was even more invested than the Tudors in the notion of sacred monarchy.

Thanks to the Van Dyck portraits that hang in the Louvre, we have clear, close-up images of Charles I: pale visage; cavalier moustache and goatee; long, dark hair; nervous expression. Physically diminutive at five foot four, Charles had been sickly from childhood and spoke with a stammer. He was not born to be king. His older brother, Henry, was Prince of Wales, but died of typhoid fever at age eighteen in 1612. The poet John Donne composed an elegy "On the Untimely Death of the Incomparable Prince Henry." Now the much-loved Henry's sickly twelve-year-old brother Charles was heir to the throne.

Charles succeeded his father James I—son of Mary Stuart, Queen of Scots—in 1625 at age twenty-five. Almost from the start, Charles's assertion of divine-right monarchy put him on a collision course with his own parliament. English parliamentarians already suspected him of harboring the Roman Catholic views of his French wife, Henriette-Marie de Bourbon. As the daughter of French king Henri IV and Marie de Medici, Henriette-Marie (called "Queen Mary" in England) was the sister of France's king Louis XIII and aunt of the Sun King, Louis XIV. Henriette-Marie was said to have great influence over her husband, Charles I, who built her a private Roman Catholic chapel, designed by Inigo Jones, next to St. James Palace in London. This only further exacerbated suspicions that the Stuart monarchy was Catholic. Charles didn't help matters by appointing William Laud, a strident anti-Calvinist, as Archbishop of Canterbury. Laud's religious policies antagonized English Puritans, who would soon be the king's adversaries in parliament and, finally, on the battlefield.

The first phase of the English Civil War was fought on the battlefield of public opinion. The printing press had already been a formidable weapon of protest during the Tudor era, especially by religious reformers. By the early seventeenth century, pamphleteering was a free-for-all combat sport.[15] One of England's leading Puritans of the day was William Prynne, an Oxford-educated lawyer on the radical fringe of Calvinist theology. Prynne virulently opposed religious feasts, including Christmas, and used the press to fulminate against worldly distractions as wicked and sinful. He opposed, among other things, long hair on men and make-up on women, but he was particularly incensed about stage plays as "pernicious recreations." In late 1632, Prynne published an inflammatory book, *Histriomastix: The Player's Scourge*, a tirade against English theaters. This was only seventeen years after the death of England's greatest playwright, William Shakespeare. For Prynne, however, the theater was an abomination. Many did not fail to detect in Prynne's diatribe an implicit attack on the king's Catholic wife, Henriette-Marie, who had taken up drama at court and was a well-known patron of the theater. Prynne's invective, in other words, was a Puritan political assault on the Stuart monarchy.[16]

Prynne was arrested and thrown into the Tower awaiting charges for publishing unlicensed tracts. The king's infamous Star Chamber court, guided by Archbishop Laud, sentenced him to prison, fined him £5,000, stripped him of his Oxford degree, and disbarred him from the law. He was also sentenced to physical mutilation through loss of his ears. Prynne was put in the pillory, his ears were sliced off, and he was forced to watch a bonfire of his own books burning.[17] It was said that he almost suffocated to death from the smoke bellowing up from the flames. Undeterred, Prynne continued to publish invectives denouncing Archbishop Laud. Arrested again in 1637, this time he was sentenced to another £5,000 fine. That wasn't the end of his punishment. Laud ordered that Prynne's cheeks be branded "SL" with a hot iron. "SL" stood for "seditious libeler." Showing an unusual sense of humor in an otherwise painful situation, Prynne claimed "SL" stood for *Stigmata Laudis*, or the "mark of Laud."

Charles I moved to tighten up publishing laws. The Star Chamber issued a decree in 1637 making it an offense to print, sell, or import any books that contained "seditious, schismatic or offensive books or pamphlets." Also, no books could contain any views "contrary to Christian Faith, and the Doctrine and Discipline of the Church of England, nor against the State or Government, nor contrary to good Life, or good Manners."[18] In sum, it was henceforth illegal to publish anything contrarian about religion, politics, and most other topics of controversy. Public debate was being shut down in books and pamphlets. When foreign news journals reached England's shores in the form of *corantos*—single sheet, printed on both sides—they were at first censored, then banned altogether as "unfit for popular view and discourse."[19]

These censorship measures, while draconian, were not easy to implement. Enforcement proved utterly futile after the standoff between Charles and parliament broke down. In 1642, civil war broke out between Oliver Cromwell's New Model Army and Charles's royalist "Cavalier" forces. Vitriolic pamphlets spread like wildfire throughout the kingdom—sold in stalls, hawked in streets, passed from hand to hand. Most of the pamphleteering during the Civil War was religious and political invective. As one chronicler observed, England was filled "with so many Books, and the Brains of the People with so many contrary Opinions, that these Paper-pellets became as dangerous as Bullets."[20] The most effective propagandists were the anti-royalist Levellers, a well-organized populist movement calling for equality and religious tolerance. They polemicized in their own publication, *The Moderate,* and were remarkably skilled at smuggling printing presses and foreign publications from Amsterdam.[21] The Levellers also led iconoclastic attacks on the established Church's tradition of displaying idols, icons, altars, and crosses, practices that were condemned as "popery." The issue of idolatry was highly charged among Puritan parliamentarians. In 1643, parliament had ordered bonfires of idols, icons, and crucifixes ripped out of royal chapels at Somerset House and St. James Palace in London. These iconoclastic campaigns against "superstition and idolatry" would be stepped up throughout the Civil War.

Civil War pamphleteering kicked off what would become a well-established newspaper tradition: partisan journalism. Newspapers (called "news-books") served as partisan mouthpieces for the royalist and parliamentary causes. The royalist paper *Mercurius Aulicus* combined vicious attacks on parliamentary leaders with fawning items about Charles I. Each edition began with a regular feature called "London Lies," documenting all the falsehoods emerging from the parliamentary party. The anti-royalist organ of the "Roundheads" was the *Mercurius Britanicus.* It accused royalist papers of "lies, forgeries, insolencies, prophanations, blasphamies, and Poperie"—the final dig, "Poperie," an allusion to the Stuart monarchy's suspected affinities for Catholicism.[22] In this outpouring of partisan venom, factual truth was a secondary consideration. Pamphlets and papers published all manner of brazen lies, including misinformation about the outcome of battles. In one pamphlet in 1642, poet John Bond published a letter purporting to have been written from Holland by Henriette-Marie to her husband Charles I, warning the king of a foreign invasion of England by the French, Spanish, and Danish fleets. The letter was forged. When arrested, Bond confessed and pleaded that he had published the letter purely for profit. He was put in the pillory and imprisoned. Many forged letters were published in pamphlets and circulated widely. The problem of truth versus lies was apparent to many observers at the time. In 1644, William Collings, editor of the *Kingdom's Weekly Intelligencer*, observed: "There were never more pretenders to the truth than in this age, nor ever fewer that obtained it." A London pamphlet called *The Poets Knavery Discovered* catalogued the number of lies in other pamphlets. Making a distinction between "Lyes" and "Real Books," it described pamphleteering as a "Laborinth of inumerous fictions."[23]

The pamphleteering fury grew so overheated that, in 1643, parliament enacted press controls through a licensing order that subjected publications to prior censorship. Not surprisingly, enforcement once again proved ineffective in the middle of a civil war. The censorship measure did, however, ignite an impassioned debate about censorship and press freedoms. That debate produced a literary classic on freedom of speech: John Milton's *Areopagitica*, published in 1644. Milton, famous for his epic poem *Paradise Lost*, was in his lifetime known as a rhetorician engaged in the great issues of his day. During the Civil War, he sympathized with the Puritan cause opposed to Charles I and published tracts attacking High Church Anglicanism. In *Areopagitica*, Milton associated censorship and repression with Catholicism. Freedom of the press, he argued, was an inherently Protestant principle because it allowed for the open expression of ideas in a society where God's people possess the powers of reason. On the possibility of falsehoods and lies proliferating, Milton asserted that falsehoods will always be defeated by truth in reasonable minds. In a famous phrase, he declared "let truth and falsehood grapple," unhindered by prior restraint. People are rational and can make up their minds about what is true and false.[24]

Despite Milton's rhetorical powers, his famous *Areopagitica* had little impact in the middle of a civil war. The licensing order remained in force. That hardly mattered, however. Not even laws could restrain the feverish pamphleteering that continued to rage in England until Charles I was finally defeated on the battlefield, then arrested, tried, and executed.

On January 30, 1649, the morning of his execution, Charles I was given permission to take exercise in St. James's Park with his toy spaniel named Rogue. He was then escorted to Whitehall, where he spent some time in prayer in Banqueting Hall, whose ceiling fresco featured his father, James I, portrayed as God. The apotheosis on that ceiling was one of the last things Charles looked at before being led outside, where a huge throng was gathered to witness the beheading of their king.

Charles was said to have worn an extra shirt under his pale blue silk waistcoat that morning. He didn't want to shiver in the sharp cold lest the assembled crowd believe he was trembling from fear. He was also wearing his teardrop-shaped pearl earring embedded in a gold crown and cross, hanging from his left ear. When he stepped out of a first-floor window onto the scaffold erected in front of Banqueting House, the crowd stared in expectant silence.

"I go from a corruptible to an incorruptible Crown, where no disturbance can be," declared the king.[25]

Charles turned toward a bishop and removed the George medallion from his neck. He began to pray, his eyes open, as he put his head down on the block. When he stretched out his arms, the executioner brought down the axe and severed his head with one blow.

The crowd let out a horrible groan and fell into a heavy silence. Some approached the scaffold and dipped their handkerchiefs in the king's blood. Others took away pieces of the boards stained with blood as morbid relics. The soldiers present were ordered to scatter and disperse the crowd to avoid disturbances. Charles's severed head was sewn back onto his body so his corpse could be put on display in a room in Whitehall and viewed by the public for several days. Nobody could claim that the king was not dead.

The king was dead. After nearly a decade of civil war, the monarchy in Britain was abolished. Oliver Cromwell was the new republic's lord protector.

Deposing and executing a sacred monarch was an extraordinary event that, throughout England, was immediately felt as a tremendous shock. The principle of divine-right kingship had been decapitated. The king's adversaries understood, however, that the republic still needed to be accepted as legitimate. To achieve that, the monarch's image had to be thoroughly discredited and his execution received as a liberation. The king was dead, but there was still a public relations war to win. This was accomplished by a concerted propaganda campaign in newspapers and pamphlets whose purpose was to transform the image of Charles I from sacred monarch into detestable tyrant.

Charles, it turned out, had written his own pamphlet in the final days of his life. Titled *Eikon Basilike*, the king's memoir was published in early February 1649, only ten days after his execution. The title in Greek translated as "royal portrait," the word *eikon* signifying "icon" or "image." It was Charles I's final self-portrait, the image he was leaving to posterity. Part confession and part self-justification, *Eikon Basilike* revealed a king who admitted his failings as a man but stubbornly insisted on his sacred right as a monarch. Above all, Charles portrayed himself as a martyr. A remarkable document, *Eikon Basilike* was perhaps the first literary attempt by a monarch to establish a posthumous cult of royal veneration.[26]

Eikon Basilike became an instant bestseller, going through at least twenty printings in one year. It is doubtful, however, that Charles I was its author. It was royalist propaganda written inside the king's inner circle. Its impact on the English public was so powerful, however, that Cromwell's regime grew worried about a monarchist backlash. The poet John Milton was hastily commissioned to write a response to the "King's Book," as *Eikon Basilike* was called. Milton's rebuttal, titled *Eikonoklastes* (Greek for "iconoclast"), was published nine months later in October 1649. In the tract, addressed to "the seduced people of England," Milton attempted to smash apart the image of Charles I as a martyr by portraying him as a tyrant. Milton's Puritan counter-propaganda, by the semantics of its title, was playing out the old icon-versus-icon-smashing battles. Puritan iconoclasm was assailing the king's icon. But the *Eikonoklastes* riposte backfired. The English were too shocked by the execution of their monarch to countenance the defiling of his name.

Britain's republican experiment did not survive its Puritan leader. When Oliver Cromwell died in 1558, the republic fell into chaos. The executed monarch's heir, Charles II, returned triumphantly from exile in the French court of Louis XIV. Following the Restoration in 1660, the new royalist parliament ordered the arrest of those responsible for Charles I's trial and public beheading. Twelve regicides were apprehended, sentenced to death, hanged, drawn and quartered, disemboweled, decapitated, and dismembered. Oliver Cromwell was already dead—he had died in 1658—so his corpse was disinterred so he could be tried and sentenced posthumously. Exhuming Cromwell's corpse was a delicate matter, for he had been buried in Westminster Abbey. His body was entombed next to the crypt of the Tudor king Henry VII.

On January 30, 1661—the anniversary of Charles I's execution—the English monarchy orchestrated a macabre spectacle of royal vengeance. Cromwell's body was exhumed from Westminster Abbey and publicly dragged through the streets of London to the Tyburn gallows at present-day Marble Arch. His corpse was strung up in chains until four o'clock that afternoon, then struck down and decapitated. Cromwell's head was impaled on a twenty-foot pole and displayed in front of Westminster Hall, the place of Charles I's trial and death sentence. Rumors circulated for years that the body disinterred and decapitated had not been the corpse of Oliver Cromwell—and, if not, his body was still enshrined in Westminster Abbey. An even more horrible thought was that, if the mutilated corpse was not Cromwell's, it had possibly belonged to a king of England entombed nearby in Westminster Abbey. There were even claims that Cromwell was still alive.

All these rumors were false. Cromwell's head remained gruesomely displayed on a pike for about twenty years, until one day a storm blew it off. The grotesque skull fell into the hands of private collectors, who sold it as a macabre relic that passed through successive generations as an object of curiosity. It was finally buried, this time for good, at Sydney Sussex College, Cambridge, in 1960.

***

In the early evening of July 17, 1676, a massive crowd of more than 100,000 Parisians came out to watch the execution of Marie-Madeleine de Brinvilliers.

At about six o'clock, Madame de Brinvilliers was dragged from the prison cell in the Conciergerie where she had been confined following her death sentence. Dressed in a white chemise, barefoot, and hands bound, she was placed on a cart to be led to the place of execution at Place de Grève along the Seine. A throng of morbidly curious Parisians lined the bridge crossing the Seine, hoping to get a glimpse of the wicked woman found guilty of abominable crimes. When she passed by on the tumbril, the crowd was stunned. Madame de Brinvilliers was an attractive lady with a trim figure, dark gold hair, white skin, a delicate nose, and large blue eyes. Not the heinous monster they had imagined, her appearance was almost angelic. Her escort stopped in front of Notre Dame, where she made a public confession of her unspeakable crimes and demanded pardon.

The famous French woman of letters, Madame de Sévigné, noted in a letter: "Here, we talk only of the deeds, the speeches, and the exploits of la Brinvilliers."[27] For most Parisians, Marie-Madeleine de Brinvilliers's execution was the most sensational event in living memory.

The Marquise de Brinvilliers is remembered not for the circumstances of her execution. Her name still resonates because the terrible crimes for which she was put to death exposed dark secrets extending right into King Louis XIV's most intimate circles at Versailles palace. At the dawn of the Age of Reason, the "Affair of the Poisons" scandal surrounding Madame de Brinvilliers exposed the vices of a French ruling class in the thrall of alarming superstitions, sorcery, and criminal rituals. The affair shook Louis XIV's court like no other controversy in the Sun King's long reign. The scandal was so shocking that many, including the king himself, were anxious to erase the sordid episode from the pages of history.

Marie-Madeleine de Brinvilliers was the daughter of Antoine Dreux d'Aubray, one of the most influential magistrates in France. She was raised in a rarefied atmosphere of wealth and privilege. The family owned a house in Paris and a chateau in the country, and the household counted carriages and a retinue of servants. As befitting a young woman of her station, she was married off, with a substantial dowry, to a suitable husband with a handsome fortune, Antoine Gobelin, marquis de Brinvilliers. A scion of a wealthy family belonging to the lower nobility, his family owned the famous Gobelin dye manufacture that made the king's tapestries. Gobelin and his new wife, established at their own *hôtel particulier* in Le Marais, entered the highest ranks of Parisian society as the Marquis and Marquise de Brinvilliers.

Things quickly turned sour, however. Antoine Gobelin was not a particularly attentive husband. He made the mistake of introducing his neglected wife to an old friend, Jean-Baptiste Godin de Sainte-Croix, who had served in the same cavalry regiment. Sainte-Croix was a murky figure with an unknown past, though it was rumored he was the bastard son of a grand family in Gascony. A charming bounder with a bad gambling habit and mounting debts, he was always on the make. He quickly installed himself in the Brinvilliers residence as a permanent house guest. It didn't take long for Sainte-Croix to see that his fellow cavalry officer Gobelin, after eight years of marriage, wasn't paying much attention to his young wife. Sainte-Croix wasted no time in exploiting Madame de Brinvilliers's emotional void with Tartuffian flattery intended to seduce. She quickly fell passionately in love with the beguiling cavalier, apparently without much opposition from her indifferent husband. The adulterous affair consummated, Madame de Brinvilliers began lavishing huge sums on Sainte-Croix to support his extravagant lifestyle in gambling salons. The adulterous couple was seen together at Place de Grève for the annual "feu de Saint-Jean" fête on June 21. Both were drinking and dancing, waving champagne bottles as a basket full of screaming cats was torched in a bonfire, as was customary in this superstitious ritual inherited from medieval times when cats were hated as incarnations of the devil. [28]

The cuckolded Marquis de Brinvilliers appeared to accept his humiliation, doubtless because he was distracted by his own mistresses. But the gossip in Parisian society about Marie-Madeleine de Brinvilliers's strange ménage-à-trois was too much for her distinguished family. They were particularly shocked when Marie-Madeleine took legal steps to separate her own fortune from her husband's capital. It was clear that Sainte-Croix was attempting to ensure that he had all her money for himself. Her well-connected father, Antoine Dreux d'Aubray, had a long arm in the Paris power elite. He used his considerable influence to have Sainte-Croix arrested with a *lettre de cachet*, allowing for the arrest and detention of anyone at the king's pleasure. Sainte-Croix was promptly locked up in the Bastille prison. When he was released six weeks later, he moved on with his life and even married another woman. But Madame de Brinvilliers, still subjugated by her lover's charms, did everything to win back his affections. She was certain that Sainte-Croix was the father of her youngest child, conceived during a passionate afternoon of love-making when her dissolute husband was away.

When he eventually returned to the Marquise de Brinvilliers, Sainte-Croix had bigger plans this time. He enlisted his pliable mistress in a lethal scheme to get his hands on her family's entire fortune. Marie-Madeleine was susceptible to any scheme to despoil her family. Although she was the eldest child, as a daughter she came after her younger brothers in line for the inheritance. Sainte-Croix's plot was to eliminate the Brinvilliers family by poison. Among his many sidelines, Sainte-Croix was an amateur chemist who concocted bogus potions that he flogged to naïve ladies looking for remedies to real and imagined ailments. This was an era when chemistry, like medicine, was still emerging from medieval practices of alchemy and sorcery. Thanks to his network of louche connections in the alchemy underworld, Sainte-Croix had been introduced to the secret marketplace for *poudres de succession* ("inheritance powders"), deadly poisons procured by ladies to dispose of their rich husbands. There were already murmurs in Paris, through indiscretions made by confessors at Notre Dame Cathedral, about high-born ladies admitting to poisoning their husbands. Having murdered their rich spouses, these ladies evidently still wanted absolution for their mortal sins. Luckily for them, there had been no formal police investigation into their alarming claims made in confessionals.

Sainte-Croix managed to lay his hands on lethal "inheritance powders" for his mistress. Madame de Brinvilliers began poisoning her father, Antoine Dreux d'Aubray, who soon enough fell ill at his chateau in the country. She moved him to her residence in Le Marais to watch over while furtively hastening his death. He finally died mysteriously in September 1666, the same month of the Great Fire of London. An autopsy was performed, but, luckily for Madame de Brinvilliers, nothing suspicious was found. The father was soon followed to the grave by the two d'Aubray brothers. Madame de Brinvilliers planted a manservant in her brother Antoine's household to execute the deadly plot. The manservant was a rogue named Jean Hamelin, known as "La Chaussée." He poisoned the older brother Antoine before performing the same deadly service on the younger sibling, André, who evidently quite liked the valet who was adding poison to his wine. The sudden deaths of the two d'Aubray brothers, like the mysterious expiry of the father, went unexplained.

The family now out of the picture, the fortune was left to the daughter Marie-Madeleine. Madame de Brinvilliers and her scheming cavalier once again threw themselves into extravagant excesses. But Sainte-Croix quickly squandered her money and did a runner. Their dangerous liaison was over. Within a few years, the Marquise de Brinvilliers was broke.

She had participated in the poisoning of her entire family, only to find herself alone, destitute, and suicidal.

It is doubtful that the Marquise de Brinvilliers would ever have been caught for her odious crimes if her scoundrel lover Sainte-Croix had not had the misfortune of dying accidently, probably the victim of his own lethal potions. At the end of July in 1672, his body was discovered at his Paris lodgings in the Latin Quarter. Despite his shameless swindling, there apparently had been a residue of Catholic guilt in Sainte-Croix's cold heart. He had left a written confession of all his worldly sins, including the names of the victims he'd bumped off by poisoning. He also named his accomplices in these deadly conspiracies. Madame de Brinvilliers's passionate love letters, with references to their lethal plots, were also found in his papers. So were samples of Sainte-Croix's potions. Police, curious about the substances in the phials and packets of powder, tested them on two dogs and a cat. The two dogs died immediately; the cat vomited and died the next day. The compounds contained calcinated vitriol, potassium sulphate, and arsenic.

Police promptly arrested the treacherous manservant, La Chaussée, who had administered the poisons on the d'Aubray brothers. Madame de Brinvilliers, for her part, fled to London. She was eventually tracked down in a Belgian convent, arrested, and escorted back to Paris for trial. The fact that the Marquise de Brinvilliers was rich, aristocratic, and well-connected—Madame de Sévigné remarked that she was "related to half the lawyers in Paris"—would normally have been greatly advantageous in such circumstances. But this case was too shocking. The Marquise de Brinvilliers was branded the "wickedest woman in the world."[29]

One reason for the morbid fascination was undoubtedly the Marquise de Brinvilliers's title, social position, and great beauty. In seventeenth-century France, it was difficult to believe that a noblewoman could be guilty of such horrendous wickedness. This perception was hypocritical, of course, for the court of Louis XIV was infamous for vicious intrigues, especially among aristocratic ladies competing for position at Versailles. Still, the combination of rank, beauty, and evil made Madame de Brinvilliers the object of intense public curiosity. The aristocracy was no less absorbed by the scandal, if only because her rank brought discredit to the reputation of the entire nobility.

The fact that Marquise de Brinvilliers was a woman added to her legend as a wicked sorceress. In the educated classes in late-seventeenth-century France, lethal poisoning evoked the ancient Greek mythological figure of Medea. In the Greek myth, Medea helped her lover Jason capture the Golden Fleece, but after their marriage he abandoned her for the king of Corinth's daughter. Medea took revenge on her love rival by sending the princess a dress dipped in poison that, when she put it on, consumed her in flames. The myth of Medea was widely known among the French aristocracy, which was steeped in Greek and Latin culture. Medea was a familiar figure in plays, operas, and court ballets, including Corneille's tragedy *Médée*, first performed in 1635 and revived by Molière's theater company in 1677. In educated Parisian society, the Marquise de Brinvilliers corresponded to the Medea archetype. Madame de Sévigné thought her crimes surpassed those in the ancient Greek myth. "Medea did not do so much," she wrote to her daughter.[30] Little wonder that so much of the gossip about the Marquise de Brinvilliers was myth. It was rumored that, before using her poisons on her family, she had tried them on paupers in public hospitals to ensure they produced the desired deadly effect.

In police custody, the treacherous manservant La Chaussée was tortured to wring a confession. The torture method used on him was known as *brodequins*, sometimes referred to as the "Spanish boot." Wooden boards were attached to his limbs and, as wedges were hammered into the "boot," the bones of his limbs were shattered. He was then tortured on the rack, where this time he confessed all—and implicated Madame de Brinvilliers. Found guilty, his execution was even more gruesome than his torture. Spread eagled on a cartwheel, his limbs and torso were bludgeoned with iron bars until his bones broke and his internal organs were mortally damaged. He was left to die in agony.

Madame de Brinvilliers, after her arrest and trial, was also tortured before her execution. She avoided the *brodequins*, however. Instead, she was subject to the dreaded "water torture." Strapped backwards on a wooden trestle, she was forced to take twenty pints of water funneled down her throat through a cow's horn. Despite the unbearable agony, she refused to admit guilt. She remained obstinate throughout her trial before prosecutors. During her interrogation, she claimed that, at the age of seven, she had been raped by a male domestic servant.

On the day of the Marquise de Brinvilliers's execution, the crowds were so massive that Madame de Sévigné wrote that she couldn't get any closer than the Notre Dame bridge. When the forty-six-year-old marquise mounted the scaffold at Place de Grève, a Jesuit priest was at her side murmuring prayers. She bent on her knees, putting her head on the block. The executioner brought down his sword at once, severing her head so cleanly that it didn't budge. Many in the crowd believed the head was still intact. As all watched expectantly, it finally rolled off the block. Her body was thrown into a bonfire until burned to cinders. Ironically, Madame de Brinvilliers had once drunk champagne and reveled at this very spot with her scoundrel lover, both dancing around a Saint-Jean bonfire as the flames consumed a basket full of screaming cats, agonizing as they were burned alive.

"It's finally over, Madame de Brinvilliers is now in the air," wrote Madame de Sévigné. "After the execution, her poor little body was tossed into an enormous fire, and then her ashes scattered to the wind. We are inhaling her."[31]

The Marquise de Brinvilliers was dead. But Affair of the Poisons was just beginning.

At Versailles Palace, rumors and tales about poison plots were now starting to reach the ears of the king. The police had arrested two Parisian fortune-tellers, Madame de la Grangeon and Marie Bosse, whose confessions opened a Pandora's box of revelations that made the Brinvilliers case seem like child's play. Louis XIV was horrified to learn that many high-ranking officials and nobles throughout his kingdom had been, like Madame de Brinvilliers, using "inheritance powders" to poison rivals and relatives. A vast network of soothsayers, palm readers, fortune-tellers, and astrologists were operating in Paris. There was also a thriving market for love charms and poisons sold to ladies of exalted rank in the king's court. Members of the nobility were paying large sums to fortune-tellers who claimed to be able to predict the outcome of their adulterous love affairs—and, if desired, procured poisons to bring their marriages and other romantic entanglements to a desired conclusion.

How Louis XIV had remained ignorant of these intrigues in his own court at Versailles is difficult to fathom. The king was interested in gossip, always insisting on knowing everything about everyone at court. The culture of superstition at court was hardly a secret. As Voltaire remarked about the era: "The former habit of consulting diviners, to have one's horoscope drawn, to seek secret means of making oneself loved, still survived vivid among the people and even in the highest of the kingdom."[32] In Louis XIV's court, many in the French nobility were under the spell of an Italian seer named Primi Visconti, who foretold the future of his high-born clients by reading their handwriting or examining their facial features. Carriages of many exalted personages could be seen lined up outside his lodgings. Among them were the Comtesse de Soissons and the Duchesse de Vitry. The king's flamboyantly homosexual brother, the Duc d'Orléans—known officially as "Monsieur"—was another of Visconti's regulars.

Louis XIV was resolutely hostile to superstitions. He certainly had religious grounds for being repulsed by stories of fortune-telling, sorcery, and poison plots. As a divine-right monarch, his piety was not to be questioned, even if his personal vices, including many mistresses and bastard offspring, kept his priestly confessors in a constant state of alarm. The king would have been genuinely alarmed by scandalous rumors of sorceresses and alchemists engaged in criminal acts. Louis XIV embraced the spirit of his era with its emphasis on science and reason. His symbol was Apollo, the god of knowledge and light. The king regarded himself as a man of science. He had long cultivated the image of Sun King to associate his reign with the Age of Reason in an era of great scientific discoveries. His epoch was the century of Galileo, Sir Isaac Newton, and René Descartes. In 1666, the king established France's National Academy of Sciences.[33] Following the death of his famous African elephant in the Versailles Palace menagerie—a gift from the king of Portugal—he personally attended the animal's autopsy and dissection as testimony to his interest in biological science.

Louis XIV was the first French monarch not to have a court astrologer. When he was a small boy, his mother, Anne d'Autriche, kept a court astrologer, Jean-Baptiste Morin, near her own chambers to provide regular predictions about the fate of her son. Morin, who was a professor at the Collège Royal, later published a book, *Astrologia Gallica*. The young dauphin, who became king at age four under his mother's regency and the guidance of Cardinal Mazarin, grew up in an atmosphere of superstition. Later in life, however, Louis XIV had little patience for things like astrology and fortune-telling. As a great believer in science, he surrounded himself with physicians, surgeons, and so-called *empiriques* with their latest nostrums to cure ailments.

In the late seventeenth century, medicine was making great strides forward but was still on the cusp between the medieval and modern age. Despite great advances in medicine, such as William Harvey's discovery of blood circulation, medical practices in Louis XIV's day were still influenced by the "Galenist" system of balancing the body's humors—blood, phlegm, and biles. Even a scientific rationalist like Descartes made false assertions about the human anatomy, including his claim that the pineal gland in the human brain was the seat of the soul.[34] Molière's comedy *Le Malade Imaginaire*, first performed at the Palais Royal in 1673, satirized the state of medicine of his day. Louis XIV and Molière were close, and the king certainly knew that play. It was the king who put the Palais Royal theater at the disposition of Molière's troupe. The king knew from personal experience that the greatest physicians of the day believed that diseases were cured by bloodletting and bowel purges. Frequently, these practices produced the opposite effect of hastening the patient's demise.

Louis XIV himself was subject to numerous bloodletting procedures that caused him tremendous physical suffering. It was said that his bowel purges were so aggressive that his stool was often red with blood. He also underwent a ghastly anal fistula operation whose excruciating pain can scarcely be imagined (though after the operation, such was the slavish culture of royal emulation at Versailles that anal fistulas became fashionable among male courtiers). Neither was the king well served by his court dentists. He lost all his teeth by his fortieth year. Behind Louis XIV's haughty bearing in the great royal portraits of the mature Sun King was an iconic fiction. Under the massive black coils of his wig cascading down his back, the king was concealing a prematurely balding pate. And behind the Sun King's majestically disdainful expression was a sorry mouth without any teeth. If he could do little to cure his baldness, Louis's tooth decay was likely caused by his love of sweetmeats, especially candied fruit.[35]

When Louis XIV's heir to the throne, the dauphin, fell ill with the ague, or fever, the king turned to a renowned English physician, Sir Robert Talbor, sent to the French court by his cousin Charles II. The English king had knighted Talbor for curing his own case of the ague (probably malaria), and subsequently dispatched Talbor to France to treat his niece, Marie Louise d'Orléans, who was to marry the king of Spain. Talbor soon became rich and famous as an in-demand physician at the courts of Europe, including Versailles. When the dauphin fell ill with fever, the king called on Talbor to administer his medicaments. Louis was astounded when the dauphin quickly recovered and showed tremendous gratitude to Talbor (including an offer to buy the patent for his secret medicine). Sir Robert Talbor's miracle medicine was known at the French court as the "Englishman's cure." Talbor went to great lengths to keep the details of his elixir a secret. The main ingredient, in fact, was quinine, made from cinchona bark. Talbor suffered some medical setbacks, however. He treated the great French writer La Rochefoucauld when he fell ill in 1680, but this time the patient died. Still, Talbor's quinine-based medicine marked great progress over bleeding and purging to cure malaria fevers.[36]

Despite his Sun King image as a great believer in reason and science, Louis XIV was a monarch who embodied puzzling contradictions. One was his devotion to the royal cult of miraculous healing by touching the afflicted. French monarchs had long observed the occult practice, especially at Easter and Christmas, of meeting victims of scrofula and "healing" them with a "royal touch"—in essence, performing a Christ-like miracle. Louis XIV carried on this tradition—it was also practiced by English kings—of meeting sick pilgrims who came to Versailles hoping to be healed of the gangrenous lesions on their lymph glands (from tuberculosis). The king met them at the Orangerie and uttered the following words as he touched their lesions: "*Le Roi te touche. Dieu te guérit*" ("The King touches you. God heals you"). Scrofula was called the "king's evil" precisely because it was believed the monarch's royal touch could cure the disease. Louis XIV was said to have touched some 200,000 victims of scrofula during his reign. The Sun King, though attached to the principles of reason, remained devoted to his own exalted status as a king whose legitimacy came from God.

When the king discovered the full extent of criminal plots and intrigues at his court, he reacted with cold fury against what he called "this miserable commerce in poisons." These superstitious practices were an affront to the rationalist order that Louis XIV personally embodied. Louis XIV's centralized state was, like the geometrical gardens at Versailles palace, founded on principles of rational design. The king's lieutenant governor of police, Nicolas de la Reynie, established the first modern police force—and would use it to aggressively prosecute the accused in the "Affair of the Poisons" case. The king ordered La Reynie to arrest and investigate anyone, whatever their rank, suspected of involvement in these abominable activities.

La Reynie established a special tribunal, called a *Chambre Ardente* (or "burning court," usually used for the trials of heretics) for judicial proceedings prosecuting the case. Several aristocratic ladies, including the Comtesse de Soissons, were promptly arrested. The Comtesse de Soissons was one of the so-called Mazarinettes, a nickname for the nieces of the king's powerful mentor, Cardinal Mazarin. While not a great beauty, she had seductive eyes and immense charm. She had also shared Louis's bed in his younger days. He had even wanted to marry her, but his mother, Anne d'Autriche, set him straight on that question (he married his cousin, Marie-Thérèse, daughter of the king of Spain, who spoke French poorly and suffered the king's many mistresses). At court, the Comtesse de Soissons, while a notorious *intrigueuse*, enjoyed the king's favor and attentions. When the scandal erupted, she was suspected not only of attempting to poison feminine rivals, including the king's mistress Louise de La Vallière, but also of using poison to murder her own husband, the Comte de Soissons. There was even reason to suspect, post-facto, that the mysterious death of the king's sister-in-law, Henriette-Anne (daughter of English king Charles I and his French queen Henriette-Marie), had been caused by a poisoned cup of chicory.

The most shocking allegations concerned Louis XIV's court favorite, the beautiful, charming, and witty Marquise de Montespan. The king's official *maîtresse-en-titre* for more than a decade, Madame de Montespan was from one of the oldest aristocratic families in France. While she had two children with her cuckolded husband, the Marquis de Montespan, she was the mother of seven of Louis XIV's illegitimate offspring. Such was her influence at court that many considered the Marquise de Montespan—her real name was Françoise-Athénaïs de Rochechouart de Mortemart—as the de facto queen of France. It was alleged that Madame de Montespan, increasingly anxious about her sexual appeal to the king, had been attempting to poison her main rival for the king's affections, the pretty Mademoiselle de Fontanges. Louis was smitten with Mademoiselle de Fontanges, who was more than twenty years younger than the Marquise de Montespan. Anxious about being usurped by her younger rival, Madame de Montespan visited a fashionable sorceress in Paris for help. The Marquise de Montespan had been a regular client of Catherine Monvoisin, known among her aristocratic clientele as "La Voisin." La Voisin supplemented her activities as a fortune-teller with other services, including procuring poison powders, arranging black masses, and providing abortions. La Voisin supplied the king's mistress with "Spanish fly" love potions that Madame de Montespan sprinkled on the king's food to excite his sexual desires for her. It was La Voisin's arrest that blew open La Reynie's investigation. She confessed and revealed everything. She also disclosed the names of her illustrious clientele, including the king's official mistress, Madame de Montespan.

The revelation that most horrified the king was that Madame de Montespan had participated in a black mass at which an infant had been sacrificed. Madame de Montespan's sorceress La Voisin had been organizing so-called amatory masses, performed by a renegade occultist priest, Etienne Guibourg, who ceremoniously sacrificed infants (they were usually the unwanted newborns of prostitutes). It was believed that La Voisin had incinerated the bodies of hundreds of babies sacrificed in black masses. At the black mass attended by Madame de Montespan, the baby's blood had allegedly been used to make a communion wafer that was mixed with the love potions that she later put in the king's food. There was even a suggestion that Madame de Montespan had once attempted to poison the king.

Louis XIV was horrified by what he learned, especially the implication of Madame de Montespan. These scandals revealed a murky underworld in the upper reaches of French society where the line between Catholic sacerdotal rituals and black demonic rites was shockingly indistinguishable. Louis XIV could not allow the reputation of his court to be tarnished by these accusations of sacrilege. He gave strict orders for all details of the investigation to be kept from the public.

In seventeenth-century France, information was under tight censorship. Unlike in England, where the sacred monarchy had been decapitated in 1649, in France the principle of divine right remained unmolested. Any criticism of the monarch was tantamount to sacrilege. Louis XIV was revered almost as a deity, which was conveyed by his radiant Apollo iconography. From his earliest childhood as boy king, his portraits in almanacs circulated throughout the kingdom to spread his image. He posed for magnificent portraits, including an equestrian painting presenting him as a warrior king with Victory holding a crown of laurels over his head. Louis used the French Academy of Painting and Sculpture, directly under his control, as an official instrument of his personal propaganda to create icons and idols around his own cult of personality. When the English philosopher John Locke visited the Gobelin tapestry manufacture in Paris—owned by the Marquis de Brinvilliers's family—he noted that the central figure in most of the images was Louis XIV.

Louis XIV's obsession with controlling information was undoubtedly a reaction to the emotional shock of the "Fronde" rebellion against the monarchy during his regency as a boy king. That turbulent period was France's version of the English Civil War—and came close to producing the same result. The Fronde unleashed a fury of pamphleteering against the monarchy. One powerful weapon was the so-called *libelles* (from Latin *liber* for book, though interestingly the word *libel* comes from the same root). Most *libelles* were quarto pamphlets that contained either satirical or polemical writing, often scandalous and sometimes defamatory. Other pamphlets attacked the reputation of the young king's powerful minister, Cardinal Mazarin. Known as *mazarinades*, they were hawked at specific locations in the streets of Paris. Some made sarcastic references to Mazarin's status as a foreigner, others ridiculed his Italian accent, and still others alluded to his mistresses. Cyrano de Bergerac wrote several *mazarinades* against the cardinal; others were penned by well-known burlesque authors of the day. It is estimated that some 1,500 pamphlets were circulating in France during this period, half of them against the king despite the draconian regime of censorship.[37] Following the Fronde, Louis XIV moved his court to Versailles, centralized power in his own hands, and subordinated the aristocracy by keeping them bowing and curtseying to gain royal favor.

That is not to say that pamphlets did not circulate under Louis XIV. There was a market for so-called *canards sanglantés* filled with stories of lurid crimes. *Canards* were printed quickly and hawked on the streets of Paris to a readership ranging from literate artisans to the uncultured bourgeoisie. Another type of publication was called *histoires tragiques*, which spun tales of strange and violent deaths combined with propaganda, news, and tales that were largely indifferent to factual truth. News about the monarchy, on the other hand, was never critical. It ranged from unctuous fawning in the *Mercure Galant* to royal propaganda in the *Gazette de France*. La Reynie's police force was aggressive in repressing any seditious speech or writing. La Reynie commonly imposed severe punishments, from hard labor to death by hanging, on printers convicted of publishing words or caricatures that defamed the king. Two printers were sentenced to death by hanging for publishing an engraving showing Louis XIV enchained by the four women in his life: Madame de Montespan, Mademoiselle de Fontanges, Madame de Maintenon, and Madame de la Vallière.[38]

During the judicial investigation into the poisons affair, the French press was virtually silent on the matter. The court's official *Mercure Galant* paper published no articles about the case. But gossip was more powerful than the press. People from all walks of life learned the juicy details from word-of-mouth accounts that leaked out through the grapevine. As the letters of Madame de Sévigné attest, the Affair of the Poisons was the worst-kept secret of Louis XIV's reign. The 100,000 people who came out to watch Madame de Brinvilliers being led to her gruesome execution—the population of Paris was only 500,000 in the late seventeenth century—was another testimony to the intense public fascination with scandal and lurid tales. The number of people arrested and interrogated during the ensuing criminal investigation made it simply impossible for the French state to conceal the affair from the public. Everybody was talking about it.

In the end, more than four hundred suspects had been rounded up and interrogated. Many were tortured to extract confessions. Dozens had fled the country to escape prosecution. The Comtesse de Soissons, once the king's much-admired mistress, was disgraced and exiled. Thirty-six other suspects were found guilty and executed. One of them was La Voisin, who in 1680 was found guilty of witchcraft and burned at the stake at Place de Grève, where Madame de Brinvilliers had been decapitated and burned four years earlier. Others were sent to fortresses to spend the rest of their lives in solitary confinement chained to walls. These were mostly witnesses whose testimony was so scandalous that Louis XIV took no risk of their accounts ever reaching the public.

In 1682, Louis XIV shut down the judicial inquiry altogether. The reputational risk for his court was too great. The king ordered his ministers to have every record of the trials suppressed. All documents were put under seal. He was especially fearful that further revelations would uncover illegal activities committed by Madame de Montespan. She was the mother of the king's favorite son, Louis-Auguste de Bourbon (named after his father and the Roman emperor Augustus), known by his title, Duc du Maine. The king nonetheless put an end to Madame de Montespan's status as his official mistress. She remained at court, increasingly showing the ravages of age, disgraced in the eyes of the monarch. The Marquise de Montespan never again enjoyed the attentions of Louis XIV.

Perhaps most significantly, when the affair concluded, Louis XIV issued an edict that declared all acts of witchcraft and magic fraudulent. The word *witchcraft* ("*sorcellerie*") was not used. The royal edict preferred more indirect language, "diviners, magicians, and enchanters." Anyone engaged in such practices was ordered to leave the kingdom on threat of punishment, which was the death penalty in cases involving sacrilege, blasphemy, or poisoning. By declaring "so-called acts of magic" fraudulent, Louis XIV was asserting that no such thing exists. Anyone claiming to perform acts based on magic or superstitions was prosecuted. The edict also brought in a new regime of regulation for the sale of poisons. In the end, the Sun King came down on the side of reason.

Many years later in 1709, Louis XIV ordered every record related to the Affair of the Poisons burned. He wanted the whole sordid business consigned to "eternal oblivion." The last of the prisoners, a woman, expired after thirty-seven years confined at the Villefranche fortress. When she died in 1717, she had outlived the king himself. What we know about the Affair of the Poisons today is thanks mainly to the work of historians who managed to reconstitute details through copies of interrogation minutes and other documents that slipped through the official cover-up.

At the end of Louis XIV's seventy-year reign, poison plots were no longer dominating his thoughts. His mind was tortured by other regrets. The court at Versailles had become solemn as the king approached death, now under the influence of the pious Madame de Maintenon following their secret morganatic marriage. The king, his leg diseased with gangrene, continued to suffer painful bloodletting and bowel-purging procedures.

On his deathbed in 1715, the Sun King uttered a final regret: "*J'ai trop aimé la guerre et les batiments.*" He had been too fond of making war and constructing palaces.

Louis XIV recognized that his excesses had pushed his kingdom into ruin. A century later, another royal scandal would explode. This time, the Bourbon monarchy would be toppled.

9

COFFEE AND CAKE

On the first day of November in 1755, the city of Lisbon was destroyed by a massive earthquake. That devastating event not only crippled Portugal as a major colonial power but also sent a shockwave through Renaissance civilization.

It was just past nine o'clock in the morning on All Saints Day. Worshippers were arriving for morning mass in Lisbon's churches. Suddenly a massive earthquake shook the city, followed by a powerful tsunami. Within ten minutes, the city's great palaces, opera house, libraries, cathedrals, hospitals, and art galleries were decimated. What remained standing went up in flames as thousands looted and pillaged in the ruins. The death toll was estimated at more than 40,000, roughly a fifth of Lisbon's population. The shock was felt in other parts of Europe and northern Africa. In Morocco to the south, some 10,000 were killed.[1]

The French philosopher Voltaire, shocked by the devastating news, followed the aftermath of the Lisbon earthquake with great interest. Lisbon was a major European city in the eighteenth century, rivaling London and Paris and Naples. News of the disaster was on everyone's lips for months. A great deal of the reporting of the catastrophe was sensationalized second-hand accounts published in newspapers and pamphlets. The expected arrival of Halley's Comet two years later added to the widespread belief that the disaster had been caused by a supernatural force—specifically, God's wrath. Voltaire was particularly intrigued by the religious reasons given for the catastrophe. The Catholic Church declared it had been divine retribution against sinners, or *theodicy*. Pamphlets claimed that survivors of the Lisbon disaster had been saved by an apparition of the Virgin Mary. For many, believing that the catastrophe had been an act of God was a cultural coping mechanism.

Voltaire saw something else at work. Born at the end of the seventeenth century, Voltaire was the embodiment of Enlightenment suspicion of supernatural explanations for the condition of humankind. In the aftermath of the Lisbon earthquake, he published his famous satire, *Candide*, in which he seized on the disaster to attack the naïve belief that everything in this world is God's work—or, to quote the French philosopher's famous phrase, "all is for the best in the best of all possible worlds." Voltaire refused to accept that a good God could be responsible for such unspeakable human suffering. At the end of the book, the protagonist Candide abandons his naïve faith and realizes that life must be approached with pragmatic understanding of the world.

The Lisbon earthquake tragedy, which occurred only three decades before the French Revolution, brought into focus the necessity of Enlightenment values. Following centuries of obscurantism, the French *philosophes* asserted the primacy of reason, science, and objective truth as the basis of knowledge. Insisting on the existence of universal values and laws, Enlightenment humanism rejected the authority of revelation, scripture, dogma, and the supernatural or transcendent. Enlightenment values of universality, objectivity, and rationality challenged and discredited superstition, ignorance, barbarism, fanaticism, cruelty, intolerance, and oppression. Humankind was finally unburdened of supernatural explanations for events in this world. After centuries of darkness, Western civilization had reconnected with the virtue that ancient Romans called *humanitas*. Wherever reason triumphed over superstition, people lived freely and without fear of persecution from laws based on supernatural authority. Thanks to the progress of science and industry, the human well-being of its beneficiaries improved in virtually every category. No previous era had ever rivaled the modern world's achievement of prosperity and happiness.

The seeds of the Enlightenment's high-flowering in the eighteen century had germinated a century earlier. In Britain, its origins are often traced to the Revolution of 1688, when divine-right monarchy was overthrown for good. Even before 1688, English philosophers such as Thomas Hobbes championed a mechanistic view of nature and realism in human affairs. Like Machiavelli, Hobbes understood that we must take man not as he should be, but as he really is. When social order breaks down, he famously observed, life degenerates into a lawless state of nature in which "the life of man is solitary, poor, nasty, brutish and short."[2] Hobbes argued that societies need strong states to protect people from their own passions, fears, and mutual suspicions.

Hobbes's rationalist view of society was echoed by the great scientific minds of his day on the continent. First among them was René Descartes, who argued that, to understand the world, intellect and reason must prevail over feelings and sensations. For Descartes, the world we see is not a dream or a strange hallucination, but something very real. Knowledge therefore requires intellectual methods and rules to prove "truths." Descartes's often-quoted *cogito ergo sum* ("I think, therefore I am") was an assertion that proved existence through intellect, not feelings. His rationalist ideas laid the foundation for other Enlightenment thinkers to approach all questions with skepticism.

Descartes nonetheless articulated an *a priori* argument that "proved" the existence of God. His mind-body dualism asserted that, since the mind and body are separate, our consciousness (non-physical and hence distinct from the brain) is connected to our eternal souls. The separation of mind and body, combined with the rational demonstration of God's existence, made Descartes's philosophy compatible with established Christian dogma. The merger of science and religion was not entirely new. Galileo had attempted to reconcile Scripture and science, famously observing that the Bible "tells us how to go to heaven, not how the heavens go." Galileo's heliocentric theory was more politically problematic for the Church, however, because it directly contradicted passages in the Bible stating unequivocally that God created the earth as unmovable. Descartes, for his part, used science to affirm the existence of God, and our eternal souls, without offending Scripture. Descartes believed, however, that only humans have souls. He regarded animals as mere physical objects, like machines. For Descartes, when an animal howls in agony when being butchered, the noise is no more significant morally than the sound of a clock striking the hour. Since animals do not possess reason, he believed, they were incapable of suffering. The moral hierarchy established by Descartes's rationalist vision placed humans at the pinnacle, for better or worse, as they attempt to understand the objective world around them through observation and reason.

The question of religion remained delicate. Descartes's reluctance to disprove religion with the exacting standards of rationality was typical of many philosophers of his era. In 1646, the famous physician Sir Thomas Browne published his *Pseudodoxia Epidemica*, an attack on superstition that argued truth is accessible through reason and empirical methods. Yet Brown, like other scientific thinkers of his age, remained a devout Christian. While their ideas were overthrowing the authority of religion, they personally remained faithful to religious doctrine. To the more probingly skeptical mind, this left unresolved many implausible stories in the Scriptures, such as the parting of the Red Sea, the abused donkey of Balaam given the power of speech, cherubs brandishing swords of fire at the Gates of Paradise, not to mention the myriad prophecies and miracles. Voltaire's highly educated mistress, Madame du Châtelet, found many deplorable errors in the Bible, even on matters of simple mathematics.

Some Catholic apologists attempted to reinterpret these passages, or exclude them altogether from the biblical narrative. Enlightenment philosophers, including John Locke, felt compelled to demonstrate that the Bible was, in fact, entirely "reasonable."[3] In his *Reasonableness of Christianity*, published in 1695, Locke argued that the truths of the Scriptures are accessible through human reason. Though a great liberal philosopher whose political treatises greatly influenced the French *philosophes*, Locke was profoundly influenced by traditional biblical theology. This may explain why the biblical language in Locke's political rhetoric greatly inspired the Founding Fathers of the American republic where patriotic fervor was deeply rooted in religion.[4]

In France, philosophers such as Voltaire, Montesquieu, and Diderot broke more deliberately from religious dogma. Whereas Descartes had been careful to make an ontological argument for the existence of God, the *philosophes* subjected even that question to the test of reason. Emboldened by the Roman poet Horace's dictum *sapere aude*—"dare to know"—the *philosophes* rejected the metaphysics of Descartes to embrace the natural physics of Isaac Newton. They asserted that truths are accessible by reason and hence disqualify the supernatural and religious dogma. Voltaire was even in the habit of signing letters with the words *écraser l'infâme*, an expression of his combat against superstition and religion and all forms of intolerance. The *philosophes* regarded the Bible as a collection of myths integrated into human understanding of the world—much like the ancient Greeks and Romans read the Homeric epics. For ecclesiastical authorities, the underlying threat posed by Enlightenment thinking was obvious. Pope Benedict XIV put Montesquieu's *The Spirit of the Laws*—in which he set out three kinds of regimes: republican, monarchical, despotic—on the Church's index of forbidden books. The influence of the Church and its dogmas gradually receded, usurped by the Renaissance revival of ideals from Greece and Rome celebrating the humanist pursuit of honor and glory—and, in time, by the passion for personal gain and wealth with the emergence of liberal capitalism.[5]

Despite the momentum of Enlightenment ideas, boldly expressed in the American and French constitutions, the practical task of unbending the crooked timber of humanity was an ambitious project that confronted many obstacles.[6] Superstition and religious orthodoxy, even fanaticism, continued to thrive throughout the Age of Reason. Less than a century after Voltaire, Enlightenment values confronted a rebellion from an entire movement gathered under the banner of Romanticism. For the Romantics of the counter Enlightenment, the Age of Reason's mechanistic worldview had overthrown religion only to install its own soulless cult of rationality and inflicted on the world the cold machinery of industry. The triumph of reason had furnished a rationale for selfish brutality toward the natural world in a ceaseless enterprise of pillaging, exploiting, and commercializing natural resources with little concern for the moral and material consequences. Descartes's cold indifference to the feelings and suffering of animals demonstrated the moral vacuity of the rationalist worldview. The Age of Reason was, moreover, implacable with its designated adversary: irrationality. Anything belonging to the category of "unreason" was repressed. Just as the Catholic Church had used inquisitions to censor and silence heresy, Enlightenment rationalism targeted unreason and superstition as secular heresies that needed to be corrected. The horrific excesses of the French Revolution were an early warning sign of this reaction. During the Reign of Terror, anyone found guilty of unreason was dragged to the guillotine. Soon modern asylums were built to intern those diagnosed as irrational, deviant, or insane.

The Enlightenment philosopher who most embodied the spirit of the age was also, paradoxically, its fiercest critic: Jean-Jacques Rousseau. Entombed in the Pantheon as a hero of the French republic, Rousseau is venerated as an immortal of the Age of Reason. It is often overlooked, however, that he was the Enlightenment's rebellious offspring. Rousseau was suspicious of scientific rationalism because it elevated reason over feeling. Famous for his observation that "man is born free and everywhere he is in chains," Rousseau believed that civilization had a corrupting and alienating influence on man's natural state of freedom and happiness. His concept of "general will" rearticulated freedom as citizen sovereignty in a social contract. In civilization, he contended, we lose our natural liberty but gain civil liberties. While Rousseau rejected Church dogma, he did not share the hostility of Voltaire and other *philosophes* toward religion. Rousseau advocated a "natural religion," which he claimed was not accessible through reason, but through feelings. This conception of religion anticipated the Romantic movement's fusion of spirituality and nature as an emotional experience. Rousseau also saw a place for a "civil religion" that belonged in the secular realm of human affairs. Civil religion fosters patriotic sentiments of sociability and public duty. Rousseau's religious convictions were thus essentially civic, rather than theological.[7]

Even if their worldviews were largely in harmony, Voltaire could not abide Rousseau's rejection of reason as the basis of religious knowledge. The two men enjoyed cordial relations for a time, but they gradually came to despise each other utterly. Though born into the Parisian bourgeoisie (his real name was François-Marie Arouet), Voltaire belonged to the aristocratic wing of the Enlightenment. Following early success with his play *Oedipus*, he was a rich and famous superstar for the rest of his life. He made a fortune on the stock market; he was imprisoned in the Bastille for eleven months for insulting the regent; he was exiled in England (a country whose culture of liberty he greatly admired) after challenging a French nobleman to a duel; he counted princes and kings among his admirers, including the young king of Prussia, Frederick II; he had a long and turbulent extramarital romance with the brilliant woman of science Madame du Châtelet. Jean-Jacques Rousseau, on the other hand, was an outsider who abhorred elites (he famously turned down a pension offered by Louis XV). The animosity between the two philosophers reached a low point when Rousseau publicly unmasked Voltaire as the author of a scathing anti-Christian pamphlet, *Sermon des cinquante* (*Sermon of the Fifty*), published anonymously in 1752. Infuriated, Voltaire shot back in *Sentiment des citoyens*, attacking Rousseau for abandoning his own children, though he denied being the author of the pamphlet.

Despite his superstar status at the courts of kings and emperors, Voltaire took great risks by criticizing religion. "Every sensible man," he wrote, "every honorable man, must hold the Christian sect in horror." Voltaire was a "deist," which during the Enlightenment in France was regarded as a code word for *atheist*. The foundations of deism were built on the influential scientific ideas of the age, notably those of Isaac Newton. Deists stressed the importance of rational observation of the natural world as the judge of all truths. They did not deny the existence of a Supreme Being, but insisted that religion was natural, not supernatural. Above all, deists rejected revelation and miracles as superstitions believed only by ignorant and credulous. As Voltaire famously observed about belief in miracles: "Those who can make you believe absurdities, can make you commit atrocities."[8]

The Scottish philosopher David Hume asserted that miracles were a "violation of the laws of nature." For Hume, superstitions and miracles did not belong to the natural sphere of human perception. He observed that superstitious belief in miracles, like those recounted in the Bible, were also found in pagan Rome, where it was claimed that emperors performed miracles in a Christ-like manner. The historian Tacitus reported, for example, that emperor Vespasian cured a blind man by moistening his eyes with his spittle, and on another occasion restored through his imperial touch the use of a lame man's hand. For Hume, these tales were manifestly false. Enlightenment-era deists conceived of God as a cosmic engineer, a watchmaker who designed the universe but did not intervene in human affairs. Voltaire liked to say that, unlike religion, "there are no sects in geometry." In America, several of the Founding Fathers, including George Washington and Thomas Jefferson, espoused deist beliefs. Jefferson rejected the supernatural claims in the New Testament. His famous "Jefferson Bible," assembled from selected passages from the Gospels, excluded all references to miracles, including the resurrection of Christ.

Rejection of superstition stretched back to ancient Greece, where pre-Socratic philosophers had opposed mythological and religious explanations in favor of a rational understanding of the world. Several centuries later, the Epicureans took a similar empirical view, though they emphasized human sensations as the basis for knowledge. While the word *Epicurean* would later be associated with hedonism, it was in fact a philosophy that advocated moderation of human appetites. Rejecting the transcendental metaphysics of Plato, the Epicureans argued that the soul does not survive the body and hence cannot be punished after death. Epicureans advocated the maximization of "pleasure" in this world—not hedonistic indulgence, but happiness—by eliminating pain and anxieties about death and, above all, seeking the life-affirming virtues of friendship. The Epicureans were ancient Greek humanists who repudiated the notion of divine interventions in human affairs.

The Age of Reason constantly grappled with these same questions, especially the persistent hold of superstition on people's beliefs. There can be no doubt that the Enlightenment's rational culture of scientific enquiry succeeded in dispelling many beliefs in old legends and fables. People no longer followed the ancient Roman custom of predicting events by reading the warm entrails of slaughtered animals. Still, fascination with the supernatural and occult persisted throughout the Age of Reason. Irrational fear of omens was widespread. Many consulted fortune-tellers, and the sale of astrology almanacs was booming in the eighteenth century, boasting quasi-scientific claims to outlandish predictions based on readings of the stars. The practice of necromancy was also common. In 1761, the queen of Sweden, Louisa Ulrika, consulted the famous theologian-turned-psychic Emanuel Swedenborg for news about her deceased brother, Crown Prince Augustus William—and was astonished by his insights into her sibling relationship. Witchcraft was declining, but there were still claims of demonic possession. One was the famous semi-public exorcism of a beautiful teenaged French girl, Marie-Catherine Cadière, in the town of Toulon in 1730 (signs of her demonic possession emerged after her sexual affair with her Jesuit confessor, Father Jean-Baptiste Girard). In England thirty years later, two Bristol girls, Molly and Dobby Giles, were said to have been violently possessed, including beatings and chokings, by the demon Malchi (though there was reason to believe that the Giles family was being harassed). Stories of vampires also proliferated throughout the continent, despite Voltaire's impatient dismissal of them as superstitious fantasies. While belief in the occult and supernatural was held in contempt by the French *philosophes* who wrote in the *Encyclopédie*, their deep skepticism was not widely shared among common people.[9]

Medical knowledge was progressing in the eighteenth century, but quackery was still rampant. Ignorance about diseases made people turn to bogus remedies that promised to cure ailments for everything from scurvy and gout to venereal disease and evil cancers. In the year 1700, the population of London was roughly a half million, but there were only sixty certified doctors and about one thousand apothecaries dispensing medicine. Many turned to unqualified practitioners working outside the profession. Some were "empirics" who made serious claims for their remedies and published books and pamphlets as marketing tools. Others were fraudulent quacks flogging cure-all elixirs. Some prescriptions were folk medicines with a good chance of producing desired results, for example, treating a toothache with cotton soaked in oil of cloves and opium. Other cure-all remedies produced no medicinal effects. One of the most popular remedies of this period was tar water—one quart of tar stirred into a gallon of water and left to stand for forty-eight hours—which was believed to cure smallpox, scurvy, typhus, and other ailments. The English aristocrat Lady Mary Wortley Montagu, famous for her letters, remarked in 1747: "We have no longer faith in miracles and relics, and therefore, with the same fury run after receipts and physicians; the same money which three hundred years ago was given for the health of the soul, is now given for the health of the body, and by the same sort of people, women and half-witted men."[10]

Even the mighty and powerful were convinced by the efficacy of quack medicines. A well-known empiric of the era, Miss Joanna Stephens, came up with a remedy for kidney stones, a common ailment in the eighteenth century known as "the stone." Miss Stephens counted many influential figures among her patients, including the Duke of Richmond and the Bishop of Oxford. Another was the prime minister, Sir Robert Walpole, who swore by Miss Stephens's secret remedy, which claimed to dissolve kidney stones, or *vesical calculi*. Miss Stephens was so famous in her day that Parliament awarded her £5,000—a substantial sum in the early eighteenth century—for the ingredients of her medicine. Her nostrum turned out to be a concoction consisting primarily of soap, honey, and calcined egg shells. Walpole may have felt cured by Miss Stephens's remedy, but when he died in 1745, three large stones were found in his bladder.[11]

An equally vital question that divided leading figures of the Enlightenment was the role of our senses and perception in understanding the world. Rationalists such as Descartes argued that objective truth is independent of our sensory experience. Innate knowledge of things is acquired through reason, not through subjective experience. To demonstrate this, Descartes used his famous "wax argument," observing that a ball of wax, when melting, is transformed in all its sensory aspects (size, shape, color, texture, fragrance)—thus proving that we cannot trust our sensory experience as a source of knowledge. Empiricists such as David Hume argued, on the other hand, that knowledge is acquired through our senses and experience of the world. Whereas Descartes put reason before passions, Hume asserted that reason is "a slave to the passions." Enlightenment rationalists and empiricists were united against superstitions as sources of knowledge, but they diverged on the role of human experience.

The quintessential Enlightenment figure from the empirical school was, ironically, a protagonist from fantasy literature: Robinson Crusoe. Daniel Defoe published his famous *Robinson Crusoe* travelogue to explore the question of perception and truth. Defoe was a prolific author who wrote books, pamphlets, and journals on a wide array of subjects that frequently courted controversy. In 1703, he was arrested on charges of seditious libel for publishing a pamphlet that was a *faux* tirade against religious dissenters (Defoe was one himself, and his satire was in fact mocking the extremism of High Anglican political views). The following year, he founded the *Weekly Review*, a journal that provided insightful commentary on everything from contemporary English society to foreign relations with France. His book *Robinson Crusoe,* often described as the first novel in English, was an instant success when published in 1719 under the title *The Life and Strange Surprizing Adventures of Robinson Crusoe.* Its great success was owed, in part, to its narrative tension between fact and fiction. *Robinson Crusoe* was a work of fiction, but many readers took Defoe's travelogue for a true story.

The widespread perception that *Robinson Crusoe* was factual was not unusual in Defoe's day, when tales about voyages to exotic places were popular. *Robinson Crusoe* was probably inspired by the real-life adventures of Scottish sailor Alexander Selkirk, who in 1704 had washed ashore on an island off the coast of Chile. On a deeper level, the novel was an innovative form of English literature in the early eighteenth century. Novels were consequently regarded as morally suspect. They were books filled with lies. When clergyman John Bunyan published *The Pilgrim's Progress* in 1678, he felt compelled to apologize to his readers for his fictional story, insisting that it contained valuable life lessons. When Defoe was writing a generation later, authors had found a way around apology by disguising their fictional tales as factual accounts of real events. Defoe championed this literary device, not only in *Robinson Crusoe* but also in *Diary of a Plague Year*, *Moll Flanders*, and *Roxana: The Fortunate Mistress.* In the preface to *Roxana*, Defoe advised his readers that "the foundation of this is laid in truth of fact; and so the work is not a story, but a history." To make his work socially acceptable, Defoe dressed up his fiction as fact. [12]

Robinson Crusoe took philosophical inspiration from John Locke's notion that human knowledge is gained from perception of our surroundings. In the novel, the character of Robinson Crusoe, marooned on a distant island, survives through his powers of perception and reason. Through personal experiences in his unique predicament, he achieves a deeper understanding of the meaning of life. No wonder Rousseau was a fan of the novel. In his classic book on education, *Emile*, Rousseau recommended Defoe's novel as necessary reading and advocated following Robinson Crusoe's model of self-sufficiency. But while Crusoe confronts life's challenges with tools of reason supplied by experience, his moral posture was more controversial, especially his master-slave relationship with his noble savage called Friday, who Crusoe converts to Christianity. Many have seen in Crusoe the embodiment of Western imperialism. Crusoe's colonialist impulses, taking possession of his island and exploiting it through the labor of a native servant, illustrated what many foid contestable in the Enlightenment project. The era's cult of material progress legitimized values based on civilizational hierarchies. [13]

On his desert island, Crusoe failed to grasp that morality is more than religious sentiments of pity and compassion. The principles of moral law command duty and conduct. Crusoe was not alone in his moral ambiguity. Defoe himself, though he felt compassion for slaves and had ethical qualms about their mistreatment, was an advocate of trade and commerce and, in the final analysis, supported colonialism as an economic enterprise. The greatest minds of the era—including Voltaire and Immanuel Kant—faced the same dilemma. They privately expressed attitudes about the inferiority of *les nègres*, who, like Crusoe's savage Friday, needed to be improved through religion and civilization; but publicly they were resolutely opposed to slavery and colonialism. The practice of slavery was eventually abolished, starting in post-revolutionary France, mainly thanks to the enduring force of Enlightenment principles. Still, the noble purpose of the Enlightenment's universalist values was frequently contradicted by the imperfect men who professed them. Slavery, it should be noted, continued in the non-Western world into the twentieth century, notably in the Ottoman Empire where it had cruelly thrived for centuries (the Ottomans forced eastern European Christians into slavery throughout their empire, hence "Slav" as the origin of the word slave).

Two products imported from the colonies—coffee and tea—played a key role in fueling the intellectual energy of the Enlightenment. England is often considered a nation of tea drinkers. Tea, which was initially introduced as a medicinal drink, would eventually triumph over coffee as the British drink of choice. [14] In the early Enlightenment, however, it was coffee, not tea, that fueled the liberal revolution led by the greatest minds of the era. And coffee, like tea, was initially marketed as a medicine before it became a stimulating beverage. By the early eighteenth century, coffeehouses were enjoying massive success in England. They were especially popular with scribes and politicians.

The first London coffeehouse was opened in St. Michael's Alley in 1652 by Pasqua Rosée, who had brought his knowledge of coffees from his time living in the Ottoman Empire. The first Ottoman coffeehouse, or *kahvehane*, was founded in Constantinople by Syrian merchants in 1555. A century later in England, coffeehouses were sober alternatives to licentious taverns during the Puritan interregnum under Cromwell. Pasqua Rosée, a shrewd businessman, made various claims about coffee's medicinal powers, including its potency against drowsiness, headaches, dropsy, gout, and scurvy.

By the end of the eighteenth century, educated men in England were meeting in coffeehouses to discuss the great issues of the day. Authorities quickly realized that these new public meeting places could be potential hotbeds of dangerous ideas. Charles II had attempted to suppress coffeehouses entirely with a Royal proclamation in 1675 declaring that coffeehouses were producing "diverse False, Malicious, and Scandalous Reports" that were being spread abroad "to the Defamation of His Majestie's Government and to the Disturbance of the Peace and Quiet of the Realm."[15] The king backed down after a loud protest, though the government extorted £500 licenses from coffeehouse owners and forced them to swear allegiance to the crown and promise to prevent the reading, perusing, or divulging of any "scandalous" information that defamed or libeled the government. The controversial reputation of coffeehouses continued well into the eighteenth century. Those who praised them as beacons of civilization regarded the Restoration regime's reaction as an attempt to extinguish the light of reason. Royalist apologists saw things differently, of course. They validated the view that coffeehouses were mischievous places that facilitated the spreading of false rumors and seditious libels.

In the early eighteenth century, the biographer Roger North expressed the regret that Charles II had not succeeded in shutting down coffeehouses. "Now the mischief has arrived to perfection," observed North, "and not only sedition and treason, but atheism, heresy, and blasphemy are publicly taught in diverse of the celebrated coffee-house. . . . It is as unseemly for a reasonable, conformable person to come there, as for a clergyman to frequent a bawdy house."[16]

For those who frequented coffeehouses, these establishments not only were temples of liberty but also conferred social cachet. Spending time at a coffeehouse, which was usually appointed with good furniture and well-stocked bookshelves, was a mark of social sophistication. While male-only establishments, coffeehouses shunned distinctions based on social class. Old values around rank as a measure of the "quality" of a person, though not altogether extinct, were not enforced in London's coffeehouse culture. If anything, coffeehouses were avowedly egalitarian in spirit. They admitted a great diversity of profiles—from merchants and sailors to lawyers and judges. As the poet Samuel Butler noted, in coffeehouses "gentleman, mechanic, lord, and scoundrel mix, and are all of a piece."[17] The Turk's Head coffeehouse in London advertised itself as a "free and open academy unto all comers" where the talk was "contentious but civil, learned but not didactic."[18] Coffeehouses were sometimes referred to as "penny universities" to convey their openness despite social class. In one London establishment, the printed rules included: "No man of any station need give his place to a finer man."[19] Entry was based on wit, not rank.

Some observed however that coffeehouses were a massive time-waster that undermined learning. A pamphlet published in 1673 noted that coffeehouses were "the ruin of many serious and hopeful young gentlemen and tradesmen." One seventeenth-century grumbler was Oxford academic Anthony Wood, who observed: "Why doth solid and serious learning decline, and few or none follow it now in the University? Answer: Because of Coffee Houses, where they spend all their time."[20] The famous novelist Daniel Defoe was another critic, though mainly for partisan reasons. Not only did his government-friendly *Review* target coffeehouse readers, Defoe also went on circuit tours of provincial coffeehouses to pick up political gossip and spread propaganda favorable to the ruling Whigs. Defoe was, in effect, a coffeehouse spy for the Whig government. He saw firsthand how false information was planted at coffeehouses— including by himself—to manipulate and deceive on every subject. His role as coffeehouse propagandist made him inclined to take a dim view, at least rhetorically, of their culture of gossip and innuendo.

Defoe observed:

> The tea-table among the ladies, and the coffeehouse among the men, seem to be places of new invention for a depravation of our manners and morals, places devoted to scandal, and where the characters of all kinds of persons and professions are handled in the most merciless manner, where reproach triumphs, and we seem to give ourselves a loose to fall upon one another in the most unchristian and unfriendly manner in the world.[21]

Defoe's opinion reflected the prevailing establishment view in early eighteenth-century England. Coffeehouses, like newspapers, were regarded with suspicion as potential threats to the affairs of state. If the suspicions were sometimes well-founded, that was precisely the purpose of the coffeehouse. More than places of idle distraction and vicious gossip, they provided a public space where men could share ideas, opinions, and gossip on every subject—including politics. The negative reactions to coffeehouses only confirmed their influence. Some attacked them as hubs of untrustworthy gossip, yet the government was also keen to keep coffee houses on the short leash of the law through licensing.

The English coffeehouse as Enlightenment public sphere was famously theorized by the modern German philosopher Jürgen Habermas. He observed that the coffeehouse-driven public sphere served the interests of the rising liberal bourgeoisie. In previous epochs, characterized by no separation of private and public spheres, the Church and state had monopolized power through propaganda, censorship, and repression. The emergence of a public sphere during the Enlightenment signaled the arrival of a new bourgeois class of private subjects who depended on a free flow of information and news for their own prosperity and power. With the power shift in favor of the emerging bourgeoisie, authority was no longer articulated by rituals of *representation*; it now relied on the power of public *discourse* produced by private citizens and political parties. Habermas's theory has been challenged and revised. Some argue that the influence of the coffeehouse culture is exaggerated because its political autonomy was constrained by state controls, infiltration by elites, and political manipulation. Others note that the Enlightenment public sphere was, in fact, largely restricted to bourgeois white men—in short, that it was socially restricted. Still, it cannot be doubted that the English coffeehouses played an important role in driving the Enlightenment agenda forward. [22]

For most of the eighteenth century, coffeehouses in England were the intellectual engine of the country's news-driven political culture. It was a time when everybody was in search of the latest "news," and the best place to find it was at coffeehouses. When a patron arrived in a coffeehouse, he was often greeted with the query, "What news have you?" In his famous *Dictionary*, Samuel Johnson defined *coffeehouse* as "a house of entertainment where coffee is sold, and the guests are supplied with newspapers." [23] The famous diarist Samuel Pepys noted many times in his journal, "Thence to the coffee-house." [24] Sir Isaac Newton wrote his *Principia* in a coffeehouse. Adam Smith's great work, *The Wealth of Nations,* was born in one. It was in coffeehouses that men read and shared copies of journals and periodicals such as Defoe's *Review.* The *Spectator* boasted that it had "brought philosophy out of closets and libraries, schools, and colleges, to dwell in clubs and assemblies, at tea-tables and coffee–houses." [25] The *Spectator*, whose motto was "to enliven morality with wit, and to temper wit with morality," printed three thousand copies per issue, though it was estimated that each issue reached sixty thousand readers as copies were passed hand to hand in coffeehouses. [26] It is doubtless testimony to the pervasiveness of this news culture that periodicals of the day, including Defoe's *Review* and the *Spectator*, sometimes treated "newsmongering" and the proliferation of false information with satirical condescension. While journals such as the *Spectator* and *Tatler* appealed mainly to "public-spirited" men, they endeavored to attract female readers. As the *Tatler*'s Richard Steele put it, condescendingly: "I resolve also to have something which may be entertainment to the fair sex, in honour of whom I have invented the title of this paper."[27] At the *Spectator*, Joseph Addison noted that "there are none to whom this paper will be more useful than to the female world."[28] In 1709, the *Tatler* launched a women's periodical, *Female Tatler*, but it lasted only one year. In 1744, the *Female Spectator* had a more successful run of twenty-four numbers over two years.[29]

Most of the best-known journals and periodicals were affiliated on partisan lines to the two established political parties, Whig and Tory. Daniel Defoe's *Review* was allied with the Whigs, in keeping with his longstanding opposition to High Tories. The *Spectator*, too, was considered a Whig periodical. When the *Examiner* recruited Jonathan Swift to its pages, his voice added Tory authority to the debate with its Whig rivals. It would be erroneous, however, to characterize these journals as little more than house organs. They attracted the era's sharpest wits—from Defoe and Swift to Samuel Johnson and Alexander Pope—who wrote elegantly on a wide array of subjects. In literature, the period is often called the Augustan age, a reference to the flourishing of classical poetry and novels under Roman emperor Augustus.

The great satirists of this Augustan renaissance often targeted charlatans and quacks who profited from the enduring culture of superstition and credulity. The greatest satirist of the age was Jonathan Swift, essayist, pamphleteer, master of irony, famous for his masterpiece *Gulliver's Travels*. That book, first published in 1726, is often interpreted as an attack on the cult of rationalism that Swift observed all around him in the eighteenth century. Swift, it must be remembered, was a High Church Anglican who was dean of St. Patrick's Cathedral in Dublin. He was not attacking Enlightenment values. He was looking with the disapproving eyes of a moralist on the obsession with Newtonian physics and its culture of measuring and quantifying everything.[30] In *Gulliver's Travels,* rationalism is famously symbolized by the magnetically levitated island of Laputa, which is inhabited by devotees of sciences such as mathematics and astronomy. Alert readers of the day would have understood Laputa to represent the Royal Society and its illustrious academicians. Lost in their abstractions, the inhabitants of Laputa are hopeless with life's more pragmatic challenges. Nothing works on their island, including their ill-fitting clothes.

Gulliver's Travels is marvelous satire of rationalism, but it should not be assumed that Swift was more indulgent with superstition. He was under no illusion that quackery and credulity were the greater menace to the intelligence of his era. Swift was quick to expose lies, duplicity, and deceit. As he observed in an essay titled "The Art of Political Lying" in 1710: "Falsehood flies, and truth comes limping after it, so that when men come to be undeceived, it is too late, the tale is over, and the jest hath had its effect." This was the satirical point in *Gulliver's Travels:* it was a "lie" presented to the public as an authentic experience.[31]

Swift hid behind his pseudonym, Isaac Bickerstaff, Esq., to launch his most famous satirical attack on superstition and quackery. His target was a bogus astrologer named John Partridge. Partridge was famous for his almanac, *Merlinus Liberatus.* Almanacs were booming business during the Enlightenment. In the seventeenth century, there were some two thousand titles written by three hundred different compilers known by pseudonyms such as "Lily," "Dove," "Pond," and "Poor Robin." Many of these writers, like Partridge, were famous and attracted a large following. Some almanacs featured information about husbandry and other practical advice. Partridge's *Merlinus Liberatus* exploited the gullibility of readers with lists of alarming predictions, including the imminent deaths of notable people. His almanac also sold purging pills and offered to cast nativities to private patients. Partridge, who was known to be quarrelsome, boasted that he had a medical degree. He also claimed that his astrological predictions were based on "science" founded on Ptolemaic principles that, needless to say, only he understood. For the end of March in 1708, Partridge predicted a double eclipse followed by great troubles in London, whose inhabitants would be subject to "divisions and fears and differences, attended by a spring of distemper, that will arise from a cold and putrefaction, and seems likely to be a tertian ague, and fever with a disorder in the bowels."[32]

Having followed Partridge's outlandish predictions, Swift decided to expose him as an utter fraud. His weapon, as always, was satire. He slipped into his Bickerstaff persona to pose as another astrologer with his own prognostications. One notable prediction was the imminent demise of John Partridge. In a pamphlet titled *Predictions*, Swift gave a precise date for Partridge's death: March 29, 1708. On that day, Bickerstaff predicted, John Partridge would die of a "raging fever." Swift's pamphlet was such a massive success, selling thousands of copies, that rival publishers lifted the contents of the Bickerstaff predictions to rush out halfpenny pirate editions. Town wits jumped into the fray, replying to Bickerstaff with more published predictions. Some even pretended to be Isaac Bickerstaff.

John Partridge, the target of Swift's satire, publicly denounced Bickerstaff as a fraudulent "rascal." Attempting to turn the tables on Bickerstaff, Partridge riposted with more astrological warnings for his readers: "Much lying news at this time; and also Scandalous Pamphlets."[33] Unwittingly, Partridge had fallen into Swift's carefully laid trap. Swift now took his Bickerstaff hoax a step further. In a new pamphlet following the predicted date of Partridge's death, he informed his readers that, on April Fool's Day, poor John Partridge had indeed died of a raging fever. And to bury him once and for all, Swift published an elegy to the deceased John Partridge. Partridge angrily protested in print that he was still alive. He even included a rhyming couplet to counterattack Swift's prediction: "*His whole Design was nothing but Deceit, The End of March will plainly show the Cheat.*"[34] Too late: it was widely believed that the astrologer John Partridge was no more.

Unrepentant and indefatigable, Partridge attempted a comeback with a new almanac, *Merlinus Redivivus*, in which he described himself, without irony, as a "Lover of Truth." He died in 1715, however, this time for real. Seven years after Jonathan Swift had killed him off, the infamous astrologer John Partridge was now truly dead and in his grave.

By the end of the eighteenth century, coffeehouses had evolved into hubs for published news that were an early form of journalism. Reporters, called "runners," did the rounds of coffeehouses to announce news to the patrons. The *Tatler* depended heavily on gossip and news from coffeehouses for its editorial content. Some coffeehouses eventually cut out the middleman publisher by printing their own journals. Meanwhile, so-called "paragraph men" picked up gossip in coffeehouses, scribbled a few sentences on a scrap of paper, and turned in the text to publishers, who printed collections of news items. The term *paragraph writer* soon became associated with scribes who published slander, dubious news, and unfounded claims. As periodicals throughout Europe and America copied and pasted (often translated) paragraphs from other publications, it became impossible to distinguish between fact and fiction.[35]

Still, paragraphs were so influential that political leaders in England, while they knew that paragraphs had a reputation for inaccuracy, couldn't afford to ignore them. Papers such as London's *Morning Post* learned that there was money to be made in abusing the reputations of the powerful with intrusive stories about their private lives. The paragraph system was even based on bribery. When a paragraph writer became privy to a salacious story about a political leader or member of the aristocracy, the target was approached and asked to pay up to have the article suppressed.[36] In this journalistic climate, a long way from Enlightenment values, important figures had no choice but to pander to the paragraphs. The Whig politician Charles Fox noted in 1785: "Subjects of Importance should be first treated gravely in letters or pamphlets or best of all perhaps a series of letters, and afterwards the Paragraphs do very well as an accompaniment."[37] The bribery went both ways. Sir Robert Walpole, the longest-serving Whig prime minister of the century, was in the habit of bribing scribes (including Daniel Defoe) not only to write positive opinions about him, but also to criticize him when it was expedient.

Paragraph writers didn't shy from gossiping about foreign leaders, or even monarchs, including the Queen of France. In December 1784, the *Morning Post* reported that Marie Antoinette kept an English gigolo named "Mr. W." The paragraph read:

> The Gallic Queen is partial to the English. In fact, the majority of her favourites are of this country; but no one has been so notoriously supported by her as Mr. W—. Though this gentleman's purse was known to be *dérangé* when he went to Paris, yet he has ever since lived there in the first style of elegance, taste and fashion. His carriages, his liveries, his table have all been upheld with the utmost expense and splendor.[38]

This scurrilous piece of news about Marie Antoinette's sexual *anglophilie* has never been verified by historians or biographers. In 1784, however, many must have read and believed it.

But across the channel in France, scurrilous news in the English press was the least of Marie Antoinette's worries.

***

"Let them eat cake."

That familiar expression is perhaps the most famous, or infamous, remark in history. It is so embedded in our popular culture that it has become a catchphrase to convey haughty indifference to the misfortune of others.

It is not even necessary to name the historical figure who uttered it. Marie Antoinette, the frivolous French queen, was dismissing news that the peasants were starving due to the high price of bread.

In the original French, Marie Antoinette allegedly said, *"Qu'ils mangent de la brioche!"* That doesn't quite translate to "let them eat cake." *Brioche* is sweet, eggy bread that tastes vaguely like cake. The translated English word *cake* made Marie Antoinette seem even haughtier than in French. More to the point, Marie Antoinette never said "let them eat cake" in any language. There is no historical evidence that she ever uttered that phrase. The story is pure invention. It's a historical legend that rivals the myth of Nero "fiddling" while Rome burned. And yet this outlandish fabrication that has shaped our image of Marie Antoinette for more than two centuries.

As a historical falsehood, this one is easy to trace to the source: it was the French philosopher Jean-Jacques Rousseau. In book 6 of his *Confessions* written in 1767, Rousseau wrote of a "great princess" who had, when told that the peasants had no bread, replied, "*Qu'ils mangent de la brioche!*"[39]

Was Rousseau referring to Marie Antoinette? This is impossible. When he wrote that passage, Marie Antoinette was a girl living at the Habsburg court in Vienna. Rousseau's story was entirely invented, probably borrowed from another source. What's more, his book was published in 1782, and thus had been in circulation seven years before the French Revolution began. Finally, the first time someone put the words "let them eat cake" in Marie Antoinette's mouth was in another book, *Les Guêpes*, published in 1843—a half century after her death.

That we are still attributing this supercilious remark to Marie Antoinette reveals how historical falsehoods can become embedded in popular culture, especially when they confirm collective bias. Following the French Revolution, portraying Marie Antoinette as a supercilious queen offended no one, especially as republican values took hold in France. She and her Bourbon husband, Louis XVI, had been tried and executed. To believe that Marie Antoinette had been treated abominably was too great a moral burden on the French national conscience. So she was transformed into a haughty and extravagant Austrian princess who had shown only contempt for the French nation. People believed the "let them eat cake" myth because they wanted to believe it. Marie Antoinette was not entirely innocent in her lifetime; in fact, she was guilty of many extravagances. But she was a much more complex character than the "let them eat cake" cliché suggests.

When Marie Antoinette first arrived in Paris in 1770, she was tremendously popular as the teenage bride of the French *dauphin*. The French papers described her as a glowing goddess of youth. "Born high above all ordinary thrones," the official court paper, *Mercure de France*, declared, "to her belongs all the radiance of Divinity." Four years later, when old king Louis XV died after a long reign, the French nation celebrated the ascension to the throne of the youthful Louis XVI and Marie Antoinette. This was still the era of strict controls on the press in France under Louis XV. The police had even cracked down on public poetry readings after it was discovered that students were reading a poem critical of the king. Still, well-connected Parisians picked up gossip at court by attending salons and meeting at cafés and other public places designated for the trading of information. One meeting place was under the famous "tree of Cracow," a massive chestnut in the Palais Royal gardens. While the *Mer-*

cure de France reported where the queen was spending Easter, the *mauvais propos* and *bruits publics* circulating in salons and at these public locations revealed juicy tidbits like news of the king's latest mistress.[40]

Marie Antoinette arrived in Paris at the end of this era of strict censorship. Her honeymoon with French public opinion was short-lived. The official press, notably the *Mercure* and *Gazette,* continued churning out puffery and snippets of society news about the royal couple's diary. By the 1780s, however, the French had ready access to scandalmongering *libelles* and pamphlets, not to mention the gossip and rumors circulating in the streets of Paris. The French papers had their own paragraph men, called *nouvellistes*, who picked up "news" from well-informed sources posted on benches in the Tuileries, Luxembourg Gardens, and, of course, under the tree of Cracow. Police efforts to repress *nouvellistes* gossip proved futile in the face of high demand for their eyebrow-raising tidbits. One famous *libelle* of the era, *Le Gazetier cuirassé,* promised "scandalous anecdotes about the French court."[41] It was printed in London, out of reach of official French censors. Another publication printed in London starting in the 1760s was the famous *Mémoires secrets,* an anonymous chronicle of insider gossip and anecdotes from Parisian high society. A scurrilous book about Louis XV's mistress, Madame du Barry, also appeared as a collection of gossip that *nouvellistes* had picked up around Paris.

Despite the gossip and *libelles* circulating in Paris, the Bourbon monarchy was still relatively protected compared with the hurly burly culture of public opinion across the channel in London, where coffeehouses buzzed with political innuendo and intrigue. Some French *philosophes*, it is true, attempted to replicate London's coffeehouse culture at Parisian cafés, such as the Procope on the Left Bank. Voltaire frequented the Procope, where he liked to add chocolate to his coffee. Other regulars at the Procope—named after the Byzantine writer Procopius, famous for his *Secret History*—were Rousseau, Danton, and Robespierre, as well as Americans Benjamin Franklin and Thomas Jefferson. The Parisian equivalent of the coffeehouse, however, was the salon. French salons were not, strictly speaking, a genuine public sphere where debate flourished independent of the French state. Salons were frequented by Parisian elites closely connected to the court. Still, the salon was a unique social institution that gave birth to a genuine "Republic of Letters" in pre-revolutionary France.[42]

Parisian salons were different from London coffeehouses in both ambiance and function. Whereas London coffeehouses were boisterously public, salons were essentially closed spaces, usually held in private homes. Most were "invitation only," not public places where people could come and go. Many salons were held by women, usually titled or wealthy ladies with an interest in culture and politics. This gave the salon a discreetly feminine dimension that was absent in the masculine ambiance of the London coffeehouse. A small number of influential French women were famous for their salons, such as the Marquise du Deffand, Madame de Rambouillet, Madame Necker, Madame Geoffrin, and Mademoiselle Lespinasse. Their salons attracted the great minds of the day. The Marquise du Deffand, for example, was a friend to Voltaire and the English man of letters Horace Walpole, to whom she bequeathed not only her papers, but also her pet dog, Tonton.

As these rarefied spaces increasingly became elitist symbols of social success, access became tightly controlled. Madame Geoffrin expelled Diderot from her salon because she found his conversation "quite beyond control." Still, those who frequented salons represented a great diversity within the elites—from rising young writers and established authors to powerful politicians and eccentric aristocrats. The tacit rule at Paris salons was, as in London coffeehouses, that wit was more important than rank. Many great French writers launched their careers thanks to their admittance into Parisian salons. One was the philosopher Montesquieu, who found success at the salon of Madame Lambert. [43]

It could hardly be claimed, however, that Parisian salons were dangerous hotbeds of political unrest. Neither were London coffeehouses, for that matter, though the British monarchy's spies were sufficiently worried to show up incognito to listen in. In Paris, the Procope had a similar reputation for subversive gossip. Conversation in Parisian salons, by contrast, was relatively restrained, though some salons were known to be tolerant of opinions critical of the royal family. In their function, salons were not "news" hubs like London coffeehouses; they tended to produce writing in the form of epistolary correspondences. Some salons produced weekly newsletters, though they often read like the society pages of a newspaper—announcements of engagements and deaths, information about government proclamations, and the like. It can nonetheless be argued that, over time, the ideas and values that emerged from Parisian salons created an intellectual culture hostile to divine-right monarchy. It took generations for these ideas to germinate. Voltaire's *Lettres philosophiques* was published in 1734, Montesquieu's *The Spirit of the Laws* in 1748, and Rousseau's *The Social Contract* in 1762—all decades before the storming of the Bastille. In comparison to England, where a divine-right monarchy had been toppled a century earlier, the French were slowly catching up in the mid-eighteenth century.

When Rousseau published his *Confessions* in 1782, it is doubtful that Marie Antoinette was even aware of the book. She had more pressing things on her mind. Revolution was still seven years away, but there were already rumblings of discontent. The pamphlets in France were increasingly impudent and fearless about satirizing the royal family. Marie Antoinette's extravagant tastes and spending habits were the subject of spiteful gossip and commentary. The fact that she was a foreigner did not help. Many at court resented her for that reason alone. Austria was a longstanding enemy of France (her marriage to the future Louis XVI had been meant to patch up diplomatic tensions). Marie Antoinette was described in pamphlets as *"l'Autrichienne"*—a proper feminine noun for Austrian, but the suffix *chienne* also meant "bitch." There was speculation, fueled by poisoned gossip, about her sexual dalliances, notably with the Swedish ambassador to the French court, Count Axel de Fersen. Insinuations of infidelity were made plausible by rumors that Louis XVI was impotent (*"mauvais fouteur"*). When Marie Antoinette became pregnant, the pamphlets speculated on the real identity of the biological father.

Things took a turn for the worse for the foreign-born Queen of France when, in 1785, the so-called Diamond Necklace scandal erupted. It hit the Bourbon monarchy much like the poisons scandal had destabilized the court of Louis XIV a century earlier. As the great French diplomat Talleyrand remarked at the time, "Watch out for this diamond necklace business, it may well rock the throne of France."[44]

Today, the Diamond Necklace affair has been relegated to the status of sensational footnote in history books about the French Revolution. Throughout the nineteenth century, however, the Diamond Necklace scandal was widely believed to have been a major factor in the overthrow of the Bourbon monarchy. Decades after the French Revolution, Napoleon observed from the vantage point of his post-Waterloo exile: "The Queen's death must be dated from the Diamond Necklace trial." In Germany, the poet Goethe wrote a play based on the scandal, titled *Der Grosse Cophta*. "The history of the 'Necklace' had made an unspeakable impression on me," Goethe recalled.[45]

While the Diamond Necklace affair was the scandal that most tarnished Marie Antoinette's reputation, it was the one in which she was almost certainly guiltless. The origins of the affair stretched back to Louis XV, who wished to lavish on his mistress, Madame du Barry, a splendid diamond necklace containing 647 stones and weighing 2,800 carats (worth roughly $15 million today). Louis XV died, however, and the sale of the necklace was never concluded. When young Louis XVI succeeded his grandfather, the Paris jewelers Boehmer and Bassenge hoped the new king would purchase the same necklace for his queen, Marie Antoinette. She refused, however, to accept a piece of jewelry that had been created for the previous king's mistress.

Meanwhile, a socially ambitious minor aristocrat named Jeanne de la Motte was plotting to get her hands on the necklace. Married to the Comte de la Motte, she was also the mistress of Cardinal de Rohan, the former French ambassador to Marie Antoinette's native country, Austria. Madame de la Motte managed to convince Cardinal de Rohan, who was head of the Church in France, that Marie Antoinette wished to possess the necklace. He could ingratiate himself at court, she insisted, by obtaining the necklace for the queen. Madame de la Motte persuaded de Rohan that she was personally acting on behalf of Marie Antoinette. Cardinal de Rohan, who was besotted with the manipulative Madame de la Motte, foolishly purchased the necklace on credit in the naive belief that he would be repaid by Marie Antoinette. The scam concluded with Madame de la Motte stealing the necklace from the cardinal and, using her husband's louche connections, selling it in pieces through fences in England.

This tawdry business was closer to comic opera than an affair of state. But when the fraud was discovered, the scandal gripped Parisian society. Louis XVI was so infuriated that he had Cardinal de Rohan arrested and imprisoned in the Bastille. That only heightened public interest in the affair. Marie Antoinette was already being caricatured in pamphlets as a depraved nymphomaniac. It was now open season on her. In some caricatures, she appeared as a wild beast, a tiger feeding on the French nation. In others, she was depicted as an ostrich, a French wordplay with her home country "Autriche" for Austria, which reads like *autruche* for *ostrich*. Even worse, she was depicted in pornographic postures, legs open and genitals gaping, cuckolding her obese husband with a succession of lovers, including lesbian trysts.[46] Allusions to her sexual appetites suggested a carnal relationship with Satan. Robespierre's publication *Le Journal des hommes libres* described her as "more bloodthirsty than Jezebel, more conniving than Agrippina."[47] The pamphlets blamed Marie Antoinette for all the nation's misfortunes, including economic recession. She was so hated by the French public that there were serious concerns for her physical safety.

An attempt at damage control was made by commissioning an official portrait of Marie Antoinette to be displayed in the Grand Salon of the Louvre. The painting by Élisabeth Vigée Le Brun showed the Queen as loving *mater familias* surrounded by her children. As a PR strategy, the portrait was too little, too late. Its completion was delayed by two years, during which time an empty frame was displayed in the Louvre. When the painting finally appeared, the public was indifferent. The portrait was removed from the Louvre and placed in a remote wing of Versailles palace.[48]

Cardinal de Rohan, meanwhile, was tried for his role in the Diamond Necklace affair. Astonishingly, he was acquitted. The scheming Madame de la Motte met a different fate. She was found guilty of theft and sentenced to be whipped and branded on the shoulder with the letter *V* for *voleuse* (thief). She was also incarcerated in the Salpêtrière prison in Paris but escaped to London. In 1789, she published a book, *Mémoires justific-atifs*, a scathing tell-all memoir against Marie Antoinette. It was a good year to attack the French monarchy, for the revolution was just getting going with the storming of the Bastille. Madame de la Motte was never returned to France to face justice. Exiled in London, she died in 1791 after falling from a window, apparently fleeing debt collectors. She was buried in St. Mary's Churchyard in south London.

Though totally innocent, Marie Antoinette had already been found guilty in the court of public opinion. The damage to the French monarchy was irreparable. Knocked off their pedestal by pamphlets and porno-graphic caricatures, the Bourbons became objects of public scorn. The desacralization of the monarchy made it possible for Louis XVI and Marie Antoinette to be arrested, prosecuted, and carted off to the guillo-tine. One hundred and forty years after the execution of Charles I in London, the French nation made the same dramatic rupture with divine-right monarchy.

On the morning of her execution in October 1793, Marie Antoinette's hair was shorn, and her hands were tied behind her back. At her prison in the Conciergerie along the Seine, she was put on an open cart and drawn through the streets of Paris. Throngs of people jeered and insulted her. At the Place de la Concorde, where her husband Louis XVI had been exe-cuted nine months earlier, a massive crowd was waiting. The mob watched in silence as Marie Antoinette mounted the steps of the scaffold. According to legend, she accidently stepped on the foot of the execution-er, Henri Sanson, and humbly apologized: "*Monsieur, je vous demande pardon, je ne l'ai pas fait exprès.*" Those were her last words. When the guillotine blade came slicing down, Sanson picked up the head by the hair and, holding it up for the crowd to see, shouted, "*Vive la République!*" Marie Antoinette's decapitated corpse was later thrown into an unmarked grave in the nearby Madeleine cemetery.

From the instant she was beheaded, Marie Antoinette became a figure of myth. Her portraits—alabaster complexion, rosy cheeks, powdered bouffant hair—became instantly recognizable. She was, in many respects, the first iconic celebrity of the modern world. Successive generations projected onto her legend their inner-most fantasies, fetishes, and delu-sions.

Undoubtedly the strangest tale about Marie Antoinette dates to the late Victorian period. Two English women visiting Versailles Palace in 1901 claimed to have met the French queen in the flesh. The two middle-aged women, Anne Moberly and Eleanor Jourdain, were from educated fami-lies. Moberly's father was headmaster at Winchester College and later Bishop of Salisbury. Miss Jourdain, the daughter of a vicar, wrote several books and became vice principal of St. Hugh's College, Oxford. In August 1901, they were in Paris together and decided to take the train out to Versailles. At the palace, they were walking through the gardens near the Petit Trianon, the small chateau on the grounds favored by Marie Antoinette. They suddenly came upon the strange figure of a black-haired, pock-faced man dressed in the attire of a bygone era. Near the Temple de l'Amour, Miss Moberly caught sight of a fair-haired lady dressed in a full white shirt. She was sitting on the grass sketching. Miss Jourdain saw nothing. Suddenly, the two Englishwomen were overcome with powerful feelings of fatigue and melancholia. Later, when they reached the Petit Trianon, a wedding party was being held inside the chateau, though everyone appeared dressed from another epoch.

Miss Moberly and Miss Jourdain realized later that the people they had seen at the Petit Trianon did not belong to the present. The two women must have traveled back in time to the late eighteenth century. Miss Moberly had laid eyes on Marie Antoinette, the fair-haired lady in white on the lawn.

But they still needed proof. So they threw themselves into obsessive research, combing the archives to discover everything they could find on Marie Antoinette's life at the Petit Trianon. Everything they came upon corresponded to what they had witnessed with their own eyes. There was no doubting their paranormal experience. They had slipped through time and seen the real Marie Antoinette in the gardens of the Petit Trianon.

In 1911, the two English women recounted their experience in a book, *An Adventure*, using the pseudonyms Elizabeth Morison and Frances Lamont.[49] The book immediately caused a sensation. Among those who were gripped by their time-travelling tale was a young J. R. R. Tolkien, who would later write his fantasy epic, *Lord of the Rings*. So was Tolkien's friend, fantasy writer C. S. Lewis, whose later book about time travel, *The Dark Tower,* referred to "the ladies of the Trianon." At the turn of the century in England, there was great interest in the paranormal, whose leading proponents included the eccentric occultist Aleister Crowley, author of *The Book of Lies*. It was an era when fascination with spiritualism created a culture of credulity in the face of fantastic fictions and clever hoaxes.

One of the most famous hoaxes of that era was the so-called Cottingley Fairies. Two girls in Yorkshire, cousins Elise Wright and Frances Griffith, took a series of five photos in 1917 showing themselves near a stream in the presence of tiny fairy-like creatures. Elsie's father Arthur Wright, an amateur photographer, never doubted that the photos were fabricated. But the girl's mother Polly was more credulous. The pictures became public when Polly Wright attended a lecture on "fairy life" at a Theosophical Society meeting in Bradford. The pictures were quickly circulated among the group's adherents, who found the photographed fairies consistent with their theosophical beliefs. The extraordinary photos soon came to the attention of the famous author Sir Arthur Conan Doyle, an ardent spiritualist who was writing an article on fairies for the *Strand Magazine*.[50] Conan Doyle, the creator of Sherlock Holmes, was convinced the fairies were real. His article was published under the headline "Fairies Photographed," describing the Cottingley Fairies as an "epoch-making event." "The recognition of their existence will jolt the material twentieth century mind out of its heavy ruts in the mud, and will make it admit that there is a glamour and mystery to life," wrote Conan Doyle. "Having discovered this, the world will not find it so difficult to accept that spiritual message supported by physical facts which has already been put before it."[51]

In 1922, Conan Doyle followed up with a book, *The Coming of the Fairies,* in which he announced that proof of fairy existence was a blow to cold Victorian science, which "would have left the world hard and clean and bare, like a landscape in the moon." He added: "There is nothing scientifically impossible, so far as I can see, in some people seeing things that are invisible to others."[52] Conan Doyle was wrong of course. Like many other spiritualists at the time, he'd been taken in. The photos were fake. The two girls Elsie and Frances both lived into their eighties. Toward the end of their lives in the 1980s, they admitted that they'd fabricated the fairy photos using paper cutouts. At the outset of the century, however, the public mood was receptive to paranormal stories about fairies and a time slip back to the court of Louis XVI and Marie Antoinette.

Like skeptics who doubted the authenticity of the fairy photos, critics argued that the two authors of *An Adventure* were plainly deluded about seeing Marie Antoinette. Miss Moberly and Miss Jourdain fiercely answered these skeptics in a second edition, insisting that everything they had recounted was completely factual. The mystery surrounding their outlandish claims continued after their deaths—Miss Jourdain died in 1924, Miss Moberly in 1937—as biographers and psychologists attempted to understand what could have happened at Versailles Palace back in 1901. One author, looking for a banal explanation, conjectured that the two English ladies had simply come across a costume party thrown by the famous dandy, Robert de Montesquiou, the aristocratic friend of Marcel Proust. Montesquiou was known to have given lavish fancy-dress parties at the Petit Trianon in the summer of 1901. Another theory, more psychoanalytical, claimed that the two women had a homoerotic fixation on Marie Antoinette. Their hallucination at Versailles Palace was an expression of repressed sexual desires—a homosexual legitimation fantasy. It is also possible that both women had been aware of other Marie Antoinette apparition stories published in the previous years, including one titled "Dream Romance." In the Victorian period, many of the books written bout Marie Antoinette were romanticized apologies that idealized the French queen—and, paradoxically, invited the suggestion of feminine homoeroticism by dismissing claims that she had lesbian affairs. It may well be that Annie Moberly and Eleanor Jourdain, two respectable middle-aged English ladies at the end of the Victorian era, were the first obsessed fans in modern history.[53]

After the decapitations of Louis XVI and Marie Antoinette, the French Revolution took deism to its rational conclusion by abolishing religion altogether. Rousseau's term *civic religion* was now institutionalized. The first French republic converted Catholic churches into humanist "Temples of Reason" inscribed with the motto *liberté, égalité, fraternité*. Catholicism was toppled by a new atheist religion, called the "Cult of Reason," celebrated by civic *fêtes de la Raison*.

In 1791, the massive neo-classical church on the Left Bank of Paris was repurposed as a Greek-style Pantheon dedicated to the glory of France's great men (*"Aux Grands Hommes la Patrie Reconnaissante"*). One of first great men entombed there, in 1794, was Jean-Jacques Rousseau. Not far away was the crypt of his great intellectual adversary, Voltaire. The transfer of Voltaire's remains to the Pantheon in July 1791, thirteen years after his death, was a great national ceremony of celebration in Paris. Thousands watched the magnificent procession carrying Voltaire's coffin through the streets, stopping at the Bastille, where he had once been imprisoned, before the cortege arrived at the Pantheon.

Finally, reason had triumphed. But the victory would be short-lived. The volatile *sturm und drang* turbulence of the romantic counter-Enlightenment was just around the corner.

Part IV

Empire of Lies

10

ALL THE NEWS THAT'S FIT TO FAKE

The name Theodor Fontane is largely unknown today except among admirers of late nineteenth-century German fiction.

As a novelist, Fontane's realist style and sharp observations of daily life in Brandenburg society earned him comparisons with Charles Dickens and Emile Zola. One critic described Fontane's novels as "the most completely achieved of any written between Goethe and Thomas Mann."[1] High praise indeed, especially since Fontane was in his sixties when he began writing the novels for which he is remembered, notably *Effie Briest*, a tragic tale about a seventeen-year-old girl forced into an unhappy marriage to a much older aristocrat who was once her mother's lover. The novel is considered a masterpiece comparable to Gustave Flaubert's *Madame Bovary*.[2]

Theodor Fontane left another, more puzzling, legacy. He occupies a controversial place in the history of journalism as a pioneer of fake news.

Fontane was born in Prussia in 1819. His French name came from his Huguenot origins; his ancestors had fled France after Louis XIV's expulsion of Protestants in the seventeenth century. Fontane followed in his father's footsteps by apprenticing as an apothecary, but quickly abandoned that profession to pursue a career as a writer. In his early twenties, he wrote a novella and translated Shakespeare's *Hamlet* into German. In 1844, at age twenty-five, he traveled briefly to London, where he cultivated a deep interest in English history, culture, and folklore, especially Old English ballads and the novels of Sir Walter Scott.

By 1852, Fontane was back in London for another stay, this time bringing his wife Emilie (a Huguenot like him) and children to live with him. Despite his earlier liberal leanings and enthusiasm for the German revolutions of 1848, he was in London as a press officer for the Prussian intelligence agency, *Zentralstelle*. His knowledge of the English language and culture made him eminently qualified for his assignment, which was to plant stories in the British press that were favorable to Prussia's foreign policies. Working directly for the Prussian ambassador in London, Fontane was in effect a foreign intelligence agent in England. He found himself back in London in 1855, this time writing stories in the newspapers *Neue Preussische Zeitung* and *Die Zeit*, both controlled by the Prussian government. He also busied himself writing books, including *A Summer in London* and a travelogue book about Scotland titled *Beyond the Tweed*. In Fontane's day, there was a strong appetite in Prussia for novels about England and Scotland due to the success of Walter Scott's historical novels translated into German.

Fontane's job in London was low paid and money was always tight. At the end of the 1850s, he was back in Berlin with his family looking for stable employment. He found another job at the conservative *Neue Preussische Zeitung*—known as the *Kreuzzeitung* ("Cross Newspaper") for its iron cross emblem—as the paper's London correspondent. He threw himself into the job, filing dispatches from London on diverse stories that gripped his German readers. In 1861, he covered the devastating Tooley Street fire that ripped through much of the Thames's south bank. The conflagration, which started near Saint Olave's Church, burned for two weeks and was long remembered as one of the most traumatic events in Victorian London.

As the *Kreuzzeitung*'s man in London, Fontane reported to his Prussians readers: "I went to the scene today, and it's a terrible sight. One sees the burned buildings like a city in a crater. . . . Fires live on eerily in the deep, and at any moment a new flame can burst forth out of every mound of ash."[3] Fontane's absorbing coverage of the Tooley Street fire, like his other dispatches from London, put his German readers in the thick of English current events, great and small.

There was just one hitch: Fontane was not in London. For an entire decade in the job, he worked as the *Kreuzzeitung*'s "London correspondent" sitting at his desk in Berlin. Every story he filed about England was fabricated—either cobbled together from wire dispatches, or cut-and-pasted from other newspapers. Fontane invented countless stories to create the impression he was on the front lines of turbulent events in London. But everything he wrote was fabricated.

Years later, Fontane was unembarrassed about his newspaper work. In his autobiographical writings, he claimed to have exercised "poetic license" as a journalist. The "truth" about events did not necessarily depend on objective facts. Truth was accessed through imaginary constructions. "Fifteen kilometers or a hundred and fifty miles make no difference," wrote Fontane. "It's just like with anecdotes about Frederick the

Great. The fake anecdotes are just as good as the real ones, and some-times a little bit better."[4]

In the wider scope of Theodor Fontane's prodigious literary output, it's perhaps unfair to focus on his early hack years in journalism. Fontane wasn't the only fake newspaperman of his day. In the late nineteenth century, there were so many bogus correspondents working for German papers that, in the news trade, a term was coined for it: *unechte Korres-pondenz*—"fake foreign correspondent." Fake news was standard journa-listic practice, in Prussia and elsewhere.

It could be argued that Fontane's work as a correspondent was a precursor of the "New Journalism" movement a century later in the 1960s, when renowned American writers employed subjective perspec-tives and literary techniques to reveal the "truth" behind events. Among the leading proponents of New Journalism—Truman Capote, Tom Wolfe, Norman Mailer—many were, like Fontane, respected writers of fiction. At the height of the trend in the 1970s, New Journalism was hailed as innovative and ground-breaking. Truman Capote and Norman Mailer owed a great deal to the nineteenth-century journalists who mixed fact-gathering and fictional techniques—and who, in England, also called their style the "New Journalism."

Fontane was a literary realist but a journalistic fabulist. The movement of literary realism—associated with the novels of Flaubert and Emile Zola in France and George Eliot in England—belonged to the nineteenth-century tradition when writers, breaking from the idealized Romantic conventions, endeavored to represent objective reality based on plain factual observations. As a novelist, Fontane was part of this movement. He was a realist because he didn't start writing his novels until toward the end of the century when realism had supplanted romanticism. Working as a journalist earlier in his career, he was an intellectual product of the German Romantic era that inspired the nationalist movement culminating in the emergence of a united Germany. His journalism career corre-sponded to the period when Richard Wagner was composing his mesmer-izing operas inspired by medieval Teutonic myths. During those same years, Otto von Bismarck was consolidating a Prussian-controlled Ger-man Empire. Fontane worked as a journalist covering Bismarck's mili-tary aggressions.

The Romantic movement was a rebellion against the rationalist de-signs of the Enlightenment—hence its description as a "Counter Enlight-enment." For Romantic artists, Enlightenment rationalism had produced the dehumanizing bleakness of the Industrial Revolution. They sought truths in powerful subjective feelings and mysticism, frequently evoking the myths and legends of ancient Greece and the heroic individualism of the medieval epoch. Advocates of the Romantic ethos revisited the old

Renaissance quarrel between the relative virtues of ancients versus moderns, coming down resolutely on the side of antiquity. They eschewed religious orthodoxy, and its church institutions, in favor of a pantheistic spirituality seeing manifestations of God in all things—or what some called "deism." That notion was aligned with the deist cult of the "Supreme Being" in France following the Revolution. Friedrich Nietzsche rejected the idea that the French Revolution had been inspired by rationalist Enlightenment ideas. In *Human, All Too Human*—which he dedicated to Voltaire—Nietzsche described the French Revolution as "the last great slave revolt."[5]

The Counter Enlightenment is usually associated with German romanticism. Described by Nietzsche as *Gegen aufklärung* ("against the Enlightenment"), the German Romantic movement embraced the irrational, emotional, supernatural, and mythological.[6] The era's greatest poets were Goethe and Schelling. Goethe's sturm und drang novel, *The Sorrows of Young Werther*, was the quintessentially Romantic tale of a melancholic young man driven to suicide by a failed romance. Goethe's *Werther* was a massive success and read throughout Europe, including by Napoleon, and inspired a rash of copycat suicides. The era's most famous German composers were Beethoven and Wagner. In painting, the Gothic landscapes of Caspar David Friedrich captured the spirit of the age in Germany. But the Romantic movement was pervasive throughout Europe. Early in the century, the English poets Wordsworth, Keats, and Byron rejected modernity and evoked a mystical connection with nature. Byron wrote, "I love Man not the less, but Nature more." The poet Shelley, who was sent down from Oxford in 1811 for writing a tract titled "The Necessity of Atheism," was the most religiously skeptical among the major Romantic poets. Their professed faith in subjective feelings as the source of truth was not devoid of a religious sentiment, however. The Danish philosopher Soren Kierkegaard rejected cold rationalism and argued for subjective truths as a spiritual connection to God. In his 1846 work, *Concluding Unscientific Postscript*, Kierkegaard asserted the dictum, "Subjectivity is truth." He did not reject objective truths; he argued that they are "outward," while subjective truths are the result of "passionate inwardness." For Kierkegaard, subjective truths are more important because they connect us to God. Faith affirms the truth of subjectivity.[7]

In England, the spirit of the Romantic age had been anticipated, perhaps ironically, by the conservative political philosopher Edmund Burke. Though a product of the Enlightenment, Burke was an empiricist who did not share the rationalist humanism of Descartes. Burke believed that we see and understand the world through our feelings and passions. His most powerful pre-Romantic idea was the notion of the "sublime," which he articulated in 1757, at age twenty-eight, in a treatise titled *A Philosophi-*

cal Inquiry into the Origins of Our Ideas of the Sublime and Beautiful.[8] Burke associated the sublime with the awesome power of nature—for example, a thunderstorm—that incites wonder and terror in our hearts. "The passion caused by the great and the sublime in nature, when those causes operate most powerfully, is astonishment," wrote Burke. "And astonishment is that state of the soul, in which all its motions are suspended, with some degree of horror."[9] Burke believed that great works of art and poetry—for example, John Milton's *Paradise Lost*, which Burke admired—could incite these same emotions. These emotions are necessary, he argued, because they commanded humility before the force that he called "Infinity." Burke's connection of nature, emotion, and imagination was a quintessentially Romantic idea that, a half century later, would be embraced by the poets Wordsworth, Coleridge, Keats, Shelley, Byron, and others.

The Romantic movement's boldest Counter-Enlightenment clarion call came from the visionary poet William Blake. Blake studied under the Enlightenment painter Sir Joshua Reynolds but rebelled against his teacher. At London's Royal Academy, Reynolds lectured on the high classical style of painting, but as a pupil Blake was impatient and loathed Reynolds's *Discourses on Art.* He was too distracted by the cults of Druids, millenarian prophecies, and the mystical visions of John Milton and Emanuel Swedenborg. Blake was notoriously opposed to the instruments of science, an attitude evoked in his famous painting of Sir Issac Newton, who like Reynolds was an icon of the Enlightenment. Blake portrayed Newton naked at the bottom of a sea, hidden from all light, gazing down and drawing on a scroll with a compass. Blake's Newton was like a scientific inhabitant of Jonathan Swift's island Laputa in *Gulliver's Travels*, disconnected from life by abstract mathematical thoughts. Blake refused to give Newton the last word on the cosmos. As a visionary poet, Blake looked up at the stars to see the infinite map of eternity.

The words of Blake's famous poem known as "Jerusalem" are familiar around the world in the hymn that has achieved the status of England's unofficial national anthem. Blake's poem, taken from a longer work titled *Milton*, was inspired by an apocryphal story about Jesus setting foot on English soil in his early years. Christ's visit to England is expressed in the line: "And did those feet in ancient times walk upon England's mountains green; and was the Holy Lamb of God on England's pleasant pastures seen." For Blake, the vision of Christ appearing in England was an apocalyptical revelation associating the nation with the New Jerusalem. The bucolic paradise evoked in the poem is contrasted to the grim reality of the Industrial Revolution's "dark Satanic mills" that Blake saw everywhere in early nineteenth-century England. Inspired by the Book of Revelation, "Jerusalem" was an illuminated vision that expressed the Romantic spirit of the times. The hymn version of "Jerusalem" was not, in fact, composed until a century later when, in 1916, Sir Hubert Parry put the words to rousing patriotic music to embolden British spirits during the First World War. Today, England's most famous hymn, sung in churches throughout the country, is inspired by a myth with no basis in historical fact.

Romantic fascination with myths, especially from the Middle Ages, inspired a Gothic revival movement in literature and architecture. In 1818, Mary Shelley published her classic Gothic horror story, *Franken-stein*, about a scientist who creates a monster. *Frankenstein*, which Shelley wrote while staying at a villa in Switzerland with her husband Percy Shelley and Lord Byron, was followed in 1819 by their friend John William Polidori's *The Vampyre*. The same Gothic style inspired Emily Bronte three decades later when she wrote *Wuthering Heights*. The Gothic influence crossed the Atlantic in the works of Edgar Allan Poe, whose stories were translated into French by the poet Charles Baudelaire. In France, Baudelaire and Arthur Rimbaud were steeped in mystical Gothic symbolism. Rimbaud's prose poem, "Les Illuminations," was a visionary expression of the connection between emotional subjectivity and truth. Rimbaud's illuminations would inspire many avant-garde musical artists a century later—from Bob Dylan and Allen Ginsberg to Jim Morrison, Lou Reed, and Patti Smith. Thus an artistic connection can be made between the nineteenth-century Romanticism and the counter-culture pop music movement of the 1960s.

In the early nineteenth century, the Romantic rebellion against the Industrial Revolution was accompanied by a fascination with the cosmos. While dark satanic mills blighted England's once-verdant landscapes, all eyes turned mystically toward the heavens. Visionaries like William Blake gazed up and saw the clouds open for the burning chariots of fire from the Book of Kings. Others studied the celestial bodies through the cold lens of a telescope, the sort of scientific instrument that Blake detested. In 1781, when William Herschel's telescope discovered a new planet, Uranus, he became famous overnight. King George III appointed him court astronomer and financed the construction of even more powerful telescopes. When Hershel died in 1822, his epitaph was inscribed: *Coelorum perrupit claustra* ("He broke through the barriers of the heavens").

Widespread fascination with celestial bodies provided a timely pretext for the first great newspaper hoax in history. The "Great Moon Hoax," as it was known, stunned the world in 1835. In August of that year, the *New York Sun*, a penny paper struggling to make a name for itself, astonished readers with astounding news. The eminent British astronomer, Sir John Herschel—son of William Herschel who had discovered Uranus—had just found life on the moon. Not primitive forms of microscopic life, but a lunar world thriving with exotic plants and strange animals. The *Sun* reported that Sir John Herschel had made this extraordinary discovery with a massive telescope pointed at the moon from the Cape of Good Hope in South Africa. Herschel had observed with stunning clarity a lunar landscape where oval-shaped mountains and extinct volcanoes were teeming with life—bison, goats, unicorns, and two-legged beavers. Even more amazing, Herschel's high-powered telescope had spotted human-like creatures that resembled large bats about four feet tall. Herschel called this new extraterrestrial species *Vespertilio-homo.*

While the story seemed almost unbelievable, there was no reason to doubt its veracity. Sir John Herschel, author of *Treatise on Astronomy* published in 1833, was a world-famous scientist and founder of the Royal Astronomical Society. The *Sun*'s headline listed his impressive credentials: "*Great Astronomical Discoveries Lately Made by Sir John Herschel, LL.D. F.R.S.*" It was known, moreover, that Sir John Herschel had recently traveled to South Africa to catalogue the stars and track the return of Halley's Comet later that year. The *Sun* also reported that Herschel had published news of his discovery in the respected *Edinburgh Journal of Science.* The *Sun*'s article provided details, including elaborate descriptions of Herschel's telescope (twenty-four feet in diameter). The scientific tone of the article, which ran over six installments, reinforced its credibility.

The story was a massive PR coup for the *Sun.* Crowds in New York rushed to the newspaper's offices to get their hands on a copy of the paper. Other American newspapers scrambled to cover the story. The *New Yorker* declared: "The promulgation of these discoveries creates a new era in astronomy and science generally."[10] The *Daily Advertiser* called the story the "gospel truth" and extolled its author for adding "a stock of knowledge to the present age that will immortalize his name and place it high on the page of science."[11] Foreign papers offered the *Sun* huge sums to reprint the original six-part series. News of Sir John Herschel's historic discovery of life on the moon was soon appearing in newspapers throughout Europe. In New York, the *Sun*'s circulation soared to more than forty thousand copies, making it the biggest-selling newspaper in the world.[12]

The story was, of course, an outlandish hoax. Sir John Herschel was real, but he had never made any claims about finding life on the moon. The prestigious *Edinburgh Journal of Science* was real, too, but it had folded and stopped publishing. Some rival New York papers, it is true, doubted the story—and felt vindicated when the hoax was found out. But most newspapers, not to mention thousands of readers, were taken in by the *Sun*'s fake news.

Why so many people in the 1830s believed that life had been discovered on the moon has been the subject of much study, analysis, and speculation. The cultural fascination with celestial bodies—including an expected appearance of Halley's Comet—provides one clue. The discovery of new planets and stories about the cosmos excited imaginations in the early nineteenth century. The Great Moon Hoax was not the first moon story of the era. The outlandish tales of the famous Baron Munchausen were widely familiar at the time. The published Munchausen tales, written by Rudolf Erich Raspe and published in 1785, were inspired by the vaunted exploits of a real German aristocrat, Hieronymus Karl Friedrich, known as the "baron of lies." The word *Munchausen* would later be used as a medical term describing psychological disorders—notably "Munchausen Syndrome"—related to exaggerated claims and pathological lying. In the early nineteenth century, Munchausen was the famous fictional character who boasted of implausible exploits, including riding a cannonball and traveling to the moon.[13] Other lunar fantasies were George Fowler's *A Flight to the Moon* in 1813, and *A Voyage to the Moon*, a science fiction satire by American congressman George Tucker published under a pseudonym in 1827. While these incredible tales undoubtedly were read as fantasies, they tapped into pervasive fascination with the cosmos after great scientific discoveries in astronomy.

Another reason for widespread credulity was the recent emergence of a large reading public easily taken in by tales like the Great Moon Hoax. During the Industrial Revolution, masses of people flocked into cities to work in factories and shops. The existence of a new urban working class brought political and social reforms, including mandatory schooling. Increased literacy created a new market for newspapers and low-end books such as dime novels and penny dreadfuls. At the same time, new technologies such as the steam-powered press, replacing the old hand-crafted presses, allowed for higher newspaper print runs at much lower cost. The explosion of mass-market newspapers created a new phenomenon: public opinion. Owners of commercial newspapers, having established a relationship of trust with their readers, were keen to pander to popular tastes with outlandish stories that sold papers.

The trust factor is important to understanding hoaxes, for their success is based on a betrayal of trust. Consumers in the early nineteenth century had no reason to distrust the newspapers that they bought as loyal readers. In that respect, newspapers such as the *Sun* were playing a dangerous game with hoaxes, for they were setting up their own readers for humiliation by playing on their ignorance. A hoax is a form of trickery that counts on the gullibility of those it targets. The word *hoax* derives from "hocus pocus," believed to come from *hoc est enim corpus meum* ("this is my body," uttered by Catholic priests when raising the host during mass as the Eucharist is transubstantiated from bread into the body of Christ). [14]

In the 1830s, most people in America were unsophisticated readers of the press. The recent scientific revolution, especially in astronomy, was beyond their comprehension. Astrology and astronomy were still blurred concepts in their minds. People were nonetheless aware of the great advances in scientific knowledge in their time. When reported in newspapers, it seemed possible that science could furnish proof of things in spheres of knowledge beyond their own experience—including life on the moon. In early nineteenth-century America—with its growing problems of urban crowding, social inequalities, and slavery—the *Sun*'s idyllic descriptions of the verdant valleys on the moon held out an Eden-like promise of a pastoral paradise. In a single leap of the imagination, modern scientific discoveries were taking American newspaper readers to a New Jerusalem in the heavens. The *Sun*'s series of stories about life on the moon indeed was rolled out like a Biblical act of creation over six days. [15]

The instigator of the Great Moon Hoax was an Englishman called Richard Adams Locke. Born in 1800, Locke was something of a disappointment to his prosperous Somerset family when he failed to follow in his father's footsteps by attending Cambridge. Instead, he drifted into journalism in Bristol and London and became known for his republican political views. At age twenty-six, he married a fifteen-year-old girl named Esther Bowring. In 1832, Locke was finding it difficult to make a living in British journalism, doubtless due to his radical politics. That year, he moved to New York with his wife and baby daughter, Adelaide. Despite the impact of the Industrial Revolution transforming America, the United States in the 1830s was still a frontier society with a total population of only 13 million. When Locke arrived in America, populist politician Andrew Jackson, who owned slaves and removed Indians from their lands, was the anti-establishment president in the White House.

Soon after arriving in New York, Richard Adams Locke immediately showed formidable talents for fictitious invention—starting with his own credentials. He told potential employers that he had attended Cambridge (which was untrue) and boasted that he was a direct descendant of the English philosopher John Locke (only partly true, his great-great-great-grandfather was John Locke's uncle). In an era before rigorous background checks, Locke's false claims went unquestioned. New Yorkers in the 1830s were easily impressed by a well-spoken Englishman who displayed a remarkable vocabulary and extraordinary erudition. A later photograph of Locke shows a man with penetrating self-confidence, his high forehead balding, deep-set eyes, long aquiline nose, and trimmed mutton-chop beard. If he wasn't always truthful, he possessed impressive intelligence and exceptional talents.

Locke quickly landed a job as a New York court reporter for the *Courier and Enquirer.* His stories stood out for their sharp writing and insightful perspectives, especially his coverage of the high-profile trial of Robert Matthews, known as "Matthias the Prophet." A precursor of the modern-day religious cult leader, Matthews was a down-and-out carpenter from small-town New York who had been driven out of a Methodist church after accusations of assault and battery on his wife. He was soon sporting a religious beard and claiming to be the incarnation of the thirteenth apostle Matthias. Remarkably, he attracted a coterie of devout followers who lived together in a religious commune, called Mount Zion, on the Hudson River in Ossining, New York.

Self-styled religious prophets were not uncommon in early nineteenth century America. This was the period of the so-called Second Great Awakening, when an evangelist revival was embracing the Romantic spirit of the age by appealing to ecstatic emotions, supernatural forces, and evoking the Second Coming. Religious revivalism in America was a reaction to the deist skepticism of Enlightenment theology based on reason.

Illuminated religious prophets were not restricted to evangelical America. A generation earlier in Richard Adams Locke's home country of England, a self-styled millenarian prophet named Richard Brothers declared that he was descended directly from James, the brother of Jesus. In 1794, Brothers published *A Revealed Knowledge and Prophecies of the Times,* whose title page claimed his book had been written "under the direction of the Lord God." Brothers claimed that the world was 5,913 years old since the Creation, that the tribes of Israel would return to Palestine in the year 1798, and that the wrath of God was about to destroy London, which he compared to Sodom. He also warned that the House of Commons (which had 666 members) would be destroyed by an Armageddon-like earthquake. Brothers claimed, however, to have postponed the destruction of London after direct negotiations with the Almighty in the presence of angels. In a follow-up to the book, Brothers prophesied the death of King George III and warned that the four beasts in the Bible's Book of Daniel were four ruling crowned heads: George III, the Empress of Russia, Louis XVI, and the Emperor of Germany. He added that the French monarchy, recently toppled, would never return; and the British monarchy might soon be extinguished.

Astonishingly, the book made Richard Brothers extraordinarily famous. Copies of *Revealed Knowledge* were distributed in political and diplomatic circles, and he quickly attracted a large following. His prophecies tapped into widespread belief in England that the French Revolution was God's work to rid the world of the pope. Brothers attempted to take his prophecies directly to the prime minister, William Pitt. When his overture was spurned, he complained that he'd been treated with "unfeeling contempt and incivility."[16] In 1795, he was arrested, charged with treason, declared a lunatic, and imprisoned. The *Times* applauded his imprisonment, noting that Brothers was "the tool of a faction, employed to seduce the people, and to spread fears and alarms."[17] And yet his cause was taken up in parliament by an MP called Nathaniel Brassey Halhed. An Oxford-educated philologist and expert in Hindu religious writings, Halhed believed Brothers's prophecies. He moved in parliament that Brothers's revelations should be printed and distributed to all MPs. He even obtained Brothers's release from prison and transfer to an asylum— from where, undeterred, Brothers continued churning out prophetic writings.

In antebellum America, the Second Great Awakening movement was particularly strong in New England and upstate New York, where the construction of the Erie Canal was driving a population and urbanization boom. Robert Matthews was born and raised in the town of Cambridge, New York. While he was setting up his Mount Zion commune on the Hudson River north of New York City, another upstate religious prophet, Joseph Smith, was laying the foundations of a new sect called the Mormons. Like Matthews, Smith made extraordinary claims about religious illuminations, including a visitation by an angel who directed him to the golden plates that he translated into the Book of Mormon. The French political philosopher Alexis de Tocqueville was, by a coincidence of history, making the trip through America in the 1830s that would produce his masterpiece *Democracy in America*. Tocqueville observed firsthand American culture's feverish religious fundamentalism everywhere he looked. He was especially struck by the Enlightenment paradox of democratic liberty mixed with religious orthodoxy, in contrast to the rise of religious skepticism in undemocratic Europe. Enlightenment philosophers had asserted that religious passions would decline with the rise of scientific knowledge and democratic institutions. Yet this did not appear to be so in the young American republic, where religion was a powerful political institution. "In America, one of the freest and enlightened nations in the world," he observed, "the people fulfill with fervor all the outward duties of religion." Tocqueville noted that an American politician could attack a particular religious sect without damage, but if he attacked all Christian sects, the population would abandon him.[18]

A darker side of the Matthews Mount Zion sect north of New York City soon surfaced. Local residents became aware of strange sexual practices going on at the commune. Matthews had taken up sexually with Mount Zion devotee Ann Folger, who happened to be the wife of another follower named Benjamin Folger. Deprived of his spouse, he accepted Matthews's own daughter, Isabelle, as a consolation prize. Another Mount Zion follower was Elijah Pierson, a rich businessman who was also a devout Presbyterian. He and his wife Sarah were Christian perfectionists who worked tirelessly as religious reformers, especially with poor child prostitutes in New York. When his wife died of consumption, Pierson was emotionally traumatized, and began attempting to bring Sarah back from the dead. It was undoubtedly her death that made Pierson, a broken man, vulnerable to the religious dogmas and financial manipulations of Robert Matthews. The people living near Mount Zion, hearing rumors about abusive behavior at the commune, began regarding Matthews with suspicion and antipathy.

In New York, the prophet "Matthias," aka Robert Matthews, met a similar fate. He was eventually arrested and charged for defrauding Benjamin Folger and other Mount Zion followers of huge sums and deeds to real estate on the promise of greater riches in the kingdom of heaven. Matthews himself had been living high on the hog, taking sexual advantage of his female followers. More seriously, Elijah Pierson had died in suspicious circumstances. Matthew was accused of murdering Pierson with a dish of poisoned blackberries.[19]

Robert Matthews's widely publicized trial, at which the accused appeared in the box swaggering confidently, was a media circus. Medical witnesses called to testify stated that Matthews, given his hysterical language and fanatical religious claims, was almost certainly insane. Others who knew him told the court that Matthews was an imposter, though not insane, for he was razor sharp with his financial affairs. Some who had lived at Mount Zion described him as an abusive tyrant. When Elijah Pierson had fallen gravely ill, Matthews refused to send for a doctor. The court ordered Elijah Pierson's body exhumed to be examined for traces of poison, but results were inconclusive.

The trial provided fabulous material for Richard Adams Locke's sharp eye for theater of the absurd. Benjamin Day, publisher of the fledgling *Sun*, was so impressed by Locke's gripping coverage that he offered him the colossal sum of $150 (several months' salary for a journalist at the time) to defect from the *Courier and Enquirer* to cover the trial for the *Sun*. Locke accepted the offer. His reports produced a quickie book for the *Sun*, titled *Memoirs of Matthias the Prophet, with a Full Exposure of His Atrocious Impositions, and of the Degrading Delusions of His Followers*. The title left little doubt about Locke's view of the man in the dock claiming to be a prophet.

Despite damning evidence against him, Matthews was acquitted on the murder charge. He was, however, sentenced to three months for assaulting his daughter Isabelle with a whip, plus an additional thirty days for contempt due to his loud outbursts in the courtroom. After his release from prison, he continued undeterred making claims about religious illuminations, now calling himself "Joshua." He visited Mormon leader Joseph Smith, who at first received Matthews as a fellow prophet; but the two men parted ways in a climate of mutual distrust. While Smith founded the Church of Jesus Christ of Latter-Day Saints, Matthews, reviled in the American press, vanished into semi-obscurity as an itinerant preacher until his death several years later. Locke, meanwhile, was appointed as the *Sun*'s editor—an extraordinary promotion for a foreigner who had arrived off the boat only three years earlier. Benjamin Day was hoping Locke would use his talents to come up with more human-interest stories.

Locke did not disappoint. The "Matthias the Prophet" trial, exposing the dark zones of religious fanaticism, had given him insights into the perverse psychology of human credulity. He was now ready to put the credulity of the *Sun*'s readers to the test with his outlandish tale about life on the moon.

***

As an upstart newspaper struggling to make itself known in the crowded New York newspaper market, the *Sun*'s primary motive in publishing the Great Moon Hoax was financial. The 1830s was a period of explosive growth for American newspapers. The business was shifting from its old highbrow model of biased partisan allegiances toward a more non-partisan, advertising-driven strategy of attracting larger mass audiences with sensationalized stories. At the beginning of the decade, there were some 850 newspapers boasting a combined circulation of 68 million copies. By 1840, that figure had doubled to 1,630 newspapers with a total circulation of 196 million copies.

Established newspapers were stuck in the editorial formula of politics and financial news in papers priced at six cents a copy. Papers like the *Sun* aggressively catered to the tastes of working-class readers and charged only one cent (hence the name "penny" paper). The cut-rate, one-cent price meant that penny papers had to sell many more copies to make a profit. This basic economic reality put pressure on the penny press to sensationalize stories with quirky, outlandish, and shocking angles. The penny papers also revolutionized how newspapers reached readers. They hired newsboys to hawk copies in the streets. For papers like the *Sun*, each edition contained attention-grabbing headlines for the newsboys to shout out. The clichéd image of boys flogging papers on street corners shouting "Extra! Extra! Read all about it!" dates to the 1830s. In New York, many of these newsboys were homeless children. One of the *Sun*'s

first newsboys was a ten-year-old Irish immigrant named Bernard Flaher-
ty (he later went into the theater under the stage name Barney Williams),
who could be seen on Manhattan corners shouting out *Sun* headlines such
as "Awful Occurrence!" and "Infamous Affair!" While this early phase of
modern journalism witnessed the growth of unpartisan news based on
facts, the competition to attract readers meant that liberties were frequently taken with the truth.

The penny press formula was a huge commercial success. In the five
years following the Great Moon Hoax, thirty-five penny papers launched
in New York alone. The *New York Times* debuted as a penny paper in
1851. Few survived, but penny papers proliferated. For the penny papers
that did survive and thrive, one of the reasons for their success was
advertising. The established papers had long been fussily middle class
about advertisements, rejecting adverts for patent medicines, lotteries,
theater shows, and shops that opened on Sunday. The penny papers took
an amoral, laissez-faire attitude toward advertising. The *Sun* was brazen
about its open-door commercial approach to journalism. At the top of its
front page, the *Sun*'s long-winded motto was: "The object of this paper is
to lay before the public, at a price within the means of everyone, all the
news of the day, and at the same time offer an advantageous medium for
advertisements."[20]

The Great Moon Hoax succeeded far beyond Locke's expectations.
Beyond its impact on the market for American newspapers, Locke's hoax
unmasked deeper truths about social psychology in the early nineteenth
century. It was so convincing that it led to the discovery of a new phenomenon called "spontaneous mendacity." When the story first appeared
in the *Sun*, many attempted to claim a personal connection with Sir John
Herschel's amazing lunar discovery. One old gentleman, dressed in a
broadcloth Quaker suit, told crowds gathered outside the *Sun*'s offices
that he'd recently been to London and was at the East India Docks when
Sir John Herschel's seven-ton lens and telescope were loaded aboard a
ship bound for South Africa. It turns out that Locke was standing outside
the *Sun* building listening to this old chap boasting of having seen the
famous telescope with his own eyes.

Locke was not the first to try his hand at satirical hoax. A century
earlier in Britain, Jonathan Swift had used the same weapon as Isaac
Bickerstaff, Esq., to expose and ridicule frauds such as the astrologist
John Partridge. In America, Benjamin Franklin had likewise used
pseudonyms—Alice Addertongue, Anthony Afterwit, Silence Dogood—
to publish hoaxes satirizing superstitions. The hoax indeed is often associated with the Enlightenment when science was challenging accepted
sources of knowledge. This made it possible for sharp-witted satirists
such as Swift to mock not only old superstitions (as he did with astrolo-

gers) but also the new sciences (as he did with Laputa island in *Gulliver's Travels*).

In the 1830s shortly before the Great Moon Hoax, nothing much had changed. People were still consulting astrologers and buying quack medicines that had no effect on their ailments. This was the great era of traveling medicine shows and snake oil salesmen flogging their cure-all remedies to the gullible public. In Locke's day, however, science was much more advanced than a century earlier when Jonathan Swift was skewering the astrology quack Partridge. Following the Industrial Revolution, humankind was pushing the limits of knowledge in every field of scientific inquiry—biology, zoology, botany, geology, engineering. The popular imagination followed this great burst of technological progress with curiosity, fascination, and wonder. New inventions, from the steam engine to the telegraph wire, were driving human progress. In astronomy, scientists were declaring the certainty of life on other planets. In 1824, a decade before the Great Moon Hoax, the German astronomer Franz von Gruithuisen published a paper, "Discovery of Many Distinct Traces of Lunar Inhabitants, Especially of One of Their Colossal Buildings," that asserted the existence of life on the moon.

The unstoppable progress of science was so persuasive that religious doctrines, no longer powerful against the claims of science, felt they had to keep up. In previous centuries, the language of science was obliged to show deference to Scripture and theology. Now the tables were turned.[21] Churchmen were using the language of science to legitimize their religious claims. The first signs of this reversal dated to the seventeenth century, when the respected Anglican cleric and biblical scholar Bishop James Ussher calculated with astounding precision the date of God's creation of the universe: October 23, 4004 BCE. That meant that the history of the world dated back only four thousand years before Christ. In Ussher's time, his dating of creation was commonly accepted. The German theologian Martin Luther had put the date of creation at about 4000 BC. In Shakespeare's play *As You Like It*, the heroine Rosalind says, "The poor world is almost six thousand years old." Even the astronomer Johannes Kepler asserted that the world was probably created around 3992 BC. After Ussher's death, his creation chronology was included in annotations of most editions of the authorized King James Bible.[22] By the nineteenth century, the iron laws of science were establishing with greater precision what was true and false about the universe. Church leaders had no choice but to make efforts to reconcile science and faith—or, rather, to adapt religious doctrines to scientific truths.

In 1817, the Scottish theologian Thomas Chalmers, an advocate of natural theology, published a collection of sermons under the title *Astronomical Discourses*, which reconciled theology and astronomy. Chalmers argued that, since God would not have created the rest of the universe in vain, there must be a multitude of worlds with life such as our own. In short, humankind must humbly accept that we are not God's chosen people. Chalmers's claims were so popular in his day that his book went through nine editions and sold a total of twenty thousand copies. He became a superstar on the lecture circuit, giving electrifying sermons in London on his astronomical theology. Other Christian preachers soon jumped on the scientific bandwagon with books that belonged more to the realm of science fiction than to theology. Notable among them was Reverend Thomas Dick, another Scottish churchman making a connection between astronomy and religion. Whereas the poet William Blake stridently opposed the measures of science in religious passions, preachers like Dr. Dick appropriated the language of astronomy. His books, boasting titles such as *The Christian Philosopher* and *Celestial Scenery*, were enormously popular in the United States. The subtitle of the latter work was *The Wonders of the Planetary System Displayed, Illustrating the Perfections of Deity and a Plurality of Worlds.* Dr. Dick claimed with scientific precision, using a calculation based on the population density of England, that our solar system counted more than 21 trillion inhabitants. He put the population of the planet Jupiter at 6 trillion, 967 billion. The Earth's moon, he claimed, had a population of 4,200,000,000.[23] All the inhabitants in our solar system, he said, were God's creatures. Dr. Dick insisted, however, that there could be no volcanoes on the moon. His reasoning was religious: volcanoes were a sign of God's displeasure, and since lunar inhabitants were innocent, the moon could not be punished with natural agents of physical destruction. Dr. Dick was taken so seriously that, in Britain, he was inducted into the Royal Astronomical Society.

Richard Adams Locke was familiar with Dr. Dick's books and frankly considered him a fraud. The Great Moon Hoax didn't specifically target Reverend Dick, but there can be little doubt that Locke was mocking characters of his ilk. His satirical point was that, in an era when everything seemed possible, it was difficult to distinguish between fact and fiction, between reality and fantasy, between truth and lies. It was this culture of credulity, Locke believed, that made religious quacks like Reverend Dick internationally famous. With Swiftian skill, Locke's hoax satirized the hocus pocus, mumbo jumbo of false prophets who were promoting the "plurality of worlds" theory of alien life. As Locke confided in an article in the *New World* five years after his famous hoax, he had been "resolved to throw a pebble at this Colossus, not, certainly, with the hope of rivalling David, but merely to express my independent and utter contempt for the imaginative and canting school, by endeavoring to out-imagine it, and ape its solemn cant, under the mask of dignified and plausible science."[24]

Locke's choice of Sir John Herschel as the famous astronomer who discovered life on the moon was probably not a coincidence. Herschel's famous father, astronomer William Herschel, had claimed that not only was there was life on every planet, but the sun too was inhabited.[25] William Hershel died in 1822, making him an impossible target for Locke's Great Moon Hoax in 1835. Locke kept it in the family by targeting his illustrious son, Sir John Hershel. The younger Herschel was fair game. In his *Treatise on Astronomy,* published only a year before the Great Moon Hoax, the younger Hershel weighed the evidence about life on the moon and concluded that it was possible. Telescopes, he noted, needed to be "greatly improved before we could expect to see signs of inhabitants as manifested by edifices or by changes on the surface of the soil."[26] The Great Moon Hoax haunted Hershel for decades, though he was more amused than outraged by the publicity. Many years later, he confided in a letter, "I have been pestered from all quarters with that ridiculous hoax about the Moon—in English French Italian & German!"[27]

The Great Moon Hoax spawned a new genre in journalism. Hoax stories flourished for decades in American newspapers. Many have been forgotten today, but some were so outlandish that social historians dissected them for decades. One of the most famous hoaxes of that era was the tale of the so-called Cardiff Giant. In 1869, it was claimed that a ten-foot-tall petrified man, believed to come from a lost race, had been exhumed behind the barn of William "Stub" Newell in Cardiff, New York. After benefiting from a flurry of hype in the newspapers, Newell took the petrified body on the road as a paid curiosity attraction. Some 60,000 Americans paid to see the Cardiff Giant exhibition. Even eminent personalities such as Ralph Waldo Emerson and Oliver Wendell Holmes went to get a look at the corpse. So did P. T. Barnum, the great impresario famous for his remark that "there's a sucker born every minute." Barnum was sniffing out a business opportunity. He offered Newell the extraordinary sum of $50,000 for the giant. Newell turned him down. Barnum, faithful to another of his adages—"every crowd has a silver lining"—made his own petrified giant and hyped it as the authentic one. The real petrified giant was a fake; so was the fake claiming to be the real one.

Another famous hoax was concocted by one of America's greatest writers of the nineteenth century. In 1863, a newspaper in Virginia City, Nevada, published a blood-curdling story about a man named Philip Hopkins who had killed his entire family. After losing everything through bad stock market investments in a San Francisco utility company, Hopkins went insane and murdered his wife and seven children (two daughters survived the slaughter). Following this horrific act, Hopkins rode horse-back into town with his throat cut ear-to-ear, brandishing the long, red-haired scalp of his wife, before collapsing dead in front of the Magnolia saloon. The newspaper story provided gut-wrenching details: "The scalp-less corpse of Mrs. Hopkins lay across the threshold, with her head split open and her right hand almost severed from the wrist. Near her lay the axe with which the murderous deed had been committed. In one of the bedrooms six of the children were found, one in bed and the others scattered about the floor. They were all dead. Their brains had evidently been dashed out with a club, and every mark about them seemed to have been made with a blunt instrument."

The story horrified readers. The writer, it turned out, was a young reporter named Samuel Clemens, soon to change his name to Mark Twain, author of the great American literary classic *The Adventures of Tom Sawyer*. Twain owned up to the hoax with an explanation. His grue-some tale was intended to shock San Francisco newspapers into sending reporters to cover the story—and by doing so, expose corruption at the city's Spring Valley Water Company, which was suspected of cooking its books. Twain's hoax was fake news with a political agenda, a well-spun lie that exposed an uncomfortable truth about financial corruption. As Twain later remarked: "A lie can get halfway round the world while the truth is still getting its shoes on."[28]

Perhaps the greatest hoax writer of the era was Edgar Allan Poe. Two months before Locke's Great Moon Hoax, Poe had published his own astronomical hoax in the *Southern Literary Messenger*. Titled "Hans Pfaall, a Tale," Poe's "true" story was about a Dutchman who traveled to the moon on a balloon craft and returned home to tell his tales.[29] But while Locke's life-on-the-moon story in the *Sun* stunned the world, hard-ly anyone read Poe's tale. Poe was bitter, and even threatened to sue the *Sun* for plagiarism. He grudgingly praised Locke's exploit, however, as "decidedly the greatest *hit* in the way of sensation—of merely popular sensation—ever made by any similar fiction either in America or in Eu-rope."[30] Poe even penned a profile of Locke in the woman's magazine *Godey's Magazine and Lady's Book*. Poe was clearly impressed by his subject. "Like most men of true imagination, Mr. Locke is a seemingly paradoxical combination of coolness and excitability," wrote Poe.

> He is about five feet seven inches in height, symmetrically formed; there is an air of distinction about his whole person, the air of noble genius. His face is strongly pitted by the smallpox and perhaps, from the same cause there is a marked obliquity in the eyes; a certain, calm, clear luminousness, however, about these latter, amply compen-sates for the defect, and the forehead is truly beautiful in its intellectu-

ality. I am acquainted with no person possessing so fine a forehead as
Mr. Locke. He is married and about forty-five years of age, although
no one would suppose him to be more than thirty-eight. He is a lineal
descendant of the immortal author of the *Essay on Human Understanding*.[31]

The last sentence revealed that Locke was still spinning his exaggerated
boast about being a direct descendant of philosopher John Locke.

Not all fake news stories of the era aspired to satire. Some were
intended to terrify. In November 1874, the *New York Herald* published a
ten-thousand-word story headlined "A Shocking Sabbath Carnival of
Death," about wild animals escaping the Central Park Zoo. The story's
subheading warned "Savage Brutes at Large" and "Awful Combats between Beasts and Citizens." The beasts—Numidian lions, panthers, Ben-
gal tigers, polar bears, hyenas—had broken free after a rhinoceros tram-
pled and killed a zookeeper by plunging its horn into his head. The
Herald story, written by Irish American journalist Joseph Clarke, reported that wild animals rampaging through the streets of Manhattan had
killed two hundred people. "Men and women rushed in all directions
away from the beast, who sprang upon the shoulders of an aged lady,
burying his fangs in her neck and carrying her to the ground." A panther
was spotted gnawing on its victim; another had attacked worshippers in a
church on West 53rd Street.

The *Herald*'s reports of "terrible scenes of mutilation" provoked
widespread panic. Men were seen racing around the streets of Manhattan
carrying rifles. Parents rushed to retrieve their children from school. To
reassure readers, the *Herald* announced that the National Guard had converged on the city to confront the uncaged beasts.[32]

Why did people believe it? One reason was ignorance about zoos and
wild animals. Zoos were a relatively new phenomenon in the 1870s. The
Central Park Zoo had opened as a menagerie only a decade earlier in
1864. Most people in cities like New York were unfamiliar with exotic
beasts and knew nothing of their behavior. It was entirely plausible that
lions and tigers could escape and attack humans. Most readers—including editors at rival papers—failed to spot the newspaper's disclaimer,
tucked away at the bottom of the story: "The entire story given above is a
pure fabrication. Not one word of it is true." The *Herald*'s competitors
were quick to denounce the story, though their moral outrage concealed
competitive jealousy. Fake news sold papers.

It's easy to disparage penny papers like the *Sun* and the *Herald* for
pandering to the bottom of the market with outlandish fake news stories.
It must be remembered, however, that these papers invented modern journalism. True, they were the precursors of modern tabloids that continued

the tradition of scandal-mongering and fake news. But they were also the first papers to hire reporters to find stories and cover the news. As astonishing as it may seem, early newspapers didn't have their own reporters. New York papers covered Washington, DC, by reprinting official documents and publishing reports written up by members of Congress—in effect, free political publicity. This was much like the European tradition, where editors like Theodor Fontane in Germany pinched stories from other papers and invented details to create the impression that they were real foreign correspondents. It was the penny press, not the broadsheets, that invested in newsgathering and hired reporters to dig for news.

On both sides of the Atlantic, the penny press's focus on the "human angle" helped bring public attention to serious social issues such as child labor. In Britain, influential editor William Thomas Stead's *Pall Mall Gazette* and its competitor the *Star* pioneered modern investigative journalism. Highly personalized, this style of reporting was called "New Journalism." Stead wrote a manifesto on the future of journalism in which he declared: "Everything depends upon the individual—the person. Impersonal journalism is effete."[33] Some of Stead's journalistic campaigns produced important social changes in Victorian society. Most famous among them was an exposé in 1885 on the brutality of child prostitution, under headlines such as "The Violation of Virgins" and "How Girls Were Bought and Ruined." The public was shocked by the revelations in the *Pall Mall Gazette.* The result was a new law, referred to as the "Stead Act," raising the age of consent from thirteen to sixteen. Stead called his approach "government by journalism." His own tragic death was the stuff of sensational journalism. Stead was a passenger on the ill-fated *Titanic* on its maiden voyage across the Atlantic in 1912. Some reported that, when the ship started to sink, Stead was seen helping women and children into lifeboats. It was also claimed that he retired to the first-class smoking room and, while the ship slipped into the depths, sat quietly in a leather chair reading a book. Perhaps both are true. His body was never recovered.

In New York, Richard Adams Locke retired from the penny press knowing he had pulled off the greatest journalistic hoax of the century. After editorial jobs at other papers following his departure from the *Sun*, he left journalism for good in 1842 to take a sinecure as an inspector for the Customs Service in New York, which in Locke's day was rife with bribery and political patronage. As a Briton who never naturalized as a U.S. citizen, Locke would have been disqualified for the job, but he probably used his professional connections with the local Democratic Party to pull strings. This doubtless explains why he lied to U.S. census inspectors in 1850 and 1860, giving his place of birth as New York.

Locke appears to have led a relatively anonymous life, living modestly on Staten Island with his wife Esther and their six children. As Locke retreated into retirement, the public fascination with fantastic tales about life on other planets increased. The writings of astronomer Richard Anthony Proctor were particularly popular with the public in the late nineteenth century, notably his *Other Worlds Than Ours* in 1870.[34] Locke died a year later, in 1871, at age seventy. When he died, there were no obituaries in the newspapers—not even in the *Sun*, the newspaper he had made world famous with the Great Moon Hoax.

In Germany, meanwhile, Prussia's "fake correspondent," Theodor Fontane, left journalism the same year as Locke's death to devote the last two decades of his life to writing novels. His final journalistic assignment was the Franco-Prussian War. After France declared war on Prussia in 1870, Fontane went to the front as an observer-journalist for the *Kreuzeitung*. This time he wasn't a fake correspondent; he was reporting from the front lines. He was even taken prisoner by the French and remained in captivity for a few months. The Prussian chancellor, Otto von Bismarck, personally intervened to secure his release, a sign that Fontane had friends in high places.

It's ironic that Fontane played a minor role in the Franco-Prussian War. That war was the first major military conflict in modern history to be provoked by fake news. The author of the disinformation was none other than Fontane's protector, Otto von Bismarck.

11

BISMARCK'S FAKE NEWS

In the autumn of 1865, Otto von Bismarck traveled to the seaside resort of Biarritz as a guest of French emperor Napoleon III.

Finding himself in Biarritz evoked poignant memories for Bismarck. Three years earlier, as Prussian ambassador to France, the forty-seven-year-old Bismarck had spent the summer in the French spa town with his twenty-one-year-old Russian mistress, Katharina Orlov. Bismarck was smitten with Katharina despite the great age difference—and the inconvenient fact that she, like him, was married. The wife of Nikolai Orlov, the aristocratic Russian ambassador to Belgium, Katharina—whom Bismarck affectionately called "Katch"—had a lively intelligence and played the piano. Bismarck wrote enthusiastically to his wife Johanna about the Russian countess, describing her as "amusing, intelligent, kind, pretty, and young." Johanna, who was far away in Pomerania with the three Bismarck children, did not seem to resent her husband's romantic interlude in the French spa town. Neither apparently did Katharina's husband, Prince Orlov.

One day during their summer tryst, Bismarck and Katharina were bathing in the sea. Despite the calm weather, both were suddenly swept out by a strong current. A quick-thinking lighthouse keeper named Pierre Lafleur swam out and rescued Katharina. Bismarck, a massive walrus-like figure who weighed more than two hundred pounds, was still frantically waving his arms for help. Lafleur swam back out to the deep waters and managed to bring the six-foot-two Prussian back to shore. Bismarck was unconscious, but Lafleur revived him. Four weeks later, Lafleur tragically drowned at the very same spot where he'd rescued Bismarck and Katharina Orlov. Bismarck and his Russian mistress showed their gratitude by becoming godfather and godmother to Lafleur's orphaned baby boy.[1] Shortly after his trip to Biarritz, Bismarck became president of Prussia.

It was later remarked that Pierre Lafleur's heroism changed the course of history. If he had let Bismarck sink and drown, there would have been no German Empire, perhaps no First World War, nor a Second World War.

Bismarck returned to Biarritz three years later, but this time it was not for a romantic dalliance. He was back in the spa town to meet with the French emperor, Napoleon III. While the two leaders strolled together along the beach, a great deal was at stake.

As Prussian president, Bismarck's ambition was to consolidate Prussia's control over the remnants of the Holy Roman Empire and forge a modern German nation. Ironically, the Holy Roman Empire—which Voltaire famously described as "neither holy, nor Roman, nor an empire"—had been dissolved in 1806 by the French emperor's uncle, Napoleon Bonaparte, following his military victory at Austerlitz. It was now a patchwork of German kingdoms and duchies in a loosely woven confederation stretching from Prussia to Bavaria. In the mid-nineteenth century, Germany was a nation without a state, neighboring the powerful Austro-Hungarian Empire. Bismarck, the embodiment of Prussian militarism, was determined that a modern German nation should be ruled from Berlin, not Vienna. He believed that German unification could not be achieved with speeches and diplomacy. German nationhood, he famously asserted, could be forged only through the *Blut und Eisen* (blood and iron) of war.

That *realpolitik* imperative brought Bismarck to Biarritz for his meeting with Napoleon III. The Prussian leader was about to make a move on Austria and wanted reassurances from the French emperor that France would remain neutral. Napoleon III, though seven years older, was no match for Bismarck in statesmanship, stature, and cunning. Bismarck was a disciplined Prussian tactician, hardened by long experience in politics. Napoleon III, by contrast, was a dilettante, a rakish character from *opéra bouffe*, fond of twirling his moustache and chasing fleshy courtesans in opulent Parisian ballrooms.[2] While Napoleon III's handling of domestic affairs in France was well-meaning and sensible, his foreign policies were invariably disastrous adventures, including a failed attempt to install a puppet emperor in Mexico. Though a case can be made that Napoleon III has been cruelly judged by history, he wasn't quite made of the same stuff as his illustrious uncle Napoleon Bonaparte. At best, Napoleon III was an intriguing enigma; at worst, he was an incompetent muddler. The great French writer Victor Hugo famously dismissed him as "Napoléon le Petit." Bismarck, in the same ungenerous spirit, called him "a sphinx without a riddle."[3]

A year after his seaside meeting with Napoleon III at the Villa Eugénie in Biarritz, Bismarck lured Austria into a war that resulted in a decisive Prussian victory. Napoleon III, as promised, stood by and did nothing. Austria was defeated. Prussia annexed Frankfurt, Hanover, Hesse-
Kassel, Schleswig, Holstein, and Nassau. Most of Germany was now
under Prussian control. Power in the German sphere shifted from Vienna
to Berlin.

Bismarck needed just one more war to unite the remaining German
states under Prussian leadership. But this time, he needed a common
enemy outside of Germany. He chose France.

Bismarck had known for years, even when he was meeting Napoleon
III in Biarritz, that a war with France was inevitable. "I took it as assured
that a war with France would necessarily have to be waged on the road to
our national development," Bismarck wrote later. "I did not doubt that a
Franco-German war must take place before the construction of a united
Germany could be realized."[4]

In 1868, Bismarck unexpectedly had a timely pretext for war with
France. In Spain, Queen Isabella II abdicated after a long and unsteady
reign. The Spanish throne was suddenly vacant. The stability of Spain
depended on a judicious selection of a new monarch. Bismarck saw an
opportunity in Spain's power vacuum. He immediately proposed a German prince, Leopold of Hohenzollern, as Spain's new king. Prince Leopold, a Roman Catholic, happened to be a relation of the Prussian kaiser,
Wilhelm I.

Bismarck's maneuver was a deliberate provocation. He knew France
would never agree to a German royal sitting on the throne of Spain.
Napoleon III's hand would be forced. If he accepted a German monarch
as king of neighboring Spain, he would be humiliated and his Bonapartist
regime in France would be destabilized. His only option would be to
declare war against Prussia. That was precisely what Bismarck wanted.

Bismarck knew that the French emperor—who, unlike his uncle Napoleon Bonaparte, had never commanded armies—had an exaggerated
opinion of French military strength. Bismarck was moreover convinced
that France's Second Empire was a house of cards that would collapse at
the first sound of Prussian cannons. He was also certain that a man of
Napoleon III's personal vanity could easily be provoked into war. He had
already witnessed that when the French emperor was manipulated by his
seductive Italian mistress, Countess of Castiglione, into declaring war on
the Austrians to drive them out of Lombardy—a war that led to the
creation of modern unified Italy. Bismarck didn't have a perfumed
courtesan to excite Napoleon III's passions. But he was armed with a
provocation that promised to be just as effective: a fake news story in the
newspapers.

Napoleon III's greatest character flaw was pride. Despite his own limited abilities, he believed too ardently in the aura of his illustrious name. He was the son of Napoleon's younger brother Louis, parachuted as king of Holland from 1806 to 1810 at the height of the Napoleonic era when Bonaparte siblings were imposed as monarchs on European thrones. Louis had married his brother Napoleon's stepdaughter, Hortense de Beauharnais. Thus, when the future Napoleon III was born in 1807, he was related to his uncle Napoleon Bonaparte through both his father and mother. His parents' marriage was loveless, however, and the couple was quickly estranged.

Young Louis, as he was called, was only seven years old when his uncle was defeated at Waterloo and sent into exile. With the restoration of the Bourbon monarchy, the entire Bonaparte clan was banished from France. Louis spent much of his youth in Switzerland and Bavaria, which accounted for his slow Germanic accent in French later in life. While his family was living in exile, nostalgia for the glorious legend of his uncle Napoleon Bonaparte was soaring. Europe was at the height of the Romantic era. Heroic nationalism was the dominant theme for an entire generation of poets, novelists, composers, and painters. The Romantic poets were obsessed with Napoleon as a symbol of heroic grandeur, even the personification of personal liberty. Lord Byron penned an "Ode to Napoleon Bonaparte."[5] The German philosopher Hegel, who witnessed Napoleon with his own eyes marching victoriously into his Prussian town after the French victory at the Battle of Jena, described the emperor as a "world-historical figure" driven by the *weltgeist* of the age. In Stendhal's classic novel *Le Rouge et le Noir*, the protagonist Julien Sorel worships Napoleon Bonaparte. Young Louis, who had memories of his uncle at the Tuileries Palace in Paris, grew up acutely aware of the mythology attached to his family name. He knew from an early age that his own name, Louis-Napoleon Bonaparte, held out the prospect of an exalted destiny.

By early adulthood, Louis was concocting implausible plots to overthrow the French government and restore the Bonapartes to the imperial throne. Despite his lack of preparation, events paradoxically conspired in his favor. In 1830, only fifteen years after Waterloo, the restored Bourbon monarchy fell. While the romantic legend of Napoleon Bonaparte was powerful, the timing was not right for France's return to an imperial regime. A constitutional monarchy was proclaimed instead. Another Bourbon, Louis-Philippe, became "*roi des Français*"—not "*roi de France*"—to underscore that constitutional monarchy was replacing divine-right kings in France. Louis-Philippe, descended from the junior Orléanist branch of the Bourbons, had spent much of his life in exile, during which he visited the United States and met George Washington and Alexander Hamilton. Installed as France's constitutional monarch,

Louis-Philippe ruled as a bourgeois king who promoted the interests of the rich while the inequalities grew in France. Considered weak, he was satirized by French writers and defamed in caricatures. When the English novelist William Thackeray visited Paris in the 1830s, he wrote of drawings plastered on public walls depicting Louis-Philippe with a pear-shaped head. The French word for *pear* is *poire*. The image of Louis-Philippe as *roi-poire*—or pear-headed king—was a commentary on his perceived stupidity.[6]

In the early years of Louis-Philippe's reign, Louis Napoleon was living in London with his mother, Hortense, in a rented furnished house near Regent Street. Regarded by the London elite as an intriguing celebrity with an exalted name, Louis's life in the English capital was glamorous and filled with distractions. Many well-wishers came to the house to express their support for his political claims in France. Louis also displayed a keen interest in attractive ladies in London society, though he understood that marrying an English woman was out of the question if he wished to fulfill his political destiny. Both mother and son were aware that they were being watched—not only by King Louis-Philippe's spies in London, but also by British government agents.

A life-changing moment for Louis came in 1832. His uncle Napoleon's only son, Napoléon François Bonaparte, suddenly died of tuberculosis at age twenty-one. Napoleon II, known familiarly as "Franz," had been living in Vienna with his mother, emperor Napoleon's second wife, Marie-Louise of Austria. Following Napoleon II's death, London-based Louis suddenly became the Bonaparte's legitimate dynastic pretender.

Now the serious plotting began. Louis's mother, Hortense, took charge of a well-orchestrated publicity campaign to promote the Bonaparte name and drum up financial support in England. Her son Louis, when he wasn't seducing rich English women, spent a great deal of time entertaining leading English political figures of the day—including a rising star named Benjamin Disraeli—at his rented house in Carlton House Terrace. While a passionate anglophile immensely enjoying his life in London, Louis became increasingly focused on his political destiny. He used his London base to publish books and pamphlets—with titles such as *Rêveries politiques* and *Lettre de Londres*—to keep his name in public view back home in France. As a man of action, however, Louis was a bumbler. After clumsily plotting one failed coup d'état attempt against Louis-Philippe, he tried again in 1840 by crossing the English Channel with a group of mercenaries. Quickly arrested, he was imprisoned in a French fortress guarded by four hundred soldiers. Prison life didn't prevent Louis from seducing an attractive chamber maid, Éléonore Vergeot, who produced two illegitimate sons during his incarceration.

Imprisonment should have put an end to Louis Bonaparte's imperial ambitions, but circumstances were on his side. The French king, Louis-Philippe, had decided to return emperor Napoleon's remains to Paris in a grand public ceremony. Huge crowds greeted Napoleon's coffin with rejoicing as it proceeded down the Champs-Elysées toward its final resting place in Les Invalides. The public outpouring of national pride confirmed that the Napoleonic myth was still beating in the hearts of the French. Still locked up, Louis managed to bribe his way out of prison and make his way incognito—under the name "Badinguet"—across the English Channel. Back in London, he resumed his glamorous life as a dashing society figure, going about in a carriage with the imperial Napoleonic eagle emblazoned on the door panels. He accepted invitations to parties at country houses and in London attended the Anglo-French salon in the Kensington home of the Comte d'Orsay and his English wife, Lady Blessington, who had known the poet Lord Byron. Louis's own house in St. James was transformed into a Bonapartist shrine filled with family memorabilia about emperor Napoleon Bonaparte. He joined the Army and Navy Club, and in 1848 served as a special constable who helped put down the failed working-class Chartist demonstration on Kennington Common in south London. Louis also took up with a wealthy English woman, Harriet Howard, whose massive fortune proved useful in financing his renewed campaign to return home triumphantly as the legitimate emperor of France.[7]

In 1848, Louis got lucky—again—when Louis-Philippe was toppled in a revolution that ushered in the Second Republic. It was the moment Louis Bonaparte had been waiting for. He no longer had to overthrow Louis-Philippe; the people of France had done it for him. It was later remarked that, when Louis heard the news in his London house, he rushed back to France with such haste that his bed was discovered unmade and his marble bath was still full of water.

Eschewing his reputation as an opportunist *putschist*, this time Louis played the democracy card by standing for election as an MP in the new Second Republic parliament. French political elites were initially surprised, and somewhat relieved, at the modesty of his ambitions. Leftist politician Alexandre Ledru Rollin called him an "imbecile." Conservative Adolphe Thiers, who initially supported Louis-Napoleon, dismissed him as a "cretin who will be easily led." They were underestimating Louis's cunning and determination.[8]

When French presidential elections were held the same year, Louis announced his candidacy to become the Second Republic's head-of-state. Thanks largely to the awe that the Bonaparte name still inspired in France, he won in a landslide victory with 74 percent of the vote. Louis-Napoleon Bonaparte had finally triumphed. The perpetual dynastic pretender, whose hare-brained schemes had long been ridiculed, was now the first elected president of the Second Republic. His mother, Hortense de Beauharnais, was no longer alive to see her son restore the Bonaparte name. She had died more than a decade earlier in 1837. His rich English mistress, Harriett Howard, discreet financial backer of his political adventures in exile, quietly took up residence near the presidential Elysée Palace.

It turned out that Louis didn't have much of a head for democracy. One irritating obstacle was the Second Republic's constitution, which limited his time in office to a single four-year term. He had no intention of stepping down. In late 1851, when the clock was running out, Louis turned for advice to his half-brother, the Duc de Morny, who was the extramarital son of Napoleon III's mother Hortense and the French general Charles de Flahaut.

Morny orchestrated one of the strangest events in French history: Louis-Napoleon Bonaparte staged a coup against his own government. On December 2, 1851—the anniversary of Napoleon Bonaparte's coronation as emperor in 1804—Parisians awoke to discover posters plastered all over the city announcing that parliament had been dissolved and a state of siege had been proclaimed. Opposition to the coup quickly organized. A public revolt erupted. French army troops numbering thirty thousand crushed the uprising, killing four hundred protestors. More than two hundred members of parliament were arrested.

In the aftermath of the coup, a referendum was hastily organized to demonstrate Louis-Napoléon Bonaparte's popular support—and to extend his mandate by ten years. He easily won the vote. Later that year, following another referendum, the Second Empire was proclaimed.

Louis-Napoleon Bonaparte was now Napoleon III. France was no longer a republic; the National Assembly was dissolved. France was, once again, an imperial Bonapartist regime. Power was concentrated in the hands of the emperor. Louis cast aside Harriett Howard to find himself an empress, finally deciding on Spanish countess Eugénie de Montijo. One of his first acts was to declare August 15—normally a Catholic *fête* marking the Assumption—as a national civic holiday called "Saint-Napoleon" to commemorate Napoleon Bonaparte's birthday. The re-Bonapartization of the French state had begun.

The Second Empire was, in design and practice, a populist dictatorship. Napoleon III moved quickly to eliminate all dissent. The public sphere of debate that had flourished under the short-lived Second Republic was shut down. Political opposition was repressed. The press, too, was muzzled. All republican newspapers were banned, and new papers required prior authorization. The writer Victor Hugo, after publishing his *Napoléon le Petit* invective, was forced into exile on the islands of Jersey and Guernsey in the English Channel. Remembering the *roi-poire* image of Louis-Philippe, the imperial regime was particularly paranoid about caricatures. Popular theatrical productions were suspect, for they appealed to the uneducated masses, who could, as recent events in 1848 had demonstrated, overthrow a regime with mob violence. Parisian theater came under strict surveillance and controls. Only a small selection of theaters staging classic plays were authorized. Café-concerts, also suspect because they appealed to working-class audiences, were required to submit proposed songs for authorization. Second Empire drama censors were vigilant about any attacks against the state, the army, the courts, the family, and religion.[9] When Baudelaire published *Les Fleurs du mal* in 1857, several poems were expurgated because they offended "public decency." Flaubert's classic novel *Madame Bovary* was also accused of indecency.

These strict controls of public morals were paradoxical, if not hypocritical. While the Second Empire stood for public order and strict morality, the emperor and his court engaged in unbridled decadence. Powerful aristocrats, financiers, and politicians lavished fortunes on voluptuous courtesans—so-called *grandes horizontales*—who ruled over Parisian society like spoiled princesses. Napoleon III himself, an inveterate womanizer, had many mistresses, including the actress Marguerite Bellanger, the Italian Countess of Castiglione, and the English-born courtesan Cora Pearl. Napoleon III was by temperament, if not an intellectual, open minded toward the artistic world. When Manet's painting *Déjeuner sur l'herbe* caused a nudity scandal and was rejected by the stuffy Salon, the emperor ruled that the painting should be displayed so the public could decide for themselves.

Napoleon III's most enduring legacy was the physical transformation of Paris. Before 1850, Paris was still a medieval city with narrow alleys and squalid living conditions. During his London exile in the 1840s, Louis had admired the British capital's wide avenues and lush public parks, especially Hyde Park, where he often took strolls. Once enthroned as emperor, he wanted Paris to rival London as a great modern city. To this end, he commissioned prefect Georges-Eugène Haussmann, a Protestant from Alsace, to oversee the city's massive facelift. For most of the Second Empire, Paris was a vast construction site as engineers annexed suburbs to expand the city from eleven to twenty arrondissements. Haussmann demolished the old Parisian quarters and cut wide boulevards lined with six-story residential buildings featuring cream-colored façades and black iron balconies. Lush green spaces, modeled after London squares, were built into the city's new design—and the English word *square* was retained. Haussmann also modeled public parks—Parc Monceau and Parc

Montsouris, to name two—on the *jardin anglais* style. Paris was, in effect, remodeled as the new London.

It was claimed that Napoleon III's grand vision for Paris was a bourgeois project that displaced the poor to make room for the thriving bourgeoisie inhabiting the smart addresses along the city's elegant boulevards. It was also claimed that Napoleon III built wide avenues so troops and cannons could be rapidly deployed against the unruly Parisian mob. While this may have been partly true, there were other, more compelling, reasons to redesign Paris. One was public hygiene. In the mid-nineteenth century, the city's exploding population living in cramped conditions was exposed to disease. Victor Hugo's classic novel *Les Misérables* painted a graphic portrait of abject poverty and shocking disregard for social justice under Louis-Philippe. In the cholera outbreak of 1832, some 20,000 Parisians had perished out of a total population of 650,000. During the Second Empire, Haussmann installed sewers and water-supply systems to improve hygiene conditions. For all his character defects, Napoleon III was genuinely committed to improving the living conditions of the poor. While in exile, he had published populist tracts, including *Extinction du paupérisme*, influenced by the economic ideas of the Comte de Saint-Simon and the philosophical movement that took his name. *Saint-simonisme* embraced industrialization and economic progress as the best possible means to alleviate poverty. Napoleon III pursued a state-backed industrial policy driven by massive public investments in infrastructure such as railways, roads, canals, and ports. Some of France's biggest banks, such as the Crédit Lyonnais and Société Générale, were created during the Second Empire to finance these industrial projects. While they did indeed boost France's economic performance, the main beneficiaries were the Second Empire's capitalist bourgeoisie.

From his imperial rooms in the Palais des Tuileries, Napoleon III must have heard the loud sounds of digging and construction along the newly carved rue de Rivoli. In his palace boudoir, two paintings were prominently displayed on the walls. One was a portrait of his mother, Hortense de Beauharnais. The other was a portrait of Julius Caesar. Given his imperial ambitions, Napoleon III's admiration for Caesar was not surprising. He even published a book, *Histoire de Jules César,* to make that imperial connection explicit. His own authoritarian regime in France—like Bismarck's leadership style in Prussia—was frequently described as "Caesarism." His fascination with Julius Caesar led him inevitably to another mythic figure in France's ancient history: Caesar's Celtic enemy, Vercingetorix.

For most of pre-revolutionary French history, the ancient Gallic warlord who had marshalled his armies against Caesar was largely unknown in France. Vercingetorix was a pagan barbarian from the Roman period pre-dating France's royalist history as a Catholic nation. The country's official heroes, such as Clovis and Charlemagne, were sacred monarchs from the early Christian period. For nearly fifteen centuries, Vercingetorix had been largely cut out of France's historical narrative. The major role from that period had been attributed to Julius Caesar as the conqueror of Gaul. Voltaire had remarked, approvingly, that "uncivilized France needed to be subdued, and the Gauls were fortunate to be conquered by the Romans."[10] This was the prevalent historical view in France until the Revolution in 1789. Even after the revolution, Napoleon Bonaparte was a great admirer of Caesar, and modeled his own ambitions after those of the Roman dictator. It wasn't until after Napoleon's defeat in 1815 that a revival of Vercingetorix as a hero of the ancient Gallic people began to gain momentum. In the French popular imagination, Julius Caesar was increasingly cast in the role of foreign aggressor.[11]

In the 1860s, French archaeologists excavated the site of the Battle of Alesia where Caesar had defeated Vercingetorix in 52 BC. Napoleon III immediately took keen interest in these discoveries. His interest in archeology demonstrated his credentials as a modern ruler with a strong belief in scientific progress. He even paid for further excavations out of his own pocket. In 1867, he financed the erection of the massive statue of Vercingetorix that still stands today on the Alesia site with the inscription: "United Gaul, in a single nation, fired by a single spirit, can defy the world."

On the surface, Napoleon III's fascination with Vercingetorix was puzzling. Like his uncle Napoleon Bonaparte, he admired Julius Caesar, the victor at Alesia, model for a Caesarist regime. Vercingetorix was the defeated loser. On closer examination, however, the revived interest in the ancient Gallic warrior fit perfectly with the Second Empire narrative. Napoleon III grasped Vercingetorix's potential for founding a new national *mythos* in France. The legend of Vercingetorix connected the French with their ancient Gallic roots. He was also a more fitting symbol for Napoleon III's populist authoritarianism. In the past, France's national mythology had legitimized the Bourbon monarchy descended from the Franks. An old dichotomy in French society had long separated the ruling Franks and the peasant Gauls. Napoleon III was a populist emperor, not a sacred monarch. Vercingetorix gave French Gallic national identity a powerful new icon. For the first time in their history, the French regarded themselves as descendants of the Gauls. It was during the Second Empire, indeed, that the term *nos ancêtres les Gaulois* became a popular refrain throughout France.[12]

In the end, Napoleon III ended up like his Gallic hero Vercingetorix, crushed and humiliated by a foreign power.

For a French emperor whose slogan had initially been a promise of peace—"*L'Empire, c'est la paix*"—it was a tragic irony that he provoked a conflict with Prussia that ended in France's defeat and his own ruin. Empire wasn't peace; it was war. Napoleon III's obsession with emulating his uncle Napoleon Bonaparte was too strong. Throughout the Second Empire, France never ceased intruding in the affairs of other nations— Mexico, Algeria, Crimea, Italy.

Napoleon III's fatal mistake was declaring war on Prussia. He fell straight into Bismarck's trap.

***

In 1870, when Bismarck proposed Prince Leopold of Hohenzollern to occupy the empty throne of Spain, Napoleon III predictably saw the Prussian move as a provocation. He could not accept a German prince sitting on the Spanish throne.

The Spanish succession issue quickly poisoned relations between France and Prussia. Geopolitically, Napoleon III could not allow France to be surrounded on both sides by Prussian-allied German monarchs. Prussian control of the Spanish monarchy threatened the balance of powers system that had kept the peace in Europe for much of the century. The gathering strength of Prussia was a direct threat to France. It had been obvious for several years that Bismarck was empire-building by consolidating a united Germany under Prussian domination. France was an imperial power too. Napoleon III's Second Empire was nearly two decades old. The imperial pretentions of both France and Germany put the two nations on a collision course.

Against this backdrop of geopolitical tensions, the mood in France was turning bellicose. In Paris, the hawkish French foreign minister, Agénor de Gramont, was giving belligerent anti-Prussian speeches in parliament. The most influential newspapers in Paris, notably *Le Figaro* and *Le Gaulois*, were also calling for war. Newspapers in neutral European countries—including the *Times* in London—were reporting that French public opinion was enflamed against Prussia.[13]

Napoleon III felt compelled to act. He dispatched French diplomat Comte Vincent Benedetti to Prussia to make France's views on the Spanish succession issue known. This French chess move produced the desired effect. Prince Leopold of Hohenzollern got cold feet and withdrew his candidacy for the Spanish throne. Bismarck was infuriated.

But Napoleon III didn't stop there. He instructed Benedetti to present the Prussians with an ultimatum. They must guarantee that Prussia would never put forward another Hohenzollern candidate as king of Spain.

In early July 1870, Benedetti traveled to the small German spa town of Ems to meet the Prussian kaiser, Wilhelm I. Ems was at the height of its popularity as a resort town in the nineteenth century, attracting Europe's crowned heads every summer. One morning during their talks, Benedetti intercepted the kaiser on the Ems promenade. As the two men strolled together in the public gardens—Wilhelm I was seventy-three, Benedetti twenty years his junior—they engaged in an exchange that was more casual conversation than a formal diplomatic negotiation. Benedetti pushed France's ultimatum. The old kaiser took umbrage at the French ambassador's insistence but remained formally courteous. He refused to cede to the French demands.

Bismarck promptly received a telegram from Ems providing an account of the views exchanged between Napoleon III's emissary and the Prussian king. He must have been elated by what he read. The dispatch handed Bismarck a crucial weapon against the French. He could doctor the telegram, put his own spin on Prussia's position, and release it to the newspapers. When the fabricated story appeared in European papers, he would have his *casus belli* with France.

Bismarck knew exactly what he was doing. This was an era when newspapers played a powerful role in shaping public sentiments, especially when nations were on the verge of going to war. In the 1850s, the Crimean War—famous for Florence Nightingale and the Charge of the Light Brigade—had been the first major war to be photographed and covered by foreign newspaper correspondents. Horrific reports in the *Times* had turned British public opinion against the Crimean War, which pitted allies Britain and France against Russia. The *Times*'s reports from the front were so shocking that they contributed to the fall of Lord Aberdeen's government in 1855. For European rulers, the lesson of the Crimean War was that the press needed to be controlled to manipulate public opinion.

In both France and Prussia, the press operated in a political culture of servility and venality. Bismarck was masterful at manipulating the news. His power depended on personal loyalties, political cooperation of liberals, and an intricate network of press infiltration that spread and reinforced his ideas. The compliant German press—editorialists, cartoonists, photographers—had made him so famous by the 1860s that he often complained about not being able to step outdoors without being treated like a public event, often with spontaneous ovations. Leaving those frustrations aside, Bismarck understood that the press was key to achieving his political goals. He tightly controlled his own press bureau, which he used as an instrument of Prussian foreign policy, sometimes personally dictating articles word for word. [14]

With the Ems dispatch in hand, Bismarck took out his editing pencil. He sharpened the language to make it appear that Benedetti had been an ill-mannered interloper with the effrontery to importune the Prussian king on the Ems promenade. Bismarck's doctored narrative left the impression that Wilhelm I had coldly rebuffed the French ambassador's demands and, what's more, personally insulted Benedetti by "refusing to receive him again." Bismarck dispatched his carefully edited telegram for wide circulation in European newspapers. And to ensure maximum impact, he sent the same dispatch to all Prussian foreign embassies. [15]

On July 14, 1870, Bismarck's fabricated "Ems Dispatch," as it became known, appeared in the *North German Gazette* and other papers. The false news story was a stinging rebuke to France. To make matters worse, the French news agency Havas mistranslated the German in a way that made it seem that Kaiser Wilhelm I's rebuff of Benedetti had been even more insulting. By using the translated word *adjudant*, the French story gave the impression that the kaiser had treated Napoleon III's emissary with the contempt reserved for a low-ranking officer. When the story appeared in European newspapers, the reaction in France was outrage. And it appeared to have been sparked by the mistranslation of a single word.

Bismarck officially denied tampering with the dispatch. He insisted that he'd only made a few minor edits. But as he later confided in his memoirs, he knew the Ems Dispatch would sting the French, notorious for their "overweening and touchiness." The dispatch, he said, was like "a red rag upon the Gallic bull." [16]

In 1870, Napoleon III was no longer the dashing young Bonaparte who had been proclaimed emperor two decades previously. He was diminished both physically and politically. Suffering from a bladder infection and gallstone attacks, he was in a constant state of agonizing pain. Politically, he had encountered an embarrassing setback after his cousin, Prince Pierre Bonaparte, shot and killed a journalist named Victor Noir to settle a personal score. Pierre Bonaparte claimed self-defense in court, but Noir's death provoked a massive scandal, and 100,000 mourners attended his funeral. The republican movement against the Second Empire had been gathering momentum for several years. It was now at fever pitch. Napoleon III and his imperial regime were unpopular in France.

Bismarck's "red rag" timing was perfect. Napoleon III's honor was stung. The French emperor gave a mobilization order for the army to call its reserves. With war in the air, crowds in Paris were chanting down with the Prussian king and chancellor: "*À bas Guillaume! À bas Bismarck!*"

On July 19, 1870, France declared war on Prussia.

Despite his lack of military experience, Napoleon III insisted on personally taking command of the French armies. He believed that a French victory under his command would avenge his uncle Napoleon Bonaparte's defeat by the Prussians at Waterloo. Irrational motivations, driven by wounded honor and a lust for vengeance, were a factor on both sides of the Prussian-French hostilities. The backstory to the Franco-Prussian War of 1870 stretched back to the outset of the century, when Napoleon Bonaparte invaded and crushed the Prussians at Jena in 1806. The Queen of Prussia, Louise of Mecklenburg-Strelitz, personally appealed to Napoleon, even dropping to her knees before the victorious French emperor and begging for mercy on behalf of Prussia. Napoleon was unmoved. He dissolved the Holy Roman Empire, stripped Prussia of half its territory, and created three new vassal states, including the Kingdom of Westphalia ruled by the French emperor's brother Jerome Bonaparte. He also fixed a massive tribute to be levied on Prussia and reduced the size of its army. The defeat was a crushing humiliation for Queen Louise and her husband, Kaiser Frederick William III. Their ten-year-old son was also deeply traumatized by the French humiliation of his parents. That little boy, Wilhelm, became Kaiser Wilhelm I, the Prussian king who, as a seventy-three-old monarch, had met with Napoleon III's ambassador in Ems. Napoleon III, for his part, had been a seven-year-old boy when his uncle Napoleon Bonaparte was defeated by the British and Prussians at Waterloo. Both the Prussian king and French emperor had been scarred by early childhood memories of defeat and humiliation. Both had grown up during the Romantic period when, in parallel, the legend of Napoleon was soaring and German nationalism was rising like a turbulent crescendo in a Wagnerian opera. And now, in 1870, France and Prussia were at war again.

Blinded by injured pride, Napoleon III made a critical error of judgment. Not only did he overestimate his own military capacities, but he was also greatly mistaken about the strength of the French army. It was badly organized and poorly commanded. The French also underestimated the strength of the Prussian army, dismissing it as a bourgeois "army of lawyers and oculists." In fact, the Prussian military machine was well-trained and highly disciplined.[17] Bismarck, for his part, was elated when France declared war. Now he could rally all the German states against the French aggressors.

Bismarck had outmaneuvered Napoleon III diplomatically, and now he was ready for him on the battlefield. The Germans rolled through eastern France in only a few weeks. Following the Battle of Sedan in September 1870, Napoleon III surrendered. The French emperor was taken prisoner along with more than 100,000 French soldiers. The Second Empire collapsed immediately, overthrown by an uprising in Paris. A provisional government was installed while the Prussians advanced on the city. For Parisians, the worst was yet to come.

During the Prussian siege of Paris at the end of 1870, cannons inflicted devastating destruction on the French capital. The Prussians destroyed communications and transportation networks connecting Paris to the outside world. Inside the French capital, the population innovated by using balloons and carrier pigeons to send and receive news and information. Some London newspapers managed to get into the city via diplomatic post, but Bismarck moved to prevent this.[18]

As the siege ground on through the winter, Paris was hit with a smallpox outbreak that killed thousands. Hospitals were crowded with the sick suffering from typhoid fever, dysentery, and pneumonia. Parisians were also running out of food. Rich Parisians could rely on their personal finances to pay for exorbitantly priced food, but supplies were limited. The diarist Edmond de Goncourt wrote, "People are talking only of what they eat, what they can eat, and what there is to eat. Conversations consist of this and nothing more. . . . Hunger begins and famine is on the horizon."[19] Bismarck was said to have remarked, "Eight days without *café au lait* will suffice to break the Parisian bourgeoisie."[20] At the Paris Jockey Club, the menu featured "rat pie." Poor Parisians were harder hit. Malnourished children were suffering from vitamin A deficiency. Funeral processions with small coffins for infants were a common sight in the streets. Ordinary Parisians were so famished that many slaughtered dogs, cats, pigeons, and rats. It was said that domestic dogs and cats became suspicious of caresses in the streets, instinctively fearing they would end up in the cooking pot. The painter Edouard Manet despaired when his pet cat went missing.

Unlike fellow Impressionist artists Monet and Pissarro, who had fled to London to wait out the war, Manet stayed in Paris to join the National Guard and defend Paris against the Prussians. After sending his family to safety in southwestern France, he wrote letters dispatched by balloon to his mother, wife Suzanne, and pupil Eva Gonzalès. As the starvation set in, he wrote to Eva: "We are beginning to suffer here, horse meat is regarded as a delicacy, donkey is wildly expensive, there are dog, cat, and rat butcher shops." In the streets of Paris, the sight of horses being slaughtered and hacked to pieces for meat was common. It is estimated that some 65,000 horses were slaughtered, including two of Napoleon III's stallions given as a gift by the Russian czar. The animals in the Paris zoo were also slaughtered for food. The two elephants, Castor and Pollux, were hugely popular with Parisian crowds. No matter, Castor and Pollux were shot and eaten. Only the monkeys and lions, and the hippopotamus in the Jardin des Plantes, were spared slaughter.[21]

Following massive Prussian shelling to break the city's morale, Paris finally capitulated in late January 1871. In early March, some thirty thousand Prussian, Bavarian, and Saxon troops marched down the Champs-

Elysées in a victory parade. When they departed, the defeated French were left to fight a bloody civil war as leftist Commune rebels defended the city in an insurrection against French government forces. The massacres and summary executions were horrific. Much of the city was destroyed in the bloodshed. The Tuileries Palace—where French monarchs, including Napoleon III, had lived for centuries—was burned to the ground. Napoleon III's great cultural capital, freshly reconstructed during the previous two decades of the Second Empire, now lay in ruins.

The Franco-Prussian War was the most humiliating defeat France had ever suffered. The battlefield death toll on the French side was nearly 140,000. There were nearly fifty thousand civilian casualties during the siege of Paris as the city was pounded by Prussian canons. After the victorious Prussians retreated, some twenty thousand were massacred during the Paris Commune insurrection.

The French capital's destruction was even the subject of fake news reports outside of France. The German philosopher Friedrich Nietzsche, living in the Swiss town of Basel, where he was a professor of philology, read alarming accounts in German newspapers of the Louvre having been set ablaze and destroyed in the Paris uprisings. Nietzsche was so devastated by this news that he canceled his university lectures. "When I heard the news of the fires in Paris," he wrote, "I felt for several days annihilated and was overwhelmed by fears and doubts. The entire scholarly, scientific, philosophical and artistic existence seemed an absurdity if a single day could wipe out the most glorious works of art, even whole periods of art."[22] Fortunately, those news reports were false. The frenzied destruction of Paris's museums and palaces had not spread to the Louvre. While the Palais des Tuileries was burned to the ground, the Louvre itself was intact. Its great works of art were unmolested. It nonetheless took Parisians decades to recover from the psychological trauma of the catastrophe.

Bismarck, meanwhile, had finally realized his dream of German unification. As spoils of victory, Prussia annexed the French territories of Alsace and Lorraine and attached them to the newly proclaimed German Empire. Bismarck added insult to injury by having Wilhelm I crowned emperor of Germany in the Hall of Mirrors at Versailles Palace. The German Empire was born in the palace of the Sun King, Louis XIV.

Napoleon III, a prisoner of the Prussians, at first attempted to negotiate his return to power as a puppet emperor. Bismarck would have none of it. Disavowed by the French parliament, Napoleon III was forced into exile, once again in England, but this time for good. A sad and forlorn figure, he and his Spanish empress Eugénie retreated to a country house, Camden Place, southeast of London. His health deteriorated rapidly when his gallstone attacks returned. He underwent two painful operations but never recovered. He died in January 1873—only two years after his abdication—and was buried in the local Catholic Church. In 1888, his body was moved to St. Michael's Abbey in Farnborough. His remains have never been returned to France.

Napoleon III had a mythic name that took him far—all the way to defeat and humiliation. Otto von Bismarck toppled his Second Empire with a false news story in the newspapers.

France's Napoleonic saga was over. As Karl Marx put it, history had repeated itself—first as tragedy, second as farce.

But the battlefield slaughter between France and Germany was not over. The five-act cycle that began with Napoleon's victory over Germany in 1806, and continued with the battle of Waterloo followed by the Franco-Prussian War, still had two more acts before the final curtain.

For both France and Germany, the two world wars of the twentieth century, fueled by the same irrational passions of mutual hatred, would be far more devastating.

12

TO HELL WITH SPAIN

The Spanish-American War is arguably the most forgotten war in American history. Squeezed between the Civil War and the First World War, the brief flurry of belligerence between the United States and Spain in 1898 has been relegated to the status of historical footnote.

Yet a century ago, the Spanish-American War put the United States on the global map as an imperial power. It was the war that gave America overseas territories, and led to the annexation of Hawaii. It marked the beginning of the "American Century."

Like the Franco-Prussian War three decades earlier, the war between the United States and Spain was sparked by fake news. In this case, however, the false news wasn't a press release doctored by a cunning statesman. It was a relentless campaign of emotionally inflamed anti-Spanish reporting in American newspapers, especially William Randolph Hearst's *New York Journal* and Joseph Pulitzer's *New York World*. At the end of the nineteenth century, the rivalry between those two newspapers was so intense that it inspired a new term for sensationalized news: yellow journalism. The Spanish-American War also spawned one of the most tenacious media myths in American journalism. William Randolph Hearst's famous line, "You furnish the pictures, I'll furnish the war!" is still cited as historical fact. And yet it's entirely apocryphal, a fabricated tale transformed into historical truth.

The backdrop to this false legend was the brutal Spanish repression of an insurgency movement in colonial Cuba off the coast of Florida. American newspaper reports of terrible suffering in Cuba began turning the public mood in the United States against Spanish rule on the island. In the vanguard of this press campaign was Hearst's *New York Journal*. Hearst wanted the United States to declare war on Spain.

In late 1896, Hearst dispatched artist Frederic Remington to Cuba to draw sketches of the rebellion against Spain's colonial rule. When Remington arrived on the island, however, he found it remarkably calm. There was no uprising, no insurrection, no repression. No sign of any war of independence. Remington purportedly sent a telegram back to Hearst: "Everything is quiet. There is no trouble here. There will be no war. I wish to return."

According to legend, Hearst cabled Remington, telling his man in Cuba, "Please remain. You furnish the pictures, I'll furnish the war!"

The point of that familiar quote, which has the timeless appeal of being easily remembered, was to underscore the tremendous power of press moguls. Hearst wanted a war. And in the end, he got his war.

Hearst was a powerful figure who made many flamboyant statements during his long and colorful career. But he never dispatched a message claiming he would "furnish the war." The famous telegram has never turned up in any archives; its existence has never been documented. Its origin is easy to trace, however. The quote was made up in a slim 1901 memoir by a Canadian-born journalist, James Creelman, reputed for his bombast and exaggeration. He had been the *New York Herald*'s correspondent in Europe, where he'd shown remarkable skills at landing interviews with important figures, including Russian literary giant Leo Tolstoy and Pope Leo XIII. He later covered the Sino-Japanese War for Pulitzer's *World* before accepting a job offer from Hearst to cover the American war with Spain for the *Journal*.

Ironically, Creelman fabricated the "I'll furnish the war" quote to show his approval for Hearst. At first, nobody paid attention to the published anecdote. It didn't attract attention until 1906, when the *Times* of London correspondent in America came across Creelman's memoir, which was titled *On the Great Highway: The Wanderings and Adventures of a Special Correspondent.* Astonished, the *Times* journalist wrote an article asking, "Is the press of the United States going insane?"[1] It was this *Times* article that caught Hearst's attention. He personally responded to the *Times* with a resolute denial, stating categorically that he'd never written or said, "You furnish the pictures, I'll furnish the war!" Hearst dismissed the story as "ingeniously idiotic" and "frankly false."[2]

"This kind of clotted nonsense," added Hearst, "could only be generally circulated and generally believed in England, where newspapers claiming to be conservative and reliable are the most utterly untrustworthy of any on earth. In apology for these newspapers, it may be said that their untrustworthiness is not always due to intention, but more frequently to ignorance and prejudice."[3]

The story of Hearst's "I'll furnish the war!" outburst quickly fizzled and was forgotten. It was revived decades later, in the 1930s, when public opinion in America was turning against Hearst and media magnates like him.

The term *yellow journalism* has more factual basis. While still employed as a catchphrase for scandal-mongering tabloids, it refers specifically to the sensationalistic reporting style in Hearst's *Journal* and Joseph Pulitzer's *World*. The coining of the term was an accident that, in fact, had nothing to do with scandal and sensationalism. It started with a comic strip.

In the 1890s a popular Sunday cartoon called "Hogan's Alley" featured a famous character known as the Yellow Kid. A barefoot street urchin from the wrong side of the tracks, the Yellow Kid wore a yellow hand-me-down nightshirt, his head was shaved bald (probably due to lice infestation), and he spoke with coarse urban dialect. The character was recognizable to newspapers readers in late-nineteenth-century America, when thousands of poor children were abandoned to the squalid streets of major cities. The Yellow Kid was not unlike the boys that New Yorkers saw hawking penny newspapers on Manhattan street corners. As his creator, cartoonist Richard Outcault, later recalled: "The Yellow Kid was not an individual but a type. When I used to go about the slums on newspaper assignments, I would encounter him often, wandering out of doorways or sitting down on dirty doorsteps. I always loved the Kid. He had a sweet character and a sunny disposition, and was generous to a fault. Malice, envy, or selfishness were not traits of his, and he never lost his temper." At the outset, many Yellow Kid fans believed he was Chinese due to his appearance, until Outcault made his identity clear by giving him a name, Mickey Dugan.[4]

The "Hogan's Alley" comic strip was a phenomenal success in the New York newspaper market. It was the first comic strip character to become a merchandising icon. His snaggle-toothed grin was seen everywhere in New York—on billboards, buttons, cigarette packs, cracker tins, chocolate figures, cigars, matchbooks, chewing gum cards, even ladies' fans. The strip was so popular in Pulitzer's *New York World* that Hearst was constantly attempting to poach it away to the Sunday comics page in his *Journal*. The intense rivalry for the Yellow Kid initially branded the two papers as "yellow kid journalism"—later shortened to "yellow journalism."[5] Thus, a comic strip about a New York street urchin gave its name to a new style of modern journalism. The only connection between the two was that both were jaundiced.

The Pulitzer name today is associated with prestigious prizes in journalism and literature. In the nineteenth century, the name was intimately connected to the explosion of yellow journalism in America. Joseph Pulitzer was a Hungarian Jew who, arriving in America with his family as a teenager, served in the Civil War in an all-German-speaking cavalry unit in the Union Army. He didn't become an American citizen until after the war, in 1867, when he started working at a German-language newspaper in St. Louis. A decade later, he bought another paper in town, the *St. Louis Dispatch*, for the bargain price of $2,500. That purchase marked Pulitzer's debut as a newspaper publisher. By the early 1880s, he was the owner of the *New York World*, which he used in his progressive campaigns against city corruption. Pulitzer's motto, announced in his paper's inaugural edition, was "to fight all public evils" and "to expose all fraud and sham." The *World* had only 23,000 readers, but Pulitzer quickly built up the paper's readership with sensational, attention-grabbing stories. Editorial crusades became part of the Pulitzer formula. One was the *World*'s crusade on behalf of the Statue of Liberty, a gift from France that was languishing in crates while the U.S. Congress balked at the cost and finding a location for the statue remained unresolved. Pulitzer used the *World* to challenge New Yorkers to donate to the Statue of Liberty campaign, kicking off the fundraising drive with a $250 donation from the newspaper. The crusade was a massive success. On October 26, 1886, when the Statue of Liberty was finally inaugurated in New York Harbor, Pulitzer was among the dignitaries invited. He watched the ceremony from a boat in the harbor.[6]

Pulitzer's *World* also pioneered exposés—or what would later be known as investigative journalism—with stories about corruption and social issues. The legendary reporter Nellie Bly, who became famous for her first-person exposé about conditions in New York asylums, worked at Pulitzer's *World*. But the yellow press, like the penny papers a few decades earlier, also pandered to popular tastes with publicity stunts, wild exaggerations, fabricated stories, and outright lies. The *World*'s editorial credo was that "news" was defined as any violation of one of the Ten Commandments, preferably numbers five to nine—and especially if it involved celebrities.

Thus, the yellow press formula was a mixture of social crusades and shameless sensationalism. The difference was that, by the end of the century, American newspapers were no longer small operations shaped by editors with a flair for human-interest angles, gruesome crime stories, and the odd hoax. Newspapers were massive industrial operations fueled by robust advertising revenues. Their huge daily circulations gave their owners tremendous influence on public opinion. This was also the tradition in Britain, where press barons such as Lord Northcliffe, Lord Rothermere, and Lord Beaverbrook shaped public opinion with their mass-circulation papers—*Daily Mail*, *Daily Mirror*, *Evening Standard*, *Sunday Express*, and the *Times*. Newspapers magnates shaped "truth." The truth was what their newspapers said it was.

In New York, a measure of the press magnates' power was the height of their headquarters in "Newspaper Row" across from City Hall. The *New York Sun* building next door occupied the former headquarters of Tammany Hall where the Democratic machine controlled local and state politics through corrupt party bosses. In 1890, Pulitzer's sixteen-story, brick and terra cotta building at 99 Park Row was the tallest building in the world. William Randolph Hearst, a newcomer from San Francisco, muscled into the New York newspaper cabal by purchasing the decrepit *Journal* around the corner and poaching away top writers from the competition. When he finally pinched "Hogan's Alley" from Pulitzer's *World*, his circulation soared from 20,000 to 150,000. Hearst's *Journal* was still losing money, however, mainly because of the hefty sums paid to lure Pulitzer's staff. Hearst tried other stunts and gimmicks to boost publicity for his paper—everything from fireworks to parades. But nothing worked to stem the losses. He needed something much bigger, a great cause to rally public opinion around his newspaper. Something like a war.

The upheaval in Cuba arrived just in time. The Cuban independence movement was widely regarded in America as a just cause. Three centuries of slavery in Cuba had finally come to an end in 1886 following a ten-year rebellion. In the United States, a country that itself had thrown off colonial rule, sympathy for Cubans was a natural reflex. There were other, more calculated, considerations. The annexation of Cuba had been on the American political agenda for decades. The United States had declared Latin America as a key strategic zone of influence in 1823 with the "Monroe Doctrine," named for President James Monroe. That coincided with the "Manifest Destiny" period in America, when the country's westward and southward expansion was evoked as pre-ordained by providence. The obstacle to American expansion in the north was Britain. To the south, the obstacles were Mexico, which possessed Texas, and Spain, which controlled Florida, Cuba, and Puerto Rico. The United States acquired Florida from Spain in the 1820s, followed by Mexico's surrender of Texas two decades later.

Cuba remained under Spanish colonial control. In the United States, Southern Democrats with a keen eye on Cuba's plantation economy advocated annexing the island and turning it into another slave state. In 1848, President James Polk was prepared to pay Spain $100 million for Cuba, considerably more than the $7 million paid to Russia for Alaska. Following the Civil War, however, annexing Cuba as a slave state was off the political agenda. Instead, American business interests invested massively in Cuba's sugar industry. Most of Cuba's exports went to the United States.

Cuban rebels ignited a war for independence in 1868, but it ended after a decade with little resolved, though slavery was finally abolished in

1886. The war of independence from Spain was revived in 1895, this time fought as a guerilla war destroying sugar cane fields, railroads, and telegraph infrastructure. Many of the Cubans revolting against Spain were poor black laborers. Spain dispatched 200,000 troops to Cuba to put down the insurgency. Spanish troops forced Cuban peasants off their lands, burned their crops, and killed their livestock to cut off food supplies to rebels. The impact of the belligerence was devastating. With food and medical shortages, hunger and disease spread through the island. Cuba's population was 1.6 million when the war began in 1895. It was estimated that 240,000 Cubans died of disease and starvation.[7]

William Randolph Hearst, following these events from his *New York Journal* headquarters, finally found his newspaper's next big cause: the liberation of Cuba. Spanish aggression in Cuba needed to be stopped. Also, a splendid little war promised to boost newspaper sales.

There was one major obstacle to a war with Spain, however: President William McKinley. As the last American president to have fought in the Civil War, McKinley had witnessed firsthand the horrors of military conflict. He was also sensitive to the negative economic consequences of war with Spain. The United States was still emerging from a severe depression that had provoked social unrest, including protests, strikes, and riots. Powerful industrialists such as Andrew Carnegie, J. P. Morgan, and John D. Rockefeller were also anxious about the economic impact of war. Some American companies, on the other hand, had invested massively in Cuban sugar cane plantations that were being destroyed by rebels. Their business interests were aligned with the Spanish colonial power attempting to put down the violent rebellion. The political dilemma was between ending the Cuban crisis by force or through peaceful diplomacy. Most of the American business establishment was opposed to a direct U.S. military intervention in Cuba. President McKinley, too, favored peaceful negotiation.

In New York, meanwhile, Hearst was growing frustrated with McKinley's cautious approach. Hearst was prepared to send reporters to Cuba and fabricate a fake war until McKinley declared a real one. While Hearst never made the infamous "I'll furnish the war!" comment, it reflected the kind of febrile journalism that his papers practiced. Hearst called it "journalism of action."[8] Newspapers had a duty to fill the void of government inaction.

The Cuban crisis provided a glorious opportunity for Hearst to put his motto into practice. Before his reporters arrived in Cuba, his editors at the *Journal* offices in New York were making up stories and publishing them as dispatches filed from Cuba. One authentic scoop was a leaked private letter by the Spanish ambassador to the United States, Enrique Dupuy de Lôme, in which he disparaged President McKinley as indecisive and weak. Hearst published the letter in the *Journal* under the headline: "The Worst Insult to the United States in Its History." The leaked letter was a hugely embarrassing incident. President McKinley demanded that the Spanish government apologize. Dupuy de Lôme resigned, but it was too late. The damage was done.

When Hearst's team of reporters finally arrived on the island, they bribed their way into rebel army camps with medicines and kegs of rum to get front-line stories. Hearst upped the ante by sending a ceremonial sword with a diamond-studded ivory handle as a gift to rebel commander General Máximo Gómez. The bribe worked. Hearst's paper got great scoops, most based on unverified information, that portrayed the Spanish overlords as monsters guilty of gruesome acts of torture, pillaging, murder, and mass slaughter. Most of these tales were gleaned from third-hand accounts and false testimonies given by Cuban revolutionaries who, like Máximo Gómez, had an interest in spreading lies.

Fueled by these stories on the ground in Cuba, Hearst's paper portrayed Spain as a dark villain raping a distressed damsel in need of a white knight to rescue her. The white knight, of course, was the United States. A real Cuban damsel in distress was found in the figure of Evangelina Cisneros, a teenage daughter of a Cuban rebel. She had taken part in the uprisings and, following her arrest, was languishing in prison. Hearst saw a sensational story in the girl's rescue. He needed a white knight in the flesh, however. Hearst hand-picked Karl Decker, a handsome, six-foot-tall son of a Confederate cavalry colonel. His selection for the role was akin to the casting of the lead role in a Hollywood motion picture.

Decker was dispatched to Cuba to rescue the girl from prison and bring her back to the United States. Hearst's *Journal*, reporting the story it had orchestrated, recounted Decker's swashbuckling rescue of Evangelina by scaling the prison wall and sawing through the bars of her jail cell. She was spirited out of Cuba and smuggled disguised in men's clothing onto the steamer *Seneca*. When the heroic couple returned triumphantly to America, the *Journal* drummed up jubilant celebrations with a self-congratulatory headline: "EVANGELINA CISNEROS RESCUED BY THE JOURNAL." The public rejoicing in New York was crowned with a massive reception for Evangelina in Madison Square Garden. She also traveled to Washington, DC, to meet President McKinley before embarking on a fundraising tour for Cuban independence.

The truth of the girl's escape was much less dramatic than the accounts trumpeted on Hearst's front page. There were suspicions that Decker had simply bribed the prison guards to set her free. Also, after Evangelina arrived in America, she did not fall in love with her white knight. She ended up marrying a dentist nearly three decades her senior and vanishing into obscurity. No matter, Hearst had his thrilling exclusive splashed on the front page of the *Journal*.

By 1898, New York's yellow press had so successfully turned American public opinion against Spain that it had become a hair-trigger issue in Congress. Hearst also had an influential ally in the capital: Theodore Roosevelt, the hard-charging assistant secretary of the Navy. Hearst and Roosevelt were on the same page on the Cuban crisis. Roosevelt advocated war with Spain as a pretext to assert American power in the region. His boss in the White House, William McKinley, remained cautious, however. McKinley continued to believe that Spain, a tired and weak empire, was willing to bring reforms to Cuba and had no desire to draw the United States into a war. He even considered offering Spain $300 million for the island.

In early 1898, violent riots erupted in Cuba. Now the McKinley administration had a pretext to act. It sent a Navy warship, the USS *Maine*, to Havana to take a measure of the situation and, if necessary, to protect American interests. The decision to send a battleship to Cuba was later described as "waving a match in an oil well." The metaphor was fitting. In February 1898, the *Maine*, anchored in the Havana harbor, blew up and sank. Some 260 American seamen aboard, most of them sleeping, were killed in the blast.

The death toll on the *Maine* shocked American public opinion. While the exact cause of the blast was not immediately known, the yellow press cranked up inflammatory front-page headlines blaming Spain. Pulitzer's *World* claimed the *Maine* had been sunk by a "bomb or torpedo."[9] Hearst's *Journal*—already attacking President McKinley's caution on Cuba—ran the following banner headline: "THE DESTRUCTION OF THE WAR SHIP MAINE WAS THE WORK OF AN ENEMY."

There was no evidence to support these claims. In fact, the explosion was likely caused internally by a coal-bunker fire near the *Maine*'s ammunition magazine. But inconvenient facts were disregarded by the New York papers. Some rival newspapers denounced the yellow press for their bellicose sensationalism. "Nothing so disgraceful as the behavior of these two newspapers has ever been known in the history of journalism," wrote E. L. Godkin, the Irish-born editor-in-chief of the *New York Evening Post* who had covered the Crimean War for the London *Daily News*.[10] Godkin denounced the Hearst and Pulitzer papers' "gross misrepresentation of the facts, deliberate intervention of tales calculated to excite the public, and wanton recklessness in construction of headlines." Godkin's admonitions had no effect. The *World* and *Journal* kept inflaming public opinion with anti-Spanish diatribes and cartoons. The battle cry that went up in pubs and taverns across America was "*Remember the* Maine! *To Hell with*

Spain!" Tin Pan Alley also stoked public ire with popular songs such as "My Sweetheart Went Down with the *Maine*."

Following on Karl Decker's starring role in the rescue of Evangelina Cisneros, the yellow press found another leading-man hero for the next phase of the Cuban narrative: private William Anthony. A broad-shouldered, six-foot-tall graduate of the West Point military academy, Anthony had been on watch on the *Maine* and sounded the alarm after the explosion. Celebrated as "Brave Bill" in the New York papers, he was quickly promoted to sergeant for his quick-thinking heroism. Anthony was so famous upon his return home that he was receiving fan mail from throngs of female admirers. One was Adela Maude Blancet in Philadelphia. After their courtship and engagement, their nuptials made newspaper headlines. The couple settled down and had a son, but Anthony had trouble finding work. Also, his old habit of hitting the bottle caught up with him. In November 1899, less than two years after his heroic burst of fame, police found him in Central Park in a life-threatening state of intoxication. He had apparently taken cocaine too. Rushed to Presbyterian Hospital, Anthony refused to identify himself. He died in hospital. Police found a suicide note in his pocket along with a photo of his wife. One sentence read: "I am discouraged and disconsolate, it is better to end it all." Nobody came to claim his body.[11] William "Brave Bill" Anthony was the *Maine*'s last casualty.

In the aftershock of the Maine explosion, President McKinley was under tremendous pressure to declare war. He nonetheless continued to negotiate for Cuban independence, hoping for a diplomatic solution. The European side to the crisis was another important factor. Most of Europe's great powers supported Spain. The German kaiser, while diplomatically neutral, took the Spanish side in the dispute if only because Spain's queen regent was a Habsburg from the Austrian royal family. France was also sympathetic to the Spanish position because major French banks owned Spanish bonds and did not want to see the country in bankruptcy after a war. The only European power that sympathized with the United States was Britain, a colonial rival with Spain, which the UK government regarded as a declining power.

When Spain rejected President McKinley's proposals to end the crisis, he turned the matter over to Congress. This was good news for Teddy Roosevelt. As assistant secretary of the Navy, he had been lobbying Congress to declare war. Roosevelt's pro-war stance was undoubtedly based on principle and patriotism. He also knew, however, that a military conflict with Spain would boost U.S. naval expenditures and enhance his own public profile.

By this point, it was impossible for Congress to ignore American public opinion inflamed against Spain. Anti-Spanish rallies broke out in towns throughout America. A Spanish general in Cuba, Valeriano Weyler, was burned in effigy in the streets. Spanish-flag toilet paper was sold and used in American homes. In the American press, the pro-war sentiment spread beyond the yellow newspapers. *Cosmopolitan* magazine declared: "The time is right for the interference of the United States in the affairs of Cuba."[12]

In April 1898, Congress voted a joint resolution in favor of Cuban independence from Spain. The vote—311 to 6 in the House of Representatives, 42 to 35 in the Senate—authorized President McKinley to use military force against Spain. A week later, McKinley issued an ultimatum to Spain to withdraw from Cuba. Spain refused and declared war on the United States.

On April 25, McKinley announced that the United States was at war with Spain. The declaration of war expanded hostility beyond Cuba to Puerto Rico and other Spanish overseas territories including the Philippines.

New York's yellow press had been clamoring for war. Now they got it. The splendid little war was on.

***

Once war was declared, the American yellow press pulled out all the stops on anti-Spanish propaganda. They portrayed war with Spain as a morality tale of good versus evil.

The war's villains, of course, were the island's Spanish oppressors, depicted in the American papers as vicious monsters who had imprisoned innocent girls such as Evangelina Cisneros. The heroes were courageous Americans soldiers like Karl Decker and William "Brave Bill" Anthony. The war's greatest American hero was Teddy Roosevelt. Though assistant secretary of the Navy, Roosevelt quickly switched roles and took command of the First Volunteer Cavalry of a thousand men. They were known as the "Rough Riders," a term borrowed from the legendary Buffalo Bill, named for the huge number of buffalo he massacred on the American frontier. Roosevelt's Rough Riders regiment played a crucial role in the American victory in Cuba, notably in the Battle of San Juan, where the brigade charged up Kettle Hill to take the Spanish positions. Roosevelt emerged from the war as a virile national hero, the embodiment of an ideal of fearless American masculinity.

The fact that the enemy Spanish were Catholics added another dimension to the propaganda campaign in the American press. Anti-Catholic bigotry was virulent in the United States throughout the nineteenth century. American newspapers, magazines, and books stoked the flames of anti-Catholic hatred. In 1835, Rebecca Reed's book *Six Months in a*

Convent recounted a tale of young girls forced into Roman Catholicism in an Ursuline convent near Boston. Even before the book was published, rumors convinced locals that women were being held in the convent against their will. The local papers, virulently anti-Catholic, had already been publishing false stories about Protestant children vanishing into the nunnery in nearby Charlestown. The well-known Boston preacher Lyman Beecher—father of Harriet Beecher Stowe—fueled anti-Catholic attitudes in his sermons and a nativist tract titled "A Plea for the West." In 1834, an angry Protestant mob burned down the convent. When Reed's book came out, it quickly became an anti-Catholic blockbuster, selling 200,000 copies within a month. A year later, the *American Protestant Vindicator* gave massive publicity to a similar book, *The Awful Disclosures of Maria Monk*, a memoir about a woman who had escaped from the iniquities of a Catholic nunnery in Montreal. Like Rebecca Reed's gothic exposé of the turpitudes inside a nunnery, Maria Monk's book was a huge bestseller, selling twenty thousand copies within a few weeks and some 300,000 by 1860. The book was so successful, in fact, that it was followed by a sequel, *Further Disclosures of Maria Monk*. Reed's *Six Months in a Convent* and Monk's *Awful Disclosures* had one thing in common: they were both untrue. Both stories were fabrications. Rebecca Reed had never been a nun; she had entered the convent as a student postulant but left after only a few months. Maria Monk, too, was a fraud whose story was invented (and possibly written by two anti-Catholic ministers). Both books, written in the Gothic style, exploited the anti-Catholic "escaped nun" theme that easily found a receptive audience in early nineteenth-century America.[13]

Catholics in antebellum America suffered the same discrimination as Jews and Quakers. Immigrant Irish Catholics, stereotyped as thieving drunkards, were reviled and excluded as they settled in American cities. According to a familiar legend, job adverts regularly added "No Irish need apply," though there is evidence that so-called NINA signs were a cliché imported from England where, in the 1820s, handwritten signs in wealthy London insisted on non-Irish maids. That is not to say that Irish Catholics did not suffer discrimination in America. In Philadelphia, newspaper stories reported false rumors about Irish Catholic immigrants removing Bibles from public schools. In 1844, local Protestants held rallies calling on fellow American citizens to "throw off the bloody hand of the Pope." The rallies provoked riots in which more than twenty people were killed, dozens injured, and Catholic churches destroyed. Thousands of militiamen were called in to quell violent attacks on Catholic homes and churches.[14]

America's xenophobic culture was, in part, the result of the country's territorial expansion in the early nineteenth century following the Louisiana Purchase and the annexation of Texas. These new territories attracted massive inflows of foreign immigrants to settle the frontier. Many were Catholics, especially from Ireland following the potato famine in the 1840s. The huge surge of immigration, while needed to populate new lands, provoked the antipathy of native-born Americans loyal to the Protestant heritage of America stretching back to the Pilgrims. These tensions gave rise to a "nativist" movement hostile to Catholics and Jews.[15] Secret nativist organizations, boasting names such as Order of the Star-Spangled Banner, sprang up and mobilized electoral support for anti-Catholic politicians.

One of the leading voices of the nativist movement was Samuel Morse, more famous as the inventor of the telegraph. Virulently anti-Catholic and pro-slavery, Morse believed the Catholic Church had a secret plan to take over America. In 1834, he penned "A Foreign Conspiracy against the Liberties of the United States" in the anti-Catholic *New York Observer* under the pseudonym Brutus. His message: America needed to be protected from the pope.[16] Two years later, Morse ran for mayor of New York on the nativist ticket. Because nativist organizations were secret, its members were instructed, if asked about their activities, to say, "I know nothing." When newspaper editor Horace Greeley of the *New York Tribune* dismissed them as "know nothings," nativists seized on that label to found the Know Nothing Party advocating limited rights for immigrants. The Know Nothings, re-baptized as the American Party, briefly became a powerful political brand in American politics, electing seven governors, controlling eight state legislatures including Massachusetts, and establishing a strong presence in Congress. In the 1856 presidential election, former president Millard Fillmore ran under their banner—but came in third with 21.5 percent of the popular vote (James Buchanan was elected president). At the end of the century, the nativist movement was still going strong through organizations such as the American Protective Association, a secret fraternal organization with links to masonic lodges with a strong anti-Catholic agenda. In the tense period before the Spanish-American War broke out, Catholic newspapers felt compelled to come out strongly in favor of the war to prove that they were true Americans.[17]

Teddy Roosevelt, born into a New York patrician family, personally had little time for the bigoted ravings of American nativists. But he wasn't above exploiting their sentiments for political purposes. In his speeches, he talked about the necessity to promote the "American race stock" and opposed unregulated immigration as "race suicide." He was against "hyphenated" Americans, insisting that immigrants to the United States must assimilate and show loyalty to no other nation or flag. In his four-volume *The Winning of the West*, published over the decade preceding the Spanish-American War, Roosevelt portrayed the Spanish as a deceitful and treacherous race who used "every species of bribery and corrupt diplomacy" to turn the native Indians against American settlers on the frontier. His books expressed a worldview that contrasted civilized races and "savages." Roosevelt was an advocate of a "strenuous life" philosophy whose values of toil, effort, labor, and strife defined the quintessential American. He believed in the principle of Manifest Destiny as moral justification for the domination of the white race. As Roosevelt put it himself: "It is of incalculable importance that America, Australia, and Siberia should pass out of the hands of their red, black, and yellow aboriginal owners, and become the heritage of the dominant world races." At the end of the nineteenth century, such statements were uncontroversial.[18]

The war against Spain was a tremendous career opportunity for Roosevelt to act out his self-image as a virile warrior. He seized on the conflict with exceptional self-promotional skills, taking his own press agents to Cuba to maximize his publicity. Reporters covering the war were embedded with troops. Roosevelt, a politically savvy New Yorker, knew many of them personally and could count on their favorable accounts of his exploits. His leading the Rough Riders up San Juan Hill was immortalized in a painting by Frederic Remington, the same artist sent to Cuba by William Randolph Hearst. Roosevelt personally commissioned that painting. He also grasped that the new medium of motion pictures could be used to publicize his exploits in Cuba. He made sure that Thomas Edison's camera crews documented his battlefield heroism. That the films were faked did not matter. Edison's movie crews did shoot films of Roosevelt and his cavalry "riding like demons, yelling and firing revolvers" while engaging in skirmishes with the enemy in Cuba. The films were staged, however, shot in the Orange Mountains of New Jersey. The enemy Spaniards were played by African Americans. Other film footage of Roosevelt and his Rough Riders charging into battle was shot on Long Island, New York.[19]

Faked film footage of wars was the accepted standard in the early days of motion pictures. French film pioneer Georges Méliès, famous for his classic *A Trip to the Moon* made in 1902, also produced "reconstructed newsreels" about historic events and wars. When commissioned to make a film about the Greco-Turkish War in 1897, Méliès didn't bother traveling to the battlefields in Greece. He used his studio in Paris to shoot fake footage showing the Turks committing atrocities in Crete. From the same studio in Paris, Méliès shot films about the Spanish-American War, including one showing the sinking of the *Maine*. He also made reconstructed newsreels about France's "Dreyfus Affair" and the coronation of King Edward VII. Early American filmmakers were using the same techniques to fake newsreels. When the Spanish-American War broke out, an

American Vitagraph crew traveled from New York to Cuba, but quickly realized it was difficult to get good footage with bulky camera equipment. When they learned of an American naval battle victory in the Philippines, they opted to emulate Georges Méliès's trick of producing reenactments. These fake Spanish-American War films played in theaters in New York and other American cities. Packed houses cheered fake footage showing American soldiers climbing up a mast, hauling down the Spanish flag, and replacing it with the Stars and Stripes. Another newsreel, *Shooting of Captured Insurgents,* showed Spanish soldiers lining up four Cuban rebels and executing them by firing squad. A hint that the film was fake was provided by the Cuban actors who, when struck by the bullets, dramatically threw up their arms and fell backward. If further proof were needed, another staged newsreel, *Cuban Ambush,* was shot against the very same backdrop where the firing squad execution occurred. Remarkably, nearly everyone who watched these fake newsreels—including government officials on both sides of the war—regarded them as authentic. [20]

In the final analysis, the Spanish-American War was more sordid than splendid. It was also brief. The outcome could have been predicted. America was a robust young republic aggressively expanding its territories. In 1850, the population of the United States had been only 23 million; by the end of the century it had more than tripled to 76 million. Spain, with a population of only 18 million in 1898, was a weak colonial power ruling over a collapsing empire. Only a few months into the war, Spain sued for peace. Some three thousand American lives had been lost (most of them from malaria and typhoid and other infectious diseases in the Philippines). Spain lost sixteen thousand men, most to disease. The total death toll on the island of Cuba was roughly 400,000, more than half from disease and starvation.

A peace treaty, signed in Paris in 1898, triggered the collapse of the Spanish Empire and the birth of American imperialism. Spain gave up its rights to Cuba and lost all its overseas territories. The United States took control of Puerto Rico, Guam, and paid Spain $20 million for the Philippines. President McKinley seized on the treaty to annex Hawaii. The United States didn't annex Cuba outright, but the island fell into the American sphere of influence as a protectorate, and the United States built a naval base on Cuba's Guantanamo Bay.

Teddy Roosevelt emerged from the war as the great victor. When McKinley won re-election in 1900, war hero Roosevelt was his running mate on the Republican ticket. The following year, a national tragedy propelled Roosevelt even higher. McKinley was assassinated by an anarchist in Buffalo while attending the Pan-American Exposition celebrating America's industrial progress. Radical anarchism was a well-organized revolutionary movement in the late nineteenth century. When McKinley had been negotiating with Spain's prime minister, Antonio Cánovas, to find a peaceful end to the Cuban crisis, Cánovas was assassinated by an Italian anarchist named Michele Angiolillo. Angiolillo, who shot Cánovas dead at a spa in the Basque country, was avenging the Spanish government's imprisonment of hundreds of anarchists. Angiolillo was arrested and executed by garrote. Three years later, President McKinley himself was dead, shot by an anarchist in upstate New York. The assassin, a Polish American steelworker named Leon Czolgosz, had been inspired by the famous anarchist Emma Goldman. In Buffalo, he shot McKinley twice in the abdomen while the president was greeting and shaking hands with members of the public at a reception. Czolgosz was arrested and executed by electric chair several weeks later. Some blamed William Randolph Hearst for McKinley's assassination. Despite the United States' victory over Spain, Hearst's *Journal* continued its attacks on McKinley. One of Hearst's columnists had called for the same bullet that had just assassinated the governor of Kentucky to be used on President McKinley. A few months before McKinley's visit to Buffalo, the *Journal* published an editorial stating: "If bad institutions and bad men can be got rid of only by killing, then the killing must be done."[21]

When President McKinley succumbed to his bullet wounds, Vice President Theodore Roosevelt was sworn in as twenty-sixth president of the United States. His period in the White House marked the dawn of the American Century. The United States was now a global power. Faithful to his image as a virile national icon, Teddy Roosevelt walked lightly but carried a big stick.

America's problems in Cuba were just beginning, however. They would end six decades later with another Cuban revolution—and the assassination of another American president, John F. Kennedy.

Part V

Supermen, Supermyths, Superpowers

13

THE GUN THAT KILLED THE HUN

Edith Cavell, daughter of a Church of England vicar, is still remembered as a heroic martyr of the Great War.

For an entire generation following the First World War, the brave English nurse's execution by a German firing squad was a horrific act of barbarity that signaled the passing of civilization from light to darkness. When the "war to end all wars" ended in 1918, it seemed that an entire moral order had collapsed.

Edith Cavell was also a tragic symbol in a new era of propaganda and lies. More than a century later, we still don't know the whole truth about her life and death.

Cavell was born in 1865 near Norwich, the eldest daughter of Reverend Frederick Cavell. She was educated at boarding schools and raised with a strong sense of duty commanded by her Christian faith. As a young woman, she worked as a governess in Brussels before returning to England to care for her ailing father. That experience gave her a passion for nursing that soon became a career. She took a job at Fever Hospital in Tooting, followed by stints in east-end London infirmaries. She also tended to the sick in their homes, administering morphine to relieve pain. [1]

In 1907, Cavell returned to Brussels to take a job as matron of a new nursing school called L'École Belge d'Infirmières Diplômées. Photographs of Cavell from this period, when she was in her forties, show a handsome woman with strong, angular features and intelligent eyes. She obviously had formidable leadership abilities. Soon after arriving in Belgium, she launched a nursing journal, L'Infirmière, and was training nurses at three separate hospitals.

When war broke out in August 1914, Cavell found herself on the front lines in Belgium. By November, the Germans had invaded the country and occupied Brussels under a military governor, General von Sauberzweig. The British Expeditionary Force of 150,000 troops was forced to retreat hastily. Hundreds of seriously wounded soldiers were left stranded behind enemy lines. New military techniques in the First World War—mustard gas, machine guns, armored tanks—inflicted horrific injuries. British soldiers who had escaped injury hid in the countryside to avoid capture by the Germans. Some who surrendered pretended to be deaf mutes to conceal their nationality. The lucky ones ended up at Edith Cavell's clinic operating under the auspices of the Red Cross. She also took in a stray mongrel, named Jack, that one day arrived on her doorstep.

While tending to wounded soldiers, Cavell used her good offices to facilitate their escape from Belgium via the neutral Netherlands. Soon her hospital was serving as a way station in an underground network, spiriting British, French, and Belgian soldiers out of occupied territory. Cavell was eventually outed, however, betrayed by a Frenchman spying for the German occupiers. The Germans suspected the English nurse of working on behalf of British intelligence. She defended her actions on moral grounds: "I cannot stop while there are lives to be saved."[2] The Germans who arrested her were unmoved. They charged her with treason under German military law. She was placed in solitary confinement at St. Gilles Prison near Brussels. A few weeks later, she was found guilty and sentenced to death by firing squad.

Cavell's death sentence sparked indignation and outrage in the international press. The execution of a woman, even in time of war, was morally repugnant in the early twentieth century. The United States, still not engaged in the war, used diplomatic channels in Germany in a last-ditch attempt to spare her life. But these pleas for clemency fell on deaf German ears. From her prison cell, Cavell declared: "Standing as I do in view of God and eternity, I realize that patriotism is not enough. I must have no hatred or bitterness toward anyone."[3]

The night before her execution, Cavell read from the devotional book, *The Imitation of Christ*, in which she marked the following passage: "Vanity it is, to wish to live long, and to be careless to live well."

At dawn on the morning of October 12, 1915, Cavell was led from her cell. She said prayers with a British chaplain, Reverend Stirling Gahan, who later reported that her last words to him were, "We shall meet again." Moments later, she was executed by a sixteen-man firing squad of German soldiers.

If the German army hoped Cavell's execution would serve as an example to others assisting enemy soldiers, it backfired catastrophically. The German volleys at her execution immediately echoed around the world. Cavell's death was front-page news for weeks, provoking outrage and indignation. The international press portrayed Edith Cavell as a heroic Florence Nightingale, a victim of German barbarity, a martyr for the Allied cause. The *Manchester Guardian,* which published a story under the headline, "Merciless Execution of Nurse Cavell," denounced the "callousness" and "brutality" of the Germans for carrying out a death sentence on a woman.[4] The *New York Herald* wrote that the English nurse's execution would cause "a wave of horror to sweep over the world."[5] Horrifying details of her death reinforced the image of Germans as monstrous "Huns." Newspapers reported that, on the morning of her execution, Cavell had fainted before the firing squad. After her execution, the German commanding officer stepped over to her collapsed body and finished her off with a single bullet in the ear. A Dutch newspaper added that the coup de grâce was delivered only because most of the soldiers in the firing squad, taking pity on the poor woman, had aimed wide, and she was only wounded. The German foreign ministry denied reports that Cavell had been shot in the head when collapsed on the ground, insisting that the execution was conducted properly. The Germans made no apologies, however. The German undersecretary of foreign affairs, Alfred Zimmermann, stated: "We must travel the hard road of duty."[6]

Whatever the legalities of Edith Cavell's trial and execution, the Germans were losing the propaganda war. The international outrage over Cavell's death came on the heels of other newspaper stories recounting German atrocities. There were reports of German soldiers raping Belgian women, cutting off the breasts of nuns, thrusting bayonets into children, hacking off the heads of babies in front of their parents.[7] The portrayal of Germans as a barbaric race of "Huns" exploited xenophobic stereotypes that were rife in the decades before the war. When war broke out in 1914, it was only forty-five years since Bismarck had forged a united German nation in his "blood and iron" military campaigns. Germany's triumphant nationalism had come at a great cost to the French, who suffered the most crushing military defeat in their history. Memory of these humiliations was still festering in the years before the First World War. National hatreds were at a fever pitch.

The image of Germans as "Huns" came, ironically, from Kaiser Wilhelm II. Historically, the Huns were not German at all. They were a nomadic Central Asian race that, under their leader Attila, invaded the declining Roman Empire in the fifth century. The Germanic races of that period—Ostrogoths, Visigoths, Vandals—fought and defeated the Huns. Many centuries later, in July 1900, Wilhelm II was addressing his German troops before they set sail for China to quell the anti-colonial Boxer Rebellion. In extemporized remarks, the kaiser commanded his soldiers to show the Chinese no mercy. "Pardon will not be given, prisoners will not be taken," he declared. "Whoever falls into your hands will fall to your sword." The kaiser added, using grandiose language with racist terms that have been diversely translated: "Just as one thousand years ago the Huns under Attila made a name for themselves for their ferocity which tradition still recalls, so shall the name of Germany become known in China for one thousand years. No Chinaman will ever again dare to look a German in the eye with even a squint."[8] The word *squint* was also translated as "slit-eyed" and "cross-eyed." The kaiser's infamous "yellow peril" speech evoked the Huns as ancient enemies to be emulated against China. By the outbreak of the First World War, the notion of "Hun" and "German" had merged.[9]

The English poet Rudyard Kipling was largely responsible for spreading the German-as-Hun conflation. A year before the kaiser's infamous speech, Kipling published an anti-German poem, "The Rowers," railing against "the shameless Hun" as "the breed that have wronged us most."[10] Anti-Germany xenophobia was rife in Britain at the turn of the century, especially in magazines such as *John Bull*. In 1900, T. W. Offin published *How the Germans Took London*, describing how the "Teutons" had "year by year, crept into our employ."[11] Over the next decade, journalist William Le Queux published stories in the same invasion fantasy genre, notably *The Invasion of 1910*, which was serialized in the *Daily Mail* in 1906 and became a huge bestseller. Three years later in 1909, Le Queux published *Spies of the Kaiser: Plotting the Downfall of England*. At the outbreak of war in 1914, Kipling published his famous poem, "For All We Have and Are" to rally the British spirit against the German aggressors. One stanza of that poem reads: "For all we have and are; for all our children's fate; stand up and take the war. The Hun is at the gate!"[12] Thanks to Kipling's cultural influence in Edwardian England, the word *Hun* entered usage to designate and stigmatize Germans as barbarians. In British wartime propaganda after 1914, Germans were routinely portrayed as spiked-helmeted Hun-beasts. Anti-German posters used slogans such as "Keep Out the Hun!" and "Halt the Hun!" The German Hun became the destructive beast that needed to be slain. Kipling personally amplified the "man against beast" theme in his wartime speeches. At one public event, Kipling stated that "there are only two divisions in the world today, human beings and Germans.[13]

The First World War was the first "total war" in history. In the past, warfare had been confined to military confrontations between armies combatting on fixed territories. In 1914, the scope of war was broadened to society as a whole. Total war required total mobilization—not only of soldiers to engage the enemy on the battlefield but also of public opinion to hate the enemy in their hearts. Beyond the spirited patriotism of writers such as Rudyard Kipling, states deployed their own resources in the propaganda war. A half century after Bismarck doctored a news dispatch to trigger a war with France, state propaganda techniques were more sophisticated than falsified telegrams. Modern states could now put massive bureaucratic resources behind propaganda campaigns. The goal was twofold: to stir patriotic emotions and to recruit soldiers for the war effort. The truth of the message was irrelevant. The propagation of falsehoods was necessary to boost morale, demonize the enemy, and summon men to the colors.

From the outset of war in 1914, the British government asserted direct control over news and information through a secret agency called the War Propaganda Bureau. Operating from Wellington House in London, it was headed by Liberal politician Charles Masterman, known for his solid connections with figures such as Winston Churchill and David Lloyd George.[14] Masterman's propaganda unit was said to be so secret—it used the National Insurance Department as a front—that even Members of Parliament did not know it existed. Masterman, who had literary ambitions, took a highbrow approach to propaganda. He held secret meetings with noted writers of the day, including Arthur Conan Doyle, John Masefield, Arnold Bennett, Ford Madox Ford, Thomas Hardy, G. K. Chesterton, John Galsworthy, H. G. Wells, and, of course, Rudyard Kipling. These esteemed men of letters put their narrative skills to work for the war effort, writing propaganda pamphlets printed by the finest publishers of the day, including Oxford University Press, Methuen, Macmillan, and Hodder & Stoughton.

When David Lloyd George became prime minister in 1916, he took a much more pragmatic approach. Unlike other British politicians of his day, Lloyd George was a strong advocate of propaganda. Once in Downing Street, the first thing he did was enlist the support of powerful British press barons. On the day George V asked him to form a government, Lloyd George went straight from his meeting with the king at Buckingham Palace to a private dinner with two newspaper magnates: George Riddell, owner of *News of the World,* and *Daily Telegraph* proprietor Lord Burnham. He offered other press barons—Lord Beaverbrook (proprietor of the *Daily Express*) and Lord Northcliffe (owner of the *Times* and *Daily Mail*)—key roles in the government's propaganda bureaucracy. The British government also took control of the Reuters news agency, headed by Sir Roderick Jones, and passed a Defence of the Realm Act that put limits on freedom of the press. Dissident and pacifist newspapers, such as the suffragette paper *Britannia*, were prosecuted or suppressed. The *Labour Leader,* read by working-class Britons who voted for the Labour Party, was too popular to censor. Lloyd George took a more diplomatic approach to blunt criticism. He invited Labour leader Arthur Henderson to join his government as a minister.[15] With these legal and media powers behind the war effort, the British government exercised total control over all news and information. Most British newspapers—especially the *Times*, *Daily Mail*, and *Daily Express*—served as mouthpieces for official propaganda. Wellington House had two dozen reporters on its payroll working as "special correspondents" for several leading newspapers. One of the most talented among them, Major Hugh Pollard, worked in Lloyd George's propaganda department while writing for the *Daily Express*. There was no distinction between journalism and propaganda.

Wellington House also produced films to boost public morale, notably *Battle of the Somme* released in 1916. The *Times* reported that cinema audiences were "thrilled to have the realities of war brought so vividly before them."[16] British propaganda films also traveled to America to build support for the war in the United States. In May 1916, the film *How Britain Prepared*, billed as "a motion picture lesson for America," played for a four-week run at the Lyceum Theatre in New York. It was also screened in Washington, DC, at an event sponsored by the National Press Club. The audience of top figures from Washington politics included the U.S. secretary of war, Newton Baker, and thirty-four-year-old Franklin Delano Roosevelt, who was assistant secretary of the Navy during the war. Roosevelt wrote afterward that he greatly enjoyed the film, which was shown at the Belasco Theater for a week. The British propaganda film provoked the ire of German American lobbies, however, and four German members of the National Press Club threatened to resign.[17]

Call-to-arms posters plastered in the streets throughout Britain were also used as part of the British propaganda strategy. The most famous was the "Lord Kitchener Wants You" poster, featuring the mustachioed face of the British war secretary, pointing his finger above the words "Join Your Country's Army! God Save the King!" Other slogans used emotional blackmail to encourage men to sign up. One famous poster depicted two children asking their father: "Daddy, what did YOU do in the Great War?" Others exploited anti-German emotions with "Halt the Hun!" messages. One poster showed a heroic Saint George slaying a German dragon. Cartoons depicted Kaiser Wilhelm II as a satanic figure. Even children were targeted in propaganda campaigns. Wellington House subsidized the publication of children's books, such as Henry Newbolt's *Tales of the Great War*, which portrayed Germans as a "ferocious wicked people." Old nursery rhymes such as "This Is the House That Jack Built" were transformed for propaganda purposes to demonize the Germans as "Huns":

> This is the house that Jack built.
> This is the bomb

> that fell on the house that Jack built.
> This is the Hun
> who dropped the bomb
> that fell on the house that Jack built.
> This is the gun that killed the Hun
> who dropped the bomb
> that fell on the house that Jack built.

Wellington House also launched an "atrocity propaganda" campaign to shock public opinion with horror stories about German barbarity.[18] Following the German invasion of Belgium in 1915, the British government published a *Report on German Outrages* that documented horrific atrocities committed by German soldiers. The report, translated into thirty languages and distributed worldwide, claimed Germans had murdered six thousand Belgians and destroyed twenty-five thousand homes. The German invasion of the small neutral country was dubbed the "Rape of Belgium." The cataloguing of these horrors triggered a flurry of front-page headlines in the British, American, and other foreign newspapers. One story in Lord Northcliffe's *Times* claimed that Germans had crucified a Canadian army officer after the Battle of Ypres by impaling him on a barn with their bayonets. The infamous "Corpse Factory" story was atrocity propaganda at its most gruesome. The *Times* published a story, "The Germans and Their Dead," which reported that the German army had built a *Kadaververwertungsanstalt,* or "corpse utilization factory." In the corpse factory, the Germans boiled the bodies of their own soldiers so they could be used for fat in the manufacture of nitroglycerine and candles for the war effort. The *Daily Mail*'s story, "The Huns' Corpse Factory," claimed that revelations of German body factories had caused "universal horror."[19] The *Daily Express* story "The Kaiser's Ghouls" accused the Germans of "cannibalism" and "systematic desecration of their dead." [20] American and French papers also picked up these stories portraying Germans as diabolical monsters.

Most of these stories about German atrocities were false. While some barbarities had doubtless occurred, there was no evidence of babies being impaled. The "corpse factory" story was deliberate false news, counterpropaganda concocted by the chief of British Army Intelligence, Brigadier General John Charteris. After learning that the Germans were incinerating dead horses, he swapped *soldiers* for *horses* to create the impression that the hated Huns were monstrous beasts. Charteris's main goal in fabricating the "corpse factory" story was to incite China to join the war on the Allied side, which explains why the story was planted in Chinese newspapers. The German government protested that "corpse factory" stories were false, dismissing them as "loathsome and ridiculous."[21] No matter, the Chinese declared war on Germany a few months later.

British propaganda also took a highbrow turn against Germany philosophy. Virulent Teutonic aggression was blamed on the dangerous ideas of Friedrich Nietzsche. The link between Nietzsche's thinking and German nationalism would be widely known two decades later during the Nazi period. Hitler greatly admired Nietzsche and took inspiration from his works, especially *Will to Power*. Less known is that Nietzsche's ideas were associated with German nationalism even before the Nazi era. During the First World War, when Hitler was a low-ranking corporal in the kaiser's army, British propagandists claimed Nietzsche's thinking infused the German ethos with megalomania, the gospel of power, and a cult of master morality. By attacking Nietzsche's ideas, British propagandists advanced the argument that virulent aggression was intrinsic to the German spirit. This provided justification for war because it demonstrated that the Germans were a dangerous race who must be stopped.

A month after war was declared in 1914, *Times* published an article, "The Great Illusion," blaming the "unconscious followers of Nietzsche" for the war. The *Times* wrote: "The peculiarity of Germany is that this notion of war as an end in itself has taken hold of the intelligence of the country, that her idealists now are not peace-loving but war-loving, her national conscience has undergone the change of moral values which Nietzsche desired."[22] The same theme was picked up by a London bookshop, whose window display in Piccadilly featured editions of the philosopher's works with a sign: "The Euro-Nietzschean War. Read the Devil in order to fight him the better."[23]

The drama critic William Archer, who worked for the British Propaganda Bureau, believed the war was not being fought against a German nation, but against a German philosophy. In an essay published in 1915 titled "Fighting a Philosophy," Archer wrote:

> There is not a move of modern Prussian state craft, not an action of the German army since the outbreak of the war, that could not be justified by scores of texts from the Nietzschean scriptures. In many cases, no doubt, it would also be possible to find texts of an opposite tendency; for few philosophical rhapsodists have been more fertile than Nietzsche in self-contradictions. But the dominant ideas of his philosophy, the ideas most frequently and emphatically expressed—the ideas, in a word, that get home to the mind of nine readers out of ten—are precisely those which might be water-marked on the protocol paper of German diplomacy and embroidered on the banners of German militarism. This is certainly no mere coincidence.

He concluded with the warning: "In a very real sense it is the philosophy of Nietzsche that we are fighting."[24]

The anti-Nietzsche campaign, whatever its merits as propaganda, was based on a distorted reading of his ideas. For one thing, Nietzsche abhorred German nationalism and advocated a pan-European civilization. He was fiercely critical of Bismarck's blood-and-iron nationalism, and would have been horrified by the aggressive German spirit that provoked two world wars in the decades after his death.[25]

In Britain, the martyred English nurse Edith Cavell inevitably became an iconic figure in British propaganda. Not only did the British government seize on Cavell's death as shocking evidence of German barbarity, but also her image was used on army recruitment posters to boost enlistments. One featured a photo of Cavell with the words "Murdered by the Huns." Postcards showed a German officer wearing a spiked helmet, pointing his revolver at Cavell's dead body splayed on the ground, a red cross on her white uniform, under the words: "Miss Edith Cavell murdered Oct. 12, 1915—Remember!" Sherlock Holmes creator Arthur Conan Doyle wrote, "Everybody must feel disgusted at the barbarous actions of the German soldiers in murdering this great and glorious specimen of womanhood."[26] In the two months following Cavell's execution, British army enlistments doubled.

Edith Cavell's legend took on mythic dimensions after the war. She was posthumously decorated by foreign governments, including France, which awarded her the Légion d'Honneur. Cavell was celebrated as a martyr of the war just as much by the French as by the British. In France, the humiliation of their Franco-Prussian War defeat was still stinging. After her execution, French newspapers joined the chorus of outrage at the hated German "Boches" (from the pejorative, *alboche*, joining *Allemand* for German and *caboche* for head). Edith Cavell's name was so famous in France that mothers named their female newborns Edith after the martyred English nurse. One was a baby girl born in Paris only two months after Cavell's execution. Her name was Edith Piaf.

In 1919, Edith Cavell's body was exhumed from her grave in Belgium to be returned home to England. When her coffin was opened, witnesses were astonished that Cavell's body was remarkably intact. They described her as wearing a calm expression, serene as a saint. Her gold collar-stud and a hat-pin made of tortoiseshell were preserved like sacred relics. When the body was escorted by boat to London, huge crowds were amassed in the streets for the funeral procession. Film footage of the London event still exists—it's authentic, not a "reconstructed newsreel"—showing a solemn ritual befitting a deceased monarch or fallen national hero. The oak coffin, draped in the Union Jack, made its way on a horse-drawn gun carriage through the London streets lined with mourners. King George V attended the memorial service at Westminster Abbey.[27]

The following year, a large memorial statue of Edith Cavell was erected near London's Trafalgar Square. Her dog Jack, meanwhile, had been adopted by Belgian princess Marie de Croÿ, who like Cavell had smuggled Allied soldiers out of her country. Jack lived several more years, dying in 1923. But the dog's fame was only beginning. Jack's body was stuffed for posterity. Today, Edith Cavell's dog is still on display at the Imperial War Museum in London.

In the century following her execution, biographical treatment of Edith Cavell was largely hagiography, portraying her as Britain's "Joan of Arc." Eleven streets in London were named after Cavell, and Oxford baptized both an Edith Road and a Cavell Road. There was a new Edith Cavell Hospital in Peterborough and an Edith Cavell School of Nursing in Bedfordshire. In Canada, a mountain was named after Edith Cavell.

On the centenary of her death, however, new revelations questioned Cavell's image as a heroic martyr. Perhaps she had been a spy after all. Stella Rimington, ex-head of the British MI5 spy agency, produced documents that gave reason to believe Edith Cavell was indeed part of an organized network engaged in espionage in Belgium. Cavell knew that the soldiers she was helping escape from Belgium were carrying information, often hidden in shoes or sewn into clothes.

"We may never know how much Edith Cavell knew of the espionage carried out by her network," said Rimington, whose startling revelations were part of a BBC Radio Four documentary, *Secrets and Spies: The Untold Story of Edith Cavell.* "She was known to use secret messages, and we know that key members of her network were in touch with Allied intelligence agencies. Her main objective was to get hidden Allied soldiers back to Britain but, contrary to the common perception of her, we have uncovered clear evidence that her organization was involved in sending back secret intelligence to the Allies."[28]

These claims, while intriguing, have done little to damage Cavell's reputation as a martyred British icon. To mark the one hundredth anniversary of her death in 2015, Cavell's final resting place at Norwich Cathedral was restored, while the British government gave grants of nearly £100,000 to explore stories about her life. The same year, a commemorative £5 coin was issued in her honor.

Edith Cavell remains a mystery. It would appear that, like all mythic heroes, she was all too human.

***

In the United States, President Woodrow Wilson showed no interest in Europe's war.

Only a week after the assassination of Archduke Franz Ferdinand in Sarajevo in late June 1914, Wilson didn't even mention that shattering event in a speech. When war broke out two months later, he said, "The United States has never attempted to interfere in European affairs."

Americans were in no mood for a war. In 1915, the most popular song in the United States was "I Didn't Raise My Boy to Be a Soldier." That song, publicized as an "anti-war hit," captured the isolationist spirit in America.

German Americans, loyal to their ancestral homeland, were especially against the war. German immigration to states such as Pennsylvania had been so massive in the early nineteenth century that, in 1850, German was the second most-spoken language in the United States. Abraham Lincoln had his own German-speaking secretary for correspondences with German American voters. During the Civil War, the Union army counted eighteen German-speaking regiments. The press magnate Joseph Pulitzer, a Jewish immigrant from Hungary, fought in one of them as a young man. In 1910, four years before the First World War, some 2.3 million Americans had been born in Germany, and 10 million claimed German ancestry.

In 1916, Wilson won re-election to the White House on the slogan "He Kept Us Out of War." Wilson was the peace candidate. "Governments have gone to war with one another," he declared. "Peoples, so far as I can remember, have not, and this is a government of the people, and this people is not going to choose war."[29] It was the message many Americans wanted to hear.

Wilson wasn't lacking a strong pretext to declare war on Germany. In May 1915, a German U-boat's sinking of the ocean liner *Lusitania* had outraged American public opinion. More than 1,100 passengers, including 128 Americans, had perished in the Atlantic. Anti-German emotions in America were stoked by false news stories claiming that schoolchildren in Germany were given a holiday to celebrate the *Lusitania*'s sinking. Later that year, American newspapers were filled with heart-wrenching reports about the brave English nurse Edith Cavell's execution by a German army firing squad.

Another factor in favor of war was military. In early 1917, British intelligence deciphered an encrypted German foreign office memo—the so-called Zimmermann Telegram—revealing a planned German military alliance with Mexico, a country bordering the United States. The incentive for Mexico to declare war on the United States was the recovery of the lost territories of Texas, New Mexico, and Arizona.

Yet even when Wilson was receiving these alarming intelligence reports, he remained cautious. He cut off diplomatic relations with Germany, but in an address to a joint session of Congress in February 1917, he was careful to placate German Americans.

"We do not desire any hostile conflict with the Imperial German Government," declared President Wilson in his speech to Congress. "We are the sincere friends of the German people and earnestly desire to remain at peace with the government which speaks for them. We shall not believe they are hostile to us unless and until we are obliged to believe it."[30]

Theodore Roosevelt, the former president who had occupied the White House a decade earlier, wrote in a letter: "I don't believe Wilson will go to war unless Germany literally kicks him into it."[31]

The German kick came sooner than Roosevelt expected. In March, only weeks after President Wilson's speech to Congress, German U-boats sank more merchant American ships with loss of life. Wilson suddenly changed his mind about the war. The peace president was now a war president.

On April 2, 1917, Woodrow Wilson was back in Congress, this time to seek a declaration of war against Germany. Four days later, Congress voted for war.

Wilson was not a politician from the *realpolitik* school. He was a moral idealist. If the United States was going to get involved in Europe's war, he believed America must set an example for the world. American resolve needed to be justified with high purpose. Guided by that principle, Wilson struck on a slogan, perhaps his most famous: "The world must be made safe for democracy." Wilson's moral idealism was sincere. It was even quasi-religious. He believed America had a moral obligation to spread what he called the "Gospel of Americanism."

The American gospel needed a compelling narrative. It was one thing to mobilize American troops; an even greater challenge was to mobilize American public opinion to support the war effort. This wasn't easy given the pervasive anti-war mood in the country.

The first signs of change were noticeable in American music halls. Songs like "I Didn't Raise My Boy to Be a Soldier" quickly disappeared, replaced by more patriotic tunes such as "America Needs You" and "You're in the Army Now." Other popular pro-war songs were imported from Britain, such as "Pack Up Your Troubles in Your Old Kit Bag" and "Keep the Home Fires Burning." The mood in America was shifting from pacifism to belligerence.

President Wilson needed more than Americans whistling a new tune. He needed a well-organized government propaganda machine. Within two weeks of declaring war on Germany, Wilson set up a propaganda unit called the Committee for Public Information. The unit was informally known as the "Creel Committee" because it was run by George Creel, a journalist who was close to Wilson and had played a key role in his presidential re-election campaign in 1916. Wilson also reached out to the Hollywood studios to join the propaganda blitzkrieg against Germany. Fortuitously, the motion picture industry, still in its infancy, was producing globally popular films starring Charlie Chaplin and Douglas Fairbanks. Wilson quickly grasped that Hollywood films could be used as the storytelling factory for his Gospel of Americanism. The studios set up a structure called the National Association of the Motion Picture Industry, or NAMPI, whose board members included movie moguls Samuel Goldwyn and Adolph Zukor and director D. W. Griffith.

"The film has come to rank as the very highest medium for the dissemination of public intelligence," Wilson wrote in a letter to NAMPI president William Brady. "And since it speaks a universal language, it lends itself importantly to the presentation of America's plans and purposes."[32]

Some Hollywood directors were already producing pro-war films for the British propaganda effort. D. W. Griffith had made *Hearts of the World*—starring Lillian Gish and Noël Coward—about young lovers in a French village torn apart by the war. British prime minister David Lloyd George even played himself in that film. Now Hollywood started cranking out even more pro-war movies. One film was about the martyred English nurse Edith Cavell. Another film, *The Star Bangled Banner,* was released as part of the U.S. Army's recruitment drive. The studios also enlisted their biggest stars in pro-war publicity campaigns. Charlie Chaplin, Douglas Fairbanks, and Mary Pickford addressed massive crowds in Manhattan to sell Liberty war bonds. In a short Chaplin film to sell war bonds, audiences cheered as lovable Charlie hit a figure of the kaiser over the head with a mallet inscribed with the words "Liberty Bonds." Douglas Fairbanks sent President Wilson a movie projector for private screenings in the White House. One film Wilson watched at a special White House screening was D. W. Griffith's historical epic *Birth of a Nation,* which romanticized the Ku Klux Klan and denigrated blacks in post–Civil War America. The film was based on a novel, *The Clansman*, by Thomas Dixon Jr. Woodrow Wilson and Dixon were good friends.

Wilson's handpicked propaganda chief, George Creel, took on his assignment not as a government bureaucrat, but as an advertising executive selling a product.[33] Creel, a well-connected journalist who had once worked for William Randolph Hearst's *New York Journal*, drew on his extensive connections to recruit battalions of marketing executives, journalists, filmmakers, and playwrights to promote the war effort via newsprint, posters, radio, and movies. Creel's campaigns had three main goals: to turn American public opinion in favor of the war and drive army recruitment, to discredit anti-war activists, and to portray the enemy Germans as beasts. Creel's poster campaign, like propaganda images in Britain, was explicitly anti-German. A typical poster slogan was "Stop the Hun!" A familiar sight at Independence Day parades throughout America was a man dressed as Kaiser Wilhelm with a noose around his neck.[34]

Creel's most powerful weapon was motion pictures. Such was his influence that Creel was, in effect, a Hollywood studio boss during the war. He had the power, through the U.S. War Trade Board, to determine which Hollywood movies were fit for export to foreign countries. Strict standards ensured that films spread positive narratives about America. Hollywood faithfully churned out a raft of anti-German movies—*The Hun Within*, *The Claws of the Hun*, *The Prussian Cur*—that played on stereotypes of the detested German Huns. Kaiser Wilhelm II was portrayed as a demonic figure in a spiked helmet in films such as *To Hell with The Kaiser* and *The Kaiser: The Beast of Berlin*.

The campaign of Germanophobia proved tremendously effective, as anti-German emotions spread like wildfire in American towns. Some towns with German names—especially if the name was "Germantown"— rebaptized themselves to remove the stigma. Street names such as Kaiser, Bismarck, and Berlin were changed. Dachshund dogs, used by cartoonists as the symbol for the German threat, were called "liberty pups." Sauerkraut was renamed "liberty cabbage." And German measles became "liberty measles." Many schools stopped teaching the German language.[35]

Anti-German propaganda was reinforced by statutory measures that limited freedom of speech. In 1917, Congress passed the Espionage Act, which made it illegal to hinder U.S. Army recruitment efforts, fly enemy flags, or hinder the government's war efforts in any way. A year later, the Sedition Act made it illegal to "willfully utter, print, write, or publish any disloyal, profane, scurrilous, or abusive language about the form of government of the United States, or the Constitution of the United States, or the military or naval forces of the United States." These new laws were vigorously enforced. German aliens in the United States were arrested and deported. In some towns, German Americans were harassed in their daily lives, some beaten, even tarred and feathered. Many changed their German-sounding names to seem more American. For example, the surname Schmidt became "Smith," Müller became "Miller," and Drumpf became "Trump." Some German-Americans, to avoid stigma and ostracism, claimed they were Dutch, Swiss, or Scandinavian. A tragic case of anti-German violence was the lynching of Robert Paul Prager in Collinsville, Illinois. Born in Germany in 1888, Prager immigrated to the United States in 1905 and was working as a coal miner when war broke out in 1914. After a dispute over his rejection from the union, other workers accused Prager of loyalty to his native Germany. A Collinsville mob of some two hundred men harassed and beat him and forced him to kiss the

American flag. He was dragged to a local bluff and lynched. All eleven men indicted for his hanging were acquitted.[36]

The most famous case of wartime anti-German persecution was Karl Muck, the German-born conductor of the Boston Symphony Orchestra. One of the most renowned maestros of his day, Muck had a prestigious international reputation for conducting Wagner's operas. He had been music director of the Boston Symphony for several years when war broke out in 1914. At the outset of the war, it was a practice for American symphonies to strike up "The Star-Spangled Banner" as a patriotic finale. At a concert in Providence, Rhode Island, the Boston Symphony did not play the future national anthem with Muck at the podium, though there was no evidence that he had refused to play "The Star-Spangled Banner." The local newspaper nonetheless attacked him as a German, and soon it became a full-blown scandal. The newspaper magnate Joseph Pulitzer, the symphony's chief patron, refused to attend concerts. Mrs. William Jay, a wealthy and influential socialite and board member of the New York Philharmonic, actively campaigned to have Muck driven out of the American classical musical scene. She had been instrumental in getting German works banned from the Metropolitan Opera stage. Former U.S. president Theodore Roosevelt added fuel to the fire by telling the newspapers that any conductor who refused to play the national anthem should be deported. At other symphonies, conductors and musicians of German origin were pressured to retire or take a hiatus during the war. Some American orchestras banned all German music from their programs. The controversy swirling around Muck became so tense that protestors shouted "Kill Muck!" at his concerts. A concert at New York's Carnegie Hall required a heavy police guard.[37]

In March 1918, U.S. federal agents finally arrested Muck as an enemy alien and ransacked his house. Police found a cache of love letters between the married, fifty-eight-year-old Muck and a teenaged Boston heiress, Rosamond Young, who was an up-and-coming mezzo-soprano. The *Boston Post* splashed the contents of the letters in a series of articles that portrayed Muck as a sexually depraved Hun who had deflowered a virtuous American girl. Many unpleasant revelations were made about Muck, including that his cufflinks featured the kaiser's coat-of-arms. His lawyer attempted to argue that Muck was in fact Swiss, which was technically true, but this was of no importance to U.S. authorities, for he had been born in Germany. Even worse, it was discovered that Muck was carrying an honorary German passport personally signed by the kaiser. Muck was interned at Fort Oglethorpe, Georgia, for more than a year as an enemy alien before being deported back to Germany. He later took up a conducting position at Bayreuth, where he was close to the Wagner family. In 1933, when he conducted a concert in Leipzig on the fiftieth anniversary

of Wagner's death, Adolf Hitler was in the audience. On Muck's eightieth birthday in 1939, Hitler sent him a Plaque of the German Eagle with
the personal inscription "To the great conductor."[38]

Given the powerful influence of newspapers at the outset of the century, one of George Creel's biggest propaganda divisions was news. A U.S.
government-run wire service cranked out press releases and spread
American "news" stories that were either exaggerations or fabricated. A
Creel news report claimed, falsely, that American planes were on their
way to France. Another reported that ships escorting American troops had
sunk German submarines. Most American journalists played along with
the official propaganda line, if only to preserve their high-level contacts.
The *New York Times*, a rare voice of skepticism, dubbed Creel's news
unit the "Committee on Public Misinformation." Newspapers that criticized the war effort were targeted by Creel in poster campaigns intended
to damage their reputations. One Creel press pillory announced an "Official Condemnation of the *New York Tribune*." The poster accused the
Tribune of giving "aid and comfort to the enemy." Its message, signed by
George Creel, stated that the *Tribune* "has been busy for some time with a
campaign to make the War Department ridiculous in the eyes of the
American people, and to that end the *Tribune* has not hesitated to publish
any story that came to hand, whether it was true or not."[39] At the top of
the poster, instructions were given: "Please post in a conspicuous place."

Ironically, Creel's news unit attracted some of the most progressive
journalists in America. Among them were idealistic "muckrakers," such
as Ida Tarbell and S. S. McClure, famous for their crusading investigative
journalism exposing social injustices and excessive corporate power in
the first decade of the century. George Creel had been a muckraking
journalist himself. The U.S. government's department of misinformation
was staffed not by soulless bureaucrats in a Kafka-esque dystopia, but by
liberal-minded, progressive journalists on the left. They regarded propaganda and censorship as justifiable to combat German militarism and,
faithful to President Wilson's slogan, to keep the world safe for democracy. The crusading journalistic voices that once had spoken truth to power
were now propagandists on the state payroll.[40]

Creel also recruited seventy-five thousand volunteers to deliver pro-
war speeches in churches, synagogues, movie theaters, labor union halls,
masonic lodges—anywhere they could find an audience. They were
called "Four-Minute Men" because they were instructed to speak for only
four minutes, keeping their message snappy and compelling. The Four-
Minute Men were the pioneers of the sound bite. The topics they covered
ranged from patriotic morale-boosting to more pragmatic subjects such as
selling war bonds. In less than two years, Four-Minute Men delivered
some 7.5 million speeches to an estimated 314 million people. George

Creel noted that the Four-Minute Men program had the "sweep of a prairie fire."

George Creel's propaganda unit folded soon after the Allied victory in 1918, but its impact was enduring. The success of wartime propaganda attracted widespread post-war interest in the techniques employed. Some warned of the grave dangers of state-mobilized misinformation. British politician Arthur Ponsonby—whose father Sir Henry Ponsonby had been Queen Victoria's private secretary—published a widely ready book titled *Falsehood in War-Time.* "There must have been more deliberate lying in the world from 1914 to 1918 than in any other period of the world's history," wrote Ponsonby, who catalogued all the falsehoods that had circulated during the war, including many by eminent writers and clergy working for the British government. "Falsehood is a recognized and extremely useful weapon in warfare, and every country uses it quite deliberately to deceive its own people, to attract neutrals, and to mislead the enemy," he observed. "The ignorant and innocent masses in each country are unaware at the time that they are being misled, and when it is all over only here and there are the falsehoods discovered and exposed. As it is all past history and the desired effect has been produced by the stories and statements no one troubles to investigate the facts and establish the truth."[41]

In America, a prominent critic of wartime propaganda was Harold Lasswell, a law professor at Yale University and a pioneer of the social science known as behavioralism. Lasswell published a seminal work in 1927, *Propaganda Technique in the World War,* in which he argued that modern communications had profoundly transformed how democracies conducted war. "Not bombs nor bread," he wrote, "but words, pictures, songs, parades, and many similar devices are the typical means of making propaganda."[42] The well-known journalist Walter Lippmann, founder of the *New Republic,* echoed these warnings. Lippmann had been a supporter of Woodrow Wilson and accepted a presidential appointment as a wartime propagandist. Once on the inside, however, Lippmann was alarmed by the lies and falsehoods fabricated by fellow journalists in George Creel's propaganda machine. Lippmann eventually quit the Propaganda Board.[43]

After the war, Lippmann exacted revenge on Creel with blistering attacks on propaganda, notably in his 1922 book, *Public Opinion,* which is credited, ironically, with inspiring the PR profession. Lippmann took a pessimistic view of people's capacity to distinguish between truth and lies, especially in modern society where issues were complex and difficult for ordinary citizens to understand. This was dangerous for democracy, he argued, because modern societies demand that citizens be informed on important issues of the day. News consumers, he observed, were a "bewildered herd" easily manipulated. The public was "slow to be aroused and quickly diverted . . . and is interested only when events have been melodramatized as a conflict." Journalists, he argued, had abandoned truth for propaganda in the arrogant belief that "edification is more important than veracity.[44]

"In so far as those who purvey the news make of their own beliefs a higher law than truth," wrote Lippmann, "they are attacking the foundations of our constitutional system. There can be no higher law in journalism than to tell the truth and shame the devil."[45]

Other members of Woodrow Wilson's wartime propaganda machine took a more business-like attitude toward new mass communication techniques. Among them was Vienna-born Edward Bernays, the nephew of Sigmund Freud. Only an infant when his Jewish family moved to New York, Bernays graduated from Cornell and worked as a publicist for famous performers including Russian ballet star Vaslav Nijinsky and opera tenor Enrico Caruso. During the First World War, his knack for publicity landed him a job working for Creel's propaganda unit, where he gained valuable experience using media as tools of mass persuasion. Bernays didn't share Lippmann's anxiety about propaganda's threat to democracy. He saw mass media manipulation as an exciting business opportunity.

"It was, of course, the astounding success of propaganda during the war that opened the eyes of the intelligent few in all departments of life to the possibilities of regimenting the public mind," wrote Bernays in his book, *Propaganda*. "It was only natural, after the war ended, that intelligent persons should ask themselves whether it was not possible to apply a similar technique to the problems of peace."[46]

Bernays's definition of *peace* was conveniently all-encompassing. For him, peace meant business as usual. He was principally interested in using propaganda techniques to manipulate consumers. He explicitly outlined this in another book, *Crystallizing Public Opinion*, published five years after the war. In that work, Bernays helped himself liberally to Walter Lippmann's insights to formulate his own theories about human behavior (the title of his book was a marketing ploy borrowing two words from Lippmann's bestselling book, *Public Opinion*, published a year earlier). On some points Bernays agreed with Lippmann. Bernays argued that people are motivated by primal emotions and urges whose origins they don't understand. These impulses lead to a "herd mentality" and mob behavior during times of political unrest. The same impulses influence how people make political and consumer choices. He argued that public opinion is shaped by educated elites. If you can influence these elites, he believed, you can shape public opinion. Walter Lippmann, for his part, advocated for professionally trained elites—journalists—to inform public opinion with facts. Bernays believed that these elites, too, were subject to manipulation.

The political propaganda tricks learned during the war were still being used in the immediate post-war years. The most infamous example of post-war political disinformation was the "Zinoviev letter" scandal in Britain during the general election of 1924. At the outset of that year, British voters elected the country's first socialist government. Less than a decade after the Bolshevik revolution in Russia, the British intelligence agency MI6 was anxious about a socialist government in the United Kingdom. The Labour prime minister, Ramsay MacDonald, recognized the Soviet Union diplomatically and dropped prosecution of a communist newspaperman for a pacifist article in the *Workers' Weekly*. When MacDonald's minority government fell several months later, fresh elections were called. During the election campaign, MI6 leaked a letter purportedly written by Grigory Zinoviev, head of the Communist International, to the British Communist Party calling for its members to enlist "sympathetic forces" inside the Labour Party to support an Anglo-Soviet treaty and to incite "agitation-propaganda" in the British armed forces. Published by the conservative *Daily Mail* only four days before the election, the leaked letter produced its intended effect. The headline on the *Daily Mail* scoop was: "Civil War Plot by Socialists' Masters." British public opinion abruptly polarized, pushing Liberal support to the Conservatives. Labour was crushed at the polls. The Conservatives took power under Stanley Baldwin, who immediately announced that he would not ratify the trade treaty with the Soviet Union. Baldwin's government maintained that the Zinoviev letter had been genuine, but it was later discovered to have been forged by the UK secret service. For anyone looking for a historical precedent to fake news manipulation of national elections, they need look no further than the British general election of 1924.[47]

The greatest casualty of the First World War had been truth. The shock of nearly 20 million dead was so horrific that the Great War was called, naively, the "war to end all wars." In the aftermath, an entire generation capitulated to despair and resignation. Their once-unshakeable values crumbled like a handful of dust. It is no coincidence that T. S. Eliot's "The Waste Land" and William Butler Yeats's apocalyptic poem "The Second Coming" were published in the immediate post-war years. During the same period, Dada avant-gardists, Cubists, and surrealists, artistic precursors of the postmodern world, were fracturing, deconstructing, and distorting reality. This was the "Lost Generation" who, having abandoned faith in moral truths, escaped into a culture of aesthetic dissent and hedonistic distraction during the reckless post-war years known as *les Années Folles*.

It was in this godless world, devoid of moral purpose, that new ideologies slithered up from the murky swamp, tempting a generation of lost souls with bold and exhilarating lies that would lead them to an even greater catastrophe. The shaky pillars of this brave new world were embedded in an irrational rejection of Enlightenment values of reason. Throughout the Roaring Twenties, while Scott and Zelda Fitzgerald sipped gin fizzes and danced till dawn in the nightclubs of Montparnasse, ominous rumblings could be heard on the horizon.

It was the hypnotic sound of Teutonic jack-boots goose-stepping with cold and fierce determination.

14

TRIUMPH OF THE WILL

Adolf Hitler proved that a lie, when too big to be doubted, can convince an entire nation to march toward its own destruction. The Nazi "big lie" left a death toll of 100 million, 6 million killed in genocidal mass murder.

Countless books, many by eminent historians, have attempted to explain how Hitler rose from impoverished obscurity to mesmerize the entire German nation with his demented ideology. Did Hitler's rise to power find its origins in Germany's weak historical experience with healthy democratic institutions in the nineteenth century, leading to the collapse of the Weimar Republic—the so-called *Sonderweg* thesis? Was it revenge for Germans' national humiliation after their defeat in the First World War? Was it the disastrous post-war economic conditions that crippled the German economy in the 1920s? Or was it something intrinsic in the German national spirit, a lust for power and domination following Bismarck's "blood and iron" consolidation of the German Empire?

Without the turbulent post-war backdrop in Germany, Hitler probably have would remained an anonymous Austrian drifter who had fought in the kaiser's army as a lowly corporal. From the rubble of the war, Hitler emerged from the shadows in a disgraced German society and, putting to use his mesmerizing talents as an orator, built a political movement inspired by a Teutonic myth of ethnic grandeur. In an era already poisoned by anti-Semitism, his ultra-nationalist ideology targeted Jews as the scapegoat for Germany's national dishonor.

Hitler's timing was perfect for another reason. In the early 1920s when he drifted into meetings of the upstart National Socialist Party, the new science of propaganda was just gaining momentum. Adolf Hitler did not invent mass propaganda. Its techniques had been perfected during the Great War by the British and American governments, which mobilized massive resources behind propaganda campaigns to manipulate public opinion. In the post-war years, the UK government used its control of the BBC's airwaves to subordinate radio broadcasting to political objectives. In America, where radio was in the hands of private enterprise, wartime propagandists such as Edward Bernays took their techniques to the private sector to develop finely honed tools of mass persuasion for consumer advertising. When Hitler was building the Nazi Party in the 1920s, he had already learned valuable lessons from the British and Americans about how propaganda worked. Their instruments of mass manipulation were fit-for-purpose for the Nazi ideology.

"Ever since I have been scrutinizing political events, I have taken a tremendous interest in propagandist activity," confided Hitler in *Mein Kampf,* written in prison after his failed Munich Beer Hall Putsch in 1923.[1]

Hitler was convinced that the British and Americans could not have won the war on the strength of their armies alone. The effectiveness of Anglo-American propaganda, which he described as "weapons of the first order," explained the Allied victory against Germany. He had contempt for German wartime propaganda, which he dismissed as "the last resort of unemployed politicians and a haven for slackers."[2] He believed that British portrayals of Germans as barbarian Huns worked because they appealed to primitive tribal instincts.

"What we failed to do, the enemy did with amazing skill and really brilliant calculation," wrote Hitler. "I, myself, learned enormously from this enemy war propaganda."[3]

Hitler grasped, above all, that propaganda is not rational. It succeeds when it reaches the deep recesses of the human psyche. "The art of propaganda lies in understanding the emotional ideas of the great masses," he wrote in *Mein Kampf.*[4] Propaganda was like total war: every medium had to be mobilized. "From the child's primer down to the last newspaper," he added, "every theater and every movie house, every advertising pillar and every billboard must be pressed into the service of this one great mission."[5]

Hitler's most far-reaching, and disturbing, insight was the "big lie"—in German, *grosse Lüge.* Hitler believed that the masses fall victim to big lies easier than they do to little lies. People tell little lies, but would be ashamed to tell a big lie. Consequently, they don't doubt big lies because they cannot believe that others would distort the truth so impudently. "In the big lie there is always a certain force of credibility," wrote Hitler, "because the broad masses of a nation are always more easily corrupted in the deeper strata of their emotional nature than consciously or voluntarily; and thus in the primitive simplicity of their minds they more readily fall victims to the big lie than the small lie."[6]

The Nazi big lie was a toxic alchemy mixing historical vengeance and racist ideology. The first lie was constructed around Germany's collective humiliation. At the end of the Great War in 1918, the victorious Allied powers amputated parts of Bismarck's German Empire, which had expanded through the annexation of territories including Alsace and Lorraine. After 1918, both were French again. The loss of these two territories was a devastating blow to German pride. Nazi ideology asserted that Germany needed to be restored to its rightful place in history with re-expanded borders—or *"Lebensraum"*—to bring the entire German race together in one Deutschland. That meant territorial expansion in both the east and west.

The second lie was based on racist ideology backed up by a conspiratorial fiction. Nazis depicted the Jew as a serpent that had slithered into Christian civilization and contaminated the purity of the Aryan race. Hitler blamed "international Jewry" for the bourgeois capitalism that had produced the materialistic values that were thwarting the spiritual aspirations of the German nation. Only through the eradication of Jews could the German *Volk* purify its blood and achieve cultural transcendence.

The notion of *Volk* in Nazi ideology, evoking a mystical Teutonic past, was based on a rejection of reason and an irrational glorification of national identity. Hitler made this explicit when setting down his views on propaganda in *Mein Kampf*, stressing the importance of appealing to the "primitive simplicity" of the emotional and unconscious zones in people's minds. Nazi ideology's celebration of a mythic Germanic identity was, in keeping with Hitler's convictions about human nature, essentially a Counter-Enlightenment project inspired by German romanticism.

Nazi ideology found expression in German literature, art, and music. It could even be argued that, for Hitler personally, *völkisch* mythology was essentially aesthetic in its inspiration. Everything about Hitler's personal tastes revealed a contempt for Enlightenment values and a fascination with mythic romanticism. Hitler's early biographer, Allan Bullock, described his early reading habits as "indiscriminate and unsystematic," showing interest in subjects such as "ancient Rome, eastern religions, yoga, occultism, hypnotism, astrology, Protestantism."[7] The philosophers that interested Hitler in his youth were Schopenhauer and Nietzsche. While it is difficult to know the impact of specific ideas on Hitler's early thinking, there was a clear intellectual orientation toward fantasy, supernatural, and nonrational themes and a lack of strong interest in Enlightenment values based on reason.

In music especially, the Nazis showed an ideological preference for Romantic composers admired by Hitler, especially Wagner but also Beethoven. Modern musical styles—particularly jazz, based on free improvisation—were despised as decadent and degenerate (in German, *Entartete*

Musik). The German historian Oswald Spengler, famous for his classic *Decline of the West*, wrote in 1933 that "jazz music and nigger dances are the death march of a great civilization."[8] Hitler, who met Spengler the same year, agreed with this view. Under the Nazis, what was considered acceptable German music was determined by the *Reichsmusikkammer*, set up by Hitler's propaganda chief, Joseph Goebbels, in 1933. Jewish composers such as Felix Mendelssohn were proscribed. So was Gustav Mahler, also Jewish, even though he was a late Romantic composer. Another late Romantic, Richard Strauss, flourished under the Nazis and even became head of the *Reichsmusikkammer*. When the Nazis took power in 1933, Strauss was an eminent German composer. Hitler knew and greatly admired his operas. He had even attended the première of Strauss's *Salomé* in Austria in 1906. The two were also connected intimately with the Wagner family and their Bayreuth festival. They moreover shared an interest in Nietzsche. Strauss's Nietzsche-inspired work *Also Sprach Zarathustra*, composed in 1896, would later become internationally famous in the Hollywood science fiction film *2001: A Space Odyssey*.

Hitler was obsessed with the music of Wagner, whose mythical glorification of German culture was elevated to the status of Nazi theme music. The Führer had been a rapturous admirer of Wagner since his youth. In *Mein Kampf,* he recounted his epiphany-like discovery of Wagner at age twelve when he attended his first opera, *Lohengrin*. "In one instant I was addicted," he wrote. "My youthful enthusiasm for the Bayreuth Master knew no bounds."[9]

Lohengrin, first performed in 1850, was based on the German medieval romance of *Parzifal*, one of the greatest German epic poems. Parzifal (called Percival in English) was a knight from the court of King Arthur on a quest for the Holy Grail. Like most of Wagner's operas, *Parzifal* borrowed mythic characters and themes from medieval romance as a bold assertion of German national grandeur. The historical backdrop to Wagner's operas was the German nationalist movement that reached a crescendo in the 1848 revolutions. Wagner personally took part in these events on the side of German nationalism, and avoided arrest for treason by escaping to Switzerland.[10] He lived long enough to witness German national unity achieved following Bismarck's military victory over France in 1871. While Wagner believed the mythical themes in his operas transcended the facts of history, his works were widely interpreted as an expression of Germany's national aspirations. When young Adolf Hitler was growing up in Austria on the Bavarian border, Richard Wagner was the "German" composer par excellence. Hitler was mesmerized by the mythological connection between Wagner's operatic narratives and Germany's national grandeur.

Everything about Wagner, from the soaring cadences in his operas to his published political opinions, made the composer perfect for Nazi propaganda. His operas evoked Teutonic mythology; his personal views about German purity resonated with the Nazi ideology of the Aryan master race. In *Art and Revolution* in 1849, Wagner wrote: "Into the ebbing veins of the Roman world, there poured the healthy blood of the fresh Germanic nations. Despite the adoption of Christianity, a ceaseless thirst of doing, delight in bold adventure, and unbounded self-reliance, remained the native element of the new masters of the world."[11] Wagner was also a virulent anti-Semite. His anti-Semitism was a matter of public record in his own lifetime, perhaps best summed up by his dictum: "The Jew is the plastic demon of the decline of mankind."[12] In 1850, the same year *Lohengrin* was first performed, Wagner wrote a treatise titled *Jewishness in Music* (*Das Judentum in der Musik*), initially published in the *Neue Zeitschrift für Musik* under the pseudonym K. Freigedank ("Free Thought"). Wagner claimed that Jews lacked passion and had never produced a great poet. "We have to explain to ourselves," he wrote, "the involuntary repellence possessed for us by the nature and personality of the Jews."[13] In the realm of music, Wagner took aim at fellow composer Felix Mendelssohn, who was Jewish. "Mendelssohn has shown us that a Jew can have the richest abundance of talents and be a man of the broadest culture," he observed, "but still be incapable of supplying the profound, heart-seizing, soul-searching experience we expect from art."[14] In a letter in 1881 to his patron, King Ludwig of Bavaria, Wagner expressed himself more explicitly: "I hold the Jewish race to be the born enemy of pure humanity and everything noble in it."[15]

The connection between Wagner's opera and Hitler's Nazi ideology is a dark zone in the history of music. Some claim that Wagner's personal views, however despicable, must not be confused with the greatness of his musical works. Wagner's anti-Semitism, it is argued, must be understood in the historical context of nineteenth-century Europe. When Wagner was writing his pamphlets in the late 1840s, many in Europe were blaming Jews for propping up bourgeois capitalism while revolutions swept across the continent. Wagner was a product of his age. Others claim that Wagner's anti-Semitism was born of rancor and opportunism. In the 1840s, Wagner spent time in Paris attempting to make his name in musical circles, but he failed to find success and felt shunned. He came to the view that the music profession in the French capital was controlled by Jews. He also bore a jealous hatred of the operetta composer Jacques Offenbach, who enjoyed great success in Paris. Offenbach was Jewish.

Wagner died in 1883, six years before Hitler was born, so their lives never converged. Wagner's heirs embraced Hitler and his Nazi regime, however, making a posthumous connection historically indisputable.

When Hitler took power in 1933, it was the fiftieth anniversary of the composer's death. Hitler organized a magnificent Wagner celebration in the composer's birthplace, Leipzig. The event was attended by Wagner's daughter-in-law, English-born Winifred Wagner, and her son Wieland. At the podium for the Wagner concert was world-renowned German conductor Karl Muck, the maestro who had been deported from the United States as an enemy alien during the First World War. Throughout the Nazi era, Hitler assiduously cultivated the Wagner family and stayed at Richard Wagner's villa, Wahnfried. He was on such close personal terms with Winifred Wagner that she affectionately called him "Wolf." Her four children called him "Uncle Wolf." Winifred Wagner remained loyal to the Nazi legacy even after the war. She was often called "the last Nazi."[16]

For the composer Richard Strauss, accepting the position of *Reichsmusikkammer* in the Nazi regime turned into a poisoned chalice. Strauss was playing a dangerous game when he effectively became the Nazis' top musical official. His daughter-in-law, Alice von Grab-Hermannswörth, was a Jewish heiress who married the composer's son Franz in 1924. Through Alice, Strauss's grandchildren were also Jewish, a fact that, given his position as the head of the Nazi regime's *Reichsmusikkammer*, he attempted to conceal. He was eventually rebuked and fired by Hitler's propaganda chief, Joseph Goebbels, for hiring the Jewish writer Stefan Zweig as a librettist and, even worse, writing Zweig a letter in which he criticized the Nazis. Strauss managed to use his name and influence to protect his daughter-in-law Alice and her family when the Nazis began persecuting and sending Jews to concentration camps. Alice was eventually detained, but Strauss managed to secure her release. A different fate met her Jewish family, who were arrested and sent to the Theresienstadt concentration camp. None of them survived.

Strauss's reputation was forever tarnished by his links to the Nazis. After the war, he managed to escape Germany to Switzerland to avoid prosecution for his proximity to the Nazis, and died in 1949 at age eighty-five. The great Italian conductor Arturo Toscanini remarked: "To Richard Strauss, the composer, I take off my hat. To Richard Strauss, the man, I put it on again."[17]

Joseph Goebbels, the top Nazi who fired Strauss, was by far the most educated Nazi, holding a doctorate from the University of Heidelberg. He had been an early recruit to the Nazi party in 1924. Hitler trusted him unquestioningly. Goebbels was the rationalist at the top of the ideologically charged Nazi hierarchy. Other high-ranking Nazis, including Hitler's right-hand man Rudolf Hess, were deeply engaged with astrology. They belonged to the Thule Society, which promoted Aryan race theories. The word *Thule* came from ancient Greek and Rome for "Scandinavia," which the Romans called "Ultima Thule." For nationalist Germans, Thule was a mythic northern nation that inspired the early Nazi *völkisch* mythology. Goebbels was indifferent to the occult and Aryan mythology and the mystical aspects of Nazi sorcery. A small man with a deformed right foot, he was an unlikely specimen of the master Aryan race. Goebbels proved himself to the Führer as a remarkably skilled technocrat of modern bureaucracy. As head of the Nazi Ministry of Propaganda and Popular Enlightenment, Goebbels was the man in charge of spinning and propagating the Nazi big lie.[18]

"If you tell a lie big enough and keep repeating it, people will eventually come to believe it." That axiom is often attributed to Goebbels, though there is no historical evidence that he ever made the much-quoted assertion. Even Nazis, it would appear, were sometimes victims of false news. Goebbels could very well have said it, for it corresponds perfectly to his thinking about propaganda. He attempted to argue that big lies were the mental habit of the English. "The English follow the principle that when one lies, it should be a big lie, and one should stick to it," he wrote. "They keep up their lies, even at the risk of looking ridiculous."[19] Goebbels regarded Winston Churchill as the embodiment of the English penchant for lies. "The astonishing thing is that Mr. Churchill, a genuine John Bull, holds to his lies, and in fact repeats them until he himself believes them," wrote Goebbels in 1941. "That is an old English trick. Mr. Churchill does not need to perfect it, as it is one of the familiar tactics of British politics."[20]

Goebbels was disingenuously blaming the English for something at which he was himself an unrivaled master. His philosophy of propaganda could best be described as an "illusion of truth" paradox. To succeed, it required people to accept unquestioningly an illusion for the truth. As Goebbels put it: "Propaganda works best when those who are being manipulated are confident they are acting on their own free will." It was, in a word, "gaslighting" as mass hypnosis. Hannah Arendt, in her landmark book *The Origins of Totalitarianism*, analyzed the Goebbels propaganda method. "The ideal subject of a totalitarian state is not the convinced Nazi or Communist," she observed, "but people for whom the distinction between fact and fiction (that is, the reality of experience) and the distinction between true and false (that is, the standards of thought) no longer exist."[21]

When the Nazis came to power in 1933, Goebbels took control of all German media: newspapers, magazines, books, music, movies, and above all the relatively new medium of radio. Propaganda was centralized. The Nazis effectively shut down the public sphere in Germany. Labor unions were disbanded. Public meetings and rallies required official authorization. At German universities, Nazi student organizations drafted lists of books to be proscribed. Libraries were raided to purge them of "un-German" books, including works of Jewish authors such as Albert Einstein and Sigmund Freud. Ideologically incompatible books were incinerated in bonfires at night.

Visual art, due to its iconic power, was targeted for special attention by the Nazis. In other forms of art, notably music, the Nazi period did not successfully produce a unique style compatible with fascist ideology. While the Nazi regime attempted to centralize control over music through the *Reichsmusikkammer*, the historically privileged status of German music protected the art form from fascist ideology.[22] Besides, there was much in nineteenth-century German Romantic music that Hitler admired, especially the operas of Wagner. Nazi ideology in music was hostile to the modern—especially jazz. In painting and sculpture, however, the Nazis came closer to imposing an aesthetic that reflected fascist ideology. Hitler, who had been an artist in his aimless early years and was passionate about architecture, took a keen interest in the connection between Nazi ideology and visual aesthetics.

In painting and sculpture, as in music, Hitler knew what he did not like. Under the Nazis, so-called degenerate works (often a code word for *Jewish*) were expunged from German society. Anything "modern" was deemed degenerate and un-German—more proof that Nazi ideology was profoundly anti-modern. Nazi aesthetics were a reaction to the avant-garde art movement—Expressionism, Cubism, Dadaism, Surrealism—that had been popular in Germany during the Weimar Republic in the 1920s. Nazi art, by contrast, conveyed a "blood and soil" aesthetic that turned back to ancient Greece and Rome for ideal forms of human perfection that Hitler praised as "Greco-Nordic." The Führer's hosting of the 1936 Olympic Games in Berlin made the Third Reich's connection to ancient Greece symbolically explicit before the eyes of the world. In *Mein Kampf*, Hitler argued that the Greeks, Romans, and Germans were linked by "racial unity"—or *Rasse-Einheit*—due to common Nordic origins. The aesthetic worship of ancient ideals of physical beauty and strength was an artistic expression of Nazi ideology's Greco-Nordic identity myth. From the Romans, the Germans had inherited the title "Kaiser" from Caesar. In the tradition of Charlemagne—in German, "Karl der Grosse "—Hitler's Third Reich would achieve a *restauratio imperii* as a new Aryan empire. This elaborate historical fiction was grounded in aesthetic principles borrowed from the Greeks and Romans. The reconnection with these ancient civilizations promised to remedy Germany's identity crisis following Napoleon's dissolution of the Holy Roman Empire. And above all, it would erase the national humiliation of Germany's defeat in 1918.[23]

Joseph Goebbels was tasked with the aesthetic housecleaning. In 1937, he ordered the confiscation of sixteen thousand works of "modern" art from public museums. These "un-German" works were not hidden from public view. On the contrary, Goebbels wanted Germans to see the artistic styles to be regarded with disgust. He put a selection on display in a "Degenerate Art" (*Entartete Kunst*) exhibition that traveled to eleven cities in Germany and Austria, including Munich, Berlin, Weimar, Vienna, and Leipzig. The show's publicity pitch was "German *Volk*, come and judge for yourselves!"[24] More than 2 million visited the exhibition in Munich alone over its four-month run in that city, roughly twenty thousand visitors per day. The traveling exhibition was organized thematically for visitors to guide their reactions. Themes included: "Revelation of the Jewish Racial Soul," "An Insult to German Womanhood," and "Nature as Seen by Sick Minds." Among the "degenerate" works displayed were paintings by Picasso, Chagall, Paul Klee, and Kandinsky. The exhibition was timed as a counter-program to another art show, "Great German Art" (*Große Deutsche Kunstausstellung*), of Nazi-approved works in the Romantic realist style showing idealized Aryan nudes inspired by classical Greece and heroic figures of medieval mythology. Hitler personally attended the Great German Art exhibition's inauguration in Munich and gave a speech attacking modern art for its degeneracy and depravity. Degenerate art, he said, was an insult to "German feeling."[25]

Goebbels was also a skilled manipulator of journalists. Like Hitler, he was an admirer of Anglo-American propaganda techniques using the press. Goebbels had closely followed American public relations pioneers in the vanguard of mass persuasion in the 1920s. He notably studied the techniques of American public relations pioneer Edward Bernays (even though Bernays was Jewish and moreover the nephew of Sigmund Freud). After the Nazis came to power, Goebbels actively cultivated journalists and spared no expense in bribing them with luxury hotel accommodations. He hired an American public relations firm, Carl Byoir & Associates, to plant pro-Nazi stories in the American press. Carl Byoir, an influential PR executive in America, had worked earlier in his career, like Edward Bernays, in Woodrow Wilson's propaganda unit during the First World War. Goebbels also paid another top American PR executive, Ivy Lee, an annual fee of $25,000 (a huge sum in the early 1930s) to provide advice on how to promote Germany in the United States. Lee, who had worked for John D. Rockefeller to soften the billionaire's public image, traveled to Germany and met with Hitler. Part of his paid work for the Nazis included cultivating American journalists in Germany to spin positive stories about Hitler.[26]

The foreign press had been naïve about Hitler from the earliest days of the Nazi movement. In 1922, the *New York Times* published a fawning profile of Hitler under the headline "New Popular Idol Rises in Bavaria," by the *Times* correspondent in Germany, Cyril Brown. Brown noted that, while Hitler used anti-Semitic rhetoric, it was merely a political posture. "Several reliable, well-informed sources confirmed the idea that Hitler's anti-Semitism was not so genuine or violent as it sounded," wrote Brown, "and that he was merely using anti-Semitic propaganda as a bait to catch masses of followers and keep them aroused, enthusiastic, and in line for the time when his organization is perfected and sufficiently powerful to be employed effectively for political purposes."[27] One American reporter who was more critical was Edgar Ansel Mowrer at the *Chicago Daily News.* Mowrer fearlessly sent dispatches back to his newspaper documenting the brutality of the rising Nazi movement. In 1933, just as Hitler was coming to power, Mowrer published a book critical of the Nazis titled *Germany Puts the Clock Back.* He was promptly expelled from Germany after Hitler's inauguration.[28] The Nazis weaponized an old term in German politics to attack stories in the foreign press as falsehoods: *Lügenpresse,* or "lying press"—a word that would resurface decades later in English as "fake news." In the nineteenth century, the word *Lügenpresse* had been used by Catholic polemicists against the liberal press (implying they were controlled by Jews or Freemasons). During the First World War, the kaiser's government attacked international media stories about German atrocities in Belgium as propagandistic lies perpetrated by the foreign *Lügenpresse.* For the Nazis, the term was used against foreign, communist, and Jewish-owned media.[29]

While the Nazis regularly denounced the communist press, they actually had few problems with accredited foreign correspondents in Germany. Most foreign reporters largely bought the official PR line supplied by Nazi propagandists. American newspapers and magazines consistently published stories that, while expressing some reservations about Nazi ideology, generally portrayed Hitler in a favorable light. Shortly after the Nazis came to power, a writer for the *Christian Science Monitor* reported that "I have so far found quietness, order, and civility," adding "not the slightest sign of anything unusual afoot."[30] The American press continued in this indulgent tone toward the Führer for the next few years. When the Nazis opened the "Degenerate Art" exhibition in Munich in 1937, an American art critic wrote in the *Boston Globe:* "There are probably plenty of people—art lovers—in Boston, who will side with Hitler in this particular purge."[31] Even after it was known that the Nazis were persecuting Jews, many American papers preferred to look the other way. The *New York Herald Tribune*'s correspondent in Berlin reported that, while the plight of Jews in Germany was "an unhappy one," many atrocity stories reported in the international press were "exaggerated and often unfounded."

On American editorial boards, there was a reluctance to believe reports of Nazi molestation of Jews, if only because eyewitness accounts could not be verified. Even Walter Lippmann, the respected dean of American journalism, argued that Adolf Hitler was a great statesman and "the authentic voice of a genuinely civilized people." Lippmann dismissed rumors of "uncivilized things" happening in Germany, adding that they were no worse than the Terror in revolutionary France, the British atrocities in Ireland, the Spanish Inquisition, and the Ku Klux Klan in America. Nazi officials routinely denied rumors of violence against Jews, claiming these reports were lies. Some American reporters, such as Karl von Wiegand from the Hearst newspapers, were regarded as openly sympathetic to the Nazis (he was granted a personal interview with Hitler).[32] In late August 1939, less than two weeks before Hitler triggered the most cataclysmic war in human history, the *New York Times Magazine* published what can only be described as a glowing puff piece on the Führer's domestic life and home decor at his Berghof mountain retreat. Under the headline "Herr Hitler at Home in the Clouds," readers learned that "high up in his favorite mountain he finds time for politics, solitude and frequent official parties."[33] The article, written by experienced British foreign correspondent Hedwig Mauer Simpson, gave a detailed account of the Führer's daily life—his breakfast routines, his walks with his beloved Alsatian dog, his fondness for chocolate. Not a hint that Hitler was planning to invade Poland in eleven days.[34]

The reasons for the American media's blind-eye approach to Nazi Germany—described as a "moral failing"—has been the subject of much debate and soul-searching.[35] Some have suggested that an uncomfortable truth is that Hitler regarded America in the 1930s as not much different from his vision for Nazi Germany. Hitler had long greatly admired America. As a child, he was a voracious reader of Karl May's cowboy-and-Indians books set in America's Wild West. Some have pointed out that Nazi racist ideology was not only similar to American racism and segregation in the early twentieth century, but that the Nazis even looked to America's Jim Crow laws as a model for building a society based on racial supremacy.[36] Also, America's "Manifest Destiny" of conquering the West, and slaughtering everything that got in the way of settlers, was a Nazi model for Hitler's "*Lebensraum*" policy of aggressively invading territories that he claimed belonged to the German nation. As an article in the *New Yorker* titled "How American Racism Influenced Hitler" put it: "Scholars have long been aware that Hitler's regime expressed admiration for American race law, but they have tended to see this as a public-relations strategy—an 'everybody does it' justification for Nazi policies."[37]

For the foreign media in Germany, alarm bells should have sounded in November 1938 with the violent brutality of the *Kristallnacht* pogroms. The outbreak of organized violence against Germany's Jews occurred only weeks after British prime minister Neville Chamberlain met with Hitler in Munich to sign the "peace in our time" agreement to appease the Führer. Throughout Germany, Nazi SA storm troopers destroyed hundreds of synagogues, smashed Jewish-owned shops, and forced thousands of Jews into concentration camps. If there had been any doubt previously, the Nazis' plans for Jews in Germany were now shockingly obvious. The timing of the *Kristallnacht* ("Night of Broken Glass")—on German theologian Martin Luther's birthday—was not a coincidence. Luther had written virulently anti-Semitic tracts believed to have inspired Nazi ideology. Shortly after taking power in 1933, the Nazis celebrated the 450th anniversary of Luther's birthday by declaring November 10 as *Der Deutsche Luthertag* (German Luther Day). Five years later, the *Kristallnacht* violence against Jews occurred on the same date. The "broken glass" destruction of Jewish property was an echo of the fanatical icon-smashing done in Luther's name four centuries earlier.[38]

The *Kristallnacht* pogroms, while alarming, did little to turn international opinion against Nazi Germany. Much of the world was distracted by a severe economic depression in the 1930s. Also, anti-Semitism was widespread in the early twentieth century. In most countries, Jews suffered systematic discrimination and exclusion. In the United States, President Franklin Roosevelt's New Deal was described by the American far-right as a "Jew Deal." The eminent American journalist Walter Lippmann's uncritical commentary on Hitler included a reference to Jews as "parvenus." Father Charles Coughlin, a famous Catholic priest in the 1930s, used his popular radio broadcast in America to deliver virulently anti-Semitic speeches. Automaker Henry Ford, one of the richest men in America, was an outspoken anti-Semite whose newspaper, the *Dearborn Independent,* blamed the "International Jew" for undermining the American way. Ford distributed 500,000 copies of the notorious anti-Semitic document, *The Protocols of the Elders of Zion*, which claimed to provide proof of a Jewish plan for world domination (it was in fact a forged text first published in Russia in 1903 during the pogroms). Another American hero, aviator Charles Lindbergh, famous for his trans-Atlantic flight in 1927, was an avowed Nazi sympathizer. In 1936, Lindbergh traveled to Germany to receive the Order of the German Eagle, conferred on him personally by Hitler's right-hand man, Hermann Goering.

World leaders, too, were disinclined to confront Adolf Hitler over the persecution of Jews in Germany. Many important figures who met Hitler—including Britain's future king, Edward VIII, and his American wife, Wallis Simpson—fell under the Führer's spell. The American ambassador in Britain, Joseph Kennedy—father of John F. Kennedy—was an outspoken pro-German pacifist who publicly criticized Winston Churchill and declared that "democracy is finished in England." Kennedy attempted to seek personal meetings with Hitler without authorization from President Roosevelt. In London, Kennedy murmured to senior UK government officials that Roosevelt's foreign policy was controlled by Jews (whom Kennedy regularly called "kikes"). Kennedy suggested to the American press that the best solution for German Jews was to ship them to Africa. In 1939, both the American and Canadian governments turned away a ship carrying more than nine hundred Jews fleeing Hitler's Germany. After being refused entry to Cuba, the Jewish passengers on the MS *St. Louis* sought safe haven in the United States and Canada, but were similarly turned away and returned to Germany. Many later perished in Nazi concentration camps.

Throughout the 1930s, most of the world failed to see the dark storm clouds on the horizon. The Nazi big lie had not only convinced the German people but also deceived world opinion. The deception would not be exposed until it was too late.

***

The most famous work of Nazi propaganda was Leni Riefenstahl's classic film *Triumph of the Will.*

The date of Riefenstahl's mesmerizing film, shot in 1934, reveals that Hitler was aware of the power of cinema from the earliest days of the Nazi regime. Riefenstahl masterfully transformed a Nazi rally into a Wagnerian operatic spectacle. Hitler was in the starring role as a Teutonic god venerated by his people chanting, *"Ein Volk, Ein Führer, Ein Reich!"* Riefenstahl's cinematic mythologizing of Hitler was the first time in history that motion pictures had been used to create a cult of personality. [39]

Riefenstahl, who died in 2003 at the grand age of 101, spent most of her long life denying that she had been an active Nazi sympathizer. That she was part of Hitler's inner circle cannot be disputed. She enjoyed a close relationship with both the Führer and Goebbels. In press interviews during the 1930s, she effusively praised Hitler. "To me, Hitler is the greatest man who ever lived. He truly is without fault, so simple and at the same time possessed of masculine strength," she said on a tour of America in 1938. [40] Riefenstahl was, like the composer Richard Strauss, an artistic genius who was willing to put her brilliant talents at the service of an evil ideology. There was one important difference, however. Riefenstahl produced Nazi propaganda. She was, more than anyone else, the creator of the Führer myth that enraptured millions.

Riefenstahl's film techniques—soundtrack, camera angles, slow panning on her subject—had never been seen before on the big screen. In the early 1930s, motion pictures with sound were in their awkward infancy. Sound had only recently been added to movies with the birth of "talkies" in the late 1920s. Most world leaders were still communicating through short newsreels and scripted addresses before immobile cameras. When Riefenstahl turned her cameras on Hitler at a Nuremberg rally, her filmmaking talents transformed political propaganda into visual poetry. Two years later, her filming of the Berlin Olympics in 1936 was such a masterful work of cinematic pageantry that it influenced how the games were filmed for decades.

The title of Riefenstahl's film, *Triumph of the Will,* was an allusion to Friedrich Nietzsche's final book, *The Will to Power.* The connection between Nazi ideology and Nietzsche's philosophy was controversial even in Hitler's lifetime. Nietzsche had been dead for more than three decades when Hitler came to power, and there can be little doubt that he would have been horrified by the Nazi project. The connection between his ideas and Nazi ideology was made by the philosopher's younger sister, Elisabeth Förster-Nietzsche, who posthumously published *The Will to Power* in 1901. It was Elisabeth who, three decades after her brother's death, marketed Nietzsche's work as philosophical inspiration for Nazi ideology.

Elisabeth Förster-Nietzsche was a virulent anti-Semite. She had married a German nationalist named Bernhard Förster, who launched a short-lived plan to establish a "pure German" colony called Neuva Germania in Paraguay. Nietzsche ridiculed his younger sister's Aryan paradise in South America and railed against her husband's anti-Semitism. Following Bernhard Förster's suicide by poison, Elisabeth hastily returned to Germany. At this point, her philosopher brother Friedrich had lapsed into a comatose state after suffering a nervous breakdown. He had collapsed in the street in Turin after seeing a man whipping a horse in Piazza Carlo Alberto. Nietzsche had thrown his arms around the horse before falling to the ground in a convulsion of sobs. For the final decade of the philosopher's life, Elisabeth was her brother's caregiver, guardian, executor, and editor of his works. Though the philosopher was in a vegetative state, she invited people to their house in Weimar to observe the famous Friedrich Nietzsche close up, the way one might gaze with fascination at an exotic zoo animal. Even more controversially, when she arranged for the publication of *The Will to Power,* the edited book based on her brother's notes reflected many of her own views.

Whatever her intentions, Elisabeth Nietzsche's talents for publicity proved tremendously successful. Even before the First World War, Friedrich Nietzsche was regarded as an influential philosopher whose name was associated with German hubris and megalomania. A decade later, the Nazis embraced the themes in Nietzsche's posthumous book that were compatible with their own ideology. Hitler befriended Elisabeth Nietzsche and visited the philosopher's home in Weimar. His visit was captured by the Führer's personal photographer, showing Hitler in profile contemplating a bust of Nietzsche. The widely circulated photo appeared in German newspapers with the caption: "The Führer before the bust of the German philosopher who spawned two great popular movements: the National Socialism one in Germany and the Fascist one in Italy."[41] As a gift, Elisabeth Nietzsche gave the Führer her brother's favorite walking stick. Hitler put Elizabeth Nietzsche on the German state's payroll with a monthly allowance, ostensibly to maintain the Nietzsche archives with an adjoining library. When she died in 1935, Hitler attended her funeral accompanied by other high-ranking Nazi officials. The official Nazi propaganda organ, *Voelkischer Beobachter,* eulogized Elisabeth Förster-Nietzsche as the "Mother of the Fatherland."[42]

On the surface, it's not difficult to understand how the Nazis found in Nietzsche's work inspiration to legitimize their own doctrines. Nietzsche's celebration of Dionysus and his admiration for ancient Greek tragedy were compatible with the Nazi veneration of Greek cultural models and pagan symbols. Nietzsche also admired warrior cultures, praised Caesar and Napoleon, and expressed contempt for democracy and modernity. He repudiated Christianity, with its life-denying morality preaching worldly escape into suffering and salvation, and called for a new order governed by an aristocracy of "great men." These ideas, even if misinterpreted, powerfully resonated with the ethos of Nazi doctrine.

Yet at the same time, Nietzsche was profoundly opposed to the entire thrust of Nazi ideology. He expressed revulsion for *völkisch* notions of "race" and tribal nationalisms. He was critical of Bismarck's construction of a new German empire. He was opposed to the subordination of the individual to the state. He believed, above all, that we all must shape our own personal morality, not fall in with mass hysteria. Nietzsche's philosophy was fundamentally life-affirming, emphasizing the vitality of individual human will in a constant state of becoming. He believed in the necessity of throwing off the burdens of existing moral codes by challenging all assumptions about truth, beliefs, culture, values, and history. Nietzsche's Übermensch was not a blond beast German warrior. The Übermensch was the embodiment of a philosophy driven not by a will to dominate others but by personal achievement and self-fulfillment unrestrained by Christian morality.

The most obvious contradiction between Nietzsche's philosophy and Nazi doctrine was the question of Jews. Nietzsche would have been horrified to see his name associated with an ideology based on anti-Semitism. His quarrels with his sister Elisabeth revealed Nietzsche's contempt for anti-Semitic opinions. He also had a famous falling out with Richard Wagner over the composer's virulent hostility toward Jews. Having praised Wagner's operas in his early work, *The Birth of Tragedy,* Nietzsche later turned on him in *Nietzsche Contra Wagner.* Nietzsche was resolutely opposed to Wagner's romantic celebration of German nationalism. Decades later, Nazi ideology owed more to the Teutonic legends in Wagner's operas than to the pan-national values espoused by Friedrich Nietzsche. Still, there was just enough in Nietzsche's ideas that could be interpreted as compatible with the Nazis' clarion call for a revitalized German nation rooted in a "blood and soil" life force. Nietzsche's rhetorical excesses, his bold aphorisms, and his self-proclaimed status as a prophet also made his powerful ideas attractive to new ideologies seeking sources of truth. Even his rebellion against the restraints of Christian morality would have appealed to Nazi ideologues, including Hitler, who were seeking to construct a new society founded on veneration of *Volk* and the cult of the Führer.

The conflation of Nietzsche's thinking and Nazi ideology, which persisted beyond the Third Reich, was embodied by another German philosopher, Martin Heidegger. Often regarded as the greatest philosopher of the twentieth century, Heidegger was hugely influenced by Nietzsche's thinking. But their connection to Nazi ideology was different. Nietzsche went insane in 1889, the year Adolf Hitler was born; and he died in 1900 when Hitler was an eleven-year-old boy. Nietzsche had been dead for more than three decades when Hitler came to power in 1933. Heidegger, who published his greatest philosophical work *Being and Time* in 1927, was a contemporary of Hitler. More controversially, he became a card-carrying member of the Nazi Party in 1933. Appointed rector of Freiburg University, Heidegger swore allegiance to the Führer, wore a swastika pin, demoted academic colleagues who were not toeing the Nazi line, and implemented a policy of discrimination against Jewish students because they were "non-Aryan." Heidegger told his students: "Let not theories and 'ideas' be the rules of your being. The Führer himself and he alone is German reality and its law, today and for the future."[43] He also presided over a student bonfire of "un-German" books, though it was apparently dampened by rain.

Heidegger was indisputably a Nazi. His commitment to the Nazi movement was even more affirmed than that of the composer Richard Strauss. Like Heidegger, Strauss accepted a patronage post from the Nazis for selfish career reasons. But Strauss remained ambivalent about Nazi ideology if only because his son was married to a Jewish woman. Heidegger was a more committed Nazi. In a 1935 lecture, he referred to "the inner truth and greatness of National Socialism."[44] He advocated

Führer prinzip, or the principle of leadership, over the principle of democracy. Even after he left the university rectorship, he remained a member of the Nazi Party until the end of the war in 1945. He told his students that the "nomad Semite" was foreign "to the nature of our German space."[45] He kept "black notebooks" (they remained unpublished for more than a half century) filled with anti-Semitic observations. He wrote, for example, that "the Jews, with their marked gift for calculating, live, already for the longest time, according to the principle of race, which is why they are resisting its consistent application with utmost violence."[46]

How a philosopher of Martin Heidegger's immense stature could have been attracted to the Nazi ideology has been debated for decades. Some argue that there were two Heideggers: philosopher and Nazi. Others claim that, if Heidegger were a great philosopher, he would never have been attracted to Nazi ideology; and conversely, if he was a genuine Nazi, he could not have been a great philosopher.

After the war, Heidegger was stripped of his academic titles and banned from teaching in Germany. In the post-war years, he oriented his career toward France, where his work was tremendously influential, notably on Jean-Paul Sartre, whose *Being and Nothingness* was heavily influenced by Heidegger's *Being and Time*.[47] He scrupulously avoided the issue of his Nazi past. In 1953, however, a twenty-four-year-old German intellectual named Jürgen Habermas directly challenged him on the Nazi question. Habermas was unknown in the early 1950s, his international fame would come later. As a German in the post-war years, Habermas did not show the same indulgence toward Heidegger as French philosophers. Habermas called on Heidegger to explain what he had meant in *Introduction to Metaphysics* (based on his lectures from 1935) when referring to the "inner truth and greatness" of the Nazi movement. Heidegger remained silent. He observed the same evasive silence until his death in 1976. Habermas concluded that Heidegger "exhibited a conflation of philosophical theory with ideological motifs."[48] Three decades later, Habermas observed that it was only after the war that German culture began to assimilate the philosophical values of the Enlightenment.

Another mystery to the Heidegger affair were the indefatigable post-war efforts of his protégée, Hannah Arendt, to exculpate him and restore his name. There can be little doubt that Arendt, who in the post-war decades enjoyed the status of revered German intellectual in America, was largely responsible for Heidegger's absolution. On the philosopher's eightieth birthday in 1969, Arendt gave a radio address in West Germany defending Heidegger's reputation. She also wrote a birthday tribute to her mentor in the *New York Review of Books*, titled "Martin Heidegger at Eighty." Arendt compared Heidegger to Plato, lamenting that both philosophers, when they shifted their thoughts to the sphere of politics, resorted to "tyrants and Führers." She argued that Heidegger's past links to the Nazis had been merely an "escapade" during which he had naively succumbed to the temptation of getting involved in the world of human affairs. His tragic error, to use terms associated with Arendt's thinking, was that he crossed over from the intellectual realm of his *vita contempla-tiva* to the *vita activa* of the political sphere. She argued that Heidegger's political activities must be considered as autonomous, distinct from the man Martin Heidegger.[49]

The reasons behind Arendt's steadfast loyalty to her intellectual mentor were complex. In the 1920s, when she was an impressionable student at Marburg University, she had a romantic relationship with Heidegger, who was her professor. Arendt gravitated toward Heidegger after hearing rumors that he was the "hidden king" of philosophy. When their affair began, she was nineteen and he was a married man of thirty-six. In a small university town, they kept their adulterous affair secret, meeting in Arendt's attic apartment. His love letters to his young student were passionate. In one, he confided: "After the concert, I was so moved by being near you that I could not bear it any longer—and left, when I would have much rather have wandered through the night with you, walking silently beside you."[50] In 1933 when Hitler came to power, Heidegger joined the Nazi Party and was promoted to rector at Freiberg; while Arendt, as a Jew, fled Germany for Paris. After the war, Arendt became a famous intellectual who coined the term *banality of evil* in her controversial book *Eichmann in Jerusalem*.[51] Yet throughout all those years, Arendt remained in contact with Heidegger and worked tirelessly to restore his tarnished reputation. It wasn't until their love letters were published in the 1990s—two decades after both Heidegger and Arendt were dead—that the depth of their secret romance became known. Some have argued that Arendt maintained a lifelong "schoolgirl crush" on Heidegger; others claim Heidegger was a fox who manipulated Arendt. Whatever the dynamic that bonded them, she was faithful to a man who, far from banal, was both an eminent philosopher and a card-carrying Nazi. In maintaining her personal loyalty, she put feelings before facts. As an intellectual, Arendt was fearlessly engaged in a quest for truth, except on the subject of Martin Heidegger.[52]

Arendt's attempts to absolve Heidegger, while successful in her lifetime, failed in the decades following their deaths. Most books on Heidegger have demolished Arendt's forgiving portrait of her mentor, arguing that Heidegger was not just a philosopher and a Nazi, but a Nazi philosopher.[53] The rehabilitation of Friedrich Nietzsche was much more successful. It was easier to be forgiving toward Nietzsche, if only because he was dead when the Nazi movement was born. Despite the opportunism of his sister Elisabeth after his death, it is almost certain that Nietzsche would have found German fascism repugnant. More unexpectedly, after the war, Nietzsche's ideas found favor with the postmodernist movement rebelling against established truths. In the 1960s, his philosophy proposed a do-it-yourself Dionysian moral relativism that, after a quick rinsing through campus Marxism, powerfully resonated in the leftist counter-culture and the postmodernist ethos that frothed in its wake.

"My time has not yet come either," wrote Nietzsche in *Ecce Homo.* "Some men are born posthumously."[54] Among all his predictions, that one was undoubtedly the most accurate. Yet Nietzsche would be horrified to learn that his ideas inspired two diametrically opposed movements—one on the fascist right, the other on the radical left—both of which he would have regarded with scorn.[55]

The Nazi big lie died with Adolf Hitler in a carbonized Berlin bunker in 1945. Before his suicide, Hitler had issued the "Nero Decree"—a scorched-earth destruction of Germany like the burning of Rome in 64 AD—but his orders were not carried out. With the defeat of Nazi Germany, the entire saga of aggressive German nationalism—from Bismarck and the kaiser to Hitler—was now truly dead, buried in shame. Germans retreated into painful soul-searching, forced to confront the truth of the horrors they had inflicted on Western civilization. For other nations, the triumph of victory spared them the necessity of confronting their own uncomfortable truths—namely, that fascism had not been restricted to Germany.

In the United States, the pro-Nazi German American Bund had been launched in 1936 as "an organization of patriotic Americans of German stock." It operated twenty youth camps and seventy regional divisions across the United States. In February 1939, the Bund held a pro-fascist mass rally in New York's Madison Square Garden. The event attracted some twenty thousand fascist supporters who came to hear anti-Semitic speeches, including one by the Bund leader, German-born Fritz Kuhn, who railed against "Jewish-controlled media." The Bund's so-called pro-America rally in New York, which was filmed for posterity, featured a massive image of George Washington flanked by American flags and Nazi swastikas. Banners held aloft in the arena were emblazoned with slogans such as "Stop Jewish Domination of Christian America." A dramatic moment came during Kuhn's speech, when a twenty-six-year-old Jewish plumber from Brooklyn named Isadore Greenbaum rushed the stage and shouted, "Down with Hitler!" Kuhn's security guards tackled, punched, and kicked Greenbaum before he was dragged out of the arena by New York police officers. Greenbaum was arrested and charged with disorderly conduct and, later in court, fined $25. The outbreak of war with Germany several months later year marked the end of the Bund, which was outlawed in 1941. Kuhn meanwhile had been arrested for tax fraud and imprisoned. During the war he was arrested, this time as an enemy agent, and interned again until September 1945 when he was deported to Germany.[56]

In Britain, meanwhile, the influential *Daily Mail* and *Daily Mirror* newspapers ran articles that praised Hitler and supported British fascist leader Oswald Mosley. The owner of the *Daily Mail,* Lord Rothermere, published a story under his own name titled "Hurrah for the Blackshirts." Lord Rothermere even went to Germany to meet Hitler. After the war, those voices fell silent, their fascist outbursts conveniently swept under history's rug. Oswald Mosley exiled himself in France upon his release from prison. His choice of France was fitting. He escaped to a country that, more than any other, was in collective denial about its conduct during the war.

The Nazi occupation of France, though traumatic, provided many French with an opportunity to settle old scores festering since the Dreyfus Affair in the 1890s. Even though Jewish army captain Alfred Dreyfus had been exonerated, the civil war for France's soul raged on, pitting secular republicans against Catholic nationalists.[57] In the early decades of the twentieth century, the political elites who dominated the secular Third Republic effectively marginalized far-right nationalists attached to traditional Catholic values. In the 1920s, while Hitler's Nazis were plotting putsches in the Weimar Republic, ultra-nationalists in France were deploying similar tactics to destabilize the Third Republic. The French far-right movement's big moment came when Hitler invaded in 1940. The collaborationist Vichy regime under Marshal Pétain replaced the republican motto *"Liberté, Egalité, Fraternité"* with *"Travail, Famille, Patrie"* (Work, Family, Homeland). Under Pétain, the enemies of the French *patrie* were the old targets of the Catholic right: Jews, communists, and freemasons. The Vichy regime, under no pressure from the Germans, passed an infamous "Jewish Statute," banning Jews from the civil service, professions, teaching, journalism, and show business. Vichy's Commission for Jewish Affairs confiscated the properties of Jewish-owned businesses. More than forty thousand foreign Jews were placed in concentration camps under French control. Some three thousand died over the winter of 1940. Mass arrests and deportations soon followed. In July 1942, French police rounded up more than thirteen thousand Jews in Paris, including four thousand small children, many of them separated from their mothers. They were sent via rail in cattle cars to extermination camps in Germany. In total, the French state sent more than seventy-five thousand Jews to Nazi death camps. Fewer than three thousand returned.

In the immediate aftermath of the war, the most despicable Nazi collaborators were tracked down and executed in merciless purges. Marshal Pétain was tried for treason and sentenced to death (his sentence was later commuted, and he spent his remaining years in a comfortable prison). The celebrated novelist Louis-Ferdinand Céline, whose *Voyage au bout de la nuit* had won the prestigious Renaudot prize in 1932, was arrested after the war for three virulently anti-Semitic pamphlets published in the late 1930s. He was sentenced to "national disgrace." For the rest of the French who had collaborated with the Nazis, the Vichy years were erased from their memories like an unpleasant event that had never happened. While Germans were forced to confront the truth about the Holocaust, the French took refuge in revisionist history that became a collective lie. The stigma of Nazi collaboration became a taboo subject in France, plastered over by a heroic myth of national resistance against the Nazis. The shameful truth was buried deep in the national psyche. France's collective lie put the nation on the right side of history with the Allied victors.

The official lie was sanctioned, and enforced, by the French state. When Marcel Ophuls's documentary about the Vichy collaboration, *The Sorrow and the Pity,* was released in 1969, it was banned from French television. The truth emerged slowly, not on television but in literature and cinema. The French writer Patrick Modiano, born during the war to Jewish parents who had barely escaped deportation, wrote novels—*Place de l'Étoile* in 1968 and *Dora Bruder* two decades later—that explored the theme of memory and shame during the Nazi occupation. In the early 1970s, director Louis Malle broke the official taboo with his film *Lacombe, Lucien*, based on Modiano's novel about a French adolescent during the Occupation who joins the Gestapo but falls for a Jewish girl whose family he is terrorizing.

François Mitterrand was the most troubling embodiment of France's collective lie. He had been a right-wing activist in his youth in the 1930s opposing the Third Republic. During the Vichy interlude, he worked directly for Marshal Pétain. Mitterrand even received the Vichy regime's *Francisque* medal for his loyal services. After the war, Mitterrand enjoyed a long and successful political career, including many ministerial posts in the Fourth Republic, never molested by his dubious past. A close friend during his political ascent was René Bousquet, a wealthy corporate director. Bousquet had been head of the Paris police during the German occupation. He had authorized the roundups of thousands of Jews, including children, who were sent to extermination camps in Germany.

Mitterrand later became the Socialist leader and ran for the French presidency three times. In 1981, he finally won at age sixty-four. During his two-term, fourteen-year presidency, not a single article in the French press surfaced about Mitterrand's connections to the Vichy regime. Mitterrand was also keeping two parallel families, and a secret daughter, living in separate official residences at taxpayer expense. This, too, was known in media circles but never reported. Shortly after his election in

1981, Mitterrand learned that he had prostate cancer but kept that secret from the French public. For years, official bulletins about the president's health indicated that he was in excellent condition. The tacit *omerta* about his Vichy past had protected him for half a century; and the media kept knowledge of his personal life from the public. In a culture with an ambiguous relationship with the truth, Mitterrand knew that his secrets were safe.

Finally, at the end of his second term, when Mitterrand was dying of cancer, French journalist Pierre Péan published a book, *Une Jeunesse française*, about the president's far-right youth and Vichy activities.[58] Mitterrand did not dispute the facts in the book, but refused to acknowledge any guilt. He went to his grave unrepentant. His lie was France's lie.

In 1995, France finally faced the shame of its Nazi collaboration. Mitterrand's successor, Jacques Chirac, the first president too young to have fought in the Second World War, publicly admitted that the French state had played an active role in the deportation of French Jews to Nazi extermination camps.

It took fifty years for the French state to admit its role in the Holocaust. Collective lies can be kept as secrets for generations, even centuries, before uncomfortable truths are finally revealed.

15

SHAKEN, NOT STIRRED

The Cold War, which opposed Western liberalism and Soviet communism for the last half of the twentieth century, contained two unique paradoxes.

First, it was a "war" but not a military conflict; it was an ideological confrontation about values. Second, while the Cold War was a rivalry between two competing claims on truth, the weapons deployed on both sides were lies.

In hindsight, it could be argued that the United States and its Western allies never should have bothered fighting the Cold War in the first place. Soviet communism was an oppressive totalitarian system doomed to fail. Confronted with a moral dilemma between the two opposing models—liberal democracy and communist dictatorship—the choice should have been easy. In the beginning, however, it wasn't so obvious.

When the Cold War broke out in the early post-war years, the populations of many European countries were drawn to the Soviet model. From the 1930s, influential artists and philosophers, including Picasso and Jean-Paul Sartre, were attracted to Stalinism. They openly declared themselves to be communists and supported the Soviet Union. Karl Marx had observed that religion was the opiate of the people; but communism, it turned out, was the opiate of the intellectuals. The horrors of the gulags, purges, and mass murder committed in the name of Marxist ideology were still not widely known.

In 1944, when George Orwell was seeking a London publisher for his anti-Stalinist book, *Animal Farm,* he met only rejection. The book was too politically sensitive. One publisher that turned him down was Faber and Faber, whose editor-in-chief was the poet T. S. Eliot. In his rejection letter, Eliot wrote to Orwell that he was not convinced that "this is the thing that needs saying at the moment." Eliot was not a communist. But in 1944, the Soviet Union was Britain's wartime ally against the Nazis. Eliot was reluctant to cause offense. Orwell couldn't get *Animal Farm* published until after the war, when a small publisher, Secker and Warburg, paid him £100 for the manuscript. In the book's preface, titled "Freedom of the Press," Orwell called out the "intellectual cowardice" of the publishers who had rejected his manuscript. One of those publishers, Jonathan Cape, had turned it down after being warned off the book by the UK government's Ministry of Information. Orwell observed that, in British books and periodicals, "hardly anyone will print an attack on Stalin, but it is quite safe to attack Churchill.

"If publishers and editors exert themselves to keep certain topics out of print, it is not because they are frightened of prosecution, but because they are frightened of public opinion," wrote Orwell in the *Animal Farm* preface. "In this country intellectual cowardice is the worst enemy a writer or journalist has to face, and that fact does not seem to me to have had the discussion it deserves. . . . At this moment what is demanded by the prevailing orthodoxy is an uncritical admiration of Soviet Russia. Everyone knows this, nearly everyone acts on it. Any serious criticism of the Soviet regime, any disclosure of facts which the Soviet government would prefer to keep hidden, is next door to unprintable."[1]

The tacit rules of the game quickly changed after the Soviet Union annexed much of Eastern Europe after the war. An Iron Curtain fell on the continent. The Cold War was officially declared. The Russians were now the enemy. Joseph Stalin was the incarnation of communist brutality and lies.

Right from the start, the American president, Harry Truman, framed the Cold War against Soviet communism as a moral choice for the world. In his famous "Truman Doctrine" address to a joint session of Congress in March 1947, President Truman declared:

> Nearly every nation must choose between alternative ways of life. . . .
> One way of life is based upon the will of the majority, and is distinguished by free institutions, representative government, free elections, guarantees of individual liberty, freedom of speech and religion, and freedom from political oppression. The second way of life is based upon the will of a minority forcibly imposed upon the majority. It relies upon terror and oppression, a controlled press and radio; fixed elections, and the suppression of personal freedoms.[2]

For President Truman, the conflict with Soviet communism was a war between truth and lies. The United States, he declared, was leading a "campaign of truth" to combat Soviet "deceit, distortion, and lies." The

Soviets, for their part, asserted the same position. They claimed that communist "truth" would defeat the "lies" at the rotten core of the capitalist system.

It could be argued that Soviet communism was, like Nazi ideology, based on a big lie; the Soviet Union, like Nazi Germany, had no civil society, no public sphere, no civic discourse, no public opinion, no competing ideas. But there was one important difference. The Nazis articulated an explicit propaganda strategy around their big lie. For the Soviets, on the other, propaganda was instrumental in spreading their "truth." Under Soviet communism, there was only one truth: Marxist-Leninist ideology. Indoctrination began in early childhood through schooling and Communist Party youth organizations. Even the advanced sciences were subjected to the test of communist "truth." The Soviet state rejected empirical sciences as "bourgeois." Scientific truths were merged with ideological truths. The name of the Communist Party's propaganda newspaper, *Pravda* (Russian for "truth"), revealed the depth of Soviet cynicism. For lies to be accepted as true, words had to be divorced from their meaning.

Pravda was founded by Lenin in 1912, five years before the Russian Revolution. Stalin was an early member of the *Pravda* editorial team and kept the paper on a tight leash after taking control of the Communist Party in the 1920s. *Pravda* pioneered the construction of alternative truths—what today we could call "alternative facts." The newspaper praised the Soviet gulags where more than a million perished. While Stalin was announcing a new democratic Soviet constitution in 1936, he was also ordering mass executions in the Great Purge. *Pravda* published phony letters to the editor calling for the death penalty for "enemies of the people." In a society where anything can signify its opposite, a newspaper titled "Truth" could be filled with lies.

All media in the Soviet Union—newspapers, radio, cinema—were mobilized into the service of official propaganda. In Russia's large cities, subway commuters were bombarded with radio propaganda. In movie theaters, they watched Soviet propaganda newsreels. When a member of the Soviet leadership was disgraced or pushed out—or, like Trotsky, assassinated —their images were cropped from photographs. Condemned to *damnatio memoriae* like a disgraced Roman emperor, they were expurgated from Soviet history.

Astonishingly, Western media were largely uncritical of Stalin's atrocities, just as they were indulgent toward Hitler during the same period in the 1930s. Stalin's most ardent cheerleader in the West was the Moscow correspondent for the *New York Times*. Walter Duranty, a Cambridge-educated Englishman, had been the paper's correspondent in Moscow since 1922. He was a loyal Stalin apologist in the pages of the *Times* for nearly fifteen years. When the British press revealed the existence of

Soviet labor camps and sent shocking reports of famine, Duranty told his *New York Times* readers that these claims were false: "Any report of famine is today an exaggeration or malignant propaganda."[3] He also defended Stalin's brutal show trials when the Soviet dictator was purging his enemies in the Communist Party. "Most of the accused, I am convinced, deserve their fate," he wrote.[4] His favorite catchphrase to qualify Stalin's brutal repression was "You can't make an omelet without breaking eggs."[5]

Back in America, Duranty's reports were tremendously influential in shaping President Franklin Roosevelt's foreign policy toward the Soviet Union. Among his fellow journalists, Duranty's reports from Moscow were highly praised, and even earned him the Pulitzer Prize. The *Nation* described Duranty's reporting as "the most enlightened, dispassionate dispatches from a great nation in the making which appeared in any newspaper in the world." Liverpool-born Duranty, notorious for his skirt-chasing despite having only one leg (the other had been amputated after a train crash), remained in his Moscow bureau chief job until 1936. He lived in a well-appointed four-room Moscow apartment stocked with fine liquors and caviar—and sometime opium, to which he had become addicted after losing his leg. He also had his own cook and a chauffeur.

A different fate was reserved for Gareth Jones, the British journalist who exposed the Soviet-inflicted famine in Ukraine. He was expelled from the Soviet Union. Other British journalists in Moscow saw through Walter Duranty. Malcolm Muggeridge, the Moscow correspondent for the *Manchester Guardian* who had witnessed the mass starvation in Ukraine with his own eyes, called Duranty "the greatest liar of any journalist I have ever met."[6] Three decades after Duranty's death in 1957, a critical biography of him was published, aptly titled *Stalin's Apologist*. The *New York Times* admitted that his stories from Moscow in the 1930s were "some of the worst reporting" ever to appear in the paper. "Taking Soviet propaganda at face value this way was completely misleading," stated the *Times*.[7] There was a move to strip Duranty of his Pulitzer Prize. But in 2003, the Pulitzer Prize board refused to revoke the award, concluding that "there was not clear and convincing evidence of deception" in Duranty's reporting from Moscow.[8]

Duranty's success in Moscow was owed largely to his personal relationship with Stalin. He fell under the spell of the Soviet dictator. Stalin, like Hitler, carefully constructed a cult of personality around his own image. In the atheist Soviet state, the personality cult around the leader was crucially important. Unlike religion, Marxism didn't hold out the promise of eternal salvation; it offered the proletariat a utopia in the here and now. Veneration of icons therefore was directed toward revered "great leaders"—Lenin, Stalin, followed by Mao Zedong and the Kim dynasty in North Korea. Following Lenin's death in 1924, Stalin created a personality cult around his predecessor. Lenin became a Bolshevik icon. Against the wishes of Lenin's widow, Stalin ordered Lenin's body embalmed and displayed in public to be venerated like a sacred relic. Lenin thus became the first Soviet saint, resistant to putrefaction, worshipped in perpetuity by the proletariat.

The British economist John Maynard Keynes insightfully made the connection between religion and Soviet ideology a year after Lenin's death. In an essay on the Soviet Union, Keynes observed:

> Leninism is a combination of two things which Europeans have kept for some centuries in different compartments of the soul—religion and business. We are shocked because the religion is new, and contemptuous because the business, being subordinated *to* the religion instead of the other way round, is highly inefficient. Like other new religions, Leninism derives its power not from the multitudes but from a small number of enthusiastic converts whose zeal and intolerance make each one the equal in strength of a hundred indifferentists. . . . Like other new religions, it persecutes without justice or pity those who actively resist it. Like other new religions, it is unscrupulous. Like other new religions, it is filled with missionary ardor and ecumenical ambitions. But to say that Leninism is the faith of a persecuting and propagating minority of fanatics led by hypocrites is, after all, to say no more or less than that it *is* a religion, and not merely a party, and Lenin a Mahomet, and not a Bismarck. [9]

Stalin did not neglect, of course, to fashion his own image as Lenin's legitimate successor. Soviet newspapers published fake photographs showing the two great leaders together. Gradually, Stalin appropriated Lenin's personality cult as he transitioned the Soviet Union from its revolutionary phase to consolidate his power over a coercive security state. Unlike Hitler, whose Nazi ideology was fused with soaring Teutonic mythology, there was nothing romantically operatic about Stalin's personality cult. Soviet propaganda portrayed him as a modest cobbler's son who, by the strength of his will, rose in the Communist Party to become the "Father of Nations."

After 1934, when Stalin added to his titles "Commissar for Cultural Enlightenment," his iconography was ubiquitous. Enormous statues of Stalin and Lenin were erected in Soviet cities, where public squares were festooned with massive portraits of Marx and Engels. Compared with statuary propaganda in ancient Rome, when statues of emperors were eight meters high, Soviet iconography was megalomaniacal. Statues of Stalin and Lenin reached heights of forty meters. Lenin's statues invariably showed him in dramatic oratorical poses, an arm stretched out to a

mass gathering. Stalin was portrayed in less histrionic postures. His iconography conveyed the quasi-sacred image of a Savior among his people,
comforting, blessing, and healing. Images of Stalin were in every home.
It was said that, in times of deprivation, there was "no bread on the table,
but Stalin on the wall." On his seventieth birthday, a massive portrait of
Stalin was hung in Red Square. *Pravda* devoted the entire newspaper to
his veneration. A short man who stood only five foot seven inches, Stalin
was sensitive about his physical stature—and painters who failed to de-
pict him as tall with powerful hands risked execution.[10]

Beyond the Soviet Union's borders, communist propaganda was weaponized to spread lies—or *dezinformatsiya*—targeting Western capitalism. The KGB covertly funded trade unions, women's movements, and
other protest groups, though their members were never made aware of the
Soviet financing. Soviet spies also cultivated leftist intellectuals in the
West to mobilize them as instruments of dissidence. These infiltration
campaigns exploited Orwellian weasel words and phony causes to attract
leading Western intellectuals and artists. The most successful was the so-
called "peace" movement. For three decades, the KGB infiltrated and
financed "peace" movements throughout the West, including the United
States. The main goal of the Soviet "peace" offensive—which portrayed
Russia as a peace-loving nation, in contrast to Western imperialist capitalism—was to turn public opinion against the American nuclear missile
build-up in Europe. Soviet "peace" propaganda worked through KGB-
infiltrated front organizations with names such as World Peace Council,
Christian Peace Conference, and International Institute for Peace.

One Soviet-sponsored "peace" meeting was the five-day Cultural and
Scientific Conference for World Peace, held at New York's Waldorf
Astoria in 1949. Among the event's attendees were famous names from
the arts and sciences: Leonard Bernstein, Marlon Brando, Charlie Chaplin, Lillian Hellman, Aaron Copland, Thomas Mann, Dorothy Parker,
and Albert Einstein. A Russian delegate at the conference was internationally renowned composer Dmitri Shostakovich. The conference, which
attracted nearly three thousand attendees, was picketed by several hundred protestors on the pavement outside the hotel. The *New Yorker* reported that one protestor was holding a placard that read: "Join Communism. You Have Nothing to Lose But Your Brains." Another man was
brandishing a banner reading, "Shostakovich Jump Through a Window."
While many attendees were genuinely interested in the cause of world
peace, the event degenerated when Shostakovich launched into an attack
on the United States, which he said was building weapons of mass destruction. Some of the American artists joined the Soviet denunciation of
"American warmongering." The composer Aaron Copland declared that
the United States was pushing the planet toward a third world war. Writ-

ers Norman Mailer and Mary McCarthy countered by denouncing Stalinism. [11]

In Britain, where Soviet intelligence had recruited spies such as Kim Philby and Anthony Blunt at Cambridge in the 1930s, the KGB covertly orchestrated high-profile protest movements such as the Campaign for Nuclear Disarmament. A "ban the bomb" movement, the CND attracted many famous British writers and actors, including the philosopher Bertrand Russell, playwright John Osborne, writer Doris Lessing, and filmmaker Lindsay Anderson. Among British politicians, future Labour Party leaders Michael Foot and Jeremy Corbyn were also supporters. The CND staged highly publicized demonstrations, including one in Trafalgar Square in 1961 at which hundreds of protestors were arrested. The CND reached the height of its influence two decades later in the 1980s, when conservative hardliners Margaret Thatcher and Ronald Reagan were in power in Britain and America. In March 1981, 150,000 protestors in London marched on Hyde Park. The *New York Times* correspondent in London reported: "The protesters, most of them apparently middle class and under the age of forty, came from all over Britain on special trains and buses. Many brought babies or young children, their carriages bearing such slogans as 'Let Me Be Allowed to Grow Up' and 'I Want to Live.'" [12]

The Soviets also used art—painting, sculpture, music, literature—as propaganda tools. The officially sanctioned Soviet style reflected an aesthetic known as "socialist realism." This was not to be confused with the wider international movement in art, including in America, called *social* realism. *Socialist* realism was Soviet-controlled propaganda. *Pravda,* always vigilant about ideological truth, guided Soviet artists with a strict definition:

> Socialist realism, the basic method of Soviet artistic literature and literary criticism, demands truthfulness from the artist and a historically concrete portrayal of reality in its revolutionary development. Under these conditions, truthfulness and historical concreteness of artistic portrayal ought to be combined with the task of the ideological remaking and education of working people in the spirit of socialism. [13]

In short, socialist realism strictly adhered to Soviet doctrine. Its function was the glorification of every aspect of communist society. In painting and sculpture, socialist realism shared common traits with the Nazi art connection between ideology and an ideal of the perfect human specimen. While Nazi art depicted an Aryan ideal, Soviet art portrayed the perfect communist worker. It provided the iconography for the Soviet "New Man" inhabiting a Marxist utopia.

If Soviet socialist realism was not terribly uplifting as an art form, its aesthetic ideology mobilized the talents of Russia's most renowned artists, writers, and composers. The movement's founder and leading voice was writer Maxim Gorki, who had known Tolstoy and Chekhov in his early pre-Soviet career before befriending Stalin. In the 1930s, Stalin built a propaganda plane called the "Maxim Gorki," outfitted with printing presses to churn out newspapers distributed by the aircraft to remote corners of the Soviet Union. The plane, said to be the biggest aircraft in the world at the time, was typical of the Soviet "futurist" movement rejecting the past and embracing modernity. The plane made only twelve flights, however. In 1935, it crashed, killing everyone on board. Gorki himself died, less dramatically, at his Moscow villa the following year. Stalin was a pallbearer at his funeral.

In music, the Russian composer Sergei Prokofiev spent many years abroad in Paris and the United States, but eventually returned to the Soviet Union under Stalin to compose "Soviet operas." Why Prokofiev, famous for the "Classical" Symphony and *Peter and the Wolf*, chose to return to Russia at the height of Stalin's brutal purges remains a mystery. A greater enigma are Prokofiev's propaganda compositions. His cantata celebrating the twentieth anniversary of the Bolshevik revolution featured texts by Stalin, Marx, and Lenin. Prokofiev had the misfortune to die on the same day as Stalin—March 5, 1953—earning him the reputation as "Stalin's last victim."

Another great Russian composer of the same period, Dmitri Shostakovich, was a darling of the Soviet establishment early in his career. Like Prokofiev, Shostakovich enjoyed international celebrity. When his opera *Lady Macbeth of the Mtsensk District* debuted in 1934, it was a huge success and toured the world. In the Soviet Union, *Lady Macbeth* was hailed as a "chef-d'oeuvre of Soviet creativity." Two years later, however, Stalin attended a performance of the opera and hated it so much that he left early. When *Pravda* dismissed the work as "muddle instead of music," it was believed Stalin himself had dictated the negative review. Worse, *Pravda* accused Shostakovich's opera of being "bourgeois," the ultimate disgrace for any artist in the Soviet Union. Shostakovich fell into disgrace, terrified, especially since Stalin had just unleashed the Great Terror in which more than a million perished. "From that moment on," Shostakovich wrote toward the end of his life, "I was stuck with the label 'enemy of the people' and I don't need to explain what the label meant in those days."[14]

Shostakovich redeemed himself the following year with his Fifth Symphony, a more conservative work composed within the expectations of socialist realism. In 1949, he traveled with Stalin's blessing to the famous "world peace" conference in New York at the Waldorf Astoria

Hotel. Shostakovich did his Stalinist duty at the conference by denouncing the United States. At a press conference later, however, a reporter asked him if he supported the Kremlin's denunciation of Igor Stravinsky's music. Shostakovich, a great admirer of Stravinsky, was mortified by the question. Nervously twitching, he gave an embarrassed answer in the affirmative. He toed the party line.

When he returned home to Russia, Shostakovich composed an oratorio, *The Song of the Forests*, to celebrate the reforestation of the Russian steppes. The work gained notoriety for its lines praising Stalin as "the great gardener." Two years later, Stalin appointed Shostakovich to the Supreme Soviet. Following Stalin's death, Shostakovich enjoyed even greater triumphs in the Soviet Union. He joined the Communist Party in 1960 and, the following year, composed his Twelfth Symphony to glorify the Bolshevik Revolution. In 1973, he provoked widespread criticism in the West when he signed a Soviet denunciation of dissident Andrei Sakharov.

Shostakovich finally spoke truth from the grave when his memoirs were published posthumously in the West in the late 1970s.

"Awaiting execution is a theme that has tormented me all my life," he wrote. "The majority of my symphonies are tombstones."[15]

Shostakovich's memoirs, whose authorship was contested by some scholars, were translated into thirty languages—but were not published in Russian.

***

Compared with sterile Soviet propaganda, the Americans had a much more appealing Cold War message with the promise of life, liberty, and the pursuit of happiness.

Still, the United States needed a compelling narrative to sell the American way. That was the purpose of President Truman's "campaign of truth," launched after the war to win the hearts and minds of Europeans.

The American truth campaign combined several approaches. Part of it operated in broad daylight, such as the Fulbright Program, established in 1946, to finance educational exchanges. On the economic front, the Marshall Plan was aimed at sandbagging Soviet expansion through economic aid to Western Europe. The cash inflows of U.S. dollars to prop up European economies were accompanied by a massive wave of American pop culture—movies, jazz music, bubble gum, Coca Cola, Lucky Strike cigarettes. This was a highly visible marketing campaign promoting the American way of life.

Other aspects of Truman's "truth" campaign were more covert. To counter Soviet attempts to co-opt Western artists and intellectuals, the CIA secretly financed highbrow art and publications—about theater, music, and books—that were promoted throughout Europe. The American intelligence agency also infiltrated intellectual circles to sponsor debates about liberal democracy versus communism. The CIA deliberately targeted leftist elites to make the case that it was possible to be liberal-minded and anti-communist. While the Soviets were covertly manipulating leftist intellectuals through "peace" conferences in the West, the CIA set up a "Congress for Cultural Freedom," bringing together a diverse group of writers, historians, poets, and artists. Some of the West's best-known intellectuals were indirectly on the CIA payroll through published work in periodicals including *Encounter* and *Partisan Review*. The list of eminent writers who indirectly received CIA funding was impressive: Isaiah Berlin, Stephen Spender, Daniel Bell, Robert Lowell, Irving Kristol, Hannah Arendt, Mary McCarthy, Arthur Koestler, Raymond Aron, Anthony Crosland, and George Orwell.

The CIA also paid for the Russian translation of books that presented a negative image of the Soviet Union. Some 10 million copies of CIA-financed books were secretly distributed behind the Iron Curtain. One of them was Boris Pasternak's *Doctor Zhivago,* published in 1957 but banned in the Soviet Union because of the novel's grim portrayal of the Russian Revolution and disillusionment with communist dogma. As a declassified CIA memo observed: "Pasternak's humanistic message—that every person is entitled to a private life and deserves respect as a human being, irrespective of the extent of his political loyalty or contribution to the state—poses a fundamental challenge to the Soviet ethic of sacrifice of the individual to the Communist system." The author of the memo, John Maury, head of the CIA's Soviet Russia Division, added: "There is no call to revolt against the regime in the novel, but the heresy which Dr. Zhivago preaches—political passivity—is fundamental. Pasternak suggests that the small unimportant people who remain passive to the regime's demands for active participation and emotional involvement in official campaigns are superior to the political 'activists' favored by the system. Further, he dares hint that society might function better without these fanatics."[16]

The Kremlin, infuriated by the worldwide success of *Doctor Zhivago*, denounced the book as a "malicious libel." When Pasternak won the Nobel Prize for literature in 1958, his initial response to the Swedish Academy was: "Thankful, glad, proud, confused."[17] His mood changed, however, when *Pravda* denounced him as a "malevolent Philistine."[18] His fellow Russian writers dismissed him as a "literary weed."[19] The Kremlin warned Pasternak that if he went to Oslo to receive the Nobel

Prize, he would never be allowed back into Russia. Pasternak declined the prize. In a telegram to the Nobel committee, he wrote: "Considering the meaning this award has been given in the society to which I belong, I must reject this undeserved prize which has been presented to me. Please do not receive my voluntary rejection with displeasure."[20] He died from lung cancer two years later.

The Congress for Cultural Freedom was just one of many propaganda conduits that received CIA funding. Others included the Rockefeller Foundation, Ford Foundation, Time Inc., PEN, and the Metropolitan Opera. The Metropolitan Museum of Modern Art (MOMA) in New York proved especially effective as an institutional weapon in the American "truth" campaign. By shifting its focus toward modern art, the CIA moved into a different sphere of propaganda. Promoting Hollywood movies, jazz music, and bubble gum was effective on the level of popular culture. Modern art exhibitions elevated the CIA's initiative to an oysters-and-champagne campaign. Avant-garde American paintings promised to appeal to European cultural elites and opinion leaders. This strategy led to one of the most improbable—and inspired—propaganda campaigns of the Cold War. Just as it had promoted works of literature such as Pasternak's *Doctor Zhivago*, the CIA played a key role in launching Abstract Expressionism as a modern art movement.

Before the CIA's involvement, the U.S. State Department had assembled a traveling exhibition in 1946 called "Advancing American Art," featuring forty-nine paintings purchased with government money for a total of $49,000. The show, including works by Georgia O'Keeffe, Edward Hopper, Robert Motherwell, and Stuart Davis, opened at the Metropolitan Museum in New York to positive reviews. Influential art critic Clement Greenberg, writing in the *Nation,* described the exhibition as "a remarkable accomplishment, and its moral should be taken to heart by those who control the public destiny of art in our country."[21] Flush with that critical success, the exhibition moved to Paris and Prague on a planned five-year tour of Europe and Latin America.

The tour was abruptly canceled, however, after American artists back home in the United States condemned the works as "un-American." The conservative American Artists Professional League criticized the exhibition as representing the "radicalism" of European trends in art. These criticisms got picked up in the American press. One magazine published photos of the works under the derisory headline "Your Money Bought These Paintings." An American congressman wrote a blistering letter to secretary of state George Marshall, complaining that the paintings were a "travesty" that would "make the United States appear ridiculous." Another congressman suggested that the paintings were the work of communists. President Truman, no fan of modern art, was happy to see the exhibition canceled. He gave his own appraisal of the work with a famous remark, "If that's art, then I'm a Hottentot." With congressmen threatening to withdraw funding for the exhibition, George Marshall canceled the show. All the paintings were auctioned off. They sold for a total of $5,544—a fraction of the purchase price.[22] One Georgia O'Keeffe canvas fetched fifty dollars. In 2014, a similar Georgia O'Keeffe floral painting from the same era set a record price of $44.4 million at auction.

After this aborted attempt via State Department channels, the modern art offensive was turned over to the CIA. Nelson Rockefeller, who had high-level connections inside both the CIA and MOMA, became a key player in this phase of the campaign. His family had financed the MOMA (he called it "mummy's museum"). Rockefeller, who would later serve as U.S. vice president under President Gerald Ford, was perfect for the job. He was an art lover and a resolute anti-communist. In the 1930s, he had ordered the removal of a Diego Rivera mural from New York's Rockefeller Center because one of the panels depicted Vladimir Lenin and a Soviet May Day parade. In the post-war years, Rockefeller greatly admired the new Abstract Expressionist style, which he called "free enterprise painting."

Through the MOMA, the CIA funneled large sums into promoting American painters, including Jackson Pollock and Mark Rothko, in the vanguard of Abstract Expressionism. Their artistic style, dazzlingly modernist, was a perfect antidote to the rigid and drab socialist realism of officially sanctioned Soviet paintings. The MOMA was also working with the U.S. State Department to promote American industrial design concepts, especially mid-century furniture, as a contrast to the austerity of Soviet design styles, which in architecture was associated with the urban utopia "brutalist" movement (from French *béton brut,* for raw concrete). The MOMA's "Good Design" exhibitions, which traveled Europe after the war, promoted aesthetically pleasing and functional furniture and objects that were an expression of the American ideal.[23]

The MOMA's promotion of Abstract Expressionism followed the same propaganda playbook. The first phase of the campaign was aimed at getting the two most influential American art critics, Clement Greenberg and Harold Rosenberg, behind Abstract Expressionism (Ab Ex). Both praised the Ab Ex style as pure expression. Greenberg, a member of the CIA-funded Congress for Cultural Freedom, championed the work of Pollock. Rosenberg, the most powerful art critic in America during the 1950s, was a former Marxist associated with the *Partisan Review* who had turned against Soviet aesthetics and worked for the U.S. government's propaganda unit during the Second World War. He lauded Abstract Expressionism as American "action painting," which he admired for its unique style of spontaneous splash, dribble, and smear that transformed canvases into "events."

On the strength of accolades at home in America, the Congress for Cultural Freedom sponsored a "New American Painting" touring exhibition featuring the works of Pollock, Willem de Kooning, Robert Motherwell, and other artists. In 1958, the Ab Ex exhibition travelled to Paris, Berlin, Brussels, Milan, and Basel. The Tate Gallery in London desperately wanted the show, too, but couldn't afford it. That was no obstacle. The CIA arranged financing through wealthy individuals—notably well-connected American philanthropist Julius Fleishmann—so the exhibition could travel to London. The Tate had no idea that the show had been financed by the CIA. Nor did the Ab Ex artists know that they were being coopted as Cold War crusaders. The European tour of "New American Painting" put Ab Ex on the map in the international art market. It's scarcely an exaggeration to claim that the CIA created the booming market for Abstract Expressionist painting. As British historian Frances Stonor Saunders put it: "In the manner of a Renaissance prince—except that it acted secretly—the CIA fostered and promoted American Abstract Expressionist painting around the world for more than twenty years."[24]

In the 1950s, President Dwight Eisenhower took a more liberal, and pragmatic, view toward modern American art than his predecessor Harry Truman. "As long as our artists are free to create with sincerity and conviction, there will be healthy controversy and progress in art," Eisenhower said in 1954. "How different it is in tyranny. When artists are made the slaves and tools of the state; when artists become the chief propagandists of a cause, progress is arrested and creation and genius are destroyed."[25] Eisenhower stepped up the American "truth" offensive with American music, movies, and even news broadcasts. Radio Free Europe, created by a CIA front organization, sent American news broadcasts into Soviet-bloc countries via transmitters in Germany. At the same time, Voice of America and U.S. Army radio stations throughout Europe played jazz to spread American popular culture. The Eisenhower administration sponsored jazz tours, featuring African American musicians and George Gershwin's opera *Porgy and Bess*, to counter Soviet propaganda about racism in America. A Voice of America radio show called *Music USA* was so popular that its host, Willis Conover, became one of the best-known American names in Soviet-bloc countries. *Look* magazine wrote that jazz was "full of friendliness that totalitarians won't easily be able to close." As the popularity of jazz spread in Europe, the State Department financed world tours of Dizzy Gillespie and Louis Armstrong. In 1956, *Saturday Review* published an article titled "Is Jazz Good Propaganda?" Everyone knew the answer.[26]

The Hollywood studios also joined the Cold War propaganda juggernaut. After churning out a raft of anti-Hitler films during the war, the script switched to anti-communist films such as *The Red Menace, I Married a Communist,* and *Pickup on South Street.* Hollywood's strong output of Biblical epics in the 1950s—*Quo Vadis, The Ten Commandments, Ben-Hur*—reinforced the American perception of the Cold War as a moral choice not only between capitalism and communism, but between Christianity and atheism. The U.S. government wanted to contrast the values of God-fearing American society with those of anti-religious Soviet communism. Cecil B. DeMille's *Ten Commandments* was released in 1956, the same year the U.S. Congress adopted the motto "In God We Trust" as the official United States motto, replacing the Latin phrase *E pluribus unum* ("out of many, one"). While "In God We Trust" had appeared on American currency for nearly a century, the shift from secular to pious language in the national motto underscored the profoundly religious dimension of American patriotism. In the 1950s, American evangelists such as Bill Graham preached that the Ten Commandments were the bedrock of America's moral code. Some believed that the commandments should be posted in every American school classroom.

A Hollywood blockbuster titled *The Ten Commandments* was bound to succeed in America in the 1950s. When the film was released, there could be no mistake that it was a propaganda movie. In the movie's prologue, producer Cecil B. DeMille appeared to deliver the following message to movie audiences: "The theme of this picture is whether men are to be ruled by God's law or whether they are to be ruled by the whims of a dictator. . . . Are men the property of the state? Or are they free souls under God? This same battle continues in the world today."[27] At the box office, *The Ten Commandments* was the highest-earning film of the decade, and one of the most successful movies in Hollywood history.

The most famous anti-Soviet movie hero of the era was the dapper British spy James Bond, agent "007." Ian Fleming's famous Cold War spy worked for Her Majesty's government to thwart the sinister world-domination plots of a Russian spy agency, SPECTRE (in Fleming's books, it's called SMERSH). In early Bond films—such as *Dr. No* and *From Russia, With Love*—James Bond drove an Aston Martin, took his martinis "shaken, not stirred," and canoodled with sultry Russian beauties working for Soviet counter-intelligence. Bond's memorable lines—especially, "The name's Bond, James Bond"—became among the most famous in the history of cinema.

Off screen, the Hollywood studios were purging their own ranks of suspected communists during the "red scare" sweeping through the industry in the 1950s. This was the period of anti-communist senator Joe McCarthy's show trials and the U.S. Congress's House Un-American

Activities Committee. Among the Hollywood stars suspected of being communists were Orson Welles, Lucille Ball, and Charlie Chaplin. Even Groucho Marx—famous for his line "Whatever it is, I'm against it!"—was suspected of communist sympathies. Reputations were ruined, and lives were broken. During the dark Hollywood "blacklist" period, scriptwriters and directors were run out of the industry and never worked again. In television, the so-called Red Channel purges saw dozens of industry figures blacklisted. When actor Philip Loeb, star of a popular CBS situation comedy *The Goldbergs*, was identified as a communist, the show's sponsor, General Foods, ordered him to be fired. The program's producers refused. In 1951 General Foods canceled the show. The following season, *The Goldbergs* moved to NBC—but Loeb was replaced in the starring role. Depressed, he committed suicide in 1955.

The persecution of suspected communists went beyond Hollywood. The American composer Aaron Copland, famous for classic works such as *Appalachian Spring* and *Rodeo*, was put under surveillance by the FBI as a suspected communist. Ironically, Copland was a quintessential American composer, the first to write classical music in a uniquely American idiom. His works, notably *Fanfare for the Common Man*, became patriotic American classics. During the Cold War, however, Copland was a suspected traitor. In 1936, he had supported the Communist candidate for president, Earl Browder, against Franklin Roosevelt. For more than two decades, the FBI monitored Copland's whereabouts and used informants to collect detailed information about him. In 1953, Copland's orchestral work, *A Lincoln Portrait,* was withdrawn from the program at President Eisenhower's inauguration due to his alleged communist sympathies. One accusation against him was his presence as a speaker at the Soviet-friendly "peace" conference at the Waldorf Astoria in 1949. Summoned before Joe McCarthy's Government Operations Committee, Copland denied he was a communist, adding, "I spend my days writing symphonies, concertos, ballads."[28]

Americans who believed in the "fourth estate" role of the press must have been sorely disappointed during the Cold War. Very few newspapers were critical of U.S. government surveillance and harassment of suspected radicals. Most journalists were faithful to the anti-communist red scare script and lavished an extraordinary amount of publicity on figures like Joe McCarthy and his anti-communist hearings. However repugnant, McCarthy's shrill message resonated with the prevailing political culture in America. That came sharply into focus when Julius and Ethel Rosenberg—both children of Russian immigrants—were arrested and tried for passing nuclear secrets to the Soviets. Despite judicial improprieties and due process violations, the only American media outlets that spoke up for the Rosenbergs were radical leftist papers such as the

National Guardian. The American media were overwhelmingly hostile, covering the story through an ideological prism of anti-communism. Even the American Civil Liberties Union spurned the Rosenbergs. Their case was more controversial in Europe, especially in France, where protest movements rallied to support the Rosenbergs. In America, the only debatable question was whether the Rosenbergs should get the death sentence, mainly because it would leave their two children orphaned.

The court sentenced both Rosenbergs to die in the electric chair. When all appeals were exhausted, the execution was set for June 1953. In the French communist newspaper *L'Humanité*, Pablo Picasso published a drawing of the Rosenbergs holding hands seated on electric chairs. "The hours count, the minutes count," wrote Picasso. "Do not let this crime against humanity take place."[29] Pope Pius XII pleaded for clemency, but to no effect. President Eisenhower rejected these appeals, refusing to exercise his executive powers to commute the death sentences.

The Rosenbergs were executed in the electric chair in Sing Sing prison on June 19, 1953. Ethel Rosenberg's death was particularly gruesome. Electricity had to be sent through her body a few times, sending smoke from the top of her head, before she finally died. French philosopher Jean-Paul Sartre thundered at America in the newspaper *Libération*: "Your country is sick with fear. You are afraid of the shadow of your own bomb."[30] Commentators in the American media did not share Sartre's outrage. When the American press did cover the issue, it was to express scorn. The *New York Post* dismissed Rosenberg supporters as a "monstrous example of communist doublethink."[31] The Rosenberg case, whatever the facts, was far from a highpoint for "objectivity" in American journalism.

When the Soviet Union collapsed at the end of the 1980s, it was a great victory for liberal democracy. The Cold War had begun as an ideological confrontation between two opposing systems. A half century later, it ended on the same battlefield of ideas. Communism was exposed as an economic failure wrapped in evil ideological packaging. The West's triumph was a victory for the values underpinning liberal democracy. Liberalism had both facts and values on its side. Above all, it was a victory of truth over lies—or, at the very least, of liberal truths over Soviet lies.

In the 1990s, the world entered a new era of Pax Americana. The decade's triumphant catchphrase was "the end of history," an old term revived by Francis Fukuyama in a famous essay bearing the same title. Fukuyama turned Marxism on its head by declaring that Karl Marx's historical materialism had been tragically wrong. "The triumph of the West, of the Western idea, is evident first of all in the total exhaustion of viable systematic alternatives to Western liberalism," wrote Fukuyama.[32] The prospect of a Marxist paradise had been a cruel fantasy. Communism in practice was a grim dystopia of gulags, purges, and mass murder. Liberal democracy had prevailed because, whatever its defects, it was morally and functionally superior.

"What we may be witnessing is not just the end of the Cold War, or the passing of a particular period of post-war history, but the end of history as such," observed Fukuyama. "That is, the end point of mankind's ideological evolution and the universalization of Western liberal democracy as the final form of human government."[33]

Fukuyama's triumphalism was regarded by many as a clarion call for a glorious new epoch in human history. Fukuyama was careful, however, to caution against simplistic interpretations of his theory. History was not over, he stressed; there would still be historical events, but the *idea* of liberal democracy had triumphed. "At the end of history it is not necessary that all societies become successful liberal societies," he observed, "merely that they end their ideological pretensions of representing different and higher forms of human society."[34]

The end-of-history celebrations turned out to be premature. Fukuyama may have been correct in asserting that liberal ideas had triumphed, but he could not have predicted that liberal democracy would quickly show deep cracks and fissures. In the first decade of the new century, an international financial crisis triggered widespread disillusionment with capitalism. Anti-globalization protest movements mobilized against the grotesque inequalities produced by a free-market system and the destructive impact of modern industrialism on the planet's climate. War and its tragic consequence of refugee migrations triggered a backlash of reactionary populism in countries—including the United States—once considered model democracies. Only two decades after the "end of history," liberal democracy and capitalism were under attack again. History was not over; it was roaring back with a vengeance, this time on a wave of religious fanaticism and populist demagoguery.

In this tense global climate, a serious external threat to the liberal West came, not unexpectedly, from post-Soviet Russia. After a decade of casino capitalism that witnessed oligarchs loot and pillage the Russian economy, Vladimir Putin asserted order as a new Kremlin strongman attached to old authoritarian methods. That wasn't surprising given his background as a KGB spy under the Soviet regime. Putin didn't restore Soviet communism. He borrowed bits and pieces from several ideological currents—liberalism, conservatism, nationalism, Russian Orthodoxy, anticosmopolitanism—in a new regime of authoritarian populism. One thing Putin did restore, however, was the old Soviet propaganda game of Orwellian double-speak.

Putin's model of "managed democracy" was inspired by a little-known Russian philosopher named Ivan Ilyin.[35] A fierce early critic of

Bolshevism, Ilyin was among the intellectuals expelled from Russia in 1922 on the so-called philosophers ship. Exiled in Germany, he became a great admirer of fascism, first under Mussolini in Italy and then its German version under Hitler. Ilyin advocated a brand of fascism custom made for his Russian homeland. He held up the "Russian spirit" as the ideal for a potently masculine form of nationalism whose enemies were both communism and liberalism. Though he died in obscurity in 1954, Ilyin's works experienced a revival in Russia after the collapse of the Soviet Union. Under Putin, he was described as the Kremlin's court philosopher.

Putin borrowed two of Ilyin's key ideas. First, the Kremlin must destroy all decadent enemies threatening to "sodomize" the Russian spirit. As the embodiment of Russia's virile nationalism, Putin's cult of personality was constructed around masculine iconography.[36] He was photographed shirtless on fishing and hunting expeditions. He stripped down for the cameras to immerse himself in icy waters to mark the Russian Orthodox feast of the Epiphany—thus associating traditional religion with Russia's virile national spirit. Second, the most outrageous official lies produce the most unquestioning loyalty. This was a Putin-era Russian update on the Nazi big lie. Putin's *dezinformatsiya* tactics, weaponizing lies against Russia's designated enemies, were described as a "firehose of falsehood." The Kremlin continuously sprayed lies, fictions, and partial truths on social media with no regard for objective reality. As a RAND report observed in 2016, the Russian firehose tactic had two distinctive features: first, a high number of channels and messages; and second, a shameless willingness to disseminate partial truths or outright fictions.[37]

Under Putin, nothing was true, and everything was possible. Accused of ordering Russian missiles to shoot down a Malaysia Airlines flight over eastern Ukraine, Putin denied it. The same denials were issued in response to every accusation even when backed up by factual evidence. Accused of using Russian trolls to spread disinformation on social media during the American presidential election to favor Donald Trump, Putin flatly denied it. When two Russian agents were caught red-handed using a nerve agent to murder a former Russian double agent living in England, the Kremlin denied that the two men were spies. The two Russian agents, caught on camera near the crime scene in Salisbury, even appeared on Russian television claiming they were merely tourists visiting England. Their extraordinary denial was almost ludicrous. Nobody outside of Russia believed them. But that didn't matter. Putin didn't revive the old Soviet system, but he kept its worst habits—including the communist regime's utter disregard for truth.[38] As George Orwell observed, a useful lie is preferable to a harmful truth.

Today, while these external threats attempt to destabilize the West, liberal societies are tearing themselves apart in an internal culture war that has little to do with Russian trolls or Islamic terrorism. As these culture wars rage, the question of truth is far from settled. We have simply changed battlefields. Today, the fight over truth has become a civil war.

Part VI

The War on Truth

16

GUARDIANS OF THE TRUTH

In November 1902, *McClure's Magazine* published the first installment of a nineteen-part series titled "The Rise of Standard Oil." More than a century later, those articles are still considered a stellar example of American investigative journalism at its best.

"The Rise of Standard Oil" was written by a woman, Ida Tarbell, one of the most famous journalists of her day. Born in 1857 in Hatch Hollow, Pennsylvania, Tarbell was raised with a family legend claiming they were descended from Sir Walter Raleigh (her maternal grandfather was named Walter Raleigh McCullough). Her father, Franklin Tarbell, was a teacher-turned-oilman during the Pennsylvania petroleum boom of the 1860s. When Ida was growing up in the years following the Civil War, her Methodist family was intellectually sophisticated and socially active. After graduating with an MA degree from Allegheny College, she moved to Paris in 1890 to research the lives of the women who had played a role in the French Revolution. While in France, she worked as a correspondent for *Scribner's Magazine* and, after meeting Samuel McClure in Paris, began writing for his new magazine, *McClure's*. Her high-profile feature articles for *McClure's*, including a biographical series on Napoleon Bonaparte, helped boost the monthly magazine's subscriptions to 250,000 copies.

Back in the United States in 1900, Tarbell began researching the life of another powerful figure: the richest man in the world, John D. Rockefeller. While Tarbell had already established a solid reputation at *McClure's* as a biographer, including a series on Abraham Lincoln, her interest in Rockefeller had a more personal dimension. When she was fourteen, Rockefeller's Standard Oil aggressively cornered the oil market in Ohio by buying up all the competition. The buyouts in 1872 were so devastating for small oil refinery operators that it was dubbed the "Cleveland Massacre." One of its victims was the small oil refinery owned by Ida Tarbell's father in nearby Pennsylvania. Crushed by the Rockefeller steamroller, Franklin Tarbell's business partner committed suicide, and Tarbell was forced to mortgage his house to pay company debts.

It was later speculated that Ida Tarbell's journalistic investigation into Standard Oil was a personal vendetta against Rockefeller. It's an intriguing theory, and may be partially valid. But Tarbell's meticulous research into the Rockefeller dynasty was unimpeachable. Her nineteen-part investigation into Standard Oil was a painstakingly documented, rigorously fact-checked exposé of the business methods exploited by John D. Rockefeller to consolidate control of the American oil industry. Tarbell's feature articles about Rockefeller were revolutionary. It was the first time in American journalism that the public and private life of a business tycoon had been the object of such scrutiny.

Tarbell argued that John D. Rockefeller was fair game. He was not only tremendously rich but also "an inspirer of American ideals." Rockefeller was an icon for industrial capitalism in the Gilded Age. "A man who possesses this kind of influence cannot be allowed to live in the dark," wrote Tarbell. "The public not only has the right to know what sort of man he is; it is the duty of the public to know."[1]

Tarbell's portrayal of Rockefeller in *McClure's* was part investigative reportage, part psychological portrait. Probing into Rockefeller's strict religious upbringing, she recounted how, from an early age, he was maniacally obsessed with earning money. Tarbell even attended service at Euclid Avenue Baptist Church in Cleveland to secretly observe John D. Rockefeller during the sermon. She noted that he was restless and agitated, always looking around him from his pew, as if consumed by a terrible guilt about his tremendous wealth. She speculated that Rockefeller had a dual personality that allowed him to compartmentalize two opposing aspects of his character. One was a pious Baptist; the other was a ruthless capitalist.

Tarbell's articles on Standard Oil won widespread praise from American newspapers, including the *New York Times*. The original *McClure's* series was turned into a bestselling book, *The History of the Standard Oil Company*. The book's impact on public opinion was massive, triggering a public outcry against Rockefeller's monopoly power.

John D. Rockefeller, not surprisingly, was displeased with *McClure's* investigation into his life history and business dealings. He referred to Ida Tarbell as "that poisonous woman" and ordered everyone at Standard Oil to refuse to comment on her exposé. But the impact of Tarbell's series in *McClure's* could not be ignored. Rockefeller realized he needed to improve his image. He hired a public relations adviser to plant favorable articles about him in the press. His choice of PR man was intriguing: Joseph Clarke, an Irish American newspaper editor who, thirty years earlier, had written the famous hoax in the *New York Herald* about wild animals on the loose in Manhattan after escaping from the Central Park Zoo. The affable Clarke called on his contacts and cronies in the press and offered them direct access to John D. Rockefeller. The plan was to bring out the oil magnate's "human side."

The PR offensive wasn't enough to placate U.S. trust busters. Ida Tarbell's unflinching journalism had set in motion judicial proceedings against Standard Oil. In 1911, following a Supreme Court decision ruling that Standard Oil was an illegal monopoly, the company was split up into thirty-four smaller, independent firms. It was a watershed moment in the history of American capitalism. It was also a proud moment in the history of American journalism. Tarbell's fearless exposé of corporate power became known as "muckraking."

The term *muckraking* is seldom used today, except nostalgically. In Ida Tarbell's day, it was a new kind of investigative reporting that revitalized American journalism following the shameful era of penny press hoaxes and yellow press stunts. Journalism in the United States was finally adopting ethical codes based on standards of evidence and verifiable facts. Journalists in America were pursuing objective truth.

American journalism's transformation in the early twentieth century was not a historical accident. It was during this era that modern states were setting up bureaucracies and hiring experts to manage the complexities of advanced economies. New professions were pushing out amateurs and asserting monopoly control over spheres of knowledge based on credentials, expertise, and ethical standards. At American universities, the "scientific" movement was carving out new disciplines in pharmacy, law, medicine, accounting, and other fields. The quaint, gentlemanly tradition of "amateur expert" (think Sherlock Holmes) was being phased out. Society needed qualified experts (think forensic science) armed with scientific knowledge. Credentials-based professions were the modern-day equivalent of monks in the monasteries who had once monopolized truth through tight control of the production and diffusion of knowledge. Unlike the monastic spinners of religious dogma, however, modern professionals were specialists in highly focused areas of expertise. In the modern economy that empowered managerialism and technocracy, they were the new power elite. Journalists in America became part of this movement.

Professionalization brought many benefits in spheres cluttered with amateurs, dilettantes, and frauds. In medicine, for example, quacks had for decades been flogging bogus nostrums as bona fide remedies. The claims of patent medicines were a major issue in America at the end of the nineteenth century. Coca-Cola, for example, initially marketed itself as a "brain tonic," a boast that customers didn't doubt due to the powerful effect of its main ingredient: cocaine. In 1903, the U.S. government forced Coca-Cola to remove cocaine from the drink. All cocaine-based products—tablets, pastilles, tooth drops—were made illegal in the United States in 1914. Thanks to the advances of science and medicine, other bans would follow: arsenic to treat malaria, heroin lycetol for coughs, and radium salts in toothpastes. It was thanks to the work of muckraking journalists working for *McClure's* and *Collier's* that many quack remedies—fake antiseptics, headache powders, cures for consumption—were exposed as fraudulent. Investigative series such as Samuel Hopkins Adams's "The Great American Fraud: The Patent Medicine Evil," published in *Collier's* in 1906, were instrumental in prodding the U.S. government to pass the Pure Food and Drug Act.[2]

American journalism was not, strictly speaking, a profession, but aspired to that status by providing training and credentials. American universities started educating a new generation of graduates in the field. At the height of the muckraking era, the University of Missouri opened its School of Journalism in 1908, followed by Columbia University in 1912. These schools inculcated new empirical values and practices in the presentation of fact-based news as objective truth.[3] This was a uniquely American approach to newsgathering. In Europe, journalism practices remained largely amateur and politically partisan. In America, journalists aspired to a higher calling as guardians of the truth.

Most muckraker journalism appeared in monthly magazines—the *Nation*, *McClure's*, the *New Republic*, *Collier's*, *Ladies' Home Journal*—that enjoyed wide circulation among middle-class consumers of information. Sales of top-selling titles such as *Cosmopolitan* and *Collier's* soared in the first decade of the century to more than 500,000 copies. While the liberal-minded journalists writing for these magazines used investigative techniques to bring attention to the pressing issues of the day, it would be difficult to argue that they were purely dispassionate pursuers of objective truths. The muckrakers were frequently criticized, as the yellow press had been previously, for sensationalism. Their journalistic crusades were undoubtedly supported by facts, but they were often driven by a partisan political agenda. Their cause may have been noble, but their work was filtered through a bias that was unmistakably progressive.[4]

The historical context of the Progressive era was indeed key to their success. In the early twentieth century, America was grappling with difficult social issues brought on by rapid industrialization, urbanization, and immigration. The Progressive movement advocated bold reforms to tackle problems ranging from urban poverty and child labor to political corruption. The investigative reporting of muckraker journalists—such as

Samuel Hopkins Adams's "The Great American Fraud" exposé in *Collier's* on patent medicines—provided evidence-based impetus for these reforms. In the same spirit, Lincoln Steffens wrote a series in 1902 for *McClure's* exposing graft and corruption in America's big-city political machines. Two years later, his series was published as a book, *The Shame of the Cities,* which won widespread accolades.

The term *muckraker* was coined by Theodore Roosevelt, the battle-ready hero of the Spanish-American War who became president following William McKinley's assassination in 1901. In the White House, Roosevelt was a progressive reformer whose ideas were in tune with muckraking journalistic practices. He was also a politician, however, and was sometimes irritated by aggressive press inquiries. In a speech in Washington, DC, in 1906, Roosevelt alluded to the "Man with the Muck-rake" in John Bunyan's *Pilgrim's Progress* to express his vexation. "The men with the muck-rakes are often indispensable to the well-being of society," he said, "but only if they know when to stop raking the muck." Roosevelt was not opposed in principle to muckraking. "There should be relentless exposure of, and attack upon, every evil man whether politician or business man; every evil practice, whether in politics, in business, or in social life," he declared. He insisted, however, that its standard should always be truth. "I hail as a benefactor every writer or speaker, every man who, on the platform, or in book, magazine, or newspaper, with merciless severity makes such attack, provided always that he in his turn remembers that the attack is of use only if it is absolutely *truthful*."[5]

Muckraking, despite its tremendous influence on American society, was a short-lived trend in journalism. By the end of the First World War, the movement had largely disappeared. Some claim muckraking vanished because its social reform agenda had succeeded, especially through progressive legislation under Teddy Roosevelt and Woodrow Wilson. By the First World War, muckrakers were no longer needed. Mission accomplished. Their work was done.

A more material reason for muckraking's demise was economic. While magazines such as *McClure's* and *Collier's* were highly successful, they depended mostly on subscriptions. But revenues were not sufficiently robust to fund costly investigative journalism. Their finances became even more vulnerable when corporations, wary of the muckrakers' crusading social agenda, withdrew their advertising. *McClure's* was financially strapped even at the height of its power and fame. In 1906, its top writers, including Ida Tarbell, defected to start their own magazine. Sold to creditors in 1911, *McClure's* was transformed into a women's magazine.

The main reason for the death of muckraking, however, was war. When the United States entered the First World War, the media had a new cause. American journalism shifted its focus to the war against the German "Huns." Pursuing the "truth" based on objective facts was no longer a priority. American newspapers became part of Woodrow Wilson's war effort as tools of persuasion, manipulation, and deception. What's more, some prominent muckraker journalists—including Ida Tarbell—joined the U.S. government's propaganda unit. Before the war, they had published investigative stories that pushed a liberal social agenda that advocated progressive legislation to make food and drugs safe for Americans. In the war years, their work upheld President Wilson's credo about keeping the world safe for democracy. The man who ran Wilson's wartime propaganda unit, George Creel, was himself a former muckraker. When war was declared, the brightest minds in American journalism abandoned standards of truth to embrace the wartime necessity of propaganda.

After the war, hard-hitting investigative journalism had lost its cachet. The American economy was booming, the stock market was soaring, and Flappers were dancing in fountains of champagne. In the sparkling effervescence of the Jazz Age, another powerful new profession emerged with its own gospel of truth: public relations. The new science of propaganda had proved itself as a powerful weapon against the kaiser. Now its tools were refined and aimed at persuading American voters and consumers. As public relations took off in the post-war years, journalists would quickly find themselves out-gunned by battalions of PR hacks and spin doctors working for governments, corporations, and Madison Avenue advertising agencies. It was in this booming post-war culture that modern consumer society was born. Truth would never be the same.

The American public relations industry was founded by Ivy Lee. The son of a Methodist preacher, Lee was a Georgian who had graduated from Princeton and worked as a business reporter at Joseph Pulitzer's *New York World* during the heyday of the yellow press. Lee had witnessed firsthand the rise of Progressivism and simmering class war in America as public opinion turned against corporate robber barons. As a newspaperman, Lee understood the power of the press in shaping public opinion. He saw an opportunity in American businesses' failure to address negative press coverage. Big corporations needed to tell their story. They needed a narrative. And Ivy Lee was the man for the job.

In 1905, Lee set up a PR firm with partner George Parker, but quickly struck out on his own with Ivy Lee & Associates. His motto was "Tell the truth because sooner or later the public will find out anyway."[6] His first big break came on October 28, 1906. That afternoon, a newly built drawbridge connecting Atlantic City to the mainland lifted to allow a small vessel to pass under. But the electric signals malfunctioned. An eastbound train from Philadelphia hurtled onto the bridge, derailing and scudding over the rail ties before plunging into the river. The first two cars were completely underwater, their passengers trapped and unable to escape. Fifty-three people drowned.

The shocking tragedy put the Pennsylvania Railroad in the media spotlight. In panic mode, railroad executives hastily called Ivy Lee. He convinced them to be up front with facts about the accident. Lee's public statement about the Atlantic City train wreck was the first press release in history. His stick-to-the-facts approach worked. The *New York Times* published Lee's press release word for word.

His reputation now established, Lee put his skills to work for powerful American corporations in steel, banking, tobacco, cars, rubber, and meat packing. His most famous client was billionaire John D. Rockefeller, who had hired newspaperman Joseph Clarke to clean up his image following Ida Tarbell's investigative series in *McClure's* about Standard Oil. When Rockefeller called on Ivy Lee a decade later, the billionaire was confronted with an even greater crisis. In 1914, Rockefeller dispatched armed guards to attack 1,200 striking miners at the family's coal mines in Ludlow, Colorado. More than fifty people were killed in the violence, including twelve children of miners. The event, known as the "Ludlow Massacre," shocked American public opinion. It also exposed the appalling conditions in which men and children worked at Rockefeller-owned mines.

The Rockefellers desperately needed help. John D. Rockefeller Jr.—the son of the seventy-six-year-old family patriarch—wanted to buy advertising to get the family's story out. Ivy Lee advised against this. The best approach, he argued, was a public relations strategy based on honesty and compassion. He convinced John D. Rockefeller Jr. to cancel a family holiday and personally visit the Ludlow coal mine. Lee personally escorted Rockefeller out to Colorado to meet with miners and their wives. The press naturally was invited to cover the event. Lee's strategy worked. Newspaper coverage of John D. Rockefeller Jr.'s visit to Ludlow was overwhelmingly favorable.[7]

Ivy Lee's role as an "honest broker" had its limits, however. He wasn't above spreading egregious falsehoods on behalf of corporate clients. During the Ludlow Massacre crisis, he planted a defamatory story about the Irish-born union organizer named Mary Harris Jones, claiming she was a prostitute and brothel-keeper. The accusation seemed absurd. At the time, Mary Jones—known as "Mother Jones"—was an old lady of nearly eighty. Lee's attempts to portray Mother Jones as the most dangerous woman in America was character assassination of the worst kind. It was the sort of dirty tricks that earned Ivy Lee his derogatory nickname, "Poison Ivy." No matter, the Rockefellers were grateful. Lee's handling of the crisis was so successful that the Rockefellers retained him as their PR counsellor at $1,000 a month—a huge sum at the time.

One of Ivy Lee's early competitors was Edward Bernays, a rival for the title of "founder" of public relations. Bernays, like Lee, had started off as a journalist but quickly drifted into the publicity side of the business before working on President Wilson's wartime propaganda unit. After the war, he wrote books—including *Propaganda* in 1928—in which he formulated his ideas about influencing public opinion. Whereas Ivy Lee liked to say that PR professionals were "honest brokers" between their clients and the public, Bernays took a uniquely different approach. He regarded the public as essentially emotional and highly susceptible to influence and manipulation. Bernays regarded PR as a form of social psychology. Inspired by Freud's theories about dreams and repressed sexual desires, Bernays believed that truth was subjective perception filtered by deeply embedded impulses and emotions.[8]

Bernays quickly built a blue-ribbon client list of major American brands such as Proctor & Gamble, United Fruit Company, General Electric, and Lucky Strike cigarettes. He gained fame (and later infamy) as the man who made smoking in public fashionable for American women. In a notorious publicity stunt in 1919, Bernays paid a dozen attractive debutantes to smoke Lucky Strike cigarettes while marching in New York's Easter Sunday parade. He made sure, of course, that newspaper photographers showed up to snap photos of the girls. It worked like magic. Bernays even succeeded in making the color of Lucky Strike packages—green—popular with women by organizing balls at which green gowns were worn. Following the success of Bernays's pseudo-events to promote Lucky Strike, the number of American women smoking in public soared. In the Roaring Twenties, cigarettes became a feminine symbol of emancipation. Bernays had another trick up his sleeve: he dubbed cigarettes "torches of freedom."

It occurred to Bernays that cigarettes could not only make women free but also make them thin. So he launched another campaign encouraging women to smoke Lucky Strike cigarettes to lose weight. The billboard slogan was "Reach for a Lucky, instead of a sweet." For Bernays—who died in 1995 at the grand old age of 103—the millions of cigarette-addicted women who would die of lung cancer were not his problem. His wife, Doris Fleischman—who had joined her husband's PR firm after an early career as a newspaper reporter—smoked Parliament cigarettes. In many respects, Doris Fleischman was the perfect feminine consumer according to her husband's own advertising slogans. An early feminist, she was a highly independent woman who, in fact, became famous in 1923 as the first American woman issued a U.S. passport with her maiden name. Doris was also a heavy smoker. Bernays didn't approve. He was constantly attempting to get her to kick the habit. Through his work for the American tobacco industry, he was privy to secret reports linking cigarette smoking to cancer. Doris nonetheless lived to age eighty-eight, though was outlived by her husband by fifteen years.[9]

For corporate America, the public relations industry was great for business. The tools of mass persuasion were helping sell their products to consumers, and the tools of media manipulation were helping spin their story. The success of PR also brought far-reaching consequences for cultural perceptions of truth and falsehood. While American journalism was attempting to professionalize with rational standards of objectivity, public relations was a counter-force appealing to deeply subjective and emotional truths. The PR industry's mission was to undermine the status of objective facts by demonstrating the powerful influence of sensations and feelings on both individual and collective behavior.

The cultural zeitgeist was more favorable to PR spin. At the end of the nineteenth century, Friedrich Nietzsche had declared that "there are no facts, only interpretations." A generation later, in the aftershock of the First World War, it seemed Nietzsche had been right. People were desperately looking for answers to comprehend the world and understand themselves. Religion had been overthrown by science (and pseudo-science), driving many to seek refuge in superstitions, astrology, spiritualism, and the occult. Sigmund Freud meanwhile was exploring the significance of dreams, hysteria, and neurosis. Avant-garde artistic movements of the era—Expressionism, Cubism, Dada, Surrealism—took inspiration from the same ideas in their anti-bourgeois revolt against the rationalism of the modern world. This movement traced its origins to the Parisian bohemian culture in the latter half of the nineteenth century, when avant-garde French artists were rebelling against traditional authority, culminating with the Paris première of Alfred Jarry's absurdist play *Ubu Roi* in 1896.[10] The avant-garde spirit marked the autonomy of artistic creation vis-à-vis prevailing "bourgeois" norms and values. By the 1920s when PR spin was taking off, celebrating the irrational zones of the human psyche was very much in vogue.

Edward Bernays wasn't an artist; he took a more scientific approach to these trends. He had witnessed firsthand during the war how mass persuasion techniques could make Americans irrationally hate Germans. He understood that the same tools could make consumers succumb to other irrational impulses—for example, buying cigarettes.

Ivy Lee, for his part, never swerved from his conviction that there is no such thing as objective truth. When called before a U.S. congressional inquiry probing his PR practices, Lee was startlingly candid about his disregard for facts.

"What is a fact?" he asked. "The effort to state an absolute fact is simply an attempt to give you my interpretation of the facts."

Friedrich Nietzsche could not have put it better. The deconstruction of truth was a pre-condition to building the postmodern consumer society.

***

For those who were nostalgic about the values of truth that animated the muckrakers, the Depression brought some hope.

In the 1930s, corporate-owned media in America were so powerful that many believed the social contract between the press and public was broken. The influence of corporate media was reminiscent of the old days of yellow press magnates Joseph Pulitzer and William Randolph Hearst. Pulitzer had died before the war, but Hearst was still a powerful force, having added *Cosmopolitan* to his stable of titles in 1905. A decade later, novelist Upton Sinclair published an exposé, *The Brass Check,* denouncing the corporate control and conservative bias of American newspapers. The investigative zeal of the muckraking era had largely disappeared in the post-war years, but the issue of corporate power was back in the spotlight following the Wall Street stock market crash of 1929. During the Depression, the corporate-owned press was overwhelmingly hostile to President Franklin Roosevelt's interventionist New Deal policies. Following Roosevelt's re-election in 1936, media owners feared he would attempt to regulate them. Their suspicions were based on more than paranoia. One of Roosevelt's closest political allies, Democratic senator Sherman Minton, initiated hearings into press conglomerates. Senator Minton proposed, among other things, a new press law that would make it illegal "to publish information known to be false." His Senate investigation was a shot across the bow of powerful press moguls, most of them Republicans, such as Hearst, Henry Luce, and Frank Gannett.

Media magnate Luce was especially worried about the political climate during the Depression. He was a formidable figure, admired or feared according to where you stood with him. Tall with heavy eyebrows, Luce oversaw his powerful media empire—including *Time* and *Life* magazines—with commanding personal authority. As one of his editors observed, Henry Luce "lived well above the tree line on Olympus."[11] A strong critic of President Roosevelt, he used his clout as a media proprietor to pursue a staunchly conservative political agenda. He had no time for journalistic notions of objective truth. He regarded newspapers as private property, not guardians of truth.

"We tell the truth as we see it," he once remarked. "Show me a man who claims he is objective and I'll show you a man with illusions."[12]

Luce preferred only certitudes. And he had no illusions about America's status in the world. Having grown up in China as the child of Presbyterian missionaries, Luce believed he was invested with a mission to preach the gospel of the American way of life. It was Luce who, in 1941, coined the term *American Century* in a *Time* editorial calling on the United States to enter the Second World War.[13] He believed that the United States had succeeded Britain as the next global superpower. The main adversary to American power in the world, he believed, was communism.

When the United States declared war in late 1941, President Roosevelt was politically strengthened as the nation rallied around his leadership. He now had the upper hand against Henry Luce and other American media tycoons who feared he would curb corporate concentration. Luce decided to get out in front of the issue. In 1942, he set up a private-sector body of eminent Americans to deliberate on the role of the press in a democratic society and release its findings to the public. Luce handpicked his old Yale classmate Robert Hutchins, who was now president of the University of Chicago, as chairman for his "Commission on Freedom of the Press." The commission was composed of sixteen members, including scholar Harold Lasswell, philosopher William Hocking, historian Arthur Schlesinger, and poet Archibald MacLeish. The commission deliberated over four years, meeting seventeen times and interviewing fifty-eight witnesses, at a total cost of $200,000 to Henry Luce.

When the Hutchins Commission report was finally published in 1947, the major issues facing the American press were dramatically different in the post-war years. FDR had died in office two years earlier, the Nazis had been defeated, and the United States had emerged—as Henry Luce hoped—as a global superpower fighting Soviet communism. In the boom years following the war, American media magnates like Luce were less anxious about government regulation. The Hutchins Commission's report, titled *A Free and Responsible Press,* reflected this new political climate. It focused on the role of the media in promoting liberal democracy. But the report issued some warnings. "No democracy will indefinitely tolerate concentration of private power, irresponsible and strong enough to thwart the democratic aspirations of the people," it stated. "If these giant agencies of communication are irresponsible, not even the First Amendment will protect their freedom from government control."[14]

Henry Luce must have received the Hutchins Commission findings as a poisoned chalice. He was not alone. Many American newspapers harshly criticized its recommendations, dismissing them as a call for state interference with a free press. The *Chicago Tribune* described the Hutchins Commission members as "a determined group of totalitarian thinkers" who were calling for a "Hitler-style" press in America. Those who read the Hutchins report carefully, however, grasped that it was handing American journalism an unbelievable gift. It called for not only a *free* press, but also a *responsible* one. It advocated putting power into the hands of professional journalists to promote the public interest. The report rejected the libertarian "free marketplace of ideas" and warned of the dangers of totalitarian and communist models of media. Between these two extremes of unbridled liberty and state control, the Hutchins Commission advocated a *social responsibility* model of journalism as the best way to defend democratic values in a free society. The social responsibility model was, in effect, an endorsement of professional journalists as information gatekeepers—or guardians of the truth.[15]

The principles underpinning the Hutchins report, conferring the duty of professional responsibility on the press, had a far-reaching impact on American journalism in the decades following the war. Some describe this period—roughly the second half of the twentieth century—as a golden age in American journalism. Journalists began to assert themselves as confident professionals who, standing above social and political divisions, enjoyed the status and independence to pursue objective truths. The economics of the industry undoubtedly helped boost this professional self-assurance. In the second half of the century, an immensely profitable business model provided the profession with the autonomy to uphold values of facts and objectivity without fear or favor.

Journalism's "high-modernist" period, as it has been called, was unique to the United States.[16] In America, there was a broad political consensus with limited ideological diversity and contestation around accepted facts and values. These were ideal conditions for journalism to thrive as a powerful profession with cohesive occupational values. In Europe, by contrast, a wider political spectrum reinforced old partisan connections between newspapers and political parties. In the United States, the profession's ideological consensus coalesced around what can broadly be described as liberal values, especially in contrast to right-wing ideological postures by Cold War firebrand politicians such as the fiercely anti-communist senator Joseph McCarthy. Like the muckrakers at the outset of the century, American journalists in the high-modernist period were largely progressive.[17]

High modernism in American journalism gained momentum in the 1960s against the turbulent backdrop of civil rights, the Vietnam War, and youth counter-culture rebellion. These disruptive events did fracture the wide consensus in American society, though divisions were more generational than ideological. In newsrooms, a new generation of journalists reconnected with muckraking methods of the early century to investigate important social issues. Their professional credo was that truth is objective and discoverable through facts. At prestigious American newspapers such as the *New York Times* and *Wall Street Journal,* objectivity was so sacrosanct that the Op-Ed department was separated from the newsroom. Columnists wrote opinion. Reporters pursued facts.

As American journalists gained more institutional power, they arrogated an increasingly adversarial "fourth estate" role. This pushed the profession toward an approach based more on interpreting the news. Reporting methods were rigorously fact-based, but journalists relied on their own professional judgment to set the news agenda.

The Watergate scandal in the early 1970s marked the apogee of the high-modernist period in American journalism. Through tireless evidence-gathering and fact-checking (and an indispensable "deep throat" insider source), *Washington Post* reporters Bob Woodward and Carl Bernstein uncovered the truth about abuse of power in the White House. It was the scoop of the century. President Richard Nixon, disgraced and facing impeachment, had no choice but to resign in 1974. In the wake of Watergate—and the Hollywood film about the scandal, *All the President's Men*—journalism was no longer merely a trade for ink-stained wretches. The profession could now make a legitimate claim on its self-designated status as a "fourth estate." Journalists were a power in the system. [18]

Journalism also became glamorous. In the post-Watergate years, applications to American journalism schools skyrocketed. Young aspiring journalists charged out of American universities armed with credentials, trained in media law and ethics, steeped in values of objectivity, and determined to become the next Woodward and Bernstein. For successful journalists working in the high-modernist era, it must have seemed like their monopoly as guardians of the truth would go on forever. But like the heyday of muckraking at the outset of the century, the power and glory would not last. Only a decade after Watergate, the profession was already undergoing a profound transformation.

A powerful factor driving change in the profession was technology. The rise of cable TV in America, followed by direct-to-home satellite television, was a technological big bang that created the so-called five-hundred-channel universe.

This triggered a major revolution in the news business. Suddenly, there was hugely expanded room on the dial for a multitude of new channels—including round-the-clock news. Competition for viewers was cutthroat, so cable channels produced fast-paced news with high-volume opinion. Facts were out; opinions were in. CNN launched a show called "Crossfire," which staged debates with voices on each end of the spectrum. Fox News followed with its own right-wing point of view on politics and world events, while MSNBC offered its loyal viewers a more left-leaning perspective.

The crowded field of all-news channels, and the multitude of different perspectives, was undoubtedly more entertaining for viewers—hence the derogatory term *infotainment*. It also promoted values of pluralism: many more different viewpoints across the spectrum could now be heard. But it produced other unintended consequences. First, journalists gradually shifted away from fact-based reporting in favor of more emotionally driven, first-person news. As subjective storytelling flourished, the line between fact and fiction became increasingly blurred. Second, it fractured the cohesion of the profession. Whereas journalists had been bonded by high-modernist values based on objectivity, the profession was now divided on the impact of these new trends on standards of objective truth.

This state of affairs was nothing new in Europe, where journalism had never observed a strict division between news and opinion. In Britain, blatant slanting was pushed to absurd extremes by the tabloids, which routinely passed off partisan opinion as news. The problem was not restricted to the gutter press. Roy Greenslade, a veteran media columnist for *The Guardian*, observed that mixing news and opinion was a longstanding practice in British journalism. "No one reading newspapers down the years can have been in any doubt how their political stance has influenced their content," noted Greenslade.

> Our press has been proudly partisan. The result has been blatant bias. It is an understatement to call it spin. Heavily angled stories and headlines are the norm. Comment articles merely underline the prejudice in the so-called news items. They are indistinguishable. Nor is there the slightest embarrassment about omission, about failing to inform readers about news that, for one reason or another, fails to fit the editorial agenda. Almost everyone involved in producing papers—publishers, editors and journalists—has been relaxed about this situation.[19]

A more serious issue was the impact on journalistic ethics. At the height of the high-modernist period, journalists were acutely aware of their monopoly power as news agenda-setters. They consequently became smug and self-important. Many enjoyed the status of well-connected "insiders," cozy members of the power elite they were supposed to be holding to account. Their professional culture of smug complacency, along with commercial pressures, gradually compromised professional ethics. The revolving door between journalism and politics and PR was constantly turning. There were murmurs and gossip about ethical lapses, and the odd reproach in a newspaper column that dared to break ranks, but no major alarm bells. The corrosive breach of public trust was discreetly imperceptible. It was a crisis slowly building, creeping through the profession.

For critics outside journalism, the mainstream media's credibility crisis was hardly surprising. Its main cause, they argued, was the fundamental contradiction at the core of mass media: corporate ownership. So long as the media are controlled by capitalist corporations, journalists will serve and protect the interests of their owners. The leading voice of this critique was Noam Chomsky, who in the 1960s achieved celebrity status on university campuses worldwide. Chomsky agreed that mass media were powerful shapers of "truths" that influenced public opinion. He argued, however, that the media presented only one "truth," namely the one dictated by their corporate owners.

Chomsky constructed a "propaganda" model to demonstrate how journalists, despite their pretensions to professional standards of "objective" truth, were in fact filters of bias, persuasion, propaganda, and control. The function of media, he contended, was not to hold power to account, as journalists often claimed, but rather to "manufacture consent" of citizens. The role of the media, he argued, was to propagate the illusion that consumer society was a desirable model. Chomsky called this a "necessary illusion"—a sort of neo-liberal capitalist version of Plato's "noble lie." The illusion was necessary because, if the majority grasped the uncomfortable truths about winners and losers in society, the result would be upheaval, instability, and uncertainty. The media, argued Chomsky, contained debate about political options, keeping acceptable discourse within a limited middle ground, never integrating more radical opinions. This was accomplished by ensuring that those given a voice in the media—sources, commentators, columnists—were members of established elites from academia, think tanks, political parties, and so on. And to make sure the media stayed on message, battalions of PR men and spin doctors worked their dark arts to shape the "truth," which of course was dutifully reported in the mainstream media.[20] Chomsky had many critics and detractors. Some dismissed him as a radical anti-capitalist with his own ideological agenda. Still, his critique of mainstream media as establishment glove-puppets resonated with an entire generation of leftist activists.

If one were searching for case-study evidence to support Chomsky's critique, there would be no better place to look than journalist Nick Davies's book, *Flat Earth News*. Davies, a British investigative journalist from the high-modernist era, committed the unpardonable by breaking ranks with his journalist colleagues with a candid confession: "Finally I was forced to admit that I work in a corrupted profession."[21] Journalists, observed Davies, work in a closed system lubricated by PR hacks and spin doctors on the payroll of corporations and governments. The result is a phenomenon he called "churnalism." Journalists churn out story after story about "pseudo-events" manufactured by the PR industry. Newsrooms are awash in freebies. Journalists themselves play fast and loose, and break ethical rules, to get scoops. In sum, while professional journalists pretend to hold others to account, they are silent on their own questionable ethics. Too frequently, they get sucked in by hype and lies served up by PR hacks and spin doctors—everything from the "millennium bug" to Iraq's "weapons of mass destruction." Davies called this system of professional hypocrisy "flat earth news." A planted story could be as false as news that the earth is flat, but journalists would still show up and cover it.

These professional sins can be castigated, or indulged, depending on the weight one attributes to external pressures that reshaped journalism at the end of the twentieth century. A severe judgment would be that journalists, corrupted by hubris, abandoned their own professional standards and practices. A more indulgent view would be that they were forced to adjust to the structural transformation of the industry that employed them. Technological and commercial factors indisputably put pressures on the profession.

Another factor had an even more powerful impact on journalism: the wider cultural zeitgeist of postmodernist values. The influence of postmodernism on journalism is less understood because it is much more difficult to measure. It has nonetheless been profound and enduring.

The term *postmodern* invariably incites acrimonious debate. Using the term is like kicking a political hornet's nest, certain to provoke a buzzing ideological frenzy. There is fierce debate about what *postmodern* means, let alone what its consequences have been. Leaving aside these pitched ideological battles, it is possible to situate postmodernism historically. It was a philosophical movement whose influence extended far beyond the precincts of academia into every aspect of late-twentieth century culture—from literature, cinema, television, and music to trends in lifestyle and social movements such as feminism. It is this dimension of postmodernism that is pertinent to understanding the transformation of journalism over the same period.[22] Postmodernism's influence on popular culture permeated the media, including the values and practices of journalists.

The term *postmodern*, as noted, is difficult to define with precision. As philosopher Michael Lynch observed: "Pretty much everyone admits that it is impossible to define postmodernism. This is not surprising, since the word's popularity is largely a function of its obscurity."[23] The purpose here is not to open the can of worms over the term's definition. It is nonetheless possible to outline postmodernism's core beliefs and assumptions. At the risk of oversimplifying, postmodernism is a philosophical movement founded on a skeptical rejection of Enlightenment values and rationalist claims on truth based on reason, science, and objective knowledge. In that respect, postmodernism is subversive because it opposes established structures of knowledge and authority and the norms that have legitimized them. Postmodernists argue that Enlightenment rationalism—which overthrew the power structures of feudalism and religion and their claims on "truth"—was simply a new, modernist system of power with its own self-legitimizing narratives about "truth." Postmodernists regard the legacy of the Enlightenment (colonialism, capitalism, patriarchy) as a system of cultural and economic domination that has marginalized and oppressed. Postmodernists reject the Enlightenment assertion that values are universal, that rights are natural, and that truths are objective. These claims, they argue, are simply instruments of power. According to postmodernists, there is no such thing as objective truth; the only truths are subjective. Some postmodernists make the more controversial assertion that there is no such thing as "truth," period. This leaves us only with nihilism and despair in a world devoid of meaning beyond our narcissistic self-satisfactions. In sum, postmodernists reject the entire epistemological and moral foundations of the Enlightenment. They rejoice in the collapse of the Enlightenment's universalist claims on truth, morality, and aesthetics because it promises to open opportunities for new forms of human creativity, freedom, and truths based on personal narratives.

Postmodernism took off in the decades following the Second World War, though the term was not coined until 1979 in French philosopher Jean-François Lyotard's *The Postmodern Condition*. The movement found deeper origins in the ideas of earlier philosophers, especially in the works of Friedrich Nietzsche. Nietzsche is remembered mostly for his rejection of transcendent morality—hence his famous "God is dead"— and his affirmation that we must break free from the constraints of religious doctrine to achieve the true possibility of human excellence. Inspired by the ancient Greek poet Pindar's injunction, "Become who you are," Nietzsche urged us to love our own fate, to stop kicking against life, to embrace everything and erase nothing. His other legacy was a philosophical hostility to the notion of truth. In his work *On Truth and Lying*, he asserted that "truths are illusions which we have forgotten are illusions."[24] There are no facts, only interpretations. Nietzsche's rebellion against the grand narratives of religion and their moral strictures, and his passionate embrace of individual truth, laid the philosophical cornerstones of the postmodernist movement that emerged a century later.

If Nietzsche was postmodernism's patron saint, the movement's apostles were mostly French thinkers, especially Lyotard, Michel Foucault, and Jacques Derrida. There was some irony in this: the Enlightenment had essentially been inspired by French philosophers from Descartes to Voltaire and Rousseau; and three centuries later, postmodern French philosophers set about deconstructing the entire Enlightenment project. Lyotard described postmodernism as "incredulity toward metanarratives"[25] —in short, don't believe the modern doctrines of Enlightenment truths. French postmodernists claimed that truths are partial, subjective, open to interpretation. Foucault warned that all claims on truth conceal power agendas. The American postmodernist philosopher, Richard Rorty, put it this way: "Truth is what your contemporaries let you get away with."[26] Any assertion of objective truth is automatically suspect. All assertions of truth, and the structures that support them, need to be challenged, deconstructed, and dismantled. Postmodernists didn't have their own normative project to propose to society. They were essentially hostile skeptics subverting all systems of authority. Their mission was deconstruction and demolition.

Postmodernist thinking gained momentum in the 1960s when it was taken up by the neo-Marxist left. Following the exposure of the Soviet Union's totalitarian "big lie" under Stalin—oppression, gulags, mass murder, genocide—leftists could no longer make a moral case for communism. New Left intellectuals abandoned old Marxist doctrines and embraced postmodernism as an ideological coping strategy. Postmodernism, in some respects, was a reformulation of Marxist tenets but oriented more toward social activism on a wider range of goals beyond class struggle. Not all postmodernists were Marxists, and some Marxists did not identify with the postmodernist movement. Still, postmodernism armed the left with new rhetorical weapons in its combat against Western "neo-liberal" power structures.

By the 1980s, French postmodernist ideas were sweeping through American university campuses where they resonated with the youth culture rebelling against the political establishment and modern consumer society. There was some irony in the popularity of French postmodernism in America. The movement's biggest names—including Jacques Derrida and Gilles Deleuze—were celebrated as intellectual superstars in America but were less revered in their home country. In France, the philosophical current had been moving in the opposite direction with the rise of the *nouveaux philosophes*, including Bernard-Henri Lévy and André Glucksmann, who turned against Marxism as a totalitarian system. In France, anti-Marxist philosophers were attracting all the attention, while their Marxist-inspired postmodernist compatriots were venerated as intellectual rock stars in America.

French historian François Cusset analyzed this paradox in his book *French Theory.* He argued that American academics, especially in the humanities, appropriated French postmodernist thinking for their own ideological purposes.[27] French postmodernist theory was, in effect, "displaced and reconstructed" in the United States, where it became a politically motivated movement disconnected from its philosophical origins in

France. A small clique of celebrity intellectuals in the United States—one was Susan Sontag, who had lived in Paris for a time—cultivated and popularized French postmodernist ideas. But things got lost in translation. The "denationalization" of French postmodernism resulted in a misunderstanding in the American cultural context dominated by identity politics, political correctness, anti-colonialism, and an ideological revolt against Western civilization. In sum, American intellectuals appropriated French postmodernism and used it for their own ideological agendas.

Leaving aside this question of cultural mistranslation, French postmodernism had tremendous intellectual cachet in America in the 1980s. The result was a proliferation of niche fields in the American humanities, many under the umbrella of "Cultural Studies" or "Comparative Literature," deeply permeated by French critical theory. By the end of the 1990s an entire generation of American students had been profoundly influenced by postmodernist claims, especially its assault on universal values, scientific knowledge, and objective truths. They learned to suspect Enlightenment values as a power system of colonial oppression of marginalized groups based on class, race, gender, sexual orientation, and so on. They were taught that all claims on fact and truth are suspect and must be critiqued, challenged, and deconstructed. This reflex to deconstruct turned postmodernism in America into a movement of political activism. While it was initially associated with the radical left, the far-right too eventually embraced many of postmodernism's assumptions. The joining up of far-left and far-right, while on the surface paradoxical, was not as contradictory as it appeared. Both extremes rejected liberal values and natural rights in favor of group identity based on ethnicity, race, gender, and sexual orientation. Both also rejected reason, science, and objective truths as the basis for knowledge. Most importantly, both the far-right and the far-left were hostile, albeit for different reasons, to the entire Enlightenment project of modernity.

Despite its massive influence in America, postmodernism was controversial and frequently contested. Major philosophers including Jürgen Habermas frontally critiqued the movement as essentially irrational. This reproach was easy to grasp given that postmodernism was a counter-Enlightenment rebellion against reason. Habermas defended the "project of modernity" against attacks by postmodernists (and by neo-conservatives who made common cause with postmodern intellectuals against modern values). Habermas argued, among other things, that postmodernists were guilty of a performative contradiction by employing modern concepts—subjectivity, freedom, creativity—that they otherwise attempted to undermine in their assault on modernism. He regarded postmodernism as a sort of latter-day avant-garde movement. Postmodernism proclaimed the same radical aesthetics that emerged in the late nineteenth century in opposition to prevailing bourgeois norms and established forms of authority. It had started with the Parisian bohemian culture in which poets such as Baudelaire and Rimbaud thrived. Later advocates included the Parisian avant-garde scene gathered around theater, including Alfred Jarry's *Ubu Roi* and artists at the Cabaret Voltaire in Zurich in the First World War era.[28] Many decades later, some of postmodernism's apostles grew disenchanted with the movement's affiliation with "political correctness" and other forms of activism. Others observed that postmodernism had become the same kind of system of intolerance that it claimed to oppose. Still others argued, following on Habermas, that postmodernism was not a philosophy at all, but more an aesthetic movement of radical skepticism animated by critique, protest, and subversion.

The movement's leading advocates were, in some instances, its worst publicists. At the height of its influence, postmodernism was tarnished by scandals that cast discredit on the entire movement. The most infamous controversy surrounded postmodernist guru Paul de Man. From the 1960s till his death in 1983, Belgian-born de Man was the leading postmodernist thinker in the United States. De Man boasted a PhD from Harvard and was a distinguished professor at Yale University. At Yale, he was a charismatic figure preaching the gospel of postmodern criticism to a whole generation of brilliant students who venerated him as a superstar. It was de Man who brought Jacques Derrida to America and had his works translated into English. Four years after his death, however, de Man's fraudulent past caught up with him. It was revealed that he had consistently lied about his past and had falsified his credentials. He had also committed bigamy by seducing and marrying a Bard College undergraduate even though he had another wife.

Worst of all, it was discovered that, during the war years after the Nazis occupied his native Belgium, de Man had written several anti-Semitic articles for the collaborationist newspaper, *Le Soir*. In one article, de Man referred to the "Semitic interference in all aspects of European life" and proposed, as a solution to the "Jewish problem," the creation of a colony for Jews "isolated from Europe."[29] After the war, a Belgian court convicted de Man on several counts of forgery, falsifying records, and financial malfeasance. He was sentenced to five years in prison. But de Man was not present in court. He had already skipped the country for New York.

In America, de Man's beguiling talents as a con man helped him insinuate himself into the highest spheres of the academic establishment, including Yale. He became the leading voice of postmodern philosophy in the American cultural elites. Many regarded him as one of the intellectual giants of his time. When he died at age sixty-four in 1983, de Man was hailed as the "father of deconstruction." The *New York Times* reported his death on the front page.

Five years later, when de Man's shameful fascist past was exposed, his name was on the front page the *New York Times* again—although this time for different reasons. The reaction in American intellectual circles was oddly in keeping with postmodernist thinking. Instead of condemning his academic fraudulence and anti-Semitic opinions, his illustrious defenders—including Jacques Derrida himself—attempted to "deconstruct" de Man's language to prove that he didn't mean what he had written. One de Man supporter dismissed the criticism about his criminal past, claiming that it "repeats the well-known totalitarian procedures of vilification it pretends to deplore."[30] De Man wasn't a fascist, they claimed; his critics were fascists. In the final analysis, the exposure of de Man as a fraud with a murky past did little to blunt the postmodernist movement. Years after the scandal, deconstructionist thinkers were still writing scholarly articles and books lauding Paul de Man's intellectual legacy. In the academic establishment that had built up around "deconstruction" theory, too much was at stake. One of de Man's old friends in Belgium had a much clearer memory of him: "Swindling, forging, and lying were, at least at the time, second nature to him."[31]

A decade after Paul de Man's posthumous disgrace, postmodernism suffered another high-profile setback with the Sokal Affair. In 1997, Alan Sokal, a professor of physics at New York University, published a book titled *Fashionable Nonsense: Postmodern Intellectuals' Abuse of Science.* It was a blistering attack on the most illustrious postmodernist thinkers of the day, including Jacques Lacan, Jean Baudrillard, Jacques Derrida, Michel Foucault, and Julia Kristeva. Sokal's book, released in Britain under the title *Intellectual Impostures,* was based on the results of an elaborate hoax he had perpetrated on a leading postmodernist journal, *Social Text.* The hoax was oddly reminiscent of Jonathan Swift's Bickerstaff satire targeting astrology fraudsters in the eighteenth century. Sokal's targets were what he considered to be postmodernist quacks: the editors of academic journals that, like eighteenth-century astrologers, promoted pseudoscientific claims based on unverifiable theories.

To expose the "fashionable nonsense" of postmodernist ideas, Sokal drafted a paper titled "Transgressing the Boundaries: Toward a Transformative Hermeneutics of Quantum Gravity." The title, while satirical, was sufficiently pretentious for the editors at *Social Text* to take the bait. Sokal wrote later that his paper, while "liberally salted with nonsense," contained just enough buzzwords to flatter the journal's ideological biases. *Social Text*, a prestigious review that had helped launch the new field of "cultural studies," published the paper in the spring of 1996.[32] A few weeks later, Sokal revealed in another journal, *Lingua Franca,* that his paper had been an elaborate hoax intended to expose the intellectual fraudulence of postmodernist thinking.

"While my method was satirical, my motivation is utterly serious," wrote Sokal, who earned his PhD at Harvard. "What concerns me is the proliferation, not just of nonsense and sloppy thinking per se, but of a particular kind of nonsense and sloppy thinking: one that denies the existence of objective realities."[33]

Like Jonathan Swift's scathing satire of eighteenth-century astrologists, Sokal's attack on postmodernist academics was fundamentally about truth. As the *New York Times* reported shortly after the scandal erupted:

> This is one more skirmish in the culture wars, the battles over multiculturalism and college curriculums and whether there is a single objective truth or just many differing points of view. Conservatives have argued that there is truth, or at least an approach to truth, and that scholars have a responsibility to pursue it. They have accused the academic left of debasing scholarship for political ends.[34]

In the short term, the Sokal Affair dealt a serious blow to the credibility of leftist theorists in academia. Panicked and embarrassed, they furiously counter-attacked Sokal, both intellectually and personally. Literary theorist Stanley Fish fired off a rebuttal in the *New York Times* titled "Professor Sokal's Bad Joke."[35] The Sokal Affair was great fun while it lasted—attracting praise and fury—but it wasn't sufficient to stop postmodernism's cultural juggernaut. When the Sokal Affair died down, its academic targets brushed off the incident as a mishap and carried on preaching the postmodernist gospel hostile to objective truths.

Beyond the confines of academia, the postmodernist ethos was permeating the cultural zeitgeist. In the creative spheres of literature, cinema, television, theater, and the visual arts, the exploration of subjective narratives and fractured perspectives was a fascinating way of exploring the question of truth. It was precisely this aesthetic dimension of postmodernism that Jürgen Habermas identified, if not entirely approvingly, when he compared it to the radical avant-garde movements such as Dada at the end of the nineteenth century.

The Marxist critic Fredric Jameson similarly attempted to understand postmodernism as a movement of aesthetic production, which he unflatteringly described as "the cultural logic of late capitalism."[36] Jameson situated the postmodern aesthetic within a specific historical context. Realism in art corresponded to early capitalism in the nineteenth century, followed by modernism in the first half of the twentieth century. The aesthetic of the postmodern movement, he argued, was an expression of late capitalism's phase of multinational corporations and consumer society. In this period, aesthetic production was integrated into commodity production. A familiar illustration of this commodity aesthetic was Andy Warhol's pop art. Jameson compared Van Gogh's painting *A Pair of Shoes* with Warhol's *Diamond Dust Shoes* to make his point about the authenticity of modern art versus the depthless superficiality of the postmodernism aesthetic. That was perhaps the point of Warhol's pop art, including his famous Campbell's soup cans. His works conferred an aesthetic iconography on commercial products and famous people as an illustration of consumer society's commodity and celebrity fetishism. For Jameson, it was a cultural symptom of late capitalism.

Whatever the merits of Jameson's Marxist critique of postmodern aesthetics, he succeeded in framing debate and discussion about the movement's influence on popular culture. One of Jameson's key insights was that postmodern aesthetics were characterized by the alienation of the self. In the visual arts, images were without depth; in narratives, the subject was fragmented. Whereas modern art rebelled against the past and promised a radiant future (think Le Corbusier's modernist architecture), the postmodernism ethos was perpetually stuck in the present, devoid of memory and hope. In architecture, Jameson cited the Pompidou Center in Paris as an illustration of the cold postmodern aesthetic. In literature, he regarded E. L. Doctorow's historical metafiction, *Ragtime*, as a quintessentially postmodern novel due to its impersonal style "in which neither author nor public could be felt present." Other American works of fiction considered emblematic of the postmodern style were Thomas Pynchon's complex, multi-narrative novel, *Gravity's Rainbow*, published in 1973; and Don DeLillo's satire, *White Noise*, which appeared a decade later in 1985.

A distinguishing feature of postmodernism in art, as noted, is fractured perspective. Stories are subjective; narrators are unreliable. In cinema, this became known as the "Rashomon effect," taken from Japanese director Akira Kurosawa's film *Rashomon*, in which a murder is described differently by four witnesses. The message: knowledge of facts is uncertain. In literature, the same ideas inspired a flurry of novels based on the same premise of partial truths. One was David Foster Wallace's *Infinite Jest,* published in 1996. It features four intermingled narratives, hundreds of endnotes, and many narrative digressions—a playful deconstruction of standard literary structure. *Infinite Jest,* which made Wallace famous, is sometimes described as the "last postmodern novel." That may be so, but the so-called unreliable narrator became a familiar technique in many subsequent novels—such as Gillian Flynn's *Gone Girl* and Lauren Groff's *Fates and Furies*—in which facts and truth are uncertain and open to question. In television, the cult series *Twin Peaks* played on audience expectations by mixing genres. More recently, the drama *The Affair*, which explored the destruction of a marriage after a spontaneous act of adultery, followed this trend by questioning the reliability of any single point of view. The message was the same: If you are expecting established structures and reliable narratives, think again. The "truth" comes in different versions and competing narratives. Objective truths are elusive. Subjective truths may be imprecise and unreliable, but to interpret reality, we have only our perceptions, feelings, and unreliable memory.[37]

Now to the question of postmodernism's influence on journalism, which raises issues that go beyond aesthetics. Journalism is not usually considered art, and journalists are not generally regarded as artists. Most journalists are trained professionals whose business is news and information. Professionally trained journalists espouse values and ethics based on fact, evidence, objectivity, and impartiality. This is the antithesis of the postmodern ethos rejecting objective facts and truth and emphasizing the subjective. And yet the impact of postmodernist assumptions on journalism, while not generally understood, was just as profound as its influence on other spheres of popular culture.

As with everything regarding postmodernism, it's difficult to pinpoint when exactly it began exerting an influence on journalistic practices. The first obvious sign of journalists integrating postmodernist approaches to their work dates to the 1960s, when many began using subjective perspectives and literary techniques as innovative methods to get at the "truth." They called their movement "New Journalism." The name was borrowed from the penny press exposés of the late nineteenth century, when the *Pall Mall Gazette* in London tackled issues such as child prostitution. A century later, the revival of literary techniques in journalism had a major impact on storytelling in American magazines. The best work appeared in the *New Yorker*, *Esquire*, the *Nation,* the *Saturday Evening Post*, *Harper's,* the *Atlantic Monthly*, and *Rolling Stone.* The New Journalism's leading proponents were among the most successful writers in America: Truman Capote, Tom Wolfe, Gay Talese, Joan Didion, Norman Mailer, Hunter S. Thompson. Among the best-known examples of the genre was Truman Capote's book *In Cold Blood*, about the real-life murder of an entire family in Kansas (it first appeared in the *New Yorker* in 1965), and Joan Didion's collection of essays, *Slouching Toward Bethlehem* (the *Saturday Evening Post,* 1966). The biggest names in the New Journalism wave saw their work—such as Tom Wolfe's *The Right Stuff*—adapted as Hollywood movies.

Employing fiction-writing techniques in nonfiction journalism presented ethical dilemmas. Reliance on literary devices abandoned a strict adherence to facts. For writers working in this style, truth wasn't necessarily factual; it was accessible through fictional accounts of reality. Some even called the New Journalism genre "nonfiction novels." Advocates of the New Journalism style argued that objectivity is impossible and misleading. Subjective narratives, on the other hand, present authentic truths. "One of the greatest changes brought about by this new breed of journalists," observed the movement's high priest, Tom Wolfe, "has been that the proof of one's technical mastery as a writer becomes paramount and the demonstration of moral points becomes secondary."[38] While often dazzling, the New Journalism movement was criticized for pure invention and outright fabrication. If the style was lively and engaging, the story was often too good to be true. Recent evidence suggests that Truman Capote's *In Cold Blood*, while he claimed it was "immaculately factual," was an elaborate work of fiction in which the author changed facts to suit his narrative.[39]

In the 1980s, the blurred distinction between facts and fiction sparked even more serious scandals. The first one hit the *Washington Post*, the same newspaper that, only a decade before, had broken the Watergate story. In 1981, reporter Janet Cooke won a Pulitzer Price for her emotionally poignant story "Jimmy's World," about an eight-year-old heroin addict. It was later discovered, however, that Cooke had fabricated the entire story. Jimmy did not exist; the story was pure fiction. Cooke was forced to return the prize, and the *Washington Post* made an abject public apology. Her editor on the "Jimmy's World" story, it turned out, was Bob Woodward, the star investigative reporter famous for his Watergate scoop. More than a decade later at the *New Republic*, reporter Stephen Glass was forced to resign when it was discovered he had invented characters in dozens of articles. One story, "Hack Heaven," recounted the life of a fifteen-year-old computer hacker. Like Janet Cooke's eight-year-old heroin addict, Glass's fifteen-year-old hacker did not exist. Glass admitted that he had fabricated characters and events in twenty-seven other stories. An even worse scandal rocked the *New York Times* in 2003, when star reporter Jayson Blair was exposed for fabricating or plagiarizing many of his stories, including details from places that he had never visited. In the fallout to that scandal, two senior editors at the *New York Times* resigned.

It is impossible to know with certainty what pushed these journalists to break basic ethical codes. The common thread in most cases of fabrication and plagiarism, however, was a combination of personal careerism and a professional culture of permissiveness and negligence. It could also be argued that these highly publicized scandals happened squarely in the period when professional journalism was turning increasingly toward subjective storytelling based on emotion. These journalists, while each had their own motives, were working in a larger professional culture that did not actively discourage personal narratives and fictional techniques. These practices had even been popular, and celebrated, during the New Journalism of the 1960s. But unlike Truman Capote and Tom Wolfe, who won celebrity for their compelling fictional devices, Janet Cooke and Stephen Glass were driven out of the profession in disgrace.

The "postmodernist turn" in journalism, as it is sometimes called, didn't happen overnight, like the storming of the Bastille.[40] The postmodern capture of the mainstream media fortress occurred gradually, over many years, through the permeation of its core assumptions and values into the decision-making machinery of newsrooms. The influence of the New Journalism, though it petered out at the end of the 1970s, was a key factor in changing the rules. Journalism was becoming more personal, adversarial, and activist. While journalists themselves were not necessarily activists, news angles and story-sourcing frequently revealed activist agendas. The structural transformation of the news business made these changes possible. After the explosion of television channels and the emergence of round-the-clock news, new channels needed to fill their schedules with talking heads. Journalists needed to find articulate voices for interviews. This widened the media space to include new voices who now enjoyed access to op-ed pages and TV studios. Some were PR flaks, political spin doctors, and lobbyists carrying a brief of activist causes. Others were academics carrying heavy ideological baggage. These newcomers networked and socially mingled with journalists, editors, and television producers. They enjoyed cordial relations, and a certain degree of mutual dependence, based on shared attitudes and values—including intellectual skepticism, a critical perspective, and hostility to established power structures. There was one important difference, however. Whereas journalists were trained to value facts and objectivity, academics, PR flaks, and activists were, for the most part, adversaries of objective truths. They were in the business of opinion, persuasion, and protest.[41]

Generational factors also pushed postmodernist values into newsrooms through the front door of recruitment and hiring. Most major news organizations hired on university campuses. By the 1980s, an entire generation of students had been profoundly influenced by postmodernist thinking in classrooms that were activist laboratories for social change. Among the best and brightest of this generation, many went into journalism and the media more generally. They brought with them not only an intellectual skepticism and hostility to power structures, but also an ideological conviction that objective truths do not exist, that all truths are based on subjective perception, experience, and identity. These attitudes fit perfectly with new trends in journalism favoring subjective storytelling and clashing opinions. By the 1990s, the journalism profession had absorbed the pervasive values of the wider postmodernist culture. Postmodernism was now the cultural zeitgeist. It was not surprising that its ideological miasma crept into newsrooms.

The postmodernist penetration of the media space was also facilitated by technology. Ready access to low-cost digital tools undermined the mainstream media's monopoly power as news gatekeepers. PR flaks, spin doctors, advertisers, even politicians could use digital tools to produce their own spin, advocacy, and propaganda. Technology made the merger of activism and journalism possible. The term *advocacy journalism* emerged as a legitimate professional activity. Working as an activist reporter for Greenpeace was just as professionally validating as landing a job at the *New York Times*. There were ethical consequences, however. The blurred distinction between journalism and advocacy erased the line between objectivity and subjectivity, between facts and opinion, between truth and falsehood. If journalism and activism are the same thing, then its goal is no longer truth, but power.

Journalism's growing emphasis on subjective storytelling was compatible with a postmodernist revisionist movement frequently described as the "affective turn." As the influence of postmodernism began to wane, especially in literature, some challenged its cold aesthetics and called for a revival of genuinely human stories based on feelings and emotions. In literary criticism, the "affective turn" shifted attention toward moods, feelings, and emotions. In 2010, a *New York Times Book Review* critic hailed Jonathan Franzen's new novel, *Freedom,* as a great literary achievement. It followed on Franzen's earlier novel, *The Corrections,* which the same critic, Sam Tanenhaus, praised as "a new kind of novel that might break the suffocating grip of postmodernism" by celebrating the "warm beating heart of an authentic humanism."[42] Franzen's literary achievement, it seemed, was his rejection of postmodern coldness to plunge into the human warmth of the "affective turn." [43]

The notion of "affective turn" was largely a refinement of the ideas of the seventeenth-century philosopher Baruch Spinoza. He established three main categories of affect: desire/appetite (*cupiditas*), pleasure/joy (*laetitia*), and pain/sorrow (*tristitia*). As a theory, the "affective turn" spurned the steady light of Apollonian reason to embrace the dark and turbulent Dionysian zones of feelings, emotions, bodily impulses, and irrationality. In academia, "affect" theory took off in the humanities where it reflected interest in critical theory and Freudian psychoanalysis exploring issues related to passions, fears, dreams, religions, gender, sexuality, identity, and conspiracy theories.[44] It also offered explanations for the rise of emotions and anger in democratic politics, especially with the explosion of social media and the success of populist demagogues— especially Donald Trump. The phenomenon was called the "Trumping of politics."[45]

In the cognitive sciences, where "affect" theory was sometimes called the "introspective turn," the movement was influenced by neuroscientist Antonio Damasio's book *Descartes' Error*, published in 1994. The book's title made it clear that affect theory was repudiating centuries of cold rationalism. Specifically, Damasio challenged Descartes's notion of mind-body dualism that separated reason and emotion, arguing that emotions are cognitively embedded in rational processes in the brain. Affect theory asserted, in essence, that emotions are not an "irrational" dysfunction of the human mind, but deeply integrated into the human experience and the lives of other mammals in the animal kingdom. We are bonded by common emotions: fear, lust, desire, rage, care, play, panic, grief. Emotional introspection finds expression in our greatest works of art, for example, in the literary works of Virginia Woolf, Henry James, Fyodor Dostoyevsky, and Edgar Allan Poe. However intriguing the innovations of artificial intelligence may be, they are disconnected from basic emotional components of biology.[46]

The "affective turn" is more than a theory debated in the ivory tower. Some have claimed that affect theory predicted the post-truth era, its volatile culture wars, and the rise of Donald Trump.[47] It also provides insights into the transformation of journalism in the postmodern era. The same core arguments about the importance of feelings and emotions were borrowed to promote a new normative model for journalists. Indeed, some have called for an "affective turn" away from the rational high-modernist model of journalism and its claims on fact-based objective truth. They advocate a greater role for emotions, feelings, fears, and sensations in journalistic practices.

In 2003, the *Columbia Journalism Review* published an article titled "Rethinking Objectivity," stating: "Journalists (and journalism) must acknowledge, humbly and publicly, that what we do is far more subjective and far less detached than the aura of objectivity implies—and the public wants to believe. If we stop claiming to be mere objective observers, it will not end the charges of bias but will allow us to defend what we do from a more realistic, less hypocritical position."[48] A decade later, the same journal published an ambitious clarion call for emotion in journalism titled "Journalism and the Power of Emotions." In this article, the authors cited scientific studies about empathy and the human brain to call for a new form of journalism based on emotions. Emotional journalism was nothing new, they noted; its origins stretched back to the first-person storytelling in nineteenth-century newspapers and the New Journalism of the 1960s. "Stories have powerful effects on us," the article noted. "We feel empathy for characters just as we do for flesh-and-blood people, and the act of reading about them might even make us more empathetic in real life, change our opinions, and push us to action."[49] In short, emotional journalism is necessary because it appeals to our deep-seated need for narratives that inspire human empathy.

An articulate voice in the "affective turn" school is Charlie Beckett, a professor at the London School of Economics. He calls for "emotionally networked journalism." Citing the examples of *Teen Vogue*, Vice, and BuzzFeed, Beckett argues that a shift toward "affect" in journalism should be encouraged. "This is more than a shift in style towards the personal," he observes. "It is a structural, cultural and ethical change in the operation and public value of journalism. It has positive aspects. Journalism that actively includes emotion as part of its networked creation and distribution is more engaging and shared, and offers opportunities for greater empathy, agency and relevance."[50] Another academic, Antje Glück, takes a similar position in an article titled "Should Journalists Be More Emotionally Literate?" Boasting a scientific rationale for her argument, Glück cites four reasons justifying a more emotional approach to journalism: neuro-biology, moral decision-making, professionalism, and the changing role of journalism in a society that encourages a more open expression of emotions. She argues that journalists have a moral duty to abandon the professional ethics of impartiality. "When commercial pressures make audience engagement an essential requirement, when populist leaders hijack the public sphere by riding a wave of collective emotions," she observes, "quality journalism needs to seek new paths beyond the purely cognitive-focused information dissemination and inverted pyramid models."[51] Both Beckett and Glück appear to be making the claim that, since the social media and political spaces are increasingly emotional, journalists needs to get emotional too.

The "turn" toward subjectivity and emotion undoubtedly has produced many excellent examples of compelling reportage and investigative journalism. Personal storytelling and emotional narrative have indeed become the norm in television news, especially on major networks such as CNN. It is difficult to argue against appeals to human empathy. At the same time, the influence of postmodernism has brought serious risks to the profession. Empathy may create the appearance of authenticity, but it puts emotion before reason, and sometimes fiction before fact. When journalists present subjective narratives, it may be getting close to a certain kind of truth, but they are abandoning their core professional values based on impartiality, facts, evidence, and objective truths. By doing so, they risk playing by the same rules as those who have utterly no regard for facts and truth.

Looking back, it can hardly be claimed that the twentieth century was a glorious epoch for objective truth in journalism. It began optimistically with the rise of the muckrakers and the emergence of strong professional standards of facts and objectivity, but that era quickly disintegrated as journalists became willing mouthpieces in the propaganda wars. They made a sincere attempt, it cannot be doubted, to fulfill their "fourth estate" function during the high-modernist period in the last half of the century. That era was a shining moment for the profession. But journalists' professional monopoly as news gatekeepers was always fragile, undermined by commercial pressures, PR spin, professional complacency, ethical breaches, and storytelling misadventures that corroded public trust. Journalism began the twentieth century upholding professional values and practices dictated by reason and objectivity, but by the end of the century had capitulated to the postmodernist culture of subjectivity and emotion.

At the outset of the twenty-first century, professional journalism's prestige and power were already in decline. The coup de grâce was the social media explosion. It destroyed the business model that had provided the profession with stability and self-confidence for decades. It also shattered journalists' cherished status as guardians of the truth.

The high-modernist period was over. The mainstream media fortress gates had been stormed and demolished. The closed media sphere, once reserved for professionals, was now overwhelmed. Everyone had shown up. Literally everyone.

17

THE DIGITAL TOWN SQUARE

All revolutions, history has demonstrated without exception, are initially resisted by those who have the most to lose.

Their first instinct is to deny the impetus for change. Their second is to diminish its importance. When violence finally erupts, their third instinct is to underestimate its impact—until it's too late.

Recall that on the day the Bastille was stormed—on July 14, 1789— Louis XVI wrote only one word in his diary: *"Rien."* Nothing. Just another day at Versailles Palace.

The digital revolution followed the same pattern.

When the World Wide Web lit up the world in the early 1990s, techno-prophets predicted the arrival of a bold new age. In the short term, however, nothing much changed. Email replaced the fax machine. Other than that, business as usual.

By the end of the decade, however, hype about the internet was gaining momentum. Investment bankers began earning big fees on dot-com start-ups. One of them, America Online, stunned the world in early 2000 by buying Time Warner for $165 billion—the biggest media mega-merger in history. An internet start-up had swallowed a global media conglomerate. There could be no doubt about it: the web was going to change the world. Everybody wanted to get a piece of it.

The hype didn't last. When the dot-com bubble burst a few months later, it wiped out billions on stock markets. The internet hype had triggered a spiral of irrational exuberance. Digital tulip mania. In the old media fortresses, journalists who had been feeling anxious about the impact of the web could now relax. There would be no digital revolution.

But the web, it turned out, was a smart long-term bet. Companies like Amazon proved they had solid business fundamentals. Google was becoming an indispensable search engine. Apple, meanwhile, was disrupting the music industry with its online retail store iTunes. Other new online networks—YouTube, Facebook, Twitter—would soon launch with plans to turn the web into a social space for connecting and sharing (and, of course, selling advertising).

The web revolution's second coming was fittingly called "Web 2.0." The Silicon Valley techno-evangelists who had proclaimed a new digital age finally felt vindicated. Their bible was *The Cluetrain Manifesto*, a Martin Luther–style "95 Theses" tome that announced the arrival of the networked age. The Web 2.0 era promised to revive "conversations" as the dominant form of communication. Logging on to the internet would be like going to the Greek agora or Roman forum to engage in dialogue with fellow citizens. Techno-evangelists hit the speaking circuit to preach the Web 2.0 gospel. Some published books filled with exciting buzzwords—*groundswell, smart mobs, naked conversations, wisdom of crowds*—to describe the toppling of old vertical hierarchies. The "truth" was no longer dictated by elites. Truth was in numbers. Mobs were smart; crowds were wise. Citizens, consumers, employees, and customers always knew what was best. And thanks to the web, they were now empowered.[1]

Among the digital prophets was Clay Shirky, an academic at New York University who had been following the Web 2.0 revolution with an astute eye. In 2008, Shirky published a book on the internet revolution, aptly titled *Here Comes Everybody*. His key insight was this: the web was empowering individuals to do things without organizations. The internet's open-access architecture gave everyone the tools to write, work, create, and collaborate. There were no more barriers to creativity and collaboration. If you wanted to be a journalist, you didn't need to earn a degree at a journalism school. You just created a blog and started writing. On the internet, everybody was a journalist.[2]

That assertion sounds banal today. But back in the heyday of Web 2.0, circa 2008, it was bold talk. It was also threatening. And not surprisingly, news gatekeepers in professional journalism didn't embrace the techno-optimism of web evangelists with unrestrained enthusiasm.

Media executives at first dismissed Web 2.0 as a non-event. At best, they claimed, the internet was an intriguing sideshow. Nothing to see here; move along. When Facebook, Twitter, and blogging started taking off, however, the doubters began feeling the groundswell rumbling under their feet. The anxiety level in newsrooms mounted a notch. Attitudes changed from condescension to caution. Instead of dismissing the internet, news executives wanted to know how Web 2.0 worked so they could understand the dynamics of its threat.

Bill Keller, executive editor of the *New York Times*, was a prominent voice among the internet skeptics in the news industry. In 2007, he delivered a well-publicized speech in London on the state of American newspapers. The title of his speech, "Not Dead Yet: The Newspaper in the Days of Digital Anarchy," left little doubt about his point of view. Keller acknowledged that the web was breaking down barriers through blogging and "citizen journalism," a term he described as having a "sweet, idealistic ring to it."[3] He nonetheless rejected any suggestion that the internet was a "self-regulating democracy of voices that would replace professional journalism."[4] Newspapers like the *New York Times*, he argued, possessed two key advantages that could not be matched by web-based rivals. First, professional journalists were rigorously trained and highly skilled. Second, they adhered to ethical standards of accuracy and fairness. On the second point, Keller admitted that the *New York Times* had been embroiled in embarrassing scandals over plagiarism and fabrications. Still, he insisted that only newspapers possessed the financial resources to produce journalism that met standards of objective truth. Professional journalists possessed expertise. Citizen journalists were unschooled amateurs.

The first wave of bloggers and citizen journalists were indeed amateurs. Most had not attended journalism school and did not work for traditional media outlets. They had no access to the media sphere controlled by professional journalists, whose monopoly on the news had long been protected by high entry barriers. But those barriers were crumbling. The internet allowed bloggers to bypass media gatekeepers. They could now, as Clay Shirky argued, do things without organizations. You could now produce journalism without belonging to the profession. This technological fact triggered a wave of amateur journalism on blogs. Some bloggers attracted massive followings and went on to carve out high-profile careers as respected voices in their areas—fashion, food, travel, politics, celebrity news. In the early days of the internet revolution, however, the "amateur" stigma persisted.

A notable critic of the new web culture was Andrew Keen, author of *The Cult of the Amateur*. Watching the Web 2.0 revolution, Keen was disturbed by what he saw everywhere. The internet had unleashed amateur chaos on the media space. Masses of people were going online, he lamented, to publish "everything from uninformed political commentary, to unseemly home videos, to embarrassingly amateurish music, to unreadable poems, reviews, essays, and novels."[5] Trusted professionals— journalists, editors, educators, librarians—were being undermined by what Keen described as a "democratization of information." He dismissed user-generated content as "ignorance meets egoism meets bad taste meets mob rule."[6]

What troubled Keen most was the democratic dynamic of the internet. "Democratization, despite its lofty idealization," he argued, "is undermining truth, souring civic discourse, and belittling expertise, experience, and talent."[7] Democracy, in short, was the enemy of truth. Mobs were not smart; they were dangerous. Crowds were not wise; they were irrational. Society needed professional experts to establish the truth. Beneath the petulance of his observations, Keen was resurrecting an old debate about the status of experts in democratic societies. He was also raising a deeper philosophical reflection about perceptions of truth. Both questions were particularly relevant in the digital age.

During the Enlightenment, empiricists such as David Hume argued that all knowledge comes from human experience. In complex societies, however, we cannot possibly navigate through life, like Daniel Defoe's Robinson Crusoe, trusting our own perceptions to understand the world. We must put trust in others who possess a greater knowledge of things in many different areas. Knowledge, therefore, is not only direct experience, but also secondhand. Experts are necessary, and it is important that they benefit from acceptance and trust.[8] When we go to the doctor for a vaccination or prescription, most of us cannot scientifically verify the precise nature of the molecules used to prevent disease and remedy our ailments. We trust medical doctors to know these things. Even John Stuart Mill, the classic liberal philosopher who argued for the primacy of individual liberty, advocated a voting system in which the educated classes have more votes than uneducated citizens. While Mill's ideas on plural voting seem unacceptably elitist today, in the nineteenth century his argument that democratic participation must be linked to competence did not seem unreasonable. It was assumed that the public needed to defer to the educated classes. Hierarchies were necessary to avoid mob rule.

Fear of the mob stretched back to ancient Greece, when power struggles opposed ruling oligarchs and democratic orators such as Pericles and Demosthenes. Athenian oligarchs considered mob rule—or ochlocracy, from *ochlos* for crowd—as a dangerous form of government. The ancient Romans called it *mobile vulgus,* which gave us the word *mob*, or mobocracy. In ancient Rome, the plebeian mob could overthrow an emperor. The most desirable form of government—despite Plato's distaste for it— was democracy (from *demos*, "rule by the people"). Democracy was not mob rule; it was representative government through elected politicians. Emperors such as Augustus understood the virtue of this elitist system that favored the senatorial class. Despite his authoritarian rule, he always claimed to be restoring the republic.

The notion of democratic truth—or "common sense"—inspired English common law, the Protestant Reformation, and was embedded in the founding principles of the American and French Revolutions. In America, the Founding Fathers were nonetheless confronted with the old dilemma about who should be empowered with a voice in a democratic society. Benjamin Franklin argued for free speech as a fundamental principle because intellectual freedom was a pre-condition of political freedom. The people must have the right to speak and share their own knowledge, opinions, and beliefs. In Thomas Paine's famous pamphlet, *Common Sense*—published at the same time as America's declaration of independence in 1776—he argued for plain facts and simple truths as the basis for egalitarian government. This view was supported by Thomas Jefferson, who asserted that the common good required a "diffusion of knowledge" toward the people so common sense could prevail. The vitality of republics depended on democratic truths established by freedom of speech and robust participation in politics.[9] This is precisely what distinguished new republics from monarchical regimes, where power was invested in aristocratic and clerical oligarchies who determined and dictated truth. A fundamental principle of democracy was popular sovereignty.

James Madison, one of the authors of the U.S. Constitution, took a slightly more cautious approach. Madison had carefully studied the failure of democracy in ancient Greece and Rome and was concerned about the danger of mobs and demagogues. In the *Federalist Papers*, he warned against the potential violence of the "majority faction." Alexander Hamilton echoed these concerns, especially the danger of the majority electing a demagogue. The remedy against populist passions was a system of representative democracy in which the U.S. president was not directly elected by the people, but indirectly by an electoral college. "The process of election affords a moral certainty, that the office of President will never fall to the lot of any man who is not in an eminent degree endowed with the requisite qualifications," wrote Hamilton.

> Talents for low intrigue, and the little arts of popularity, may alone suffice to elevate a man to the first honors in a single State; but it will require other talents, and a different kind of merit, to establish him in the esteem and confidence of the whole Union, or of so considerable a portion of it as would be necessary to make him a successful candidate for the distinguished office of President of the United States.[10]

In short, American democracy needed an institutional check on the majority.

These ideas framed the original design of the American republic. But even though an Electoral College was instituted, values and practices changed over time. As early as the 1830s, when the French political philosopher Alexis de Tocqueville visited America, he observed in *Democracy in America* that the young republic, when compared with old

European societies burdened by tradition, was characterized by a great egalitarian spirit. Tocqueville expressed concern that American democracy might succumb to a "tyranny of the majority." Two centuries following Tocqueville's warning, America has not succumbed to tyranny or dictatorship. There have been turbulent periods when the American republic's democratic institutions were put to the test. At the end of the nineteenth century, for example, strong populist movements were sweeping through the American political landscape. In the early twentieth century, American presidents such as Teddy Roosevelt and FDR could appeal directly to public opinion thanks to mass media. In our own era, Donald Trump's populist Twitter presidency was, for many, the nightmare that James Madison dreaded.[11] While Trump's supporters undoubtedly regarded his victory as a democratic renaissance, his adversaries had reason to believe that Tocqueville's warning about a tyranny of the majority was prescient. Trump was, as Alexander Hamilton had described, a populist demagogue with "talents for low intrigue and the little arts of popularity." America's political institutions were supposed to prevent his rise to power.

Many believe Trump's victory can be understood as part of the wider culture of animosity toward elites and experts and their monopoly on truth. Attacks on elites are part of a larger war on dominant power structures being waged on many fronts. Trump shrewdly understood—or at least his political strategists did—that the winds were changing in America. His promise to "drain the swamp" was an attack on the corruption of the established elites that ordinary Americans had come to distrust and despise. Above all, Trump grasped that the digital Twittersphere, which is fundamentally egalitarian, was a perfect public square for his brand of populism. Social media allowed Trump to bypass the old media elites and connect directly with American public opinion. For the mainstream media, which had enjoyed a monopoly on the news agenda for more than a century, the frenzied opinion on social media was akin to mob rule. Online networks such as Twitter empowered the icon-smashers of the digital age.

If journalists' reservations about the irrational dynamics of social media were often justified, their disdain for social media did little to mitigate the impact of the digital vortex. After nearly a decade of denial, it was no longer credible for journalists to dismiss the web as an online amateur hour. Old boundaries between the mainstream media and web journalism had been knocked down. It had begun with the upstart news site the Huffington Post, which quickly gained just as much credibility—and web traffic—as its mainstream media revivals. The site's founder, Arianna Huffington, had boldly challenged the old media's "veneer of unassailable trustworthiness" and won. Other sites followed—BuzzFeed, Vice,

Vox, Politico, ProPublica—and became respected sources of news. Influential fashion bloggers, once dismissed by top-drawer professionals at *Vogue*, now sat in front-row seats at Paris and New York catwalks. Only a few years earlier, most professional journalists would not have even considered working for an online news startup. Today, many are making long-term career bets by defecting to digital-only news sites.

"The open web created genuinely new possibilities for journalism," acknowledged Katharine Viner, editor of the *Guardian*. "And journalists who resisted the technological revolution would damage both their own interests and the interests of good journalism."[12]

The *Guardian* had worked harder than most newspapers to harness the web's democratic dynamics. The paper had, among other things, opened its opinion section to a wider range of contributors under the rubric "Comment Is Free"—an allusion to legendary *Guardian* editor C. P. Scott, who wrote in 1921, "Comment is free, but facts are sacred."[13] He also declared that the duty of journalists was to ensure that the "unclouded face of truth" suffers no wrong. Scott, who died in 1932, would have been disappointed to see how cloudy the truth became throughout most of the twentieth century.

Katharine Viner conceded that "truth" was a notion with which journalists often took liberties. The printed word, she noted, encouraged readers to believe in stable and settled truths—whether they were true or not. "This settled 'truth' was usually handed down from above: an established truth, often fixed in place by an establishment," wrote Viner in 2013. "This arrangement was not without flaws: too much of the press often exhibited a bias toward the status quo and a deference to authority, and it was prohibitively difficult for ordinary people to challenge the power of the press." She argued that, in the digital age, journalists need to break out of old attitudes and reflexes. The journalist today must be three things: truth-teller, sense-maker, explainer.[14]

Viner's candid assessment of the profession's past sins was undoubtedly sincere. And her vision for the future was a noble goal. Her case for professional journalism was based essentially on values and practices. It wasn't surprising that, in turbulent times, senior journalists were attempting to reassert the legitimacy of the profession. Still, it seemed too late to salvage the "high-modernist" model of professional journalism that had prevailed for the previous half century. That era was gone. The technological forces of "creative destruction"—to employ the famous term coined by Austrian economist Joseph Schumpeter—had shattered the profession's pretensions, prestige, and power.[15] First, it destroyed the business model that created the conditions of financial stability and independence for the profession to prosper. Second, it toppled the profession's monopoly gatekeeper power by lowering the barrier to entry to anyone who wished to produce news and voice their opinions, thus redefining the boundaries of journalism. Third, it upended journalism's claim on fact-based truth by blurring the lines between objectivity and subjectivity. In sum, the radically egalitarian dynamics of the internet dispossessed professional journalists' status as guardians of the truth. Journalists still enjoyed an influential place in the digital media landscape, but they no longer exercised a monopoly on news agenda setting.

If the digital media sphere is a free-for-all where everyone can have a voice, without any professional oversight, what are the implications for truth? Professional journalists may not have always been trustworthy guardians of the truth, but the alternative has often been alarming. Social media networks, many claim, are a cauldron of slander, rumors, innuendo, and lies. Facebook and Twitter feeds are overwhelmed by a bewildering onslaught of rage and hatred. As the *Guardian*'s Katharine Viner put it, our digital town squares are "mobbed with bullies, misogynists and racists who have brought a new kind of hysteria to public debate."[16] In debates about the digital sphere, the same word keeps returning: *mob*. The implication here, as elsewhere, is that professional journalists are defenders of democracy, whereas the social media sphere is a *mobile vulgus* that promotes mobocracy.

Some claim that the mob effect on social media illustrates the unintended consequences of the "tragedy of the commons." The term was first coined in 1833 by British economist William Forster Lloyd, who cited the example of the common as a shared resource for grazing herds. If one farmer acts in his own self-interest by putting all his cows on the common, he will benefit in the short term. However, if all cattle owners do the same, over-grazing will deplete the common to the detriment of everyone. In short, selfish individual behavior acts against the common good. When applied to online social networks, the same negative consequences can result. It becomes overpopulated, overrun with trolls; intelligent discourse is overwhelmed, rendered inaudible. The result is that democracy suffers, destroyed by the mob. *Financial Times* columnist John Gapper put it this way:

> Here lies the threat to social networks. They set themselves up as commons, offering open access to hundreds of millions to publish "user-generated content" and share photos with others. That in turn produced a network effect: people needed to use Facebook or others to communicate. But they attract bad actors as well—people and organizations who exploit free resources for money or perverted motives. These are polluters of the digital commons and with them come over-grazers: people guilty of lesser sins such as shouting loudly to gain attention or attacking others.[17]

The "tragedy of the commons" metaphor, while intriguing, doesn't rigorously apply to social media. For one thing, Facebook is not a publicly owned resource, though admittedly it could be regulated as one. Also, social media space is not a scarce resource. If one person uses a social media network, it does not deplete resources for others to do so. Though, morally speaking, it could be argued that social media constitutes a sphere in which individuals can seek to harm others. That raises the question of free speech in the digital sphere. In an open public sphere, should every opinion be allowed? If not, who establishes what is permissible and what is offensive? Who determines what is true and what is false? And once we have designated digital-era guardians of the truth, we must find an answer to the time-honored question posed by the ancient Roman poet Juvenal: "*Quis custodiet ipsos custodes?*" Who guards the guardians?

The digital town square's critics should remember that it is not as overcrowded as many claim. The image of Twitter being stormed by hordes of barbarian trolls is powerfully evocative, though wildly overdramatic. True, in theory anyone can show up on the web. There are no more barriers to entry, except a computer and internet connection. But hard statistics reveal that the digital sphere is still a relatively exclusive club. Worldwide, Twitter boasts roughly 330 million monthly active users. Facebook counts roughly 2.5 billion users. Those are impressive figures, but they represent only a fraction of the global population of nearly 8 billion.

For professional journalists who are nostalgic for the monopoly days when the media space was a closed shop, the digital town squares may seem chaotically mobbed. But this was precisely what established elites in the sixteenth century said about pamphleteering, which was unleashed by the printing press revolution. Gutenberg's invention empowered a new class of scribes who previously had no access to the public sphere. Renaissance authorities (state and ecclesiastical) regarded these upstarts as intolerable fanatics who perpetrated slander, defamation, sedition, and heresy. Many were arrested and punished—put in the pillory, stigmatized by branding, hands chopped off, even drawn and quartered. The professional journalists today who rail against amateur mobs overwhelming the digital town square should be reminded that they trace their origins to these radical pamphleteers who were the contemptible trolls of their day. The printing press was a Renaissance Twitter.

These history lessons do little to assuage the anxiety of professional journalists as they confront a serious identity crisis. Dispossessed of their monopoly power, they find themselves competing in a cluttered information marketplace buzzing with activists, hacktivists, spin doctors, and crusaders of every stripe on both left and right. Their professional values and practices have been profoundly affected by forces beyond their control that have pushed journalism from fact-based objectivity toward opinion-based subjectivity. They are struggling to stand out in a digital sphere where millions of grappling voices are engaged in a cacophonous ideological combat. Some claim that the battle over professional values has been lost. In a politically polarized society, journalism has been drawn onto the political battlefield. Journalism today, in one way or another, is activism. If you can't beat them, join them. Others agree with *Guardian* editor Viner's claim that in a digital media sphere in upheaval, professional journalism can regain public trust in values based on fact and objective truth.

An optimist from a different perspective is journalism educator Jeff Jarvis, who advocates for a new kind of journalism that engages and seeks the truth by using the internet as digital commons. Jarvis, author of *Geeks Bearing Gifts*, is a member of the media old guard who today is critical of the profession's conservativism. Jarvis calls on journalists to move beyond high-modernist, mass media concepts and their underlying values of monopoly control. The web has blown open the sphere of public discourse. Journalism is now a conversation. And while conservations in the digital sphere are often loud and messy, for Jarvis it is ultimately a good thing. The voiceless now have a voice.

"Never before in history could millions of citizens talk back to institutions," observed Jarvis, director of the master's program at the CUNY journalism school in New York. "Never before could they air their frustrations. Never before could they find each other to do so. That's now possible."[18]

Jarvis challenges journalism's obsession with the concept of the "story." The story, he says, is a construct that both comforts our cultural biases and suits the commercial necessity to assemble, produce, package, and sell "stories" to consumers of news. That was the industrial model that financed journalism's high-modernist phase. "What if the story as a form, by its nature, is often wrong?" he asks. "What if we cannot explain nearly as much as we think we can? What if our basis for understanding our world and the motives and behaviors of people in it is illusory? What would that mean for journalism and its role in society?"[19]

Jarvis brings to his analysis the same critique that some reserve for the wider study of historical narratives—namely, that they come with cultural baggage, that history is inherently biased by its chosen form of storytelling. If we can't trust narrative history to explain what really happened in the past, the same can be said of the storytelling structure of journalism. The journalistic story is a construct with its own codes and conventions, including personality and drama. There is nothing that guarantees its reliability in discovering the truth. In journalism, as in history, storytelling is frequently an act of seduction. But seducers invariably feel compelled to lie. That is precisely why, in Plato's *Republic*, Socrates warns against storytellers as mythmakers. In ancient Greece, *logos* represented the philosophy-based power of reason; while *mythos* inspired the poetry of stories and tales. In journalism today, the fabrication scandals that have tainted the profession's most prestigious publications over the years prove that storytelling is too frequently closer to tales than truth.

Jarvis's solution is to re-engineer journalism's mission by pragmatically empowering people to engage in the sphere of public discourse. Jarvis calls it journalism that values listening over lecturing, conversation over content, collaboration over consumption, service over product. On the last point, he regards news not as a packaged product, but as a public service. On the internet, journalism should be a networked process that engages people—professionals and non-professionals—in relationships with their communities to solve common problems. Jarvis's concept of journalism's mission as democratic engagement echoes the thinking of the American philosopher John Dewey. In his book *The Public and Its Problems*, published in 1927, Dewey advocated for collective problem-solving through open citizen communication. Dewey shared Walter Lippmann's concerns about the ability of average citizens to grasp complex issues, but he did not embrace Lippmann's prescription for professional journalists to give the public guidance. Lippmann was essentially an elitist, in the tradition of Plato's *Republic*, who believed that society needs a class of guardians. Lippmann was attached to values of fact and objectivity and resolutely opposed to opinions masquerading as truth. He believed that professionally trained journalists were the best guardians of the truth. In short, Lippmann advocated a powerful role for experts in modern democracies. John Dewey disagreed. "A class of experts is inevitably so removed from common interests as to become a class with private interests and private knowledge," he argued. "The man who wears the shoe knows best that it pinches and where it pinches, even if the expert shoemaker is the best judge of how the trouble is to be remedied."[20] Dewey was a great believer in the democratic practices of citizens engaged in collective dialogue and civic action. Dewey was, in sum, an advocate of pragmatic truths.

"There is no limit to the intellectual endowment which may proceed from the flow of social intelligence when that circulates by word of mouth from one to another in the communications of the local community," wrote Dewey in *The Public and Its Problems*. "That and that only gives reality to public opinion. We lie, as [Ralph Waldo] Emerson, said, in the lap of an immense intelligence. But that intelligence is dormant and its communications are broken, inarticulate and faint until it possesses the local community as its medium."[21]

The Lippmann-Dewey debate raised the familiar issue of the status of experts in democratic societies. Attempts to resolve this question had far-reaching consequences for values about truth in American society and, more specifically, for the role of journalism in producing public knowledge. In the short term, Lippmann's ideas prevailed. He was the intellectual father of the high-modernist pretention of professional journalists as guardians of the truth. That model prevailed for most of the twentieth century, when professional journalism was organized around the industrial production of news packaged as stories. In America, the profession's values were anchored in notions of facts, objectivity, impartiality, and fairness. Cracks began to appear in that model, however, after the 1960s with the rise of the postmodernist ethos and its challenges to established structures of authority. The "New Journalism" movement, which championed subjective perspectives and literary techniques, was an attack on established journalistic practices based on seeking truth through objective facts.

Dewey's democratic vision, advocated by practitioners such as Jeff Jarvis, has regained momentum in the social media era. Journalism today is no longer monopolized by a closed profession, whatever its virtues and vices. It has become diffused over many spheres of information gathering, civic engagement, and democratic activism. Digital platforms such as Twitter and Google may be a disruptive threat to the established profession, but for the wider community they provide platforms for a new model of public discourse. Proponents of this model share John Dewey's faith in "the capacity of human beings for intelligent judgment and action if proper conditions are furnished."[22] People are reasonable and can seek the truth by themselves; they simply need to be encouraged and empowered. If this model has the virtue of being fundamentally optimistic, it is not without consequences. One is the obsessiveness of digital engagement. We are too immersed in clicking, sharing, liking, tweeting, and retweeting. Or to put it more bluntly, we spend too much time on social media. More troubling, the same digital tools that promote civic engagement are available to adversaries of democracy, including foreign states with an interest in undermining our political institutions.[23]

Opponents of the Dewey vision, following on Walter Lippmann's pessimism about people's capacity to understand complex problems, hold fast to the tenets of journalism's high-modernist values. They insist on the recognized status of journalists as professional experts whose gatekeeping power is necessary. For them, the influence of social media has been destructive because it has undermined fact-based truths by unleashing a frenzy of uninformed opinion, trolling, misinformation, and "fake news." In short, the web has not empowered people to seek truth; it has given them an unregulated platform to spread lies.

The rivalry between these two models won't likely produce a decisive winner. Professional journalists are, perhaps understandably, cautiously embracing change while jealously protecting the remnants of their privileges and power. Their semantic weaponization of the term *fake news*—an update on *digital anarchy* and *mob rule*—provides a revealing illustration of that coping strategy. Even if warnings about "fake news" need to be heeded; stubbornly clinging to old values while denouncing new turpitudes is not the way forward. The grass-roots democratic model, for its part, may succeed in mobilizing collective action around common problems, but how does it reconcile activist goals with professional values of fact, evidence, and impartiality? Is journalism's primary mission to discover truths or engage in political problem-solving?

Perhaps it can be argued that the former is a necessary precondition to accomplishing the latter, but the question remains intact.

***

Despite its imperfections, the industrial model of high-modernist journalism was a great success.

Throughout the twentieth century, advertising produced robust profits that gave media companies a solid economic foundation that afforded journalists the confidence to fulfill their "fourth estate" duty. True, journalists constantly had to deal with pressures from corporate owners, advertisers, PR flaks, and spin doctors. But overall, the business model worked. Revenues were abundant and diverse, providing journalists the autonomy they needed to uphold their professed values of fact-based newsgathering and objective truth.

In hindsight, it's astounding how quickly that model collapsed. In the pre–social media days, circa 2002, American newspapers and magazines were flush with cash. Advertising revenues were roughly $70 billion. Google was a little-known search engine scarcely on the advertising industry radar. A decade later, Google's revenues had surpassed the combined American newspaper and magazine industry revenues, which were only $20 billion—a $50 billion drop from a decade earlier. By 2018, the lion's share of advertising revenues was going to two companies: Google and Facebook. Together, they controlled more than 60 percent of global online advertising revenue. As these two web giants soaked up most of the advertising juice, the financial lifeblood was squeezed from the news industry.

The industry's first reaction was massive downsizing and layoffs. The journalism profession started shrinking. On the corporate side, some panicked owners opted for asset shedding. Newspapers and magazines went under the hammer at rock-bottom prices. In 2013, Amazon owner Jeff

Bezos bought the *Washington Post*—the prestigious paper that broke the Watergate story—for $250 million. Chump change for an internet multi-billionaire. In the same fire sale, *Newsweek* magazine was sold for a symbolic one dollar.

A more humiliating blow for news organizations was loss of gatekeeper power over their own content. Most consumers were now accessing news via Google searches and on their Facebook timelines. This shift toward "search" and "social" gave Google and Facebook tremendous power as distribution systems. Since news reached audiences thanks to searches, clicks, likes, shares, and—if you add Twitter—tweets and retweets, the success or failure of a story was determined by algorithms. For powerful news brands that once ruled the media space—*New York Times*, the *Guardian, Daily Telegraph, Vogue, Vanity Fair, Le Monde, Wall Street Journal*—the shift from editorial to algorithmic gatekeeping was catastrophic. They were still producers of news, but they no longer controlled the distribution platforms to reach consumers.

Also, algorithms rewarded social media engagement that attracted the most clicks. Now the game was clickbait to generate viral buzz. This was not to say that newspapers and television networks had never indulged in sensationalism before Facebook and Twitter. But social media networks pushed journalists to "game" the algorithms with stories that elicited strong reactions. Paradoxically, the hyper-rationalist logic of algorithms drove and rewarded journalistic practices favoring emotion. If journalism had reluctantly made the "affective turn" in the past, now it was embedded in their business model. The subordination of the profession to technology was double: journalists lost gatekeeper power to Google and Facebook as distribution systems connecting to consumers, and they lost control over content to the logic of the algorithm in determining what kinds of stories they produced.

For some in the news industry, this trend promised an apocalyptical endgame. The four horsemen of the Apocalypse, charging through the media landscape and slaying everything in sight, were Facebook, Google, Twitter, and YouTube. These four behemoths were henceforth keepers of the gates. As Emily Bell, director of Columbia University's Tow Center for Digital Journalism, observed: "We are seeing massive changes in control, and finance, putting the future of our publishing ecosystem into the hands of a few, who now control the destiny of many. Social media hasn't just swallowed journalism, it has swallowed everything. It has swallowed political campaigns, banking systems, personal histories, the leisure industry, retail, even government and security."[24]

The news industry had no choice but to play by the new digital rules. Editorial strategies were retooled to game Google and Facebook algorithms. This entailed restructuring the basic plumbing of newsrooms.

They hired SEO experts to boost search engine optimization results on Google. They recruited videographers to edit and package clickable videos for Facebook and Twitter. As SEO and video editors marched into newsrooms, the ink-stained wretches from the old days were quietly escorted out the back door. The ordeal was painful.

Upstart news sites such as BuzzFeed and Mashable, meanwhile, had already been gaming the algorithms with no damage to their self-esteem. They had built their entire business model on it. A sizable portion of their revenues came from "native advertising" and "branded content," which was effectively paid advertising dressed up as news. This strategy would have been ethically questionable during journalism's proud high-modernist period, when so-called advertorials were a stigma that offended professional values. In digital journalism, however, driving revenues with branded content was shamelessly out in the open. It shaped editorial strategy. And it wasn't only clickbait sites like Mashable and BuzzFeed that were using branded content to attract revenues. Many prestige news organizations—the *New York Times, Wall Street Journal, Time*, the *Guardian*—began launching their own branded content divisions. The old "church and state" wall, which had once separated editorial from advertising, was discreetly dismantled.

More troubling, some of the world's most respected newspapers struck "sponsored content" deals with the Chinese to publish propaganda supplements that portrayed China's communist regime in a flattering light. For the Chinese, buying editorial space in major Western newspapers was part of their "borrowed boats" soft power strategy. China was using Western media to target global audiences with its propaganda. For the newspapers who accepted cash to publish Chinese-produced editorial supplements—including the *New York Times, Washington Post, Wall Street Journal,* and the *Daily Telegraph* and *Daily Mail* in Britain—the financial benefits clearly outweighed the questionable optics. By accepting these financial inducements, American and British newspapers gave credibility to Chinese propaganda while undermining their own reputations as trusted sources of news. But with their traditional business model collapsing, it was a risk they were prepared to take.

For some observers, more was at stake than a redistributed media advertising pie. The future of democracy was hanging in the balance. "Facebook has become the richest and most powerful publisher in history by replacing editors with algorithms—shattering the public square into millions of personalized news feeds, shifting entire societies away from the open terrain of genuine debate and argument, while they make billions from our valued attention," observed *Guardian* editor Katherine Viner. "This shift presents big challenges for liberal democracy."[25] Viner's observation about the shattered "public square" was doubtless accurate. Her point about the new economics and their consequences was also correct. Facebook and Google had not only destroyed journalism's business model but also usurped the profession's status as guardians of the truth. It was less than certain, however, that Facebook and Google accepted the ethical responsibility that came with their gatekeeper power.

Politicians, not surprisingly, were quick to understand that the digital dynamics of social media had disrupted the news hierarchy. The first was Barack Obama. Before his first presidential bid in 2008, Obama had been a junior senator with little name recognition in American politics. Thanks to his skillful use of the internet to raise money and mobilize voters, he outmaneuvered Hillary Clinton for the Democratic nomination before defeating Republican candidate John McCain for the presidency. Following Obama's spectacular victory, the *New York Times* published a story titled "How Obama's Internet Campaign Changed Politics."

"One of the many ways that the election of Barack Obama as president has echoed that of John F. Kennedy is his use of a new medium that will forever change politics," noted the newspaper. "For Mr. Kennedy, it was television. For Mr. Obama, it is the Internet."[26]

In the White House, Obama did not forget how he had won. He shrewdly grasped that the best way to reach young American voters was to find them where they spent most of their time—on social media. In the past, old media competed for consumers' attention and sold it to advertisers. Social media hyper-accelerated the economics of attention. Smartphones and laptops transformed users into always-on media consumers— liking, sharing, commenting, retweeting. Americans were increasingly getting their news via Facebook, Twitter, and other online networks. Obama was the first world leader to understand the dynamics of the "attention economy."

In the White House, Obama's fourteen-member digital team posted YouTube videos, created infographics for WhiteHouse.gov, and manned social media accounts on Facebook, Twitter, Instagram, and Pinterest. When dealing with the media, Obama put online news outlets such as BuzzFeed and Vox in the same league as the *New York Times* and *Washington Post*—a gesture that displeased the established White House press corps. He also granted interviews to YouTube stars who never talked about politics. "The reason we did it is because they're reaching viewers who don't want to be put in some particular camp," Obama said in a Vox interview in early 2015. On using social media in office, Obama had a message for his successors in the White House: "My advice to a future president is increasingly try to bypass the traditional venues that create divisions and try to find new venues within this new media that are quirkier, less predictable."[27]

Donald Trump, who would move into the White House at the end of the following year, was listening and watching.

As soon as he entered the White House, and even before, Trump attracted criticism for his narcissistic obsession with social media. It is forgotten however that, before Trump, Obama had been criticized for his social media tactics. When Obama was still in office, critics observed that he was primarily interested in social media for branding and marketing. He masterfully used social networks to fashion his "cool dad" image, but did little to harness the internet as a platform to strengthen democracy. At the end of Obama's second term, the *Atlantic* magazine observed, "As Obama leaves office, the digital tools he quietly celebrated have also hollowed out American life."[28]

Today, many argue that public discourse on social media oversimplifies complex ideas and problems. On social networks, there are no barriers, no filters, no gatekeepers. Every conceivable voice can seek an audience and be heard, even those with questionable motives. The digital sphere favors emotion over reason. Voters are moved more by tweeted indignation than by considered argument. Online networks, it is argued, exacerbate social divisions and polarize opinion. People go online to connect with like-minded opinions in "echo chambers" and "filter bubbles" that confirm their own subjective biases. Worse, the web is overpopulated with hatemongering trolls. Genuine democratic debate is overwhelmed and undermined.

Many of these concerns—which incidentally echo the accusations made against pamphleteers in the seventeenth century—are undoubtedly valid. There is reason to believe, however, that arguments about "polarization," "echo chambers," and "filter bubbles" are overstated. A study by scholars at Oxford University's Reuters Institute found that social media networks do not, as is often claimed, facilitate mono-think "echo chambers" where people confirm existing biases. Empirical research across thirty-six countries found that social media users, compared with non-users, are in fact more engaged in news across a wider range of sources. "Not everything that social media is accused of stands up in our research," notes David Levy, head of the Reuters Institute when the study was published in early 2018. "One thing people accuse it of is creating an echo chamber. We actually discovered in our research that people using social media or search [engines, such as Google] for news online actually see more news sources each week than people who don't."[29] Another seven-country study conducted at Michigan State University arrived at similar findings. It concluded that claims of "echo chambers" and "filter bubbles" were "under-researched and overhyped."[30]

Other empirical studies refuted exaggerated claims casually attributed to social media. One was that people are prone to a "backfire effect." A cognitive phenomenon related to confirmation bias, the "backfire effect" holds that when people encounter evidence that contradicts their beliefs, they reject it and retrench even more resolutely in their own beliefs. Empirical evidence suggests, however, that the "backfire effect" is a myth. People with zealous beliefs—religious or political—will doubtless reject evidence that challenges their deeply held convictions. People hold steadfastly to their fundamental worldview. Most of the time, however, facts and evidence are convincing. Parents who refuse to have their children vaccinated against measles are usually motivated by either religious conviction or misinformation. Those in the former category often reject the facts of science; those in the latter group are more likely to be convinced that they are in error.

Why are many myths about social media accepted as true? One reason is that they are generated by academics and activists with ideological agendas and then circulated in the mainstream media where they gain credibility. As Jeff Jarvis at the CUNY graduate journalism school notes, media coverage about the web is too often founded on "assumptions, fears, theories, myths, mere metaphors, isolated incidents, and hidden self-interest, not evidence." "The discussion about the internet and the future should begin with questions and research and end with demonstrable facts," adds Jarvis, "not with presumption or with what I fear most in media: moral panic."[31]

Even if online "echo chambers" and confirmation bias do exist, are they any different from newspapers and magazines that attract millions of readers according to their political leanings? For decades, newspapers shouted out partisan bias from their front-page headlines and news angles to the columns on their opinion pages. In Britain, *Daily Mail* and *Telegraph* readers are overwhelmingly Tory voters; and *Guardian* and *Daily Mirror* readers are largely Labour supporters. In France, *Le Monde* attracts readers on the left, while *Le Figaro*'s readership is conservative. Are these newspapers not print media "filter bubbles"? And what about all-news television channels such as Fox News on the right and MSNBC on the left? Surely, they are cable news "echo chambers."

Critics nonetheless insist that social media polarization presents a greater danger than old media bias. Some blame digital advertising metrics. Facebook and Google are not interested in truth, it is claimed; their motivation is maximizing advertising revenues. Social media algorithms don't reward journalism in the public interest; they boost articles and videos that get the most clicks—even ones that spread falsehoods and lies. Consequently, social media networks polarize opinions on the radical extremes—toxic trolls, conspiracy theorists, white supremacists, antivaxxers, flat-earth loonies—where reason and factual truth are unimportant. This critique undoubtedly has some merit and should not be casually dismissed—indeed, social media networks are starting to regulate their platforms more aggressively, though that sometimes creates other problems related to arbitrary censorship. It could also be argued that bringing previously marginalized voices into the public sphere is not a bad thing. The internet has provided a platform to the voiceless in many countries where authoritarian regimes suppress free speech. Arguments that characterize free speech on social media as "mob rule" risk legitimizing censorship and repression. Like Roman emperors, modern-day dictators fear the "mob."

What is the solution? Will a quick fix to Google's algorithm make "fake news" and online trolls disappear? Not likely. Some argue that we need to enhance "media literacy" at an early age so young people can learn how to decode information in the digital sphere. It's a noble goal, in theory. But media literacy projects have been around for a long time, stretching back decades before the internet era. They produced few measurable benefits then, so how are they going to work today in a much more complex digital sphere? Also, media literacy is a field that is often heavy with normative baggage. As internet scholar Danah Boyd notes, a contestable brand of media literacy, while it doesn't always use that name, is already taught in American schools.

"Students are asked to distinguish between CNN and Fox," observes Boyd. "Or to identify bias in a news story. When tech is involved, it often comes in the form of 'don't trust Wikipedia; use Google.' We might collectively dismiss these practices as not-media literacy, but these activities are often couched in those terms." Boyd argues that these pedagogical practices in schools promote "a form of critical thinking that asks people to doubt what they see."[32] Fox-versus-CNN media literacy is simply shifting familiar partisan battles to the classroom. That is ideology, not pedagogy. At a time of heightened anxiety about "polarization" of opinion in liberal democracies, surely the purpose of media literacy should not be to pour fuel on the fire. This is the fundamental problem with postmodern culture's rejection of facts and objective truths. If we are going to promote critical thinking, it should take us toward truth, not teach us to doubt its existence or suspect its motives.

Perhaps we need to stop fixating on the worst dysfunctions of the digital sphere. By constantly calling out "fake news" and shouting down slimy trolls, we are in fact amplifying their messages and extending their audience. "Fake news" and "polarization" are not technology problems for experts to fix. Their causes lie in human values, attitudes, and behavior. It is worth asking ourselves why we are so focused on the dangers of "fake news" when astrology, fortune-telling, palmistry, and cartomancy are a billion-dollar industry in the United States—and even bigger in many other countries. We are astounded American voters believe a viral news story on Facebook claiming the pope endorsed Donald Trump, yet are indifferent to the fact that millions of Americans believe astrology is a science.[33]

With so much turmoil and uncertainty in the digital sphere, one can understand nostalgia for the old high-modernist model of professional journalists setting the news agenda. Nostalgia is a powerful sentiment. But the old era of media elitism is over. Today, everyone can have a voice. For those who fear a digital mobocracy, the challenge is to foster a public sphere that enriches the quality of civic discourse around values of open debate and truth. We need to boost the level of trust in society—trust in facts, trust in expertise, trust in institutions. Trust creates stable societies; distrust leads to social instability. A society based on trust is a society that values facts as the source of truth.[34]

The level of trust in American society was put to the test in the presidential election of 2016. The result stunned the world. And yet it was entirely predictable.

18

LORD OF THE LIES

A few months after Donald Trump moved into the White House, he produced a paid television commercial that listed his major accomplishments after one hundred days in office.

The gesture, if typical of Trump's penchant for self-admiration, was extraordinary. The boastful television advert was oddly "unpresidential," even in a country whose political culture is driven by paid advertising.

To nobody's surprise, right-wing Fox News channel faithfully aired the Trump commercial. But the other major networks—ABC, NBC, CBS, CNN—flatly rejected it. Their rationale: it contained falsehoods. The Trump ad, it turned out, not only boasted his achievements in office but also attacked the mainstream media. It featured a graphic that labeled network news anchors—including NBC's Andrea Mitchell, CNN's Wolf Blitzer, MSNBC's Rachel Maddow, ABC's George Stephanopoulos, and CBS's Scott Pelley—as "fake news."

By refusing to air the ad, the main networks were reminding Trump that it was their job—not his—to determine what was true and false.

Trump's daughter-in-law Lara Trump jumped into the fray by denouncing the television networks. "Apparently, the mainstream media are champions of the First Amendment only when it serves their own political views," said the wife of Trump's son Eric. "Faced with an ad that doesn't fit their biased narrative, CNN, ABC, CBS, and NBC have now all chosen to block our ad. This is an unprecedented act of censorship in America that should concern every freedom-loving citizen."[1]

Trump's first term thus began with a declaration of war on the news media. He called the media "fake news." The media, for their part, called Trump a liar.

Relations between an American president and the mainstream media had never been so acrimonious. Even Richard Nixon, in the darkest hours of the Watergate scandal, did not suffer this kind of naked media animosity. Journalists disdained George W. Bush, but in retrospect he was regarded as an affable figure of affection. Trump made all his predecessors seem honest and likeable. From the moment he walked into the White House, the media treated Trump as illegitimate, a con artist, a usurper of high office. Some stories intimated that he suffered from mental illness. Inevitably, impeachment proceedings were initiated against Trump. The message was implicit but unequivocal: Donald Trump was unfit to govern.

That Trump was a unique figure in American politics was disputed by nobody. Most politicians are narcissistic, but Trump stood in a category of his own. His tirades on Twitter revealed a self-besotted man tortured by paranoia and incapable of handling any degree of narcissistic injury. He was intellectually shallow, self-reverential, and obsessed with his television ratings. His blustery manner and tangerine soufflé hairdo made him an easy target for satire. The mockery reached a grotesque moment when a large "Baby Trump" balloon was floated over London during Trump's visit to England in July 2018. He was so thin-skinned about the Ubu-esque blimp that he refused to visit the city.

The extravagant traits of Trump's over-sized persona did little to win the media's affection. But it was his penchant for exaggeration and falsehoods that came under the most serious scrutiny. Trump was vulgar, but he was above all a liar. "If he has a particular untruth he wants to propagate—not just an undifferentiated barrage—he simply states it, over and over," writes a pundit for *Politico Magazine*, drawing a parallel between Trump's lies and Nazi propaganda. "As it turns out, sheer repetition of the same lie can eventually mark it as true in our heads."[2] In April 2017, a *Los Angeles Times* editorial, bluntly titled "Why Trump Lies," stated: "Truth is as vital a part of the civic, social and intellectual culture as justice and liberty. Our civilization is premised on the conviction that such a thing as truth exists, that it is knowable, that it is verifiable, that it exists independently of authority or popularity and that at some point— and preferably sooner rather than later—it will prevail."[3]

Trump's irrational rants on Twitter attracted special scrutiny. His tweetstorms had begun before the presidential election in 2016. He had tweeted, for example, that Barack Obama was not born in the United States (and hence was disqualified from office) and moreover was a Muslim. Once in the White House, Trump stepped up his assaults on his predecessor, claiming that Obama had ordered the wiretapping of his Trump Tower offices in New York. While some of Trump's outlandish statements were difficult to disprove, many could be fact-checked. The

Washington Post calculated that Trump made 492 false or misleading statements in his first three months in office—an average of 4.9 false claims per day. There were only ten days when Trump did not make a false claim. The media's scorecard of Trump's first hundred days was a striking contrast to the one presented in his boastful television commercial aired on Fox News. Two years later, the *Washington Post* was still tracking Trump's false and misleading statements: he crossed the ten thousand threshold on April 26, 2019.[4]

Donald Trump was not, of course, the first president in American history who ever uttered a falsehood. Politicians lie, and do so frequently. It is the nature of public life. Lying in politics stretches back to Machiavelli's counsel to the prince, if not all the way to Plato's "noble lie" in ancient Greece.

In the United States, one does not have to search far back in history to find evidence of presidential mendacity. Harry Truman once described his predecessor Franklin Roosevelt this way: "He lies." When Richard Nixon was in the White House, political correspondent David Wise published a book, titled *The Politics of Lying*, in which he observed: "By 1972 the politics of lying had changed the politics of America. In place of trust, there was widespread mistrust; in place of confidence, there was disbelief and doubt in the system and its leaders."[5] Two decades after Nixon's impeachment, Bill Clinton not only lied but also lied to the entire world on live television when angrily denying a sexual affair with a White House intern. Clinton confessed later that he had lied. When George W. Bush was in the White House, the *Atlantic* magazine published an article titled "Untruth and Consequences." It acknowledged that American presidents since George Washington had uttered lies—but George W. Bush's lies were different. Books about Bush invariably featured the word *lie* in the title, including *The Lies of George W. Bush*, *When Presidents Lie*, and *Lies and the Lying Liars Who Tell Them*. In 2004, the *New York Times* published an article, "Calling Bush a Liar," which began: "So is President Bush a liar? Plenty of Americans think so." In 2012, the American media were calling out falsehoods during the election campaign opposing Barack Obama and Mitt Romney. *Time* magazine published a cover story showing Obama and Romney under the headline: "Who Is Telling the Truth: The Fact Wars." The Obama-Romney televised debate provoked an outpouring of negative commentary about the "decline of facts."[6]

Four years later, Americans were being told—again—that the lies of the man in the White House set a shocking new precedent. Previous presidents lied, but Donald Trump's lies were different. His falsehoods had the ring of a huckster, a circus impresario, a confidence trickster. Trump's bling-bling bombast made the media nostalgic for the golden age of noble lies when American presidents deceived with decorum. Trump's lies were ignoble.

Either Donald Trump was indeed the worst pathological liar who had ever set foot in the Oval Office, or the media were prosecuting him with extraordinary zeal. His detractors overlooked the inconvenient fact that he won the presidency fair and square, following the established rules—Republican primary, presidential election, Electoral College vote. His critics claimed, however, that Trump had "gamed" the electoral system. That may be so, but previous presidential elections were won and lost according to the same rules without the same negative reaction from the media. In that respect, Trump was different. He had disrupted the entire system, including the media.

That may explain, at least in part, why the American media's reaction to Trump was so hostile. Prestigious papers such as the *New York Times*, proud of their tradition of objective journalism, dropped all pretenses of impartiality. In news stories, slanted words used to describe Trump—*bluster, tirade, swagger, brag, boast, rant*—revealed unequivocal bias. As an article in the *Nation* observed, the media's aggressive coverage of Trump became an obsession that backfired by boosting his standing with his anti-establishment base of supporters:

> In many ways, the press has become the main check on Trump, hold-ing him accountable at a time when Congress is paralyzed, Republi-cans are cowed, and Democrats are fractured. Yet even as news organ-izations perform this valuable function, they have shown some serious weaknesses, including bias, insularity, groupthink, and condescension, which have provided ammunition to Trump and his supporters as they seek to discredit the press.[7]

Trump's victory was predictable for anyone who was paying attention. There had even been a dress rehearsal earlier that year across the pond in the United Kingdom. British voters spent months in the grip of a Brexit referendum campaign filled with blatant falsehoods. Among the outra-geous claims by pro-Brexit politicians, notably Boris Johnson, was a "fact" that received widespread media coverage: the UK was paying an eye-popping £350 million a week—or £20 billion a year—to keep the Brussels bureaucracy running. Fact-checked, this claim was a lie. An-other false claim was that the UK could not stop Turkey from joining the EU, raising the dreaded prospect of hordes of Muslims arriving on British shores. Other false claims belonged to the realm of farce—for example, that the EU would regulate the curvature of bananas and ban British tea kettles. Though patently ludicrous, these lies produced a powerful impact on British public opinion. The referendum result proved it.

A few months later, the American presidential election campaign served up another carnival of deception from the Trump campaign. Trump's critics in the media failed to grasp that many American voters didn't believe that Trump was lying. They believed that the media were the liars. Distrust in elites was widespread in the American hinterlands. Voters were tired of the lies and corruption of the entire establishment— Wall Street, Washington, the media, all of it. When Trump promised to "drain the swamp," they applauded and cheered. If Trump was lying, they didn't care. They liked what he was saying. Finally, they believed, an American political leader was on their side.

Political sociologists have described this phenomenon as the "authentic appeal of the lying demagogue."[8] In the past, many American politicians were guilty of "insider" lies. An insider (or "special access") lie is defined as a deliberately false statement based on facts that the speaker knows. This type of lie is perpetrated, for example, by politicians who fail to state publicly what they know privately to be the truth. A classic example of a "special access" lie was Bill Clinton's famous declaration that he "did not have sexual relations" with a White House intern. Clinton was lying, and he knew he was lying (he had special access to the truth). Trump's false statements, by contrast, are categorized as "common knowledge" lies, defined as flagrant violations of the norm of truth-telling that appeal to non-normative private prejudices. When Trump boastfully exaggerated the crowd size at his inauguration, the inaccuracy of his claims was largely irrelevant. Trump had no special access to the truth of his claims; he was simply indulging in what he liked to call "truthful hyperbole." His supporters didn't care if he was being untruthful; they made up their own minds. Another "common knowledge" lie was Boris Johnson's Brexit referendum claim that Britain was sending "£350 million a week" to the European Union. British voters didn't care if it was true or false. It sounded true, and that was all that mattered. Voters usually resent skilled "insider" liars such as Bill Clinton or Tony Blair, but they are more willing to indulge the bluster of "common knowledge" liars such as Donald Trump and Boris Johnson. The brashness of Trump's lies is seductively authentic.

Lies are expected during election campaigns. The American presidential campaign of 2016, however, was also riddled not only with false and misleading statements but also with bogus news stories—or "fake news." Many of them, favorable and unfavorable, were about Donald Trump. Among them was breaking news that the pope had endorsed Trump. That story, manifestly false, received nearly 1 million engagements on Facebook. Some fake news stories targeted Trump's personal conduct. One claimed he had once "groped" drag queen RuPaul at a party—and was furious when he reached up his skirt to discover male genitals. That story, pure fabrication, attracted more than 300,000 engagements on Facebook. Yet another story reported that President Trump, after moving into the White House, intended to continue as executive producer of his reality TV show, *Celebrity Apprentice*. That, too, was false.

The most revealing false story about Trump's election was the widely circulated news that he had won the popular vote. This news appeared at the top of Google search rankings. But it was false. Trump won the Electoral College vote—that is why he was elected. But he lost the popular vote. Hillary Clinton won nearly 3 million more votes than Donald Trump. This statistical fact clearly irritated Trump. After the election, he insisted that he'd won the popular vote too. In this case, Trump was committing a "special access" lie. It's difficult to believe he did not know the statistical result of the popular vote. Trump conceded as much when he tweeted: "In addition to winning the Electoral College in a landslide, I won the popular vote if you deduct the millions of people who voted illegally." Trump was, in effect, accusing Hillary Clinton of voter fraud. Many Americans didn't seem to care about the veracity of his claim. Polls indicated that roughly half of Americans who voted for Donald Trump believed he won the popular vote.

Few argued that "fake news" was not a problem. But who was to blame? The media and Trump accused each other. Throughout Trump's first term, journalists aggressively fact-checked his statements for falsehoods. The *New York Times* observed that "the presidency has served as a vehicle for Mr. Trump to construct and promote his own narrative, one with crackling verve but riddled with inaccuracies, distortions and outright lies."[9] Trump, for his part, excoriated the press for publishing lies about him. His tweets constantly dismissed the mainstream media as "fake news" (a term he claimed to have coined). In Twitter tirades, he angrily castigated the media as "the enemy of the people."[10] He was so infuriated at CNN that, during a press conference, he refused to answer a question put to him by the network's White House correspondent. Trump snapped, "You are fake news!"[11]

Trump's fulminations against the "fake news" media were consistent with his populist, anti-establishment rhetoric about "draining the swamp." In that respect, his accusation resonated with the postmodernist ethos hostile to powerful institutions including the media. Distrust of the mainstream media stretched back to the counter-culture 1960s, when protestors opposed to the Vietnam War accused the media of acting as mouthpieces of the military-industrial establishment. At that time, distrust of the media was on the anti-establishment left. A half century later, the distrust had spread and crossed the political spectrum to the conservative right. Trump skillfully harnessed that distrust for his own political purposes.

Trump did not coin the term *fake news*. It was one of his claims that, like others, was simply untrue. But he used the term so frequently that it became identified with his uniquely volatile rhetoric. By effectively claiming ownership of the term *fake news*, Trump deprived his adversaries of employing it. Journalists had attempted to deploy the term to disparage "fake news" spread on social media by nonprofessional sources. They used the term to distinguish themselves ("real news") from the cacophony of lies and falsehoods on the internet ("fake news"). But their semantic strategy backfired. Trump called *them* "fake news." His accusation, not theirs, stuck in the public's mind. In the battle for ownership of the term, Trump won. Some journalists even urged colleagues to stop using the term. Some began using the term *junk news*, possibly due to the association with junk bonds. [12]

The term *fake news*, whatever its origin, is overused and oversimplified. "Fake news" has morphed into a hydra-headed monster with many faces, some more alarming than others. For some, "fake news" is any story that is knowingly false, like the news about the pope endorsing Trump. For others with more exacting standards, it is any story that is false or inaccurate, period, even unknowingly—though the word *false* is probably more appropriate in this case. Also labeled "fake news" are manipulated reports, phony photos, and videos posted online to create misleading impressions. So are false stories planted in the news cycle by states and their proxies, such as alleged Russian meddling in the American elections. This type of fake news is state disinformation. Stories spun by PR firms and spin doctors are also considered "fake news." [13]

Finally, satire produced by parody sites and television comedians who mock public figures is also classified as "fake news." While this may seem ludicrous, political satire is often taken seriously—and, indeed, mistaken for the truth. When the *Onion* reported that North Korean dictator Kim Jung-Un had been named "Sexiest Man Alive," the story was picked up as real news in the Chinese and South Korean media. Parody and satire as "truth" established a connection between "fake news" and the avant-garde movements in the late nineteenth and early twentieth century when artists mocked bourgeois social norms with the irrational aesthetics of the absurd. The gigantic "Baby Trump" blimp floating over the streets of London during his official visit could be regarded as an absurdist Ubu Roi satire of the culture of power and greed that Donald Trump's critics claim he represents. On American television, the satirical impersonations of Trump—notably by Hollywood actor Alec Baldwin on *Saturday Night Live*—created a jarringly comic confusion between the fake and real. The real Donald Trump, infuriated at the mockery, even took to Twitter to vent his exasperation at the fake version of himself.

Beyond the comic aspect of the parody, the tension between "fake" and "real" revealed something deeper about American society. As the Italian critic Umberto Eco observed, Americans are obsessed with realism. "The American imagination demands the real thing," he noted, "and, to attain it, must fabricate the absolute fake."[14] For any reconstruction to be credible, it must be a perfect copy of the original. Imitations are not just an attempt to reproduce reality, but an attempt to improve on it. The fake replaces the authentic as more genuine. The result is a "hyper-reality" in which fake becomes real—or "authentic fake." The American cultural landscape is cluttered with "authentic fakes." Think Disneyland as fake reality. Or Las Vegas with its replica of the Eiffel Tower. In the classic American novel *The Great Gatsby*, the tragic hero Jay Gatsby owns a lavish mansion on Long Island described as "a colossal affair by any standard—it was a factual imitation of some Hôtel de Ville in Normandy." In a culture where the copy seems genuine, the invisible line between imitation and original in political comedy creates a bizarre hyper-reality in which the fake gets closer to the truth. On American television, the satirical Trump-l'oeil made viewers want to believe that the fake Trump was the real thing.

Before Alec Baldwin's impersonation of Trump on *Saturday Night Live*, other American comedians were playing on the same tension between fake and real. The most famous example was Jon Stewart's *The Daily Show*, which began in 1999, and its spinoff show, *The Colbert Report*. Both shows were based on the "fictional anchorman" concept. Stewart and Colbert were fake anchormen satirizing authentic news shows. But for many viewers, they were the real thing. Stewart and Colbert were comedians making fun of the news cycle, but millions of Americans trusted their "fake news" more than they believed real news networks. Opinion polls consistently listed *The Daily Show* as one of the "most trusted" news sources in America. One study concluded that "the fake news of Jon Stewart and Stephen Colbert may be more real than today's 'real' news shows."[15]

The influence of Jon Stewart and Stephen Colbert could be measured by the constant stream of political guests who jockeyed to appear on their shows—Barack Obama, Hillary Clinton, Joe Biden, even Tony Blair. It was said that appearing on *The Colbert Report* gave an American politician a "Colbert bump" in the polls. After Colbert took over as host of *The Late Show*, one of his guests was the real Donald Trump. Among other guests was a fake First Lady played by Laura Benanti doing a pitch-perfect comic impersonation of Melania Trump's thick eastern European accent. Real or fake—it didn't seem to matter. Like the Baby Trump blimp, this form of "authentic fake" satire was, even if unconsciously, reconnecting with the avant-garde aesthetic rebellions—Dada, surrealism, theater of the absurd—a century earlier in Europe. That connection invites us to understand "fake news" satire as postmodernist deconstruction of reality through skepticism, mockery, and subversion.

As the brief taxonomy above reveals, "fake news" comes in many packages. It can mean what you want it to mean. It has been so overused in liberal democracies that news consumers have grown impervious to its weaponization. Few regard "fake news" as a serious problem; many believe the term itself is overhyped. "Despite a certain degree of moral panic, fake news itself does not pose an existential threat either to democracy or the free press," writes Tim Harford in the *Financial Times*. "The free press—and healthy democratic discourse—faces some existential problems. Fake news ain't one."[16] The same cannot be said in the non-democratic world, however. Trump's outbursts against "fake news" in America have given foreign despots a pretext to censor press criticism of their own regimes. In Syria, Bashar al-Assad declared, "We are living in a fake news era." The leaders of Russia, China, Turkey, Burma, Venezuela, the Philippines, Angola, Singapore, Cambodia—none of them paragons of liberal democracy—also chanted Trump's "fake news" mantra to crack down on dissent.

The media attacks on Trump, even armed with facts, entailed a serious risk. Open hostility made it appear that the media were acting like a partisan opposition to the Trump presidency. Journalists in America are supposed to function as a "fourth estate," not an official opposition. More importantly, an ideologically biased media, whether on the left or right, can make no claim on objectivity. That point was made from the highest echelons of the *New York Times* itself, when former executive editor Jill Abramson observed that her former employer had become "unmistakably anti-Trump." In her book, *Merchants of Truth,* Abramson praised some aspects of the *Times*'s coverage of Trump. She noted, however, that while the paper claimed it didn't want to set itself up as an "opposition party" against Trump, headlines and news stories contained "raw opinion."[17]

"Given its mostly liberal audience, there was an implicit financial reward for the *Times* in running lots of Trump stories, almost all of them negative," observed Abramson. "They drove big traffic numbers and, despite the blip of cancellations after the election, inflated subscription orders to levels no one anticipated. But the more anti-Trump the *Times* was perceived to be, the more it was mistrusted for being biased."[18] Abramson added that young "woke" *Times* staffers, in particular, favored a more adversarial stance vis-à-vis Trump because "urgent times called for urgent measures; the dangers of Trump's presidency obviated the old standards."[19] Those who disagreed with Abramson noted that there was a difference between being "pro-truth" and "anti-Trump."[20]

In the final analysis, Trump didn't need the mainstream media. He had the cultural zeitgeist on his side. His electoral victory in 2016 proved that. Trump won the White House without the media.

A billionaire reality TV star, Trump was a perfect celebrity icon in a culture that worships success and fame. Before he declared his candidacy, he was world famous on *The Apprentice* for uttering the words "You're fired!" His brash manner won him few admirers in the liberal media. They cringed at his vulgar tastes displayed in his fantasyland penthouse high in Trump Tower with a fake Renoir on the wall. Trump seemed like a man devoid not only of refined tastes but also of personal morality, compassion, and human sympathies. In the White House, he confessed to an un-presidential aversion to dogs and pets of any kind. Trump didn't seem to love anyone but himself. Still, millions of Americans venerated his celebrity persona—his money, his private jets, his mansions, his glamorous lifestyle. For the average American voter, Trump was a self-made billionaire celebrity. He was the embodiment of the free-market America they cherished.

Trump not only had the cultural zeitgeist on his side but could also count on support from an even high place: God. The evangelical Christian vote was crucial to Trump's election victory.

Why fundamentalist Christians supported a figure like Donald Trump was, on the surface, profoundly perplexing. As a business tycoon, Trump had cultivated the image of a flashy jet-setting playboy hanging out in chic Manhattan discotheques. Later as a reality TV celebrity, he was known as a "grab-them-by-the-pussy" philanderer who burned through two trophy wives before marrying Slovenian fashion model Melania Knauss, who was twenty-four years younger. He also became famous as a casino operator in Atlantic City and impresario of body-slamming Wrestlemania spectacles. Church-going piety seemed far from Donald Trump's preoccupations.

Trump could nonetheless claim a longstanding connection with a brand of Christianity that was perfectly compatible with right-wing evangelical politics. He was an adherent to the so-called prosperity gospel movement.[21] According to the prosperity gospel, wealth and fortune are rewards from God. The stronger your faith in God, the richer you will become. Trump had been introduced to this doctrine early in his life when attending the services of Norman Vincent Peale, his family's pastor at Marble Collegiate Church on Manhattan's Fifth Avenue. Peale's credo was simple: If you believe in something enough, and you have faith in it, it will be so. His memorable slogan was "Prayerize, picturize, actualize." Peale's motivational doctrine was elaborated in his book, *The Power of Positive Thinking*, published in the 1950s. That book laid the foundations for the "health, wealth and prosperity" movement in Christian evangelical ministries. It also tremendously influenced the thinking of the young Donald Trump. He refined Peale's prosperity gospel into the "truthful hyperbole" credo that drove his fast-talking, deal-making career in business.

The salesman in Trump instinctively understood his own appeal to evangelical Christians. He had learned early in his business career that people aren't interested in the truth, even in matters of religious faith. They are compelled by great stories. Trump's political slogan, "Make America Great Again," summoned a providential vision of America as God's paradise. His promise to "drain the swamp" evoked Christ's cleansing of the temple. It was a metaphor that tapped into American values about sin, redemption, and salvation. The evangelical Christian connection also explained why fact and evidence held little sway with Trump's supporters. Believing that Trump would "drain the swamp" and "make America great again" was an article of faith. Religious faith is impervious to contradiction by factual evidence. If people believe that God created the world in six days, no amount of evidence is going to persuade them that the scripture is false. If anything, evidence will trigger a "backfire effect" and make them even more convinced that their beliefs are true. Religious passions are powerful. For Trump's zealous supporters, he was sent by God to clean the stables and restore American godliness and greatness. Some evangelicals likened Trump to the great Persian king Cyrus who, in the Bible, conquered corrupt Babylonia, ended the captivity of the Jews, and rebuilt the Temple in Jerusalem. Cyrus was the same biblical king that the Florentine monk Savonarola prophesied would scourge the corrupt Italian elites and purify the depraved Babylonian papacy in Rome. For evangelical Christians in America, the Whore of Babylon was the liberal establishment that controlled the country. They hailed Trump as the "modern Cyrus."

While Trump was tapping into the religious right, the same messianic rhetoric could also be found on the left in American politics. Its main proponent was the self-help guru Marianne Williamson, a candidate for the Democratic presidential nomination in 2020. Famous for her bestselling "New Age spirituality" books with quasi-religious titles—such as *The Law of Divine Compensation* and *The Age of Miracles*—Williamson's message resonated with Hollywood celebrities and trendy leftists in search of spiritual meaning in their lives. She had soared into the public spotlight, thanks largely to appearances on Oprah Winfrey's television show, at the same time as other spiritual gurus, including Deepak Chopra and Tony Robbins. When she unsuccessfully ran in 2014 for Congress in California, her supporters included Kim Kardashian. In her bid for the Democratic nomination against Trump in 2020, she received widespread media coverage that was focused on her rhetoric of spirituality. Though her message was not explicitly evangelical, she exploited the same imagery and emotions. In television debates with other Democratic candidates, Williamson vowed to practice the "politics of love." In one debate, she scored points by delivering a direct challenge to Donald Trump that she also posted on Twitter.

"So, Mr. President—if you're listening—I want you to hear me, please: You have harnessed fear for political purposes, and only love can cast that out. So I, sir, I have a feeling you know what you're doing. I'm going to harness love for political purposes. I will meet you on that field, and sir, love will win."[22]

The fact that Williamson's candidacy attracted so many cheerleaders demonstrated that her unique brand of pop religion resonated just as much on the progressive left as fundamentalist evangelism did on the political right. The *New York Times* even published an opinion column by David Brooks titled "Marianne Williamson Knows How to Beat Trump."[23] Trump was a moral threat to America, and she was calling for a moral uprising against him. Williamson's critics observed, however, that she embodied the same kind of suspicion toward facts and science that was pervasive on the religious right. She had once called mandatory vaccinations "Orwellian."[24] She also stated that "the AIDS virus is not more powerful than God."[25] Some observed that Williamson was merely a left-wing, Hollywood-friendly version of Donald Trump. They both belonged to the "New Thought" movement that promoted the prosperity gospel of positive thinking. Or as Tara Burton observed in the *Washington Post*: "For Marianne Williamson and Donald Trump, religion is all about themselves. The conviction that you can shape the world with your mind is an American tradition."[26] Williamson was exploiting the same self-centered spiritual rhetoric of unreason to beat Trump at his own game. And in American politics, religion is a winning card.

The Christian evangelical vote was crucial to Trump's election victory in 2016. A key player in mobilizing fundamentalist Christian support for Trump was evangelical Jerry Falwell Jr., president of evangelical Liberty University in Virginia. One of the most politically influential Christian colleges in the United States, Liberty counts fifteen thousand students on campus with an additional ninety thousand taking online courses. Falwell endorsed Trump for president after he attended the school's convocation in early 2016. Trump's un-Christian past, including controversies about his sexual adventures, shocked some Christians at the school, including a board member who resigned. But Falwell was unapologetic about his support for Trump. "We're never going to have a perfect candidate unless Jesus Christ is on the ballot," he said. It was estimated that Falwell delivered more than 80 percent of the evangelical vote to Trump in the 2016 election.[27]

After Trump's victory in 2016, powerful evangelical Christians enjoyed open access to the White House. Trump's hand-picked spiritual adviser in the White House was Pastor Paula White, a controversial figure known for her Pentecostal ministry in Florida called the New Destiny Christian Center. Without any formal religious training, White began preaching after receiving a vision from God at age eighteen. She opened a storefront church in Tampa and gradually built it into one of the biggest "megachurches" in the United States. Her evangelical television show was available throughout Florida, where Trump spent time at his Mar-a-Lago residence. She later bought a luxury apartment in Trump's building on New York's Park Avenue. Described as Trump's link to the evangelical Christian community, White claimed to influence him on important policy decisions, such as moving the U.S. embassy in Israel from Tel Aviv to Jerusalem. White stated that her position as Donald Trump's spiritual advisor was a direct "assignment" from God.[28]

Evangelical Christians were also powerful figures in Trump's cabinet. His vice president, Mike Pence, was an ultra-conservative fundamentalist Christian. So was his secretary of state, Mike Pompeo, who once declared in a speech: "I keep a Bible open on my desk to remind me of God and his word, and the truth." Earlier in his career, Pompeo had publicly evoked the "rapture," an apocalyptical Second Coming vision of the faithful ascending to heaven while sinners went to hell. As secretary of state on an official visit to Israel in early 2019, Pompeo cited the Bible's Book of Esther to affirm his belief that God had raised Donald Trump to save the people of Israel from the Persian menace of Iran. Trump's White House spokesperson Sarah Sanders went further. She claimed that the Trump presidency was an act of God.

"I think God calls all of us to fill different roles at different times," said Sanders. "And I think that he wanted Donald Trump to become president."[29]

That claim was as close to the principle of divine right as any modern democracy has ever come. And yet Sarah Sanders was saying what millions of white evangelical Christians in America already believed.

Trump's transformation from casino operator to biblical icon was a remarkable performance. While he hardly embodied the Christian ideal, Trump proved his undeniable credentials as a devoted worshipper at the altar of winning. He won 80 percent of the white evangelical vote in 2016 by casting himself in the role as messianic ruler promising to drain the liberal swamp and bring the Christian right's political agenda to Washington. For ordinary churchgoing Americans who felt marginalized and disenchanted with the establishment, this was the kind of rapturous message they wanted to hear.

That's why they put Donald Trump in the White House. And that's why Trump was convinced he needed evangelical Christian support to win a second term.

***

The buzzword most associated with Donald Trump's presidency is *post-truth*. For many, the post-truth era began on the day Trump was elected.

Like *fake news*, *post-truth* is an elastic term that can mean what you want it to mean—and consequently risks ending up entirely devoid of meaning.

Journalists weaponized the term *post-truth* to describe an Orwellian political culture in which deceit and lies are indistinguishable from truth. News organizations also grasped that *post-truth* was a timely opportunity to reboot their financial fortunes. The *New York Times* seized on the word *truth* as its own slogan. The newspaper took out adverts—on billboards, in newspapers, on YouTube—with a succinct message: "The truth is hard." A *Times* television commercial, broadcast during the Academy Awards in 2017, concluded with the words: "The truth is hard to find. The truth is hard to know. The truth is more important now than ever." In the post-truth era, the *New York Times* was committed to the truth. The marketing gambit worked. In the first six months of Trump's presidency, the newspaper's digital subscriptions soared. The more Trump railed against the *New York Times* as "fake news," the higher its digital revenues climbed. The revenue boost was called a "Trump bump." If Donald Trump was bad for America, he was good for the *New York Times*. It might be argued, however, that the more newspapers such as the *New York Times* pandered to paid-up anti-Trump subscribers, the greater the danger of falling into the partisan trap that transgresses journalistic values of impartiality. If newspapers were increasingly partisan, it was due in part to their new economic model based more on subscriptions than on advertising. In some respects, American journalism was returning to the days of the partisan press in the eighteenth century.

The arrival of a "post-truth" era was comforting for some, especially those who espoused morally relativist beliefs that there is no such thing as "truth." On university campuses, academics churned out papers attempting to shoehorn the "post-truth" concept into theories attacking the foundations of the Enlightenment. The question was now settled: there is no such thing as truth. Some critical theorists argued that *post-truth* describes a cultural shift toward a narcissistic consumer society (think "selfie culture" and Instagram "influencers") in which we are all producers of narratives of deception and self-delusion. In short, *post-truth* blurs reality with fiction—and we are all its authors. This view was quintessentially postmodernist. It entrapped all perception and knowledge in the confines of subjectivity and, by doing so, remained skeptical toward the possibility of objective truth.

Leaving aside marketing slogans and academic theories, the term *post-truth* remains semantically problematic. When we refer to a "post-war era," the meaning is clear: the period following the end of the war. By the same logic, *post-truth* should signify the period immediately following the end of truth. Truth once existed but it is over, part of the past. We are living in an age after truth. That meaning, however, doesn't stand up to serious scrutiny. Like the postmodernist rejection of truth, it is logically self-defeating. If one asserts that there is no such thing as truth, that assertion itself cannot be true. It is *ipso facto* false. Similarly, the claim that we are living in a post-truth era cannot be true. If truth exists, it cannot *no longer* exist. *Post-truth*, in sum, is a self-refuting concept that disqualifies itself.

The editors at the *Oxford English Dictionary*, doubtless grasping that their buzzword-of-the-year was logically contestable, opted for a more flexible definition: "Relating to, or denoting, circumstances in which objective facts are less influential in shaping public opinion than appeals to emotion and personal belief." That meaning, while interesting, has nothing to do with truth. Perhaps the *Oxford English Dictionary* should have declared the dawn of a "post-fact" era. The OED editors added a post-truth proviso, however. Comparing *post-truth* with *post-national* and *post-racial*, they clarified that the prefix *post* signifies "belonging to a time in which the specified concept 'truth' has become unimportant or irrelevant." That nuanced definition tells us something about people's attitudes toward the truth, but nothing about truth itself. It is moreover hardly reassuring. A civilization that considers truth "unimportant" and "irrelevant" is condemned, in a world devoid of meaning, to fall into an abyss of moral chaos.

In contemporary politics, the term *post-truth* was first used to describe alleged lies coming out of Ronald Reagan's White House in the 1980s. President Reagan was a paradox in office. While his foreign policy was implacably realist, Reagan was open to the suggestions of astrological predictions. Following the assassination attempt on his life in 1981, Reagan's wife Nancy hired a White House astrologer, Joan Quigley, who was henceforth consulted on key presidential decisions, including Cold War foreign policy regarding the Soviet Union. As Donald Regan, the top White House adviser, recalled in his memoirs: "Virtually every major move and decision the Reagans made during my time as White House Chief of Staff was cleared in advance with a woman in San Francisco who drew up horoscopes to make certain that the planets were in a favorable alignment for the enterprise."[30] In 1988, *Time* magazine published an exclusive cover story titled "Astrology in the White House."[31] If Reagan's spin doctors were taking liberty with facts, the man sitting in the Oval Office was putting faith in the outlandish claims of unreason.

Twenty years after the Reagan presidency, during George W. Bush's second term in office, *post-truth* took on a slightly different meaning. In 2005, television satirist Stephen Colbert coined the term *truthiness*, defined as "truth that comes from the gut."[32] Colbert was criticizing the Bush White House's justifications for policies, notably the rationale to invade Iraq. "We're not talking about truth," he said. "We're talking about something that seems like truth—the truth we want to exist."[33] *Truthiness* meant emotion over reason.

Five years later, *post-truth* reappeared in a different context during the Obama presidency, this time to describe the debate about climate change. Once again, the "truth" about a vitally important issue triggered fractious debate between two adversarial camps. On one side were climate change deniers with strong emotions and personal opinions on the question; on the other were those warning of the disastrous consequences of climate change as demonstrated by hard scientific facts. Each side was certain of their certitudes.

During the 2016 election campaign, the media dusted off the term *post-truth* and repurposed it with a new spin. While journalists used the term *fake news* to discredit information circulating on social media, they deployed *post-truth* as an indictment of the false statements coming from the Trump campaign. The term *post-truth* flattered the media's professional pretensions. In the previous era of "truth," when the media were still powerful agenda-setters, Trump never would have been elected. Now that social media had usurped their gatekeeper power over the news cycle, look at the result. Donald Trump was sitting behind the presidential desk in the Oval Office.

Trump gave the media good reason to label him a post-truth president. As soon as he moved into the White House, it often seemed he was still inhabiting the celebrity persona from his reality TV show, *The Apprentice*, performing for the cameras in a fantasy bubble, disconnected from facts and evidence. When facing judicial proceedings investigating alleged links between his election campaign and Russian operatives, Trump angrily denied everything while his legal team attacked the idea of truth itself. In an astounding outburst that could have been lifted from the pages of Friedrich Nietzsche, Trump's lawyer, Rudy Giuliani, declared on national television, "Truth isn't truth." That statement seemed to capture the essence of the Trump presidency. He was a post-truth president for the postmodern age.

Declarations like "truth isn't truth" make for great headlines. But the plain fact is that we are not living in a "post-truth" era. Even if it did exist, it certainly did not begin with the election of Donald Trump. Long before he was elected to the White House, the truth had been abused over many centuries of myths, legends, falsehoods, and lies. The institutionalized deception of the twentieth century was particularly overwhelming: mass manipulation, propaganda, disinformation, PR spin, corporate advertising, infotainment. And yet, remarkably, truth managed to withstand the ordeal—until today, when values of fact and truth are under attack yet again.

The prophets of "post-truth" never believed in truth in the first place. Donald Trump and social media chaos are merely the latest pretexts to carry on their attacks on the entire Enlightenment legacy of reason and liberal democracy. The first salvo in this assault on reason was, as has been previously noted, Friedrich Nietzsche's famous declaration that "there are no facts, only interpretations." A century later, postmodernist thinkers including Michel Foucault made Nietzsche's ideas fashionable among intellectuals on the radical left. Reformulating Marxist ideology with a critique of bourgeois truths, they argued that claims on truth are a form of domination, usually of the Western capitalist variety. Thanks to French thinkers, the ideas of Nietzsche conquered America.[34]

By the 1980s, postmodern ideas had armed a generation of university students waging a culture war against the entire edifice of Western civilization. In 1987, students at Stanford university chanted, "*Hey hey, ho ho, Western Civ has got to go!*" They were protesting the inclusion of Western classics—Plato, Saint Augustine, Rousseau, John Stuart Mill—on their reading lists. These authors, they claimed, represented "European-Western male bias." The enemies of these culture warriors were neoliberalism, capitalism, science-based truths, freedom of speech, even democracy itself.

Foucault and his postmodernist disciples had articulate critics. One was Allan Bloom, whose bestselling book *The Closing of the American Mind*—published the same year as the Stanford student protests—attacked the pervasive culture of moral relativism in the United States. Bloom argued that while relativist values claimed to be open and inclusive, they in fact created a dogmatic culture of close-mindedness. He put the blame squarely on American universities and the radical leftist culture inherited from the counter-culture 1960s. Bloom even compared the fevered activism on American campuses during that period with the ideological hysteria under the Nazis in the 1930s. He was thinking, in particular, of philosopher Martin Heidegger, who joined the Nazi Party as rector of Freiburg University and professed allegiance to the Führer.

Bloom observed:

The fact that in Germany the politics were of the right and in the United States of the left should not mislead us. In both places the universities gave way under the pressure of mass movements, and did so in large measure because they thought those movements possessed a moral truth superior to any the university could provide. Commitment was understood to be profounder than science, passion than reason, history than nature, the young than the old. In fact, as I have argued, the thought was really the same. The New Left in America was a Nietzscheanized-Heideggerianized left. The unthinking hatred of 'bourgeois society' was exactly the same in both places. . . . Heidegger himself, late in his life, made overtures to the New Left. The most sinister formula in his rectoral address of 1933 was, with only the slightest of alterations, the slogan of the American professors who collaborated with the student movements of the sixties: "The time for decision is past. The decision has already been made by the youngest part of the German nation."[35]

A generation after Allan Bloom's critique of the intellectual climate in America, the chorus of attacks on Western philosophy and literature had become even more politicized to include identity issues focused on subjective feelings and emotions. Students demanded that schools provide "safe spaces" to protect them from threatening ideas, often those found in Western classics. Instead of being taught to discover truth through reason, students were encouraged to interpret reality through *emotional reasoning*. When studying works of literature in their classes, students demanded "trigger warnings" alerting them to "microaggressions" in books that might upset, offend, or cause them emotional stress. The books targeted included *The Great Gatsby, Huckleberry Finn,* Virginia Woolf's *Mrs. Dalloway*, even Shakespeare's plays. University campuses, it might be argued, were the first to make the "affective turn" toward feelings and emotions.[36]

Academics who puppeteered the culture wars were also busy battling truth on another front: social science. Denialism about scientific truths—from climate change and vaccinations to the genetics of gender—became zealously proclaimed dogma. Some refuted scientific truths not because they were empirically false, but because they were ideologically threatening. They angrily called for scientific findings on gender and identity issues to be censored because they were ideologically censored. The rational tools of empirical science were suspect as instruments of Western oppression. These reactions were reminiscent of the Soviet Union, where empirical science was dismissed as "bourgeois." On Western university campuses, truth was now ideology. Prestigious universities sacrificed values of open inquiry to appease ideological indignation. They used doublespeak, of course, to assure critics that they resolutely supported the principle of academic freedom, while in practice abandoned it with astounding cowardice.

Activists meanwhile were reengineering the language to create a political vocabulary of accepted and banished terms. A strict distinction between "correct" and "incorrect" language was imposed and enforced. Like hostility to empirical science, this too was reminiscent of Soviet propaganda, which used specific terms—*bourgeois, decadent, imperialist*—to discredit Western values. Linguistic engineering on the politically correct left, in like manner, deployed designated words to challenge the dominant power structure. The adversary was the "patriarchy" dominated by "white males." Their "white privilege" was owed to oppressive "neoliberalism" that must be opposed and dismantled. Linguistic policing was not restricted to the left. The same semantic tactics were used on the far right. Conservatives described leftist activists as "social justice warriors" and abbreviated their postmodern neo-Marxist movement as "PMNM."

Inevitably, the mainstream media got dragged into these culture wars. When the *New York Times* invited a Harvard-educated Korean American journalist, Sarah Jeong, to join the newspaper's editorial board, her hiring provoked an outcry on the conservative right. It was discovered that, in a barrage of tweets, Jeong had been using racist language—for example, "dumbass fucking white people" and "#CancelWhitePeople." If directed at any other race, her tweets would have been denounced as despicable, but Jeong kept her job at the *New York Times*. He defenders claimed she was the victim of "alt right" trolls; her detractors pointed out the hypocrisy of discounting anti-white racism. Jeong wasn't fired, in the final analysis, because her language, however provocative, conformed to accepted semantics in an ideological culture that evidently included the *New York Times*.

Jeong's hashtagging of the word *cancel* was an act of linguistic violence in the new "cancel culture." It had begun with the "no platforming" movement. Its adherents mobilized vocal protest to insist that campus events featuring undesirable speakers be cancelled—and shouted them down if they showed up. Ideological adversaries were targeted and deprived of their free speech rights. Jeong took cancel culture even further. White people were to be "canceled" altogether, boycotted, their existence erased. Again, the echoes of Soviet repression were impossible to miss. Under Stalin, enemies of the state became "unpersons." Their images were cut from photos, their names never mentioned again. They no longer existed. They were condemned, as in ancient Rome, to *damnatio memoriae*. In the politically correct twenty-first century, cancel culture has adopted the same rules. It is a culture devoid of tolerance. As philosopher John Gray observed: "Nothing is more authentically of our time than the spectacle of people being banished from public discourse for the crime of using forbidden words, and pleading for rehabilitation in humiliating Mao-style internet struggle sessions with their liberal accusers."[37]

It is important to underscore that cancel culture is not unique to the radical left. It is a broad church in which right-wing extremists feel equally at home. The irrational politics of intolerance is precisely where far-left and far-right find common ground—terrain on which, ironically, they are often engaged in pitched ideological battle. In *The Closing of the American Mind*, Allan Bloom described this paradox as the "fatal old alliance" between traditional conservatives and the radical left. "They had nothing in common but their hatred of capitalism," observed Bloom, "the conservatives looking back to the revival of throne and alter in the various European nations, and to piety, the radicals looking forward to the universal homogenous society and to freedom—reactionaries and progressives united against the present. They feed off the inner contradictions of the bourgeoisie."[38]

The culture wars have spread well beyond America. The British actor Stephen Fry, in a speech in Australia in late 2018, denounced the culture of toxic politics on both ideological extremes: on the right, Christian fundamentalists with their libertarian values; and on the left, "illiberal liberals" obsessed with identity politics and cultural appropriation. "A great canyon has opened up in our world," observed Fry. "Is this what is meant by the fine art of disagreement? A plague on both their houses."[39]

This house divided is impossible to broker because belligerents on both sides are hostile to reason and truth. For both camps, truth resides in righteous emotions of indignation, which mask desperate pleas for recognition and empowerment. These pleas need to be recognized. In a culture that has disavowed truth, however, there is little possibility for open dialogue based on mutual acknowledgment. When one has rejected the belief that rational discourse leads to truth, the principle of free speech is easily abandoned along with it. Each side, retrenched in their own subjective truths, devotes their energies to shutting down their adversaries[40]

Many dismiss postmodernist thinking as a convoluted ideology whose influence is largely restricted to leftist precincts of academia. Others argue that the influence of postmodernist values, especially moral relativism, has spread throughout Western culture far beyond university campuses. That is a considerable achievement for a system of ideas flawed by so many internal contradictions. For example, postmodernists argue that all truths are socially constructed and hence relative, yet assert their own claims as true —thus boxing themselves inside a self-defeating paradox from which there is no escape. Also, while postmodernists adhere to values of cultural relativism, they consistently attack Western values as destructive. But if all cultures are relative, Western values cannot be any better or worse than any other values. Similarly, postmodernists claim all values are relative, yet they denounce sexism, racism, homophobia, and fascism as abhorrent. These values are indeed repugnant, but if you assert that all values are relative, you cannot condemn some values as bad and others as good. Finally, while they claim to espouse diversity and inclusiveness, they attack opposing viewpoints as offensive, thus exposing themselves to the criticism that they are neither inclusive nor open to diversity. Perhaps these internal contradictions explain why the philosopher Jürgen Habermas took sides with modernity against postmodernist assaults on the Enlightenment's legacy of reason.[41]

Harvard psychologist Steven Pinker, in his book *Enlightenment Now*, argued that postmodernism has corroded our culture with bogus ideas and pseudo-assertions. Pinker is also scathing toward the notion of post-truth. "The term is corrosive," he argues, "because it implies that we should resign ourselves to propaganda and lies and just fight back with more of our own. We are not in a 'post-truth' era. Mendacity, truth-shading, conspiracy theories, extraordinary popular delusions, and the madness of crowds are as old as our species, but so is the conviction that some ideas are right and others are wrong."[42]

Pinker's point raises an issue that moral relativists have difficulty addressing regarding Donald Trump. If all values are relative, it cannot be argued that Trump's supporters are wrong, or bad; they simply have their own values. Their perceptions and beliefs are just as valid as anyone else's. Similarly, the values of white supremacists in America must be regarded as no less legitimate than those of far-left "social justice warriors." Trump's supporters on the far right doubtless would have no difficulty accepting this premise. For his adversaries on the left, it would likely be received with less enthusiasm. In the "post-truth" world, the postmodernist left got hoisted with their own relativist petard.

American philosopher Rebecca Newberger Goldstein, author of *Plato at the Googleplex*, has argued that the post-truth debate isn't even about truth—it's about political ideology. "The repurposing of truth-valued propositions for political ends isn't exactly new under the sun, but its prevalence today does seem like a genuinely new phenomenon," she observes. "They don't just describe the structures of power they have supposedly discovered—they defiantly oppose them. How this normative imperative arises out of the theory isn't clear, but it may be that leftist politics comes first for postmodernists and their theory dutifully follows after. As a political matter, the difficulty with the postmodernist vision—of truth supplanted by power struggles—is that it can just as easily fit with any right-wing view. If truth has no deeper basis than power, who's to say that the assertions of Trump supporters are wrong? They won, after all, and isn't that what truth, ultimately, is about?"[43]

That is where we are left today: truth reduced to the raw friction of a power struggle. To the victor go the spoils. Even more despairing, the dogmatic certitudes of identity politics have transformed warring political tribes into quasi-religious cults. Perhaps Nietzsche was right after all: science usurped religion as truth, but it left a nihilistic void that people would inevitably seek to fill with new religions. Today it's the political religion of identity. As political commentator Andrew Sullivan observes: "Now look at our politics. We have the cult of Trump on the right, a demigod who, among his worshippers, can do no wrong. And we have the cult of social justice on the left, a religion whose followers show the same zeal as any born-again Evangelical. They are filling the void that Christianity once owned, without any of the wisdom and culture and restraint that Christianity once provided."[44]

Donald Trump was not the architect of the post-truth era's divided house. Its shaky cornerstones had been laid by the postmodern disciples of cultural relativism long before he sought political office. Trump was not the fork-tongued prophet of a brave new post-truth world. He was its inevitable political apotheosis in a culture that had already rejected and abandoned the possibility of truth. The relativist orthodoxies that had been disparaging truth for decades made the political triumph of a figure like Donald Trump possible.

As David Frum observed in his book *Trumpocracy*: "Donald Trump did not create the vulnerabilities that he exploited. They awaited him."[45] In a culture that put feelings, emotions, and opinions before reason and facts, the distinction between truth and falsehood no longer mattered. Everyone had their own truth. Trump filled the truth vacuum with populist slogans, inspired by his old "truthful hyperbole" credo, that appealed to the biases and harnessed the anger of ordinary Americans who felt shafted by the system.

Trump's blustery disregard for the truth was part of his persona. His tirades against the "fake news" media were a verbal prop in the celebrity act that he had been perfecting for decades. Hyperbole and bombast were his way of getting attention—and it worked every time. His penchant for hype had served him well as a playboy real-estate tycoon; and it proved indispensable to his political ambitions.

The media pundits who pinned the *post-truth* label on Trump's presidency made much of his fawning cheerleaders on Fox News. But Trump's critics were, with very few exceptions, products of the same media culture as their colleagues at Fox, owned by Rupert Murdoch, who also owned the *Wall Street Journal, New York Post*, and the *Times*, Sky News, and the *Sun* in Britain. Trump's critics conveniently overlooked that, years earlier, he had become a superstar icon largely thanks to the media. Major media corporations, not far-right populists, had signed

Trump to a blockbuster book deal, put his face on the covers of glossy magazines, and gave him his own prime-time reality TV show. Trump was a great story. In a culture that venerates celebrity icons, the media created Trump's cult of idolatry. If Trump was a monster, he was their monster. When the media finally realized he was an abomination—a gargantuan Ubu Roi version of a nihilist Nietzschean blond beast—it was too late. Their monster had turned on them.

So what is the truth about Trump? That depends on how you perceive him—a statement that, by definition, gives primacy to opinion, emotion, and subjective values. There are facts about Trump, of course, and many are not to his credit—everything from his attitude toward women to his past business practices. But facts alone are not enough to discredit Trump. His zealous supporters have already made up their minds about him, just as his fiercest critics don't need any more convincing that he was unfit for public office. Trump is such a divisive figure in American democracy that he appeals to instinctive confirmation bias at both ends of the ideological spectrum. More intriguing, each side believes they possess facts to support their beliefs. The "dueling facts" theory of American democracy argues that our values shape not only our opinions about politics but also how we perceive reality.[46] Our political opinions are not determined by partisan loyalties; they find their source in the deepest layers of our underlying values. Our values channel what we see as important issues. Values and facts, often regarded as distinct, are blurred in people's minds. They start with values to find facts. Values motivate facts. No set of opposing facts will move people off emotionally held opinions—about race, climate change, vaccinations—that have already been determined by their values. That explains Donald Trump's electoral success. A powerful measure of Trump's *mythos* is his capacity to withstand an onslaught of facts against him. Trump is fact-proof.

Political observers are meanwhile struggling to understand Trump's place in American history. Some hope his presidency will be regarded as a lapse into temporary madness, while others argue that Trump has transformed American politics. His critics claim he has debased the "magisterial presidency" by turning the White House into a vapid reality TV show. Many evangelical Christians, on the other hand, see Trump as a modern Cyrus who came to drain the swamp and take his people to a New Jerusalem. Others contend that those who expected Trump to build a God-fearing theocracy ended up with a vulgar "kakistocracy"—from the Greek *kakistos* for government by the least suitable, least qualified, and least competent. The celebrity charade of the Trump presidency, with his daughter Ivanka and son-in-law Jared Kushner swaggering like global power brokers, reveal a level of shallow amateurism never witnessed in American diplomacy. In its grotesque indulgence in shameless nepotism, they argue, the Trump presidency rivals the corrupt Borgia papacy. Despite his "Make America Great Again" slogan, Trump has made the United States weaker on the world stage.

Other political observers are more favorably disposed. They claim Trump's bully pulpit tirades on Twitter, far from alienating him from voters, have made him accessible to average Americans who are receptive to his message. Despite his extravagant personality, Trump genuinely embodies the spirit of a moment in American history. Some even argue that he could well be remembered as a "great man" embodiment of a "world spirit"—or *weltgeist* to utilize the term used by the German philosopher Hegel. If so, that puts Trump in exalted company along with Alexander the Great and Julius Caesar.

In the *Financial Times*, foreign affairs columnist Gideon Rachman argued that Trump could well turn out to be a "truly historic president"— what Hegel called a "world-historical figure." The world-historical figure is the forceful, charismatic leader who embodies the hopes and fears of his age, sometimes virtuous, sometimes vicious, but driven by the *weltgeist*—and thus inevitable. In the early nineteenth century, Hegel's ideal of the world-historical figure was Napoleon. The German philosopher actually saw Napoleon with his own eyes, following the Battle of Jena in 1806. Hegel looked up in wonder as the French emperor, astride his horse, marched victoriously through his local Prussian town. Hegel described Napoleon as a "world spirit on horseback."

"I doubt Mr. Trump has much to say about Hegel," observed Rachman. "But he may be the kind of instinctive statesman that Hegel described—a figure who has harnessed and embodied forces that he himself only half understands."[47]

Those who see Trump as a tyrant inevitably turn to more unflattering parallels than Julius Caesar and Napoleon Bonaparte. If Trump is like Julius Caesar, he is the Caesar who destroyed Rome's democratic institutions. Others see similarities between Trump and emperor Commodus, whose narcissism drove him to the delusion that he was a god; but ended up assassinated and remembered as the unhinged emperor who turned Rome "from gold into iron and rust." Still others compare Trump with Caligula, the young emperor who succumbed to insanity and was assassinated. The suggestion is that Trump, like Caligula, is mentally unbalanced. Nobel Prize–winning economist Paul Krugman wrote a column in the *New York Times* under the headline "Trump Makes Caligula Look Pretty Good." Krugman suggested that the U.S. Senate needed to do to Trump what the Roman Senate did to Caligula. "When his behavior became truly intolerable, Rome's elite did what the party now controlling Congress seems unable even to contemplate: it found a way to get rid of him."[48]

These analogies are intriguing. But Donald Trump is not a military commander like Julius Caesar. And whatever one thinks of Trump's frame of mind, it could hardly be argued that he is insane like Caligula. The Roman emperor with whom Donald Trump shares the most attributes is, inevitably, Nero.

Like Nero, Trump is driven by narcissistic self-reverence and a profound emotional need for approval. Above all, Trump—like Nero—is more interested in performing than in governing. Nero spent much of his reign racing chariots and acting in Greek dramas to seek applause and admiration. Trump displays the same obsession with performance and approval. Before throwing his hat into the political ring, he was grandstanding in Wrestlemania rings where, escorted by Playboy bunnies, he performed fantasy matches before hysterically cheering crowds. After his election, he demonstrated the same craving for veneration, appearing at political rallies where grassroots voters cheered his bluster and bombast. Trump is, like Nero, more actor than statesman, more performer than ruler, more celebrity than commander-in-chief. And like the ill-fated Roman emperor, Trump is disdained by elites but supported by common people. Even Trump's bizarre tweetstorms are oddly Neronian. As David Remnick observed in the *New Yorker*: "Future scholars will sift through Trump's digital proclamations the way we now read the chroniclers of Nero's Rome—to understand how an unhinged emperor can make a mockery of republican institutions, undo the collective nervous system of a country, and degrade the whole of public life."[49]

Perhaps there is a warning for Donald Trump in Nero's tragic final act. At the end of his troubled reign, the Roman Senate declared Nero *hostis publicus*, or public enemy. Trump's fiercest critics would be satisfied to witness a Neronian downfall, though through congressional impeachment, not imperial suicide.

We cannot know whether Donald Trump will be remembered by future generations as the president who destroyed American democracy or made America great again. There can be no doubt, however, that his brash style and cult of personality make Trump a president like no other in American history.

We can also say with certainty that Trump's presidency did not mark the beginning of a "post-truth" era. That term tells us less about the truth than it does about our own attitudes toward the truth. If Trump's presidency has taught us anything, it's that we need to re-evaluate our values about truth.

We are not living in a post-truth world. Truth is still with us; it simply has been neglected, manipulated, and abused. Truth is remarkably resilient. The fact that we are debating truth so fiercely is a sign that we recognize its vital importance. We must affirm truth as the highest goal of all civilized societies.

CONCLUSION

If the preceding chapters have demonstrated anything, it's that the truth about truth is complicated. Our relationship with truth has been a tumultuous saga, fraught with tensions, ambiguity, contradictions, and sometimes violence.

We argued at the outset of this book that truth and lies have been intricately woven into our historical narrative. They cohabit the same space in our collective psyche, each making claims on our values, loyalties, commitments, and conduct with immediate and far-reaching consequences. From ancient Greece and Rome to our modern age, we have struggled to reconcile conflicting tensions between reason and unreason, between truth and falsehood, between power and dissent. Myth, legend, superstition, religion, philosophy, science, ideology, and propaganda have proclaimed their rival truths in virtually every epoch. Divisions over truth and falsehood have triggered great upheavals, ignited revolutions, toppled monarchies, shaken civilizations, and inflicted horrendous suffering on the world. As the chapters in this book have illustrated, the history of these tensions has not followed a course of constant moral progress. We don't always advance toward greater knowledge and wisdom. Civilizations are fragile. They decline and collapse, surrendering to chaos and barbarism.

Not so long ago, the values of liberal democracy were unassailably triumphant. It seemed impossible that we would ever again fall into the abyss of the vile ideologies, cataclysmic wars, and horrific atrocities of the last century. In our optimism about an ever-brighter and more prosperous future, we neglected fundamental lessons of the past. Human folly is stubborn; we keep making the same mistakes, sometimes with even more horrendous consequences. We are learning those lessons today.

Everywhere we look, there are disturbing signs—the Trump presidency, the Brexit crisis, the fevered pitch of political populism and religious fanaticism—that we are in the grip of collective folly. Once-stable societies are being torn apart by ideological divisions that are corroding trust, polarizing opinion, and fueling the acrimonious politics of anger and violence. The pendulum has swung in favor of truth's most passionate adversaries. Truth has fallen into disrepute.

For many, the most alarming symptom of our "post-truth" age is contempt for the values underpinning of liberal democracy. Tyrants and despots thrive in societies where truth is rejected as suspect, where facts are scorned, and where lies are asserted as truth. Many believe we are sinking into dark days reminiscent of the mass hysteria of the 1930s, when "big lies" were irrationally embraced as unquestioned truth. Today, authoritarian leaders such as Russia's Vladimir Putin openly claim that the debate about liberal democracy is irrelevant because liberalism itself is obsolete.[1] The liberal model is no longer workable, they argue, because the complex problems facing the world—for example, global population migrations—cannot be efficiently managed by democratic regimes based on consensus. Faced with the grim realities of a turbulent and violent world, liberalism is paralyzed. Authoritarian efficiency is an attractive model for those who have retreated into collective identities based on nation, race, and religion. If the authoritarian temptation is understandable, we know it almost always ends in tragedy. As historian Timothy Snyder observes in his book *On Tyranny*: "To abandon facts is to abandon freedom. If nothing is true, then no one can criticize power because there is no basis upon which to do so." In sum, "post-truth is pre-fascism."[2]

Perhaps the problem, as we suggested in the final chapter of this book, is the term *post-truth* itself. It suggests that we live in an age when truth no longer exists, or at a minimum no longer matters. Capitulating to that idea only empowers those who exploit lies for their own ends. If there are no truths, it is impossible to expose lies as false. Accepting the notion of "post truth" is to surrender to the claim that truth has been defeated—or worse, that it never existed in the first place. Those who believe this are condemned to moral nihilism. If there are no truths, and all values are relative, even the most horrendous atrocities cannot be judged morally. They cannot be judged because there is no good or bad, no right or wrong, no truth or lies—only different perspectives, diverging beliefs, diverse points of view.

Moral chaos is a despairing reality. If we surrender to it, existence is ultimately devoid of meaning, and survival is a constant struggle. It rewards the guile of the fox that uses cunning to compensate for its lack of a coherent vision of life. In the face of harsh realities, existence in its most elemental form becomes how the philosopher Thomas Hobbes famously described it: nasty, brutish, and short. No wonder authoritarian regimes appeal to those who have disavowed values of truth and accepted the limitations of their own knowledge. Surely a wiser approach is to defer not to authority out of fear, but to reason out of a desire to seek truth. As philosopher Julian Baggini observes: "The claim that we live in a post-truth world is the most pernicious untruth of them all. It serves the interests of those who have the most to fear from the truth."[3]

Today, we are confronting these fundamental choices with great urgency, especially after the alarming spectacle of the Trump presidency. Yet as we argue in the book's final chapter, Donald Trump's political triumph was the symptom of a much deeper malaise in society. Our truth-disparaging culture made a figure like Trump possible. He was not its prophet; he was its product. Still, we can draw lessons from the Trump presidency to understand our cultural disavowal of truth and its consequences. Trump forced us to reflect on fundamental values about facts and truth—and, above all, on their vital importance for a healthy liberal democracy. Authoritarian regimes are based on lies and propaganda; liberal democracy is founded on values of fact and truth. In open societies where citizens enjoy rights and freedoms, wide acceptance of collective truths is established by public discourse based on reason and sound judgment. Truth is public knowledge whose broad recognition cements trust. A society devoid of trust is condemned to be ruled by lies.

Despite widespread pessimism about the status of truth today, there is reason for optimism. We must, however, commit to revitalizing our approach to questions about truth and falsehood. We must affirm values of fact and truth through reasoned discourse that openly acknowledges diverse voices. Make no mistake: we must affirm truth as something that exists beyond our subjective beliefs, opinions, and perceptions. Equally important, we need to carve out a public space for civic engagement—not pitched battles on the ideological extremes, but reasoned debate based on common values. We must also, however, acknowledge that reason alone is not the only way to understand the world. We must not abandon reason; we must accept that it has limits. Rationalism must be balanced with acknowledgment of our subjective experience of the world we inhabit. As we observe at the outset of this book, the world would be poorer without the passionately personal visions of poets, painters, playwrights, novelists, and composers. As commanders of our values, they are the unacknowledged legislators of the world.

How wide an inclusive public sphere should be—especially in our internet age—is the subject of fierce debate. On social media, everyone has the power to assert what they believe to be true—and to spread falsehoods. Many argue that the web is a toxic cauldron overwhelmed with hate-filled trolls whose unreasoned discourse is beyond the acceptable parameters of public discourse. Establishing the boundaries on the public sphere is not an easy task. It is worth remembering, however, that the seventeenth-century pamphleteers who were castigated in their day as irrational and seditious were the precursors of modern journalism. As a general principle, empowering the voices of all citizens must be regarded as a desirable goal, especially at a time when so many feel disaffected with established elites. We must affirm shared values around truth in a public sphere in which many diverse voices and values can be acknowledged. By listening to those on the margins, or to rival viewpoints with which we profoundly disagree, we are filling in pieces of a larger objective reality in the world.

The best institutional means to foster shared values is education. At the most basic level, education must encourage skepticism while promoting an intellectual culture of open and rational inquiry. Our children must learn that knowledge is accessible through reason and experience, and that superstition and obscurantism do not form a rational basis for discovering truths. Teaching young people to distrust factual truths—or worse, telling students that there is no such thing as truth—only reinforces an intellectual culture in which they will be prepared to believe anything. We will have defeated obscurantism when no person on this planet believes that the earth is flat, that climate change is unproven, that vaccinations are dangerous to our health, and that powdered rhino horns, bear bile, and donkey-hide gelatin are medicines that cure ailments, real or imagined. If our youth are taught that there is no such thing as facts, that all truths are social constructs, and that all values are relative, they will be condemned to live in a world in which there is no distinction between right and wrong.

In our age of resurgent fanaticism, religion is the most sensitive challenge to truth. Freedom of conscience is a fundamental right in all civilized societies. The cruel lessons of history, however, demonstrate that religions tend to assert dogmas as truth. When religious orthodoxies have been imposed as the sole basis for truth, the result has been intolerance, persecution, and atrocity. Religious truth is supernatural, accessible through faith; it does not reside in this world. Religion, therefore, must remain in the private sphere of personal belief. For personal liberties to flourish, bonfires of vanities cannot be permitted in public squares in the name of religion. The stories told in sacred texts, myths, legends, and epic tales should inspire our imaginations; they should not, however, be erected as doctrines that dictate our laws and actions. To quote the Gospel of Matthew: "Render therefore unto Caesar the things which are Caesar's; and unto God the things that are God's." We must approach civic discourse in a spirit that, while acknowledging the existence of spirituality, excludes religious dogma from political discourse and collective action. We must also be vigilant about dogmatic secular faiths—from irrational identity politics to political correctness—asserted with quasi-religious fervor. They too inevitably produce a culture of intolerance and persecution.

Another challenge is restoring trust in our institutions. Distrust of professions and expertise undermines values based on facts and truth. Corroded trust finds its origins in a pervasive belief that experts and institutions are complacent and corrupt. They are regarded as selfish elites motivated primarily by the maintenance of their own status, privilege, and power. All professions—law, medicine, accountancy, journalism, public relations—must reaffirm their commitment to integrity and transparency. They can do so by embracing values of fact and truth and, above all, aligning their professional practices with them.

The institutions of liberal capitalism, in particular, are under attack everywhere, often with good reason. Despite hype about corporate social responsibility, it remains little more than a hollow PR slogan. The reality of corporate behavior is too frequently associated with opacity, dishonesty, and malfeasance. The global crisis in trust is aggravated by corporations that pollute the environment, destroy the world's rainforests, behave obnoxiously in the marketplace, adopt fiscal strategies to avoid taxes, and use money and lobbyists to seek unfair advantages from states. Business, like science, is increasingly accused of being disengaged from basic duties of social responsibility. When the logic of capitalism serves only the rational interests of profit, divorced from moral responsibility, the results are inevitably disastrous—shocking social inequalities, forest and wildlife destruction, horrors of factory farming, long-term consequences of climate change. The failure of capitalism will only make the authoritarian temptation more appealing to those who are disaffected with the entire liberal legacy.

This is why states, too, must uphold values of fact and truth. We cannot in good conscience insist that business and science integrate ethics into their practices without placing the same moral burden on states. For centuries, the conduct of governments has been guided by the dictates of opacity, deception, even criminal conduct. The international state system was constructed with a tacit acknowledgment that lies and falsehoods are acceptable forms of discourse. States lie to one another; and, worse, they lie to their own citizens. The institutionalized mendacity of states can no longer be considered acceptable. States must abandon the logic of raison d'état that gives them license to manipulate and deceive. They must embrace values of openness, transparency, and truth—factual and moral—in their relations with other states and, above all, with their own citizens. States as technocratic systems of power, disengaged from the populations they govern, are condemned to be overthrown. Populist backlashes, as noted, are already erupting throughout the world in countries where authoritarian efficiency is regarded as a more attractive model. Some will persist in the belief that liberal democracy needs to be dismantled. Those voices are already active on many fronts advocating illiberal alternatives. All the more reason for those who believe in reason and truth to defend the values that underpin liberal democracy. The alternative is living under the authority of states that are the most adept at lying, manipulating, and repressing human freedoms.

Finally, and most importantly, each one of us, individually, must reaffirm our commitment to values of fact and truth. These values must reside deeply not only within the institutions that govern our societies, but in our personal relations with one another every day.

Truth exists. We need to seek, discover, and cherish it.

NOTES

INTRODUCTION

1. Hannah Arendt, "Lying in Politics," *New York Review of Books,* November 18, 1971.

2. "Hillary Clinton Attacks Trump for Waging 'All-Out War on Truth, Facts, and Reason,'" *Guardian,* April 23, 2018.

3. The last line in Shelley's "A Defence of Poetry," written in 1821 and published posthumously in 1840. The text is available via the Poetry Foundation online at www.poetryfoundation.org/articles/69388/a-defence-of-poetry.

4. See Isaiah Berlin, *The Hedgehog and the Fox* (London: Weidenfeld, 1953). For a defense of hedgehogs, see Ronald Dworkin, *Justice for Hedgehogs* (Cambridge, MA: Harvard Belknap, 2011).

5. See Christine Smallwood, "Astrology in the Age of Uncertainty," *New Yorker*, October 21, 2019.

6. See Timothy Levine, *Duped: Truth Default Theory and the Social Science of Lying and Deception* (Tuscaloosa: University of Alabama Press, 2019).

7. For a critique of narrative history, see Alex Rosenberg, *How History Gets Things Wrong: The Neuroscience of Our Addiction to Stories* (Cambridge, MA: MIT Press, 2018).

8. Steven Levitsky and Daniel Zibblatt, "This Is How Democracies Die," *Guardian,* January 21, 2018.

1. I CAME, I SAW, I PUBLISHED

1. Julius Caesar, *The Conquest of Gaul* (London: Penguin Books, 1982).

2. For a biography of Julius Caesar, see Adrian Goldsworthy, *Caesar: Life of a Colossus* (New Haven, CT: Yale University Press, 2006).

3. For an account of Caesar's early life, see "The Ambitious Upstart" in Robert Garland, *Julius Caesar* (Liverpool, UK: Liverpool University Press, 2004).

4. Mary Beard, *SPQR: A History of Ancient Rome* (London: Profile Books, 2015), 9.

5. See Tom Standage's book, *Writing on the Wall: Social Media—The First 2,000 Years* (London: Bloomsbury, 2013). On Roman publishing methods, see Rex Winsbury, *The Roman Book* (London: Bloomsbury, 2013).

6. On Caesar's strategic use of his chronicles, see Kathryn Welch and Anton Powell, eds., *Julius Caesar as Artful Reporter: The War Commentaries as Political Instruments* (Wales: Duckworth & Classical Press of Wales, 1998); and Andrew Riggsby, *Caesar in Gaul and Rome: War in Words* (Austin: University of Texas Press, 2006).

7. On Caesar's moral justifications, see Michel Rambaud, *L'Art de la déformation historique dans les Commentaires de César* (Paris: Audin, 1953). See also Lincoln MacVeagh, "Caesar, De Bello Gallico, the Attack at Gergovia: A Case of the 'Limited Objective,'" *Classical Weekly* 21, no. 23 (April 23, 1928): 177–81.

8. See Jane Bellemore, "The Roman Concept of Massacre: Julius Caesar in Gaul," in *Theatres of Violence: Massacre, Mass Killing and Atrocity throughout History*, ed. P. G. Dwyer and L. Ryan (New York: Berghahn Books, 2012). Also see, "Julius Caesar Battlefield Unearthed in Southern Netherlands," *Guardian,* December 11, 2015.

9. Kathryn Welsh, "Caesar and His Officers in the Gallic War Commentaries," in *Julius Caesar as Artful Reporter: The War Commentaries as Political Instrument*, ed. Kathryn Welch and Anton Powell (Wales: Duckworth & Classical Press of Wales, 1998), 86.

10. Suetonius quotes Cicero in the chapter on Julius Caesar in his classic work, *The Twelve Caesars* (London: Penguin, 2007), available online at http://penelope.uchicago.edu/Thayer/E/Roman/Texts/Suetonius/12Caesars/Julius*.html.

11. See Suetonius, *Life of Julius Caesar* (London: Loeb Classical Library, 1913), available online at http://penelope.uchicago.edu/Thayer/E/Roman/Texts/Suetonius/12Caesars/Julius*.html.

12. See Lucian, *The Way to Write History*, available online at https://ebooks.adelaide.edu.au/l/lucian/works/chapter24.html.

13. See chapter 2 in Beard, *SPQR: A History of Ancient Rome*.

14. See Michael Grant's introduction to Tacitus, *The Annals of Imperial Rome* (London: Penguin, 1996).

15. Robert Morstein-Marx , "Caesar's Alleged Fear of Prosecution and His Ratio Absentis in the Approach to the Civil War," *Historia* 56 (2007): 159–78 .

16. Julius Caesar, *The Civil War* (London: Penguin Books, 1967). Also see Ramon Jimenez, *Caesar against Rome: The Great Roman Civil War* (London : Praeger Publishers, 2000).

17. For a life of Cato, see Rob Goodman and Jimmy Soni, *Rome's Last Citizen: The Life and Legacy of Cato* (New York: Thomas Dunne, 2012). Also

see Plutarch's life of Cato the Younger in *Parallel Lives* (London: Loeb Classical Library, 1989).

18. See the life of Julius Caesar in Plutarch's *Lives* (New York: Collier, 1909), available at www.bartleby.com/12/10.html.

19. See Suetonius, *The Twelve Caesars*; also Ida Ostenberg, "Veni, Vidi, Vici and Caesar's Triumph," *Classical Quarterly* 63, no. 2 (December 2013): 813–27.

20. Monroe Deutsch, "I Am Caesar, Not Rex," *Classical Philology* 23, no. 4 (October 1928): 394–98.

21. Petronius, *Satyricon* (London: Penguin, 2011); and *Juvenal: The Sixteen Satires* (London: Penguin, 1998). Also see the Victorian scholar James George Frazer, "Some Popular Superstitions of the Ancients," *Folklore* 1, no. 2 (June 1890): 145–71.

22. See Suetonius's chapter on Caesar in *The Twelve Caesars*.

23. See Appian's *Civil Wars*; his description of Caesar's funeral can be found online at www.livius.org/sources/content/appian/appian-caesars-funeral.

2. SHOW ME THE MONEY

1. For Plutarch's life of Mark Antony in his *Parallel Lives,* see chapter 9 in *Makers of Rome* (London: Penguin, 1965). For a modern biography, see Eleanor Goltz Huzar, *Mark Antony: A Biography* (Minneapolis: University of Minnesota, 1978).

2. For a biography of Octavian, see Adrian Goldsworthy, *Augustus: From Revolutionary to Emperor* (London: W&N, 2014).

3. See Suetonius's life of Augustus in *The Twelve Caesars,* available online at http://penelope.uchicago.edu/Thayer/E/Roman/Texts/Suetonius/12Caesars/Augustus*.html.

4. See Cicero's *Orations*, volume 4 (London: Loeb Classical Library, 1989).

5. Cicero, *Philippics 1–6* (London: Loeb Classical Library, 2010).

6. See the second oration in Cicero, *Philippics 1–6* (London: Loeb Classical Library, 2010).

7. Donald Knight, "The Political Acumen of Cicero after the Death of Caesar," *Latomus* 27, no. 1 (January–March 1968): 157–64.

8. Ancient historians who recounted the death of Cicero include Plutarch, Appian, Livy, and Cassius Dio. For a discussion of these accounts, see Andrew Wright, "The Death of Cicero. Forming a Tradition: The Contamination of History," *Historia: Zeitschrift für Alte Geschichte* 50, no. 4 (4th Quarter, 2001): 436–52.

9. For accounts of how Antony and his wife Fulvia abused and displayed Cicero's decapitated head, see Cassius Dio, *The Roman History, Book XLVII* (London: Penguin, 1987); and Plutarch, *Life of Cicero* (Liverpool: Liverpool University Press, 1989).

10. Clare Rowan, *From Caesar to Augustus: Using Coins as Sources* (Cambridge: Cambridge University Press, 2018).

11. On the political importance of Roman coinage, see Robert Newman, "A Dialogue of Power in the Coinage of Antony and Octavian 44-30 BC," *American Journal of Numismatics* 2 (1990): 37–63.

12. See chapters 7 and 8 in Thomas Hubbard, ed., *Homosexuality in Greece and Rome* (Berkeley: University of California Press, 2003).

13. Both Suetonius and Plutarch, cited above, refer to Antony's will, with slightly different interpretations. For an examination of the events surrounding the will and its disputed authenticity, see John Robert Johnson, "The Authenticity and Validity of Antony's Will," *L'Antiquité Classique* 47, no. 2 (1978): 494–503; and John Crook, "A Legal Point about Mark Antony's Will," *Journal of Roman Studies* 47, nos. 1/2 (1957): 36–38.

14. For an account of Mark Antony in Egypt and his breach with Rome, see the chapter "Breaking with Octavian" in Eleanor Goltz Huzar's biography, *Mark Antony* (Minneapolis: University of Minnesota Press, 1978).

15. On the fate of Cleopatra's children, see K. W. Meiklejohn, "Alexander Helios and Caesarion," *Journal of Roman Studies* 24 (1934): 191–95.

16. See Paul Zanker, *The Power of Images in the Age of Augustus* (Ann Arbor: University of Michigan Press, 1990); and Niels Hannestad, *Roman Art and Imperial Policy* (Aarhus: Aarhus University Press, 1986).

17. Harald Ingholt, "The Prime Porta Statue of Augustus," *Archaeology* 22, no. 3 (June 1969): 177–87. Also see Jodie Martyndale-Howard, "Augustus: Caesar and God: Varying Images of the First Roman Emperor," in Christoph Klose, Lukas C. Bossert, and William Leveritt, eds., *Fresh Perspectives on Graeco-Roman Visual Culture*, Proceedings of an International Conference at the Humboldt-Universität, Berlin, Germany, September 2–3, 2013.

18. See Suetonius's description of Augustus in his *Twelve Caesars* (London: Penguin, 2007), available online at http://penelope.uchicago.edu/Thayer/E/Roman/Texts/Suetonius/12Caesars/Augustus*.html.

19. See the chapter on Augustus in Suetonius, *The Twelve Caesars*.

20. Suetonius relates this anecdote in his "Life of Horace," see *Suetonius, Volume II* (London: Loeb Classical Library, 1914).

21. On Virgil and empire, see Daniel Mendelsohn, "Is the Aeneid a Celebration of Empire—or a Critique?" *New Yorker*, October 15, 2018.

22. See book 1 in Tacitus, *The Histories* (London: Penguin, 1995).

23. See Suetonius's life of Augustus in *The Twelve Caesars*.

24. See Suetonius's life of Tiberius in *The Twelve Caesars,* available online at http://penelope.uchicago.edu/Thayer/E/Roman/Texts/Suetonius/12Caesars/Tiberius*.html.

25. See chapter 9, "The Transformation of Augustus," in Mary Beard, *SPQR: A History of Ancient Rome* (London: Profile Books, 2015).

3. THE NERO UNREALITY SHOW

1. For a history of the Julio-Claudian dynasty, see Tom Holland, *Dynasty: The Rise and Fall of the House of Caesar* (London: Little, Brown, 2015).

2. See Suetonius's life of Nero in *The Twelve Caesars* (London: Penguin, 2007).

3. For biographies of Nero, see Miriam T. Griffin, *Nero: The End of a Dynasty* (London: Routledge, 2000); and Michael Grant, *Nero, Emperor in Revolt* (New York: American Heritage Press, 1970).

4. On Agrippina's ambitions, see Anthony Barrett, *Agrippina: Sex, Power and Politics in the Early Empire* (New Haven, CT: Yale University Press, 1996).

5. See Book XIV in Tacitus, *The Annals of Imperial Rome* (London: Penguin, 1956).

6. See Suetonius's chapter on Nero in *The Twelve Caesars*.

7. On Seneca's influence on Nero, see Elizabeth Kolbert, "Such a Stoic: How Seneca Became Ancient Rome's Philosopher-Fixer," *New Yorker*, February 2, 2015; and Emily Wilson, *The Greatest Empire: A Life of Seneca* (New York: Oxford University Press, 2014).

8. See Ulrich W. Hiesinger, "The Portraits of Nero," *American Journal of Archaeology* 79, no. 2 (April 1975): 113–24.

9. For Cassius Dio's account of Nero's feuds with his mother Agrippina, see, *Roman History,* Books 61–70 (Cambridge, MA: Harvard University Press, 1925).

10. See Book XIV in Tacitus, *The Annals of Imperial Rome*; also see Mary Frances Gyles, "Qualis Artifex?" *Classical Journal* 57, no. 5 (February 1962): 193–200.

11. See Suetonius's chapter on Nero in *The Twelve Caesars*.

12. See Suetonius's chapter on Nero in *The Twelve Caesars*.

13. See Book XVI in Tacitus, *The Annals of Imperial Rome*. Also see Holly Haynes, "The Tyrant Lists: Tacitus' Obituary of Petronius," *American Journal of Philology* 131, no. 1 (Spring 2010): 69–99.

14. On Nero's Greek tastes, see chapter 14, "The Temptation of Philhellenism," in Miriam T. Griffin, *Nero: The End of a Dynasty* (London: Routledge, 2000).

15. See Suetonius's chapter on Nero in *The Twelve Caesars*, available online at http://penelope.uchicago.edu/Thayer/E/Roman/Texts/Suetonius/12Caesars/Nero*.html#ref158.

16. See "The Death of Nero's Mother" (Tacitus, Annals, XIV, 1–13), *Latomus*, T. 33, Fasc. 1 (January–March 1974): 105–15.

17. See the chapter "Murder: Agrippina, Claudia Octavia and Poppaea," in Guy de la Bédoyère, *Domina: The Women Who Made Imperial Rome* (New Haven, CT: Yale University Press, 2018).

18. See Suetonius's chapter on Nero in *The Twelve Caesars*.

19. Mary Francis Gyles, "Nero Fiddled while Rome Burned," *Classical Journal* 42, no. 4 (January 1947): 211–17.

20. See Tacitus, *The Annals of Imperial Rome, Book XV* (London: Penguin, 1956). The Loeb Classical Library edition is available online at http://penelope.uchicago.edu/Thayer/E/Roman/Texts/Tacitus/Annals/15B*.html.

21. See Suetonius on Nero, available online at http://penelope.uchicago.edu/Thayer/E/Roman/Texts/Suetonius/12Caesars/Nero*.html#ref158.

22. See Tacitus, *The Annals of Imperial Rome, Book XV*.

23. See Tacitus, *The Annals of Imperial Rome, Book XV*.

24. See Tacitus, Part I, *The Annals of Imperial Rome*.

25. On the Nero Redivivus cult, see Marco Frenschkowski, "Nero Redivivus as a Subject of Early Christian Arcane Teaching," in *Early Jewish and Christian Responses to the Roman Power Empire*, ed. Michael Labahn and Outi Lehtipuu (Amsterdam: Amsterdam University Press, 2015).

26. Saint Augustine, *The City of God* (London: Penguin, 2003); and the chapter "Once and Future King" in Edward Champlin, *Nero* (Cambridge, MA: Harvard University Press, 2003).

27. See Book XX, chapter "Of the Endless Glory of the Church," in Saint Augustine, *The City of God* (London: Penguin, 2003).

28. New Testament, Book of Revelation 17:10, available online at https://biblehub.com/revelation/17-10.htm.

29. See Sulpicius Severus, chapter 28, *The Sacred History*, available online at www.documentacatholicaomnia.eu/03d/0360-0420,_Sulpicius_Severus,_Chronicorum_[Schaff],_EN.pdf.

30. See Henry A. Sanders, "The Number of the Beast in Revelation," *Journal of Biblical Literature* 37, nos. 1/2 (1918): 95–99.

31. Richard Bett, "Nietzsche and the Romans," *Journal of Nietzsche Studies* 42, no. 1 (Autumn 2011): 7–31.

32. Nietzsche's "become who you are" quote is from aphorism 270 in *The Gay Science*, sometimes translated as *The Joyful Science*, first published in 1882. See Friedrich Nietzsche, *The Joyful Science* (London: Penguin Classics, 2019).

4. SECRETS AND LIES

1. Procopius, *The Secret History* (London: Penguin, 2007).

2. For a portrait of Procopius and his times, see James Allan Evans, *Procopius* (New York: Twayne, 1972).

3. For a biography of Justinian, see James Allan Evans, *The Emperor Justinian and the Byzantine Empire* (Westport, CT: Greenwood Press, 2005); and for a portrait of his age, see Michael Maas, *The Cambridge Companion to the Age of Justinian* (New York: Cambridge University Press, 2005).

4. Procopius recounts this in Book IV of his *History of Wars* (London: Loeb Classical Library, 1918).

5. See Averil Cameron, *Procopius and the Sixth Century* (Berkeley: University of California Press, 1985).

6. See James Allen Evans, "Justinian and the Historical Procopius," *Greece & Rome* 17, no. 2 (October 1970): 218–23.

7. For biographies of Theodora, see James Allan Evans, *The Empress Theodora* (Austin: University of Texas Press, 2003); and Stella Duffy, *Theodora: Empress, Actress, Whore* (London: Virago, 2010).

8. On Procopius's negative portrayal of Theodora, see Elizabeth A. Fisher, "Theodora and Antonina in the *Historia Arcana*: History and/or Fiction?," *Arethusa* 11, nos. 1/2 (Spring and Fall 1978): 253–79.

9. See Nadine Elizabeth Korte, "Procopius' Portrayal of Theodora in *The Secret History*," in *Hirundo: The McGill Journal of Classical Studies*, vol. 3, 109–30 (Montréal: McGill University, 2005).

10. See Adrian Goldsworthy, *How Rome Fell: Death of a Superpower* (New Haven, CT: Yale University Press, 2010).

11. Edward Gibbon, *The History of the Decline and Fall of the Roman Empire* (London: Penguin Classics, 2000).

12. From chapter 15 of Edward Gibbon's *The History of the Decline and Fall of the Roman Empire*, available online at www.ccel.org/g/gibbon/decline/volume1/chap15.htm.

13. See Olivia Robinson, "Blasphemy and Sacrilege in Roman Law," *Irish Jurist* 8, no. 2 (Winter 1973): 356–71.

14. On the anti-pagan violence of the early Christians, see Catherine Nixey, *The Darkening Age: The Christian Destruction of the Classical World* (London: Macmillan, 2017).

15. See chapter 15 of Gibbon's *The History of the Decline and Fall of the Roman Empire*.

16. On Gibbon's Enlightenment attitudes towards Christianity, see B. W. Young, "'Scepticism in Excess': Gibbon and Eighteenth-Century Christianity," *Historical Journal* 41, no. 1 (March 1998): 179–99.

17. See Rodney Stark, *The Rise of Christianity: How the Obscure, Marginal Jesus Movement Became the Dominant Religious Force in the Western World in a Few Centuries* (Princeton: Princeton University Press, 1996); and Tim Whitmarsh, *Battling the Gods: Atheism in the Ancient World* (London: Faber and Faber, 2015).

18. See Andrew Alfoldi, *The Conversion of Constantine and Pagan Rome* (New York: Oxford University Press, 1949); and Noel Lenski, *The Cambridge Companion on the Age of Constantine* (New York: Cambridge University Press, 2007).

19. For a portrait of Constantine as defender of Christianity, see Timothy Barnes, *The New Empire of Diocletian and Constantine* (Cambridge, MA: Harvard University Press, 1982).

20. On Eusebius's portrait of Constantine, see T. G. Elliott, "Eusebian Frauds in the 'Vita Constantini,'" *Phoenix* 45, no. 2 (Summer 1991): 162–71.

21. On Constantine's coinage, see Nathaniel DesRosiers, "Suns, Snakes, and Altars: Competitive Imagery in Constantinian Numismatics," in *Religious Competition in the Greco-Roman World*, ed. Nathaniel DesRosiers and Lily Vuong (Atlanta: SBL Press, 2016).

22. See Glen Thompson, "From Sinner to Saint? Seeking a Consistent Constantine," in *Rethinking Constantine: History, Theology, Legacy*, ed. Edward Smither (Cambridge: James Clarke & Co., 2014).

23. Exodus 20:4 KJV: www.biblegateway.com/passage/?search=Exodus+20%3A4&version=KJV.

24. John 5:21 KJV: www.biblegateway.com/passage/
?search=1+John+5%3A21&version=KJV.

25. See T. C. G. Thornton, "The Destruction of Idols: Sinful or Meritorious?" *Journal of Theological Studies* 37, no. 1 (April 1986): 121–29.

26. Thomas Mathews nuances the "Emperor Mystique" theory in his book, *Clash of the Gods: A Reinterpretation of Early Christian Art* (Princeton: Princeton University Press, 1993).

27. See Glanville Downey, "Justinian as Achilles," *Transactions and Proceedings of the American Philological Association* 71 (1940): 68–77.

28. On the rise of Christian iconography, see Beata Fricke, *Fallen Idols, Risen Saints* (Turnhout, Belgium: Brepols Publishers, 2015).

29. See Leslie Brubaker and John Haldon, *Byzantium in the Iconoclast Era* (Cambridge: Cambridge University Press, 2011).

30. St. John Damascene's *Apologia against Those Who Decry Holy Images* is available online at www.documentacatholicaomnia.eu/03d/0675-0749,_Ioannes_Damascenus,_Apologia_Against_Those_Who_Decry_Holy_Images,_EN.pdf. For a textual analysis of his Apologia, see Jas Elsner, "Iconoclasm as Discourse: From Antiquity to Byzantium," *Art Bulletin* 94, no. 3 (September 2012): 368–94.

31. See Bronwen Neil, "The Western Reaction to the Council of Nicaea II," *Journal of Theological Studies* 51, no. 2 (October 2000): 533–52.

5. PR MEN IN THE MONASTERIES

1. For a biography that addresses the Charlemagne of fact and fiction, see Matthew Gabriele, *An Empire of Memory: The Legend of Charlemagne, the Franks, and Jerusalem before the First Crusade* (New York: Oxford University Press, 2011).

2. For biographies of Charlemagne, see Donald Bullough, *The Age of Charlemagne* (London: Elek Books, 1965); Derek Wilson, *Charlemagne: A Biography* (New York: Vintage, 2005); and, more recently, Janet L. Nelson, *King and Emperor: A New Life of Charlemagne* (London: Allen Lane, 2019).

3. See the chapter "The Expansion of the Frankish Kingdom in the East: Saxons, Bavarians Avars," in Matthias Becher's biography, *Charlemagne* (New Haven, CT: Yale University Press, 2003).

4. See the chapter "Scholars at Charlemagne's Court" in Douglas Dales's book *Alcuin: Theology and Thought* (London: James Clarke & Co., 2013).

5. Bede, *Ecclesiastical History of the English People* (London: Penguin, 1990).

6. See the prologue in Einhard's *Life of Charlemagne*, available online at www.yorku.ca/inpar/eginhard_grant.pdf. For a published version, see Einhard and Notker the Stammerer, *Two Lives of Charlemagne* (London: Penguin, 2008).

7. See the Prologue in Einhard, *The Life of Charlemagne,* trans. Evelyn Scherabon Firchow and Edwin H. Zeydel (Coral Gables, FL: University of Mia-

mi Press, 1972). Also see Einhard's biography of Charlemagne online at http://people.bu.edu/dklepper/RN307/einhard.html.

8. See chapter 6 in Allesandro Barbero, *Charlemagne: Father of a Continent* (Berkeley: University of California Press, 2004), 116.

9. For Einhard's life of Charlemagne, see Einhard and Notker the Stammerer, *Two Lives of Charlemagne.*

10. See Thomas Sidey, "The Government of Charlemagne as Influenced by Augustine's City of God," *Classical Journal* 14, no. 2 (November 1918): 119–27; and François Ganshof, "Einhard, biographe de Charlemagne," *Bibliothèque d'Humanisme et Renaissance* 13, no. 3 (1951): 217–30.

11. See Jace Stuckey, "Charlemagne as Crusader? Memory, Propaganda, and the Many Uses of Charlemagne's Legendary Expedition to Spain," in *The Legend of Charlemagne in the Middle Ages: Power, Faith, and Crusade*, ed. M. Gabriele and J. Stuckey (New York: Palgrave, 2008).

12. Simon Gaunt and Karen Pratt, *The Song of Roland and Other Poems of Charlemagne* (Oxford: Oxford University Press, 2016); and Marianne Ailes, "Charlemagne 'Father of Europe'—a European Icon in the Making," *Reading Medieval Studies* 38 (2012): 59–76.

13. See the chapter "Epilogue Hero and Saint: The Afterlife of Charlemagne," in Matthias Becher's biography *Charlemagne* (New Haven, CT: Yale University Press, 2003).

14. See the chapter "Between Two Empires, 461–1000," in Eamon Duffy, *Saints and Sinners: A History of the Popes* (New Haven, CT: Yale University Press, 1997).

15. On Charlemagne's relations with Pope Leo III, see the chapter "The Republic and the Franks," in Thomas Noble, *The Republic of St. Peter: The Birth of the Papal State, 680–825* (Philadelphia: University of Pennsylvania Press, 1984).

16. See the chapter "Patriot Warrior" in Harry Redman, *The Roland Legend in Nineteenth-Century French Literature* (Lexington: University of Kentucky Press, 1991).

17. See Carol Margaret Davison, *History of Gothic: Gothic Literature 1764–1824* (Cardiff: University of Wales Press, 2009); and Angela Wright and Dale Townshend, *Romantic Gothic* (Edinburgh: University of Edinburgh Press, 2016).

18. See Rosamond McKitterick, *Charlemagne: The Formation of a European Identity* (Cambridge: Cambridge University Press, 2008).

19. See Dagmar Paulus, "From Charlemagne to Hitler: The Imperial Crown of the Holy Roman Empire and Its Symbolism," Online journal of the project "Charlemagne, a European Icon" (University of Bristol, 2017); and Becher, "Epilogue Hero and Saint."

20. See Becher, "Epilogue Hero and Saint."

21. See Simon Keynes, "The Cult of King Alfred the Great," *Anglo-Saxon England*, vol. 28 (Cambridge: Cambridge University Press, 1999).

22. Simon Keynes and Michael Lapidge, eds., *Alfred the Great: Asser's Life of King Alfred and Other Contemporary Sources* (London: Penguin, 1983). Historian Alfred Smyth challenged traditional academic interpretations of Alfred's

life based on Asser's book, whose authenticity he called into question. See Smyth's *King Alfred the Great* (Oxford: Oxford University Press, 1996); and Brian Cathcart, "Historians at Odds over Claims That Alfred the Great's Life Was a Fake," *Independent*, March 24, 1996.

23. Bede, *Ecclesiastical History of the English People*.

24. Geoffrey of Monmouth, *The History of the Kings of Britain* (London: Penguin, 1966).

25. See Joanna Parker, "Turning a King into a Hero: Nine Hundred Years of Pre-Victorian Reinvention," in *England's Darling: The Victorian Cult of Alfred the Great*, ed. J. Parker (Manchester: Manchester University Press, 2007).

26. Martin Wainwright, "King Alfred's Cakes Reduced to Crumbs," *Guardian*, March 13, 2007.

27. See Keynes, "The Cult of King Alfred the Great."

28. See Clare Simmons, *Reversing the Conquest: History and Myth in 19th-Century British Literature* (New Brunswick, NJ: Rutgers University Press, 1990).

29. David Hume, *The History of England from the Invasion of Julius Caesar to the Revolution in 1688,* with a foreword by W. B. Todd, vol. 1, 63–81 (Indianapolis: Liberty Classics, 1983).

30. See chapter 3, "England Under the Good Saxon, Alfred," in Charles Dickens, *A Child's History of England* (Newcastle: Cambridge Scholars Publishing, 2008).

31. See Joanne Parker, "Medievalism, Anglo-Saxonism and the Nineteenth Century," in *England's Darling: The Victorian Cult of Alfred the* Great (Manchester: Manchester University Press, 2007). Also see John Niles, *The Idea of Anglo-Saxon England 1066-1901: Remembering, Forgetting, Deciphering and Renewing the Past* (Oxford: Wiley-Blackwell, 2015).

32. See Joanne Parker, "The Day of a Thousand Years: Alfred and the Victorian Mania for Commemoration," in *England's Darling: The Victorian Cult of Alfred the Great* (Manchester: Manchester University Press, 2007).

6. BONFIRES OF VANITIES

1. Donald E. Wilkes, "The Cadaver Synod: Strangest Trial in History," *Popular Media* 42 (2001).

2. Michael Edward Moore, "The Body of Pope Formosus," *Millennium* 9, no. 1 (2012); and Muhammad Bilal and R. Shane Tubbs, "Popes Convict Dead Pope Twice: The Unbelievable Cadaver Synod," *Clinical Anatomy* 29 (2016): 140–43.

3. See Peter Llewellyn, *Rome in the Dark Ages* (London: Constable and Robinson, 1996); and Russell Chamberlain, *The Bad Popes* (Stroud: Sutton, 2003).

4. For an analysis of the historical background to the Cadaver Synod, see Michael Edward Moore, "The Attack on Pope Formosus: Papal History in the Age of Resentment (875–897)," in *Ecclesia et Violentia: Violence against the*

Church and Violence within the Church in the Middle Ages, ed. Radosław Kotecki and Jacek Maciejewski (Newcastle: Cambridge Scholars, 2014).

5. On *damnatio memoriae* in the Formosus trial, see Laurent Jégou, "Compétition autour d'un cadavre. Le procès du pape Formose et ses enjeux (896-904)," *Revue Historique* 317, no. 3 (July 2015): 499–523.

6. On mutilation as punishment with reference to Pope Formosus, see the chapter "Insult and Injury" in Lisa Oliver, *The Body Legal in Barbarian Law* (Toronto: University of Toronto Press, 2011).

7. See Lindsay Brook, "Popes and Pornocrats: Rome in the Early Middle Ages," *Foundations* 1, no. 1 (2003): 5–21.

8. For Machiavelli on Savonarola, see J. H. Whitefield, "Savonarola and the Purpose of 'The Prince,'" *Modern Language Review* 44, no. 1 (January 1949): 44–59; also see the chapter "Afterwards," in Donald Weinstein, *Savonarola: The Rise and Fall of a Renaissance Prophet* (New Haven, CT: Yale University Press, 2011).

9. For biographies of Savonarola, see Donald Weinstein, *Savonarola: The Rise and Fall of a Renaissance Prophet* (New Haven, CT: Yale University Press, 2011); and Lauro Martines, *Scourge and Fire: Savonarola and Renaissance Italy* (London: Jonathan Cape, 2006).

10. John F. Wippel, "Truth in Thomas Aquinas," *Review of Metaphysics* 43, no. 2 (December 1989).

11. See Paul Oskar Kristeller, "The Alleged Ritual Murder of Simon of Trent (1475) and Its Literary Repercussions: A Bibliographical Study," *Proceedings of the American Academy for Jewish Research* 59 (1993): 103–35.

12. See Donald Weinstein, "Savonarola, Florence, and the Millenarian Tradition," *Church History* 27, no. 4 (December 1958): 291–305.

13. See G. A. Lindeboom, "The Story of a Blood Transfusion to a Pope," *Journal of the History of Medicine and Allied Sciences* 9, no. 4 (October 1954): 455–59.

14. See C. J. Meyer, *The Borgias: The Hidden History* (New York: Bantam, 2014); and Sarah Bradford, *Cesare Borgia: His Life and Times* (London: Penguin, 2011).

15. See chapter 11, "The Savonarolan Moment: King Christ," in Lauro Martines, *Scourge and Fire: Savonarola and Renaissance Italy* (London: Jonathan Cape, 2006); and Patrick Macey, "The Lauda and the Cult of Savonarola," *Renaissance Quarterly* 45, no. 3 (Autumn 1992): 439–83.

16. See chapter 16, "I Can't Live without Preaching" in Donald Weinstein, *Savonarola: The Rise and Fall of a Renaissance Prophet* (New Haven, CT: Yale University Press, 2011).

17. For this Savonarola text, see Margaret Bald, *Literature Suppressed on Religious Grounds* (New York: Facts on File, 2006), 53.

18. For Savonarola's collected works, see Donald Beebe, ed., *Selected Writings of Girolamo Savonarola: Religion and Politics, 1490–1498* (New Haven, CT: Yale University Press, 2006).

19. See Hyatt Mayor, "Renaissance Pamphleteers: Savonarola and Luther," *Metropolitan Museum of Art Bulletin* 6, no. 2 (October 1947): 66–72.

20. See chapter 19, "Excommunicated!" in Donald Weinstein, *Savonarola: The Rise and Fall of a Renaissance Prophet* (New Haven, CT: Yale University Press, 2011). *Triumph of the Cross* can be accessed online at https:// oll.libertyfund.org/titles/savonarola-the-triumph-of-the-cross.

21. See chapter 6 in *The Prince* (London: Penguin, 1976); and book 1, chapter 11, in *Discourses on Livy* (Oxford: Oxford University Press, 2009).

22. For Machiavelli on "unarmed prophets," see chapter 6 of *The Prince*.

7. SELLING INDULGENCES

1. See the chapter "Wittenberg 1517" in Richard Rex, *The Making of Martin Luther* (Princeton: Princeton University Press, 2017).

2. On the "Devotio Moderna" movement in Holland, see Charles Caspers, Daniela Müller, and Judith Kessler, "In the Eyes of Others. The Modern Devotion in Germany and the Netherlands: Influencing and Appropriating," *Church History & Religious Culture* 93, no. 4 (2013): 489–503.

3. For a biography of Martin Luther, see Lyndal Roper, *Martin Luther: Renegade and Prophet* (London: Vintage, 2016).

4. See Adrian Bell and Richard Dale, "The Medieval Pilgrimage Business," *Enterprise & Society* 12, no. 3 (September 2011): 601–27.

5. For an economic analysis of indulgences, see Alberto Cassone and Carla Marchese, "The Economics of Religious Indulgences," *Journal of Institutional and Theoretical Economics* (JITE)/*Zeitschrift für die gesamte Staatswissenschaft* 155, no. 3 (September 1999): 429–42.

6. See "The 95 Theses, or Disputation for Clarifying the Power of Indulgences, 1517," in Timothy Wengert, Hans Hillerbrand, and Kirsi Stjerna, eds., *The Annotated Luther: The Roots of Reform* (Minneapolis: Augsburg Fortress, 2015).

7. See "The Election of Leo X" in Anthony Cummings, *The Politicized Muse: Music for Medici Festivals, 1512–1537* (Princeton: Princeton University Press, 1992).

8. See Barbara Tuchman's portrait of Leo X, "The Protestant Break: Pope Leo X," chapter 5 in her book, *The March of Folly: From Troy to Vietnam* (New York: Random House, 1984).

9. See Jared Wicks, "Reactions to Luther, the First Year (1518)," *The Catholic Historical Review* 69, no. 4 (October 1983): 521–62.

10. See chapter 5, "Let Truth and Falsehood Grapple," in Tom Standage, *Writing on the Wall: Social Media—The First 2,000 Years* (London: Bloomsbury, 2013), 84.

11. See "How Luther Went Viral," *Economist*, December 17, 2011; and the chapter "How Luther Went Viral" in Tom Standage, *Writing on the Wall: Social Media—The First 2,000 Years* (London: Bloomsbury, 2013), 53.

12. See "Luther's Reformation: The Stand," *Economist*, November 4, 2017; and Mark U. Edwards Jr., *Printing, Propaganda and Martin Luther* (Berkeley: University of California Press, 1994).

13. See "How the 16th Century Invented Social Media," *Economist,* January 16, 2017; and "How Luther Went Viral," *Economist*, December 17, 2011.

14. See "How Luther Went Viral," *Economist*; and Colin Woodward, "The Power of Luther's Printing Press," *Washington Post*, December 18, 2015.

15. See "How the 16th Century Invented Social Media," *Economist*, January 16, 2017; Elizabeth Eisenstein, *The Printing Revolution in Early Modern Europe* (New York: Cambridge University Press, 2005); and chapter 7, "Pamphlets and Persuasion" in Andrew Pettegree, *Reformation and the Culture of Persuasion* (Cambridge: Cambridge University Press, 2005).

16. See "How Luther Went Viral," *Economist,* December 17, 2011.

17. See Andrew Pettegree, *Brand Luther: How an Unheralded Monk Turned His Small Town into a Center of Publishing, Made Himself the Most Famous Man in Europe—and Started the Protestant Reformation* (London: Penguin, 2015); and the chapter "Marketing Luther" in Steven Ozment, *The Serpent and the Lamb: Cranach, Luther, and the Making of the Reformation* (New Haven, CT: Yale University Press, 2011).

18. Larry Mansch and Curtis Peters, *Martin Luther: The Life and Lessons* (Jefferson, NC: McFarland, 2016), 77.

19. Mark U. Edwards Jr., *Printing, Propaganda, and Martin Luther* (Berkeley: University of California Press, 1994), 62.

20. See chapter 3, "The Catholic Dilemma," in Edwards Jr., *Printing, Propaganda, and Martin Luther*; also "How Luther Went Viral," *Economist*.

21. For an economic interpretation of how the Church dealt with rivals to its monopoly power, see Robert B. Ekelund Jr., Robert F. Hébert, and Robert D. Tollison, "An Economic Analysis of the Protestant Reformation," *Journal of Political Economy* 110, no. 3 (June 2002): 646–71.

22. See the chapter "Excommunications" in James M. Kittelson and Hans H. Wiersma, *Luther the Reformer* (Minneapolis: Augsburg Fortress, 2016).

23. Eric Lund, ed., *Documents from the History of Lutheranism* (Minneapolis: Augsburg Fortress, 2002), 32.

24. See the chapter "How Luther Went Viral" in Standage, *Writing on the Wall*.

25. On Luther's anti-Semitism, see Thomas Kaufmann, *Luther's Jews: A Journey into Anti-Semitism* (Oxford: Oxford University Press, 2017); and the chapter "Luther—Defender of the Jews or Anti-Semite?" in Walter Altmann, *Luther and Liberation* (Minneapolis: Augsburg Fortress, 2015).

26. See Adam Francisco, *Martin Luther and Islam: A Study in Sixteenth-Century Polemics* (Leiden: Brill, 2007); also see George Forell, "Luther and the War against the Turks," *Church History* 14, no. 4 (December 1945): 256–71.

27. Jules Michelet, *The Life of Martin Luther Gathered from His Writings* (Sydney: Wentworth Press, 2019), 76.

28. See the chapter "We Are Beggars," in James M. Kittelson and Hans H. Wiersma, *Luther the Reformer: The Story of the Man and His Career* (Minneapolis: Augsburg Fortress, 2016), 250.

8. LÈSE MAJESTÉ

1. See Lucy Beckett, "Smash and Grab," *Times Literary Supplement*, June 20, 2008. Also see R. W. Hoyle, "The Origin of the Dissolution of the Monasteries," *Historical Journal* 38, no. 2 (June 1995): 275–305.

2. See Stanford E. Lehmberg, "Henry VIII, the Reformation and the Cathedrals," *Huntington Library Quarterly* 49, no. 3, Tudor History Issue (Summer 1986): 261–70.

3. See G. W. Bernard in "The Dissolution of the Monasteries," *History* 96, no. 4 (324) (October 2011): 390–409.

4. See the chapter "The Mystic, the Monarch, and the Persistence of 'the Medieval': Elizabeth Barton and Henry VIII," in Nancy Bradley Warren, *Women of God and Arms: Female Spirituality and Political Conflict, 1380–1600* (Philadelphia: University of Pennsylvania Press, 2005).

5. See the chapter "Tudor Propaganda" in Philip M. Taylor, *Munitions of the Mind: A History of Propaganda* (Manchester: Manchester University Press, 2003).

6. See W. Gordon Zeeveld, "Richard Morison, Official Apologist for Henry VIII," *PMLA* 55, no. 2 (June 1940): 406–25.

7. See the chapter "Trial and Execution" in David Daniell, *William Tyndale* (New Haven, CT: Yale University Press, 1994); and Melvyn Bragg, "A Man of His Words: How William Tyndale Shaped Our World," *Prospect*, December 13, 2017.

8. See the chapter "Henry VIII: Syphilitic Sovereign?" in Bert Park, *Ailing, Aging, Addicted: Studies of Compromised Leadership* (Lexington: University Press of Kentucky, 1993); and J. F. D. Shrewsbury, "Henry VIII: A Medical Study," *Journal of the History of Medicine and Allied Sciences* 7, no. 2 (Spring 1952): 141–85.

9. See Robert Hutchinson, *The Last Days of Henry VIII: Conspiracy, Treason and Heresy at the Court of the Dying Tyrant* (London: Weidenfeld & Nicolson, 2005).

10. See Dora Thornton, "Her Majesty's Picture: Circulating a Likeness of Elizabeth I," British Museum blog, June 30, 2017; and Deanne Williams, "Elizabeth I: Size Matters," in *Goddesses and Queens: The Iconography of Elizabeth I*, ed. Annaliese Connolly and Lisa Hopkins (Manchester: Manchester University Press, 2007).

11. See John Cooper, *The Queen's Agent: Francis Walsingham at the Court of Elizabeth I* (London: Faber and Faber, 2011).

12. See Alice Dailey, "Making Edmund Campion: Treason, Martyrdom, and the Structure of Transcendence," *Religion & Literature* 38, no. 3 (Autumn 2006): 65–83.

13. British Parliament, *Act against Seditious Words and Rumours Uttered against the Queen's Most Excellent Majesty* (1581; 23 Eliz. c. 2).

14. See Natalie Mears, "Counsel, Public Debate, and Queenship: John Stubbs's 'The Discoverie of a Gaping Gulf', 1579," *Historical Journal* 44, no. 3 (September 2001): 629–50; and Christopher Haigh, "Puritan Evangelism in the

Reign of Elizabeth I," *English Historical Review* 92, no. 362 (January 1977): 30–58.

15. See Joad Raymond, *Pamphlets and Pamphleteering in Early Modern Britain* (Cambridge: Cambridge University Press, 2003).

16. See the chapter "In the 'Publike' Theater of William Prynne's Histrio-Mastix," in Lisa Freeman, *Antitheatricality and the Body Public* (Philadelphia: University of Pennsylvania Press, 2017).

17. See David Cressy, "Book Burning in Tudor and Stuart England," *Sixteenth Century Journal* 36, no. 2 (Summer 2005): 359–74.

18. Tom Standage, *Writing on the Wall: Social Media—the First 2,000 Years* (London: Bloomsbury, 2013), 86.

19. On the Star Chamber decrees, see Cyndia Susan Clegg, "Censorship and the Courts of Star Chamber and High Commission in England to 1640," *Journal of Modern European History* 3, no. 1, Censorship in Early Modern Europe (2005): 50–80. For the text of the 1637 Star Chamber decree, see https://archive.org/details/decreeofstarcham00englrich/page/n43.

20. Joad Raymond, *Pamphlets and Pamphleteering in Early Modern Britain* (Cambridge: Cambridge University Press, 2003), 12.

21. See chapter 1, "What Is a Pamphlet" in Joad Raymond, *Pamphlets and Pamphleteering in Early Modern Britain* (Cambridge: Cambridge University Press, 2003), 12; and the chapter "The English Civil War (1642-6)" in Philip Taylor, *Munitions of the Mind: A History of Propaganda* (Manchester: Manchester University Press, 2003).

22. Geoffrey Alan Cranfield, *The Press and Society: From Caxton to Northcliffe* (London: Routledge, 1978), 11.

23. See chapter 12, "The Search for Truth" in Andrew Pettegree, *The Invention of News: How the World Came to Know about Itself* (New Haven, CT: Yale University Press, 2014); and Jason Peacey, *Politicians and Pamphleteers: Propaganda During the English Civil Wars and Interregnum* (London: Routledge, 2004).

24. See Thomas Fulton, "Areopagitica: Books, Reading, and Context," in *Manuscript, Print, and Political Culture in Revolutionary England* (Boston: University of Massachusetts Press, 2010).

25. King Charles I's final words are published on the British monarchy's official website at www.royal.uk/charles-i.

26. See Robert Wilcher, "What Was the King's Book For?: The Evolution of 'Eikon Basilike,'" *Yearbook of English Studies* 21, Special Number, Politics, Patronage and Literature in England 1558–1658 (1991): 218–28; and Elizabeth Skerpan-Wheeler, "The First 'Royal': Charles I as Celebrity," *PMLA* 126, no. 4, Special Topic: Celebrity, Fame, Notoriety (October 2011): 912–34.

27. See Lynn Wood Mollenauer, *Strange Revelations: Magic, Poison and Sacrilege in Louis XIV's France* (University Park: Pennsylvania State University Press, 2006), 62.

28. Francis Leary, "The Wickedest Woman," *Virginia Quarterly Review* 73, no. 2 (Spring 1997): 238–56; and Georges Carrière, "Feux, bûchers, et autodafés bien de chez nous," *Revue de l'histoire des religions* 194, no. 1 (1978): 23–64.

29. See Francis Leary, "The Wickedest Woman."

30. Lynn Wood Mollenauer, *Strange Revelations: Magic, Poison and Sacrilege in Louis XIV's France* (University Park: Pennsylvania State University Press, 2006), 63.

31. See Delphine Reguig-Naya, "Rejoindre l'émotion et son public: D'une relation judiciaire par Mme de Sévigné," *Littératures classiques* 1, no. 68 (2009): 309–19.

32. On superstition under Louis XIV, see Lynn Wood Mollenauer, "The End of Magic: Superstition and 'So-Called Sorcery' in Louis XIV's Paris," in *Crime and Punishment: Perspectives from the Humanities*, ed. Austin Sarat (Bingley, UK: Emerald, 2005).

33. See James King, *Science and Rationalism in the Government of Louis XIV, 1661–83* (Baltimore: Johns Hopkins University Press, 1949).

34. See Mirko Grmek, "L'émergence de la médecine scientifique en France sous le règne de Louis XIV," *Medizinhistorisches Journal* 11, nos. 3/4 (1976): 271–98.

35. See Colin Jones, "The King's Two Teeth," *History Workshop Journal,* no. 65 (Spring 2008): 79–95.

36. On Sir Robert Talbor (sometimes referred to as "Tabor"), see T. W. Keeble, "A Cure for the Ague: The Contribution of Robert Talbor (1642–81)," *Journal of the Royal Society of Medicine* 90 (May 1997): 285–90; and François Lebrun, "Médecins et empiriques à la cour de Louis XIV," *Histoire, Économie et Société* 3, no. 4 (1984): 557–66.

37. See Pierre Bonnet, "De la critique à la satire: Trente années d'opposition pamphlétaire à Louis XIV," *Bulletin de la Société de l'Histoire du Protestantisme Français* 157 (January–March 2011): 27–64; and Linda Kiernan, "Frondeurs and Fake News: How Misinformation Ruled in 17th-Century France," *Conversation*, August 1, 2017.

38. See Pierre Clément, "La police sous Louis XIV: Nicolas de la Reynie," *Revue des Deux Mondes* 50, no. 4 (April 15, 1864): 799–850.

9. COFFEE AND CAKE

1. For a book on the Lisbon earthquake, see Mark Molesky, *The Gulf of Fire: The Destruction of Lisbon, or Apocalypse in the Age of Science and Reason* (New York: Alfred A. Knopf, 2015).

2. See the section "The Incommodities of Such a War," in Thomas Hobbes, *Leviathan* (London: Penguin Classics, 2017). The book is available online at https://philo-labo.fr/fichiers/Hobbes%20-%20L%C3%A9viathan%20(gutenberg).pdf.

3. See Bertram Eugene Schwarzbach, "Reason and the Bible in the So-Called Age of Reason," *Huntington Library Quarterly* 74, no. 3 (September 2011): 437–70.

4. For an analysis of Locke's reading of the Bible, see Ross Corbett, "Locke's Biblical Critique," *Review of Politics* 74, no. 1 (Winter 2012): 27–51.

5. Albert O. Hirschman explores these themes in *The Passions and the Interests: The Political Arguments for Capitalism before Its Triumph* (Princeton: Princeton University Press, 1977).

6. The term "crooked timber of humanity" is from Immanuel Kant, cited by the philosopher Isaiah Berlin. On Berlin's use of that phrase, see Graeme Garrard, "Strange Reversals: Berlin on the Enlightenment and Counter-Enlightenment," in *The One and the Many: Reading Isaiah Berlin*, ed. George Crowder and Henry Hardy (Amherst: Prometheus Books, 2007).

7. See Fred H. Willhoite Jr., "Rousseau's Political Religion," *Review of Politics* 27, no. 4 (October 1965): 501–15.

8. Frequently paraphrased in English, the original quote from Voltaire's *Questions sur les miracles* is "*Certainement, qui est en droit de vous rendre absurde pourront vous rendre injuste.*" See Voltaire's eleventh letter in *Questions sur les miracles* (Paris: Hachette Livre BNF, 2013).

9. See Jeffrey Hopes, "The Age of Credulity: Believing the Unbelievable in the Century of the Enlightenment," *Revue de la Société d'études anglo-américaines des XVIIe et XVIIIe siècles*, HS3 (2013): 181–91. Also see Brian Levack, "Possession in the Age of Reason," in *The Devil Within: Possession and Exorcism in the Christian West* (New Haven, CT: Yale University Press, 2013); and Kathryn Morris, "Superstition, Testimony, and the Eighteenth-Century Vampire Debates," *Preternature: Critical and Historical Studies on the Preternatural* 4, no. 2 (2015): 181–202.

10. See "Quackery in London in the Eighteenth Century," *British Medical Journal* 1, no. 2731 (May 3, 1913): 959–60; and Eric Trimmer, "Medical Folklore and Quackery," *Folklore* 76, no. 3 (Autumn 1965): 161–75.

11. For an exhaustive study of Joanna Stephens's kidney stone cure, see Arthur Viseltear, "Joanna Stephens and the Eighteenth Century Lithontriptics: A Misplaced Chapter in the History of Therapeutics," *Bulletin of the History of Medicine* 42, no. 3 (May–June 1968): 199–220.

12. On Daniel Defoe and the early English novelists, see chapter 7, "Truth within a Fable? Fiction, Truth and Post-Truth," in Stuart Sim, *Post-Truth, Scepticism and Power* (Cham: Palgrave Macmillan, 2019).

13. See Hans Andersen, "The Paradox of Morality and Trade in Defoe," *Modern Philology* 39, no. 1 (August 1941): 23–46.

14. See S. D. Smith, "Accounting for Taste: British Coffee Consumption in Historical Perspective," *Journal of Interdisciplinary History* 27, no. 2 (Autumn 1996): 183–214.

15. By the king, A Proclamation for the Suppression of Coffeehouses (1675), see text online at www.staff.uni-giessen.de/gloning/tx/suppress.htm.

16. See Brian Cowan, "The Rise of the Coffeehouse Reconsidered," *Historical Journal* 47, no. 1 (March 2004): 22.

17. See Tom Standage, "Social Networking in the 1600s," *New York Times,* June 22, 2013.

18. On the "Penny Universities," see chapter 4 in Brian Cowen, *The Social Life of Coffee* (New Haven, CT: Yale University Press, 2005): 97.

19. Tom Standage, *Writing on the Wall: Social Media—the First 2,000 Years* (London: Bloomsbury, 2013), 107.

20. See Tom Standage, "Social Networking in the 1600s."

21. See chapter 8, "Civilizing Society" in Brian Cowan, *The Social Life of Coffee: The Emergence of the British Coffeehouse* (New Haven, CT: Yale University Press, 2005), 242.

22. See Jürgen Habermas, *The Structural Transformation of the Public Sphere* (Cambridge, MA: MIT Press, 1991). For a critique of the coffeehouse "public sphere" theory, see Brian Cowan, "Mr Spectator and the Coffeehouse Public Sphere," *Eighteenth-Century Studies* 37, no. 3 (Spring 2004): 345–66. For a feminist critique, see Nancy Fraser, "Rethinking the Public Sphere: A Contribution to the Critique of Actually Existing Democracy," *Social Text*, nos. 25/26 (1990): 56–80.

23. Samuel Johnson, *A Dictionary of the English Language* (London: W. Strathan, 1755).

24. Pepys constantly recorded his presence at London coffeehouses in his famous diary; see one entry for March 28, 1665, published online at www.pepysdiary.com/diary/1665/03/28.

25. Richard Addison, *Spectator,* March 12, 1711, available online at www2.scc.rutgers.edu/spectator/text/march1711/no10.html.

26. Tom Standage, "Social Networking in the 1600s."

27. Andrew Pettegree, *The Invention of News: How the World Came to Know about Itself* (New Haven, CT: Yale University Press, 2014), 280.

28. Addison, *Spectator,* March 12, 1711.

29. See chapter 13, "The Age of the Journal" in Andrew Pettegree, *The Invention of News*.

30. See Colin Kiernan, "Swift and Science," *Historical Journal* 14, no. 4 (December 1971): 709–22.

31. For Swift's "Political Lying," see this online source at Bartleby.com: www.bartleby.com/209/633.html; also see Douglas Lane Patey, "Swift's Satire on 'Science' and the Structure of Gulliver's Travels," *ELH* 58, no. 4 (Winter 1991): 809–39.

32. See George Mayhew, "Swift's Bickerstaff Hoax as an April Fools' Joke," *Modern Philology* 61, no. 4 (May 1964): 270–80.

33. See Valerie Rumbold, "Burying the Fanatic Partridge: Swift's Holy Week Hoax," in *Politics and Literature in the Age of Swift: English and Irish Perspectives,* ed. Claude Rawson (New Haven, CT: Yale University Press, 2010); and George Mayhew, "Swift's Bickerstaff Hoax as an April Fools' Joke," *Modern Philology* 61, no. 4 (May 1964): 270–80.

34. See Mayhew, "Swift's Bickerstaff Hoax as an April Fools' Joke"; and Richard Bond, "John Partridge and the Company of Stationers," *Studies in Bibliography* 16 (1963): 61–80.

35. See Will Slauter, "The Paragraph as Information Technology: How News Traveled in the Eighteenth-Century Atlantic World," *Annales HSS* 67, no. 2 (2012): 253–78.

36. See Andrew Pettegree, "Was There an Enlightenment Culture of News?" in *Travelling Chronicles: News and Newspapers from the Early Modern Period to the Eighteenth Century*, ed. Siv Gøril Brandtzæg, Paul Goring, and Christine Watson (Leiden: Brill, 2018).

37. See Will Slauter, "The Paragraph as Information Technology: How News Traveled in the Eighteenth Century Atlantic World," *Annales HSS* 67, no. 2 (2012): 253–78.

38. See Robert Darnton, "The True History of Fake News," *NYR Daily, New York Review of Books*, February 13, 2017.

39. See Véronique Campion-Vincent and Christine Shojaei Kawan, "Marie-Antoinette et son célèbre dire," *Annales historiques de la Révolution française,* no. 327 (January/March 2002): 29–56.

40. See Robert Darnton, "An Early Information Society: News and the Media in Early Eighteenth Century Paris," *American Historical Review* 105, no. 1 (February 2000): 1–35; and Robert Darnton, *Poetry and the Police: Communication Networks in Eighteenth-Century Paris* (Cambridge MA: Harvard Belknap, 2010).

41. For the text online, see *"Le Gazetier cuirassé, ou anecdotes scandaleuses de la cour de France, 1771,"* available at https://gallica.bnf.fr/ark:/12148/ bpt6k10656221.image. On scandal and censorship in France during this period, see Robert Darnton, "The Forbidden Books of Pre-Revolutionary France," in *Re-Writing the French Revolution*, ed. Colin Lucas (Oxford: Clarendon Press, 1991); and Robert Darnton, *The Devil in the Holy Water, or the Art of Slander from Louis XIV to Napoleon* (Philadelphia: University of Pennsylvania Press, 2010).

42. See Dena Goodman, *The Republic of Letters: A Cultural History of French Enlightenment* (Ithaca: Cornell University Press, 1996).

43. On London coffeehouse versus Paris salon, see Bonnie Calhoun, "Shaping the Public Sphere: English Coffeehouses and French Salons and the Age of the Enlightenment," *Colgate Academic Review* 3 (2012): Article 7.

44. Quoted in the prologue in Jonathan Beckman, *How to Ruin a Queen: Marie Antoinette, the Stolen Diamonds and the Scandal that Shook the French Throne* (London: John Murray, 2014).

45. On the Diamond Necklace affair, see Jonathan Beckman, *How to Ruin a Queen*; and in French, Evelyne Lever, *L'affaire du collier* (Paris: Fayard, 2013).

46. See Lynn Hunt, "The Many Bodies of Marie Antoinette: Political Pornography and the Problem of the Feminine in the French Revolution," in *The French Revolution: Recent Debates and New Controversies*, ed. Gary Kates (London: Routledge, 1998).

47. See Nancy Barker, "'Let Them Eat Cake'—The Mythical Marie Antoinette and the French Revolution," *Historian* 55, no. 4 (Summer 1993), 723.

48. See Terry Castle, "Marie Antoinette Obsession," *Representations*, no. 38 (Spring 1992): 1–38; also see Nancy Barker, "'Let Them Eat Cake'—The Mythical Marie Antoinette and the French Revolution,": 709–24.

49. The 1913 edition of *An Adventure* can be consulted at this link: https:// archive.org/details/adventurewithapp00mobe.

50. See Alex Owen, "'Borderland Forms': Arthur Conan Doyle, Albion's Daughters, and the Politics of the Cottingley Fairies," *History Workshop*, no. 38 (1994): 48–85.

51. The Conan Doyle article in *Strand Magazine,* "Fairies Photographed," published in December 1920, can be found online at www.arthur-conan-doyle.com/index.php/Fairies_Photographed.

52. See chapter 2 of Conan Doyle's *The Coming of the Fairies* (London: Hodder & Stoughton 1922); it can be consulted online here: www.arthur-conan-doyle.com/index.php/The_Coming_of_the_Fairies. Also see David Barnett, "Why Do So Many People Still Believe in the Cottingley Fairies?" *Daily Telegraph*, July 17, 2017.

53. See Castle, "Marie Antoinette Obsession," 1–3.

10. ALL THE NEWS THAT'S FIT TO FAKE

1. See Daniel Mendelsohn, "Heroine Addict: What Theodor Fontane's Women Want," *New Yorker*, March 7, 2011.

2. See Daniel Mendelsohn, "Heroine Addict."

3. Petra McGillen, "Techniques of 19th-Century Fake News Reporter Teach Us Why We Fall for It Today," *Observer*, July 4, 2017.

4. See Petra McGillen, "Techniques of 19th Century Fake News Reporter Teach Us Why We Fall For It Today," *Conversation,* April 6, 2017; and Nick Fouriezos, "Tracing the Origins of Fake News Back to 19th Century Germany," *Ozy*, May 16, 2017.

5. See Graeme Garrard, "Nietzsche, for and against the Enlightenment," *Review of Politics* 70, no. 4 (Fall 2008): 595–608.

6. On the Counter Enlightenment, see Isaiah Berlin's famous essay, "The Counter Enlightenment," first published in 1973, available online at http://berlin.wolf.ox.ac.uk/published_works/ac/counter-enlightenment.pdf. Also see Zeev Sternhell, *The Anti-Enlightenment Tradition* (New Haven, CT: Yale University Press, 2010). The notion of "Counter Enlightenment" has been challenged by Robert Norton, "The Myth of the Counter Enlightenment," *Journal of the History of Ideas* 68, no. 4 (October 2007): 635–58.

7. Soren Kierkegaard, *Concluding Unscientific Postscript* (Princeton: Princeton University Press, 1968); and Michael Levine, "Kierkegaardian Dogma: Inwardness and Objective Uncertainty," *International Journal for Philosophy of Religion* 14, no. 3 (1983): 183–87.

8. The full text of Edmund Burke's treatise, *A Philosophical Inquiry into the Origins of Our Ideas of the Sublime and Beautiful,* can be accessed here: www.gutenberg.org/files/15043/15043-h/15043-h.htm.

9. See Part II, section 1, Edmund Burke, *A Philosophical Inquiry into the Origins of Our Ideas of the Sublime and Beautiful* (Oxford: Oxford University Press, 1990).

10. See Warren Bovee, *Discovering Journalism* (Westport, CT: Praeger, 1999), 95; also cited in Matthew Goodman, *The Sun and the Moon: The Remark-*

able True Account of Hoaxers, Showmen, Dueling Journalists, and Lunar Man-Bats in Nineteenth-Century New York (New York: Basic Books, 2008).

11. See Frederick Hudson, *Journalism in the United States,* vol. 1 (London: Routledge, 2000), 422; also cited in István Kornél Vida, "The Great Moon Hoax," *Hungarian Journal of English and American Studies* (HJEAS) 18, no. 1/2 (Spring–Fall 2012): 431–41.

12. For a book on the Great Moon Hoax, see Matthew Goodman, *The Sun and the Moon: The Remarkable True Account of Hoaxers, Showmen, Dueling Journalists, and Lunar Man-Bats in Nineteenth-Century New York* (New York: Basic Books, 2008).

13. See Sarah Tindal Kareem, "Fictions, Lies, and Baron Munchausen's Narrative," *Modern Philology* 109, no. 4 (May 2012): 483–509.

14. See James Fredal, "The Perennial Pleasure of the Hoax," *Philosophy & Rhetoric* 47, no. 1 (2014): 73–97.

15. See David Copeland, "A Series of Fortunate Events: Why People Believed Richard Adams Locke's Moon Hoax," *Journalism History* 33, no. 3 (Fall 2007); Paul Maliszewski, "Paper Moon," *Wilson Quarterly* 29, no. 1 (Winter 2005): 26–34; and Kevin Young, "Moon Shot: Race, A Hoax and the Birth of Fake News," *New Yorker,* October 21, 2017.

16. See Jeffrey Hopes, "The Age of Credulity: Believing the Unbelievable in the Century of the Enlightenment," *Revue de la Société d'études anglo-américaines des XVIIe et XVIIIe siècles,* HS3 (2013): 181–91.

17. Tim Fulford, "Pagodas and Pregnant Throes: Orientalism, Millenarianism and Robert Southey," in *Romanticism and Millenarianism,* ed. Tim Fulford (London: Palgrave, 2002), 124.

18. The Tocqueville quote is from book 1, chapter 17 of *Democracy in America,* cited in Richard Lee Rogers, "The Urban Threshold and the Second Great Awakening: Revivalism in New York State, 1825-1835," *Journal for the Scientific Study of Religion* 49, no. 4 (December 2010): 694–709.

19. See Paul Johnson and Sean Wilentz, *The Kingdom of Matthias: A Story of Sex and Salvation in Nineteenth Century America* (New York: Oxford University Press, 1994); and Gordon Wood, "The Wandering Jewish Prophet in New York," *New York Review of Books,* October 20, 1994.

20. On the nineteenth-century penny press, see Michael Schudson, "The Revolution in American Journalism in the Age of Egalitarianism: The Penny Press," in *Discovering the News* (New York: Basic Books, 1978), 12–31.

21. On the tensions between science and religion, see Jeff Hardin, Ronald Numbers, and Ronald Binzley, eds., *The Warfare Between Science and Religion* (Baltimore, MD: Johns Hopkins University Press, 2018); and John Hedley Brooke, *Science and Religion* (Cambridge: Cambridge University Press, 1991).

22. On Bishop James Ussher's creation chronology, see Stephen Jay Gould, "Fall in the House of Ussher," *Natural History* 100 (November 1991): 12–21.

23. See Matt Simon, "Fantastically Wrong: The Scientist Who Thought That 22 Trillion Aliens Lived in Our Solar System," *Wired,* October 12, 2014.

24. For Locke's article in *New World* and his views on Reverend Dick, see chapter 16 in Matthew Goodman, *The Sun and the Moon: The Remarkable True*

Account of Hoaxers, Showmen, Dueling Journalists, and Lunar Man-Bats in Nineteenth-Century New York (New York: Basic Books, 2008).

25. See Steven Kawaler and J. Veverka, "The Habitable Sun: One of William Herschel's Stranger Ideas," *Royal Astronomical Society of Canada Journal* 75 (1981): 46–55.

26. See Vida, "The Great Moon Hoax."

27. See Vida, "The Great Moon Hoax"; and Donald Fernie, "Marginalia: The Great Moon Hoax," *American Scientist* 81, no. 2 (March–April 1993): 120–22.

28. See Jeffrey Bilbro, "'That Petrified Laugh': Mark Twain's Hoaxes in the West and Camelot," *Journal of Narrative Theory* 41, no. 2 (Summer 2011): 204–34; and Lynda Walsh, *Sins against Science: The Scientific Media Hoaxes of Poe, Twain, and Others* (New York: State University of New York Press, 2003).

29. See Carlo Martinez, "E. A. Poe's 'Hans Pfaall,' the Penny Press, and the Autonomy of the Literary Field," *Edgar Allan Poe Review* 12, no. 1 (Spring 2011): 6–31; and Doris V. Falk, "Thomas Low Nichols, Poe, and the 'Balloon Hoax,'" *Poe Studies* 5, no. 2 (December 1972): 48–49.

30. See appendix D, "Richard Adams Locke in Poe's Literati of New York City, 1850," in *Voyage to the Moon and Other Imaginary Lunar Flights of Fancy in Antebellum America,* ed. Paul Gutjahr (London: Anthem Press, 2018), 227.

31. See the Epilogue in Matthew Goodman, *The Sun and the Moon*; and appendix D, "'Richard Adams Locke' in Edgar Allan Poe's The Literati of New York City, 1850," in *Voyage to the Moon and Other Lunar Flights of Fancy in Antebellum America*, ed. Paul Gutjahr (London: Anthem Press, 2018).

32. See Hampton Sides, "A Shocking Sabbath Carnival of Death," *Slate*, July 24, 2014; and "A Carnival of Death on New York's Streets," *Washington Post*, June 13, 2017.

33. See Richard Salmon, "'A Simulacrum of Power': Intimacy and Abstraction in the Rhetoric of the New Journalism," *Victorian Periodicals Review* 30, no. 1 (Spring 1997): 41–52.

34. See Bernard Lightman, "The Story of Nature: Victorian Popularizers and Scientific Narrative," *Victorian Review* 25, no. 2 (Winter 2000): 1–29.

11. BISMARCK'S FAKE NEWS

1. See Luke Harding, "How France Missed a Chance to Sink Bismarck," *Guardian*, August 22, 2006; and the chapter "Women, Marriage and Domestic Life" in Katherine Anne Lerman, *Bismarck: Profiles in Power* (London: Routledge, 2013).

2. For a biography of Bismarck, see Jonathan Steinberg, *Bismarck: A Life* (Oxford: Oxford University Press, 2011). For a life of Napoleon III, see Alan Strauss-Schom, *The Shadow Emperor: A Biography of Napoleon III* (New York: St. Martin's, 2018).

3. Victor Hugo wrote the pamphlet from Brussels in 1852, shortly after Louis-Napoleon Bonaparte's coup d'état. The original text of *Napoléon le Petit* is available here: https://gallica.bnf.fr/ark:/12148/bpt6k5406147k/f8.image. For

Bismarck's famous remark about Napoleon III, see the chapter, "A Bit about Personalities" in David Wetzel, *Duel of Giants: Bismarck, Napoleon III, and the Origins of the Franco-Prussian* War (Madison: University of Wisconsin Press, 2003).

4. See the chapter "The Last Straw," in Lynn Case, *French Opinion on War and Diplomacy during the Second Empire* (Philadelphia: University of Pennsylvania Press, 1954).

5. See Simon Bainbridge, *Napoleon and English Romanticism* (Cambridge: Cambridge University Press, 1995); and Paul Stock, "The Romantic Appropriation of Napoleon," *Journal of European Studies* 36, no. 3 (2006): 363–88.

6. See Fabrice Erre, *Le règne de la Poire. Caricatures de l'esprit bourgeois de Louis-Philippe à nos jours* (Paris: Champ Vallon, 2011); and Ségolène Le Men, "Calligraphie, calligramme, caricature," *Langages*, no. 75 (September 1984): 83–101.

7. See Philip Mansel, "Courts in Exile: Bourbons, Bonapartes and Orléans in London, from George III to Edward VII," in *A History of the French in London*, ed. Debra Kelly and Martyn Cornick (London: University of London, Institute of Historical Research, 2013). See also a biography of Napoleon III: John Bierman, *Napoleon III and His Carnival Empire* (New York: St. Martin's, 1988).

8. See Gérard-Michel Thermeau, "Ils étaient Présidents: Louis-Napoléon Bonaparte," *Contrepoints*, December 11, 2016.

9. See Judith Wechsler, "Daumier and Censorship, 1866-1872," *Yale French Studies,* no. 122, Out of Sight: Political Censorship of the Visual Arts in Nineteenth-Century France (2012): 53–78; and Robert Justin Goldstein, "Fighting French Censorship, 1815-188," *French Review* 71, no. 5 (April 1998): 785–96.

10. See Giuseppe Pucci, "Caesar the Foe: Roman Conquest and National Resistance in French Popular Culture," in *Julius Caesar in Western Culture*, ed. Maria Wyke (Oxford: Blackwell, 2006).

11. See Giuseppe Pucci, "Caesar the Foe."

12. See Michel Reddé, "Alésia et la mémoire nationale française," *Anabases*, no. 9 (2009): 13–24; and Michael Dietler, "'Our Ancestors the Gauls': Archaeology, Ethnic Nationalism, and the Manipulation of Celtic Identity in Modern Europe," *American Anthropologist* 96, no. 3 (September 1994): 584–605.

13. See the chapter "The Last Straw" in Lynn Case, *French Opinion on War and Diplomacy during the Second Empire* (Philadelphia: University of Pennsylvania Press, 1954); and William Halperin, "The Origins of the Franco-Prussian War Revisited: Bismarck and the Hohenzollern Candidature for the Spanish Throne," *Journal of Modern History* 45, no. 1 (March 1973): 83–91.

14. See Linda Senne and Simon Moore, "Bismarck, Propaganda and Public Relations," *Public Relations Review* 41 (2015): 326–34; Robert Keyserlingk, "Bismarck and the Press: The Example of the National Liberals," *Historical Papers* 2, no. 1 (1967): 198–215.

15. For a comparison of the original Ems telegram with Bismarck's edited version that went to newspapers, see http://germanhistorydocs.ghi-dc.org/pdf/eng/505_Orig%20Ed%20Ems%20Dispatch_148.pdf.

16. See the section on the Ems Dispatch in Bismarck's memoirs, *Bismarck: The Man & the Statesman*, vol. 2 (New York: Cosimo Classics, 2005), 101. For a historians' debate on the causes of the Franco-Prussian War, see Josef Becker, "The Franco-Prussian Conflict of 1870 and Bismarck's Concept of a 'Provoked Defensive War': A Response to David Wetzel," *Central European History* 41, no. 1 (January 2008): 93–109.

17. See chapter 2, "The Armies in 1870," in Geoffrey Wawro, *The Franco-Prussian War: The German Conquest of France in 1870-1871* (Cambridge: Cambridge University Press, 2003).

18. See Michèle Martin and Christopher Bodnar, "The Illustrated Press under Siege: Technological Imagination in the Paris Siege, 1870–1871," *Urban History* 36, no. 1 (May 2009): 67–85.

19. See chapter 12, "The Hunger," in Alistair Horne, *The Fall of Paris: The Siege and the Commune, 1870-71* (London: Penguin, 2007).

20. Chapter 12, "The Hunger," in Horne, *The Fall of Paris.*

21. See chapter 12, "The Hunger," in Horne, *The Fall of Paris*. The Manet letter citation is from the catalogue from the exhibition *Manet 1832–1883,* Metropolitan Museum of Modern Art, 1983.

22. Robert Solomon and Kathleen M. Higgins, *Reading Nietzsche* (New York: Oxford University Press, 1988), 91.

12. TO HELL WITH SPAIN

1. W. Joseph Campbell, *Getting It Wrong: Debunking the Greatest Myths in American Journalism* (Oakland: University of California Press, 2016), 13; also cited in Kenneth Whyte, *The Uncrowned King: The Sensational Rise of William Randolph Hearst* (Berkeley: Counterpoint, 2009).

2. Campbell, *Getting It Wrong*, 13.

3. See chapter 1, "I'll Furnish the War: The Making of a Media Myth," in W. Joseph Campbell, *Getting It Wrong.*

4. Bill Blackbeard, *R. F. Outcault's The Yellow Kid: A Centennial Celebration of the Kid Who Started the Comics* (Northampton, MA: Kitchen Sink Press, 1995); and Ian Gordon, "Mass Market Modernism: Comic Strips and the Culture of Consumption," *Australasian Journal of American Studies* 14, no. 2 (December 1995): 49–66.

5. See Maggie Ryan Sandford, "How the Yellow Kid Fueled the Pulitzer/ Hearst Rivalry," *Mental Floss*, February 4, 2013.

6. See the chapter "Crusaders and Conservatives, 1875–1912: Journalism in Yellow and Gray," in Christopher B. Daly, *Covering America: A Narrative History of a Nation's Journalism* (Amherst: University of Massachusetts Press, 2012); and James McGrath Morris, "Man of the World," *Wilson Quarterly* 34, no. 1 (Winter 2010): 28–33.

7. See John Offner, "McKinley and the Spanish-American War," *Presidential Studies Quarterly* 34, no. 1, Going to War (March 2004): 50–61.

8. See Joseph Campbell, "William Randolph Hearst: Mythical Media Bogeyman," BBC, August 14, 2011.

9. Clifford Krauss, "Remember Yellow Journalism," *New York Times,* February 15, 1998. For a digital archive of that *World* front page, see https://digital-collections.nypl.org/items/84ea964f-4861-b09d-e040-e00a18066a1d.

10. See Robert Love, "Before Jon Stewart: Fake News Is Back, but Our Tolerance for It Isn't What It Was before Journalism Donned the Mantle of Authority," *Columbia Journalism Review*, March/April 2007; also cited in Jonathan Ladd, *Why Americans Hate the News Media and How It Matters* (Princeton: Princeton University Press, 2012), 37.

11. See "Anthony's Body Not Yet Claimed," *New York Times,* November 26, 1899.

12. See John Maxwell Hamilton, "In a Battle for Readers, Two Media Barons Sparked a War in the 1890s," *National Geographic,* April 16, 2019.

13. See William Cossen, "Monk in the Middle: The Awful Disclosures of the Hotel Dieu Nunnery and the Making of Catholic Identity," *American Catholic Studies* 125, no. 1 (Spring 2014): 25–45; and Susan Griffith, "Awful Disclosures: Women's Evidence in the Escaped Nun's Tale," *PMLA* 111, no. 1 (January 1996): 93–107.

14. See Raymond H. Schmandt, "A Selection of Sources Dealing with the Nativist Riots of 1844," *Records of the American Catholic Historical Society of Philadelphia* 80, nos. 2/3 (June– September 1969): 68–113; and Amanda Beyer-Purvis, "The Philadelphia Bible Riots of 1844: Contest over the Rights of Citizens," *Pennsylvania History: A Journal of Mid-Atlantic Studies* 83, no. 3 (Summer 2016): 366–93.

15. Raymond Cohn, "Nativism and the End of the Mass Migration of the 1840s and 1850s," *Journal of Economic History* 60, no. 2 (June 2000): 361–83; and Michael W. Hughey, "Americanism and Its Discontents: Protestantism, Nativism, and Political Heresy in America," *International Journal of Politics, Culture, and Society* 5, no. 4 (Summer 1992): 533–53.

16. See Thomas J. Curran, "Assimilation and Nativism," *International Migration Digest* 3, no. 1 (Spring 1966): 15–25; and Thomas Gladsky, "James Fenimore Cooper and American Nativism," *Studies in the American Renaissance* (1994): 43–53.

17. See Scott Wright, "The Northwestern Chronicle and the Spanish-American War: American Catholic Attitudes Regarding the 'Splendid Little War,'" *American Catholic Studies* 116, no. 4 (Winter 2005): 55–68.

18. See Leroy G. Dorsey and Rachel M. Harlow, "'We Want Americans Pure and Simple': Theodore Roosevelt and the Myth of Americanism," *Rhetoric and Public Affairs* 6, no. 1 (Spring 2003): 55–78.

19. See J. Tillapaugh, "Theodore Roosevelt and the Rough Riders: A Century of Leadership in Film," in *Hollywood's White House: The American Presidency in Film and History*, ed. Peter Rollins and John O'Connor (Lexington: University of Kentucky Press, 2003); and David Greenberg, "Theodore Roosevelt and the Image of Presidential Activism," *Social Research* 78, no. 4 (Winter 2011): 1057–88.

20. See Mike Dash, "The Early History of Faking War on Film," *Smithsonian.com*, November 19, 2012; and Frank Kessler and Sabine Lenk, "What Is a Fake Image?," in *The Early Image in Cinema*, ed. Scott Curtis et al. (Bloomington: Indiana University Press, 2018).

21. See Jeet Heer, "America Has Always Been Violent and Angry," *New Republic,* June 15, 2017; and Eric Rauchway, *Murdering McKinley: The Making of Theodore Roosevelt's America* (New York: Hill and Wang, 2003).

13. THE GUN THAT KILLED THE HUN

1. For a biography of Edith Cavell, see Diana Souhami, *Edith Cavell* (London: Quercus, 2010).

2. See Joe Sommerlad, "Who Was Edith Cavell?" *Independent,* December 3, 2018.

3. See W. F. Deedes, "Does Cavell Give the Germans Cause for Regret?" *Telegraph*, August 25, 2006.

4. See Richard Norton-Taylor, "Edith Cavell, Shot by Germans during WWI, Celebrated 100 Years on," *Guardian*, October 12, 2015.

5. Christine Hallett, *Edith Cavell and Her Legend* (London: Palgrave, 2019), 52.

6. See the report in *Times* of London right after the execution, "Why Miss Cavell Was Shot," *Times,* October 13, 1915; and "Miss Cavell's Fate," *British Medical Journal*, 2, no. 2861 (October 30, 1915): 651.

7. See Nicoletta F. Gullace, "Sexual Violence and Family Honor: British Propaganda and International Law during the First World War," *American Historical Review* 102, no. 3 (June 1997): 714–47.

8. See the introduction in John Röhl, *The Kaiser and His Court: Wilhelm II and the Government of Germany* (Cambridge: Cambridge University Press, 1994), 14.

9. See Andreas Musolff, "Wilhelm II's 'Hun Speech' and Its Alleged Resemiotization during World War I," *Language and Semiotic Studies* 3, no. 3 (2017): 42–59.

10. Rudyard Kipling's poem, "The Rowers," is available online at www.poetryloverspage.com/poets/kipling/rowers.html.

11. T. W. Offin, *How the Germans Took London: Forewarned, Forearmed* (London: Edmund Durrant, 1900).

12. Rudyard Kipling's poem "For All We Have and Are" is available online at www.poetryfoundation.org/poems/57431/for-all-we-have-and-are.

13. See Michael Matin, "The Hun Is at the Gate: Historicizing Kipling's Militaristic Rhetoric from the Imperial Periphery to the National Center," *Studies in the Novel* 31, no. 4 (Winter 1999): 432–70.

14. See Philip Taylor, "The Foreign Office and British Propaganda during the First World War," *Historical Journal* 23, no. 4 (December 1980): 875–98.

15. See Deian Hopkin, "Domestic Censorship in the First World War," *Journal of Contemporary History* 5, no. 4 (1970): 151–69.

16. See "War's Realities on the Cinema," *Times,* August 22, 1916.

17. See Luke McKernan, "Patriotism and Profit: Charles Urban and British Official War Films in America during the First World War," *Film History* 14, nos. 3/4 (2002): 369–89.

18. See "Atrocity Propaganda," British Library, January 29, 2014, available online at www.bl.uk/world-war-one/articles/atrocity-propaganda.

19. See "The Corpse Factory and the Birth of Fake News," BBC, February 17, 2017.

20. See Joachim Neander and Randal Marlin, "Media and Propaganda: The Northcliffe Press and the Corpse Factory Story of World War I," *Global Media Journal—Canadian Edition* 3, no. 2 (2010): 67–82; and Joachim Neander, *The German Corpse Factory: The Master Hoax of British Propaganda in the First World War* (Saarbrücken, Germany: Saarland University Press, 2013).

21. See "The Corpse Factory and the Birth of Fake News," BBC, February 17, 2017.

22. See Nicholas Martin, "'Fighting a Philosophy': The Figure of Nietzsche in British Propaganda of the First World War," *Modern Language Review* 98, no. 2 (April 2003): 367–80.

23. Martin, "'Fighting a Philosophy,'" 372.

24. See Martin, "'Fighting a Philosophy'"; and William Archer, "Fighting a Philosophy," *North American Review* 201, no. 710 (January 1915): 30–44.

25. Theodor Schieder and Alexandra Hendee, "Nietzsche and Bismarck," *Historian* 29, no. 4 (August 1967): 584–604.

26. See Richard Norton-Taylor, "Edith Cavell, Shot by Germans during WWI, Celebrated 100 Years On," *Guardian*, October 12, 2015.

27. See Shane Barnay, "The Mythic Matters of Edith Cavell: Propaganda, Legend, Myth and Memory," *Historical Reflections/Réflexions Historiques* 31, no. 2 (Summer 2005): 217–33.

28. Vanessa Heggie, "Edith Cavell: Nurse, Martyr and Spy?" *Guardian*, October 12, 2015.

29. Woodrow Wilson address in Milwaukee, January 31, 1916, in *Addresses of President Wilson*, January 27–February 3, 1916, vol. 563, issue 51 (Washington, DC: Government Printing Office, 1916), 30.

30. For President Wilson's speech to Congress on February 3, 1917, see https://wwi.lib.byu.edu/index.php/President_Wilson%27s_Address_to_Both_Houses_of_Congress_in_Joint_Session,_February_3,_1917.

31. See Erick Trickey, "How Woodrow Wilson's War Speech to Congress Changed Him—and the Nation," *Smithsonianmag.com*, April 3, 2017.

32. See chapter 4, "World War I and the Triumph of the Promotional State," in Emily Rosenberg, *Spreading the American Dream* (New York: Hill and Wang, 1982).

33. See Elmer E. Cornwell Jr., "Wilson, Creel and the Presidency," *Public Opinion Quarterly* 23, no. 2 (Summer 1959): 189–202.

34. See Eric Van Schaack, "The Division of Pictorial Publicity in World War I," *Design Issues*, Vol. 22, No. 1 (Winter, 2006): 32–45.

35. See Erik Kirschbaum, *Burning Beethoven: The Eradication of German Culture in the United States during World War I* (New York: Berlinica Publishing, 2014).

36. See Donald Hickey, "The Prager Affair: A Study in Wartime Hysteria," *Journal of the Illinois State Historical Society* 62, no. 2 (Summer 1969): 117–34.

37. See Alex Ross, "The Star-Spangled Banner Hysteria of 1917," *New Yorker,* July 2, 2019; and Melissa Burrage, *The Karl Muck Scandal: Classical Music and Xenophobia in World War I America* (Rochester: University of Rochester Press, 2019).

38. See Edmond Bowles, "Karl Muck and His Compatriots: German Conductors in America during World War I (and How They Coped)," *American Music* 25, no. 4 (Winter 2007): 405–40.

39. See Krystina Benson, "Archival analysis of the Committee on Public Information: The Relationship between Propaganda, Journalism and Popular Culture," *International Journal of Technology, Knowledge and Society* 6, no. 4 (2019): 151–64.

40. See Christopher B. Daly, "How Woodrow Wilson's Propaganda Machine Changed American Journalism," *Smithsonian.com*, April 28, 2017.

41. See Arthur Ponsonby, *Falsehood in War-Time, Containing an Assortment of Lies Circulated throughout the Nations during the Great War* (London: George Allen and Unwin, 1928).

42. Harold Lasswell, Ralph Casey, and Bruce Lannes Smith, *Propaganda and Promotional Activities* (Minneapolis: University of Minnesota Press, 1935), available online at https://muse.jhu.edu/book/32847; and Harold Lasswell, "Theory of Propaganda," *American Political Science Review* 21, no. 3 (August 1927): 627–31.

43. See Heinz Eulau, "Wilsonian Idealist: Walter Lippmann Goes to War," *The Antioch Review* 14, no. 1 (Spring 1954): 87–108.

44. See chapter 1 in Walter Lippmann, *Liberty and the News* (New York: Harcourt, Brace & Howe, 1920).

45. See chapter 4, "The Task of the Public," in *The Essential Lippmann: A Political Philosophy for Liberal Democracy*, ed. Clinton Rossiter and James Lare (Cambridge, MA: Harvard University Press, 1982).

46. Alan Axelrod, *Selling the Great War: The Making of American Propaganda* (New York: St. Martin's Press, 2009), 218. The full text of Bernays's *Propaganda* can be found at www.historyisaweapon.org/defcon1/bernprop.html.

47. See Richard Norton-Taylor, "Zinoviev Letter Was Dirty Trick by MI6," *Guardian*, February 4, 1999.

14. TRIUMPH OF THE WILL

1. See chapter 6, "War Propaganda," in Adolf Hitler's *Mein Kampf* (Boston: Houghton Mifflin, 1998), another translation available online at www.hitler.org/writings/Mein_Kampf/mkv1ch06.html.

2. See chapter 6 in Hitler, *Mein Kampf*; and David Welch, *Germany and Propaganda in World War I: Pacifism, Mobilization and Total War* (London: I.B. Tauris, 2014), 264.

3. David Welch, *The Third Reich: Politics and Propaganda* (London: Routledge, 2002), 10.

4. See chapter 6, Hitler, *Mein Kampf*.

5. See chapter 6, Hitler, *Mein Kampf*.

6. See chapter 10, Hitler, *Mein Kampf*.

7. See the chapters "Books That Hitler Read Into" and "Hitler's Erudition and Reading Habits," in Ambrus Miskolczy, *Hitler's Library* (Budapest: Central European University Press, 2003).

8. On the Nazis and jazz music, see Michael Kater, "Forbidden Fruit? Jazz in the Third Reich," *American Historical Review* 94, no. 1 (February 1989): 11–43. The Spengler quote is from his 1933 book, *Jahr der Entscheidung* (Munich: C.H. Beck, 1933), published in English the following year as *The Hour of Decision* (New York: Alfred A. Knopf, 1934).

9. See chapter 1, Hitler, *Mein Kampf*.

10. See Frank Josserand, "Wagner and German Nationalism," *Southwestern Social Science Quarterly* 43, no. 3 (December 1962): 223–34; and Nicholas Vazsonyi, "Marketing German Identity: Richard Wagner's 'Enterprise,'" *German Studies Review* 28, no. 2 (May 2005): 327–46.

11. Richard Wagner, *Art and Revolution*, available online at http://www.public-library.uk/ebooks/11/97.pdf.

12. Richard Wagner, *Jewishness in Music*, available online at www.jrbooksonline.com/pdf_books/judaisminmusic.pdf.

13. Wagner, *Jewishness in Music*.

14. Wagner, *Jewishness in Music*.

15. For Wagner's letter to Ludwig II of Bavaria, see Jacob Katz, *The Darker Side of Genius* (Hanover, NH: Brandeis University Press, 1986), 35–36.

16. See Brigitte Hamann, *Winifred Wagner: A Life at the Heart of Hitler's Bayreuth* (London: Granta, 2006).

17. See Clemency Burton-Hill, "Richard Strauss, a Reluctant Nazi," *BBC Culture*, June 10, 2014. Also see Michael Kater, *The Twisted Muse: Musicians and Their Music in the Third Reich* (New York: Oxford University Press, 1997), chapter 1, available at https://archive.nytimes.com/www.nytimes.com/books/first/k/kater-muse.html.

18. See Nicholas O'Shaughnessy, *Selling Hitler: Propaganda and the Nazi Brand* (London: Hurst, 2016).

19. Goebbels made these remarks, "Churchill's Lie Factory," during the Second World War in 1941, speaking against Winston Churchill. The text is available online at https://research.calvin.edu/german-propaganda-archive/goeb29.htm.

20. Goebbels's "big lie" accusation against Winston Churchill was published in 1941 under the title "Aus Churchills Lügenfabrik" ("Churchill's Lie Factory") in Joseph Goebbels, *Die Zeit ohne Beispiel* (Munich: Zentralverlag der NSDAP,

1941). The text is available online at https://research.calvin.edu/german-propaganda-archive/goeb29.htm.

21. Hannah Arendt quoted in Paul Mason, "Reading Arendt Is Not Enough," *NYR Daily, New York Review of Books,* May 2, 2019. Original source: Hannah Arendt, *The Origins of Totalitarianism* (New York: Harcourt Brace Jovanovich, 1951).

22. See Pamela Potter, "Dismantling a Dystopia: On the Historiography of Music in the Third Reich," *Central European History* 40, no. 4 (December 2007): 623–51.

23. See Johann Chapoutot, *Greeks, Romans, Germans: How the Nazis Usurped Europe's Classical Past* (Berkeley: University of California Press, 2016).

24. See Neil Levi, "'Judge for Yourselves!' The 'Degenerate Art' Exhibition as Political Spectacle," *October* 85 (Summer 1998): 41–64.

25. See Mary-Margaret Goggin, "'Decent' vs. 'Degenerate' Art: The National Socialist Case," *Art Journal* 50, no. 4, Censorship II (Winter 1991): 84–92.

26. See Ron Torossian, "Hitler's Nazi Germany used an American PR agency," *Observer*, December 22, 2014; and Tim Morris, "'Poison Ivy' Lee and Propaganda," *Spin*, September 1, 2014.

27. Cyril Brown, "New Popular Idol Rises in Bavaria," *New York Times,* November 21, 1922.

28. See Zack Beauchamp, "The *New York Times*' First Article about Hitler's Rise Is Absolutely Stunning," *Vox*, March 3, 2016.

29. See "America's Alt-Right Learns to Speak Nazi: 'Lügenpresse,'" *Economist,* November 24, 2016.

30. See Rafael Medoff, "The American Papers That Praised Hitler," *Daily Beast,* June 26, 2017.

31. See Peter Schjeldahl, "The Anti-Modernists: Why the Third Reich Targeted Artists," *New Yorker*, March 24, 2014.

32. See chapter 1, "Dateline Berlin: Covering the Nazi Whirlwind" in Deborah Lipstadt, *Beyond Belief: The American Press and the Coming Holocaust 1933–45* (New York: Free Press, 1986); and Michael Zalampas, *Adolf Hitler and the Third Reich in American Magazines, 1923–39* (New York: Madison, 1989).

33. See Hedwig Mauer Simpson, "Hitler at Home in the Clouds," *New York Times Magazine*, August 20, 1939, available online at www.nytimes.com/1939/08/20/archives/herr-hitler-at-home-in-the-clouds-high-up-on-his-favorite-mountain.html.

34. See Jeremy Berke, "The American Media's Awkward Fawning over Hitler's Taste in Home Decor," *Atlas Obscura*, September 4, 2014; and Matt Giles, "When Newspapers Covered the Private Lives of Nazis," Longreads.com, November 30, 2017.

35. See Elisabeth Zerofsky, "The Moral Failings of American Press Coverage of Nazi Germany," *New Yorker,* March 14, 2019.

36. See James Q. Whitman's book, *Hitler's American Model: The United States and the Making of Nazi Race Law* (Princeton: Princeton University Press, 2017).

37. See Alex Ross, "How American Racism Influenced Hitler," *New Yorker,* April 23, 2018.

38. See chapter 5, "From Luther to Hitler," in Heiko Oberman, *The Two Reformations* (New Haven, CT: Yale University Press, 2003).

39. See Ken Kelman, "Propaganda as Vision: Triumph of the Will," *Logos* 2, no. 4 (Fall 2003); and Catherine M. Soussloff and Bill Nichols, "Leni Riefenstahl: The Power of the Image," *Discourse* 18, no. 3 (Spring 1996): 20–44.

40. See "The Cinematic Genius and Hitler Favourite: The Dark Story of Leni Riefenstahl," *Telegraph,* May 27, 2016.

41. See chapter 2, "Who Influenced Hitler's Religion?" in Richard Weikart, *Hitler's Religion: The Twisted Beliefs That Drove the Third Reich* (Washington, DC: Regnery History, 2016). The photo was also included in the photo book published by Hitler's official photographer, Heinrich Hoffmann, titled *Hitler Wie Ihn Keiner Kennt* (*The Hitler That Nobody Knows*).

42. See David Wroe, "Criminal Manipulation of Nietzsche by Sister to Make Him Look Anti-Semitic," *Daily Telegraph,* January 19, 2010. For a more balanced assessment of Elisabeth Nietzsche, see Robert C. Holub, "The Elisabeth Legend: The Cleansing of Nietzsche and the Sullying of His Sister," in *Nietzsche, Godfather of Fascism: On the Uses and Abuses of a Philosophy*, ed. Jacob Golomb and Robert S. Wistrich (Princeton: Princeton University Press, 2002).

43. See Joshua Rothman, "Is Heidegger Contaminated by Nazism?" *New Yorker,* April 28, 2014.

44. See Damon Linker, "We Still Need Martin Heidegger—Despite His Nazism," *Week*, March 18, 2014; also See Rothman, "Is Heidegger Contaminated by Nazism?"

45. See Adam Kirsch, "The Jewish Question: Martin Heidegger," *New York Times*, May 7, 2010.

46. See Roger Berkowitz, "Heidegger, Being Human, and Antisemitism," *American Interest*, May 3, 2014; and Jean-Pierre Hérubel, "The Darker Side of Light: Heidegger and Nazism," *Shofar* 10, no. 1 (Fall 1991): 85–105.

47. See Françoise Dastur, " Réception et non-réception de Heidegger en France," *Revue Germanique Internationale,* no. 13 (2011): 35–57. See also Hubert Dreyfus and Mark Wrathall, eds., *A Companion to Heidegger* (Oxford: Blackwell, 2005).

48. See Jürgen Habermas, "Work and Weltanschauung: The Heidegger Controversy from a German Perspective," *Critical Inquiry* 15, no. 2 (Winter 1989): 431–56. See also Michael Geyer, "The Restless Thought of Jürgen Habermas," *Times Literary Supplement,* October 4, 2017; and Peter Gordon, "A Lion in Winter," *Nation,* September 14, 2016.

49. See Hannah Arendt, "Martin Heidegger at Eighty," *New York Review of Books,* October 21, 1971. See also Daniel Maier-Katkin and Birgit Maier-Katkin, "Love and Reconciliation: The Case of Hannah Arendt and Martin Heidegger," *Harvard Review,* no. 32 (2007): 34–48.

50. Daniel Maier-Katkin, *Stranger from Abroad: Hannah Arendt, Martin Heidegger, Friendship and Forgiveness* (New York: W.W. Norton, 2010), 32.

51. See Hannah Arendt, *Eichmann in Jerusalem* (New York: Viking, 1963).

52. See Judith Shulevitz, "Arendt and Heidegger, an Affair to Forget?" *New York Times,* October 1, 1995; and Michael Jones, "Heidegger the Fox: Hannah Arendt's Hidden Dialogue," *New German Critique*, no. 73 (Winter 1998): 164–92.

53. See Adam Kirsch, "The Jewish Question: Martin Heidegger," *New York Times,* May 7, 2010.

54. This quote is from the chapter "Why I Write Such Excellent Books" in Nietzsche's *Ecce Homo,* available online at www.lexido.com/EBOOK_TEXTS/ECCE_HOMO_.aspx?S=4.

55. Allan Bloom analyzed Nietzsche's influence on leftist culture in his book *The Closing of the American Mind.* See the chapter "The Nietzscheanization of the Left and Vice Versa," in Allan Bloom, *The Closing of the American Mind* (New York: Simon & Schuster, 1987). See also Alex Ross, "Nietzsche's Eternal Return," *New Yorker,* October 14, 2019.

56. See Jason Daley, "Footage Recalls the Night Madison Square Garden Filled with Nazis," Smithsonian.org, October 13, 2017; and Sarah Kate Kramer, "When Nazis Took Manhattan," NPR, February 20, 2019.

57. See Frederick Brown's two books on France in this era, *For the Soul of France: Culture Wars in the Age of Dreyfus* (New York: Anchor Books, 2011); and *The Embrace of Unreason: France 1914–1940* (New York: Alfred A. Knopf, 2014).

58. Pierre Péan, *Une Jeunesse française* (Paris: Fayard, 1994).

15. SHAKEN, NOT STIRRED

1. See Helen Pidd, "TS Eliot's Damning Verdict on George Orwell's Animal Farm," *Guardian,* March 30, 2009; and Maria Popova, "The Freedom of the Press: George Orwell on the Media's Toxic Self-Censorship," *Brain Pickings,* August 16, 2013.

2. The text of President Harry Truman's "Truman Doctrine" speech in 1947 is available at https://avalon.law.yale.edu/20th_century/trudoc.asp.

3. See Stefan Beck, "Malignant Propaganda," *New Criterion,* June 12, 2003.

4. See Francine du Plessix Gray, "The Journalist and the Dictator," *New York Times*, June 24, 1990.

5. Sally Taylor, *Stalin's Apologist* (New York: Oxford University Press, 1990), 222.

6. See Gray, "The Journalist and the Dictator."

7. See *"New York Times* Statement about 1932 Pulitzer Prize Awarded to Walter Duranty," available online at www.nytco.com/company/prizes-awards/new-york-times-statement-about-1932-pulitzer-prize-awarded-to-walter-duranty.

8. See Gray, "The Journalist and the Dictator"; and Sally Taylor, *Stalin's Apologist* (New York: Oxford University Press, 1990).

9. See John Maynard Keynes, "Soviet Russia—I," *New Republic,* October 28, 1925, available at https://newrepublic.com/article/77318/soviet-russiai. Also

published in John Maynard Keynes, *Essays in Persuasion* (New York: Classic House Books, 2009).

10. See Carol Strong and Matt Killingsworth, "Stalin the Charismatic Leader? Explaining the'Cult of Personality' as a Legitimation Technique," *Politics, Religion & Ideology* 12, no. 4 (December 2011): 391–411.

11. See Philip Deery, *Red Apple: Communism and McCarthyism in Cold War New York* (New York: Fordham University, Empire State Editions, 2014); and John McCarten, "All Together Please," *New Yorker,* April 2, 1949.

12. See William Borders, "150,000 Rally in London against Bomb," *New York Times,* October 25, 1981.

13. See Anita Pisch, *The Personality Cult of Stalin in Soviet Posters, 1929–1953* (Canberra: ANU Press, 2016), 94.

14. See Kevin Mulcahy, "Official Culture and Cultural Repression: The Case of Dmitri Shostakovich," *Journal of Aesthetic Education* 18, no. 3 (Autumn 1984): 69–83.

15. See Edward Rothstein, "Shy Dissident or Soviet Tool? A Musical War. New Evidence on Memoirs Splits Shostakovich Scholars," *New York Times*, October 17, 1998. Also see Solomon Volkov, ed., *Testimony: The Memoirs of Dmitri Shostakovich* (New York: Harper and Row, 1979).

16. See Rebecca Renner, "The CIA Scheme That Brought *Dr. Zhivago* to the World," Lithub, April 12, 2019. The declassified CIA documents on Dr. Zhivago are available on the agency's website at www.cia.gov/library/readingroom/collection/doctor-zhivago.

17. See Ben Panko, "How Boris Pasternak Won and Lost the Nobel Prize," Smithsonian.com, October 23, 2017.

18. See Tina Jordan, "The Dr. Zhivago Novel Dust-Up," *New York Times,* October 24, 2018.

19. See Ben Panko, "How Boris Pasternak Won and Lost the Nobel Prize."

20. See Henry Shapiro, "From the Archive: 30 October 1958: Pasternak Gives Up the Nobel Prize as Attack on Him Grows," *Guardian,* October 30, 2013; and Peter Finn and Petra Couvée, *The Zhivago Affair: The Kremlin, the CIA, and the Battle over a Forbidden Book* (New York: Pantheon Books, 2014).

21. See Louis Menand, "Unpopular Front: American Art and the Cold War," *New Yorker,* October 17, 2005.

22. See Jane DeHart Matthews, "Art and Politics in Cold War America," in *Pollock and After: The Critical Debate* (New York: Harper and Row, 1985); and Irving Sandler, "Abstract Expressionism and the Cold War," *Art in America*, June/July 2008.

23. See Katherine Schwab, "The Secret History of Midcentury Modern Design as Cold War Propaganda," *Fast Company*, February 12, 2019.

24. See Frances Stonor Saunders, "Modern Art Was CIA 'Weapon,'" *Independent,* October 21, 1995; and Louis Menand, "Unpopular Front: American Art and the Cold War," *New Yorker,* October 17, 2005.

25. Greg Barnhisel, *Cold War Modernists: Art, Literature, and American Cultural Diplomacy* (New York: Columbia University Press, 2015), 80.

26. See Hugo Berkeley, "When America's Hottest Jazz Stars Were Sent to Cool Cold War Tensions," *Guardian,* May 3, 2018; and Penny Von Eschen, *Satchmo Blows Up the World: Jazz Ambassadors Play the Cold War* (Cambridge, MA: Harvard University Press, 2004).

27. See Jeremy Gunn, *Spiritual Weapons: Cold War and the Forging of an American National Religion* (Westport CT: Praeger, 2009), 71; and Tony Show, "Martyrs, Miracles and Martians: Religion and Cold War Cinematic Propaganda in the 1950s," *Journal of Cold War Studies* 4, no. 2 (Spring 2002): 3–22.

28. See Martin Kettle, "An American Life: Newly Released Files Reveal That the FBI Spied on Aaron Copland for Decades," *Guardian,* May 14, 2003.

29. See Jennifer Latson, "One of America's Most Famous Spies Didn't Do Any Spying," *Time*, March 6, 2015. Also see "Art in Defense of the Rosenbergs," *Espionart*, June 19, 2018.

30. Sartre's protest was published in French as "Les Animaux malades de la rage," *Libération*, June 22, 1953, translated as "Mad Beasts," in *Selected Prose: The Writings of Jean-Paul Sartre* (Evanston, IL: Northwestern University Press, 1974).

31. John Neville, *The Press, the Rosenbergs, and the Cold War* (London: Praeger, 1995), 83.

32. Francis Fukuyama, "The End of History?" *National Interest*, Summer 1989; and Francis Fukuyama, *The End of History and the Last Man* (New York: Free Press, 1992).

33. Francis Fukuyama, "The End of History?"

34. Fukuyama, "The End of History?"

35. See Timothy Snyder, "Ivan Ilyin: Putin's Philosopher of Russian Fascism," *New York Review of Books,* April 5, 2018.

36. See Julie Cassiday and Emily Johnson, "Putin, Putiniana, and the Question of a Post-Soviet Cult of Personality," *Slavonic and East European Review* 88, no. 4 (October 2010): 681–707.

37. Christopher Paul and Miriam Matthews, "The Russian 'Firehose of Falsehood' Propaganda Model," Rand Corporation, 2016.

38. See Peter Pomerantsev, "Nothing Is True and Everything Is Possible," Sunday Book Review, *New York Times*, November 25, 2014.

16. GUARDIANS OF THE TRUTH

1. See Ida M. Tarbell, *The History of the Standard Oil Company* (New York: Macmillan, 1904); and quoted in Steve Weinberg, "Taking on the Trust: The Epic Battle of Ida Tarbell and John D. Rockefeller," *Wall Street Journal,* March 27, 2008.

2. See Robert J. Valuck, Suzanne Poirier, and Robert G. Mrtek, "Patent Medicine Muckraking: Influences on American Pharmacy, Social Reform, and Foreign Authors," *Pharmacy in History* 34, no. 4 (1992): 183–92; and James Harvey Young, "The New Muckrackers," in *The Medical Messiahs: A Social*

History of Medical Quackery in 20th Century America (Princeton: Princeton University Press, 1967).

3. See Michael Schudson, "The Objectivity Norm in American Journalism," *Journalism* 2 no. 2 (2001): 149–70.

4. See Stanley Schultz, "The Morality of Politics: The Muckrakers' Vision of Democracy," *Journal of American History* 52, no. 3 (December 1965): 527–47.

5. Theodore Roosevelt, "The Man with the Muck-rake," speech delivered April 14, 1906, Washington, DC, available online at https://voicesofdemocracy.umd.edu/theodore-roosevelt-the-man-with-the-muck-rake-speech-text.

6. Alan Axelrod, *Selling the Great War: The Making of American Propaganda* (New York: St. Martin's Press, 2009), 37.

7. See Kirk Hallahan, "Ivy Lee and the Rockefellers' Response to the 1913–14 Colorado Coal Strike," *Journal of Public Relations Research* 14, no. 4 (2002): 265–315.

8. See Stewart Justman, "Freud and His Nephew," *Social Research* 61, no. 2 (Summer 1994): 457–76.

9. See Ron Chernow, "First among Flacks," *New York Times,* August 16, 1998. For a biography of Edward Bernays, see Larry Tye, *The Father of Spin: Edward L. Bernays and the Birth of Public Relations* (New York: Crown Publishers, 1998).

10. On the nineteenth-century bohemian movement in Paris, see Luc Ferry, *L'Invention de la vie bohème, 1830–1900* (Paris: Éditions Cercle d'Art, 2012).

11. See Alden Whitman, "Henry R. Luce, Creator of Time-Life Magazine Empire, Dies in Phoenix at 68," *New York Times*, March 1, 1967.

12. This quote was so associated with Henry Luce's thinking that it was cited in his obituary in 1967. See Alden Whitman, "Henry R. Luce, Creator of Time-Life Magazine Empire, Dies in Phoenix at 68."

13. For the text of "The American Century," see Henry Luce, "The American Century," *Diplomatic History* 23, no. 2 (Spring 1999): 159–71.

14. See the Hutchins Commission's final report, *A Free and Responsible Press* (Chicago: University of Chicago Press, 1947), 80.

15. See Margaret Blanchard, "The Hutchins Commission, the Press and the Responsibility Concept," *Journalism Monographs,* Association for Education in Journalism, Number 49 (May 1977); and Fredrick S. Siebert, Theodore Peterson, and Wilbur Schramm, *Four Theories of the Press* (Chicago: University of Illinois Press, 1963).

16. See Daniel C. Hallin, "The Passing of the 'High Modernism' of American Journalism," *Journal of Communication* 42, no. 3 (1992: 14–25.

17. See Matthew Pressman, *On Press: The Liberal Values That Shaped the News* (Cambridge, MA: Harvard University Press, 2018); and Jill Lepore, "Hard News," *New Yorker*, January 28, 2019.

18. See Michael Schudson, "When the Media Had Enough: Watergate, Vietnam and the Birth of the Adversarial Press," *Salon*, October 10, 2015.

19. Roy Greenslade, "How Blurring of Fact and Comment Kicked Open the Door to Fake News," *Guardian*, October 9, 2017.

20. See Edward S. Herman and Noam Chomsky, *Manufacturing Consent: The Political Economy of the Mass Media* (New York: Pantheon Books, 1988).

21. See Nick Davies, "Our Media Have Become Mass Producers of Distortion," *Guardian,* February 4, 2008; and Nick Davies, *Flat Earth News* (London: Chatto & Windus, 2008).

22. See Stuart Sim, ed., *The Routledge Companion to Postmodernism* (London: Routledge, 2001).

23. Michael Lynch, *True to Life: Why Truth Matters* (Cambridge, MA: MIT Press, 2004), 35–36.

24. Friedrich Nietzsche, *On Truth and Lying in a Nonmoral Sense* (1873), available online at https://archive.org/stream/NietzscheOnTruthAndLying/nietzsche%20on%20truth%20and%20lying_djvu.txt.

25. See the introduction in Jean-François Lyotard, *The Postmodern Condition* (Manchester: Manchester University Press, 1979).

26. See chapter 2 in Simon Blackburn, *Truth: A Guide for the Perplexed* (London: Penguin, 2005); and Stephen Metcalf, "Richard Rorty: What Made Him a Crucial American Philosopher?" *Slate,* June 15, 2007.

27. François Cusset, *French Theory: How Foucault, Derrida, Deleuze & Co. Transformed the Intellectual Life of the United States* (Minneapolis: University of Minnesota Press, 2008). The book was originally published in French with the title *French Theory: Foucault, Derrida, Deleuze, & Cie et les mutations de la vie intellectuelle aux États-Unis* (Paris: La Découverte, 2003).

28. See Jürgen Habermas, *The Philosophical Discourse of Modernity* (Cambridge: Cambridge University Press, 1987); and Jürgen Habermas and Seyla Ben-Habib, "Modernity versus Postmodernity," *New German Critique*, no. 22 (Winter 1981): 3–14; and Amy Allen, "Poststructuralism," in *The Habermas Handbook*, ed. Hauke Brunkorste, Regina Kreide, and Christina Lafont (New York: Columbia University Press, 2018).

29. See chapter 13, "The Jews in Present-Day Literature," in Evelyn Barish, *The Double Life of Paul de Man* (New York: Liveright Publishing, 2014).

30. See Louis Menard, "The de Man Case: Does a Critic's Past Explain His Criticism?" *New Yorker*, March 24, 2014

31. See James Atlas, "The Case of Paul de Man," *New York Times Magazine*, August 28, 1988; and Robert Alter, "Paul de Man Was a Total Fraud," *New Republic,* April 6, 2014.

32. For the text of the Sokal hoax paper, see https://physics.nyu.edu/faculty/sokal/transgress_v2/transgress_v2_singlefile.html.

33. See Alan Sokal and Jean Bricmont, *Fashionable Nonsense: Postmodern Intellectuals' Abuse of Science* (New York: Picador, 1999); and James Piereson and Naomi Shaefer Riley, "The Sokal Hoax and Its Lessons," *Weekly Standard*, January 25, 2017.

34. Janny Scott, "Postmodern Gravity Deconstructed, Slyly," *New York Times,* May 18, 1996.

35. Stanley Fish, "Professor Sokal's Bad Joke," *New York Times,* May 21, 1996.

36. See Fredric Jameson, *Postmodernism, or the Cultural Logic of Late Capitalism* (Durham, NC: Duke University Press, 1991).

37. For a more detailed analysis of postmodernism's influence on literature, cinema, television, music, architecture, art, and other aspects of popular culture, see Stuart Sim, ed., *The Routledge Companion to Postmodernism* (London: Routledge, 2001).

38. See Tom Wolfe, *The New Journalism* (New York: Harper and Row, 1973).

39. See Kevin Helliker, "Capote Classic 'In Cold Blood' Tainted by Long-Lost Files," *Wall Street Journal*, February 8, 2013.

40. On the "postmodern turn" in journalism, see Karin Wahl-Jorgensen, "Is There a 'Postmodern Turn' in Journalism?" in *Rethinking Journalism Again*, ed. Chris Peters and Marcel Broersma (London: Routledge, 2016).

41. See chapter 5, "Why the Media Worship Objectivity but the Ivory Tower Rejects Truth," in Lee McIntyre, *Respecting Truth: Willful Ignorance in the Internet Age* (New York: Routledge, 2015).

42. See Sam Tanenhaus, "Peace and War," *New York Times Book Review*, August 19, 2010.

43. See Rachel Greenwald Smith, "Postmodernism and the Affective Turn," *Twentieth Century Literature* 57, nos. 3/4, Postmodernism, Then (Fall/Winter 2011): 423–46.

44. See Patricia Clough, "The Affective Turn: Theorizing the Social," in *The Affective Turn: Theorizing the Social*, ed. Patricia Clough (Durham, NC: Duke University Press, 2007).

45. See Hua Hsu, "Affect Theory and the New Age of Anxiety," *New Yorker*, March 18, 2019.

46. See Antonio Damasio, *Descartes' Error: Emotion, Reason and the Human Brain* (New York: Penguin, 2005); Stephen Asma and Rami Gabriel, "United by Feelings," *Aeon*, August 22, 2019; and Noga Arikha, "The Interoceptive Turn," *Aeon*, June 17, 2019.

47. See Hua Hsu, "Affect Theory and the New Age of Anxiety," *New Yorker*, March 18, 2019.

48. Brent Cunningham, "Rethinking Objectivity," *Columbia Journalism Review,* July–August 2003.

49. Lene Bech Sillesen, Chris Ip, and David Uberti, "Journalism and the Power of Emotions," *Columbia Journalism Review,* May–June 2015.

50. See Charlie Beckett, "Towards an Emotional Networked Journalism," LSE Polis, August 31, 2017.

51. See Antje Glück, "Should Journalists Be More Emotionally Literate?" European Journalism Observatory, April 15, 2019.

17. THE DIGITAL TOWN SQUARE

1. Rick Levine, Christopher Locke, Doc Searls, and David Weinberger, *The Cluetrain Manifesto: The End of Business as Usual* (New York: Basic Books,

2000). See also Howard Rheingold, *Smart Mobs* (Cambridge, MA: Basic Books, 2002); and James Surowiecki, *The Wisdom of Crowds* (New York: Doubleday, 2005).

2. Clay Shirky, *Here Comes Everybody: The Power of Organizing Without Organizations* (New York: Penguin, 2008).

3. See Bill Keller, "Not Dead Yet: The Newspaper in the Days of Digital Anarchy," Chatham House lecture, London, published in *Guardian*, November 29, 2007.

4. Keller, "Not Dead Yet."

5. See the introduction in Andrew Keen, *The Cult of the Amateur* (New York: Doubleday, 2007).

6. Keen, *The Cult of the Amateur.*

7. See Andrew Keen, "The Cult of the Amateur," BBC, June 5, 2008, available online at www.bbc.co.uk/blogs/newsnight/2007/06/the_cult_of_the_amateur_by_andrew_keen_1.html.

8. See Michael Schudson, "The Trouble with Experts—and Why Democracies Need Them," *Theory and Society* 35, nos. 5/6 (December 2006): 491–506.

9. See Sophia Rosenfeld, *Democracy and Truth* (Philadelphia: University of Pennsylvania Press, 2018).

10. See Alexander Hamilton, *Federalist Papers,* Number 68, available online at https://avalon.law.yale.edu/18th_century/fed68.asp.

11. Jonathan Haidt and Tobias Rose-Stockwell, "The Dark Psychology of Social Networks," *Atlantic*, December 2019.

12. See Katharine Viner, "A Mission for Journalism in a Time of Crisis," *Guardian*, November 16, 2017.

13. See "C.P. Scott's Centenary Essay," *Guardian*, October 23, 2017, available online at www.theguardian.com/sustainability/cp-scott-centenary-essay.

14. See Katharine Viner, "The Rise of the Reader: Journalism in the Age of the Open Web," *Guardian*, October 9, 2013.

15. See Sharon Reier, "Half a Century Later, Economist's 'Creative Destruction' Theory Is Apt for the Internet Age," *New York Times,* June 10, 2000.

16. See Katherine Viner, "In Turbulent Times, We Need Good Journalism More Than Ever," *Guardian*, November 16, 2017.

17. See John Gapper, "Facebook Faces the Tragedy of the Commons," *Financial Times,* November 28, 2017.

18. See interview with Jeff Jarvis, "Media Must Help the Public Regain Trust in Facts—Jarvis," *TheMastOnline*, October 25, 2017, available at www.themastonline.com/2017/10/25/media-must-help-the-public-regain-trust-in-facts-jarvis.

19. Jeff Jarvis, "The Coming Crisis of Cognition," *Medium*, April 24, 2019.

20. See John Dewey, *The Public and Its Problems* (New York: Henry Holt, 1927), 364; and Melvin Rogers, "Dewey and His Vision of Democracy," *Contemporary Pragmatism* 7, no. 1 (June 2010): 69–91.

21. From John Dewey, *The Public and Its Problems*, quoted by John Stuhr in "Dewey's Social and Political Philosophy," in *Reading Dewey: Interpretations*

for a Postmodern Generation, ed. Larry Hickman (Bloomington: Indiana University Press, 1998), 97.

22. Robert Westbrook, *John Dewey and American Democracy* (Ithaca: Cornell University Press, 1991), 534.

23. See Oliver Berkeman, "How the News Took Over Reality," *Guardian*, May 3, 2019; and Peter Pomerantsev, "The Disinformation Age: A Revolution in Propaganda," *Guardian*, July 27, 2019.

24. Emily Bell, "Facebook Is Eating the World," *Columbia Journalism Review*, March 7, 2016.

25. See Katharine Viner, "A Mission for Journalism in a Time of Crisis."

26. Claire Cain Miller, "How Obama's Internet Campaign Changed Politics," *New York Times*, November 7, 2008.

27. See "Obama: The Vox Conversation," *Vox*, January 23, 2015.

28. See Ian Bogost, "Obama Was Too Good at Social Media," *Atlantic,* January 6, 2017.

29. See Ian Burrell, "The Evidence That Busts the Media Myths of Echo Chambers and Fake News," *Drum,* February 8, 2018; and Richard Fletcher et al., "Measuring the Reach of 'Fake News' and Online Disinformation in Europe," Reuters Institute for the Study of Journalism, University of Oxford, February 2018.

30. See William H. Dutton, "Fake News, Echo Chambers and Filter Bubbles: Under-Researched and Overhyped," *Conversation*, May 5, 2017.

31. See Jeff Jarvis, "Evidence Please," *Medium*, July 26, 2019, available at https://medium.com/whither-news/evidence-please-d794b5d21ee4.

32. See Danah Boyd, "You Think You Want Media Literacy . . . Do You?" *Data & Society,* March 9, 2018.

33. See Rachel Hosie, "Why Do So Many Millennials Believe in Horoscopes?" *Independent,* February 9, 2017; and Chris Mooney, "More and More Americans Think Astrology Is Science," *Mother Jones*, February 11, 2014.

34. See Francis Fukuyama, *Trust: The Social Virtues and the Creation of Prosperity* (New York: Free Press, 1995).

18. LORD OF THE LIES

1. See Lawrence Yee, "All Major TV Networks Block Trump's 'Fake News' Ad," *Variety*, May 5, 2017.

2. Maria Konnikova, "Trump's Lies vs. Your Brain," *Politico*, January/February 2017.

3. See "Why Trump Lies," *Los Angeles Times*, April 3, 2017.

4. See Peter Wehner, "Trump's Sinister Assault on Truth,"*Atlantic*, June 18, 2019; and "President Trump Has Made 10,796 False or Misleading Claims over 869 Days," *Washington Post,* June 10, 2019.

5. David Wise, *The Politics of Lying: Government Deception, Secrecy and Power* (New York: Random House, 1973), quoted in Carl M. Cannon, "Untruth and Consequences," *Atlantic*, January/February 2007.

6. See Adrienne LaFrance, "Calling Out a Presidential Lie," *Atlantic*, January 27, 2017; and Nicholas D. Kristof, "Calling Bush a Liar," *New York Times,* June 30, 2004.

7. Michael Massing, "Journalism in the Age of Trump," *Nation*, August 13, 2018.

8. See Oliver Hahl, Minjae Kim, and Ezra Zuckerman Sivan, "The Authentic Appeal of the Lying Demagogue: Proclaiming the Deeper Truth About Political Illegitimacy," *American Sociological Review* 83, no. 1 (2018): 1–33.

9. See Peter Baker, "For Trump, A Year of Reinventing the Presidency," *New York Times,* December 31, 2017.

10. See David Smith, "'Enemy of the People': Trump's War on the Media Is a Page from Nixon's Playbook," *Guardian*, September 7, 2019.

11. See Amber Jamieson, "'You Are Fake News': Trump Attacks CNN, BuzzFeed at Press Conference," *Guardian*, January 11, 2017.

12. See Daniel Funke, "Reporters: Stop Calling Everything Fake News," *Poynter*, August 29, 2018; and Hannah Kuchler and David Blood, "'Junk News' Still Rising, Study Finds, as US Midterms Near," *Financial Times,* November 1, 2018.

13. See Rasmus Kleis Nielsen and Lucas Graves, "News You Don't Believe: Audience Perspectives on Fake News," Reuters Institute for the Study of Journalism, University of Oxford, October 2017.

14. Umberto Eco, *Travels in Hyperreality* (London: Harcourt, Brace, 1986).

15. Mark K. McBeth and Randy S. Clemons, "Is the Fake News the Real News? The Significance of Stewart and Colbert on Democratic Discourse, Politics, and Policy," in *The Stewart-Colbert Effect: Essays on the Real Impact of Fake News*, ed. Amarnath Amarasingam (Jefferson, NC: McFarland, 2011). See also Karen Dill, *How Fantasy Becomes Reality: Information and Entertainment Media in Everyday Life* (New York: Oxford University Press, 2016).

16. Tim Harford, "Why There Is No Need to Panic about Fake News," *Financial Times,* January 3, 2019.

17. See Mariana Alfaro, "Former *New York Times* Executive Editor Criticizes Trump Coverage," *Business Insider*, January 3, 2019.

18. See Joe Concha, "Former NYT Editor Jill Abramson Takes a Jab at Paper: News Articles 'Unmistakably Anti-Trump,'" *Hill*, January 2, 2019.

19. Jill Abramson, *Merchants of Truth: The Business of News and the Fight for Facts* (New York: Simon & Schuster, 2019), 391.

20. See Joe Concha, "Former NYT Editor Jill Abramson Takes a Jab at Paper: News Articles 'Unmistakably Anti-Trump,'" *Hill*, January 2, 2019.

21. See "Why Evangelicals Love Donald Trump," *Economist*, May 18, 2017; and Molly Worthen, "A Match Made in Heaven," *Atlantic*, May 2017.

22. See Miranda Bryant, "Author Marianne Williamson on 2020 Run: 'All I Can Do Is Be Myself,'" *Guardian*, July 27, 2019.

23. David Brooks, "Marianne Williamson Knows How to Beat Trump," *New York Times,* April 1, 2019.

24. See Madeleine Aggeler, "Marianne Williamson Is Sorry for Calling Vaccines 'Orwellian,'" *Cut*, June 20, 2019.

25. See Sonia Saraiya, "Marianne Williamson Explains Her Magical Thinking," *Vanity Fair,* July 30, 2019.

26. Tara Burton, "The Self-Centered Religion Shared by Marianne Williamson and Donald Trump," *Washington Post,* August 1, 2019.

27. See Harriet Sherwood, "'Toxic Christianity': The Evangelicals Creating Champions for Trump," *Guardian,* October 21, 2018.

28. See Jessica Glenza, "Paul White: The Pastor Who Helps Trump Hear 'What God Has to Say,'" *Guardian,* March 27, 2019; and Jessica Glenza, "How the Religious Right Gained Unprecedented Access to Trump," *Guardian,* January 31, 2019.

29. Rebecca Morin, "Sarah Sanders: God Wanted Trump to Become President," *Politico,* January 30, 2019.

30. See Douglas Martin, "Joan Quigley, Astrologer to a First Lady, Is Dead at 87," *New York Times,* October 24, 2014.

31. Steven Roberts, "White House Confirms Reagans Follow Astrologer, Up to a Point," *New York Times,* May 4, 1988. See also Reyhan Harmanci, "How Nancy Reagan Became Forever Linked with Astrology," *Atlas Obscura,* March 6, 2016.

32. Jacques Steinberg, "2005: In a Word, Truthiness," *New York Times,* December 25, 2005.

33. See "Stephen Colbert's 'Truthiness' Word Describes Campaign Rhetoric," *Washington Times,* August 18, 2016.

34. See Allan Bloom, "How Nietzsche Conquered America," *Wilson Quarterly* 11, no. 3 (Summer 1987): 80–93.

35. See Allan Bloom, *The Closing of the American Mind* (New York: Simon & Schuster, 1987), 315.

36. Greg Lukianoff and Jonathan Haidt, *The Coddling of the American Mind: How Good Intentions and Bad Ideas Are Setting Up a Generation for Failure* (London: Penguin, 2018).

37. John Gray, "The Rise of Post-Truth Liberalism," *Unherd,* September 5, 2018.

38. See Bloom, *The Closing of the American Mind,* 104.

39. See Stephanie Convery, "Stephen Fry Pronounces the Death of Classical Liberalism: 'We Are All Irrelevant and Outdated Bystanders,'" *Guardian,* November 5, 2018.

40. See Jonathan Haidt, *The Righteous Mind: Why Good People Are Divided by Politics and Religion* (New York: Pantheon, 2012).

41. See Jürgen Habermas, *The Philosophical Discourse of Modernity* (Cambridge: Cambridge University Press, 1987); and Jürgen Habermas and Seyla Ben-Habib, "Modernity versus Postmodernity," *New German Critique,* no. 22 (Winter 1981): 3–14.

42. Steven Pinker, *Enlightenment Now: The Case for Reason, Science, Humanism, and Progress* (New York: Viking, 2018).

43. Rebecca Newberger Goldstein, "Truth Isn't the Problem—We Are," *Wall Street Journal,* March 15, 2018.

44. Andrew Sullivan, "America's New Religions," *NYMag*, December 7, 2018.

45. David Frum, *Trumpocracy: The Corruption of the American Republic* (New York: HarperCollins, 2018), 12.

46. David C. Barker and Morgan Marietta, "From 'Total Exoneration' to 'Impeach Now'—the Meuller Report and Dueling Fact Perceptions," *Conversation,* May 8, 2019.

47. Gideon Rachman, "Donald Trump Embodies the Spirit of Our Age," *Financial Times,* October 22, 2018.

48. Paul Krugman, "Trump Makes Caligula Look Pretty Good," *New York Times*, August 18, 2017; and Paul Krugman, "How Republics End," *New York Times,* December 19, 2016. See also Mark Brown, "Donald Trump Has 'Fascinating Parallels' with Caligula, Says Historian," *Guardian*, June 1, 2016.

49. David Remnick, "The Lost Emperor," *New Yorker,* January 15, 2018; and "Dude, Where's My Toga? The Similarities between Donald Trump's Washington and the Roman Republic," *Economist*, December 8, 2016.

CONCLUSION

1. See Lionel Barber, Henry Foy, and Alex Barker, "Vladimir Putin Says Liberalism Has 'Become Obsolete,'" *Financial Times,* June 28, 2019.

2. Timothy Snyder, *On Tyranny: Twenty Lessons from the Twentieth Century* (London: Bodley Head, 2017).

3. See the Introduction in Julian Baggini's *A Short History of Truth: Consolations for a Post-Truth World* (London: Quercus, 2017). Also see Baggini's book, *The Edge of Reason: A Rational Sceptic in an Irrational World* (London: Yale University Press, 2016).

INDEX

ABOUT THE AUTHOR

Matthew Fraser is a professor at the American University of Paris, where he lectures on communications history, political economy, media law, journalism, and the economics of the media and entertainment industries. He earned his doctorate in political science at the Institut d'Études Politiques de Paris (Sciences Po) after completing graduate studies at the London School of Economics, Nuffield College, Oxford, and Université de Paris I-Sorbonne-Panthéon. He has long experience as a journalist, as a newspaper critic, columnist, and correspondent in Paris and London. He was editor-in-chief of the *National Post* in Canada and co-host of a prime-time current affairs show, *Inside Media*, on CBC Newsworld. He is the author of five books of non-fiction, including *Weapons of Mass Distraction: Soft Power and American Empire* (2005). He lives in Paris.